物理类专业系列教材

物理学专业英语

主编 仲海洋 姚 丽 王轶卓
参编 程丽红 陈宝玖 鹿学军
　　 段 萍 孙佳石 李香萍
　　 连天雪 栾 玲 冯立军

清华大学出版社
北京

内 容 简 介

本书是一本针对高等学校的物理学及其相关专业的专业英语教材。内容主要包括：专业英语的特点、词法、语法、翻译、写作、阅读、国际会议用语等专业英语知识的介绍；运动学、质点力学、刚体的定轴转动、振动与波动、电磁学、热学、光学、原子物理、量子力学、电动力学、相对论、物理实验等内容的选读，并附有文中出现的物理专业词汇的英汉对照词汇表，便于学生课前有针对性地查阅和掌握；对物理学专业英语中的一些常用表达，在每课中也以专题的形式进行了详尽汇总和举例说明，包括工具、仪器、设备、结构、原料、精度、性能、形状、方位、用途、状态、原因、结论、学术交流、国际会议、双语教学课堂用语等 36 个专题。最后在附录部分汇总了物理专业所开设课程名称的英文翻译，教务教学管理词汇，物理学一、二级学科名称英文词汇，数学符号及其英语表达，常用物理基本常数，常用汉英物理学专业词汇表，常用英汉物理学专业词汇表，供读者使用时查阅。

本教材适用于高等学校的物理及相关专业的本科生、硕士生专业英语教学和理工科大学物理学的双语教学，也可作为科技工作者和读者自学的参考书。

版权所有，侵权必究。举报：010-62782989，beiqinquan@tup.tsinghua.edu.cn。

图书在版编目（CIP）数据

物理学专业英语 / 仲海洋，姚丽，王轶卓主编. —北京：清华大学出版社，2011.3（2024.8重印）
（物理类专业系列教材）
ISBN 978-7-302-24284-0

Ⅰ. ①物… Ⅱ. ①仲… ②姚… ③王… Ⅲ. ①物理学－英语－高等学校－教材 Ⅳ. ①H31

中国版本图书馆 CIP 数据核字(2010) 第 251376 号

责任编辑：邹开颜　李　嫚
责任校对：王淑云
责任印制：刘海龙

出版发行：清华大学出版社
　　　网　　址：https://www.tup.com.cn, https://www.wqxuetang.com
　　　地　　址：北京清华大学学研大厦 A 座　　　邮　编：100084
　　　社 总 机：010-83470000　　　邮　购：010-62786544
　　　投稿与读者服务：010-62776969, c-service@tup.tsinghua.edu.cn
　　　质 量 反 馈：010-62772015, zhiliang@tup.tsinghua.edu.cn
印 装 者：三河市天利华印刷装订有限公司
经　　销：全国新华书店
开　　本：185mm×260mm　　　印　张：26.25　　　字　数：634 千字
版　　次：2011 年 3 月第 1 版　　　印　次：2024 年 8 月第 15 次印刷
定　　价：76.00元

产品编号：032547-07

作者简介

仲海洋,大连海事大学物理系教授,美国伊利诺伊大学访问学者,辽宁省高等学校教学名师,辽宁省百万人才工程百人层次人选。多年主讲大学物理学双语教学课程,讲授过物理学专业英语、科技英语、计算机操作英语、力学、电磁学、原子物理学、量子力学等专业课程。曾经担任英语教师4年,讲授过大学英语、英语会话、航海英语会话、航海英语阅读等课程。近几年来,一直从事公共基础课大学物理的双语教学和英语教学,并积极进行大学物理双语课程的双语教学方法和模式研究,担任大学物理精品课程负责人。已经形成了一整套系统的大学物理和大学物理实验课程双语教学的模式。

负责主持辽宁省高等教育教学改革研究项目"大学物理学与物理实验双语示范课程建设与实践模式推广"等多项教改项目,教学成果获得辽宁省教学成果一等奖。

著有双语教材《University Physics》、《流行成语口语》、《新概念英语2学习辅导》、《自然科学概论》、《现代科学技术概论》、《电磁学》、《电动力学》等。

前　言

在人类追求真理、探索未知世界的过程中,物理学展现了一系列科学的世界观和方法论,深刻影响着人类对物质世界的基本认识、人类的思维方式和社会生活,是人类文明发展的基石,在人才的科学素质培养中具有重要的地位。

随着科学的发展进入 21 世纪,物理学及其相关领域的国际教育与研究合作交流更加频繁,专业英语早已经是国际上专业交流的主要语言。国家教育部也提出了高等学校各专业逐步使用英文教材,以培养和增强学生阅读英文专业文献的能力。具备良好的物理学专业英语水平和使用能力是每个物理学及其相关领域的学生和从业人员必备的素质。

本书编者在物理学专业英语教学、理工科大学物理学的双语教学和从事科研和国际交流活动的过程中发现:尽管物理学专业英语在教学和科研工作中经常使用,但是却没有一本合适而全面的参考教材和可供查阅的工具书。很多专业英语课程的学习方式仅仅停留在复印一些英文材料进行阅读、解释和翻译的阶段。学生学习后只是提高了一些专业词汇量和阅读翻译水平,而在使用专业英语进行写作和口头交流时,则力不从心。

本书编写的目的就是希望能够通过这本书的编写,总结一些专业英语和双语教学方面的经验,并将这方面的笔记、资料系统地汇编起来,以各个专题的形式总结出来,供广大物理学及其相关专业的本科生、硕士生、博士生作为教材使用,也适合物理学及其相关领域的科技工作者在使用专业英语进行学习和交流时翻阅参考。作者在写作过程中突出了以下主要特色:①内容选择注重实用性,不仅可以作为教材使用,也可以作为工具书进行查阅参考;②内容全面精练,例句的选择专业性强,并且恰当贴切;③以专题的形式进行介绍或进行汇总,便于独立学习和查询参考;④对于专业英语阅读内容中的专业词汇,在每篇后的词汇表中以中英文对照形式给出;⑤使学习者通过专业英语的学习培养和拓展实际应用英语的能力,进而掌握相应的方法和技巧。

本书共 36 课,分为 9 个单元,各单元之间既相互独立又有一定联系。每一课都包括三个部分:第一部分主要介绍有关物理学专业英语方面的知识,通过大量的例句、实例和范文介绍了包括专业英语的特点、词法、语法、句法、翻译、写作、阅读、国际会议用语等方面的内容;其中在专业英语的翻译部分,主要介绍了专业词汇、独立主格结构、名词化结构、分隔结构和长句的翻译;作者在教学和学术交流过程中,深深了解到广大学生、科技工作者在使用专业英语进行写作方面的艰难,因此在专业英语的写作部分中,主要介绍了描写文、说明文、科研论文和各种报告的写作,尤其针对科研论文和各种报告(实验报告、考察报告、工作报告、科技报告)的写作更是做了详尽的介绍,其中汇总了大量的实用句型可供参考使用;在国际会议用语方面也列举了很多实用的句型供参考使用。第二部分为专业英语的阅读内容,选择了关于运动学、质点力学、刚体的定轴转动、振动与波动、电磁学、热学、光学、原子物理、

前言

量子力学、电动力学、相对论、物理实验等专业文献的选读,为了读者查阅和节省查字典的时间,在每篇之后按照文中专业词汇出现的顺序编写了英汉对照词汇表。第三部分汇总了物理学专业英语中的一些常用表达,共36个实用的专题内容供参考查阅,包括工具、仪器、设备、结构、原料、精度、性能、形状、方位、用途、状态、原因、结论、物理实验、学术交流、国际会议、双语教学课堂用语等方面内容;尤其在每个单元的头一课中,汇总的都是在物理实验方面涉及到的工具、仪器和设备等实用的内容。附录部分共汇总了七个方面的内容:物理专业所开设课程名称的英文翻译,教务教学管理词汇,物理学一、二级学科名称英文词汇,数学符号及其英语表达,常用物理基本常数,常用汉英物理学专业词汇表,常用英汉物理学专业词汇表。

本书第一至第五单元由仲海洋编写;第七、第八单元由姚丽编写;第六、第九单元由王轶卓编写。练习和附录部分由程丽红、陈宝玖、段萍、孙佳石、李香萍、鹿学军、连天雪、栾玲、冯立军编写。杨帆参加了全书的校对工作,夏文文、谷领峥和高山水也参加了部分校对工作,深表感谢。

在本书的编写过程中,王殿夫、宓东、许雪松为我们提出了宝贵的意见,在此谨表示衷心的感谢。我们还参考了国内外出版物(见本书后面的"参考文献")中的部分观点和内容,在此谨向这些编著者致以真诚的谢意,并对未能够事先征得同意表示歉意。此外,我们还选用了互联网上的部分资料,由于这些资料涉及面广,选用时作了大量修改,在此不便一一注明,谨向有关人士深表谢意。

由于水平有限,并且是第一次进行物理学专业英语教材的编写尝试,错误和不足是难免的,请读者和同行多指教,以利于再版时修正和改进。

仲海洋
2011年1月

目 录

Unit One ··· 1
  LESSON 1 ·· 1
    1.1 物理学专业英语的特点 ·· 1
      1.1.1 物理学专业英语简介 ··· 1
      1.1.2 物理学专业英语的词汇特点 ··· 1
    1.2 专业英语阅读 ··· 5
      1.2.1 Introduction(引言) ·· 5
      1.2.2 Space and Time(时间与空间) ·· 6
    1.3 专业英语常用表达法-1 常用工具 ··· 7
  LESSON 2 ·· 8
    2.1 物理学专业英语的名词化结构 ·· 8
      2.1.1 名词化 ··· 8
      2.1.2 名词化的分类 ··· 9
      2.1.3 名词化结构的构成 ·· 9
      2.1.4 名词化的功能 ·· 10
    2.2 专业英语阅读 ·· 12
      2.2.1 Vectors(矢量) ··· 12
      2.2.2 Properties of Vectors(矢量的性质) ·· 12
      2.2.3 Unit Vectors(单位矢量) ·· 14
    2.3 专业英语常用表达法-2 仪器设备 ·· 15
  LESSON 3 ··· 17
    3.1 物理学专业英语的语法特点 ·· 17
      3.1.1 常用的动词时态 ·· 17
      3.1.2 使用介词的侧重点 ··· 18
      3.1.3 并列成分的使用 ·· 18
      3.1.4 经常使用复合修饰语 ·· 19
      3.1.5 广泛使用被动语态 ··· 19
      3.1.6 大量使用从句 ··· 20
      3.1.7 大量使用后置定语 ··· 21
      3.1.8 大量使用非限定动词结构 ··· 21
    3.2 专业英语阅读 ·· 22

    3.2.1 Linear Motion with Constant Acceleration(匀加速直线运动) …… 22
    3.2.2 Projectile Motion(抛体运动) …… 23
  3.3 专业英语常用表达法-3 技术设备的更新 …… 25
LESSON 4 …… 26
  4.1 物理学专业英语的修辞特点 …… 26
    4.1.1 多使用逻辑语法词表示各种关系 …… 26
    4.1.2 使用一些词语表示过程或顺序 …… 26
    4.1.3 下定义 …… 27
    4.1.4 分类 …… 27
  4.2 专业英语阅读 …… 28
    4.2.1 Circular Motion(圆周运动) …… 28
    4.2.2 Relative Motion(相对运动) …… 30
  4.3 专业英语常用表达法-4 组成 构成 成分 …… 32

Unit Two …… 34
LESSON 5 …… 34
  5.1 物理学专业英语中的比较 …… 34
    5.1.1 同等比较 …… 34
    5.1.2 差等比较 …… 35
    5.1.3 有额比较 …… 35
    5.1.4 递进比较 …… 36
    5.1.5 终极比较 …… 36
    5.1.6 选择性比较 …… 36
    5.1.7 表示 A≠B …… 37
  5.2 专业英语阅读 …… 37
    5.2.1 Newton's Laws of Motion(牛顿运动定律) …… 37
    5.2.2 Newton's First Law(牛顿第一定律) …… 37
    5.2.3 Newton's Second Law(牛顿第二定律) …… 38
    5.2.4 Newton's Third Law(牛顿第三定律) …… 38
    5.2.5 The Four Fundamental Forces(四种基本力) …… 39
  5.3 专业英语常用表达法-5 力学常用实验仪器 …… 40
LESSON 6 …… 41
  6.1 物理学专业英语中的举例和列举 …… 41
    6.1.1 举例 …… 41
    6.1.2 列举 …… 44
  6.2 专业英语阅读 …… 46
    6.2.1 Work and Energy(功和能) …… 46
    6.2.2 Work(功) …… 46
    6.2.3 Conservative Force and Potential Energy(保守力和势能) …… 47

6.3 专业英语常用表达法-6 原料 用途 功能或目的 …………………………………… 49
LESSON 7 ………………………………………………………………………………… 50
  7.1 物理学专业英语中的结果和结论 ………………………………………………… 50
    7.1.1 结果 ……………………………………………………………………………… 50
    7.1.2 结论 ……………………………………………………………………………… 51
  7.2 专业英语阅读 ……………………………………………………………………… 54
    7.2.1 Rigid Body(刚体) ……………………………………………………………… 54
    7.2.2 Law of Rotation of a Rigid Body about a Fixed Axis(刚体定轴转
          动定律) …………………………………………………………………………… 54
    7.2.3 Torque and Angular Momentum(力矩和角动量) …………………………… 55
  7.3 专业英语常用表达法-7 形状 …………………………………………………… 57
LESSON 8 ………………………………………………………………………………… 59
  8.1 物理学专业英语在口语体上的特点 ……………………………………………… 59
  8.2 专业英语阅读 ……………………………………………………………………… 61
    8.2.1 Oscillation(振动) ……………………………………………………………… 61
    8.2.2 Description of Simple Harmonic Motion(简谐运动的描述) ……………… 61
    8.2.3 Energy in Simple Harmonic Motion(简谐运动的能量) …………………… 62
    8.2.4 Damped Oscillations(阻尼振动) …………………………………………… 64
    8.2.5 Driven Oscillations and Resonance(受迫振动和共振) …………………… 64
  8.3 专业英语常用表达法-8 面积 体积 容量 …………………………………… 66

Unit Three ……………………………………………………………………………… 67
LESSON 9 ………………………………………………………………………………… 67
  9.1 物理学专业英语中的长句分析(一) ……………………………………………… 67
    9.1.1 长句结构的分析 ………………………………………………………………… 67
    9.1.2 简单句的分析 …………………………………………………………………… 68
    9.1.3 复合句的分析 …………………………………………………………………… 68
  9.2 专业英语阅读 ……………………………………………………………………… 70
    9.2.1 Thermal Equilibrium and Temperature(热平衡及温度) …………………… 70
    9.2.2 The Ideal-Gas Law(理想气体定律) ………………………………………… 71
  9.3 专业英语常用表达法-9 热学和波动常用实验仪器 …………………………… 73
LESSON 10 ……………………………………………………………………………… 74
  10.1 物理学专业英语中的主语从句 …………………………………………………… 74
    10.1.1 主语从句的引导词 …………………………………………………………… 74
    10.1.2 主语从句与形式主语 it ……………………………………………………… 76
    10.1.3 连词 that 的省略问题 ………………………………………………………… 77
    10.1.4 主语从句不可位于句首的五种情况 ………………………………………… 77
    10.1.5 What 与 that 在引导主语从句时的区别 …………………………………… 77
  10.2 专业英语阅读 ……………………………………………………………………… 77
    10.2.1 Heat and the First Law of Thermodynamics(热及热力学

　　　　　第一定律) ··· 77
　　　10.2.2　Kinds of Thermodynamic Processes(热力学过程的种类) ········ 79
　10.3　专业英语常用表达法-10　精度 ··· 81
LESSON 11 ··· 82
　11.1　物理学专业英语中的宾语从句 ··· 82
　　　11.1.1　宾语从句的引导词 ·· 82
　　　11.1.2　宾语从句与形式宾语 it ··· 84
　　　11.1.3　连词 that 的省略问题 ·· 84
　　　11.1.4　宾语从句与否定转移 ·· 85
　　　11.1.5　不能省略 that 的宾语从句 ······································· 85
　　　11.1.6　后边不能直接跟 that 从句的动词 ······························· 86
　　　11.1.7　不可用 that 从句作直接宾语的动词 ····························· 86
　11.2　专业英语阅读 ··· 86
　　　11.2.1　The Second Law of Thermodynamics(热力学第二定律) ········ 86
　　　11.2.2　Equivalence of the Kelvin and Clausius Statements(开尔文
　　　　　　表述与克劳修斯表述的等价性) ·································· 87
　　　11.2.3　Irreversibility and Disorder(不可逆性与无序性) ············· 88
　11.3　专业英语常用表达法-11　质量　标准 ··································· 89
LESSON 12 ··· 90
　12.1　物理学专业英语中的表语从句和同位语从句 ··························· 90
　　　12.1.1　表语从句 ··· 90
　　　12.1.2　同位语从句 ··· 92
　12.2　专业英语阅读 ··· 94
　　　12.2.1　Waves(波动) ·· 94
　　　12.2.2　Traveling Waves(行波) ·· 95
　12.3　专业英语常用表达法-12　性能和特点 ··································· 97

Unit Four ··· 99
LESSON 13 ··· 99
　13.1　物理学专业英语中的副词性从句 ··· 99
　　　13.1.1　时间状语从句 ·· 99
　　　13.1.2　地点状语从句 ·· 100
　　　13.1.3　原因状语从句 ·· 100
　　　13.1.4　目的状语从句 ·· 101
　　　13.1.5　结果状语从句 ·· 101
　　　13.1.6　条件状语从句 ·· 101
　　　13.1.7　让步状语从句 ·· 101
　　　13.1.8　比较状语从句 ·· 102
　　　13.1.9　方式状语从句 ·· 102

13.2　专业英语阅读 102
　　　　13.2.1　Introduction to Electromagnetics(电磁学引言) 102
　　　　13.2.2　Charge(电荷) 103
　　　　13.2.3　Coulomb's Law(库仑定律) 104
　　13.3　专业英语常用表达法-13　电磁学常用实验仪器1 105
LESSON 14 108
　　14.1　物理学专业英语中的形容词性从句 108
　　　　14.1.1　限制性定语从句 108
　　　　14.1.2　非限制性定语从句 110
　　14.2　专业英语阅读 112
　　　　14.2.1　Gauss's Law(高斯定理) 112
　　　　14.2.2　Conductors in Electrostatic Equilibrium(导体的静电平衡) 112
　　　　14.2.3　Capacitance and Capacitors(电容和电容器) 112
　　　　14.2.4　Dielectrics and Polarization(电介质与极化) 113
　　14.3　专业英语常用表达法-14　图的表示法 116
LESSON 15 118
　　15.1　物理学专业英语中的非谓语动词(一)动词不定式和动名词 118
　　　　15.1.1　动词不定式 118
　　　　15.1.2　动名词 121
　　15.2　专业英语阅读 123
　　　　15.2.1　Nature of Magnetic Force(磁力的本质) 123
　　　　15.2.2　The Biot-Savart Law(毕奥-萨伐尔定律) 123
　　　　15.2.3　*B* due to a Current in a Solenoid(通电螺线管的磁场) 124
　　　　15.2.4　Gauss's Law for Magnetism(磁场的高斯定理) 125
　　15.3　专业英语常用表达法-15　加减乘除　乘方　开方 126
LESSON 16 127
　　16.1　物理学专业英语中的非谓语动词(二)分词 127
　　16.2　专业英语阅读 131
　　　　16.2.1　Ampere's Circuital Law(安培环路定理) 131
　　　　16.2.2　Magnetic Field due to Varying Electric Field(与变化的电场相联系的磁场) 132
　　　　16.2.3　Effect on Magnetic Field Caused by Magnetic Media(磁介质对磁场的影响) 133
　　　　16.2.4　Ferromagnetic Materials(铁磁质) 134
　　16.3　专业英语常用表达法-16　用途　功能　目的 135

Unit Five 137
　　LESSON 17 137
　　　　17.1　物理学专业英语中的长句分析(二) 137

17.2 专业英语阅读 ·· 142
    17.2.1 Faraday's Law of Electromagnetic Induction(法拉第电磁感应定律) ·· 142
    17.2.2 Lenz's Law(楞次定律) ·· 144
17.3 专业英语常用表达法-17 电磁学常用实验仪器 2 ·· 145

LESSON 18 ·· 146
18.1 物理学专业英语文章的阅读与信息获得 ·· 146
    18.1.1 浏览 ·· 147
    18.1.2 略读 ·· 147
    18.1.3 研读 ·· 148
18.2 专业英语阅读 ·· 150
    18.2.1 Induced emf and Induced Electric Field(感生电动势和感生电场) ·· 150
    18.2.2 Eddy Currents(涡流) ·· 151
    18.2.3 Mutual Induction(互感现象) ··· 152
    18.2.4 Self-Induction(自感现象) ··· 153
18.3 专业英语常用表达法-18 物理学中常用数学运算 ·· 155

LESSON 19 ·· 156
19.1 物理学专业英语阅读能力的培养 ·· 156
19.2 专业英语阅读 ·· 160
    19.2.1 Maxwell's Equations(麦克斯韦方程组) ································· 160
    19.2.2 Electromagnetic Waves(电磁波) ·· 161
19.3 专业英语常用表达法-19 数字的增加与倍数 ·· 163

LESSON 20 ·· 165
20.1 物理学专业英语阅读时需要注意的问题 ·· 165
20.2 专业英语阅读：Introduction to Antennas(天线导言) ································ 169
20.3 专业英语常用表达法-20 分数 百分数 减少 ·· 172

Unit Six ·· 174
LESSON 21 ·· 174
21.1 物理学专业英语的翻译 ·· 174
    21.1.1 翻译的总体原则 ·· 174
    21.1.2 物理学专业术语的翻译 ·· 174
21.2 专业英语阅读 ·· 178
    21.2.1 The Nature of Light(光的本性) ··· 178
    21.2.2 The Wave-Particle Duality(波粒二象性) ······························ 180
21.3 专业英语常用表达-21 光学常用实验仪器 ·· 181

LESSON 22 182
22.1 物理学专业英语中名词化结构的翻译 182
22.1.1 动词名词化 182
22.1.2 形容词名词化 185
22.2 专业英语阅读 185
22.2.1 Reflection and Refraction(反射与折射) 185
22.2.2 Interference of Light Waves(光波的干涉) 187
22.3 专业英语常用表达-22 极值 约略数 189

LESSON 23 191
23.1 物理学专业英语中独立主格结构和分隔结构的翻译 191
23.1.1 独立主格结构的翻译 191
23.1.2 分隔结构的翻译 193
23.2 专业英语阅读:Bohr's Model(玻尔模型) 196
23.3 专业英语常用表达-23 距离 间隔 199

LESSON 24 201
24.1 物理学专业英语中长句的翻译 201
24.1.1 长句翻译的基本方法 201
24.1.2 长句的翻译技巧 203
24.2 专业英语阅读:The Elementary Particles(基本粒子) 205
24.3 专业英语常用表达-24 位置 方位 208

Unit Seven 211
LESSON 25 211
25.1 物理学专业英语写作的一般知识 211
25.2 专业英语阅读:Waves and Particles(波与粒子) 213
25.3 专业英语常用表达-25 近代物理及综合设计实验仪器 215

LESSON 26 216
26.1 物理学专业英语的段落写作 216
26.1.1 主题句 216
26.1.2 段落的展开 217
26.1.3 段落展开的常用方法 219
26.2 专业英语阅读 224
26.2.1 The Uncertainty Principle(测不准原理) 224
26.2.2 Probability Waves(概率波) 225
26.3 专业英语常用表达-26 一致 符合 227

LESSON 27 228
27.1 物理学专业英语中描写文和说明文的写作 228

目 录

    27.1.1 描写文的英语写作 ………………………………………………… 228
    27.1.2 说明文的英语写作 ………………………………………………… 229
  27.2 专业英语阅读 ……………………………………………………………… 230
    27.2.1 Bose-Einstein Statistics(玻色-爱因斯坦统计) …………………… 230
    27.2.2 Fermi-Dirac Statistics(费米-狄拉克统计) ……………………… 232
  27.3 专业英语常用表达-27 状态 状况 …………………………………… 233
 LESSON 28 ……………………………………………………………………………… 235
  28.1 物理学专业科研论文的英语写作 ………………………………………… 235
    28.1.1 科研论文的组成部分 …………………………………………… 235
    28.1.2 英文标题的撰写方法 …………………………………………… 235
    28.1.3 作者及所属单位英译 …………………………………………… 236
    28.1.4 摘要 ……………………………………………………………… 237
    28.1.5 关键词 …………………………………………………………… 237
    28.1.6 引言 ……………………………………………………………… 237
    28.1.7 正文 ……………………………………………………………… 239
    28.1.8 结论段 …………………………………………………………… 239
    28.1.9 致谢 ……………………………………………………………… 240
    28.1.10 参考文献 ………………………………………………………… 241
  28.2 专业英语阅读：Relativity(相对论) ……………………………………… 242
  28.3 专业英语常用表达-28 原因 理由 …………………………………… 246

Unit Eight ……………………………………………………………………………… 248
 LESSON 29 ……………………………………………………………………………… 248
  29.1 物理学专业科研论文中摘要的英语写作 ………………………………… 248
    29.1.1 英文摘要 ………………………………………………………… 248
    29.1.2 摘要的基本结构和内容 ………………………………………… 249
    29.1.3 英文摘要写作的常用表达方法 ………………………………… 252
    29.1.4 英文摘要写作中的常用句型 …………………………………… 254
  29.2 专业英语阅读：Lasers(激光) …………………………………………… 256
  29.3 专业英语常用表达-29 与物理学相关的词汇 ………………………… 259
 LESSON 30 ……………………………………………………………………………… 259
  30.1 物理学专业英语中报告的写作 …………………………………………… 259
    30.1.1 报告的格式 ……………………………………………………… 260
    30.1.2 报告写作的基本原则 …………………………………………… 262
  30.2 专业英语阅读：Spectroscopy(光谱学) ………………………………… 263
  30.3 专业英语常用表达-30 导致 产生 …………………………………… 265
 LESSON 31 ……………………………………………………………………………… 267
  31.1 物理学专业英语中报告写作的实例 ……………………………………… 267

		31.1.1 实验报告的写法	267
		31.1.2 观察(考察)报告的写法	270
		31.1.3 工作报告的写法	271
	31.2	专业英语阅读：Superconductivity(超导电性)	271
	31.3	专业英语常用表达-31　概括　结论	274
LESSON 32			275
	32.1	物理学专业英语中科技报告的写作	275
	32.2	专业英语阅读	285
		32.2.1 The Crystal Lattice(晶格)	285
		32.2.2 Lattice Vibrations(晶格振动)	286
		32.2.3 Band Theory of Solids(固体的能带论)	287
	32.3	专业英语常用表达-32　各种实验与试验	289

Unit Nine　　292

LESSON 33			292
	33.1	物理学国际学术会议用英语简介	292
	33.2	专业英语阅读：Errors of Observation(测量数据的误差)	302
	33.3	专业英语常用表达-33　与实验相关的词汇	306
LESSON 34			307
	34.1	物理学国际学术会议的信件交流英语	307
	34.2	专业英语阅读：Experiment of Polarization of Light(光的偏振实验)	313
	34.3	专业英语常用表达-34　观点　看法	317
LESSON 35			320
	35.1	物理学国际学术会议口头报告	320
		35.1.1 口头报告的准备(Preparation for Oral Presentation)	320
		35.1.2 开始报告(Beginning a Presentation)	322
		35.1.3 展开报告内容(Developing a Presentation)	323
		35.1.4 结束报告(Ending a Presentation)	329
		35.1.5 注意事项(Points for Attention)	330
	35.2	专业英语阅读：Measuring the Coefficient of Linear Expansion for Copper, Steel and Aluminum(铜、钢和铝的线性膨胀系数测量)	330
	35.3	专业英语常用表达-35　学术会议常用语	334
LESSON 36			335
	36.1	物理学国际学术会议的问答讨论环节口语	335
	36.2	专业英语阅读：Franck-Hertz Experiment(夫兰克-赫兹实验)	339
	36.3	专业英语常用表达法-36　双语教学课堂用语	344

翻译练习　　347

目录

Appendixes ··· 355
    附录1　物理专业所开设的课程名称汉英对照 ····················· 355
    附录2　教学教务管理常用词汇 ··· 357
    附录3　物理学一、二级学科名称英文词汇 ·························· 359
    附录4　数学符号及英语表达 ·· 359
    附录5　常用物理基本常量 ··· 364
    附录6　常用汉英物理学专业词汇表 ··································· 365
    附录7　常用英汉物理学专业词汇表 ··································· 373

参考文献 ··· 403

Unit One

LESSON 1

1.1 物理学专业英语的特点

1.1.1 物理学专业英语简介

从体裁上讲，英语主要有文学文体、政论文体、应用文体和科技文体四大类，物理学专业英语属于科技英语文体的一部分。

物理学专业英语把英语和物理学专业知识紧密结合起来，用专业语言来说明客观存在的事物或事实。专业英语的叙述要求客观、真实、明确、简洁，并大量使用科学术语和符号，也经常借用图表和插图来说明专业内容。这就决定了专业英语的文体风格：概念准确、表达正式、陈述客观、逻辑性强、专业性强、严谨周密、行文简练、重点突出、句式严整、少有变化、常用前置性陈述，即在句中将主要信息尽量前置，通过主语传递主要信息。

专业英语的语言特点表现在词汇、句法和修辞三个方面。

1.1.2 物理学专业英语的词汇特点

1. 纯科技词汇

所谓纯科技词汇是指那些只用于某个专业或学科的专门词汇或术语，如 hydroxide(氢氧化物)、diode(二极管)、isotope(同位素)等。随着物理学及其相关领域的发展，新学科、新分支的产生，这样的词汇层出不穷，其词义精确而狭窄，针对性极强。除少数术语是新造的词外，绝大多数术语都是在原有旧词的基础上，靠借用、加前后缀或合成等手段构成，其中尤以合成这种手段最为常见。专业英语中很多新术语都是用这几种手段组成的。阅读专业性强的文献，就要首先了解该领域的专门词汇和术语。

2. 通用科技词汇

通用科技词汇即不同专业都要经常使用的那些词汇，数量较大，如表示时间、空间、方位、方向、尺寸、形状、面积、体积等方面的词汇以及一批要求固定介词的形容词和动词。如 accumulate, accuracy, capital, cell, charge, current, load, intense, motion, operation, potential, pressure, react, reflection, resistance, revolution, tendency 等词汇均属于多门学科使用的半专业词汇。这类词的使用范围比纯科技词汇广、出现频率高，但在不同的专业里有较为稳定的词义。如 power 一词在物理学中的词义为"电"、"电力"、"动力"、"电源"、"功率"等，在数学中的词义为"乘方"、"功效"、"幂"等。

3. 派生词汇

派生词指在已有的词汇上加前、后缀,或以词根生成,或以构词成分形成的新词。这种词汇在物理学专业文献中占有很大的比重。例如,由前缀 hydro-,hyper-,hypo-和 inter-构成的词条在物理学专业英语中就非常多;以表示学科的后缀-logy,-ics 和表示行为、性质、状态等的后缀-tion,-sion,-ance,-ence,-ment 构成的词汇在专业英语文献中俯拾皆是。

前缀的特点:加前缀构成的新词只改变词义,不改变词类。

intergalactic	银河间的	inter＋galactic
submicroscopic	亚微观的	sub＋microscopic

另外,前缀有固定的意义。如:

multi-表示"多"　　　multimedia 多媒体
hyper-表示"超级"　　hyperelastic 超弹性的

后缀的特点:加后缀构成的新词可能改变也可能不改变词义,但一定改变词类。

infinity　无穷远(名词)＝infinite＋y(infinite 是形容词)
quantization　量子化(名词)＝quantize＋ation(quantize 是动词)

有些词加后缀后,语音或拼写可能发生变化。

electrification＝electrify＋cation
accelerator＝accelerate＋or

4. 复合词汇

所谓复合词,就是指两个或两个以上的词组合在一起构建的新词。一般来说,复合词分为复合名词、复合动词、复合形容词、复合形容动词和复合副词。有些词已经在词义上发生了变化,从意思上看不出复合的痕迹,但是从词形上仍然能够看出最初复合的痕迹。复合词常以连字符"-"连接两单词构成,或采用短语构成,但有的则去掉连字符形成一个单一的词。

以下是物理学中的一些加连字符复合词的例子:

by-pass 旁路,cathode-ray tube 阴极射线管,change-over switch 换向开关,current-carrying conductor 载流导体,digital-to-analogue conversion 数模转换,fine-adjustment 微调、细调,flat-bottomed flask 平底烧瓶,fly-back 回扫,full-wave rectifier 全波整流器,half-wave rectification 半波整流,infra-red ray 红外线,inverse-square law 平方反比定律,ion-pair 离子偶、离子对,push-button switch 按钮开关

值得一提的是,专业英语中-proof 使用的比较多,它是一个构词成分,意思是"防……的,能抗……的","完全地或成功地抵制……的;不能穿透……的"。这个构词成分能构成许多有用的单词。例如:

a water-proof material	防水材料
a bullet-proof glass	防弹玻璃
a sound-proof room	隔音室
a bomb-proof shelter	防空洞
a fire-proof material	防火材料,耐火材料
a fail-proof method	万无一失的方法
a fool-proof instrument	操作十分简便的仪器

此外还有 acid-proof 抗酸的、耐酸的,corrosion-proof 抗腐蚀的、防腐蚀的,mar-proof 耐磨损的,ozone-proof 耐臭氧的等。

以下是一些无连字符复合词的例子:

joulemeter 焦耳计,kilowatt 千瓦特、千瓦,loudspeaker 扬声器,output 输出,ratemeter 率计、率表,supersaturation 过饱和

5. 混成词

混成词指由最少两个词语或词语的一部分结合而成的词语,该新词语的意义和读音集组成部分而成。一般而言,混成词是新词,诸如 motel 汽车旅馆(motor+hotel)、smog 烟雾(smoke+fog)、brunch 早午餐(breakfast+lunch)和 cyborg 生化人(普遍代指 cybernetic organism 自动化生物)等混成词。

以下是一些物理学中混成词的例子:

potentiometer(potential+meter)	分压器,电位器,电势差计,电位差计
radioisotope(radioactive+isotope)	放射性同位素
radionuclide(radioactive+nuclide)	放射性核素
radiotherapy(radioactive+therapy)	放射疗法
sonometer(sonic+meter)	弦音计
spectrometer(spectrum+meter)	光谱仪、分光计
thermocouple(thermal+couple)	温差电偶、热电偶
telesat(telecommunication+satellite)	通信卫星

6. 缩略词

缩略词的构成有两种:将英语中较长的单词取其首部或者主干构成与原来单词同义的短单词,称为压缩或省略;将组成词汇的短语的各个单词的首字母拼接为一个字符串,称为缩写。

1) 压缩或省略

一些单词比较长,难于记忆和拼写,通过压缩或省略的方法把它们压缩成一个短小的单词,或者仅仅取其头部,或仅取关键音节。

maths(mathematics)数学,lab(laboratory)实验室,plane(airplane)飞机,ft(foot/feet)英尺,cpd(compound)化合物

2) 缩写

利用词的第一个字母代表一个词构成的缩略词,就叫做首字母缩略词。常见的有以下三类。

① 通常情况下以小写字母出现,并且已经作为常规词汇。

m(metre)公尺,cm(centimeter)厘米,g(gram)克,fm(frequency modulation)调频 scr(silicon-controlled rectifier)可控硅整流器,p.s.i.(pounds per square inch)磅每平方英寸,radar(radio detecting and ranging 无线电探测与定位)雷达,laser(light amplification by stimulated emission of radiation 受激发射光放大器)激光

② 以大写字母出现,有的具有主体发音音节,有的仅为字母缩写。

TV(television)电视,CD(compact disk)激光唱盘,CAD(computer-assisted design)计

算机辅助设计，IT(information technology)信息技术，IDD(international direct dial)国际直拨电话，PVC(polyvinyl chloride)聚氯乙烯，FRP(fiber glass reinforced plastic)玻璃钢，DNA(deoxyribonucleic acid)脱氧核糖核酸，F(fluorine)氟，U(uranium)铀，CATV(cable television)有线电视，CD-ROM(compact disk-read-only memory)光盘只读存储器(也就是光驱)，GHG(greenhouse gas)温室气体

③ 有的缩略词还可以和其他词连用，如：

E-mail (electric mail)电子邮件，H-bomb (hydrogen bomb)氢弹，CO_2(carbon dioxide)二氧化碳

7. 骈词

专业英语中有不少骈词，它们由同义词、近义词构成，两词前后顺序基本固定，中间由and连接，在语气、语调及语义方面有特殊的修辞效果。一般有以下三类：

1) 头韵类

如 effective and efficient, integral and indispensable, part and parcel, queries and questions 等。

It is clear that idealized model method provides an *effective and efficient* answer to a number of complex problems. 很明显，理想模型方法是解决许多复杂问题的一种快速高效的办法。

During the last twenty years, holography has become an *integral and indispensable* part of physics. 在最近二十年中，全息技术成为物理学不可或缺的部分。

Mechanics is *part and parcel* of physics. 力学是物理学的组成部分。

If there are *queries and questions* with laser, do not hesitate to contact us. 若对激光器有疑问，请立即和我们联系。

2) 尾韵类

如 first and most (foremost), wear and tear 等。

Calculus is the *first and most* common method of solving problems in physics. 微积分方法是最首要、最常用的解决物理问题的方法。

First and foremost, we should tackle the problem of energy sources. 首先，我们应该解决能源问题。

The *first and most* important step for learning university physics is to have a good command of calculus. 对大学物理学习来说，第一也是最重要的一步是学好微积分。

Regular maintenance of instruments reduces much needless *wear and tear*. 定期维护仪器可以大大减少不必要的磨损。

3) 无韵类

如 each and every, leaps and bounds, pure and simple, trial and error, ways and means 等。

This type of product manufacturing control ensures that consistent rare earth quality is achieved for *each and every* lot delivered to the labs. 这种产品制造控制方法，会保证发往实验室的每批稀土质量是稳定的。

Since the quantum was put forward, it has grown by *leaps and bounds* into a remarkably prosperous branch of physics. 自量子理论提出以来，它迅速发展为一个非常繁盛的物理学分支。

The operating error was due to carelessness *pure and simple*. 操作失误纯粹归因于粗心大意。

In general, the design procedure is not straightforward and will require *trial and error*. 一般来说，设计过程不是一帆风顺的，而需要反复的试验。

The object of studying thermodynamic processes was to work out *ways and means* of improvements of the efficiency of heat engines. 研究热力学过程的目的是为了找出改进热机效率的各种方法。

8. 专业词汇的隐喻

隐喻是把某种比喻意义从一个事物传给另一事物，即在两个本质不同的事物之间进行的暗含比较，是以相似和联想为基础的。

在物理领域，隐喻已经成为十分重要的形象思维手段和认知工具，词汇中充斥着大量的隐喻。原子结构理论的创立者丹麦物理学家 Henrik David Bohr（玻尔）把肉眼看不见的原子的内部结构想象成一个"太阳系"，称为 miniature solar system（微型太阳系），从大的宏观概念直至小的微观概念。与这种视微观世界为宏观世界的放大化隐喻相对应，专业词汇中也存在视宏观世界为微观世界的缩小化隐喻，如天文学家创造了 light-year（光年）这一术语作为计算星球之间距离的单位，用 crab nebula（蟹状云）来指称银河系中的某一强大射电源。当科学家发现了新的事物及其特点、规律时，他们在很多情况下不会任意杜撰或"发明"新的词汇来表示新概念，而是在原有词汇的基础上给新的概念和知识命名。这其中相当一部分是隐喻，即概念与概念之间的类比。

从已知到未知，从具体到抽象，由此及彼，相互类推，就会形成一条"隐喻链"。同一词语应用在不同学科中建构了一系列的科学概念名称，展现出隐喻思维的线索。例如从 wave（波）类推到 sound wave（声波），再到 light wave（光波）；到了电子时代，又有了 radio wave（无线电波），electromagnetic wave（电磁波），microwave（微波），ultrasonic wave（超声波）以及 long/medium/short wave（长/中/短波），及其到了量子时代的 matter wave（物质波）等。这些概念的建构一脉相承，都建立在同一喻体之上。

1.2 专业英语阅读

1.2.1 Introduction（引言）

We begin our study of the physical universe by examining objects in motion. The study of motion, whose measurement, more than 400 years ago gave birth to physics, is called kinematics.

Much of our understanding of nature comes from observing the motion of objects. In this chapter we will develop a description for the motion of a single point as it moves through space. Although a point is a geometrical concept quite different from everyday objects such as footballs and automobiles, we shall see that the actual motion of many objects is most easily described as the motion of a single point (the "center of mass"), plus the rotation of the object about that point. Postponing a discussion of rotation, let us begin here with a description of a single point as it moves through space.

1.2.2 Space and Time(时间与空间)

Kinematics is concerned with two basic questions, "Where?" and "When?". Though the questions are simple, the answers are potentially quite complicated if we inquire about phenomena outside our ordinary daily experiences. For example, the physics of very high speeds, or of events involving intergalactic distances or submicroscopic dimensions, is quite different from our common-sense ideas. We will discuss these interesting subjects in later chapters. For the present we shall adopt the space and time of Newton—those concepts we gradually developed as a result of our everyday experiences.

Space is assumed to be continuously uniform and isotropic. These two terms mean that space has no "graininess" and that whatever its properties may be, they are independent of any particular direction or location. In the words of Isaac Newton, "Absolute space, in its own nature, without relation to anything external, remains always similar and unmovable." Every object in the universe exists at a particular location in space, and an object may change its location by moving through space as time goes on. We specify the location of a particular point in space by its relation to a frame of reference.

Time, according to Newton, is also absolute in the sense that it "flows on" at a uniform rate. We cannot speed it up or slow it down in any way, in Newton's words, "Absolute, true, and mathematical time, of itself, and from its own nature, flows equably without relation to anything external, and by another name is called duration." Time is assumed to be continuous and ever advancing, as might be indicated by a clock.

Space and time are wholly independent of each other, though it is recognized that all physical objects must exist simultaneously in both space and time.

Remarkably, many of these traditional ideas turn out to be naive and inconsistent with experimental evidence. The world is just different from the picture we form from our common-sense, intuitive ideas. Space and time, by themselves, are concepts that are difficult (or perhaps impossible) to define in terms of anything simpler. However, we can measure space and time in unambiguous ways. We define certain operations by which we obtain numerical measurements of these quantities using rulers and clocks, based upon standard units of space and time.

For many years, our standard of time was based on astronomical observations of the earth's rotation. Because of the variations in the earth's rotation, in 1967 the 13th General Conference on Weights and Measures, attended by 38 nations, adopted an atomic standard for time.

Similarly, our former standard of length was the distance between two marks on platinum-iridium bar kept at Sevres, France. In 1960, the fundamental length standard was redefined in terms of the wavelength of light emitted during a transition between two atomic energy levels.

The standard units of time and length may be described as follows：

An interval of time. The fundamental unit is the **second**（s），which by international agreement is defined as the duration of 9 192 631 770 periods of radiation corresponding to the transition between the two lowest energy levels in the atomic isotope cesium 133.

An interval of length. The fundamental unit is the **meter**（m），which is defined independently of the time interval. Before 1983，by international agreement the meter was defined as exactly 1 650 763.73 wavelengths of the orange light emitted from the isotope krypton 86. In November 1983，the length standard was defined as the distance that light travels in a vacuum in 1/299 792 458 second.

Certain older units of length are still occasionally used.

$$1 \text{ angstrom}(\text{Å}) = 10^{-10} \text{ m} \quad 1 \text{ micron}(\mu \text{ or } \mu\text{m}) = 10^{-6} \text{ m}$$

Glossary

universe	宇宙	object	物体
measurement	测量	kinematics	运动学
motion of objects	物体的运动	center of mass	质心
space and time	时空	phenomena	现象
intergalactic	银河间的	submicroscopic	亚微观的
dimension	尺度	subject	研究的对象
uniform	均匀的	isotropic	各向同性的
continuously	连续地	graininess	颗粒性
direction	方向	location	位置
specify	规定	frame of reference	参考系
simultaneously	同时地	inconsistent with	与……不一致
define/definition	定义	meridian	子午线
general conference on weights and measures	国际计量大会	atomic standard	原子标准
former standard of length	长度原标准	platinum-iridium	铂铱合金
transition	跃迁	atomic energy level	原子能级
isotope cesium	铯同位素	krypton	氪
vacuum	真空	angstrom	埃

1.3 专业英语常用表达法-1 常用工具

toolbox	工具箱	nail hammer	羊角锤、拔钉锤
handsaw	手锯	sledge hammer	大锤、双手锤
ball-pane hammer	球头锤	pick	镐
ball hammer	圆头锤	double-bladed axe	双刃斧
axe hammer	斧锤	cutting nippers	剪钳、老虎钳

nipper pliers　尖嘴钳,剪丝钳
crowbar　铁锹、撬杠
nail　铁钉
coping saw　弓形锯
chisel　凿子
hand plane　刨子
screw　螺丝钉
screwdriver　螺丝刀
gimlet　手钻
scoop　铲子
triangle　三角板
protractor　量角器
curved ruler　曲尺
adjustable triangle　可调节三角板
T-square　丁字尺
angle square　角尺
drafting machine　平移角尺
dividers　两脚规

tape measure　卷尺
scissors　剪刀
wrench,spanner　扳手
adjustable spanner　活动扳手
double offset ring spanner　梅花扳手
inner hexagon spanner　内六角扳手
pipe spanner　管子扳手
connection cover cutting pliers　剥线剪钳
wire-cutting pliers　克丝钳
insulated pliers　绝缘钳
metal wire pliers　剪线钳
electric drill　电钻
hollow drill　空心钻
percussion drill　冲击钻
electric (solding) iron　电烙铁
stopwatch　秒表、跑表、停表

LESSON 2

2.1　物理学专业英语的名词化结构

2.1.1　名词化

　　物理学专业英语的两个显著特点就是广泛使用名词化结构和大量使用被动语态。名词化是指词性作用的名词性转化,比如起名词作用的非谓语动词和与动词同根或同形的名词,也包括一些形容词来源的名词。这些词可以起到名词的作用,也可以表达谓语动词或形容词所表达的内容,常伴有修饰成分或附加成分,可构成短语。名词化结构指的是大量使用名词和名词词组,即在其他功能和题材的文章里用动词、形容词等词类充当某种语法成分,而在专业英语里往往会转化为由名词充当这种语法成分。

　　专业英语的"科学性"和"说理性"是名词化大量存在的理据。因为这种结构既可减少句子或分句的出现,又能包容大量的信息,并能反映科学内容的严肃性和客观性。下面就是一个名词化的例子:

　　(1) We can assume a freely falling body moves in one dimension under constant acceleration if we neglect air resistance.

　　在专业英语中则通常说成

　　(2) The motion of a freely falling body can be assumed to be motion in one dimension under constant acceleration by negligence of air resistance.

在这组例子中,名词化发生在两个地方。首先例(1)中的谓语动词转化为(2)中的名词主语,其次,例(1)中的状语从句的谓语动词 neglect 转化为名词结构介词短语来充当状语。经过名词化处理的例(2)由含有两个主谓结构的复合句变成了只含一个主谓结构的简单句,从而使句子的结构更加精练严谨,也由于使用抽象名词替代原来的人称代词做主语而使句子的语体更加正式。

2.1.2 名词化的分类

动词的名词化具有四种形式:

1) 动作名词

在四种形式中,动作名词的名词性最强,而动词性最弱。动作名词用于一般性地叙述一个事实或概念,指出动作和技术的特点,而不强调动作本身的进行过程和时间。

Analysis of projectile motion is surprisingly simple if the following three assumptions are made.

2) 动词性名词

动词性名词的名词性稍弱一些,而动词性略强。用于把概念和动作过程联系起来的描述,时间性也不强。

The *analyzing* of projectile motion is surprisingly simple if the following three assumptions are made.

3) 动名词

动名词的动词性更强一些。在强调动作过程,概括地叙述一般行为,而不是特定行为,并且时间性也不强时,就可以使用动名词。

Analyzing projectile motion is surprisingly simple if the following three assumptions are made.

4) 动词不定式

动词不定式的名词性最弱,动词性最强。通常用动词不定式表达某一次有时间性的特定动作或过程。

Projectile motion of the ball needs *to be analyzed* now if the following three assumptions are made.

2.1.3 名词化结构的构成

名词化结构的应用使得整个句子的结构便于写作修辞,也使得词句负载信息的容量增加。经常使用的名词化结构有:

1) 名词(行为名词)+介词+名词

在此结构中,若"介词+名词"构成的介词短语在逻辑上是行为名词的动作对象或动作的发出者,行为名词的含义在深层中转换或变异,使原来的名词变为动词,构成了动宾或主谓的关系。

The acceleration of the car is due to the force applied on it. 车的加速是由于外力的作用。

此句的 The acceleration of the car=The car accelerates.

In the case of all freely falling bodies, gravity is essential in *the change of the velocity*. 所有做自由落体运动的物体,速度的改变都离不开重力。

其中 the change of the velocity＝the velocity changes.

2) 介词＋名词(行为名词)

在此结构中,行为名词的动作意义相对完整,与句中的其他部分之间存在着一定的逻辑关系,能起到时间状语、原因状语、条件状语和让步状语等作用。

A rigid body can change its position *by translation or rotation*. 刚体位置的改变可以通过平移或转动实现。

3) 谓语动词＋行为名词(＋介词短语)

此结构可以将宾语(介词宾语)转换成谓语。

Kepler's laws have *found application for* the exploration of the planets. 开普勒定律已经被用来探索行星。

此句可改变为 People have applied Kepler's laws to explore the planets.

此结构中谓语动词 find 含义空泛,只起语法作用,翻译时可以不译。类似的动词有: do, keep, have, make, take, pay, show, perform, offer 等。又如:

Friction *offers resistance to* the movement of the block. 摩擦力阻碍木块的运动。

句中 offer 几乎不表示什么意义,只起连接作用。此句可以改为:Friction resists the movement of the block.

4) 与动词构成固定搭配

名词化结构与动词构成固定搭配的常用形式为:动词＋动词名词化结构＋介词名词化结构。这种搭配大量地以一个动词短语的形式出现,约定俗成。例如:

make use of 利用,do research for 研究,lay emphasis on 强调,pay attention to 注意,等等。

5) 行为名词＋短语/从句

在此结构中行为名词可以译成动词,与后面的成分一起构成汉语的动宾结构。

I have a *doubt* whether the instrument works well. 我怀疑这仪器是否运行良好。

此句可以改换成 I doubt whether the instrument works well or not.

6) 名词＋名词(行为名词)

在此结构中,名词在表层结构上是前置定语,但在翻译过程中,其深层结构的内在含义可以译成动宾词组,行为名词转换成谓语。如:

heat conduction 导热,rust prevention 防锈,performance examination 性能检验

2.1.4 名词化的功能

名词化具有可以使语篇简洁、客观、量化、正式、严密等多种功能。

1) 简洁功能

简洁明了是物理学专业英语的重要特点之一,要求以精练的语言传达大量的信息,而名词化的使用可以使句子省去一些不必要的词语,使得结构紧凑,具有较强的可读性。例如:

Kepler's laws had been developed. For this reason, Newton could discover his laws of motion.

以上两句可用名词化结构分别表达为 the development of Kepler's laws 和 for Newton to discover his laws of motion。

若再把这两个名词化结构按句法要求组织起来，则是：

The development of Kepler's laws makes it possible for Newton to discover his laws of motion.

所以，利用名词化结构，不仅可把两个句子合二为一，使语言更简洁、更精练，而且可把更多的信息结构融合成逻辑关系明确的整体。

2）客观功能

英语中用动词体现过程，动词须有参与者，有时还须有补语。而名词化则使本来由动词体现的过程转而由名词体现，这个过程变成另一过程的参与者，与旧过程相关的参与者就可以省略掉，从而使表达显得客观、真实，避免主观因素和主观色彩。

If we substitute some rolling friction for sliding friction, we can considerably reduce the friction.

改用名词化结构后可以去掉句子的主语 we，提高了客观的程度。

The substitution of some rolling friction for sliding friction results in a very considerable reduction in friction.

3）量化功能

专业英语有时需要使用表示数量的词来表示某人做了多少事情或某物占有多少分量等，但是动词和形容词是不能被量化的，这时名词化就成了可采取的有效手段。例如：

Last year 17 major changes and improvements were made toward making the lab even more perfect.

这个句子使用了数字加动词 change 和 improve 的名词化形式，使表达准确、严谨。如果采用 Last year we changed 17 major things and improved the lab even more perfect. 则显得不够严谨，数量的概念不是很强。

4）正式功能

专业英语要求使用较为正式的语言，适当使用一些名词化结构，可以增加语篇的正式程度。

The engineers are confident about the motion of the "Shenzhou" spaceship from the very beginning.

这个句子中，使用动词 move 的名词化形式 motion，使整个句子显得很正式。如果改成 The engineers are confident how the "Shenzhou" spaceship moves…则正式程度大为降低。

5）严密功能

由于名词化结构中大量使用抽象名词，因此可以借助于抽象思维的逻辑性和概念化使科技文章的表达更确切，更严密。此外，在使用上，句子信息结构最复杂、最重要的部分往往是名词化结构。

We begin our *study of* the physical universe by examining objects *in motion*. The *study of* motion, whose measurement, more than 400 years ago *gave birth to* physics, is called kinematics. Much of our *understanding of* nature comes from observing *the motion of* objects.

2.2 专业英语阅读

2.2.1 Vectors(矢量)

Many quantities in physics have magnitude and direction. **Vectors** are quantities with magnitude and direction. Examples include velocity, acceleration, momentum, and force. Quantities with magnitude but no associated direction—for example, distance and speed—are called **scalars**.

A vector is represented graphically by an arrow drawn in the same direction as that of the vector, and with a length that is proportional to the magnitude of the vector. When the magnitude of a vector is given, its unit must also be given.

Two vectors are defined to be equal if they have the same magnitude and the same direction. Graphically, this means that they have the same length and are parallel to each other. A consequence of the definition is that moving a vector so that it remains parallel to itself does not change it. Vectors do not depend on the coordinate system used to represent them (except for position vectors, which are introduced later).

2.2.2 Properties of Vectors(矢量的性质)

In comparing vectors and performing other mathematical operations such as addition and subtraction, we may translate vectors anywhere in the coordinate space for convenience. We must be careful, however, to preserve their magnitudes and directions with respect to the axes.

Vector Addition(矢量加法)

Two vectors are added graphically by placing the tail of one, B, at the head of the other, A(Fig. 2-1). The resultant (or net) vector, $C=A+B$, extends from the tail of A to the head of B. This is the so-called **head-to-tail method**.

An equivalent way of adding vectors, called the **parallelogram method**, is to move B so that it is tail-to-tail with A. The diagonal of the parallelogram formed by A and B then equals the resultant vector C, as shown in Fig. 2-2.

Fig. 2-1 Head-to-tail method of vector addition   Fig. 2-2 Parallelogram method of vector addition

The vectors have the mathematical property of "obeying the **commutative law** in addition".

$$A + B = B + A \tag{2-1}$$

Vector Subtraction（矢量减法）

We subtract vector **B** from vector **A** by adding $-$**B** to **A**. The result is shown in Fig. 2-3. Note that vector addition or subtraction can be done only when vectors are in the same unit.

Scalar Product (Dot Product)（标积/点积）

The scalar product of any two vectors is defined as a scalar quantity equal to the product of the magnitudes of the two vectors **A** and **B** and the cosine of the angle ϕ that is included between the directions of **A** and **B**.

That is, the scalar product (or dot product) of **A** and **B** is defined by the relation

$$\mathbf{A} \cdot \mathbf{B} = AB\cos\phi \qquad (2\text{-}2)$$

where ϕ is the angle between **A** and **B** as in Fig. 2-4. A is the magnitude of **A**, and B is the magnitude of **B**, Note that **A** and **B** need not have the same unit.

Fig. 2-3　Vector subtraction

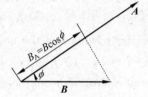

Fig. 2-4

Cross Product (Vector Product)（叉积/矢积）

The cross product of two vectors **A** and **B** is defined to be a vector $\mathbf{C} = \mathbf{A} \times \mathbf{B}$ whose magnitude equals the area of the parallelogram formed by the two vectors, as in Fig. 2-5 (a). The vector **C** is perpendicular to the plane containing **A** and **B** in the direction given by the right-hand rule, that is, as your right-hand fingers curl from the direction of **A** toward the direction of **B**, the direction of $\mathbf{A} \times \mathbf{B}$ is given by your thumb (Fig. 2-5(b)). If ϕ is the angle between the two vectors and **n** is the unit vector that is perpendicular to each in the direction of **C**, the cross product of **A** and **B** is

$$\mathbf{C} = \mathbf{A} \times \mathbf{B} = (AB\sin\phi)\mathbf{n} \qquad (2\text{-}3)$$

Fig. 2-5

If **A** and **B** are parallel, $\mathbf{A} \times \mathbf{B}$ is a zero vector.

2.2.3 Unit Vectors(单位矢量)

A **unit vector** is a *dimensionless* vector with unit magnitude. Unit vectors that point in the positive x, y, and z directions are convenient for expressing vectors in terms of their rectangular components. They are usually written as i, j and k, (or i, j, and k) respectively (Fig. 2-6). For example, the vector $A_x i$ has a magnitude $|A_x|$ and points in the positive x direction if A_x is positive (or the negative x direction if A_x is negative). A general vector A can be written as the sum of three vectors, each of which is parallel to a coordinate axis

Fig. 2-6

$$A = A_x i + A_y j + A_z k \qquad (2\text{-}4)$$

The addition of two vectors A and B can be written in terms of unit vectors as

$$\begin{aligned} A + B &= (A_x i + A_y j + A_z k) + (B_x i + B_y j + B_z k) \\ &= (A_x + B_x) i + (A_y + B_y) j + (A_z + B_z) k \end{aligned} \qquad (2\text{-}5)$$

The scalar products of the unit vectors are

$$i \cdot i = 1, \quad j \cdot j = 1, \quad k \cdot k = 1, \quad i \cdot j = 0, \quad j \cdot k = 0, \quad k \cdot i = 0 \qquad (2\text{-}6)$$

The unit vectors i, j, and k, which are mutually perpendicular, have cross products given by

$$i \times j = k, \quad j \times k = i, \quad \text{and} \quad k \times i = j \qquad (2\text{-}7)$$

$$i \times i = j \times j = k \times k = 0 \qquad (2\text{-}8)$$

Glossary

vector	矢量	magnitude	大小
velocity	速度	acceleration	加速度
momentum	动量	scalar	标量
proportional to	正比于	parallel	平行
position vector	位置矢量	coordinate system	坐标系
resultant/net vector	合矢量	addition	加法
subtraction	减法	equivalent	等价的
translate	平移	head-to-tail method	三角形法
parallelogram method	平行四边形法	diagonal	对角线
commutative law	交换律	scalar product	标积
dot product	点积	cross product	叉积
vector product	矢积	area	面积
right-hand rule	右手定则	parallel	平行
unit vector	单位矢量	unit magnitude	单位大小
dimensionless	无量纲的	respectively	分别地

2.3 专业英语常用表达法-2 仪器设备

apparatus　装置、设备、器械
appliance　器具、电器
device　装置
equipment　设备
facilities　设备、用具
gear　用具，装置
instrument　仪器、仪表
machine　机器、机械
machinery　机器设备、机械
mechanism　机械装置
plant　成套机械、装置
realia　教具、教学用品
set　（成套）设备、仪器
tool　工具
unit　装置、组件、元件

a battery supply set　电池供电设备
a device for regulating temperature　控制温度的装置
a hand-operated tool　手动工具
a remote-control gear　遥控装置
acoustic analytical instrument　声分析仪
acoustical instrument　声学仪器
adiabatic apparatus　绝热装置
adjusting instrument　调节仪器、调节装置
all-purpose instrument　多用工具、万能仪表
altitude instrument　高度仪
an air-conditioning equipment for　供……用的空调设备
an instrument for measuring the spectra　测量光谱的仪器
arc-suppressing apparatus　灭弧装置
beat measuring apparatus　拍频测试仪
bolometer　辐射热测定器
bolometric instrument　辐射热量计
calorimeter　量热计
cathode ray apparatus　阴极射线仪器
chromatographic instrument/chromatograph　色谱仪
current-measuring instrument　测流仪器
depth-measuring instrument　测深仪
detecting instrument　检测仪器、探测仪器
dial instrument　指针式仪表、有刻度的仪表
digital measuring instrument　数字式测量仪
displaying instrument　指示仪器
double-scale instrument　双标度仪表
double-range instrument　双量程仪表
dynamometer　功率计、电力测功仪、测力计、动力计
echo-sounding instrument　回声探测仪

eddy current instrument　涡流仪器
educational instrument　教学仪器
electric instrument　电工测量仪表、电表
electrical appliance　电器用具
electroacoustical instrument　电声（测试）仪器
electromagnetic acoustical instrument　电磁声学仪器
electronic measuring instrument　电子测量仪器
electronic test instrument　电子试验（测试）仪器
electrostatic acoustical instrument　静电声学仪器
electrostatic instrument　静电式仪表
electrostatic measuring instrument　静电式电表、静电式测量仪
electrothermic instrument　热电式仪表
fine measuring instrument　精密测量仪器、精密量具
first-order instrument　一阶仪器
flow instrument　流量计
humidity-measuring instrument　湿度测量仪
instructional instruments　教学仪器
insulation test instrument　绝缘（电阻）测试仪器
laboratory apparatus　实验仪器（装置）
laboratory instrument　实验室仪表
laser distance-measuring instrument/laser range finder　激光测距仪
level instrument　位面计、水平仪
levelling instrument　水准仪、水平尺、测平仪
measuring instrument　测量仪表、测量仪器
metrologic instrument　计量仪器
needle instrument　指针型仪器
optical instrument　光学仪器
photomicrographic apparatus　显微照相装置
portable instrument　便携式仪器
power plant/unit　动力装置/机组
precise instrument　精密仪器
radio instrument　无线电仪器
research instrument　试验设备、研究设备
resistance instrument　电阻式仪表
scientific apparatus/instrument　科学仪器/仪表
scientific experiment package　科学实验装置
sensing instrument　灵敏仪表、灵敏元件
spraying apparatus　喷雾器
supersonic thickness meter gauge　超声测厚仪

surveying instrument　测量仪器、测绘仪器
test instrument　试验工具、测试设备
testing instrument　试验仪器
the latest research equipment　最新研究设备
visual instrument　目视仪器
X-ray diffraction instrument　X射线衍射仪

LESSON 3

3.1 物理学专业英语的语法特点

3.1.1 常用的动词时态

专业英语在时态运用上有限，尽管英语的动词有16种时态，但在专业英语中常见的只有四种：一般现在时、一般过去时、现在完成时和一般将来时。

1) 一般现在时

在物理学英语文献资料中用得最多的时态是一般现在时，用以表述无时间性的科学定义、定理、公式、现象、过程等。究其原因可能是科学家和物理工作者都想表明他们所说的、所写的都是真理性的，都不受时间的限制。即使是叙述一个已完成的实验，或者是叙述一个将要做的实验，也大都使用一般现在时，意在表明其他人在任何时候都可以重复这样的实验而得到同样的结果。主要有以下三种用法。

(1) 表示一般叙述过程。如：

As the electrons move, the surface charge density increases until the magnitude of the internal field equals that of the external field, giving a net field of zero inside the conductor.

If we now imagine the surface to shrink to zero like a collapsing balloon, until it essentially encloses a point, the charge at the point must be zero.

(2) 叙述客观事实或科学定理。如：

A good electrical conductor contains charges (electrons) that are not bound to any atom and are free to move about within the material.

The electric field is zero everywhere inside the conductor.

Work done on a particle equals the change in its kinetic energy.

(3) 表达通常或习惯发生的行为。如：

Much of our understanding of nature comes from observing the motion of objects.

The solutions of kinematic equations are usually obtained quite easily in a direct fashion using integral calculus.

2) 一般过去时

在提到以前叙述过的事情、叙述物理学发展史时，经常使用过去时态。如：

The result is the same as Eq. (7-1), which was calculated directly from Coulomb's law.

The first capacitor was the Leyden jar, a glass container lined inside and out with gold foil. It was invented at the University of Leyden in the Netherlands by eighteenth-century experimenters who, while studying the effects of electric charges on people and animals, got the idea of trying to store a large amount of charge in a bottle of water. An experimenter held up a jar of water in one hand while charge was conducted to the water by a chain from a static electric generator. When he reached over to lift the chain out of the water with his other hand, he was knocked unconscious. Benjamin Franklin realized that the device for storing charge did not have to be jar-shaped and used foil-covered window glass, called Franklin panes.

3）一般将来时

在表示将来发生的行为或情况，或表达假设条件时，常用到将来时态。如：

In this chapter we shall use the energy concept in our study of electricity.

As we shall see in subsequent chapters, the concept of electric potential is of great practical value.

If the uncharged conductor is grounded, what will be the charge distribution and electric field near the slabs?

If a conductor is placed in an external field, the charges in the conductor will redistribute themselves, in the meantime, the external field will also be altered by the charge redistribution of the conductor.

4）现在完成时

表示已取得的成果或完成的工作。如：

We have stated that φ and E are equivalent descriptions of electric fields, and have determined how to calculate φ from E.

This problem has already been solved graphically.

So far our use of Gauss's law has been confined to the situation in which no dielectric was present.

3.1.2 使用介词的侧重点

尽管介词为英语各种文体所共用，但侧重点有所不同。如在文学英语中 with 多表示"产生某种生理或心理状态的原因（pale with anger）"，而在科技英语中更为常见的是用以表示"工具、手段"。如：

The capacitor is sprayed with aluminum to prevent rust.

Nowadays labs are built with large cranes and modern equipment.

3.1.3 并列成分的使用

在专业英语中，并列成分得到了大量的使用，下面的例句中都使用了并列的成分：

The story of the quantum is the one of a confused and groping search for knowledge *conducted by* scientists of many lands on a front wider than the world of physics had ever seen before, *illumined by* flashes of insight, *aided by* accidents and guesses, and *enlivened by* coincidences such as one would expect to find only in fiction.

Since the beginning of the present century, an increasing degree of uncertainty about the wave theory of light has been developing *due to* the discovery of the photoelectric effect, the quantum theory, and a number of allied phenomena, and *due also to* a detailed investigation into the nature and physical properties of the ether. Also, during this period a great deal has been learned about the structures of the atom which is not altogether limited to a wave picture of light. Hence the photon, or a light corpuscle, has been postulated.

In announcing that "every particle of matter in the universe attracts every other particle with a force inversely proportional to the square of the distance between the two particles", *in showing that* the one universal and comparatively simple law governs not only the motion of the planets round the sun and of the satellites round their planets but, probably, also the relative motions of all the heavenly bodies, Newton gave to the world a truth the importance of which in all branches of human thought can hardly be overestimated. Of value to science, of course, from microphysics to macrophysics. But consider the effect on man's concept of nature and of his relations thereto of realizing, indeed, of having proven to him, for the first time that the physical universe is governed by law, not by caprice; and if the physical universe, why not the biological universe, even the moral universe.

3.1.4 经常使用复合修饰语

复合修饰语的使用是为了使行文简洁,它可以由名词、形容词、副词、介词短语、从句等充当。在专业英语中,经常使用复合修饰语,通常包括以下三种情况:

1) 一个以上的修饰语同时修饰同一个中心词。如:

sound and light waves 声波和光波,*particle and wave* duality 波粒二象性

"*Absolute, true, and mathematical* time, of itself, and from its own nature, flows equably without relation to anything external."绝对的、真实的、数学的时间,就其本身而言,就其本性而言,均匀流逝,与外界任何事情都无关。

2) 一个修饰语同时修饰一个以上的中心词。如:

analyze the *efficiency and performance* of machinery 分析机械的运行情况及其效率

3) 一个以上的修饰词同时修饰一个以上的中心词。如:

Scientists always check statements and make experiments *carefully and objectively* to verify them. 科学家总是谨慎而客观地核对各种说法,并以同样的态度通过实验来加以验证。

3.1.5 广泛使用被动语态

专业英语中的谓语约三分之一是被动语态。这是因为物理文献侧重叙事推理,强调客观准确。第一、二人称使用过多时,会造成主观臆断的印象,因此尽量使用第三人称叙述,采用被动语态,例如:

Attention must be paid to the working temperature of the machine. 应当注意机器的工作温度。

而很少说：You must pay attention to the working temperature of the machine. 你们必须注意机器的工作温度。

此外，如前所述，专业文章将主要信息前置，放在主语部分。这也是广泛使用被动态的主要原因。观察并比较下列两段短文的主语：

We can store electrical energy in two metal plates separated by an insulating medium. We call such a device a capacitor, or a condenser, and its ability to store electrical energy capacitance. It is measured in farads. 电能可储存在由一绝缘介质隔开的两块金属极板内。这样的装置称为电容器，其储存电能的能力称为电容。电容的测量单位是法（拉）。

变为如下被动语态句：

Electrical energy can be stored in two metal plates separated by an insulating medium. Such a device is called a capacitor, or a condenser, and its ability to store electrical energy capacitance. It is measured in farads.

这一段短文中各句的主语分别为：electrical energy，such a device，its ability to store electrical energy 和 it(capacitance)。它们都包含了较多的信息，并且处于句首的位置，非常醒目。四个主语完全不同，避免了单调重复，前后连贯，自然流畅，充分表明被动结构可取得简洁客观的效果。

3.1.6 大量使用从句

专业英语对客观事物的描述要求准确、完整，因而各种从句用得较多，但层次清楚。以下是一些从句的例子：

1) 状语从句

The body possesses a definite store of potential energy *while it is in the elevated position*.

2) 定语从句

Switching circuits are the ones *that perform logical functions*.

3) That 引导的从句

在句子中可以起主语、宾语、补语等作用。如：

For example, in electric circuits it is often assumed *that the relations between voltages and currents are linear*.

Stated in words, Ohm's law says *that the steady current through any portion of an electric circuit equals the potential difference across that portion of the circuit divided by the resistance of that portion of the circuit*.

4) 疑问词从句

由疑问词 what, where, how, which, who, whose, whether 等引导的从句，在句子中可以起主语、宾语、补语、同位语等作用。如：

In order to determine *whether a system is performing properly and ultimately* to control the system performance, the engineer must know *what the system is doing* at any instant of time.

The question *whether the atom can or cannot be split up* is known to have interested scientists from ancient times.

3.1.7 大量使用后置定语

大量使用后置定语也是科技文章的特点之一。常见的结构有以下五种：

1）介词短语

The forces *due to friction* are called frictional forces. 由于摩擦而产生的力称为摩擦力。

2）形容词及形容词短语

In radiation, thermal energy is transformed into radiant energy, *similar in nature to light*. 热能在辐射时，转换成性质与光相似的辐射能。

3）副词

The force *upward* equals the force *downward* so that the balloon stays at the level. 向上的力与向下的力相等，所以气球就保持在这一高度。

4）单个分词，但仍保持较强的动词意义

The heat *produced* is equal to the electrical energy *wasted*. 产生的热量等于浪费了的电能。

5）定语从句

The molecules exert forces upon each other, *which depend upon the distance between them*. 分子相互间都存在着力的作用，这些力的大小取决于它们之间的距离。

关于定语从句，会在以后的章节中进一步讨论，在此不再详述。

3.1.8 大量使用非限定动词结构

专业英语文章要求行文简练，结构紧凑。为此，往往使用分词短语代替定语从句或状语从句；使用分词独立结构代替状语从句或并列分句；使用不定式短语代替各种从句；使用介词＋动名词短语代替定语从句或状语从句。这样既可将句子缩短，又比较醒目。试比较下列各组句子。

A direct current is a current which flows always in the same direction.

A direct current is a current flowing always in the same direction.

直流电是一种总是沿同一方向流动的电流。

When heat radiates from the earth, it causes air currents to rise.

Radiating from the earth, heat causes air currents to rise.

热量由地球辐射出来时，使得气流上升。

A body can move uniformly and in a straight line if there is no cause to change that motion.

A body can move uniformly and in a straight line, there being no cause to change that motion.

如果没有改变物体运动的原因，那么物体将作匀速直线运动。

Vibrating objects produce sound waves, and each vibration produces one sound wave.
Vibrating objects produce sound waves, each vibration producing one sound wave.
振动的物体产生声波,每一次振动产生一个声波。
There are different ways which change energy from one form into another.
There are different ways of changing energy from one form into another.
将能量从一种形式转变成另一种形式有各种不同的方法。
When the radio waves are made to correspond to each sound in turn, messages are carried from a broadcasting station to a receiving set.
By making the radio waves correspond to each sound in turn, messages are carried from a broadcasting station to a receiving set.
使无线电波依次对每一个声音作出相应变化时,消息就由广播电台传递到接收机。

3.2 专业英语阅读

3.2.1 Linear Motion with Constant Acceleration(匀加速直线运动)

A very common and simple type of one-dimensional motion occurs when the acceleration is constant, or uniform. Consequently, the velocity increases or decreases at the same rate throughout the motion.

For motion along a straight line, we choose a rectangular coordinate system that is oriented so that one of the axes (for example, the x-axis) is along the line. Then, components of position vector, velocity, and acceleration lie along this direction, and the y and z components are zero. The vector equations then become scalar equations. If the velocity is v_0 at time $t=0$, and v at some later time t, the corresponding acceleration is

$$a = \frac{\Delta v}{\Delta t} = \frac{v - v_0}{t - 0} = \frac{v - v_0}{t} \qquad (3\text{-}1)$$

A Case in Point—Freely Falling Bodies

It is well-known that all objects, when dropped, will fall toward the earth with nearly constant acceleration. In the idealized case, where air resistance is neglected, such motion is referred to as **free fall**.

We shall denote the *acceleration due to gravity* by the symbol ***g***. The magnitude of ***g*** decreases with increasing altitude. Furthermore, there are slight variations in g with altitude. The vector ***g*** is directed downward toward the center of the earth. At the earth's surface, the magnitude of ***g*** is approximately 9.80 m/s^2.

If we neglect air resistance and assume that the gravitational acceleration does not vary with altitude, then the motion of a freely falling body is equivalent to motion in one dimension under constant acceleration. Therefore our kinematic equations for constant acceleration can be applied. We shall take the vertical direction to be the y axis and call y positive upward. With this choice of coordinates, we have $a = -g$. The negative sign simply indicates that the acceleration is downward. We get the following expressions:

$$v = v_0 - gt \tag{3-2}$$

$$y - y_0 = v_0 t - \frac{1}{2}gt^2 \tag{3-3}$$

$$v^2 - v_0^2 = -2g(y - y_0) \tag{3-4}$$

You should note that *the negative sign for the acceleration is already included in these expressions*. Therefore, when using these equations in any free-fall problem, you should simply substitute $g = 9.80 \text{ m/s}^2$.

3.2.2 Projectile Motion(抛体运动)

Anyone who has observed a football in motion (or, for that matter, any object thrown in the air) has observed projectile motion. This very common form of motion is surprisingly simple to analyze if the following three assumptions are made: (1) the acceleration due to gravity, **g**, is constant over the range of motion and is directed downward, (2) the effect of air resistance is negligible, and (3) the rotation of the earth does not affect the motion. With these assumptions, we shall find that the path of a projectile, which we call it trajectory, is always a parabola.

If we choose our reference frame such that the y direction is vertical and positive upward, then $a_y = -g$ (as in one-dimensional free fall) and $a_x = 0$ (since air friction is neglected). Furthermore, let us assume that at $t=0$, the projectile leaves the origin ($x_0 = y_0 = 0$) with a velocity v_0, as in Fig. 3-1.

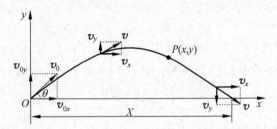

Fig. 3-1 The parabolic trajectory of a projectile that leaves the origin with a velocity v_0

If the vector makes an angle with the horizontal, then the initial velocity and acceleration have components

$$v_{0x} = v_0 \cos \theta \tag{3-5a}$$

$$v_{0y} = v_0 \sin \theta \tag{3-5b}$$

$$a_x = 0, \quad a_y = -g \tag{3-6}$$

Notice that v_x does not depend on v_y and vice versa: *The horizontal and vertical components of projectile motion are independent*. The velocity components and coordinates for the projectile at any time t are

$$v_x = v_{x0} = v_0 \cos \theta = \text{constant} \tag{3-7}$$

$$v_y = v_{y0} - gt = v_0 \sin \theta - gt \tag{3-8}$$

$$x = v_{x0}t = (v_0 \cos\theta)t \tag{3-9}$$

$$y = v_{y0}t - \frac{1}{2}gt^2 = (v_0 \sin\theta)t - \frac{1}{2}gt^2 \tag{3-10}$$

From Eqs. (3-9) and (3-10), we conclude that projectile motion is the superposition of two motions: (1) the motion of a freely falling body in the vertical direction with constant acceleration and (2) uniform motion in the horizontal direction with constant velocity.

The Total Flight Time(总飞行时间)

The total flight time T is obtained by setting $y=0$ in Eq. (3-10)

$$y = (v_0 \sin\theta)T - \frac{1}{2}gT^2 = 0, \quad T > 0$$

The flight time of the projectile is thus

$$T = \frac{2v_0 \sin\theta}{g} \tag{3-11}$$

Horizontal Range and Maximum Height(射程与最大高度)

There are two special points that are interesting to analyze: the peak with Cartesian coordinates labeled $(X/2, Y)$ and the point with coordinates $(X, 0)$. The distance X is called the **horizontal range** of the projectile, and Y is its **maximum height**.

We can determine the maximum height, Y, reached by the projectile by noting that at the peak, $v_y = 0$. Therefore, Eq. (3-8) can be used to determine time t it takes to reach the peak

$$t = \frac{v_0 \sin\theta}{g}$$

Substituting this expression for t into Eq. (3-10) gives Y in terms of v_0 and θ

$$Y = \frac{v_0^2 \sin^2\theta}{2g} \tag{3-12}$$

The range, X, is the horizontal distance traveled in the total flight time T. Using Eq. (3-9) and noting that $x=X$ at $t=T$, we find that

$$X = v_0 \cos\theta \cdot \frac{2v_0 \sin\theta}{g} = \frac{2v_0^2 \sin\theta \cos\theta}{g}$$

Since $\sin 2\theta = 2\sin\theta\cos\theta$, X can be written in the form

$$X = \frac{v_0^2 \sin 2\theta}{g} \tag{3-13}$$

The maximum value of $\sin 2\theta$ is unity, which occurs when $2\theta = 90°$. Therefore, we see that X is maximum when $\theta = 45°$, as you would expect if air friction is neglected.

Glossary

one-dimensional	一维的	corresponding	对应的
freely falling body	自由落体	air resistance	空气阻力

acceleration due to gravity	重力加速度	altitude	高度
vertical direction	竖直方向	negative sign	负号
projectile	抛体	trajectory	轨迹
assumption	假设	negligible	可忽略的
rotation	转动	air friction	空气摩擦
parabola	抛物线	parabolic trajectory	抛物线轨迹
initial	初始的	horizontal	水平的
superposition	叠加	flight time	飞行时间
horizontal range	射程	maximum height	最大高度

3.3 专业英语常用表达法-3 技术设备的更新

1. 表示"过时、陈旧、淘汰"等的词汇

obsolete 荒废的、陈旧的
old 陈旧的、古老的
old-fashioned 老式的、过时的
out-of-date 老式的、过时的

timeworn 陈旧的、老化的
behind the times 过时、落伍
fall into disuse 淘汰
out of repair 失修

2. 表示"更新、换代"等的词汇

remove 更换、升级
renew（renewal） 更新
renovate（renovation） 革新、改造
replace 取代、替换
introduce（introduction） 引进、纳入
install（installation） 安装、安置

update 使现代化、更新
upgrade 使升级、改良
in one's place 代替
in place of 代替
take the place of 代替

Thus renewal of equipment began. 就这样设备开始更新了。

These were obsolete and had to be replaced with digital technology. 这些（设备）已经陈旧不堪，将被淘汰而改用数字技术（设备）。

Many old facilities have been updated since 2005. 自2005年以来许多陈旧的设施已被更新换代。

When we arrived here we found a very congested old system which needed total renovation. 当我们到这里时，我们发现系统陈旧又拥挤不堪，需要进行彻底改造。

They had to remove many lines and exchanges which were over 20 years old and completely out of date. 他们必须把已经用了20多年的、完全过时的线路和电话交换台予以更换。

This system will most probably be upgraded in the long run to a completely fiber-optic cable route. 这套系统最终将会全部升级，改用光纤线路。

LESSON 4

4.1 物理学专业英语的修辞特点

物理学专业英语的主要作用是提供事实、数据、假设、理论、实验等信息，运用概念、判断、推理，系统论述自然科学。其内容往往是一种客观的叙述，用于描述事实、记录实验，阐明规律或探讨理论，比如经常对环境、仪器设备进行描写，对实验过程和工艺流程进行描写，对工作原理、实验结果、性能、用途、条件等进行说明。不论是科学文章、科普文章、原版专业书籍，还是技术文本，都需要把科学道理说清楚。专业英语具有平铺直叙、简洁、确切的特点，注重的是科学事实和逻辑概念等，因而其文体十分严谨，修辞比较单调。为了具有科学性、准确性、客观性和抽象性等风格特点，专业英语经常运用如下几种修辞方式。

4.1.1 多使用逻辑语法词表示各种关系

表示原因的逻辑语法词如 because, due to, owing to, as a result of, for…

表示语气转折 but, however, nevertheless, yet, otherwise…

表示限制 only, if only, except, besides, unless…

表示逻辑顺序 so, thus, therefore, furthermore…

表示假设 suppose, assuming, provided, providing…

4.1.2 使用一些词语表示过程或顺序

表示先后顺序、承上启下的词语，常用的有：first, first of all, second, secondly, third, thirdly, next, then, before, prior to, after, after that, last, lastly, finally 等，还可用 for one thing, for another, also, in addition, on top of that, more than that, furthermore 等。此外，还有如 when, where, which, and, by the time 等起连接作用的词语也经常被采用。

One must judge a model by how well it meets two standards. *First*, is the model based upon the best experimental evidence that we have? *Second*, is it good enough to allow us to predict what would happen in a new situation that has not been investigated before? 评判一个模型必须根据它在多大程度上符合下面两个标准：①该模型是不是以我们所获得的最佳实验证据为其依据？②它是不是足以使我们能预测在至今尚未研究过的新条件下将会发生什么情况？

We have decided not to import the complete plant. *For one thing*, it is expensive; *for another* its reliability is open to question. 我们已决定不进口这套成套设备了。首先，它价格昂贵；其次，它的可靠性也有问题。

Following are a set of procedures in making a scientific discovery. A problem must *first of all* be recognized. *Secondly*, existing knowledge and theories about the problem must be studies. On this basis, *the third step* is to collect factual data relevant to the problem. *Next* comes the most important step of all: the formation of a hypothesis. *After* developing a hypothesis, *the next step* is testing it. *The last step* is reporting the discovery. 科学发现的步骤是这样的:首先是确认课题,接着是研究与该课题有关的、现有的学说。在此基础上,第三步就是收集与该课题相关的资料。第四步最重要,就是形成假设。紧接着就是对该假设加以验证。最后就是把这一科学发现公之于众。

4.1.3 下定义

下定义是为了对某一科学概念或事物的本质和特征有清晰的介绍而采用的一种描述方法。一般说来定义语言都遵循一定的格式,即:被定义的事物＝被定义事物的种属、类别＋被定义事物的特殊属性(如果被定义的事物是可数名词,要用单数形式,并冠以不定冠词 a 或 an)。常用 be, be called, be known as, be defined as, be referred to as…等结构。如:

A vernier caliper is a measuring instrument consisting of an L-shaped frame with …
被定义事物　　　　　被定义事物的种属　　　　　被定义事物的特殊属性

定义通常采用关系从句(限制性或非限制性关系从句,多使用关系代词 who,which,whom,that,whose 等)或非限定动词结构,也可以采用括号或者破折号对所定义的对象进行解释,如:

The particles making up atoms are often referred to as elementary particles or fundamental particles. 构成原子的粒子通常称为基本粒子。

A force is an effect of attraction or repulsion between two bodies or particles. 力是物体或粒子之间的吸引或排斥效应。

另外,我们还会见到一句话定义后,又补充有例证、对比、说明等较长的定义形式。如:

Latent heat is the heat needed to change the state of matter of a material. While the latent heat is given to the material, its temperature remains constant. 潜热是改变物质的物态所需的热量。当物质吸收潜热时,其温度保持不变(恒定)。

4.1.4 分类

物理学中的事物错综复杂、多种多样,为研究、分析、讨论的方便,往往要对事物进行分类,找出它们之间的共同点,说明它们之间的区别。

对事物进行分类,需要三个方面的信息:①被分类的一组事物;②被分成的不同类型;③分类的标准或依据。

专业英语文本中常见的分类叙述有以下几种。

1) 完整的分类叙述:有关文字叙述直接提供上述三方面的信息。如:

Waves may be divided into two types based on the direction of the particles' oscillations relative to the wave velocity: transverse waves and longitudinal waves.

从本句可以看到:①被分类的事物为 waves;②被分成的类型为两种,即 transverse waves and longitudinal waves;③分类依据为 the direction of the particles' oscillations。

2) 不完整的分类说明:略去上述三条信息中的有关分类的标准或依据。如:

Quantities in physics can be classified as vectors or scalars.

3) 完全分类:根据某一标准把分类事物的全部归到一定数目的类型之中,加以分析讨论。如:

All the different forces observed in nature can be classified as members of one of four fundamental forces. These four fundamental forces are the gravitational force, the electromagnetic force, the strong nuclear force and the weak nuclear force. For example, the weight of the body is the gravitational force.

4) 不完全分类：在分类时，只提及有讨论价值的几种类型，而略去其余无关紧要的，或没有代表性的事物。如：

According to their shapes, capacitors can be classified into several categories: parallel-plate capacitors(平行板电容器), cylindrical capacitors(圆柱形电容器), spherical capacitors(球形电容器), etc.

在此例句中，没有说明电容器到底可以分成几种类型，只举了三种常见类型，所以我们称为"不完全分类"。

5) 多级分类：根据某一分类原则把一大类事物分成若干"子类"，然后再根据另一个分类原则把某一"子类"再分成若干更小的类别，更小的类别还可以继续分类，以此类推。我们把这种逐层分类法称为多级分类。如：

Synthesis techniques for nanomaterials, in general, can be divided into two broad categories as chemical methods and physical methods. Under chemical methods different routes, viz., colloidal, capping, cluster formation, sol-gel, electrochemical, etc., are being followed. Physical methods mostly used are molecular beam epitaxy, ionised cluster beam, liquid metal ion source, consolidation, sputtering and gas aggregation of monomers.

6) 隐含分类：在上述五种分类中，我们可以直接使用分类词，如 divide, classify 等。但有时文章中不出现这种直接提供分类信息的词语，这种情况我们称为隐含分类。如：

In physics sometimes we are concerned with the properties of substances, which may be either physical properties or chemical properties. Physical properties of a substance are those which can be observed or measured without changing it into another substance; for example, its color, form, hardness and its melting and boiling points. Chemical properties of a substance are those which describe its behavior when it changes into other substances, e.g. when it burns or is destroyed by acids.

虽然在此作者没有使用分类词语，但同样为我们提供了有关分类的三方面的信息：①被分类的事物，properties of substance；②被分成的类型，physical properties 及 chemical properties；③分类依据，whether the properties involve any change from one substance to another substance, or more substances.

4.2 专业英语阅读

4.2.1 Circular Motion(圆周运动)

Motion along a circular path, or a segment of a circular path, is called **circular motion**.

If a particle moves along a circular arc, the direction from the particle toward the center of the circle is called the centripetal direction.

LESSON 4

Angular Velocity and Angular Acceleration(角速度与角加速度)

Fig. 4-1 illustrates a particle undergoes circular motion about O. As the particle moves along the circle from point A to the point B in a time interval Δt, it moves through an arc length Δs and the radius vector sweeps out an angle $\Delta \theta$, which equals the angular displacement. We define the average angular velocity as the ratio of this angular displacement to the time interval Δt:

$$\omega = \frac{\Delta \theta}{\Delta t} \tag{4-1}$$

The **instantaneous angular velocity**, ω, is defined as the limit of the ratio in Eq. (4-1) as Δt approaches zero:

$$\omega = \lim_{\Delta t \to 0} \frac{\Delta \theta}{\Delta t} = \frac{d\theta}{dt} \tag{4-2}$$

Angular velocity has units of rad/s, or s^{-1}, since radians are not dimensional. We shall take ω to be positive when θ is increasing (counterclockwise motion) and negative when θ is decreasing (clockwise motion).

Note that angular velocity is a vector. Its direction follows the **right-hand rule**, perpendicular to the plane the particle moves in. That is, the four fingers of the right hand are wrapped in the direction of the moving particle, and the extended right thumb points in the direction of ω (Fig. 4-2). Angular velocities, when they add vectorially, follow *parallelogram rule for vectors*.

Fig. 4-1

Fig. 4-2

If the instantaneous angular velocity changes, the particle has an angular acceleration. In analogy to linear acceleration, the **angular acceleration** α is defined as

$$\boldsymbol{\alpha} = \lim_{\Delta t \to 0} \frac{\boldsymbol{\omega}_{t+\Delta t} - \boldsymbol{\omega}_t}{\Delta t} = \lim_{\Delta t \to 0} \frac{\Delta \boldsymbol{\omega}}{\Delta t} = \frac{d\boldsymbol{\omega}}{dt} \tag{4-3}$$

Angular acceleration has units of rad/s^2, or s^{-2}. Note that α is positive when ω is increasing in time and negative when ω is decreasing in time.

Circular Motion with Varying Speed(变速圆周运动)

Let us consider the motion of a particle along a circular path where the velocity changes both in direction and in magnitude. In this situation, the velocity of the particle is always tangent to the path; however, the acceleration vector $\boldsymbol{a}$ is now at some angle to the path. As the particle moves along the curved path, the direction and magnitude of the acceleration vector, $\boldsymbol{a}$, may change from point to point. This vector can be resolved into two component vectors: a radial component vector, $\boldsymbol{a}_n$, and a tangential component vector, $\boldsymbol{a}_t$. That is, the total acceleration vector, $\boldsymbol{a}$, can be written as the vector sum of these component vectors:

$$\boldsymbol{a} = \boldsymbol{a}_n + \boldsymbol{a}_t \tag{4-4}$$

The **tangential acceleration** arises from the change in the speed of the particle, and its magnitude is given by

$$a_t = \frac{dv}{dt} \tag{4-5}$$

The **radial or normal acceleration** is due to the time rate of change in direction of the velocity vector and has a magnitude given by

$$a_n = \frac{v^2}{R} \tag{4-6}$$

Since $\boldsymbol{a}_n$ and $\boldsymbol{a}_t$ are perpendicular component vectors of $\boldsymbol{a}$, it follows that $a = \sqrt{a_n^2 + a_t^2}$. As in the case of uniform circular motion, $\boldsymbol{a}_n$ always points toward the center of the circle. The direction of $\boldsymbol{a}_t$ is either in the same direction as $\boldsymbol{v}$ (if the speed v is increasing) or opposite $\boldsymbol{v}$ (if the speed v is decreasing).

Note that in the case of uniform circular motion, where v is constant, $a_t = 0$ and the acceleration is always radial. Furthermore, if the direction of $\boldsymbol{a}$ does not change, then there is no radial acceleration and the motion is one-dimensional ($a_n = 0$, $a_t \neq 0$).

4.2.2 Relative Motion(相对运动)

In this section, we describe how observations made by different observers in different frames of reference are related to each other. We shall find that observers in different frames of reference may measure different displacements, velocities, and accelerations for a particle in motion. That is, two observers moving with respect to each other will generally not agree on the outcome of a measurement.

Suppose a person on a moving vehicle (observer A) throws a ball straight up in the air according to his frame of reference, as in Fig. 4-3(a). According to observer A, the ball

Fig. 4-3
(a) Observer A in a moving vehicle throws a ball upward and sees a straight-line path for the ball;
(b) A stationary observer B sees a parabolic path for the same ball

will move in a vertical path. On the other hand, a stationary observer B, standing on the ground, will see the path of the ball as a parabola, as illustrated in Fig. 4-3(b).

In a more general situation, consider a particle located at the point P in Fig. 4-4. Imagine that the motion of the particle is being described by two observers, one in reference frame S, fixed with respect to the earth, and the other in reference frame S', moving to the right relative to S with a constant velocity $\boldsymbol{u}$. (Relative to an observer in S', S moves to the left with a velocity $-\boldsymbol{u}$.)

Fig. 4-4

We label the position of the particle with respect to the S frame with the position vector $\boldsymbol{r}$ and label its position relative to the frame S' with the vector $\boldsymbol{r}'$, at some time t. If the origins of the two reference frames coincide at $t=0$, then the vectors $\boldsymbol{r}$ and $\boldsymbol{r}'$ are related to each other through the expression

$$\boldsymbol{r} = \boldsymbol{r}' + \boldsymbol{u}t \tag{4-7}$$

If we differentiate Eq. (4-7) with respect to time and note that $\boldsymbol{u}$ is constant, we get

$$\frac{d\boldsymbol{r}}{dt} = \boldsymbol{u} + \frac{d\boldsymbol{r}'}{dt} \tag{4-8}$$

$$\boldsymbol{v} = \boldsymbol{u} + \boldsymbol{v}' \tag{4-9}$$

where $\boldsymbol{v}'$ is the velocity of the particle observed in the frame S' and $\boldsymbol{v}$ is the velocity observer in the S frame. Eqs. (4-7) and (4-9) are known as **Galilean transformation equations.** They relate the coordinates and velocity of a particle in the earth's reference frame to those measured in a frame of reference in uniform motion with respect to the earth.

Glossary

circular motion	圆周运动	centripetal	向心的
arc length	弧长	angular displacement	角位移
instantaneous angular velocity	（瞬时）角速度	radian(s)	弧度
dimensional	有量纲的	counterclockwise	逆时针
clockwise	顺时针	circle	圆
center of a circle	圆心	vectorially	矢量地
angular acceleration	角加速度	tangential acceleration	切向加速度
resolve	（矢量）分解	uniform circular motion	匀速圆周运动
radial	径向的	radial/normal acceleration	法向加速度
perpendicular	垂直的	observer	观察者
outcome	结果	measurement	测量
stationary	静止的	differentiate	微分
Galilean transformation	伽利略变换		

4.3 专业英语常用表达法-4 组成 构成 成分

常用名词有：

component　成分、组分、零件
constitution　构造、组成
content　内容、含量
ingredient　成分、配料

composition　合成、组成、成分
constituent　成分、要素
formation　形成、构成
make-up　组成、构造

常用词组有：

component assembly　零件装配
component part　成分、组分、零件
component wire　（电缆）芯线
bath composition　电解液成分
composition of forces　力的合成
alloying ingredient　合金的组分
crystal formation　结晶，晶体生成
formation of n-p-n junction　N-P-N 结结构
shock wave formation　激波系
isotopic constitution　同位素成分
molecular constitution　分子结构（构成）
chemical constitution　化学成分（结构）

microscopic constitution　显微组织
structural constitution　结构成分
component (of) velocity　分速度
component sine waves　正弦波分量
pressure component　分压力
composition metal　合金
composition of radiance　辐射谱
moisture content　湿度、含水量
formation of image　成像
pulse formation　脉冲的形成

The factory produces *components* for aircraft. 这个工厂生产飞机构件（部件）。

The *composition* of cast-iron is different for different purposes. 铸铁的成分随用途的不同而有所不同。

The carbon *content* of wrought-iron is very low. 熟铁的碳含量很低。

Ferrite and carbon are the *constituents* of mild steel. 铁氧体和碳是软钢的成分。

The moisture *content* of the cylinder increased. 汽缸的水分含量增加了。

The chemical *composition* of water remains constant whether it is in solid, liquid or gaseous state. 无论处于固态、液态或气态，水的化学成分都保持不变。

常用动词和短语有：

be combined into…　组成、构成
constitute　组成、构成
make up　组成、构成
be made up of…　由……组成
consist of…　由……组成
contain　包含、包括
be sprayed with a metal coating　喷镀一层金属

compose　组成、构成
form　组成、构成
be composed of…　由……组成
be sprayed with…　用……喷镀
comprise　由……组成

be sprayed with a coating of paint 喷镀一层涂料

A hydrogen atom *consists of* a single electron moving round a single proton. 一个氢原子是由一个电子绕着一个质子旋转构成的。

All substances on the earth, whether gaseous, liquid or solid, *are made up of* atoms. 地球上所有的物质无论它们是气态的、液态的或是固态的,都是由原子组成的。

This physical instrument *is composed of* several different parts. 这台物理仪器由几个不同的部件组装而成。

Steel *is composed of* iron and a number of other elements. 钢是由铁和若干种其他元素构成的。

Fermi-Dirac statistic is a part of the science of physics that describes the energies of single particles in a system *comprised of* many particles that obey the Pauli Exclusion Principle. 费米-狄拉克统计是物理学的一部分,它用来描述由遵守泡利不相容原理的多粒子所构成系统的单个粒子的能量。

The technician *made up* a bottle of dilute sulfuric acid. 技术人员配置了一瓶稀硫酸。

Brass *consists of* copper and zinc. 黄铜由铜和锌构成。

The atmosphere *comprises* a number of gases. 大气由许多种气体构成。

The electro-magnet *comprises* a soft iron core shaped like a horseshoe. 电磁铁包括一块马蹄形的软铁心。

Cast-iron *is made up of* about six different substances. 铸铁大约由六种不同的物质构成。

Sometimes two different types of machines *are combined into* a complex one. 有时两台不同的机器组成一台复杂的机器。

Ferrite and carbon *make up* mild steel. 铁氧体和碳构成软钢。

The alloy *contains* 10% nickel and 8% iron. 这合金含有10%的镍和8%的铁。

The rare earths *comprise* the series of elements in the sixth row of the periodic table stretching from lanthanum to ytterbium. 稀土(元素)包括元素周期表第六行中的从镧到镱的一系列元素。

Unit Two

LESSON 5

5.1 物理学专业英语中的比较

在物理学中,经常需要对所研究的事物或采用的方法进行比较说明。比较是人们认识客观事实的一个重要途径,它利用事物之间的相似或不同之处,通过类比使人们理解或接受那些不易理解或接受的东西。英语中的比较结构内容丰富,形式多样,并有其独特的表现形式,所以正确理解和表达比较结构及其相应翻译在专业英语学习中很有必要。通过比较可以发现被描述物之间的相同点和不同点,能对抽象的概念,如事物的性质、特点、功能、形状、尺寸等,有较为具体的了解。下面列举几种常见的比较和对比。

5.1.1 同等比较

表示两对象在性质、特征等方面相似或相同。其结构形式有:

1) as...as (和……一样)

The lightning rod is as good as any other. 这避雷针与其他任何一种避雷针一样好。

2) be identical with, be the same as, be equal to (和……相同)

The TV set uses the same capacitor as that one does. 这台电视机用的电容器和那台一样。

The rating of this engine is equal to that of Toyota motor. 这台发动机的额定值与那台丰田发动机的额定值等同。

3) no more(less)...than... (和……一样不……,不亚于……)

Rubber is no more conductor than glass. 橡胶和玻璃一样都不是导体。

类似的表达结构还有:

As (Just as)..., so... (和……一样,……也……)

The same thing is true of... (同样……也……)

Like (Similarly, Likewise, In the same way)... (同样……)

A and B have/share several things in common. A 和 B 有几个共同点。

A and B are alike/identical/similar/the same (in design/in every respect/in most respects). A 和 B(在设计上/在每一方面/在大多数方面)相像/一致/类似/一样。

A like/as B has/have/is/are C. A 和 B 一样,都是 C。

A bears some close resemblance(s) to B. A 和 B 有一些相似之处。

There is little resemblance between A and B. A 和 B 没有相似之处。

A do/does/be..., so do/does/be B. （A……，B 也……）

A do/does/be not..., nor do/does/be B. （A……，B 也不……）

(As ＋从句/短语)＋主句＋as 从句/短语 （和……一样……）

这些句型还可以与一些副词连用来表示程度，例如 exactly，just，precisely，more or less，almost，approximately，about，practically 等。

5.1.2 差等比较

差等比较包括两方面："优等比较"和"劣等比较"。前者表示"A 优于 B"，后者表示"A 劣于 B"。其结构形式有：

1) ...than... （比更……一些）

The carbon content of cast steel is greater than that of mild steel. 铸铁的碳含量比软钢高。

2) ...not as/so ...as （和……不一样，不如……）

Water doesn't have a boiling point as low as alcohol. 水的沸点不如酒精低。

3) be superior to /be inferior to （优于……/劣于……）

The power of the new engine is superior to that of the old one. 这台新发动机的功率优于旧的。

5.1.3 有额比较

表示具体比较结果，即"额"是多少。其结构形式有：

1) 额＋比较级＋than （比……多，是……）

Sound travels nearly three times faster in copper than in lead. 声音在铜中的传播速度几乎是铅中的 3 倍。

2) 额＋as＋原级＋as，额＋the size/weight/price/number/age/that... （是多少……）

Jupiter is 1500 times as large as/the size of the Earth. 木星是地球的 1500 倍大。

The effort is two thirds as great as the resistance. 作用力是阻力的 2/3。

3) 表示减少或增加意义的动词（decrease，increase，rise，exceed，grow，raise，expand，go up 等）＋额 （增加/减少了……）

The production of various picture tubes has increased three times as against 2003. 各种显像管的产量比 2003 年增加了 3 倍。

The new invention makes it possible that small amounts of electricity can increase hydrogen production from waste water 4 times. 这项新发明使得低耗电废水提取氢的产量提高 4 倍成为可能。

The technicians tried hard to make the balloon expand its size 6 times. 技师们尽最大努力使得气球的体积膨胀了 6 倍。

4) 表示倍数意义的动词(double，treble，quadruple)＋宾语/表语 （增加了……倍）

Production quadruples this year. 今年产量增加了 3 倍。

5.1.4　递进比较

这种比较表示一种不断递进的语义关系。其结构形式有：

1) the＋比较级＋句子/句子＋比较级，the＋比较级＋句子　（越……，越……）

The thicker the wire is, the more freely it can carry current. 导线越粗，导电就越容易。

A subject weighs less, the farther it gets from the surface of the earth. 物体离地球表面越远重量越轻。

2) 比较级＋and＋比较级　（越来越……）

More and more new knowledge is discovered in physics. 越来越多的物理学新知识被发现。

More and more scientists today work for government sponsored bodies. 今天越来越多的科学家为政府支持的机构工作。

3) never...enough, never too..., can't...over/too　（越……越……，怎么也不为过）

You can never be careful enough when operating this instrument. 操作这台仪器越小心越好。

The significance of the invention can't be overestimated. 这个发明的意义不管怎样估计都不会过高。

5.1.5　终极比较

表示某物在特定范围内显得最突出，或某一动作在一定情况下达到最高程度。其结构主要用形容词和副词的最高级。

The kilometer is the largest metric unit of measurement. 千米是最大的米制衡量单位。

注意：终级比较和差等比较也可表示完全相同的意思，只是说话者看问题的角度不同而已。这时候的差等比较结构中往往带有 other 或 else。如：

Strontium titanate is far better as a dielectric than any other ones in the group. 作为电介质，钛酸锶比其他电介质强得多。

5.1.6　选择性比较

1) more...than, less...than, better...than, not so much...as　（与其……不如……，不是……倒是……，不但没有……反而……）

His explanation about the Hall effect was more confusing than clarifying. 他对于霍尔效应的解释不但没使人明白，反而使人更糊涂了。

This material is not so much a conductor as a semiconductor. 与其说这种材料是导体不如说是半导体。

2) prefer...to..., prefer to..., rather than...　（喜欢……不喜欢……）

Physicists usually prefer idealized models to real objects when dealing with problems. 在处理问题时，物理学者通常喜欢采用理想模型取代实际物体。

He prefers to carry out experiments rather than theoretical induction. 他喜欢动手做实

验,不喜欢理论推理。

5.1.7 表示 A≠B

即 A 与 B 不相同,有差异,其常用句式为:

A is not as/so＋形容词 as B.

A is (totally/completely/entirely/quite) different from B (in every way/in every respect/in its shape/that 从句).

A (totally/completely/entirely/quite) differs from B (in every way/in every respect/in its shape/that 从句).

A can be distinguished from B (by its shape).

A unlike/as distinct from/as against B has/have C/ is/are C.

例句:

Heat waves are different/differ from light waves only in their wavelengths. 热波与光波的差异只是波长不同。

Iron,unlike glass, is a good conductor of electric current. 铁不同于玻璃,它是电流的良导体。

5.2 专业英语阅读

5.2.1 Newton's Laws of Motion(牛顿运动定律)

The purpose of classical mechanics is to provide a connection between the acceleration of a body and the forces acting on it. Keep in mind that classical mechanics deals with objects that are large compared with that dimensions of atoms ($\approx 10^{-10}$ m) and move at speeds that are much less than the speed of light (3×10^8 m/s).

In this chapter, we describe Newton's three laws of motion and begin using them to solve problems involving objects in motion and at rest.

5.2.2 Newton's First Law(牛顿第一定律)

A modern wording of **Newton's first law of motion** is:

An object at rest will remain at rest and an object in motion will continue in motion with a constant velocity (that is, constant speed in a straight line) unless it experiences a net external force (or resultant force).

In simpler terms, we can say that when the resultant force on a body is zero, its acceleration is zero. From the first law, we conclude that an isolated body (a body that does not interact with its environment) is either at rest or moving with constant velocity.

Inertial Frames(惯性系)

Newton's first law is sometimes called **law of inertia**, and it applies to objects in an inertial frame of reference.

An **inertial frame of reference** is one in which an object, subject to no force, moves with constant velocity. That is, a reference frame in which Newton's first law is valid is called an **inertial frame**.

In effect, Newton's first law defines an inertial frame of reference. A reference frame that moves with constant velocity relative to the distant stars is the best approximation of an inertial frame. The earth is not an inertial frame because of its orbital motion about the sun and rotational motion about its own axis. However, in most situations we shall assume that the earth is an inertial frame.

Thus, if an object is in uniform motion ($v=$ constant), an observer in one inertial frame (say, one at rest with respect to the object) will claim that the acceleration and the resultant force on the object are zero. An observer in any other inertial frame will also find that $a=0$ and $F=0$ for the object. According to the first law, a body at rest and one moving with constant velocity are equivalent. Unless stated otherwise, we shall unusually write the laws of motion with respect to an observer "at rest" in an inertial frame.

5.2.3 Newton's Second Law(牛顿第二定律)

Newton's second law answers the question of what happens to an object that has a nonzero resultant force acting on it.

Newton's second law of motion is:

The time rate of change of momentum of an object is equal to the resultant external force acting on the object.

$$\sum F = \frac{dp}{dt} = \frac{d(mv)}{dt} \tag{5-1}$$

where p is the momentum of the object as the product of the mass, m, and the velocity, v

$$p = mv \tag{5-2}$$

Eq. (5-1) is the most general form of Newton's second law, which is valid in any inertial frame of reference.

If m is treated as a constant, then Eq. (5-1) can be expressed

$$\sum F = \frac{dp}{dt} = \frac{d(mv)}{dt} = m\frac{dv}{dt} = ma \tag{5-3}$$

which can be stated as the acceleration of an object is directly proportional to the resultant force acting on it and inversely proportional to its mass.

5.2.4 Newton's Third Law(牛顿第三定律)

Newton's third law states that *if two bodies interact, the force exerted on body 1 by body 2 is equal to and opposite the force exerted on body 2 by body 1*. That is,

$$F_{12} = -F_{21}$$

This law is equivalent to stating that forces always occur in pairs, or that a single isolated force cannot exist. The force that body 1 exerts on body 2 is sometimes called the **action force**, while the force of body 2 on body 1 is called the **reaction force**. Either force can be labeled that action or reaction force. The action force is equal in magnitude to the reaction force and opposite in direction. In all cases the action and reaction forces act on different objects.

5.2.5 The Four Fundamental Forces(四种基本力)

All the different forces observed in nature can be explained in terms of four basic interactions that occur between elementary particles.

The Gravitational Force(引力)—the force of mutual attraction between objects

Newton's law of universal gravitation states that *every particle in the universe attracts every other particle with a force that is directly proportional to the product of the masses of the particles and inversely proportional to the square of the distance between them.*

$$F = \frac{Gm_1 m_2}{r^2} \qquad (5\text{-}4)$$

where $G = 6.67 \times 10^{-11}$ N·m²/kg² is the **universal gravitational constant.**

The Electromagnetic Force(电磁力)—the force between electric charges

This class of forces includes electric and magnetic forces. The electric force binds atoms and molecules in compounds to form ordinary matter. It is much stronger than the gravitational force. Coulomb's law states that the magnitude of the electrostatic force between two charged particles is

$$F_e = \frac{kq_1 q_2}{r^2}$$

where $k = 9 \times 10^9$ N·m²/C² is the **Coulomb constant.**

The Strong Nuclear Force(强核力)—the force between subatomic particles

This force holds the nucleus of an atom together. All nuclei except those of hydrogen contain electrically neutral neutrons and positively charged protons. The charged protons repel each other. It is the strong nuclear force that counteracts the repulsive electrical interactions. Note that the nuclear force is extremely short range and its strength decreases very rapidly outside the nucleus.

The Weak Nuclear Force(弱力)—the force between subatomic particles during certain radioactive decay processes

The weak nuclear force is a **short-range force** that is responsible for a common form of radioactivity called beta decay, in which a neutron in a radioactive nucleus is transformed into a proton while ejecting an electron and an essentially massless particle. The weak force play no direct role in the behavior of ordinary matter, but it is very important in interactions among fundamental particles.

Glossary

at rest	静止	approximation	近似
net external force/resultant force	合外力	inertial frame of reference	惯性参考系
inertia	惯性	act on＝exert	（力）作用于
unless stated otherwise	除非另有说明	nonzero	非零的
rate of change	变化率	mass	质量
directly proportional to	正比于	momentum	动量
inversely proportional to	反比于	interact	相互作用
action force	作用力	opposite	相反、相对
reaction force	反作用力	isolated	孤立的
gravitational force	引力	universal gravitational constant	万有引力常数
electromagnetic force	电磁力	electric charge	电荷
atom	原子	molecule	分子
compound	混合物、化合物	bind	约束
Coulomb's law	库仑定律	electrostatic force	静电力
charged particle	带电粒子	strong nuclear force	强力
subatomic	亚原子的	hydrogen	氢
nucleus (*pl.* nuclei or nucleuses)	原子核	neutron	中子
proton	质子	repel	排斥
repulsive	排斥的	counteract	抵抗
strength	强度	weak nuclear force	弱力
short-range force	短程力	radioactivity	放射性
radioactive decay	放射性衰变	beta decay	β衰变
electron	电子	massless	无质量的
fundamental particles	基本粒子		

5.3 专业英语常用表达法-5 力学常用实验仪器

pendulum wire	摆线	stopwatch	秒表
surface tension tester	表面张力测定仪	torsion pendulum	扭摆
dynamic meter	测力计	viscometer	黏度计
ballistic pendulum	冲击摆	gas density balance	气体密度秤
simple pendulum	单摆	balance/scale	天平
poise/weight	砝码	standard line meter	线纹米尺
(running)time meter/timer	计时器	pressure vacuum meter	压力真空表
Jolly balance	焦利秤	vernier caliper	游标卡尺
micrometer	螺旋测微仪、千分尺	pendulum weight/bob	摆锤

standard meter　标准米尺
gear　齿轮
ticker-tape timer　纸带打点计时器
spring balance　弹簧秤
analytical balance　分析天平
psychrometer　干湿计
measuring cup/graduate　量杯
densimeter　密度计、比重计
tweezers　镊子
torsion balance　扭力天平、扭秤
air track　气垫导轨
barometer　气压计
balance reading glass　天平读镜
pressure meter/gauge　压力计
Young's modulus tester　杨氏模量测定仪
balance spring/hair spring　游丝
centrifugal pendulum/centrifugal governor/centrifugal speed regulator　离心调速器
graduate, graduated/measuring volumetric cylinder　量筒
physical/compound pendulum　复摆、物理摆
target collision experiment facility　碰撞打靶实验仪
moment of inertia detector　转动惯量测定仪
new type of simple pendulum experiment facility　新型单摆实验仪
coefficient of liquid surface tension detector　液体表面张力系数测定仪
shear modulus and moment of inertia experiment facility　切变模量与转动惯量实验仪
general experimental sound velocity measurement instrument　声速测量综合实验仪
viscosity of liquid drop-ball tester　落球法液体黏滞系数测定仪
simple harmonic motion and spring stiffness coefficient experiment facility　简谐振动与弹簧劲度系数实验仪

LESSON 6

6.1 物理学专业英语中的举例和列举

6.1.1 举例

举例是专业英语中常见的表达方式。举例是作者为了更形象、更生动地揭示所表达的内容,帮助读者理解而采取的一种方法,起到进一步解释说明的作用。举例可以使抽象的内容更加具体、形象、生动,便于理解、记忆和运用。

在专业英语中,举例一般用于作者下完定义或写明某一观点之后。有时作者使用浅显的信息进一步解释抽象的概念、观点,使文章通俗易懂,表达清晰。

举例时常用到如下句型:

For example…例如……。For example 既可以放在句首,也可以放在句中。放在句首时,要大写,后面有逗号;放在句中时,前后都有逗号,形似插入语;也可以放在破折号后面,因为破折号本身表示解释说明的意思。For example 没有连接词的作用,不能连接两个分句。

e.g. …例如……。e.g. 是 for example 的缩写形式,不如 for example 正式,使用时一

般放在括号内。

  take ... as an example 以……为例

  take... for example 以……为例

  For instance... 例如……。与 for example 用法一样，但 for instance 比 for example 举例更具体些。

  Common/Typical examples are... 常见的/典型的例子是……

  An even more dramatic example is... 一个更生动的例子是……

  examples of which are... 属于此种类型的例子有……

  use an example to show... 用一个例子表明……

  an example of... 一个……的例子

  furnishes a good example of... 提供了一个……的好例子

  like... 像……

  afford an illustration of... 提供了一个……的例子

  a case in point 恰当的例子

  as an example 例如、举例来说

  as an illustration 作为实例

  as demonstrated by... 例如

  by way of example 例如、举例来说

  illustrated with... 用……举例说明

  including 包含、包括

  involving 包括

  like 类似

  range over 涉及、包括

  say 比如说

  something like... 有点像……

  specifically 具体地

  such 诸如此类的

  such as 例如、诸如

  take the case of... 以……为例

  to illustrate by an example 举例说明

以下是一些具体的例子：

  Waves transport energy and momentum through space without transporting matter. As a water wave moves across a pond, *for example*, the molecules of water oscillate up and down, but do not cross the pond with the wave. 波动只传播能量和动量而不传播媒质。例如，当水波穿过水池时，水分子上下振动，但是不随波穿过水池。

  Take the spring system *as an example*. A block attached to a spring on a frictionless track moves in simple harmonic motion. 以弹簧系统为例，一个与弹簧相连、放在光滑轨道上的木块的运动就是简谐运动。

  Mechanical waves are waves that disturb and propagate through a medium; the ripple

LESSON 6

in the water due to the pebble and a sound wave, for which air is the medium, are *examples of* mechanical waves. 机械波是扰动在媒质中传播形成的波,石头落入水中形成的波纹、以空气作媒质的声波都是机械波的例子。

To illustrate this, we *take* temperature *for example*. 为了阐明此理,我们以温度为例说明。

Another method that can be used to obtain the potential due to a finite continuous charge distribution is to start with the definition of the potential difference given by Eq. (8-7). If E is known or can be obtained easily (*e.g.* from Gauss's law), then the line integral of $E \cdot dr$ can be evaluated. 还有另外一种方法可以用来求有限连续分布电荷产生的电势,那就是利用方程(8-7)定义的电势差。如果电场 E 已知或者可以容易求得(例如利用高斯定律求得),那么 $E \cdot dr$ 的线积分就可以计算出来了。

When, *for instance*, we hit a nail with a hammer, we expect the nail to move. 比如,当我们用锤子敲打钉子时,我们可预知钉子要移动。

The mutual inductance depends on the geometrical arrangement of the two circuits. *For instance*, if the circuits are far apart, the flux through circuit 2 due to the current I_1 will be small and the mutual inductance will be small. 互感与两个回路的几何形状位置有关。例如,如果两个回路相距较远,电流 I_1 在回路 2 产生的通量就会小,从而互感就会小。

Electromagnetic waves are a special class of waves that do not require a medium in order to propagate; it is the varying electromagnetic field that propagates through space, *examples of which are* light waves and radio waves. 电磁波是一种特殊种类的波,它的传播不需要媒质;它是变化的电磁场在空间的传播,例如光波和无线电波。

An even more dramatic example of longitudinal waves is sound waves in air. 空气中的声波是纵波的一个更生动的例子。

Many machines vibrate because they have rotating parts that are not in perfect balance (observe a washing machine in the spin cycle *for an example*). 许多机器都会振动,那是因为他们的转动部分未在精确的平衡位置,作为一个例子,你可以观察一下内部旋转时的洗衣机。

A common example of the conversion of work into heat is movement with friction. 功转化为热的一个常见的例子就是摩擦运动。

Some common examples of adiabatic processes include the expansion of hot gases in an internal combustion engine, the liquefaction of gases in a cooling system, and the compression stroke in a diesel engine. 绝热过程的一些常见的例子包括:内燃机内热气的膨胀、冷却系统内的气体液化、还有柴油机内的压缩冲程。

We'll *use an example to* show that if the heat-engine statement is false, then the refrigerator statement is false. 我们可以用一个实例来说明,如果关于热机的说法是错误的,那么关于冰箱的说法也是错误的。

Another example of such a forbidden process would be if all of the air in your room spontaneously moved to one half of the room, leaving a vacuum in the other half. 另外一个不可能发生的过程的例子是:你房间内的空气自动聚集到房间的一半里边,而另一半成

了真空状态。

The result shows that the capacitance is proportional to the length of the cylinders and also depends on the radii of the two cylindrical conductors. *As an example*, a coaxial cable consists of two concentric cylindrical conductors of radii a and b separated by an insulator. 结果表明,电容正比于两个圆柱形导体的半径和长度。半径分别为 a 和 b 的两个同轴导体,中间用绝缘体隔开形成的同轴电缆就可以作为一个例子。

A nonconducting material, *such as* air, glass, paper, or wood, is called a dielectric. 不导电的物质,比如空气、玻璃、纸、木头,叫做电介质。

A water wheel, turned by water flowing over a weir, *furnishes a good example of* potential energy being turned into useful mechanical energy. 由流水过坝转动的水轮提供一个说明位能正在转变成有用的机械能的例子。

A city electric-power plant *affords an illustration of* complicated transformations of energy. 城市发电厂为能量转换复杂关系的说明提供了例子。

6.1.2 列举

物理学专业英语中经常会用到多项内容的列举,例如同一对象呈现出的多种特性、变化,支持同一结论的各种依据、原因、理论、方法等。各项内容之间的关系也不尽相同,可以是并列、递进或对比等。这些内容之间的关系可以通过使用过渡词语来更为准确、清楚地表达,同时增加了内容的条理性,不会使某些方面被忽略。这些过渡词语让我们把两个观点更好地衔接在一起,使行文或口语表达紧凑、流畅、条理清晰。

以下就是一些专业英语中常见的表示列举的过渡词语。

（1）表示并列、顺序与附加关系的

additionally 另外、加之	coupled with 连同
afterward 后来、以后	equally important 同样重要
again 再次	first of all 首先
alike 相似地、同样地	following this 之后
all the same 同样	for a start 首先
also 也、而且、此外	for one thing 首先、一则
analogous to 类似地	in addition (to) 除此之外
and 而且、亦、另外	in like manner 同样地
another 另外的、另一	in similar fashion 相似地
as well as 也、以及	in the first place 起初、首先
aside from(this) 除……以外	in the same way 同样地
at first 首先、最初	later on 后来
at the same time 同时	likewise 同样地
besides (that) 此外	meanwhile 同时
by the same token 同样地	next 其次
concurrently 同时	on top of that 最后
conjointly 相连地	once again 再次

once more　再一次
or　或者
over again　再一次
plus　并且
similarly　类似地
simultaneously　同时
so forth　等等
so on　等等
subsequently　随后、后来
then　然后
to begin with　首先
together with　连同
what is more　而且

Basically... Similarly... As well...
Both... and...
Either... or...
First... Second... Third... Next...
For one thing..., for another...
In the first place... Also... Lastly...
In the first place... Just in the same way... Finally...
Neither... nor...
Not only... but also...
To be sure... Additionally... Lastly...

例如：

Whether a physical model is good or not should be judged by how well it meets three standards. *First*, is the model similar with the original object in some specific aspects? *Second*, is it rational to neglect the difference between the model and the original object? *Finally*, is the model good enough to allow us to predict what would happen in a new situation that has not been investigated before? 一个物理模型是否完善应该通过其是否满足三个标准来判定。首先，这个模型是否与原物在某些具体方面相似？其次，对原物与模型间的差异进行忽略是否合理可行？最后，这个模型是否完善到可以使我们在尚未研究过的新环境下对未来将要发生的情况进行预测？

(2) 表示递进关系的

even more　更
further　此外、进一步
furthermore　而且、此外
more important　更重要的是
moreover　此外、加之
still　更

Clearly... Then...
Generally... Furthermore... Finally...
In the first place... In the second place... Lastly...
In the first place... Pursuing this further... Finally...
On the one hand..., on the other hand...

(3) 表示转折、让步与对照关系的

alternatively　作为选择、可选择的
although　尽管、虽然
as opposed to　与……相对比
but　但是
by comparison　比较起来
by way of contrast　两相对比

compared to 与……相比	nevertheless 仍然、不过
contrarily 反之、相反地	nonetheless 尽管如此(仍然)
conversely 相反地	notwithstanding 虽然、尽管
despite 不管、尽管	on the contrary 正相反
even so 虽然如此	otherwise 否则、要不然
even though 即使	rather than 不是……而是……
however 然而	rather 恰恰相反
in contrast 与此相反	still 仍然
in spite of 尽管	whereas 然而、反之、却
in turn 反之、反过来	yet 然而
instead 代替、也可以	

Not... but... 不是……,而是……
Not only... but also... 不但……,而且……
Sometimes... But not always... 有时……,但不总是……

6.2 专业英语阅读

6.2.1 Work and Energy(功和能)

Work and **energy** are important concepts in physics as well as in our everyday lives. In physics, a force does work if its point of application moves through a distance and there is a component of the force in the direction of the velocity of the force's point of application. For a constant force in one dimension, the work done equals the force component in the direction of the displacement times the displacement.

Energy is closely associated with work. When work is done by one system on another, energy is transferred between the two systems. For example, when you do work pushing a swing, chemical energy of your body is transferred to the swing and appears as kinetic energy of motion or as gravitational potential energy of the earth-swing system.

6.2.2 Work(功)

In dot-product notation, the element work dA done by a constant force $\boldsymbol{F}$ on a particle over a displacement $d\boldsymbol{r}$ is

$$dA = \boldsymbol{F} \cdot d\boldsymbol{r} \quad (6\text{-}1)$$

The work done on the particle as it moves from point 1 to point 2 is

$$A = \int_1^2 \boldsymbol{F} \cdot d\boldsymbol{r} \quad (6\text{-}2)$$

Work is a scalar quantity that is positive if $d\boldsymbol{r}$ and $\boldsymbol{F}$ have the same signs and negative if they have opposite signs. The SI unit of work and energy is the **joule** (J), which equals the product of a newton and a meter:

$$1\,\text{J} = 1\,\text{N} \cdot \text{m}$$

A convenient unit of work and energy in atomic and nuclear physics is the electron volt (eV):

$$1 \text{ eV} = 1.6 \times 10^{-19} \text{ J}$$

Commonly used multiples are keV (10^3 eV) and MeV (10^6 eV). The work required to remove an electron from an atom is of the order of a few eV, whereas the work needed to remove a proton or a neutron from an atomic nucleus is of the order of several MeV.

Work Done by a Variable Force (变力的功)

In Fig. 6-1 we plot a constant force F_x as a function of position x. The work done on a particle whose displacement is Δx is represented by the area under the force versus-position curve, indicated by the shading in Fig. 6-1.

Many forces vary with position. For example, a stretched spring exerts a force proportional to the distance it is stretched. And the gravitational force the earth exerts on a spaceship varies inversely with the square of the distance between the two bodies. We can approximate a variable force by a series of constant forces (Fig. 6-2). The work done by a variable force is then

$$A = \lim_{\Delta x_i \to 0} \sum_i F_x \Delta x = \text{area under the } F_x\text{-versus-}x \text{ curve} \tag{6-3}$$

Fig. 6-1 Fig. 6-2

This limit is the integral of F_x over x. So the work done by a variable force F_x acting on a particle as it moves from x_1 to x_2 is

$$A = \int_{x_1}^{x_2} F_x \mathrm{d}x = \text{area under the } F_x\text{-versus-}x \text{ curve} \tag{6-4}$$

For each displacement interval Δx_i, the force is essentially constant. Therefore the work done equals the area of the rectangle of height F_{xi} and width Δx_i. As was shown earlier, this work equals the change in kinetic energy for this displacement interval (if the force is the net force). The total work done is the sum of the areas over all displacement intervals. It follows that the total work equals the change in kinetic energy for the entire displacement. Thus, $A_{\text{total}} = \Delta E_k$ holds for variable forces as well as for constant forces.

6.2.3 Conservative Force and Potential Energy(保守力和势能)

The total work done on a particle equals the change in its kinetic energy. But we are often interested in the work done on a system consisting of two or more particles. Often, the work done by external forces on a system does not increase the total kinetic energy of the system, but instead is stored as **potential energy**—energy associated with the configuration of the system.

Potential Energy(势能)

Consider lifting a barbell of mass m to a height h. The work done by the gravitational force on the barbell starts at rest and ends at rest. Because the kinetic energy of the barbell does not change, we know the total work done on the barbell is zero. That means the work done by the force of your hands on the barbell is $+mgh$. Now consider the barbell and the earth to be a system of two particles (You are not the part of this system). The external forces on the earth-barbell system are the gravitational attraction you exert on the earth, the force your feet exert on the earth, and the force mg exerted by your hands on the barbell (Fig. 6-3). The barbell moves, but the motion of the earth is negligible, so only the force exerted on the barbell by your hands does work on the system. The total work done on the earth-barbell system by all forces external to the system is mgh. This work is stored as potential energy, which is energy associated with the position of the barbell relative to the earth. That is energy associated with

Fig. 6-3

the configuration of the earth-barbell system. This kind of energy is called **gravitational potential energy**.

Another system that stores energy associated with its configuration is a spring. If you stretch or compress a spring, energy associated with the length of the spring is stored as potential energy. Consider the spring shown in Fig. 6-4 as the system. You compress the spring, pushing it with equal and opposite forces F_1 and F_2. These forces sum to zero, so the net force on the spring remains zero. Thus, there is no change in the kinetic energy of the spring. The work you do on this system is stored not as kinetic energy, but as **elastic potential energy**. The configuration of this system has been changed, as evidenced by the change in the length of the spring. The total work done on the spring is positive because both F_1 and F_2 do positive work.

Conservative Force(保守力)

When you ride ski lift to the top of a hill of height h, the work done by gravity on you is $-mgh$ and the work done by the lift on you is $+mgh$ independent of the shape of the hill. The total work done by gravity on you during the round trip up and down the hill is zero, independent of the path you take. The force of gravity, exerted by the earth on you is a **conservative force**.

A force is conservative if the total work it does on a particle is zero when the particle moves around any closed path, returning to its initial position. From Fig. 6-5 we see that this definition implies that: The work done by a conservation force on a particle is independent of the path taken as the particle moves from one point to another.

Fig. 6-4

Fig. 6-5

Now consider yourself and the earth to be a two-particle system. (The ski lift is not part of this system.) When a ski lift raises you to the top of the hill, it does work mgh on the you-earth system. This work is stored as the gravitational potential energy of the system. When you ski down the hill, this potential energy is converted to the kinetic energy of your motion.

Glossary

work	功	point of application	作用点
joule	焦耳	notation	符号
eV	电子伏特	conservative force	保守力
potential energy	势能	positional function	位置函数
gravitational force	重力	elastic potential energy	弹性势能
independent of	与……无关		

6.3 专业英语常用表达法-6 原料 用途 功能或目的

1. 表示原料

除用 have, (be) made of, with 外,主要用"名词(或形容词)＋名词"这种结构:

a brick structure	砖结构	cut-off glass screen	玻璃隔热屏障
a concrete core	混凝土芯	a steel mast	钢柱
cast glass	压铸玻璃	a stone wall	石墙
rough-cast glass	毛玻璃	a wooden frame	木框
a glass screen	玻璃屏	tools made of iron	铁制工具

The new greenhouse *has a mild steel structure*, with glass beneath it. 这座新暖房(用的)是低碳钢结构,结构下面是玻璃。

A curved screen *is made of* steel and glass. 弧形隔热屏障是用钢和玻璃制的。

Up in the roof here, we have a 6mm thick *cast glass*. 在这里屋顶上用的是 6 mm 厚的

压铸玻璃。

Nearly 4500 square meters of space, under one low, *glass roof*. 近 4500 m² 的面积的都是在一个低矮的玻璃屋顶之下。

Locomotives *are built of* steel, and airplanes *of* aluminum. 火车头由钢制成，而飞机由铝制成。

We want *such materials as can bear high temperature and pressure*. 我们需要能耐高温高压的材料。

2．表示用途、功能或目的

（1）用 for 或动词不定式

The lab is an international centre *for physics research*. 该实验室是物理学研究的国际中心。

The institute is primarily a research establishment, but also it is there to *welcome the public*. 这个研究所主要是一个科研机构，但同时也面向公众。

（2）用 The function（或 purpose）is＋动词不定式

The rough-cast glass has several functions, and probably the main one *is to hide the internal structure*. 毛玻璃有好几个作用，主要的可能是为了把内部结构遮盖起来。

At the end we have a clear glass, and *its function* there *is* to give you a view out of the lab. 在末端用的是透明玻璃，它的作用是使你看得见实验室外边的情景。

（3）用下列词语

be designed＋动词不定式（或 for 短语）

help＋动词不定式

have the function of

serve the purpose of

The building *is designed primarily for* experiment facilities rather than people. 这座建筑是供实验仪器而不是供人们使用的。

The cast glass *helps to express* the internal configuration of the lab. 压铸玻璃有助于显露出实验室的内部结构。

It also *serves the purpose of* giving access over the roof for maintenance and for cleaning the glass. 它还起到这样的作用，使（工人）能走上屋顶，进行维修保养、清洗玻璃。

LESSON 7

7.1　物理学专业英语中的结果和结论

7.1.1　结果

在专业英语中，表示过程或计算的结果时，时态可采用一般过去时，语态可采用主动语态或被动语态。但是，被动语态的使用频率高于主动语态的使用频率。如果采用主动语态进行表达，那么，可以采用这一句型：主语＋宾语或由 that 引导的宾语从句。如：

Our final equation revealed an important general property of simple harmonic motion: the total mechanical energy in simple harmonic motion is proportional to the square of the amplitude. 最后的方程揭示了简谐运动的一个重要特点：简谐运动的总机械能与振幅的平方成正比。

展示研究结果，常用词汇有：show, result, present 等。

常见的表达方式有：…was(were)…; We found…; There was…等。

常见的用 that 从句表示结果的有：

The results indicated that … 结果表明……

The results showed that … 结果显示……

The results demonstrated that … 结果证明了……

The results revealed that … 结果揭示了……

常见的由 It 引导的 that 从句有：

It was shown that … 结果显示……

It can be seen that … 可以看出……

It was found that … 结果发现……

It was discovered that … 发现……

It was concluded that … 结论为……

It has been demonstrated that … 结果已经证明……

It was clarified that … 结果明确为……

It was revealed that … 说明/阐明……（结果），揭示了……

It is considered that … 考虑到……

It was confirmed that … 可以确信……

It is suggested that … 提出(……结果)

It was supposed that … 推测(……结果),假定(……结果)

It has become apparent that … 已经明显表明……

也可以用 to be 后面的表语成分表示测定、计算等的结果。例如

When the measured value of ε_0 and defined value of μ_0 are put into Eq. (15-1), the speed of electromagnetic waves is found *to be* about 3×10^8 m/s, the same as the measured speed of light. 当把 ε_0 的测定值和 μ_0 的定义值代入到方程(15-1)时，得到的电磁波的速度结果约为 3×10^8 m/s，这与测量所得到的光速相同。

For paramagnetic and diamagnetic materials, the magnetization is found *to be* proportional to the applied magnetic field that produces the alignment of the magnetic dipoles in the material. 对于顺磁质和抗磁质，磁化的程度正比于使磁介质产生磁偶极取向排列的外加磁场的强度。

The theoretical equation was proved *to be* correct by the experimental results. 实验的结果证实了理论方程的正确。

7.1.2 结论

结论句一般置于正文的最后，通常用于总结主要的研究成果、提出的独到见解或建议、

表明作者的观点和看法、陈述主要结论等。专业文章的结论语句简洁、突出重点。专业英文通常用完整的句子来表达结论,动词时态用一般现在时或现在完成时。在写作时通常直接写结论,也可用一些句型引出结论。介绍结论常用的词汇有:summary, sum up, introduce, conclude, as a result, in short, in a word, in brief, therefore 等。常用的英文表达方式有:

...is probably...　……或许是……

...is...　……是……

Our conclusion is that...　我们的结论是……

This study shows that...　研究表明……

This study suggests that...　研究提出……

This study confirms that...　研究确信……

These observations support...　这些观察支持(……结论)

The findings indicate that...　结果表明……

The results indicate/show that...　结果表明……

This paper concludes that...　这篇文章的结论……

This study/investigation/research leads the author(s) to conclusion that...　通过本研究作者得到的结论为……

The research enables us to conclude that...　通过研究我们得到的结论为……

It is concluded that...　结论为……

Thus, it can be concluded that...　所以,可以得出结论……

Draw the following conclusion...　得到如下结论……

The results agree with ...　这些结果与……一致

The experiment shows that...　实验表明……

It is suggested that...　可以推想(……结论),可以料想(……结论)

These results will/can be significant for...　这些结果对……来说会/可能有意义

In conclusion, ...　最后/总之,……

In general, ...　总体来说,……

To conclude, ...　总之,……

In brief, ...　简而言之,……

In a word, ...　总之,……

In short, ...　简而言之,……

In summary, ...　概括来说,……

By and large, ...　大体上/基本上……

All in all, ...　总而言之,……

Generally speaking, ...　总体来说,……

On the whole, ...　大体上……基本上……

For the above-mentioned reasons, ...　基于上述原因,……

As we have seen, ...　正如我们所知,……

As already mentioned, ...　正如已提及的一样,……

To sum up, ...　总之/总而言之,……

To summarize, ...　概括而言,……

We can easily come to the conclusion that...　我们很容易就可以得到这样的结论,……

What we can be sure of is that...　可以肯定的是……

Now it is believed that...　由此我们相信……

It is almost certainly true to say that...　几乎可以准确地说……

Clearly, ...　显然……

It may be possible to (do something)...　可能(发生……情况)

Therefore, we can find that...　因此,我们发现……

It is quite clear that...　很明显……,很清楚……

It is well-known that...　众所周知……

Now it comes to conclusion that...　可以得出结论……

There is no doubt that...　无疑……

以上句型中,措辞不同,表明对结论的肯定程度不同。

We can *draw the following general conclusion*: For any system the most probable macroscopic state is the one with the greatest number of corresponding microscopic states, which is also the macroscopic state with greatest disorder and the greatest entropy. 我们可以得到如下一般结论：任何系统的最概然宏观态就是具有最大数目对应微观态的状态,也就是具有最大无序和最大熵的宏观态。

To illustrate this further, *we can make the conclusion of* boundary conditions for Half-wave Loss... 为了进一步说明,我们可以把半波损失的边界条件的结论归纳为……

Comparing Eq.(20-23) and Eq.(20-24), we can *conclude* that when simple harmonic waves propagate, for each element of the medium, kinetic energy equals potential energy at any time. 把方程(20-23)和方程(20-24)相比较,我们得到的结论为：当简谐波传播时,媒质中的每一质元的动能和势能在任何时刻都相等。

Clearly, this inelastic collision is an irreversible process. 显然,这种非弹性碰撞是不可逆过程。

Now I would like *to sum up* what I said in a few sentences. 现在我想用几个句子来总结一下我讲过的内容。

The long and short of it is that the experimental results coincide with the theoretical speculations to a certain extent. 总之,实验结果与理论推测在一定程度上相吻合。

Thus the conclusion we can draw is that the kind of materials is not suitable to be used under high temperature. 因此我们可以得出结论,这种材料不适合用在高温环境中。

In general, all the characteristics of the ferromagnetic material come from the special internal structure of it. 总之,铁磁材料的特性都源自其内部的特殊结构。

7.2 专业英语阅读

7.2.1 Rigid Body(刚体)

In order to study some problems easily, we used to imagine some bodies as **rigid bodies**, which are idealized models of particles system. If the body is nondeformable or the separations between all pairs of particles in the body remain constant, we may look it as a rigid body, which consists of a large number of particles, each with its own velocity and acceleration.

7.2.2 Law of Rotation of a Rigid Body about a Fixed Axis(刚体定轴转动定律)

To set a top spinning, you twist it. In Fig. 7-1, a disk is set spinning by the forces $\boldsymbol{F}_1$ and $\boldsymbol{F}_2$ exerted at the edges of the disk in the tangential direction. The directions of these forces are important. If the same forces are applied in the radial direction (Fig. 7-2), the disk will not start to spin.

Fig. 7-1   Fig. 7-2

Fig. 7-3 shows a particle of mass m attached to one end of a massless rigid rod of length r. There is an axis perpendicular to the rod and passing through its other end, and the rod is free to rotate about this axis. Consequently, the particle is constrained to move in a circle of radius r. A single force $\boldsymbol{F}$ is applied to the particle as shown. Applying Newton's second law to the particle and taking components in the tangential direction gives $F_t = ma_t$. We wish to obtain an equation involving angular quantities. Substituting $r\alpha$ for a_t and multiplying both sides by r gives

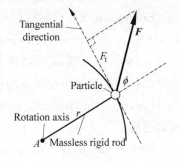

Fig. 7-3

$$rF_t = mr^2\alpha \tag{7-1}$$

The product rF_t is the **torque** M associated with the force. That is,

$$M = F_t r \tag{7-2}$$

Substituting into Eq. (7-1) gives

$$M = mr^2\alpha \tag{7-3}$$

A rigid object that rotates about a fixed axis is just a collection of individual particles, each of which is constrained to move in a circular path with the same angular velocity ω and acceleration α.

$$M_{i\text{-net}} = m_i r_i^2 \alpha$$

Applying a rigid object that rotates about a fixed axis is just a collection of individual particles, each of which is constrained to move in a circular path with the same angular velocity ω and acceleration α. Applying Eq. (7-1) to the ith of these particles gives

$$M_{i\text{-net}} = m_i r_i^2 \alpha$$

where $M_{i\text{-net}}$ is the torque due to the net force on the i th particle. Summing both sides over all particles gives

$$\sum M_{i\text{-net}} = \sum m_i r_i^2 \alpha = \left(\sum m_i r_i^2\right) \alpha = J\alpha \qquad (7\text{-}4)$$

The sum in the term on the right is the object's **moment of inertia** J for the axis of rotation.

$$J = \sum_i m_i r_i^2 \qquad (7\text{-}5)$$

In the past we saw that the net force acting on a system of particles is equal to the net force acting on the system because the internal forces (those exerted by the particles within the system on one another) cancel in pairs. The treatment of internal torques exerted by the particles within a system on one another leads to a similar result, that is, the net torque acting on a system equals the net external torque acting on the system. We can thus write Eq. (7-4) as

$$M_{\text{net,ext}} = \sum M_{\text{ext}} = J\alpha \qquad (7\text{-}6)$$

So *torque acting on a rigid body is proportional to its angular acceleration, and the proportionality constant is the moment of inertia*. This is **law of rotation of a rigid body about a fixed axis**, which is analog of Newton's second law for linear motion, $\sum \boldsymbol{F} = m\boldsymbol{a}$.

7.2.3 Torque and Angular Momentum(力矩和角动量)

Torque is expressed mathematically as the cross product (or vector product) of $\boldsymbol{r}$ and $\boldsymbol{F}$

$$\boldsymbol{M} = \boldsymbol{r} \times \boldsymbol{F} \qquad (7\text{-}7)$$

Fig. 7-4 shows a particle of mass m moving with a velocity $\boldsymbol{v}$ at a position $\boldsymbol{r}$ relative to the origin O. The linear momentum of the particle is $\boldsymbol{p} = m\boldsymbol{v}$. The **angular momentum** $\boldsymbol{L}$ of the particle relative to the origin O is defined to be the cross product of $\boldsymbol{r}$ and $\boldsymbol{p}$

$$\boldsymbol{L} = \boldsymbol{r} \times \boldsymbol{p} \qquad (7\text{-}8)$$

If $\boldsymbol{r}$ and $\boldsymbol{p}$ are in the xy plane, as in Fig. 7-4, $\boldsymbol{L}$ is parallel with the z axis and is given by $\boldsymbol{L} = \boldsymbol{r} \times \boldsymbol{p} = mvr\sin\phi \boldsymbol{k}$. Like torque, angular momentum is defined relative to a point in space.

Fig. 7-5 shows a particle of mass m attached to a circular disk of negligible mass in the xy plane with its center at the origin. The disk is spinning about its axis with angular speed ω. The speed v of the particle and its angular speed are related by $v = r\omega$. The angular momentum of the particle relative to the center of the disk is

Fig. 7-4

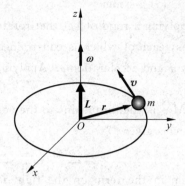

Fig. 7-5

$$L = r \times p = r \times mv = rmv\sin 90°k$$
$$= rmvk = mr^2\omega k = mr^2\omega$$

The angular momentum vector is in the same direction as the angular velocity vector. Since mr^2 is the moment of inertia for a single particle about the z axis, we have

$$L = mr^2\omega = J_z\omega$$

This result does not hold for the angular momentum about a general point on the z axis. Fig. 7-6 shows the angular momentum vector L for the same particle attached to the same disk but with L' computed about a point on z axis that is not at the center of the circle. In this case, the angular momentum is not parallel to the angular velocity vector ω, which is parallel with z axis.

In Fig. 7-7, we attach a second particle of equal mass to the spinning disk. The angular momentum vector L_1' and L_2' are shown relative to the same point O'. The total angular momentum $L_1' + L_2'$ of the two-particle system is again parallel to the angular velocity ω. In this case, the axis of rotation, the z axis, passes through the center of mass of the two-particle system, and the mass distribution is symmetric about this axis. Such an

Fig. 7-6

Fig. 7-7

axis is called a **symmetry axis**. For any system of particles that rotates about a symmetry axis, the total angular momentum (which is the sum of the angular momenta of the individual particles) is parallel to the angular velocity and is given by

$$L = J\boldsymbol{\omega} \tag{7-9}$$

There are several additional results concerning torque and angular momentum for a system of particles. The first of these is

$$M_{\text{net,ext}} = \frac{dL_{\text{sys}}}{dt} \tag{7-10}$$

The net external torque acting on a system equals the rate of change of the angular momentum of the system. This is called **theorem of angular momentum.**

Glossary

torque	力矩	axis of rotation	旋转轴
moment of inertia	转动惯量	proportionality constant	比例常数
analog	类似、相似	is proportional to	与……成正比
mass distribution	质量分布	symmetry axis	对称轴
angular momentum	角动量	theorem of angular momentum	角动量定理

7.3 专业英语常用表达法-7 形状

1. 基本形状

triangle	三角形	right triangle	直角三角形
isosceles triangle	等腰三角形	equilateral triangle	等边三角形
obtuse angle	钝角	acute angle	锐角
right angle	直角	square	正方形
rectangle	矩形	parallelogram	平行四边形
trapezoid	梯形	rhombus	菱形
polygon	多边形	quadrilateral	四边形
pentagon	五边形	hexagon	六边形
octagon	八边形	circle	圆形
semicircle	半圆	ellipse	椭圆
cylinder	圆柱	cone	圆锥
cube	正方体	cuboid	长方体
sector	扇形	cone	锥形
cube	立方形	curve	曲线
cylinder	圆柱(筒)形	sphere	球形
hemisphere	半球形	ellipsoid	椭面、椭圆形
oblong	长方形	pyramid	棱锥形

2. 描述形状常用形容词

circular 圆形的、环状的	conical 锥形的
(criss-)cross 十字形的	cubical 立方形的
curved 曲线的、弯曲的	cylindrical 圆柱形的
depressed 凹陷的	ellipsoidal 椭圆的
flat （扁）平的	half-round 半圆的
half-moon-shaped 半月形的	heart-shaped 心形的
hemispherical 半球形的	hollow 空心的
hyperbolic 双曲线的	I-shaped 工字形
oblong 长方形的	pointed/sharp 尖的
pyramidal 棱锥形的、金字塔形的	rectangular 矩形的
round/rounded 圆的	semicircular 半圆形的
spherical 球形的	spindle-shaped 纺锤形的
square 正方形的	solid 实心的
straight 直(线)的	star-shaped 星形的
triangular 三角形的	U-shaped U形的

3. 常用词组

a curved surface 曲面	a flat cable 扁平电缆
a pointed roof 尖形屋顶	rectangular timber 方木
a round box 圆盒	a spherical mirror 球面镜
triangular compasses 三角规	T-plate T字板
T-socket T形套管	I-bar 工字铁
I-steel 工字钢	cross-wire 十字线
herring bone pattern 人字形	herring bone gear 人字齿轮
Y-connection Y形连接	X-tube X形管
U-pipe U形管	Z-beam Z字梁
A-frame A形架	C-washer C形垫圈
O-ring O形环	S-wrench S形扳手
T-track 锤形径迹	U-bolt 马蹄螺栓
V-belt 三角皮带	set square 三角板
clamp 弓形夹具	U-steel 槽钢
Y-pipe 叉形管	X-type 交叉形

4. 常用词语结构

be＋adj.（＋in shape/form） （形状）是……的, 是……形的
be shaped like... 形状像……
have the shape of... 具有……形状
(be) in the shape of... 呈……的形状, 以……的形式
take the shape of... 呈……的形状

This plate is *curved/flat*.　这块板是弯的/平的。

This rod is *pointed/rounded* at one end.这根棒一头是尖/圆的。

This line is *straight/curved*.这条线是直的/弯的。

What *shape* is the top of the rocket? 火箭顶部是什么形状？

The lab building is built *in the shape of* a letter "L". 这座实验室造成字母L形。

The top of the planetarium *is like a snail in shape*.天文馆的顶部形状像一只蜗牛。

The coil *is rectangular in shape*.这线圈是矩形的。

The flask *resembles a pear in shape*.这烧瓶的外形像只梨。

The curves *are hyperbolic in form*.这些曲线是双曲线。

A wheel *has the same shape as* the letter "O"。车轮的形状与字母O相同。

The curve of normal distribution *is shaped like* a bell. 正态分布曲线的形状像一口钟。

A safety-pin *is so shaped that* it cannot easily prick you. 安全别针做成不易伤人的形状。

The simplest wave form *is a sinusoidal* curve.最简单的波形是正弦曲线。

In weightlessness, a drop of liquid *takes a spherical shape/takes the shape of a sphere*.在失重状态,一滴液体呈球形。

LESSON 8

8.1 物理学专业英语在口语体上的特点

专业英语口语体兼有专业英语及一般英语口语体的某些特点。

1) 使用大量的术语以及书面词语

例如常见的用语有 be concerned with, be subjected to, be exposed to, the order of 等。

It is well known that, different from physics, chemistry *is concerned with* the composition, properties and structure of substances and *with* the changes they undergo. 众所周知,与物理学不同,化学是研究物质的成分、(化学)性质及其结构的,还研究这些物质(在化学反应中)的变化。

The sample temperature was controlled by a thermocouple with a precision on *the order of* 0.1℃. 样品温度用热电偶控制,其精度在0.1℃左右。

2) 重在客观的叙述,较少使用人称代词

为了使内容的叙述更加客观,句子中通常不出现人称代词,如果使用也常用one或we。例如:

There is a steady loss of energy in the cycle. 在循环中能量持续损失。

In the real case *there is* a need for energy compensation. 在实际情况中需要补充能量。

As *one* shakes the end of a stretched rope, the disturbance transfers energy from the hand to the rope and a wave pulse travels down the rope. 摇动绳子的一端,扰动就会把能量从手传递给绳子,一个波脉冲就会在绳子上传播。

If *we* look into the experiment we can see the secret of what is happening. 如果我们审视一下实验,就会明白事情发生的原因。

3）用名词短语替代从句

口语使用名词短语的目的在于可以使整个句子的结构简化,易于理解。例如：

They enjoy *the newness of the building*. 相当于 They like the building *because it is new*.

These experiments demonstrated *the truth of the theory*. 相当于 These experiments demonstrated *that the theory is true*.

4）用"主语＋谓语动词的被动态＋动词不定式"替代名词从句。

例如：

An atom *is found to consist of* electrons and some other very small particles.（相当于 *It is found that* an atom consists of electrons...）。（据认为）原子是由电子及其他微粒子所组成。

这就是说,"主语＋谓语动词的被动态＋动词不定式"这种结构由于能使语言简练,在专业口语体中是常见的,能用于这种结构的谓语动词有 know, think, believe, say 等。

Alloy steel *is said to be* a carefully made steel.（相当于 *It is said that* alloy steel is a carefully made steel.）合金钢可以说是一种精细冶炼的钢。

5）对量度表达没有书面语那么确切并具体

专业英语口语在表达量度时通常不像书面语那么具体,有时只是笼统地说"高、矮、大、小、长、短"等。

The tidal range is *of the order of* 10 *meters*. 浪高在 10 m 的数量级。（书面体）

The tide is *as high as* 10 *meters*/10 *meters high*.（口语体）

Some waves have been *of heights of up to 7 or 9 meters*. 有的浪高达到 7 m 或 9 m。（书面体）

Some waves have been 7 *or* 9 *meters high*.（口语体）

6）经常使用主动语态

在专业英语书面体中常用被动语态,但在口语体中,会经常用 we 作主语的主动语态。

If the end of a stretched rope *is given* a quick shake, the disturbance transfers energy from the hand to the rope.（书面体）

If *we* give the end of a stretched rope a quick shake, the disturbance transfers energy from the hand to the rope.（口语体）

7）其他特点

一般地说,专业英语口语体还有不简练、冗余度大、用词不推敲、语法不规范、结构和层次不严密、边说边自我纠正等特点。例如：

The fact that the lab *is designing* primarily for experiment facilities rather than people, *that* makes it particularly special. 实验室的设计主要是供实验设备而不是供人使用的,这就使得它有其独特之处。

这句话是口语体,在语法和用词上不很严格。如果严格规范要求,is designing 要改为 is designed；第二个 that 要去掉。

Internally the structure is very much played down and the various instruments are beginning to dominate and it's very important, I feel, right from the outset, that the instruments should be allowed to dominate internally, especially as the spaces are relatively small and the roof is relatively low. 在实验室内,钢架结构已不占主要地位,突出的是各种仪器。我认为从一开始就要重视使各种仪器在室内居主导地位,这尤其是因为要考虑到室内的空间相对来说是少了些,屋顶也较低了些。

这是一个包含有6个子句的长句。因为属于口语体,有几层意思是反复说的,显得不够简练。其中,I feel 是一个表示态度的插入句;right 用以强调 from the outset,意思是:从一开始就……;it is important that... 是一句型,表示愿望、建议等,that 从句中的谓语用 should +v.(这是口语体),如果是书面语体,可用动词原形,即 It is important that the instruments be allowed...。

Any glassware which has a ... a delicate shape, an interesting shape, is seen very clearly against a cast glass background, it's seen in silhouette.

在口语体中,因为是即席讲话,往往不可能做到字斟句酌,于是当讲话人发现用字不当时,可随时加以修正。如这里先用了 has a... a delicate shape(有一个细小的、优美的形状),说后感到 delicate 并不达意,于是又加上了 an interesting shape,这个短语可以说是对前一个短语的修正。

8.2 专业英语阅读

8.2.1 Oscillation(振动)

Oscillation occurs when a system is disturbed from a position of stable equilibrium. There are many familiar examples: boats bob up and down, clock pendulums swing back and forth, and the strings and reeds of musical instruments vibrate. Others, less familiar examples are the oscillations of air molecules in a sound wave and the oscillations of electric currents in radios and television sets.

In this section, we deal mostly with simple harmonic motion, the most basic type of oscillatory motion. Applying the kinetics and dynamics of simple harmonic motion provides the analysis of the oscillatory motion of a variety of interesting systems. In some situations dissipative forces dampen the oscillatory motion, but in other situations driving forces sustain the motion by compensating for the damping.

8.2.2 Description of Simple Harmonic Motion (简谐运动的描述)

A common, very important and very basic kind of oscillatory motion is **simple harmonic motion**(**SHM**) such as the motion of an object attached to a spring (Fig. 8-1).

Fig. 8-1 A spring system

The **kinetic equation** for a Simple Harmonic Motion is
$$x(t) = A\cos(\omega t + \varphi) \tag{8-1}$$
where A, ω, and φ are constants. It is a mathematical representation of the position of the particle as a function of the time. For the spring system, x is the displacement of the object from its equilibrium position. In general, x can be any oscillatory quantities.

There are three property quantities for a Simple Harmonic Motion:

The maximum displacement $x_{\max}$ from equilibrium position is called the **amplitude** A. The value of the amplitude depends on initial position and the energy of the system. The constant ω is called the **angular frequency**. It has units of radians per second and dimensions of inverse time, the same as angular speed, which is also designated by ω. *The time it takes for a displaced object to execute a complete cycle of oscillatory motion—*from one extreme to the other extreme and back—is called the **period** T. The unit of the period is second. The reciprocal of the period is the **frequency** ν, which is *the number of cycle per second*
$$\nu = \frac{1}{T} \tag{8-2}$$

The unit of the frequency is the cycle per second (cy/s), which is called a hertz (Hz).

The period T is the shortest time satisfying the relation
$$x(t) = x(t+T)$$
for all t. Substituting into this relation using Eq. (8-1) gives
$$A\cos(\omega t + \varphi) = A\cos[\omega(t+T) + \varphi]$$
$$= A\cos(\omega t + \varphi + \omega T)$$
The cosine (and sine) function repeats in value when the angle increases by 2π, so
$$\omega T = 2\pi \quad \left(\text{or } \omega = \frac{2\pi}{T}\right) \tag{8-3}$$
The frequency is the reciprocal of the period
$$\nu = \frac{1}{T} = \frac{\omega}{2\pi} \tag{8-4}$$

The argument of the cosine function in Eq. (8-1), $\omega t + \varphi$, is called the **phase** of the motion, and the constant φ is called the **phase constant**, which is the phase at $t=0$. If we have just one oscillating systems, we can always choose $t=0$ at which $\varphi=0$. If we have two systems oscillating with the same amplitude and frequency but different phase, we can choose $\varphi=0$ for one of them. The equations for the two systems are then
$$x_1 = A\cos(\omega t)$$
and
$$x_2 = A\cos(\omega t + \varphi)$$
We can see by inspection that each time t increases by T, the phase increases by 2π and one cycle of the motion is completed.

8.2.3 Energy in Simple Harmonic Motion(简谐运动的能量)

When an object on a spring undergoes simple harmonic motion, the system's potential energy and kinetic energy vary with time. Their sum, the total mechanical energy $E = E_p + E_k$, is constant. Consider an object a distance x from equilibrium, acted on by a restoring force $-kx$. The system's potential energy is

$$E_p = \frac{1}{2}kx^2$$

For simple harmonic motion, $x(t) = A\cos(\omega t + \varphi)$. Substituting gives

$$E_p = \frac{1}{2}kA^2 \cos^2(\omega t + \varphi) \tag{8-5}$$

The kinetic energy of the system is

$$E_k = \frac{1}{2}mv^2$$

where m is the object's mass and v is its speed. For simple harmonic motion, $v_x = -\omega A \sin(\omega t + \varphi)$. Substituting gives

$$E_k = \frac{1}{2}m\omega^2 A^2 \sin^2(\omega t + \varphi)$$

Then using $\omega^2 = k/m$,

$$E_k = \frac{1}{2}kA^2 \sin^2(\omega t + \varphi) \tag{8-6}$$

The total mechanical energy is the sum of the potential and kinetic energies:

$$E_{\text{total}} = E_p + E_k = \frac{1}{2}kA^2 \cos^2(\omega t + \varphi) + \frac{1}{2}kA^2 \sin^2(\omega t + \varphi)$$

$$= \frac{1}{2}kA^2[\cos^2(\omega t + \varphi) + \sin^2(\omega t + \varphi)]$$

Since $\cos^2(\omega t + \varphi) + \sin^2(\omega t + \varphi) = 1$,

$$E_{\text{total}} = E_p + E_k = \frac{1}{2}kA^2 \tag{8-7}$$

This equation reveals an important general property of simple harmonic motion: the total mechanical energy in simple harmonic motion is proportional to the square of the amplitude.

For an object at its maximum displacement, the total energy is all potential energy. As the object moves toward its equilibrium position, the kinetic energy of the system increases and its potential energy decreases. As it moves through its equilibrium position, the kinetic energy of the object is maximum, the potential energy of the system is zero, and the total energy is kinetic.

As the object moves past the equilibrium point, its kinetic energy begins to decrease, and the potential energy of the system increases until the object again stops momentarily at its maximum displacement (now in the other direction). At all times, the sum of the potential and kinetic energies is constant. Fig. 8-2 shows plots of E_p and E_k versus time. These curves have the same shape except

Fig. 8-2

that one is zero when the other is maximum. Their average values over one or more cycles are equal, and because $E_{\text{total}} = E_p + E_k = \frac{1}{2}kA^2$, their average values are given by

$$\overline{E}_P = \overline{E}_k = \frac{1}{2}E$$

8.2.4 Damped Oscillations(阻尼振动)

Left to itself, a spring or a pendulum eventually stops oscillating because the mechanical energy is dissipated by frictional forces. Such motion is said to be **damped**. If the damping is large enough, as, for example, a pendulum submerged in molasses, the oscillator fails to complete even one cycle of oscillation. Instead it just moves toward the equilibrium position with a speed that approaches zero as the object approaches the equilibrium position. This type of motion is referred to as **overdamped**. If the damping is small enough that the system oscillates with an amplitude that decreases slowly with time—like a child on a playground swing when Mum stops providing a push each cycle—the motion is said to be **underdamped**. Motion with the minimum damping for nonoscillatory motion is said to be **critically damped**.

8.2.5 Driven Oscillations and Resonance(受迫振动和共振)

To keep a damped system going, mechanical energy must be put into the system. When this is done, the oscillator is said to be **driven** or **forced**. When you keep a swing going by "pumping", that is, by moving your body and legs, you are driving an oscillator. If you put mechanical energy into the system faster than it is dissipated, the mechanical energy increases with time, and the amplitude increases. If you put mechanical energy in at the same rate it is being dissipated, the amplitude remains constant over time. The motion of the oscillation is then said to be in **steady state**.

Fig. 8-3

Fig. 8-3 shows a system consisting of an object on a spring that is being driven by moving the point of support up and down with simple harmonic motion of frequency ω. At first the motion is complicated, but eventually steady state motion is reached in which the system oscillates with the same frequency as that of the driver and with a constant amplitude and, therefore, at constant energy. In the steady state, the energy put into the system per cycle by the driving force equals the energy dissipated per cycle due to the damping.

The amplitude, and therefore the energy, of a system in the steady state depends not only on the amplitude of the driving force, but also on its frequency. The **natural frequency** of a oscillator, ω_0, is its frequency when no driving or damping force are present (In the case of a spring, for example, $\omega_0 = \sqrt{k/m}$). If the driving frequency is approximately equal to the natural frequency of the system, the system will oscillate with a relatively large amplitude. For example, if the support in Fig. 8-3 oscillates at a frequency close to the natural frequency of the mass-spring system, the mass will oscillate with a much greater amplitude than it would if the support oscillates at higher or lower frequencies. This phenomenon is called **resonance**. When the driving frequency equals the natural frequency of the oscillator, the energy per cycle transferred to the oscillator is maximum. The natural frequency of the system is thus called the **resonance frequency**.

There are many familiar examples of resonance. When you sit on a swing, you learn intuitively to pump with the same frequency as the natural frequency of the swing. Many machines vibrate because they have rotating parts that are not in perfect balance (observe a washing machine in the spin cycle for an example). If such a machine is attached to a structure that can vibrate, the structure becomes a driven oscillatory system that is set in motion by the machine. Engineers pay great attention to balancing the rotary parts of such machines, damping their vibrations, and isolating them from building supports.

Glossary

oscillation/vibration	振动	oscillatory motion	振动
simple harmonic motion (SHM)		dissipative force	耗散力
	简谐运动	spring	弹簧
damping	阻尼	angular frequency	角频率、圆频率
equilibrium position	平衡位置	period	周期
radian	弧度	reciprocal	倒数
hertz(Hz)	赫兹	argument	辐角
amplitude	振幅	phase angle/(phase constant)	
phase	相、位相、周相		初相、初位相
average value	平均值	dissipate	消耗
damped oscillations	阻尼振动	submerge	浸入
molasses	糖蜜	oscillator	振子
overdamping	过阻尼	critically damped	临界阻尼的
overdamped	过阻尼的	driven oscillation	受迫振动
steady state	稳态	underdamped	欠阻尼的
resonance	共振	critical damped	临界阻尼
natural frequency	固有频率	resonance frequency	共振频率
nonoscillatory	不摆动的、不振动的		

8.3 专业英语常用表达法-8 面积 体积 容量

1. 面积的表示法

(1) 通常用 by,表示乘、除及度量关系

The room is 6 meters *by* four. 这个房间长 6 m,宽 4 m。

Multiply the base *by* the height and you have the area of a rectangle. 底乘以高,就可得出长方形的面积。

This is a room 20 by 30 feet. ＝This is a room 20 feet by 30. ＝This is a room 20×30 ft. 这是一个20 ft 宽 30 ft 长的房间。

(2) 其他表示方法

The room has an area of ten square meters. ＝The area of the room is ten square meters. ＝The room is ten square meters in area. ＝The room covers an area of ten square meters. 这个房间的面积为 10 m²。

Tianjin is about 11 760.26 square kilometers in the area. 天津面积约为 11 760.26 km²。

China's land area is 9 600 000 sq km. 我国国土面积是 960 万 km²。

2. 体积、容量的表示法

(1) 常用"基数词＋长度名词＋by＋基数词＋宽度名词＋by＋基数词＋高度名词"表示,若长、宽、高的单位一致,则通常省略后两个单位名词。如:

The box is eight inches *by* six *by* five. 这个盒子长、宽、高分别为 8 in、6 in、5 in。

The box measures three feet *by* four *by* two. 这箱子的尺寸是 3 ft×4 ft×2 ft。

(2) 用 capacity, volume 以及 cube(立方), cubed(自乘二次的), to the third power (……的三次方), liter, cubic meter, cumec, cubic centimeter 等。其结构有:The volume/capacity is…; has a capacity of…; be with a capacity of…等。例如:

The pretreatment works will *have a capacity of* 45 cumecs, or 45 cubic meters per second. 这个预处理厂将会有 45 m³/s 的处理能力。

The *capacity* of the treatment works *is approximately* 45 cumecs. 这个处理厂的处理能力约为 45 m³/s。

Before the waste joins the sea, it will pass through a large new pretreatment works *with a capacity of* 45 cumecs, or 45 cubic meters per second. 污水在流入海之前,要先通过一个容量为 45 m³/s 新建的大型预处理厂。

The formula for *the volume of* a cube with edge l is $V=l^3$. (V equals l cubed, or V equals l to the third power) 求边长为 l 的立方体的体积,其公式为:$V=l^3$。

The *volume* measuring accuracy of this system is ±0.25%. 系统容积的测量精度为 ±0.25%。

Unit Three

LESSON 9

9.1 物理学专业英语中的长句分析(一)

总的来说,专业英语文献中的句子长度呈现两种趋向:长难句多,短的简单句也多。一个句子长达一百来个单词,构成一个完整的段落的现象屡见不鲜。

物理学专业英语用于表达科学理论、原理、规律、概述,以及各事物之间错综复杂的关系,而复杂的科学思维是无法使用简单句来表达的。为了表示严谨、精确的含义,语法结构复杂的长句有较多的应用,而这种严谨周密、层次分明、重点突出的语言手段也就成了专业英语文体又一重要特征。长句由基本句型扩展而成,其方式有增加修饰成分如定语、状语的,有用各种短语如介词、分词、动名词或不定式短语充当句子成分的,也可能是通过关联词将两个或两个以上的句子组合成复合句。从句子结构来看,英语中句子可分简单句,并列复合句和主从复合句。

英语利用形态变化、词序和虚词三大语法手段可构成包孕许多修饰成分或从句的长句,句中各部分顺序灵活多样。通常英语句中的表态部分(如判断和结论)在先,而叙事部分(如事实和描写)在后,汉语则正好相反;英语句中先短后长,"头轻脚重",而汉语也正好相反;英语借助形态变化和连接手段而将句中成分灵活排列,汉语则常按时间和逻辑顺序由先到后、由因到果、由假设到推论、由事实到结论这样排列。

在专业英语的学习中,长句的分析是一个非常重要的基础,无论是专业文献阅读、翻译还是严谨精确地写作,都要从长句分析开始。长句分析既重要也有些难度。然而,无论多长的句子、多么复杂的结构,它们都是由一些基本的成分组成的。只要弄清英语原文的句法结构,找出整个句子的中心内容,理解各层意思,然后分析各层意思之间的逻辑关系,再按汉语的特点和方式表达就可以理解或译出原文了。

9.1.1 长句结构的分析

抓住主干,添枝加叶。所谓抓住主干,就是在理解长句时首先要找到主语、谓语这两个主要成分。添枝加叶,就是在主语、谓语这两个主要成分的基础上,逐个加上各种修饰语,包括定语、状语、补语、非谓语动词结构、各种从句等。比如:

In the engine, the heat required to change the water into steam is produced by the combination of the oxygen gas in the air with the fuel. 在蒸汽机中,把水变成蒸汽所需要的热是由空气中的氧气与燃料结合而产生的。

该句主语 heat 容易确定，它后面紧跟一个动词过去分词 required，这个 required 很容易误解为谓语，其实真正的谓语是 is produced。

Laser, its creation being thought to be one of today's wonders, is nothing more than a light①*that differs from ordinary lights only in* ②*that it is many times more powerful* and so be applied in fields ③ *that no ordinary light or other substance has ever been able to get in*.

此例是带有两个定语从句和一个宾语从句的主从复合句。主句为"Laser…is nothing more than a light."。定语从句①修饰主句中的名词 light，宾语从句②为介词 in 的宾语，定语从句③修饰名词 fields。另外，主句中又有一个独立主格结构"its creation…today's wonder"作状语。

The property the air has of taking up a great amount of water when heated and giving it out when cooled, is the cause of our clouds and rain. 空气所具有的这种热时吸收、冷时放出大量水汽的性能，是云和雨生成的原因。

该句主语 property 后面省略了一个 that 或 which，用来引导定语从句 the air has，修饰主语的介词短语 of taking… and giving…中又套两个用 when 引导的状语从句，显得句子结构复杂。借助 is 前面这个逗号，使我们找到了这个谓语联系动词。

在进行长句分析时，首先要理解透原文，分析句子结构，弄清语法关系。而对一个句子做结构分析，通常可采取下列步骤：通读全句，确定句子的种类——简单句或复合句，然后对句子的各种成分进行层次分析。

9.1.2 简单句的分析

对于简单句，进行句子分析时，要先找出句子的主要成分——主语、谓语，并进一步判明句中其余部分的语法成分——宾语、定语、状语、补足语、同位语、插入语等。一个简单句中只有一个主语和谓语，主谓结构是句子的骨干（主干）；其他的句子成分，如定语、状语、补语等，则是生长在这个骨干上的次要（枝叶）成分。因此，在分析简单句时，应首先找出主语和谓语，再确定其他成分跟主语和谓语之间的关系以及各次要成分之间的关系。在把原文的意思彻底弄清楚之后，再来考虑如何用中文进行表达。例如：

In order to understand the operation of a transistor, it is first necessary to be familiar with the mechanism of charge transfer across a junction formed between a piece of n-type semi-conductor and a piece of p-type semi-conductor.

分析：在这个句子中。It 是句子的形式主语，真正的主语是 to be familiar with the mechanism；is necessary 是谓语。of charge transfer across a junction 是个介词短语，作 mechanism 的定语；formed 是过去分词，作 junction 的定语；between a piece of n-type semi-conductor 是介词短语，作 formed 的状语。In order to…transistor 是个目的状语，修饰全句。这个句子有三层意思：①为了理解晶体管的工作原理；②首先必须熟悉电荷越过结的机理；③结是在一块 n 型半导体材料和一块 P 型半导体材料之间形成的。

9.1.3 复合句的分析

所谓复合句就是由两个或两个以上完整的子句组合而成的句子。一般来说，英语中一个句子只能有一个谓语,如果出现两个谓语,那么其中一个谓语只能是以从句、并列句或非谓语动词的形式出现。

把两个子句结合在一个句子中,英语需要加上连接词或加上标点符号。而由连接词 and,or,but…或标点符号结合的子句,在全句内处于并列的地位,这样的复合句称为并列复合句。这种复合句不过是简单地将两句写成一句而已,所以分析起来并不困难。

另一类复合句中的子句地位不平等,一个子句是主句,其他是从句,这样的复合句称为主从复合句。主从复合句是由主句+从句构成,它是专业英语学习中比较复杂的句子结构。所谓从句是指从属于主句的句子,由从属连词连接。从句的种类有很多,但根据其性质和作用可以分为:名词性从句、形容词性从句(即定语从句)、副词性从句(即状语从句)三大类。

在进行句子分析时,如遇到的长句为复合句,按照我们刚才介绍的方法"抓住主干,添枝加叶",应先找出主句,然后再确定各个从句的性质及其作用,判明各从句之间的关系——并列关系或从属关系,并对各成分进行层次分析。

对于结构复杂,层次纷纭的主从复合句要抓住引导各种从句的连词,弄清各种从句的性质,这样就能掌握全局结构,分清主次。

在复合句中,包含从句较多的长句又可以分为以下几种:

1) 以状语从句或含有从句的状语短语开头的长主从复合句

由于状语可以位于句首,因而很多长句是以状语从句或含有从句的状语短语开头的。在从句末尾往往有一逗号,逗号之后就是主句。这样的长句,在结构上与汉语的句子类似。例如:

①Although there exists much experimental knowledge in regard to the behaviour of bodies ②which are not in the conditions ③to which the mathematical theory is applicable, yet it appears ④that the appropriate extensions of the theory ⑤which would be needed in order to incorporate such knowledge within it cannot be made ⑥ until much fuller experimental knowledge has been obtained.

这是一个以 although 引导的让步状语从句开头的复合句。它的从句多达六个:①although 引导的修饰主句谓语的让步状语从句;②which 引导的修饰 bodies 的定语从句;③to which 引导的修饰 conditions 的定语从句;④that 引导的主语从句;⑤which 引导的修饰 extensions 的定语从句;⑥until 引导的修饰 cannot be made 的时间状语从句。

2) 以主句开头的长主从复合句

主句位于句首,后面可以接以引导词引导的各种从句,如主语从句、定语从句、状语从句等。例如:

Viscosity is a general term for all those properties of matter ①by virtue of which the resistance, ②which a body offers to any change, depends upon the rate ③at which the change is effected.

这是一个以主句开头的复合句。其中包含三个从句:①以 by virtue of which 引导的定语从句;②以 which 引导的修饰 resistance 的定语从句;③以 at which 引导的修饰 rate 的定语从句。

3) 并列成分多或长的长复合句

正确判断并列成分是能否对长句进行正确分析的重要因素。这些并列的成分,既可以是并列的分句,也可以是并列的主语、谓语、宾语、定语和状语等。而且,并列成分一般多由 and 等连词连接。在大多数情况下,根据该连词后面那个词或短语的性质到前面去找与之性质相同的词或短语,即可对并列成分做出正确判断。例如:

Such activities as investigating the strength and uses of materials, extending the findings of pure mathematics to improve the sampling procedures used in agriculture or social sciences, and developing the potentialities of atomic energy, are all examples of the work of the applied scientist.

该句中 and 后面是动名词短语 developing the potentialities of atomic energy,and 前面也有两个动名词短语 investigating…和 extending…,可以肯定这三个动名词短语并列,用作 as 引导的定语从句的主语。

4) 从句中含有从句的长复合句

在有的长句中,某个从句本身有可能也是含有一个或一个以上从句的复合句;甚至这种从句本身又含有从句。遇到这种比较复杂的现象,必须要对每个从句的性质做出正确的分析,找出与它发生关系的词。例如:

A further inference was drawn by Pascal, who reasoned that if this "sea of air" existed, its pressure at the bottom (i.e. sea-level) would be greater than its pressure further up, and that therefore the height of mercury column would decrease in proportion to the height above the sea-level.

此句中,who 引导的定语从句为一复合句,含有一个以 that 引导的宾语从句。而这个 that 引导的宾语从句又是一个复合句,其中含有一个以 if 引导的条件状语从句,and 连接的两个并列的宾语从句。

为了能够做好长句结构的分析,掌握好专业英语中关于复合句、非谓语动词的知识是非常必要的。在接下来的几课中,将介绍一下关于复合句、非谓语动词的知识。然后我们再结合实例来介绍长句结构分析的方法(见 Lesson 17,物理学专业英语中的长句分析(二))。

9.2 专业英语阅读

9.2.1 Thermal Equilibrium and Temperature(热平衡及温度)

Temperature is familiar to us as the measure of the hotness or coldness of objects or of our surroundings.

Our sense of touch can usually tell us if an object is hot or cold. Early in childhood we learn that to make a cold object warmer, we place it in contact with a hot object and to make a hot object cooler, we place it in contact with a cold object.

When an object is heated or cooled, some of its physical properties change. Most solids and liquids expand when they are heated. A gas, if its pressure is kept constant, will also expand when it is heated, or, if its volume is kept constant, its pressure will rise. If an electrical conductor is heated, its electrical resistance changes. A physical property that changes with temperature is called a **thermometric property.** A change in a thermometric property indicates a change in the temperature of the object.

Suppose that we place a warm copper bar in close contact with a cold iron bar so that the copper bar cools and the iron bar warms. We say that the two bars are in **thermal contact**. The copper bar contracts slightly as it cools, and the iron bar expands slightly as it warms. Eventually this process stops and the lengths of the bars remain constant. The two bars are then in **thermal equilibrium** with each other.

Suppose instead that we place the warm copper bar in a cool running stream. The bar cools until it stops contracting, at the point at which the bar and the water are in thermal equilibrium. Next we place a cold iron bar in the stream on the side opposite the copper bar. The iron bar will warm until it and the water are also in thermal equilibrium. If we remove the bars and place them in thermal contact with each other, we find that their lengths do not change. They are in thermal equilibrium with each other. Though it is common sense, there is no logical way to deduce this fact, which is called the **zeroth law of thermodynamics** (Fig. 9-1):

Fig. 9-1 If objects A and B are separately in thermal equilibrium with a third object, C, then A and B are in thermal equilibrium with each other

If two objects are in thermal equilibrium with a third, then they are in thermal equilibrium with each other.

Two objects are defined to have the same temperature if they are in thermal equilibrium with each other.

9.2.2 The Ideal-Gas Law(理想气体定律)

The properties of gases at low densities allow the definition of the ideal-gas temperature scale. If we compress such a gas while keeping its temperature constant, the pressure increases. Similarly, if a gas expands at constant temperature, its pressure decreases. To a good approximation, the product of the pressure and volume of a low-density gas is constant at a constant temperature. This result was discovered experimentally by Robert Boyle (1627—1691), and is known as **Boyle's law**:

$$PV = \text{constant}(\textbf{constant temperature})$$

A more general law exists that reproduces Boyle's law as a special case. As we know, the absolute temperature of a low-density gas is proportional to its pressure at constant volume. In addition—a result discovered experimentally by Jacques Charles (1746—1823) and Joseph Gay-Lussac (1778—1850)—the absolute temperature of a low-density gas is proportional to its volume at constant pressure. We can combine these two results by stating

$$PV = CT \tag{9-1}$$

where C is a constant of proportionality. We can see that this constant is proportional to the amount of gas by considering the following. Suppose that we have two containers with identical volumes, each holding the same amount of the same kind of gas at the same temperature and pressure. If we consider the two containers as one system, we have twice the amount of gas at twice the volume, but at the same temperature and pressure. We have thus doubled the quantity $PV/T=C$ by doubling the amount of gas. We can therefore write C as a constant k times the number of molecules in the gas N

$$C = kN$$

Eq. (9-1) then becomes

$$PV = NkT \tag{9-2}$$

The constant k is called **Boltzmann's constant**. It is found experimentally to have the same value for any kind of gas

$$k = 1.381 \times 10^{-23} \text{ J/K} = 8.617 \times 10^{-5} \text{ eV/K} \tag{9-3}$$

An amount of gas is often expressed in moles. A **mole** (mol) of any substance is the amount of that substance that contains Avogadro's number N_A of atoms or molecules, defined as the number of carbon atoms in 12 g of C^{12}

$$N_A = 6.022 \times 10^{23} \tag{9-4}$$

If we have ν moles of a substance, then the number of molecules is

$$N = \nu N_A \tag{9-5}$$

Eq. (9-2) is then

$$PV = \nu N_A kT = \nu RT \tag{9-6}$$

where $R = N_A k$ is called the **universal gas constant**. Its value, which is the same for all gases, is

$$R = N_A k = 8.314 \text{ J/(mol·K)} = 0.08206 \text{ L·atm/(mol·K)} \tag{9-7}$$

An **ideal gas** is defined as one for which $PV/(\nu T)$ is constant for all pressures. The pressure, volume, and temperature of an ideal gas are related by

$$PV = \nu RT \tag{9-8}$$

Eq. (9-8), which relates the variables P, V, and T, is known as the **ideal-gas law**, and is an example of an **equation of state**. It describes the properties of real gases with low densities (and therefore low pressures). At higher densities, corrections must be made to this equation. For any gas at any density, there is an equation of state relating P, V, and T for a given amount of gas. Thus the state of a given amount of gas is determined by any two of the three state variables P, V, and T.

The temperature 0℃ and the pressure of 1 atm are often referred to as **standard conditions**. Under standard conditions, a mol of an ideal gas occupies a volume of 22.4 L.

For a fixed amount of gas, we can see from Eq. (9-8) that the quantity PV/T is constant. Using the subscripts 1 for the initial values and 2 for the final values, we have

$$\frac{P_2 V_2}{T_2} = \frac{P_1 V_1}{T_1} \tag{9-9}$$

Glossary

temperature	温度	thermal equilibrium	热平衡
hotness	热	electrical conductor	电导体
coldness	冷	thermometric property	热力学特性
the zeroth law of thermodynamics	热力学第零定律	thermal contact	热接触
ideal-gas temperature scale	理想气体温标	Boyle's law	波意耳定律
universal gas constant	普适气体常量	constant volume	等体
Boltzmann's constant	玻尔兹曼常量	equation of state	状态方程
mole	摩尔	state variable	状态参量
Avogadro's number	阿伏伽德罗常量	standard condition	标准条件
carbon atom	碳原子	subscript	下标

9.3 专业英语常用表达法-9 热学和波动常用实验仪器

refrigerator 电冰箱
digital thermometer 数字温度计
heater 加热器
heat converter 热交换器
hot-water bag 热水袋
thermometer 温度计
thermal converter 热转换器
thermostat 恒温箱/温控器
thermionic tube 热离子管
calorimeter 热量表/量热器/热量计
sonometer 弦音计/振动频率计
resonance tuning forks 共振音叉
refrigerating box 冷藏箱
refrigerating fluid 冷冻液/制冷剂
thermopile 温差电堆/热电堆
heat exchanger 热交换器
thermos, thermos bottle, vacuum bottle 热水瓶
wet and dry thermometer 干湿温度计
empty box barometer 空盒气压计
magnetic barrel calorimeter 磁桶量热器
thermomotor 热力机/热气机/热发动机
boron thermopile 硼温差电堆
tuning fork 音叉
specific heat capacity converter 比热容转换器
varying-temperature viscosity coefficient tester 变温黏滞系数实验仪
single-junction vacuum thermopile 单接头真空温差电堆
sublimation and condensation of iodine demonstrator 碘的升华与凝华演示器
solid shrink force demonstrator 固体缩力演示器
interconversion of mechanical energy and heat energy demonstrator 机械能热能互变演示器
metal linear expansion demonstrator 金属线膨胀演示器
refrigerated centrifuge 冷冻离心分离机
solidification and melt of naphthalene experiment device 萘的熔解凝固实验器
experimental device for gas law 气体定律实验器

gas law demonstrator   气体定律演示器
heat conduction demonstrator   热传导演示器
thermoelectric couple, thermocouple, thermoelectric pair   热电偶/温差电偶
heat flux density converter   热流密度转换器
thermistor thermometer   热敏温度计/热敏电阻温度计
demonstrator of sound propagation   声传播演示器
quick freezing refrigeration device   速冻制冷装置
standing waves on a string instrument   弦线上驻波实验仪
harmonic wave analysis experimental instrument   谐波分析实验仪
liquid specific heat detector   液体比热测定仪
vacuum flask   真空瓶、杜瓦(真空)瓶、保温瓶、热水瓶
vacuum thermopile   真空热电堆/真空温差电堆
refrigeration compressor   制冷压缩机/冷冻机
thermal coefficient meters   导热系数测定仪
meter of metal specific heat capacity   金属比热容测定仪
meter of specific heat ratio of gas   气体比热容比测定仪
thermotics experiment facility   热学实验仪
multi-function constant-temperature controller   多功能恒温控制仪

LESSON 10

10.1 物理学专业英语中的主语从句

前面已经提到过，英语的主从复合句一般分为三大类型：名词性从句、形容词性从句和副词性从句。

名词性从句在整个复合句中起名词作用。主语、宾语、表语和同位语等各种从句统称为名词性从句，在句中起名词作用，充当主语、宾语、表语和同位语。

引导名词性从句的连接词可分为三类：

连接词：that, whether, if（不充当从句的任何成分）

连接代词：what, whatever, who, whoever, whom, whose, which

连接副词：when, where, how, why

主语从句是在复合句中充当主语的从句。

10.1.1 主语从句的引导词

主语从句通常由连词 that 和 whether，连接代词或连接副词，以及关系代词 what 引导。

1) that 引导

That each atom has a tiny but massive nucleus that contains protons and neutrons is a general phenomenon. 每个原子都有一个包含质子和中子的小而重的原子核，是个普遍现象。

That two objects carrying the same type of charge repel each other is certain. 带有同

种电荷的两个物体互相排斥，这是确定无疑的。

That she became a physicist may have been due to her father's influence. 她成为物理学家可能是受她父亲的影响。

There seems little doubt *that radar technology is a permanent and important aspect of research and development in electronics*. （That 引导的从句作实际主语）似乎没有疑问，在电子学的研究和发展中，雷达技术是一个永久并且重要的方面。

2）whether 引导

Whether the experiment of dropping bodies of different weight from the leaning tower of Pisa was performed before a multitude, as some accounts have it, was not known. 我们不知道比萨斜塔落体实验是否像某些资料记载那样在很多人目睹下进行。

Whether the plan of carrying out the experiment is feasible remains to be proved. 这一实验计划是否可行还有待证实。

Whether the discharge will do us harm remains to be seen. 放电是否有害还要看一看。

Whether the experimental result would support the theory was a problem. 实验结果是否会支持这个理论还是一个问题。

Whether a length is exactly a meter is a question no experiment can decide. 一段长度是否精确地是 1 m，没有实验能够决定。

3）连接代词引导

Whoever discovered the phenomena did not make any difference. 到底是谁发现这个现象的，没有什么分别。

Whichever of the particles gets out first does not matter. 无论哪个粒子先出来都没有关系。

Who should be responsible for the environmental degradation is still unknown. 谁对环境恶化负责还不清楚。

4）连接副词引导

When magnetism was recognized is not quite clear. 磁现象是什么时候被发现的，不是十分清楚。

How the experiment was done was a mystery. 这个实验怎样做的是一个谜。

How this happened is not clear to anyone. 这件事怎样发生的，谁也不清楚。

Where Coulomb confirmed the inverse-square law for the electrostatic force remains to be proved. 库仑到底是在哪里确定静电力的平方反比定律还有待证实。

5）关系代词 what 引导

What we need is a precision tool. 我们需要的是精密工具。

What the physicists were waiting for at that time was a solar eclipse. 那时，物理学家们等待的就是一次日食。

What make the lab more impressive are the modern instruments. 为实验室增色的是现代化的仪器设备。

10.1.2 主语从句与形式主语 it

有时为了考虑句子平衡,通常在主语从句的位置使用形式主语 it,而将真正的主语从句移至句末。用 it 作形式主语的 that 从句有以下四种不同的搭配关系:

"It＋be＋形容词＋that 从句",如:

It is necessary that …　有必要……

It is natural that…　很自然……

It is strange that…　奇怪的是……

"It＋be＋过去分词＋that 从句",如:

It is known to all that …　众所周知……

It is reported that…　据报道……

It is said that…　据说……

It has been proved that…　已证实……

"It＋be＋名词＋that 从句",如:

It is a fact that …　事实是……

It is an honor that…　非常荣幸……

It is common knowledge that…　……是常识

"It＋不及物动词＋that 从句",如:

It appears that …　似乎……

It seems that…　似乎……

It happened that…　碰巧……

It occurs that…　碰巧……

用 it 作形式主语时分以下三种情况:

1) 对于以连词 that 引导的主语从句,通常用形式主语代替主语从句:

For example, in electric circuits it is often assumed *that the relations between voltages and currents are linear*. 例如,在电路中通常假设电压和电流的关系是线性的。

It has been found repeatedly in science *that the discovery that two branches are related leads to each branch helping in the development of the other*. 在科学中经常发现,与两个分支相关的发现会导致两方相互促进发展。

It is quite clear *that the whole project is doomed to failure*. 很清楚,整个计划注定要失败。

It's a pity *that he didn't find any useful results in the experiment*. 很遗憾他在实验中没找到什么有用的结果。

It is important that *the experiment should be carried out in vacuum*. 实验必须在真空内进行。

2) 对于以连接代词(副词)引导的主语从句,可以使用形式主语代替主语从句,也可直接在句首使用主语从句:

Whether they would support us was a problem. 他们是否会支持我们还是一个问题。

It was a problem *whether they would support us*. 他们是否会支持我们还是一个

问题。

It remains to be seen *whether the material will do us harm or good*. 这材料对我们是利是害,还得看看再说。

3) 对关系代词型 what 引导的主语从句,通常直接将主语从句放在句首。如:

What we need is an inertial frame of reference. 我们需要的是惯性参考系。

What I want to know is how we apply Newton's laws to solve problems. 我想知道的就是如何运用牛顿定律解决问题。

有时也可借用形式主语。如:

It is clear enough what the results meant. 结果是什么意思很清楚。

4) 如果句子是疑问句,则必须用带形式主语 it 的结构:

Is it true *that the electric field of the source particles is present* whether or not we introduce a test particle into the field? 不论检验电荷是否放入,场源电荷产生的电场都是存在的,是真的吗?

How is it *that the two particles attract each other*? 两个粒子怎么会互相吸引呢?

10.1.3 连词 that 的省略问题

引导主语从句的连词 that 有时可省,有时不能省,其原则是:若 that 引导的主语从句直接位于句首,则 that 不能省略;若 that 引导的主语从句位于句末,而在句首使用了形式主语 it,则 that 可以省略。

That you failed to use Ampere Circuital Theorem correctly was a pity. 很遗憾你未能正确使用安培环路定理。(that 不可省)

It was a pity (that) *you failed to use Ampere Circuital Theorem correctly*。很遗憾你未能正确使用安培环路定理。(that 可省)

10.1.4 主语从句不可位于句首的五种情况

(1) if 引导的主语从句不可居于复合句句首。

(2) It is said (reported)… 结构中的主语从句不可提前。

(3) It happens…, It occurs… 结构中的主语从句不可提前。

(4) It doesn't matter how/whether … 结构中的主语从句不可提前。

(5) 含主语从句的复合句是疑问句时,主语从句不可提前。

10.1.5 What 与 that 在引导主语从句时的区别

What 引导主语从句时在从句中充当句子成分,如主语、宾语、表语,不能省略。That 不作任何成分,而只在语法上起连接作用,并且在句首使用了形式主语 it 时 that 可以省略。

10.2 专业英语阅读

10.2.1 Heat and the First Law of Thermodynamics(热及热力学第一定律)

Heat is energy that is being transferred from one system to another because of a difference in temperature. In the seventeenth century, Galileo, Newton, and other scientists generally supported the theory of the ancient Greek atomists who considered thermal energy to be a manifestation of molecular motion. In the next century, methods were developed for making quantitative measurements of the amount of heat that leaves or enters an object, and it was found that if objects are in thermal contact, the amount of heat that leaves one object equals the amount that enters the other. This discovery led to the caloric theory of heat as a conserved material substance. In this theory, an invisible fluid called "caloric" flowed out of one object and into another and this "caloric" could be neither created nor destroyed.

The caloric theory reigned until the nineteenth century, when it was found that friction between objects could generate an unlimited amount of thermal energy, deposing of the idea that caloric was a substance present in a fixed amount. The modern theory of heat did not emerge until the 1840s, when James Joule (1818—1889) demonstrated that the increase or decrease of a given amount of thermal energy was always accompanied by the decrease or increase of an equivalent quantity of mechanical energy. Thermal energy, therefore, is not itself conserved. Instead, thermal energy is a form of internal energy, and it is energy that is conserved.

We will always talk about energy transfer to or from some specific *system*. The system might be a mechanical device, a biological organism, or a specified quantity of material such as the refrigerant in an air conditioner. A **thermodynamic system** is a system which can interact (and exchange energy) with it surroundings, or environment. A process in which there are changes in the state of thermodynamic system is called a **thermodynamic process.**

In this part, we define heat capacity, and examine how heating a system can cause either a change in its temperature or a change in its phase. We then examine the relationship between heat conduction, work, and internal energy of a system and express the law of conservation of energy for the thermal systems as the first law of thermodynamics. Finally, we shall see how the heat capacity of a system is related to its molecular structure.

We describe the energy relations in any thermodynamic process in terms of the quantity of heat Q added to the system and the work W done by the system. Both Q and W may be positive, negative, or zero. A positive value of Q represents heat flow into the system, with a corresponding input of energy to it; negative Q represents heat flow out of the system. A positive value of W represents work done by the system against it surroundings, such as work done by an expanding gas, and hence corresponds to energy leaving the system. Negative W, such as work done during compression of a gas in which work is done on the gas by its surroundings, represents energy entering the system.

When the law of conservation of energy was first introduced in previous chapter, it was stated that the mechanical energy of a system is conserved in the absence of nonconservative forces, such as friction. That is, the changes in the internal energy of the system were not included in this mechanical model.

The first law of thermodynamics is a generalization of the law of conservation of energy that includes possible changes in internal energy.

It is a universally valid law that can be applied to all kinds of processes. Furthermore, it provides us with a connection between the microscopic and macroscopic worlds.

We have seen that energy can be transferred between a system and its surroundings in two ways. One is work done by (or on) the system. This mode of energy exchange results in measurable changes in the macroscopic variables of the system, such as the pressure, temperature, and volume of gas. The other is heat transfer, which takes place at the microscopic level.

To put these ideas on a more quantitative basis, suppose a thermodynamics system undergoes a change from an initial state to a final state in which Q units of heat are absorbed (or removed) and W is the work done by (or on) the system. For example, the system may be a gas whose pressure and volume change from P_i, V_i to P_f, V_f. If the quantity $Q-W$ is measured for various paths connecting the initial and final equilibrium states (that is, for various process), one finds that $Q-W$ is the same for all paths connecting the initial and final states. We conclude that the quantity $Q-W$ is determined completely by the initial and final states of the system, and we call the quantity $Q-W$ *the change in the internal energy of the system*. Although Q and W both depend on the path, the quantity $Q-W$, that is, *the change in internal energy is independent of the path*. If we represent the internal energy function by the letter E, then the change in internal energy, $\Delta E = E_f - E_i$, can be expressed as

$$\Delta E = E_f - E_i = Q - W \tag{10-1}$$

where all quantities must have the same energy units. Eq. (10-1) is known as the **first law of thermodynamics**. When it is used in this form, we must note that Q is positive when heat enters the system and W is positive when work is done by the system.

10.2.2 Kinds of Thermodynamic Processes(热力学过程的种类)

In this section we describe four specific kinds of thermodynamic processes that occur often in practical situations. These can be summarized briefly as "no heat transfer" or adiabatic, "constant volume" or isochoric, "constant pressure" or isobaric, and "constant temperature" or isothermal. For some of these we can use a simplified form of the first law of thermodynamics.

Adiabatic Process(绝热过程)

An adiabatic process is defined as one with no heat transfer into or out of a system; $Q=0$. We can prevent heat flow either by surrounding the system with thermally insulating material or by carrying out the process so quickly that there is not enough time for appreciable heat flow. From the first law we find that for every adiabatic process

$$E_2 - E_1 = \Delta E = -W \quad \text{(adiabatic process)} \tag{10-2}$$

When a system expands adiabatically, W is positive (the system does work on its surrounding), so ΔE is negative and the internal energy decreases. When a system is compressed adiabatically, W is negative (work is done on the system by its surroundings) and E increases. In many (but not all) systems an increase of internal energy is accompanied by a rise in temperature.

The compression stroke in an internal-combustion engine is an approximately adiabatic process. The temperature rises as the air-fuel mixture in the cylinder is compressed. The expansion of the burned fuel during the power stroke is also an approximately adiabatic expansion with a drop in temperature.

Isochoric Process(等体过程)

An isochoric process is a constant-volume process. When the volume of a thermodynamic system is constant, it does no work on its surroundings. Then $W=0$, and

$$E_2 - E_1 = \Delta E = Q \quad \text{(isochoric process)} \tag{10-3}$$

In an isochoric process, all the energy added as heat remains in the system as an increase in internal energy. Heating a gas in a closed constant-volume container is an example of an isochoric process. (Note that there are types of work that do not involve a volume change. For example, we can do work on a fluid by stirring it.)

Isobaric Process(等压过程)

An isobaric process is a constant-pressure process. In general, none of the three quantities ΔE, Q, and W is zero in an isobaric process, but calculating W is easy nonetheless.

$$W = P(V_2 - V_1) \quad \text{(isobaric process)} \tag{10-4}$$

Isothermal process(等温过程)

An isothermal process is a constant-temperature process. For a process to be isothermal, any heat flow into or out of the system must occur slowly enough that thermal equilibrium is maintained. In general, none of the quantities ΔE, Q, or W is zero in an isothermal process.

In some special cases the internal energy of a system depends only on its temperature, not on its pressure or volume. The most familiar system having this special property is an ideal gas. For such system, if the temperature is constant, the internal energy is also constant; $\Delta E = 0$, and $Q = W$, that is, any energy entering the system as heat Q must leave it again as work W done by the system. For most systems other than ideal gases the internal energy depends on pressure as well as temperature, so E may vary even when T is constant.

Glossary

atomist	原子学家	thermal energy	热能
manifestation	表现形式	molecular motion	分子运动
thermal contact	热接触	internal energy	内能
thermodynamic system	热力学系统	thermodynamic process	热力学过程
caloric	a. 热的;n. 热(质)	heat capacity	热容量
phase	相	heat conduction	热传导
initial state	初态	final state	末态
adiabatic	绝热的	isochoric	等体积的
isobaric	等压强的	isothermal	等温的
thermally insulating material	绝热材料	adiabatically	绝热地
compression stroke	压缩冲程	internal-combustion engine	内燃机
power stroke	做功冲程		

10.3 专业英语常用表达法-10 精度

accuracy control　精确控制
accuracy index　准确度(精确度)指数
high accuracy　高精度
percentage of accuracy　准确度百分数
order of accuracy　准确度
with accuracy　正确地、准确地
to/within accuracy of...　精度达……、准确到……
within the accuracy of...　在……的精度范围内
accurate to...　精度达……、精确到……
be accurate to dimension　符合加工尺寸
accuracy grade　准确度等级
accuracy requirements　准确度要求
per cent of accuracy　百分比精度
overall accuracy　总精度、总准确度
standard of accuracy　准确度标准
to an accuracy of...　精度达……、准确到……
with an accuracy of...　精度达……、以……的精度
the accuracy with/to which...　……的精度
accurate (to) within...　精度在……的范围之内
be accurate to/within plus or minus five per cent　精确到(精度在)±5%以内

With care a micrometer will give *an accuracy of* better than 1 part in thousand. 使用得法时,测微计能给出高于0.1%的准确度。

It is impossible to say *with any accuracy* how many are affected. 无论如何也说不准受影响的有多少。

The volume measuring *accuracy* of this system is ±0.25%. 系统容积的测量精度为±0.25%。

Readings can be obtained to *an accuracy of* one micron. 获得的读数精度可达 1 μm。

The discrepancy is *within the accuracy of* the analysis. 误差在分析精度范围之内。

The *accuracy with which* scientists can use laser can also be of help in making different kinds of measurements. 科学家使用激光所能达到的精度对进行其他各种测量也可能有所帮助。

It depends on *the degree of accuracy to which* the parts must be made. 这取决于制造零件所应达到的精度。

All input data are *accurate to* three significant figures. 所有输入的数据精确到 3 位有效数字。

This apparatus is *accurate within* microseconds. 这台装置的精确度在数微秒之内。

These parameters are known with *an accuracy of* 5%. 这些参数的已知精度为5%。

The components can be positioned *with an accuracy* better than 0.010 in. 这些部件固定的精确度可高于 0.010 in。

LESSON 11

11.1 物理学专业英语中的宾语从句

宾语从句就是在复合句中作宾语的名词性从句,通常放在主句谓语动词(及物动词)或介词之后。例如:

For a situation like this, in which the current is discontinuous in space, Ampere's law is not valid. In following, we will see *how Maxwell was able to modify Ampere's law so that it holds for all currents*. 对于像空间中电流不连续的情况,安培定律就不成立了。下面我们将看到麦克斯韦是如何修正安培定律从而使其对所有电流都适用。

This law describes *how electric field lines diverge from a positive charge and converge on a negative charge*. Its experimental basis is Coulomb's law. 这个定律说明了电场线如何发散于正电荷、聚集于负电荷,其实验基础是库仑定律。

11.1.1 宾语从句的引导词

宾语从句通常由连词 that 和 whether/if,连接代词或连接副词,以及关系代词 what 引导。

1) that 引导

It is a common fallacy to suppose *that mathematics is important for physics only because it is a useful tool for making computations*. 人们通常错误地认为数学对物理很重要仅仅因为它是一种有用的计算工具。

Stated in words, Ohm's law says *that the steady current through any portion of an electric circuit equals the potential difference across that portion of the circuit divided by the resistance of that portion of the circuit*. 欧姆定律用语言表述为：电路中任一部分的电流强度等于这部分的电势差除以这部分的电阻。

Archimedes principle states *that a body wholly or partially immersed in a fluid is buoyed up by a force equal to the weight of the fluid displaced by it*. 阿基米德原理表述为：部分或全部浸在水中的物体受到的浮力等于物体排开液体的重量。

That 引导的从句常跟在下列形容词后作宾语：afraid, anxious, aware, certain, confident, convinced, determined, glad, proud, surprised, worried, sorry, thankful, ashamed, disappointed, annoyed, pleased, hurt, satisfied, content 等。

I am afraid *that the shock waves will be very strong in this case*. 在这种情况下，恐怕冲击波会很强。

2) whether/if 引导

Before making this case a general rule, test it by experiment two or three times and see *if the experiment produces the same effect*. 在把这一情况定为常规之前，先做两三次实验看看是否产生同一效果。

In order to determine *whether a system is performing properly and ultimately to control the system performance*, the engineer must know what the system is doing at any instant of time. 为了确定系统是否准确运行以及全面控制系统性能，工程人员必须随时了解系统在做什么。

I wonder *if the voltage is high enough*. 我不知道电压是否够高。

3) 连接代词引导

Put them together and see *which is larger*. 把它们加起来看看哪个更大。

We'll do *whatever we can* to measure the magnetic force between the two parallel current-carrying wires. 我们将尽我们所能来测量这两个平行电流间的相互作用磁力。

I don't know *who/whom you mean*. 我不知道你指谁。

You can take *whichever you like*. 你爱拿哪个就拿哪个吧。

Few people knew *what the relativity meant at that time*. 那时很少有人明白相对论。

4) 连接副词引导

We often fail to realize *how little we know about a thing* until we attempt to simulate it on a computer. 在我们试图用计算机模拟一件事之前，我们通常意识不到我们对它的了解是多么少。

Our success depends upon *how well we can cooperate with one another*. 我们的成功取决于彼此间的良好合作。

The sum, difference and product of continuous functions are also continuous. The quotient of continuous functions is continuous except *where the denominator vanishes*. 连续函数的和、差、积仍然连续，连续函数的商在分母不为零时也连续。

This essay aims to explore *why quantum was put forward at that time*. 本文将探讨为什么量子的概念会在那个时候提出。

I'd like to know *when the electrification will be finished*. 我很想知道充电什么时候会结束。

5) 关系代词 what 引导

In order to determine whether a system is performing properly and ultimately to control the system performance, the experimenter must know *what the system is doing at any instant of time*. 为了确定系统在运行中是否准确全面地控制系统性能，实验人员必须随时了解系统在做什么。

First let's introduce *what the Atwood's machine is like*. 首先让我们介绍一下阿特伍德机。

【注意】 有时介词后可接一个宾语从句(但介词后通常不接 that 和 if 引导的宾语从句)：

From *what Maxwell stated*, the displacement current was reasonable. 根据麦克斯韦所说，位移电流是合理的。

有极个别介词(如 but，except)可接 that 引导的宾语从句：

The experimenters need do nothing about it except *that they should turn the power on*. 实验人员只需要通上电源，其他的什么都不需要做。

11.1.2 宾语从句与形式宾语 it

当宾语从句后跟有宾语补足语时，特别是在带复合宾语的句子中，通常在宾语从句处使用形式宾语 it，而将真正的宾语从句移至句末。

I think *it* best *that you should explain the Guass's law in detail now*. 我认为你最好现在把这个高斯定理仔细解释一下。

He hasn't made *it* known *when he is going to get started with thermodynamics*. 他还没宣布他何时开始讲热力学。

She found *it* difficult *how she could answer the question about Maxwell's Equations*. 她发现回答这个关于麦克斯韦方程组的问题很困难。

The director made *it* a rule *that every graduate student should make at least one presentation in the discussion*. 导师规定每个研究生在讨论时至少发一次言。

11.1.3 连词 that 的省略问题

引导宾语从句的连词 that 通常可以省略。

Einstein thought (*that*) the quantum theory was unreasonable. 爱因斯坦认为量子理论难以置信。

She said (*that*) the equivalent capacitance of a series combination of capacitors would be less than any individual capacitance in the combination. 她说过串联电容器的总电容会小于其中任何一个电容器的电容。

I promise you (*that*) I will be there when they maintain the equipment. 我答应你在他们维护仪器时我会去照看的。

I hoped (*that*) I would/should succeed in the experiment. 我曾希望我会在实验中成功。

He thinks (*that*) they will fix the equipment on time. 他想他们会按时安装好设

备的。

He thought (that) they would set up the equipment in time. 他本想他们会按时安装好设备的。

I expect (that) the experiment's result will turn out perfect. 我料想实验的结果将会很完美。

I suggested (that) they should handle the device carefully. 我建议他们小心操纵设备。

【注意】 有时为了强调，that 引导的宾语从句可位于句首，此时 that 不可省略。

That the electric appliance should be grounded I know. 这电器应该接地，我是知道的。

11.1.4 宾语从句与否定转移

当动词 think, believe, suppose, expect, imagine 后接一个表示否定意义的宾语从句时，其否定通常转移到主语。

I *don't* suppose *that the data they presented is true*. 我认为他们提供的数据不是真的（而不是 I suppose *that the data they presented is not true*.）。

I *don't* think *we need waste much time on the maintenance*. 我想我们不必在仪器维护上面花太多时间（而不是 I think we need not waste much time on the maintenance.）。

11.1.5 不能省略 that 的宾语从句

引导宾语从句的 that 在下列情况下一般不省略。

1) 宾语从句前有插入语。如：

We hope, *on the contrary*, *that* he can find the kinetic equation for the simple harmonic motion. 恰恰相反，我们希望他能够找到简谐运动的运动学方程。

2) 有间接宾语时。如：

He told *me that* he would apply Huygens Principle to describe the propagation of waves. 他告诉我他要用惠更斯原理来描述波的传播。

3) that 在与之并列的另一个宾语从句之后。如：

The book states (that) the standing waves are very interesting and *that*（不省略）*a standing wave does not transfer energy*. 那本书说驻波很有趣，驻波也不传播能量。

4) 在"it（形式宾语）+补语"之后时。如：

Teachers think *it* necessary *that* physics is taught with multimedia. 教师们认为利用多媒体教授物理学是必要的。

5) that 从句单独回答问题时。如：

—What did he hear? 他听说了什么事？

—*That* Kate had found a new way to prove the theory. （他听说）凯特发现了一个证明这个理论的新方法。

6) 在 except 等介词后。如：

The experimenters need do nothing about it except *that* they should turn the power on. 实验人员只需要通上电源，其他的什么都不需要做。

7) 位于句首时。如：

That the wave like this is nothing but a standing wave, I believe. 我相信像这样的波就是驻波。

8) 在较为正式或不常用的动词(如 reply，object)后。如：

The editor replied *that the paper was accepted*. 编辑回复说文章被接受了。

11.1.6　后边不能直接跟 that 从句的动词

这类动词有 allow, refuse, let, like, cause, force, admire, condemn, celebrate, dislike, love, help, take, forgive 等。这类词后可以用不定式或动名词作宾语，但不可以用 that 引导的宾语从句。

11.1.7　不可用 that 从句作直接宾语的动词

有些动词不可用于"动词＋间接宾语＋that 从句"结构中，常见的有 envy, order, accuse, refuse, impress, forgive, blame, denounce, advise, congratulate 等。例如：

He impressed the expert as an excellent experimenter.（right）

He impressed the expert that he was an excellent experimenter.（wrong）

11.2　专业英语阅读

11.2.1　The Second Law of Thermodynamics（热力学第二定律）

We are often asked to conserve energy. But according to the first law of thermodynamics, energy is always conserved. What then does it mean to conserve energy if the total amount of energy in the universe does not change regardless of what we do? The first law of thermodynamics does not tell the whole story. Energy is always conserved, but some forms of energy are more useful than others. The possibility or impossibility of putting energy to use is the subject of the second law of thermodynamics. For example, it is easy to convert work into thermal energy, but it is impossible to remove energy as heat from a single reservoir and convert it entirely into work with no other changes. This experimental fact is one statement of the second law of thermodynamics.

Kelvin statement of the second law of thermodynamics：*No system can take energy as heat from a single reservoir and convert it entirely into work without additional net changes in the system or its surroundings.*

In this chapter, we will encounter several other formulations of this law.

A common example of the conversion of work into heat is movement with friction. For example, suppose you spend two minutes pushing a block this way and that way along a tabletop in a closed path, leaving the block in its initial. Also, suppose that the block-table system is initially in thermal equilibrium with its surroundings. The work you do on the system is converted into internal energy of the system, and as a result the block-table system becomes warmer. Consequently, the system is no longer in thermal equilibrium with its surroundings. However, the system will transfer energy as heat to its surroundings until it returns to thermal equilibrium with those surroundings. Because the final and initial states of the system are the same, the first law of thermodynamics dictates that the energy transferred to the environment as heat equals the work done by you on the system. The reverse process never occurs—a block and table that are warm will never spontaneously cool by converting their internal energy into work that causes the block to push your hand around the table. Yet such an amazing occurrence would not violate the first law of thermodynamics or any other physical laws we have encountered so far. It does, however, violate the second law of thermodynamics. Thus, there is a lack of symmetry in the roles played by heat and work that is not evident from the first law. This lack of symmetry is related to the fact that some processes are irreversible.

There are many other irreversible processes, seemingly quite different from one another, but all related to the second law. For example, heat conduction is an irreversible process. If we place a hot body in contact with a cold body, heat will flow from the hot body to the cold body until they are at the same temperature. However, the reverse does not occur. Two bodies in contact at the same temperature remain at the same temperature; heat does not flow from one to the other leaving one colder and the other warmer. This experimental fact gives us a second statement of the second law of thermodynamics.

Clausius statement of the second law of thermodynamics: *A process whose only net result is to transfer energy as heat from a cooler object to a hotter one is impossible.*

We will show in this chapter that the Kelvin and Clausius statements of the second law are equivalent.

11.2.2 Equivalence of the Kelvin and Clausius Statements(开尔文表述与克劳修斯表述的等价性)

The heat-engine and refrigerator statements (or the Kelvin and Clausius statements, respectively) of the second law of thermodynamics seem quite different, but they are actually equivalent. We can prove this by showing that if either statement is assumed to be false, then the other must also be false. We'll use a numerical example to show that if the heat-engine statement is false, then the refrigerator statement is false.

Fig. 11-1(a) shows an ordinary refrigerator that uses 50 J of work to remove 100 J of energy as heat from a cold reservoir and rejects 150 J of energy as heat to a hot reservoir. Suppose the heat-engine statement of the second law were not true. Then a "perfect" heat engine could remove energy from the hot reservoir and convert it completely into work with 100 percent efficiency. We could use this perfect heat engine to remove 50 J of energy from the hot reservoir and do 50 J of work (Fig. 11-1 (b)) on the ordinary refrigerator. Then, the combination of the perfect heat engine and the ordinary refrigerator would be a perfect refrigerator, transferring 100 J of energy as heat from the cold reservoir to the hot reservoir without requiring any work, as illustrated in Fig. 11-1 (c). This violates the refrigerator statement of the second law. Thus, if the heat-engine statement is false, the refrigerator statement is also false. Similarly, if a perfect refrigerator existed, it could be used in conjunction with an ordinary heat engine to construct a perfect heat engine. Thus, if the refrigerator statement is false, the heat-engine statement is also false. It then follows that if one statement is true, the other is also true. Therefore, the heat engine statement and the refrigerator statement are equivalent.

Fig. 11-1

11.2.3 Irreversibility and Disorder(不可逆性与无序性)

There are many irreversible processes that cannot be described by the heat-engine or refrigerator statements of the second law, such as a glass falling to the floor and breaking or a balloon popping. However, all irreversible processes have one thing in common—the system plus its surroundings moves toward a less ordered state.

When real (irreversible) processes occur, the degree of disorder of chaos in the system increases. For example, consider the isothermal expansion of an ideal gas in a container with a movable piston. As the gas absorbs heat and gradually expands, it maintains a constant temperature by doing work (pushing on the piston). After the expansion, the gas occupies a greater volume than it did originally. The gas molecules become more disordered in that they are not as localized as they were originally. Left by itself, the gas will not become ordered again by giving up its thermal energy to a reservoir. Thus, the flow of heat is in the direction that increases the amount of disorder. Ordered energy is converted into disordered energy.

Suppose a box containing a gas of mass M at a temperature T is moving along a frictionless table with a velocity v_{cm}(Fig. 11-2(a)). The total kinetic energy of the gas has two components: that associated with the movement of the center of mass $\frac{1}{2}Mv_{cm}^2$, and the energy of the motion of its molecules relative to its center of mass. The center of mass energy $\frac{1}{2}Mv_{cm}^2$ is ordered mechanical

Fig. 11-2

energy that could be converted entirely into work. (For example, if a weight were attached to the moving box by a string passing over a pulley, this energy could be used to lift the weight.) The relative energy is the internal thermal energy of the gas, which is related to its temperature T. It is random, non-ordered energy that cannot be converted entirely into work. Now, suppose that the box hits a fixed wall and stops (Fig. 11-2 (b)). This inelastic collision is clearly an irreversible process. The ordered mechanical energy of the gas is converted into random internal energy and the temperature of the gas rises. The gas still has the same total energy, but now all of that energy is associated with the random motion of the gas molecules about the center of mass of the gas, which is now at rest. Thus, the gas has become less ordered (more disordered), and has lost some of its ability to do work.

Glossary

second law of thermodynamics	热力学第二定律	reservoir	热源、热库
Kelvin statement	开尔文表述	Clausius statement	克劳修斯表述
irreversible process	不可逆过程	heat-engine	热机
disorder	无序性	chaos	混乱
movable piston	活塞	inelastic collision	非弹性碰撞
random motion	无规则运动		

11.3 专业英语常用表达法-11 质量 标准

1. "质量高，优质"的常用表达

常用 fine, high, good, better, best, top, first-class, first-rate 等词，也可说

standard quality　符合标准的质量
choice quality　精选的质量
a fine quality of…　优质的……
a good quality stopwatch　一块高质量的停表
products of quality　优质产品
quality concrete　高级/优质混凝土
be superior in quality　质量好
have quality　质量好
of good quality　上等的、优质的

2. "符合质量要求"的常用表达

reach the (official) standard　达到(官方)标准
maintain the quality　保持合格质量
meet the (minimum) standard　达到(最低)标准
be up to the standard (grade, category)　达标

come up to the standard 达标
make the grade 达到(理想)标准、合乎(质量)要求

3. "质量一般"的常用表达

fair quality 质量还行
acceptable quality 可接受的质量
above the average quality 高于平均质量水平

4. "基本够格，稍有问题"的常用表达

be borderline 基本够格
have a borderline result 结果勉强够格

5. "质量次、差"的常用表达

除 bad, poor, inferior 等词外, 还可说:
off quality 品质差
below standard 低于标准
not up to standard 未达标
below the average quality 低于平均质量水平
out of grade 未达标
of poor quality 劣等的、劣质的

LESSON 12

12.1 物理学专业英语中的表语从句和同位语从句

12.1.1 表语从句

名词性从句在 be 等系动词后作表语时被称为表语从句, 可接表语从句的连系动词有 be, look, seem, sound, appear 等。

1) 从属连词 whether, as, as if/though 引导的表语从句

The question that has interested scientists from ancient times is *whether the atom can or cannot be split up*. 原子能否再分割的问题从远古就令科学家感兴趣。

The question remains *whether the experiment will be of any help*. 问题还是这个实验能否有所帮助。

The instrument looked just as *it had looked ten years before*. 这仪器看起来还与十年前一样。

It sounds as if *the argument is reasonable*. 听起来好像论证得有道理。

2) because, why 引导的表语从句

Since the weight depends on g, it varies with geographic location. This is *because g decreases with increasing distance from the center of the earth*. 因为重量与重力加速度 g 有关, 所以重量会随地理位置不同而变化。这是因为距离地心越远, g 的数值会越小。

Try opening the door by pushing at different distances from the hinges. The largest effect occurs when the force is applied farthest from the hinges. That's *why doorknobs are put there*!

【注意】 "That is because…"句型中从属连词 because 引导的名词性从句在此作表语，这也是个常用句型，意为"这就是为什么……/因为……"。"That is because…"与"That is why…"之间的不同在于"That is because…"强调原因或理由，"That is why…"则强调由于各种原因所造成的后果。"That is why…"也是常用句型，意为"这就是……的原因/因此……"，该句型通常用于针对前面已经说明过的原因进行总结。"That is why…"与"That is the reason why…"同义，只不过从语法结构上讲，"That is the reason why…"中 why 引导的是一个定语从句，将其中的 the reason 去掉则与"That is why…"结构一样。

what 引导的主语从句表示结果或名词 reason 作主语时，后面的表语从句表示原因时要用 that 引导，不宜用 because。

What causes the weight to change from position to position is *that the magnitude of **g** varies with geographic location*. 重量之所以随着位置变化，其原因在于重力加速度 ***g*** 的大小会随着地理位置发生变化。

The *reason* for capacitance's increase by a factor ε_r is *that the electric field between the plates of a capacitor is weakened by the dielectric*. 电容增长 ε_r 倍的原因是电容器极板间的电场被电介质削弱了。

3) 连接代词 who,whom,whose,what,which,whoever,whatever,whichever,连接副词 where,when,how,why 引导的表语从句

This is *what we call a sinusoidal wave* because the shape in Fig. 20-14 is that of a sinusoid. 这就是所谓的正弦波，因为在图 20-14 中，其形状就是一个正弦曲线。

The problem is *who we can get to carry out the experiment*. 问题是我们能找谁去做实验。

The question is *how we can determine the direction of each particle in the medium*. 问题是该如何确定媒质中每个粒子的（运动）方向。

The question is *who (m) the scholars should trust*. 问题是学者们应当相信谁。

What the researchers want to know is *which project they should adopt*. 研究者们想知道的是他们应采用哪个方案。

That's *why the block can stay rest on the incline*. 这就是木块能够静止在斜面上的缘故。

That's *where Aristotle was wrong*. 这就是亚里士多德的错误所在。

4) 从属连词 that 引导的表语从句

that 作为表语从句的引导词在表语从句中不充当句子成分，一般不能省略。

Galileo's greatest glory was *that in 1609 he was the first person to turn the newly invented telescope on the heavens* to prove that the planets revolve around the sun rather than around the Earth. 伽利略最光辉的业绩在于他在 1609 年第一个把新发明的望远镜对准天空，以证实行星是围绕太阳旋转而不是围绕地球的。

For example, in electric circuits the usual assumption is *that the relations between voltages and currents are linear.* 例如,在电路中通常假设电压和电流的关系是线性的。

5) 使用虚拟语气的表语从句

当句子的主语是:advice, demand, decision, desire, idea, insistence, instruction, order, plan, proposal, recommendation, request, requirement, suggestion, wish 等表示建议、劝告、命令含义的名词时,表语从句谓语动词须用虚拟语气,即:"should＋动词原形",should 可省略。如:

My advice is *that you should remember that* electric potential is a scalar quantity when handling problems involving it. 我的建议是你应该在计算与电势有关的问题时记住电势是个标量。

My suggestion *is that students (should) draw a free-body diagram showing all external forces acting on the object* when applying Newton's laws. 我的建议是学生应该在应用牛顿定律时画一个受力分析图,标明物体所受的所有外力。

12.1.2 同位语从句

在复合句中充当同位语的名词性从句称为同位语从句。

一般情况下同位语从句跟在某些名词的后面,用以说明该名词所表达的具体内容。例如:

There comes the news *that China launched its first manned spaceship on Oct* 15,2003. 消息传来,中国于 2003 年 10 月 15 日首次成功发射了载人飞船。

以下名词常用于以上句型:advice, announcement, argument, belief, claim, conclusion, decision, evidence, explanation, fact, feeling, hope, idea, impression, information, knowledge, message, news, opinion, order, probability, promise, proposal, remark, reply, report, saying, statement, suggestion, thought, treat, warning, wish, word.

1) 同位语从句的引导词

引导同位语从句的词语通常有连词 that,whether,连接代词和连接副词等。

(1) 由 that 引导

The general theory of relativity was proposed by Einstein in 1916 after nine years of grappling with the problem of formulating a theory of gravitation in agreement with the space-time symmetry of special relativity and with the experimental observation known since Galileo *that all bodies, regardless of their mass, follow the same trajectory in a gravitational field.*

(That 引导的从句作 experimental observation 的同位语)为了提出一种引力理论能符合狭义相对论的时空对称要求,同时也与自从伽利略以来就知道的实验观测一致(即,一切物体在引力场中运动都遵循相同的轨迹,与质量无关),爱因斯坦通过对此问题长达 9 年的研究,于 1916 年提出了广义相对论。

The scientists have come to the conclusion *that it was unwise to do that.* 科学家得出的结论是:这样做是不明智的。

He referred to Copernicus' statement *that the earth moves round the sun.* 他提到了哥白尼关于地球绕太阳转的说法。

They were all very much worried over the fact *that the telescope is out of order.* 对于

望远镜出故障这件事,他们都很焦虑。

(2) 由 whether 引导

The question *whether the atom can or cannot be split up* is known to have interested scientists from ancient times. 原子能否再分割的问题从远古就令科学家感兴趣。

The question *whether it is right or wrong* depends on the result. 这个是对还是错要看结果。

We are investigating the question *whether the machine works well*. 我们在调查这台机器是否运行良好。

【注意1】 whether 可引导同位语从句,但 if 不能引导同位语从句。

【注意2】 在名词 doubt(怀疑)后的同位语从句用 whether 连接;在 no doubt"不怀疑"之后的同位语从句用 that 连接。例如:

We have some doubt *whether they can complete the experiment on time*. 我们怀疑他们是否能准时完成实验。

There is no doubt *that the electric field between the plates of the capacitor is weakened by the dielectric*. 无疑,电容器极板间的电场被电介质削弱了。

(3) 由连接代词 what 引导

Have you any idea *what time the radiation will be sheltered*? 你知道什么时候辐射会被屏蔽起来吗?

I have no idea *what the equipartition theorem is about*. 我不知道均分定理是什么内容。

(4) 由连接副词 where, when, why, who, whom, whose, how 引导

His forecast *when the hurricane would come* is found entirely successful. 他对飓风何时到来的预报是完全成功的。

The reason *why the nucleus of an atom can stay together* is that the strong nuclear force holds them together. 原子内的核子之所以能够聚集在一起是由于强核力的作用。

It is a question *how he measured the angular momentum of the block*. 问题是他如何测量木块的角动量。

The question *who should do the work* requires consideration. 谁该做这项工作,这个问题需要考虑。

We haven't yet settled the question *where we are going to find suitable capacitors*. 我们还没有确定到什么地方去找合适的电容器。

2) 分隔式同位语从句

有时同位语从句可以不紧跟在它所说明的名词后,而被别的词语隔开,这在语法上叫做分隔式同位语从句。例如:

In a simulation of search and track, decisions will be made *whether we search for new targets or track existing detections on the basis of targets presently being tracked*. 在对搜索和跟踪进行仿真时,要决定去搜索新目标,还是去跟踪已有的被跟踪的目标。(decisions 和 whether 引导的从句是同位语。)

The rumour spreads *that the key lab building would be pulled down in a year*. 传言

这个重点实验室大楼要在一年后拆掉。

Report has it *that the first capacitor was the Leyden jar invented at the University of Leyden*. 据说历史上第一个电容器是莱顿瓶,那是在莱顿大学发明的。

The thought came to the experimenters *that maybe they could try to store a large amount of charge in a bottle of water*. 实验人员想到或许可以在一瓶水中储存大量电荷。

3) 同位语从句与虚拟语气

在 suggestion, advice, request, order, demand, wish, suggestion, resolution 等意为"建议、命令、要求"的名词后,同位语从句中的谓语动词通常用"should ＋动词原形"的虚拟语气结构,句中的 should 可以省略。例如:

They were faced with the demand *that this regulation（should）be abolished in the lab*. 他们被要求废除这个实验室的规定。

They expressed the wish *that they（should）cooperate in the field*. 他们表示希望在此领域合作。

There was a suggestion *that Brown should be dropped from the research team*. 建议布朗应该离开研究队伍。

Our teacher gave us some advice on *how we（should）use the demonstrative instrument*. 老师给我们提出了一些如何使用演示仪器的建议。

The head gave the order that *all these houses（should）be pulled down in three weeks*. 主任下令三个星期内所有这些房子都要拆掉。

12.2　专业英语阅读

12.2.1　Waves(波动)

Waves transport energy and momentum through space without transporting matter. As a water wave moves across a pond, for example, the molecules of water oscillate up and down, but do not cross the pond with the wave. Energy and momentum are transported by the wave, but matter is not. A rowboat will bob up and down on the waves but will not be moved by them across the pond. Water waves, waves on a stretched guitar string, and sound waves all involve oscillation.

The concept of wave is abstract. When we observe a water wave, what we see is a rearrangement of water's surface. Without the water, there would be no wave. In the case of this or any other mechanical wave, what we interpret as a wave corresponds to the disturbance of medium. Therefore, we can consider *a mechanical wave to be the propagation of a disturbance in a medium*. The world is full of other kinds of waves, including sound waves, waves on strings, seismic waves, radio waves, and X-rays. Most waves can be placed in one of two categories. **Mechanical waves** are waves that disturb and propagate through a medium; the ripple in the water due to the pebble and a sound wave, for which air is the medium, are examples of mechanical waves.

In the introduction, we alluded the essence of wave motion—the transfer of a disturbance through space without the accompanying transfer of matter. The propagation of the disturbance also represents a transfer of energy—thus, we can view waves as means of energy transfer. Two entries that depend on waves: mechanical waves and electromagnetic radiation. These are to be contrasted with another entry—matter transfer—in which the energy transfer is accompanied by a movement of matter through space.

All mechanical waves require:

(1) Some source of disturbance.

(2) A medium that can be disturbed.

(3) Some physical mechanism through which particles of the medium can interact with one another.

All waves carry energy, but the amount of energy transmitted through a medium and the mechanism responsible for the energy transport differ from case to case.

Electromagnetic waves are a special class of waves that do not require a medium in order to propagate; it is the varying electromagnetic field that propagates through space. Light waves and radio waves are two familiar examples.

Here are some common properties of waves:

(1) Waves propagate with a definite speed through the medium. This is called **wave speed**.

(2) Waves transport energy and momentum through space from one region to another without transporting matter. The medium itself does not travel through space.

(3) Waves can reflect, refract, interfere, and diffract.

12.2.2 Traveling Waves(行波)

When a medium is disturbed, energy is imparted to it. Suppose that energy is added to a material mechanically, such as by a blow or by compression (in the case of a gas). This sets some of the particles vibrating. Because the particles are linked by intermolecular forces, the oscillation of each particle affects that of its neighbors. The added energy propagates, or spreads, by means of interactions between the particles of the medium. An analogy for this process is shown in Fig. 12-1, where the "particles" are dominoes. As each domino falls, it topples the one next to it. Thus energy

Fig. 12-1 Energy transfer

is transferred from domino to domino, and the disturbance propagates through the medium.

In this case, there is no restoring force between the dominoes, so they do not oscillate as do particles in a continuous material medium. Therefore the disturbance moves in space, but it does not repeat itself in time at any one location.

Similarly, if the end of a stretched rope is given a quick shake, the disturbance transfers energy from the hand to the rope, as illustrated in Fig. 12-2. The forces acting between the rope "particles" cause them to move in response to the motion of the hand and a wave pulse travels down the rope. Each "particle" goes up and then back down as the pulse passes by. This motion and that of the wave pulse propagation can be observed by tying pieces of ribbon onto the rope (at x_1 and x_2 in Fig. 12-2). As the disturbance pass point x_1, the ribbon rises and falls, as do the rope "particles". Later, the same occurs for the ribbon at x_2, which indicates that the disturbance energy is propagating or traveling along the rope. This kind of propagation with disturbance is called **traveling waves**. It comes from the meaning of "travel".

Waves may be divided into two types based on the direction of the particles' oscillations relative to the wave velocity.

A **transverse wave** is one for which the particle motion is perpendicular to the direction of the wave velocity. As an experiment, take a string and stretch it taut across your room. If you quickly move your hand up and down once, perpendicular to the axis of the rope, the disturbance you generate propagates along the rope, see Fig. 12-3. But in this case the disturbance (the jiggling—i. e., the motion of the particles that make up the rope) is perpendicular to the direction the wave disturbance propagates.

Move your hand up and down several times quickly, and you produce multiple oscillations that propagate along the rope. Waves on a rope or string are transverse waves. But the elements do not go with the wave.

In a **longitudinal wave**, the particle oscillation is parallel to the direction of the wave velocity. A longitudinal wave may be produced in a stretched spring by moving the coils back and forth along the spring axis (Fig. 12-4). Alternating pulses of compressions and relaxations move along the spring. A longitudinal wave is sometimes called a **compressional wave**. Longitudinal waves travel by alternately compressing and rarefying (expanding) the medium, and its individual particles undergo back-and-forth motions around their equilibrium positions, but the medium itself does not travel through space.

Fig. 12-2 Wave pulse

Fig. 12-3 Transerse wave

Fig. 12-4 Longitudinal wave

Sound waves in air are another example of longitudinal waves—the molecules of a gas, liquid, or solid, through which sound travels oscillate (move back and forth) along the line of propagation, alternately compressing and rarefying (expanding) the medium.

Glossary

disturbance	扰动	propagate	v. 传播
propagation	n. 传播	medium	媒质、媒介
sound waves	声波	waves on strings	弦上波
seismic waves	地震波	radio waves	无线电波
X-rays	X 射线	mechanical waves	机械波
transmit	传输、发射、传播	electromagnetic waves	电磁波
reflect	反射	refract	折射
interfere	干涉	diffract	衍射
wave speed	波速	traveling waves	行波
intermolecular	分子间的	restoring force	回复力
domino	多米诺牌	wave pulse	波脉冲
compression	压缩	relaxation	张弛
transverse waves	横波	rarefy	使稀疏
longitudinal waves	纵波	compressional wave	压缩波
equilibrium position	平衡位置		

12.3 专业英语常用表达法-12 性能和特点

介绍仪器、设备等的性能特点是专业英语的重要功能之一，这在说明书、操作指南、产品鉴定会、学术会议等场合是常用的。其中有一些属通用词汇，对各行各业都适用，如 feature, characteristic, performance 等名词，major, main, leading, striking, unique 等形容词，以及 feature, characterize 等动词。作为口头表达，常用 The idea is …。例如：

The instrument *has several features of* … 该仪器有如下特点……

This system *features* simplicity of operation as its major design objectives. 操作简便是在设计本系统时考虑到的主要特点之一。

Operational flexibility and durable service life *feature* the equipment. 操作灵便，经久耐用是本设备的两大特色。

Micrometer *are characterized by* extreme accuracy, high reliability as well as simplicity and ease of control. 螺旋测微仪不仅操作简易，而且精密度高，性能可靠。

The rare earths *are characterized by* a partially filled $4f$ shell that is shielded from external fields by $5s^2$ and $5p^6$ electrons. 稀土（元素）的特征为：由于被 $5s^2$ 和 $5p^6$ 壳层的电子屏蔽了外场，$4f$ 壳层仅被部分填充。

Every *character* is of practical value and is based on long experience in building this type of lidar. (本产品的)每一个特点都有其实用价值,这是(本公司)在制造这类激光雷达中长期经验积累的结果。

The idea of the device is to allow the operator to perform handling and loading with the greatest convenience. (设计)这个装置的想法是使操作者能十分方便地进行装卸。

The whole idea is that ever greater attention must be paid to a better working environment. 总的想法是,必须更加重视创造一个更为良好的工作环境。

Unit Four

LESSON 13

13.1 物理学专业英语中的副词性从句

副词性从句也称为状语从句,主要用来修饰主句或者主句的谓语。大致分为九大类,分别表示时间、地点、原因、目的、结果、条件、让步、比较和方式,作什么样的状语就叫什么类型的状语从句。例如:条件状语从句就是用一个句子来作条件状语。

状语从句的起点,由状语连词标明。如果状语从句在全句的前部,则从句的结束处往往用逗号标明。在容易判别时,也可以不加标点符号。

13.1.1 时间状语从句

时间状语从句常用引导词有:when, as, while, as soon as, before, after, since, till, until, once 等。特殊引导词有: the minute, the moment, the second, every time, each time, by the time, at the time, at the moment, the day, the instant, immediately, directly, no sooner … than, hardly … when, scarcely … when 等。时间状语从句一般放在句首或句尾。特别需要注意的是,在时间状语从句中不使用将来时,而是用现在时来表示将来时。如:

The body possesses a definite store of potential energy *while it is in the elevated position*. 把物体举高时,它具有一定的势能。

When the usual road does not lead to success, one should not be content with this determination of impossibility, but should bestir oneself to find a new and more promising route. Physical thought, as such, has no end. 当寻常的方法无法成功时,(一个人)不应该就此认定不可能,而应该打起精神去寻求新的、更有希望的方法。这样的物理思想是永无止境的。

Once the overall system concept is defined, our choice becomes increasingly limited *as we proceed from general concepts to actual design details*. 一旦全系统概念定义后,当我们从一般概念进入到设计细节时,我们的选择变得越来越有限了。

When everyone is fully aware of the severity of fresh water scarcity and takes effective measures, I am convinced that we will tackle this problem constructively. 当每个人充分意识到淡水短缺的严重性,并采取有效措施时,我相信我们一定能妥善解决好这个问题。

Each time a call comes through, the signal is sent automatically from the earth station to the new digital exchange. 每当电话一打进来,从地面接收站收到的信号就会自动传到新的数字式电话交换台。

By the time the lorry arrives in the storage park, the gantry will be ready to unload the container and put it in the appropriate place. 当卡车到达货场时,吊车会等在那里把集装箱卸下,并把它堆放在合适的地方。

The engineer wants to be there, on the drill floor *at the moment the bit comes up*, to keep a close eye on things. 当钻头从海底退回到水面时,工程师希望能到现场钻台旁,这样他就能密切注视发生的一切情况。

【注意】 while 也可以作并列连词,表转折的关系,相当于 but,译为"然而"。例如:

The relationship between the transforms of source and response function is simple algebraic relationship, *while* the relationship between corresponding time functions is a differential equation. 源变换和响应函数之间的关系只是简单的代数关系,而对应时间函数间的关系却是微分关系。

13.1.2 地点状语从句

地点状语从句通常由 where, wherever 等引导。

It is well known that all objects, when dropped, will fall toward the earth with nearly constant acceleration. In the idealized case, *where air resistance is neglected*, such motion is referred to as free fall. 众所周知,所有物体被释放下落时几乎匀加速度落向地面。在理想情况下,在空气阻力被忽略的情况下,这种运动被称为自由下落。

13.1.3 原因状语从句

原因状语从句常用引导词有:because, since, as,特殊引导词有:seeing that, now that, in that, considering that, given that, inasmuch as, insomuch as,一般放在句首或句尾。如:

Because ***a*** *is a constant*, its components a_x and a_y are also constants. 因为 ***a*** 是常量,所以其分量 a_x 和 a_y 也是常量。

We call the force a linear restoring force *because it is proportional to the displacement from the equilibrium position and always directed toward the equilibrium position, opposite the displacement*. 我们把这个力称为线性回复力,因为它正比于离开平衡位置的距离并且总是指向平衡位置,与位移的方向相反。

Angular velocity has units of rad/s, or s^{-1}, *since radians are not dimensional*. 角速度的单位是 rad/s 或 s^{-1},因为弧度没有量纲。

Now that we have covered some of the tools of detailed logic design, let us look at the basic system concepts. 既然我们已经谈过了一些详细逻辑设计的工具,就让我们看看基础系统概念。

After the expansion, the gas occupies a greater volume than it did originally. The gas molecules become more disordered *in that they are not as localized as they were originally*. 膨胀后,气体占据比原来大的体积。气体分子变得更无序,因为分子已经不再局

限在原来的空间。

13.1.4 目的状语从句

目的状语从句常用引导词有：so that, in order that, 特殊引导词：lest, in case, for fear that, in the hope that, for the purpose that, to the end that 等。如：

These calculations were needed *in order that the behavior of different physical processes being studied by engineers and scientists might be understood*. 为了使工程师和科学家们明白所研究的不同物理过程的表现，这些计算是必需的。

We invent a simplified version of a problem *so that we can solve it simply and reasonably*. 为了把问题解决得简单合理，我们建立这个问题的简化模型。

13.1.5 结果状语从句

结果状语从句常用引导词有：so...that, so that..., such...that, 特殊引导词有：such that, to the degree that, to the extent that, to such a degree that 等。结果状语从句一般表示已经发生的事情。如：

Nothing is *so beautiful that it does not betray some defect on close inspection*. 没有什么能如此完美，以致严格检查也无缺陷。

A consequence of the definition is that moving a vector *so that it remains parallel to itself* does not change it. 这样定义的结果是，平行移动一个矢量并不改变这个矢量。

13.1.6 条件状语从句

常用引导词有：if, unless, 特殊引导词有：as/so long as, only if, providing/provided that, suppose that, in case that, on condition that, whereas 等。

Kinematics is concerned with two basic questions, "Where" and "When". Though the questions are simple, the answers are potentially quite complicated *if we inquire about phenomena outside our ordinary daily experiences*. 运动学探讨两个基本问题：在哪里和在何时。尽管问题简单，可是如果我们探究日常经验以外的现象，答案可能相当复杂。

Unless there is motion, however, there is no work. 除非有运动，否则不会有做功存在。

Whereas negative numbers were created to make the operation of subtraction possible without any exception, subtraction as an independent operation ceased to exist by virtue of that creation. 鉴于有了负数以后，就可以取代所有的减法运算，因而减法作为独立的运算就没有存在的必要了。

13.1.7 让步状语从句

引导让步状语从句的常用引导词有：though, although, even if, even though, 特殊引导词有：as(用在让步状语从句中必须要倒装), while(一般用在句首), no matter ＋疑问词, in spite of the fact that, whatever, whoever, wherever, whenever, however, whichever, whether...or...等。

In other words, *although the amplitude of successive harmonics may go up and down as n increases*, it will always tend to zero as *n* increases. 换言之，尽管连续谐波的振幅可能

随着 n 的增加而上下振荡，但是它最后总会随着 n 的增加而趋于零。

The computer remembers an incredible amount of data, but *no matter how large its brain becomes* it will always need help. 计算机会记住大量的数据，但是不论其记忆容量变得多大，它总是需要帮助。

It has the same result *whichever way you carry out the experiment*. 不管你怎么做实验，结果都一样。

Whatever happens everyone must be calm. 不管发生什么情况大家都要镇静。

Much as I respect him, I can't agree to his proposal. 尽管我很尊敬他，我却不同意他的建议。

Young as he is, he is quite experienced in this work. （=Though he is young）尽管他年轻，对这个工作却经验丰富。

We'll keep on *even if/though the working condition is bad*. 即使工作条件不好，我们也要坚持下去。

You'll have to attend the workshop *whether you're free or busy*. 不管你忙不忙，都要参加这个讨论会。

【注意】 有时 while 也可以引导让步状语从句，但一般要位于句首。例如：

While I like the color, I don't like the shape. 我虽然喜欢那颜色，但不喜欢那形状。

13.1.8 比较状语从句

常用引导词有：as（同级比较），than（不同程度的比较）。特殊引导词有：the more...the more..., just as..., so..., A is to B what /as X is to Y, no... more than, not A so much as B 等。

The physics lab is three times as big as the chemistry lab. 物理实验室是化学实验室的 3 倍大。

Food is to men what oil is to machine. 食物之于人，犹如油之于机器。

The more the angle of incidence increases, the farther the refracted ray diverges from the normal. 入射角增加的越大，折射线就偏离法线越远。

13.1.9 方式状语从句

常用引导词有：as, just as, as if, how, as though 等。特殊引导词有：the way.

The young man made the experiment *just as the teacher had taught him*. 年青人按照老师所教的做了实验。

Everything went on as usual *as if nothing had happened*. 每件事都一切如常，就像什么都没发生过。

13.2 专业英语阅读

13.2.1 Introduction to Electromagnetics（电磁学引言）

The laws of electricity and magnetism play a central role in the operation of devices such as radios, televisions, electric motors, computers, high-energy particle accelerators, and a host of electronic devices used in medicine. More fundamental, however, is the fact that the interatomic and intermolecular forces responsible for the formation of solids and liquids are electric in origin. Furthermore, such forces as the pushes and pulls between objects in contact and the elastic force in a spring arise from electric forces at the atomic level.

Chinese documents suggest that magnetism was recognized as early as about 2000 B. C. The ancient Greeks observed electric and magnetic phenomena possibly as early as 700 B. C. They found that a piece of amber, when rubbed, attracted pieces of straw or feathers. The existence of magnetic forces was known from observations that pieces of a naturally occurring stone called magnetite were attracted to iron. (The word electric comes from the Greek word for amber, elektron. The word magnetic comes from Magnesia, on the coast of Turkey where magnetite was found.)

In 1600, the Englishman William Gilbert discovered that electrification was not limited to amber but was a general phenomenon. Scientists went on to electrify a variety of objects, including chickens and people! Experiments by Charles Coulomb in 1785 confirmed the inverse-square law for the electrostatic force.

It was not until the early part of the 19th century that scientists established that electricity and magnetism are related phenomena. In 1820, Hans Oersted discovered that a compass needle, which is magnetic, is deflected when placed near an electric current. In 1831, Michael Faraday in England and, almost simultaneously, Joseph Henry in the United States showed that, when a wire loop is moved near a magnet (or, equivalently, when a magnet is moved near a wire loop), an electric current is observed in the wire. In 1873, James Clerk Maxwell used these observations and other experimental facts as a basis for formulating the laws of electromagnetism as we know them today. Shortly thereafter (around 1888), Heinrich Hertz verified Maxwell's predictions by producing electromagnetic waves in the laboratory. This achievement was followed by such practical developments as radio and television.

Maxwell's contributions to the science of electromagnetism were especially significant because the laws he formulated are basic to all forms of electromagnetic phenomena. His work is comparable in importance to Newton's discovery of the laws of motion and the theory of gravitation.

13.2.2 Charge(电荷)

Suppose we rub a plastic rod with fur and suspend it from a string so that it is free to rotate. Now we bring a second similarly rubbed plastic rod near it. The rods repel each other. We get the same results if we use two glass rods that have been rubbed with silk. But a plastic rod rubbed with fur and a glass rod rubbed with silk attract each other. If we repeat the experiment with various materials, we find that all objects fall into one of just two groups—those like the plastic rod rubbed with fur and those like the glass rod rubbed with silk. When materials behave this way, they are said to have become **electrically charged**.

Experiments demonstrate that there are two kinds of **charge** in nature, given the names **positive** and **negative** by Benjamin Franklin (1706—1790), these names have remained to this day. *Two objects that carry the same type of charge repel each other, and two objects that carry opposite charges attract each other.*

13.2.3 Coulomb's Law(库仑定律)

Electric forces between charged objects were measured quantitatively by Charles Coulomb (1736—1806) using a torsion balance of his own invention. In Coulomb's experiment, the charged spheres were much smaller than the distance between them so that the charges could be treated as **point charges.** Coulomb used the method of charging by induction to produce equally charged spheres. For example, beginning with charge q_0 on each sphere, he could reduce the charge to $q_0/2$ by temporarily grounding one sphere to discharge it and then placing the two spheres in contact. The results of the experiments of Coulomb and others are summarized in **Coulomb's law.**

Fig. 13-1 Coulomb's law

The force exerted by one point charge on another acts along the line between the charges. It varies inversely as the square of the distance separating the charges and is proportional to the product of the charges. The force is repulsive if the charges have the same sign and attractive if the charges have opposite signs.

The magnitude of the electric force exerted by a charge q_1 on another charge q_2 is thus given as

$$F_{21} = k \frac{|q_1 q_2|}{r_{21}^2}$$

where r_{21} is the distance between q_1 and q_2, k is an experimentally determined constant called the **Coulomb constant**, which has the value

$$k = 8.9880 \times 10^9 \text{ N} \cdot \text{m}^2/\text{C}^2 \approx 9.0 \times 10^9 \text{ N} \cdot \text{m}^2/\text{C}^2$$

Coulomb's law is given in vector equation by

$$\boldsymbol{F}_{21} = k \frac{q_1 q_2}{r_{21}^2} \boldsymbol{e}_{r21}$$

where $\boldsymbol{e}_{r21}$ is a unit vector pointing from q_1 to q_2 and $\boldsymbol{F}_{21}$ is the force exerted by q_1 on q_2. If q_1 and q_2 have the same sign, the force on q_2 is in the same direction as $\boldsymbol{e}_{r21}$, and is directed away from q_1 (Fig. 13-1). If q_1 and q_2 are of opposite signs, the force on q_2 is in the direction opposite to $\boldsymbol{e}_{r21}$, and is directed toward q_1. From Newton's third law, we see that the electric force exerted by q_2 on q_1 is equal in magnitude to the force exerted by q_1 on q_2 and in the opposite direction; that is, $\boldsymbol{F}_{21} = -\boldsymbol{F}_{12}$. The Coulomb constant k is also written as

$$k = \frac{1}{4\pi\varepsilon_0}$$

where ε_0, known as **the permittivity of free space**, has the value

$$\varepsilon_0 = 8.85 \times 10^{-12} \ C^2/N \cdot m^2$$

Therefore, in free space the expression of Coulomb's law is also written as

$$\boldsymbol{F}_{21} = \frac{q_1 q_2}{4\pi\varepsilon_0 r_{21}^2} \boldsymbol{e}_{r21}$$

Glossary

electricity	电	magnetism	磁
high-energy particle accelerator	高能粒子加速器	electronic device	电子设备
		intermolecular	分子间的
interatomic	原子间的	rub	摩擦
amber	琥珀	electrification	充电、带电、起电
magnetite	磁铁矿	inverse-square law	平方反比定律
electromagnetism	电磁学	electromagnetic waves	电磁波
magnet	磁铁	plastic rod	塑料棒
charge	电荷	repel	排斥
fur	皮革	suspend	悬挂
attract	吸引	opposite charges	相反电荷
electrically charged	带电的	torsion balance	扭秤
Coulomb's Law	库仑定律	point charge	点电荷
charged sphere	带电球	proportional to	正比于
ground	v. 接地	square	平方
discharge	放电	repulsive	排斥的
product	乘积	Coulomb constant	库仑常数
attractive	吸引的	permittivity of free space	真空介电常数
opposite signs	相反符号		

13.3 专业英语常用表达法-13 电磁学常用实验仪器 1

AC bridge experiment facility 交流电桥实验仪

AC / DC resistance box 交直流电阻箱

AC millivoltmeter 交流毫伏表

adjustable capacitor 可变电容器

adjustable inductance 可调电感

adjustable resistor　可调电阻器
air core inductance　空心电感线圈
air dielectric capacitor　空气(介质)电容器
alkaline accumulator　碱性蓄电池
ammeter/amperemeter/amperometer　安培计、电流计
analogue standard resistance　模拟标准电阻
4 and 1/2-bit DC digital voltmeter/amperemeter　4位半直流数字电压表/电流表
bridge comprehensive experiment facility　电桥综合实验仪
bridge　电桥
by-pass resistor　分路电阻器、旁路电阻器
capacitor　电容器
classical AC bridge　经典交流电桥
combined inductance box　组合电感箱
commutator modulator　换向调制器
commutator motor　整流式电动机
commutator rectifier　换向整流器
commutator　换向器、转换开关
core inductance　铁心电感
DC bridge　直流电桥
DC double bridge　直流双臂电桥
DC galvanometer　直流检流计
DC regulated power supply　直流稳压电源
DC resistance bridge　直流电阻电桥
DC single-and-double bridge　直流单双臂电桥
DC single bridge　直流单臂电桥
DC voltage divider　直流分压器
decimal capacitance box　十进式电容箱
decimal inductance box　十进式电感箱
digital micro-current meter　数字式微电流计
direct current supply　直流电源
dry accumulator　干式蓄电池
electric accumulator　蓄电池
electrical inductance　电感
electroscope　验电器
emergency supply　应急电源
experiment facility of Helmholtz coil magnetic field　亥姆霍兹线圈磁场实验仪
experiment facility of horizontal component of earth magnetic field　地磁场水平分量

实验仪
four-terminal resistor　四端电阻器
Hall Effect combined experiment facility　霍尔效应组合实验仪
heat-variable resistor　热变电阻
high potential DC potentiometer　高电势直流电位差计
hysteresis loop experiment facility　磁滞回线实验仪
Kelvin bridge　凯文电桥
low-potential DC potentiometer　低电势直流电位差计
multimeter, universal meter　万用表
non-linear circuit chaotic experiment facility　非线性电路混沌实验仪
packaged double bridge　组装式双臂电桥
photoresistor, photosensitive resistor　光敏电阻
portable DC potentiometer　便携式直流电位差计
portable universal bridge　便携式万能电桥
power supply　电源
precise DC resistance box　精密直流电阻箱
regulated power supply　稳定电源、稳压电源
resistance box　电阻箱
resistor　电阻器
RLC experiment facility　RLC实验仪
rotary resistance box　旋转式电阻箱
spherical capacitor　球形电容器
standard capacitance box　标准电容箱
standard cell, normal cell　标准电池
standard inductance box　标准电感箱
standard resistance　标准电阻
student-purpose potentiometer　学生式电位差计
switch　开关
thermal resistor, thermistor　热敏电阻
thin-film resistor　薄膜电阻器
tuning inductance　调谐电感
unbalanced bridge　非平衡电桥
variable resistor　可变电阻器
voltage dependent resistor　压敏电阻
volt-ampere characteristic tester　伏安特性实验仪
voltmeter　伏特计
Wheatstone bridge　惠斯顿电桥,单臂电桥
wire-wound resistor　线绕电阻(器)

LESSON 14

14.1 物理学专业英语中的形容词性从句

在复合句中,具有形容词功能、修饰一个名词、词组或代词的从句叫做形容词性从句或定语从句;被定语从句所修饰的词、词组叫先行词;引导定语从句的词叫关联词。定语从句通常位于先行词之后,由关系代词或关系副词引导。

定语从句有限制性定语从句和非限制性定语从句两种。

14.1.1 限制性定语从句

限制性定语从句修饰先行词,对先行词起修饰作用,紧接先行词之后,无逗号,若省去,原句意思不完整。

1. 由关系代词 who,whom,whose,that,which 引导的定语从句

引导定语从句的关系代词有 who,whom,whose,which,that,as 等。who,whom,whose 用于指人,whose 有时也可指物,相当于 of which;which 用于指物;that 既可指人也可指物,但只用于限制性定语从句中。关系代词除了引导定语从句,替代先行词外,还在从句中担任主语、宾语、定语等。

(1) 由 that 引导的定语从句

一般情况下 that 可指人或物,可以代替 who,whom 和 which,在从句中作主语或谓语动词的宾语,但不能作介词的宾语。如:

Whether a length is exactly a meter is a question *that no experiment can decide*. 一段长度是否是精确的一米,没有实验能够决定。

Switching circuits are circuits *that perform logical functions*. 开关电路就是执行逻辑函数的电路。

There is hardly a task **that** we perform **that** does not involve the generation, transmission or reaction to information in some form. 我们执行的任务几乎没有不包括以某种形式产生、传送、反应信息的(本句中有两个 that 引导的定语从句)。

【注意1】 当先行词是 all,anything,everything,something,nothing 等不定代词,或先行词前有序数词或 last,any,few,much,some,no,the only,the very 以及形容词最高级修饰时,只能用关系代词 that 引导从句。

This is the first laser *that was introduced from abroad*. 这是第一台从国外引进的激光器。

That's all *that I know about the research project*. 关于研究项目我知道的就这些。

Is there anything *that you want to put in the lab*? 你有什么东西要放在实验室吗?

【注意2】 先行词既有人又有物时,关系代词只用 that,不用 which。例如:

The scientist and his achievements *that you told me about* are admired by us all. 我们所有人都钦佩你告诉我的那位科学家和他所取得的成就。

【注意3】 关系代词在限定性定语从句中作表语并带有类比含义时,通常只用 that,

不用 which。例如：

He is no longer the scholar *that he was*. 他不再是过去的那位学者了。

The key lab is no longer the lab *that it used to be*. 这个重点实验室不再是以前的那个实验室了。

【注意4】 句中其他位置已出现 which，为避免重复，不用 which 而用 that 引导限定性定语从句。例如：

Which is the lab *that we paid a visit last year*？我们去年参观的是哪个实验室？

(2) 由 who，whom 和 whose 引导的定语从句

who 在从句中作主语，whom 在从句中作宾语，whose 在从句中作定语。如：

Madame Curie is one of the world's greatest women scientists *who will always be remembered as the discoverer of radium*. 居里夫人是世界上最伟大的女科学家之一，作为镭的发现者她被永远铭记。

He is the experimenter *whom you wanted to find*. 他就是你想要找的那个实验人员。

The cross product of two vectors A and B is defined to be a vector $C = A \times B$ *whose magnitude equals the area of the parallelogram formed by the two vectors*. 两个矢量 A 和 B 的矢积定义为 $C = A \times B$，其大小等于两个矢量形成的平行四边形的面积。

For instance, we may visualize a system as an electrical circuit *whose input is a voltage signal and whose output is a current reading*. 比如，我们可以把系统设想为一种电路，它的输入是电压信号，它的输出是电流示数。

(3) 由 which 引导的定语从句

which 指物，在从句中作主语或谓语动词的宾语。如：

A theorem is a statement *which reasoning shows to be true*. 定理是经推导得到的正确论断。

For example, in a mechanical system an ideal model may be a mass *which is concentrated at a point* such that the numerical value of the mass is independent of forces, velocities or acceleration. 例如，力学中的理想模型可以是集中于一点的质量，其数值与力、速度和加速度无关。

【注意1】 在介词提前到关系代词之前形成"介词＋关系代词"结构来修饰表示事物的先行词时关系代词必须用 which。例如：

A curve is a line *of which no part is straight* and which changes direction without angles. 曲线就是没有直的部分、转向时又没有角的线。

We regard a system as a structure *into which something (matter, energy, or information) may be put at certain times* and which itself puts out something at certain times. 我们把系统看作这样一种结构，有时可以对它输入(比如物质、能量或信息)，有时它自己也输出。

An inertial frame of reference is one *in which an object, subject to no force, moves with constant velocity*. 在一个参考系中，如果一个不受力的物体做匀速运动，那么这个参考系就是惯性参考系。

如果介词不放在修饰事物的限定性定语从句的句首，which 就可换为 that，例如：

This is the question *which/that we've had so much discussion about*. = This is the question *about which we've had so much discussion*. 这就是我们已经多次讨论过的问题。

【注意2】 先行词为"those+表示事物的复数名词"时,关系代词通常只用 which 而不用 that。例如:

Experimenters should keep in mind those regulations *which keep them off dangers*. 实验人员应牢记那些保护自己免受危险的规则。

【注意3】 关系代词在定语从句中作宾语时,关系代词常省去。如:

The device (*which/that*) *I handled just now* has been repaired twice. 我刚才使用的仪器已经维修了两次。

In this chapter, we shall take a closer look at the structure of a few particularly interesting atoms and molecules in order to see how they are fitted to the use (*which/that*) *man makes of them*. 在本章中,我们将更仔细地研究一下几个特别有趣的原子和分子的结构,看一看怎样使它们便于人类利用。

(4) as 引导的定语从句

as 引导的定语从句主要用于"such…as"及"the same…as"的结构中,代替先行词是人或物的名词。as 引导非限制性定语从句时,代替整个主句,从句可位于主句之前、之后或中间。

These are not such problems *as can be easily solved*.(as 代替先行词 problems)这是些不容易解决的问题。

2. 由关系副词 where,when 和 why 引导的定语从句

引导定语从句的关系副词 where 在从句中作地点状语,when 在从句中作时间状语,why 在从句中作原因状语。意义上相当于一个"介词+which"的结构。如:

Benjamin Franklin would never forget the moment *when*(=*at which*) *he was knocked out by the charge*. 富兰克林永远忘不了被电击昏的那个时刻。

Ever since then, Einstein has never been back to the town *where*(=*in which*) *he was born*. 从那以后,爱因斯坦再也没回过他出生的小镇。

I don't know the reason *why*(=*for which*) *the capacitor can store charge*. 我不知道电容器能够储电的原因。

14.1.2 非限制性定语从句

非限制性定语从句既可修饰先行词,也可修饰整个主句,起补充说明作用,与主句之间有逗号隔开,若省去,原句意思不受影响。不可用 that 引导非限制性定语从句。关系词不可省略。

This arises because of interference with the reflected waves, *which have the same wavelength, amplitude, and speed*. 这种现象的发生是由于与反射波的干涉,反射波具有相同的波长、振幅和速度。

Moving around the nucleus are extremely tiny particles, called electrons, *which revolve around the nucleus in much the same way as the planets do around the sun*. 围绕着原子核运动的是一些极其微小的粒子,称为电子,这些电子围绕着原子核旋转,正像行星围绕着太阳旋转一样。

For a situation like this, *in which the current is discontinuous in space*, Ampere's law is not valid. 在这样的情况下,电流是不连续的,安培定律不适用。

【注意】 as 与 which 引导的定语从句

两者均可引导非限制性定语从句,有时可以互换,但下列情况多用 as.

(1) 关系代词引导的定语从句居句首时。

As we all know, oceans cover more than 70% of the earth. 我们都知道,海洋覆盖地球表面的 70%以上。

As is known to everybody, the moon travels round the earth once every month. 众所周知,月球每个月绕地球运行一周。

(2) 当与 such 或 the same 连用时,一般用 as。

Such physics books *as you tell me* are interesting. 你告诉我的物理书很有趣。

Different statements of the second law of thermodynamic have the same meanings *as you can find*. 你会发现,关于热力学第二定律的不同表述具有等价性。

(3) 当从句和主句语义一致时,用 as,反之则用 which。

She failed again, *as was expected*.

She failed again, *which was unexpected*.

(4) as 在从句中作主语时,后面常接行为动词的被动语态,如 be known, be said, be reported 等,如从句中行为动词是主动语态,一般要用 which 作主语。

No single company or group can control what happens on the Internet, *as is mentioned above*, 如上所述,没有哪个公司和组织能够控制互联网上的事。(as 代替主语)

The model was useful, *which made us happy*. 这个模型很有用,令我们很高兴。

(5) 再看下面两个例句:

(a) This cable is like a snake, *as/which everybody can see*. =As everybody can see, this cable is like a snake. 任何人都看得出来,这电线像条蛇。

(b) Einstein's general relativity turned out to be correct, *which made the physicists very excited*. 爱因斯坦的广义相对论结果是正确的,这使得物理学家们很兴奋。

这两个例句中,as 和 which 所代表的都是整个主句所表示的内容。但有两点不同之处:

① 在形式上 as 引导的非限制性定语从句可位于主句的后面,也可位于主句的前面;而 which 引导的非限制性定语从句只能位于主句的后面,不能位于主句的前面。

② 在意义上,as 引导的定语从句和主句的关系一般为一致关系,常译为"正如……", "就像……",而 which 引导的定语从句和主句的关系是因果关系,或 which 引导的定语从句是对主句的评论。因此,在意思通顺的情况下,which 可代替 as,而 as 许多时候不能代替 which,如例句(b)。再如:

He was late again, *as/which we had expected*. = As we had expected, he was late again. 正如我们所料,他又迟到了。/他又迟到了这是我们早就料到的。

The engineer uses a lot of oil to lubricate the machine, *which makes it very dirty*. 工程师用很多油来润滑机器,结果把它搞得很脏。(which 为主动语态的主语,不用 as)

Many people ever tried hard to invent machines violating the second law of thermodynamic, *which was impossible*. 许多人曾努力想发明违背热力学第二定律的机器,

但这是不可能的。(不用 as)

He maintains the machine every month, *which has done a lot of good to its performance*. 他每月保养机器,这对它的性能很有好处。(which 为主动语态的主语,不用 as)

As has already been pointed out, the concept of idealized models is extremely important in all physical science and technology. 正如已经指出的那样,理想模型的概念在所有物理科学和技术中是极其重要的。(置于句首,不用 which)

14.2 专业英语阅读

14.2.1 Gauss's Law(高斯定理)

Gauss's law, which relates the electric field on a closed surface to the net charge within the surface, is of fundamental importance in the study of electrostatic fields. In words, *Gauss's law states that in the electrostatic field in vacuum the net electric flux through any closed surface is equal to the net charge inside the surface divided by* ε_0.

In principle, Gauss's law is valid for all surfaces and all charge distributions. In practice, however, it can be used to calculate the electric field only for charge distributions that have high degrees of symmetry. For static charge distributions, Gauss's law and Coulomb's law are equivalent. However, Gauss's law is more general in that it is always valid whether or not the charges are static.

14.2.2 Conductors in Electrostatic Equilibrium(导体的静电平衡)

A good electrical conductor contains charges (electrons) that are not bound to any atom and are free to move about within the material. When no motion of charge occurs within the conductor, the conductor is in **electrostatic equilibrium**. In this situation, every charge in the conductor is a particle in equilibrium, experiencing zero net force. As we shall see, an isolated conductor (one that is insulated from ground) in electrostatic equilibrium has the following properties:

The electric field is zero everywhere inside the conductor.

If the isolated conductor carries a net charge, the net charge resides entirely on its surface.

The electric field just outside the charged conductor is perpendicular to the conductor surface and has a magnitude σ/ε_0, where σ is the surface charge density at that point.

Every point on the surface of a charged conductor in electrostatic equilibrium is at the same electric potential, that is, the conductor is an equipotential volume and its surface is an equipotential surface.

On an irregularly shaped conductor, the surface charge density σ is highest at locations where the radius of curvature of the surface is smallest.

14.2.3 Capacitance and Capacitors(电容和电容器)

When charge is placed on an isolated conductor, the potential of the conductor increases. The ratio of the charge to the potential is called the **capacitance** of the conductor. A useful device for storing charge and energy is the **capacitor**, which consists of two conductors, closely spaced but insulated from each other. When attached to a source of potential difference such as a battery, the conductors carry equal and opposite charges. The ratio of the magnitude of the charge on either conductor to the potential difference between the conductors is the capacitance of the capacitor. Capacitors have many uses. The flash attachment for your camera uses a capacitor to store the energy needed to provide the sudden flash of light. Capacitors are also used in the tuning circuits of devices such as radios, televisions, and cellular phones, allowing them to operate at specific frequencies.

Any two conductors separated by an insulator are said to form a capacitor. In most cases of practical interest the conductors have charges of equal magnitude and opposite sign. A capacitor is usually charged by transferring a charge Q from one conductor to the other, and then leaving one of the conductors with a charge $+Q$ and the other with a charge $-Q$. The electric field in the region between the conductors is proportional to the magnitude of this charge, and it follows that the potential difference U between the conductors is also proportional to the charge magnitude Q. The capacitance of a capacitor is defined to be Q/U.

Capacitors find many applications in electrical circuits. Capacitors are used for tuning radio circuits and for "smoothing" the rectified current delivered by a power supply. A capacitor is used to eliminate sparking when a circuit containing inductance is suddenly opened. The ignition system of every automobile engine contains a capacitor to eliminate sparking of the "points" when they open and close. The efficiency of alternating current power transmission can often be increased by the use of large capacitors.

14.2.4 Dielectrics and Polarization(电介质与极化)

A nonconducting material, such as air, glass, paper, or wood, is called a **dielectric**. When the space between the two conductors of a capacitor is occupied by a dielectric, the capacitance is increased by a factor ε_r that is characteristic of the dielectric and ε_r is called the **relative dielectric constant**. The reason for this increase is that the electric field between the plates of a capacitor is weakened by the dielectric. Thus, for a given charge on the plates, the potential difference is reduced and the capacitance (Q/U) is increased.

We can understand the effects of a dielectric by considering the polarization of molecules. A dielectric weakens the electric field between the plates of a capacitor because the molecules in the dielectric produce an electric field in a direction opposite to the field produced by the plates. This electric field is due to the electric dipole moments of the molecules in the dielectric.

Although atoms and molecules are electrically neutral, they are affected by electric fields because they contain positive and negative charges that can respond to external fields. We can think of an atom as a very small, positively charged nucleus surrounded by a negatively charged electron cloud. In some atoms and molecules, the electron cloud is spherically symmetric, so its "center of charge" is at the center of the atom or molecule coinciding with the positive charge. An atom or molecule like this has zero dipole moment and is said to be **nonpolar**. Such molecules are called **nonpolar molecules** (for example, H_2 and CO_2). But in the presence of an external electric field, the positive and negative charge experience forces in opposite directions. The positive and negative charges then separate until the attractive force they exert on each other balances the forces due to the external electric field (Fig. 14-1). The molecule is then said to be **polarized** and it behaves like an electric dipole.

(a)   (b)

Fig. 14-1 Schematic diagrams of the charge distributions of a nonpolar molecule. (a) In the absence of an external electric field, the center of positive charge coincides with the center of negative charge. (b) In the presence of an external electric field, the centers of positive and negative charge are displaced, producing an induced dipole moment in the direction of the external field

In some molecules (for example, HCl and H_2O), the centers of positive and negative charge do not coincide due to a nonuniform distribution of charge even in the absence of an external electric field, so these molecules have a permanent electric dipole moment. Such molecules are called **polar molecules**.

Microwave ovens take advantage of the electric dipole moment of water molecules to cook food. Like all electromagnetic waves, microwaves have an oscillating electric field that can cause electric dipoles to vibrate. The microwaves in home ovens are tuned to the natural frequency of vibration of water molecules. The water molecules in food resonate with the oscillating electric field and absorb large amounts of energy, accounting for the rapid cooking times that make microwave ovens so convenient.

When a dielectric is placed in the field of a capacitor, its molecules are polarized such that there is a net dipole moment parallel to the field. If the molecules are polar, their dipole moments, originally oriented at random, tend to become aligned due to the torque exerted by the field (Fig. 14-2). If the molecules are nonpolar, the field induces dipole moments that are parallel to the field (as also in Fig. 14-1). In either case, the molecules in the dielectric are polarized in the direction of the external field. The net effect of the polarization of a homogeneous dielectric in a parallel-plate capacitor is the creation of a surface charge on the dielectric faces near the plates, as shown in Fig. 14-3. The surface charge on the dielectric is called a **bound charge** because it is bound to the molecules of the dielectric and cannot move about like the free charge on the conducting capacitor plates.

This bound charge produces an electric field opposite in direction to that produced by the free charge on the conductors. Thus, the net electric field between the plates is reduced, as illustrated in Fig. 14-4.

Fig. 14-2 (a) The randomly oriented electric dipoles of a polar dielectric in the absence of an external electric field. (b) In the presence of an external electric field, the dipoles are partially aligned parallel to the field

Fig. 14-3 When a dielectric is placed between the plates of a capacitor, the electric field of the capacitor polarizes the molecules of the dielectric. The result is bound charges on the surface of the dielectric are created

Fig. 14-4 The electric field between the plates of a capacitor (a) with no dielectric and (b) with a dielectric. The electric field that the surface charge on the dielectric produces weakens the original field between the plates

Glossary

Gauss's law	高斯定理	closed surface	闭合面
electrostatic field	静电场	vacuum	真空
electric flux	电通量	charge distribution	电荷分布

degrees of symmetry	对称度	equivalent	等价的
in principle	原则上	in practice	实际上
conductor	导体	electrostatic equilibrium	静电平衡
equilibrium	平衡	isolated conductor	孤立导体
insulate	绝缘	perpendicular to	垂直于
charged conductor	带电导体	electric potential	电势
equipotential	等电势的	radius of curvature	曲率半径
capacitance	电容	capacitor	电容器
flash	闪光灯	attachment	配件
tuning circuit	调谐电路	cellular phone	移动电话
electrical circuit	电路	sparking	火花
ignition system	（汽车的）点火系统	alternating current	交流
power transmission	电力传输	polarize	v. 极化
polarization	极化	polar molecules	极性分子
nonpolar molecule	非极性分子	induced dipole moments	感应电矩
permanent electric dipole moments	固有电矩	surface charge	表面电荷
align	排成一线	orient	取向
bound charge	束缚电荷	homogeneous	均匀的
free charge	自由电荷	microwave oven	微波炉
vibrate	振动	tune	调整
resonate with	与……共振	oscillating electric field	振荡电场

14.3 专业英语常用表达法-14 图的表示法

1. figure 通常指几何图形或图案；此外书中的插图不管是什么图都可以用 figure 表示。例如：

Figure 3 shows an electrics motor being used to lift a heavy object. 图 3 所示是正在起吊重物的一台电动机。

Figure 5 is the schematic diagram of a d/a converter. 图 5 是数/模转换器的示意图。

2. diagram 是专业英语中用得比较广泛的一个词，用于一般的图形、图表。例如：

schematic diagram 示意图，原理图

a diagram of the apparatus 装置简图

a diagram of a flask showing its outline 一只长颈烧瓶的轮廓简图

rough out a diagram 草拟一张图表

This simplified block diagram is valuable. 这个简化了的框图很有用。

3. graph 一般用于指曲线图、标绘图，也可指图解。例如：

relating to a graph 与图表有关

presented by a graph 用图表表达

The graph of this equation has been drawn above. 此方程所对应的曲线图已在上面

画出。

The graph showed the increase in instruments between the years 2005 and 2009. 这张曲线图所示是 2005—2009 年仪器增长的情况。

4. graphics（作单数用）制图法，制图学，图表算法，图形。例如：

specification of tables of graphics　对图表的说明

5. plot 往往可以与 graph 互换。例如：

The plot of I versus V is a straight line. I 随 V 的变化曲线是一条直线。

6. view 一般用于机械图或各种结构图中的各向视图，也用来指航海中使用的"对景图"（即实物图片）。例如：

The top and cross-sectional views of the memory structure are shown below. 这种存储器结构的俯视图和剖析图如下面所示。

A front view shows only the width and height of an object. 前视图（正面图）只给出一物体的宽度和高度。

7. profile 一般指零（部）件的外形轮廓图，剖面形状图，profile 也可指各种分布图。例如：

stratigraphic profile　地层纵断面图（剖面图）

density profile　密度分布图

pressure profile　压力分布图

8. pattern 用于指图形、图案、花纹等。例如：

diffraction/interference pattern　衍射/干涉图样

A mask with 1000 tiny individual patterns is placed over the chip and exposed to light. 将带有 1000 个微小分立图样的掩膜放在晶片上并曝光。

9. drawing 主要用于各种工程图纸及有关工程设计的附图、插图、工程图。例如：

perspective drawing　透视图，projection drawing　投影图

10. chart 多用于航线图和某种方向的图。例如：

nautical chart　航海图

flight chart　航空图

make a chart of　绘制……的图表

a chart representing numerical relationships　代表数字关系的图表

11. map 指地图、天体图、布局图以及一些专用图形。例如：

seismic map　地震图，weather map　气象图，radar map　雷达图

12. sketch 一般指粗略勾画的示意图，草图，图样。例如：

a sketch of the apparatus used for distillation　蒸馏装置的草图

13. layout 着重于被描绘对象的总体概貌，外形轮廓，总体安排和设计。例如：

Among the disadvantages are great layout difficulties. 缺点之一是（电路）排图困难。

14. line 一般仅用于线条描绘的轮廓和外形图，如船体型线图。例如：

The engineers are making the designing of the hull lines. 工程师们正在设计船体型线图。

15. scheme 指草图、示意图。例如：

wiring scheme　配线图，接线图，布线图

16. illustration 插图,图解。例如:
The colored illustrations in that book are most attractive. 那本书中的彩色插图非常吸引人。
17. image 像,图像。例如:
Project the image on a screen. 把图像投射到屏幕上。
18. outline 轮廓图,略图。
19. draft 含有底稿的意思,用得较少。
20. delineation 只用于草图、略图、示意图,用得较少。

LESSON 15

15.1 物理学专业英语中的非谓语动词(一)动词不定式和动名词

仔细分析各种物理专业英语文献,我们会发现其中的很多句子结构并不复杂,都只有一套主谓结构。前面的分析曾经提到科技英语的句子比较长,这种的现象看似矛盾,原因之一是非谓语动词的大量使用。

动词不定式、分词(现在分词,过去分词)和动名词在句中均不能作谓语用,所以统称为非谓语动词。现代英语将现在分词和动名词合为一大类叫作 $v.+ing$ 形式。这些动词的形式不能在句中单独作谓语用,因而没有语法主语,但可以有逻辑主语。由于没有语法主语,也就不受人称和数的限定,由于不是谓语,也就没有时态和语态,但这些词仍能表示动作和状态,所以仍有确定的形式,用来表示相对于其他动词的时间关系。由于具有逻辑主语,因此也有表示主动、被动的形式,同时也有自己的宾语和状语,一起构成非谓语动词短语(动词不定式短语、分词短语、动名词短语)。非谓语动词在专业英语语法中占有特殊且重要的地位。非谓语动词形式多样,应用广泛,在句中起着重要的作用。

15.1.1 动词不定式

动词不定式由"to+动词原形"构成。动词不定式虽然不能作谓语动词用,但仍保留动词的特征,它可以带有自己的宾语或状语而构成动词不定式短语,如 to locate a point in space,to be quite important。

1. 动词不定式的基本用法

动词不定式能起名词、形容词和副词的作用,可在句中作主语、表语、宾语补足语、定语和状语用。

(1) 作主语

To say that a distance is 25 is meaningless. The magnitude of the physical quantity must include both a number and a unit. 说一段距离是25是没有意义的。物理量的大小必须包括数值和单位两个部分。

动词不定式作主语时,一般可用 it 作形式主语,而将作主语的动词不定式置于句末。如:

It is convenient *to use Equation*(4-5) *in its component form*. 采用方程(4-5)的分量形

式是比较方便的。

(2) 作表语

If we wish to locate a point in space, the simplest way is *to describe* how far the point is from some other known point, and in what direction. 如果我们想在空间定位一个点,最简单的方法就是描述这个点距离某个已知的点有多远以及在哪个方向上。

(3) 作宾语

① 作动词的宾语,如:

A car starts *to move* from rest with speed increasing uniformly along a circular path. 一辆车沿着圆周从静止开始以匀加速度运动。

This relation, known as Hooke's law, turns out *to be* quite important. 这个关系,就是胡克定律,是非常重要的。

② 作形容词的宾语,如:

Space and time, by themselves, are concepts that are difficult (or perhaps impossible) *to define* in terms of anything simpler. 时间和空间,就其本身而言,是非常难以(或许也不可能)用更简单的东西来定义的概念。

③ 动词不定式一般不作介词的宾语,但动词不定式之前如有疑问词时,就可作介词的宾语。如:

Can you give us some advice on what *to do* next? 接下来怎么办,能给我们点建议吗?

(4) 作宾语补足语

Every coordinate system involves a particular point, the origin (O), and specified directions or axes that enable points in space *to be described* relative to the origin and the axes. 每个坐标系包括一个特定点(原点 O)和一些规定的方向(坐标轴),从而使空间中的点可以相对于原点和坐标轴加以描述。

We assume space *to be continuously uniform and isotropic*. 我们假设空间是连续均匀和各向同性的。

【注意】 如果句中的谓语动词为 see, hear, watch, notice, have, make, let 等,作宾语补足语的动词不定式须将 to 省去。如:

The students watch the object *fall* freely to the ground. 学生观察物体自由下落到地面。

(5) 动词不定式在句中作宾语,如带有宾语补足语时,须先用 it 作形式宾语,而将该动词不定式后置。如:

I don't think *it* right *to handle the apparatus that way*. 我认为那样操作仪器不对。

(6) 作定语

动词不定式作定语时,须位于被其修饰的名词或代词之后。如:

In this case, the particle has maximum tendency *to rotate* about the origin. 在这种情况下,粒子具有绕原点旋转的最大趋势。

(7) 作状语

动词不定式可以作下列状语:

① 目的状语

To measure the distance between two points, we need a standard unit, such as a meter. 为了测量两点间的距离,我们需要一个标准单位,例如米这个单位。

为了强调不定式表示目的的作用,可在不定式前加 in order to 或 so as to(以便或为了),但应注意 in order to 位于句首或句中均可,而 so as to 不能位于句首。如:

In order to make an idealized model of a system, we have to overlook quite a few minor effects to concentrate on the most important features of the system. 为了给系统做一个理想模型,我们不得不忽略很多不重要的因素,而把注意力集中在系统的重要特征上。

【注意】 将表示目的的不定式置于句首,也可起到强调目的的作用。

② 结果状语

We need to use some judgment and creativity to construct a model that simplifies a problem enough *to make it manageable*, yet keeps its essential features. 为了构建一个模型,我们需要发挥一下判断力和创造力,把问题简化到既能得到有效解决,又能保留必要的特征。

The electric force binds atoms and molecules in compounds *to form ordinary matter*. 电力把原子和分子约束在化合物内,形成了物质。

③ too+形容词或副词+动词不定式,表示"太……以至于不能……"的结果。如:

In physics, a model is a simplified version of a physical system that would be *too complicated to analyze* in full detail. 物理学中的模型是那些难以详尽分析的物理系统的简化描述。

2. 复合结构不定式

由 for+名词(或代词宾格)+动词不定式即构成复合结构的动词不定式。其中 for 本身无意义。for 后面的名词或代词是不定式的逻辑主语,这种不定式在句中可作主语、表语、宾语、定语或状语。如:

Note that the net external force need not be zero *for angular momentum to be conserved*. 注意:角动量守恒合外力不必为零。

It is very important *for us to get everything ready* for the experiment. 我们为实验准备好一切是很重要的。

当作表语用的形容词表示不定式的逻辑主语的性质或特征时,就用介词 of 而不用 for 引出不定式的逻辑主语,这些形容词一般有 good, nice, kind, wise, silly, stupid, foolish, right, wrong, careless, impolite 等。如:

It is very kind *of you to measure the temperature of the oil* for me every day. 你真好,每天都为我测量油温。

3. 疑问词+动词不定式

疑问代词和疑问副词后可加动词不定式构成不定式短语,在句中可作主语、表语或宾语。如:

How to prevent the temperature from getting too high in this heat engine is a problem. 如何在热机中防止高温是一个问题。

4. 动词不定式的否定式

动词不定式的否定式是由 not ＋动词不定式构成。如：

It's wrong of you *not to apply Ampere's law for a situation like this*. 在这种情况下你不应用安培定律是不正确的。

5. 动词不定式的时态所表示的时间关系

（1）一般式：动词不定式一般式所表示的动作是和谓语动词所表示的动作同时发生，但在多数情况下，是在谓语动词所表示的动作之后发生。如：

We decided *to demonstrate a standing wave* with a rope with one end fixed on the wall. 我们决定利用一根绳子，把其一端固定在墙上来演示驻波（其后）。

The assistants often watch the professor *operate the spectrograph*. 助教经常观察教授操作摄谱仪（同时）。

（2）完成式：动词不定式完成式所表示的动作发生在谓语动词所表示的动作之前。如：

I am sorry *to have kept you waiting* outside the lab. 对不起，让你在实验室外面等着。

（3）进行式：动词不定式进行式所表示的动作正在进行中，而且与谓语动词所表示的动作同时发生。如：

She happened *to be repairing a multimeter* in the room when I came in. 我进来时她正在修理万用表。

6. 动词不定式的被动语态

如果动词不定式的逻辑主语为这个不定式所表示的动作的承受者时，不定式一般就用被动语态形式。如：

Resistance welding is performed by passing a very heavy current through the pieces of metal *to be joined*. 电阻焊接是让强大电流流过待焊金属来完成的。

15.1.2 动名词

动名词是动词的一种非谓语形式。动名词的构成为：$v.$ ＋ing。

动名词具有名词的特点，可在句中作主语、宾语和表语。动名词也具有动词的某些特点，可带有宾语和状语，构成动名词短语。动名词也有主动和被动、一般时和完成时等形式。

1. 动名词及其短语在句中可以作主语、宾语和表语

例如：

Heating the water changes it into vapor. 把水加热可以使水变为蒸汽（Heating the water 在句中作主语，water 是 heating 的宾语）。

Closing the switch connects the cranking motor to the battery. 合上开关就把启动马达与蓄电池接通了（句中 closing the switch 作主语，switch 为 closing 的宾语）。

Oxygen does not burn, but does support *burning*. 氧不自燃，但能助燃（burning 是动名词，作 support 的宾语）。

This is equivalent to *stating* that it has no tendency to rotate about the origin. 这相当

于说物体根本没有绕原点运动的趋势（动名词 stating 为介词 to 的宾语）。

Energy is involved in *doing* work, or in *heating* on object. 能量与做功有关，或使物体变热（动名词 doing 和 heating 均为介词 in 的宾语）。

In the dynamo, mechanical energy is used for *rotating* the armature between the poles of an electromagnet. 在直流发电机中，机械能被用来转动电磁铁两极之间的电枢（动名词 rotating 是介词 for 的宾语）。

One way to fit the pieces of a broken iron bar together is *heating* the iron until it softens and *pounding* it with a hammer. 把一根断成数截的铁棍连接起来的一个方法就是把铁加热至软化，然后用铁锤去锻打（句中 heating 和 pounding 均为表语）。

2. 动名词的被动语态

当动名词的逻辑主体是动名词的动作对象时，该动名词通常用被动形式。例如：

When a vapor condenses, the energy that it absorbed in *being vaporized* is again released as heat. 当蒸汽冷凝时，它汽化时所吸收的能量又以热的形式释放出来（it 用来代替 vapor，it 是 vaporize 这一动作的承受者，所以要用动名词的被动形式 being vaporized）。

It is assumed that every substance which is capable of *being magnetized* consists of a very large number of molecular magnets. 人们假定，能够被磁化的各种物质都是由大量的分子磁体组成的（句中 which 用来代替 substance，which 是动词 magnetize 这一动作的对象，所以 magnetize 的动名词应用被动形式）。

3. 动名词的完成式

如果动名词的动作发生在谓语动词之前，则该动名词通常用完成式。例如：

Having discovered the property of the atom, scientists began finding ways of using atomic energy for industrial purposes. 发现了原子的特性之后，科学家们开始寻找将原子能用于工业的途径（discover 发生在谓语动词 began 之前，即先"发现了原子的特性"，后"开始寻找"用于工业的途径）。

Nuclear fuel will be used in the reactor after its *having been compressed* into the form of rods. 核燃料被压成棒状之后，可用于反应堆中（句中 having been compressed 是完成式被动语态动名词，作 after 的宾语，其行为发生在谓语动词 will be used 之前，即先"压成棒状"，后"用于反应堆"）。

4. 动名词的逻辑主体

动名词短语前面可以加一个物主代词（如 their, its 等），名词的所有格（如 teacher's）或名词的普通形式来表示这个动名词的逻辑主体。例如：

The main trouble is *their not having* enough voltage. 主要困难是他们没有足够的电压（句中物主代词 their 是动名词 having 的逻辑主体）。

Physically we understand forces as due to *matter pushing* on other matters. 在物理意义上，我们可以把力理解为一物体对另一物体的推力（句中动名词 pushing 是介词 due to 的宾语，matter 是 pushing 的逻辑主体）。

We know of the *earth behaving* as a large magnet. 我们知道，地球相当于一个大磁体

(动名词 behaving 作 of 的宾语，the earth 是 behaving 的逻辑主体)。

By using phototubes, doors can be opened without *anyone's having touched them*. 使用光电管，可以使门无人自开(having touched 是动名词完成式，在句中作介词 without 的宾语，anyone's 是 having touched 的逻辑主体)。

The process of *one substance mixing* with another because of molecular motion is called diffusion. 一物质与另一物质由于分子运动而混合的过程称为扩散(动名词 mixing 是 of 的宾语，one substance 是 mixing 的逻辑主体)。

Magnetism may be induced into an iron bar without *it touching* the magnet. 铁棒无须接触磁铁就可受到磁感应(动名词 touching 是 without 的宾语，it 是 touching 的逻辑主体)。

15.2 专业英语阅读

15.2.1 Nature of Magnetic Force(磁力的本质)

More than 2000 years ago, the Greeks were aware that a certain type of stone (now called magnetite) attracts pieces of iron, and there are written references to the use of magnets for navigation dating from the twelfth century.

In 1269, Pierre de Maricourt discovered that a needle laid at various positions on a spherical natural magnet orients itself along lines that pass through points at opposite ends of the sphere. He called these points the **poles of the magnet.** Subsequently, many experimenters noted that every magnet of whatever shape has two poles, designated the **north and south poles**, where the force exerted by the magnet is strongest. It was also noted that the like poles of two magnets repel each other and the unlike poles attract each other.

Although electric charges and magnetic poles are similar in many respects, there is an important difference: *Magnetic poles always occur in pairs*. When a magnet is broken in half, equal and opposite poles appear at either side of the break point. The result is two magnets, each with a north and a south pole. There has long been speculation as to the existence of an isolated magnetic pole, and in recent years considerable experimental effort has been made to find such an object. Thus far, there is no conclusive evidence that an isolated magnetic pole exists.

Magnetic force is the interaction between moving electric charges. This is the nature of magnetic force.

15.2.2 The Biot-Savart Law(毕奥-萨伐尔定律)

The earliest known sources of magnetism were permanent magnets. One month after Oersted announced his discovery that a compass needle is deflected by an electric current, Jean Baptiste Biot and Felix Savart announced the results of their measurements of the force on a magnet near a long, current-carrying wire and analyzed these results in terms of the magnetic field produced by each element of the current. Andre-Marie Ampere extended these experiments and showed that current elements also experience a force in the presence of a magnetic field and that two currents exert forces on each other.

The magnetic field dB produced by a current element Idl is given by

$$d\boldsymbol{B} = \frac{\mu_0}{4\pi} \frac{Id\boldsymbol{l} \times \boldsymbol{e}_r}{r^2} \tag{15-1}$$

where $\boldsymbol{e}_r$ is a unit vector that points from the current element Idl to the field point P_1 (Fig. 15-1) and μ_0 is a constant of proportionality called the **permeability of free space**, which has the value

$$\mu_0 = 4\pi \times 10^{-7} \, \text{N/A}^2$$

Fig. 15-1 The current element Idl produces a magnetic field at point P_1 that is perpendicular to both Idl and $\boldsymbol{r}$. It produces no magnetic field at P_2, which is along the line of Idl

Eq. (15-1), known as the **Biot-Savart law**, was also deduced by Ampere. The source of the magnetic field is a moving charge $q\boldsymbol{v}$ or a current element Idl, just as the charge q is the source of the electrostatic field. The magnetic field decreases with the square of the distance from the moving charge or current element, just as the electric field decreases with the square of the distance from a point charge. However, the directional aspects of the electric and magnetic fields are quite different. Whereas the electric field points in the radial direction $\boldsymbol{e}_r$ from the point charge to the field point (for a positive charge), the magnetic field is perpendicular both to $\boldsymbol{e}_r$ and to the direction of motion $\boldsymbol{v}$ of the charges, which is along the direction of the current element. At a point along the line of a current element, such as point P_2 in Fig. 15-1, the magnetic field due to that element is zero, because Idl is parallel to the vector $\boldsymbol{e}_r$.

The magnetic field due to the total current in a circuit can be calculated by using the Biot-Savart law to find the field due to each current element and then summing (integrating) over all the current elements in the circuit. This calculation is difficult for all but the simplest circuit geometries.

15.2.3 B due to a Current in a Solenoid（通电螺线管的磁场）

A **solenoid** is a wire tightly wound into a helix of closely spaced turns, as illustrated in Fig. 15-2. It is used to produce a strong, uniform magnetic field in the region surrounded by its loops. Its role in magnetism is analogous to that of the parallel-plate capacitor, which produces a strong, uniform electric field between its plates. The magnetic field of a solenoid is essentially that of a set of N identical current loops placed side by side. Fig. 15-3 shows the magnetic field lines for two such loops.

Fig. 15-2

Fig. 15-3

Fig. 15-4 shows the magnetic field lines for a long, tightly wound solenoid. Inside the solenoid, the field lines are approximately parallel to the axis and are closely and uniformly spaced, indicating a strong, uniform magnetic field. Outside the solenoid, the lines are much less dense. They diverge from one end and converge at the other end.

Fig. 15-4

15.2.4 Gauss's Law for Magnetism(磁场的高斯定理)

The magnetic field lines differ from electric field lines in that the lines of $\boldsymbol{B}$ form closed curves, whereas lines of $\boldsymbol{E}$ begin and end on electric charges (Fig. 15-5(a)). The magnetic equivalent of an electric charge is a magnetic pole, such as appears to be at the ends of a bar magnet. However, although the magnetic field lines appear to diverge from the north pole outside a bar magnet (Fig. 15-5(b)), the lines inside the magnet point toward the pole. These lines enter the south pole of the magnet from the outside, but on the inside of the magnet the lines leave the south pole. If one end of a bar magnet is enclosed by a surface, the number of magnetic field lines that leave the surface is exactly equal to the number that enter the surface. That is, the net flux of the field through any closed surface is zero.

$$\phi_{m,net} = \oint_S \boldsymbol{B} \cdot d\boldsymbol{S} = 0 \tag{15-2}$$

where the definition of the magnetic flux ϕ_m is exactly analogous to the electric flux with $\boldsymbol{B}$

Fig. 15-5

replacing **E**. This result is called **Gauss's law for magnetism**. It is the mathematical statement that there are no points in space from which magnetic field lines diverge, or to which they converge. That is, *isolated magnetic poles do not exist*. The fundamental unit of magnetism is the magnetic dipole. Fig. 15-5 compares the lines of **B** for a magnetic dipole with the lines of **E** for an electric dipole. Note that far from the dipoles the lines are identical. But inside the dipole, the lines of **E** are opposite the lines of **B**. The lines of **E** diverge from the positive charge and converge to the negative charge, whereas the lines of **B** are continuous loops.

Glossary

magnetite	磁铁矿石	magnet	磁铁
pole of the magnet	磁铁的极	magnetic pole	磁极
interaction	相互作用	the Biot-Savart Law	毕奥-萨伐尔定律
permanent magnet	永久磁铁	current-carrying wire	载流导线
current element	电流元	constant of proportionality	比例常数
permeability of free space	真空磁导率	solenoid	螺线管
turn	匝	parallel-plate capacitor	平行板电容器
diverge	发散	converge	聚合
Gauss's law for magnetism	磁场的高斯定理	magnetic flux	磁通量
		electric dipole	电偶极子
magnetic dipole	磁偶极子		

15.3 专业英语常用表达法-15 加减乘除 乘方 开方

1. 加用 plus, and 或 add 表示；等于用 is, make, equal 等词表示。

2+3=? 可表示为：How much is two plus three?

2+3=5 可表示为：Two plus three is five. 或者 Two and three is equal to five. 或者 Two and three makes five. 或者 Two added to three equals five. 或者 If we add two to/and three, we get five. 2 加 3 等于 5。

2. 减用 minus 或 take from 表示。

10-6=? How much is ten minus six?

10-6＝4 Ten minus six is four. 或者 Take six from ten and the remainder is four. 或者 Six (taken) from ten is four. 10 减去 6 等于 4。

3. 乘用 time(动词)或 multiply 表示。

3×4＝? How much is three times four?

3×4＝12 Three times four is/are twelve. Multiply three by four, we get twelve. 或者 Three multiplied by four makes twelve. 3 乘以 4 等于 12。

4. 除用 divide 的过去分词形式表示。

16÷4＝? How much is sixteen divided by four?

16÷4＝4 Sixteen divided by four is four. 或者 Sixteen divided by four equals/gives/makes four. 16 除以 4 等于 4。

When x is added to/subtracted from/taken away from/multiplied by y, the result/answer is z. 若 $x+y/x-y/x\times y/x\div y$，则结果/答案是 z。

5. 乘方、开方的表示法：指数用序数词，底数用基数词。

10^7　10 的 7 次方 the seventh power of ten(ten to the seventh power)

6^{10}　6 的 10 次方 the tenth power of six(six to the tenth power)

x^2　x square, x squared, the square of x, the second power of x, x to the second power

$5^2=25$　the second power of 5 is 25, 5 square is 25, the square of 5 is 25, 5 to the second power is equal to 25

y^3　y cube, y cubed, the cube of y, y to the third power, y to the third

y^{-10}　y to the minus tenth (power)

$\sqrt{4}=\pm 2$　the square root of 4 is/equals plus or minus 2

$\sqrt[3]{a}$　the cube root of a

$\sqrt[5]{x^2}$　the fifth root of x square

$\sqrt{518}$　the square root of five hundred and eighteen

$\sqrt[3]{930}$　the cubic root of nine hundred and thirty

$3x=5$　three times x equals 5

$\frac{x^3}{5}=y^2$　x raised to the third power divided by five equals y squared

$x^2+y^2=10$　x squared with y squared equals 10

更多关于数学符号的表示方法请参阅本书附录部分。

LESSON 16

16.1　物理学专业英语中的非谓语动词（二）分词

分词也属于非谓语动词，是动词的一种非谓语形式，分词分为现在分词和过去分词两种。现在分词表示正在进行或主动的动作；过去分词表示被动的或是已完成的动作。例如：

boiling water　沸水，boiled water　开水

developing country　发展中国家，developed country　发达国家
falling leaves　下落的叶子，fallen leaves　落叶
moving body　运动的物体，the moved body　被移动的物体

分词具有动词的某些特征，可以带宾语和状语组成分词短语。在专业英语中，分词短语在句中主要作定语和状语。过去分词在句中作某种成分时，其逻辑主语一般为该分词所表示的动作的承受者。

1. 作定语

单个分词作定语时，一般放在它所修饰的名词前（也可放在名词之后）；分词短语作定语时，一般放在它所修饰的名词后；分词在修饰由 some/any/no＋thing/body/one 所形成的不定代词时应后置。

All *moving* bodies have kinetic energy. 所有运动的物体都具有动能。

A *lifted* weight increases in its potential energy. 被举起的重物势能会增加。

The work *done* is the scalar product of the force and the displacement. 力所做的功等于力和位移的标积。

We see that impulse is a vector quantity *having a magnitude* equal to the area under the force-time curve. 我们看到冲量是一个矢量，其大小等于力-时间曲线下的面积。

When a body floats in a fluid the buoyancy is equal to the weight of the fluid *displaced*. 当物体漂浮在液体中时，浮力等于所排开的流体的重量。

A direct current is a current *flowing always in the same direction*. 直流电是一种总是沿同一方向流动的电流。

Above the troposphere is the stratosphere, *followed by the ionosphere* and *capped by the exosphere*. 在对流层上是平流层，接着是电离层，最上层是外逸层。

Heat is the energy *produced by the movement of molecules*. 热是分子运动所产生的能量。

An alloy is a substance *composed of two or more metals fused together*. 合金是由两种或两种以上融合在一起的金属所组成的物质。

2. 作状语

分词短语作状语时，往往具有时间、条件、原因、结果、让步、方式、补充说明等含义。它可以放在句首、句中或句尾，通常用逗号与句子格开。一般来说，时间、原因、条件、让步等分词短语多放在句首；而表结果、伴随的分词短语放在句尾。分词短语作状语时，前面可用 when，while，if，unless，though 等词来加强时间、条件等含义。

Being negative, an electron moves always from negative to positive. 由于电子的负电性，所以总是由负（极）向正（极）运动。（原因）

Being relatively close, the capacitor's two plates produce relatively large electric field in between. 由于两个极板距离相对较近，所以电容器极板间的电场相对很大。（原因）

Considering some common aspects of the performance of the steam engine and automobile engine, we notice that both reject heat. 在研究蒸汽发动机与汽车发动机性能的共同点时，我们注意到两者都排除热量。（时间）

All metals are fairly hard, *compared with nonmetals*. 与非金属相比，金属是相当硬的。（条件）

In a liquid or solid, the molecules are much closer together, *resulting in much more material in a given volume*. 在液体或固体中，分子结合得紧密得多，因而在一定体积内的物质也多得多。（结果）

The particle motion may be nearly circular at the surface but become more elliptical with depth, eventually *becoming longitudinal*. 粒子的运动在表面时接近圆轨道，但是随着深度加深更加椭圆化，最终变为纵向的。（结果）

Utilizing the material obtained by means of astronomical instruments, we learned more about the moon. 由于利用了天文仪器得到的资料，我们了解到了更多有关月球的知识。（原因）

Molecules vary considerably in size and weight, *ranging from the tiniest micromolecules to the largest macromolecules*. 各种分子的大小和重量都有很大的差别，范围从最小的微观分子直到最大的宏观分子。（补充说明）

Objects begin to move because a force is acting on them, *pushing or pulling them*. 物体开始运动是因为受力的作用，即受到推力或拉力的作用。（补充说明）

When heated, a body will expand. 物体受热时就会膨胀。（时间）

Iron, *when combined with carbon and other elements*, is used most widely in industry. 铁与碳和其他元素结合时，在工业上获得了极为广泛的应用。（时间）

A substance that expands *while melting* has its fusing point slightly raised by an increase of pressure. 熔化时会膨胀的物质，通过加压可使其熔点略有升高。（时间）

The photon, *while not having a material mass*, may be considered as having a radiation mass. 光子虽然没有物质质量，但可以认为它具有辐射质量。（让步）

3. 分词和分词短语作宾语补足语

在英语中，有些及物动词以分词、动词、形容词等作宾语补足语以表达完整的意思。这些动词在专业英语中也经常出现。这类动词有：see, watch, make, have, keep, start, find 等。

If we put wet clothes above the fire, we can see steam *rising from the wet clothes*. 如果把湿的衣服挂在火的上方，就会看见蒸汽从湿衣服上升起。

To keep a body *moving* on the ground, you need apply less force than you did to get it started. 保持一个物体在地面运动比启动该物体所施加的力要小。

A body at rest will remain at rest if there is no enough force to start it *moving*. 如果没有足够的力来启动静止的物体，那么静止的物体将保持静止状态。

We need to keep the temperature high enough to keep the reaction *going*. 为了使反应进行下去，我们需要保持温度足够高。

4. 分词的时态和语态

现在分词有一般式和完成式，有主动语态和被动语态。现在分词被动态所表示的动作与句子中谓语动词所表示的动作同时发生或正在进行。例如：

The Hall effect instrument *being repaired* there is ours. 正在修理的霍尔效应仪是我们的。

Being cooled in the air, the metal hardened. 金属在空气中冷却时就硬化了。

现在分词的完成时态表示的动作发生在句子谓语动词所表示的动作之前。完成时态的分词在句中只作状语用。例如：

Bound charge is deliberately ignored on the right side of this equation, *having been taken into account by the introduction of ε_r on the left side*. 方程右侧的束缚电荷被故意略掉，因为已经被考虑在左侧引入的 ε_r 中。

Having defined two units of power, the horse-power and the kilowatt, we may use these in turn to define two new units of work, the horsepower-hour and the kilowatt-hour. 在定义了功率的两种单位（hp, kW）之后，我们就可以转而用这两个单位来定义功的两个新单位（hp·h, kW·h）。

5. 分词的独立结构

分词短语作状语时，通常它的逻辑主语也就是句子中的主语。如：

Electrifying a capacitor, you store electric energy. 给电容器充电时，你就是在储存电能。

分词 electrifying 的逻辑主语就是句中的主语 you。但是，如果分词短语中的逻辑主语与句子中的主语不一致时，分词短语就可以有自己的逻辑主语。这种带逻辑主语的分词短语叫做"分词独立结构"。这种结构在句中只起到状语作用，可以表示时间、原因、条件和附加说明等。

Carbon steel being hard ferromagnetic material, we can use it for memory units. 碳钢作为硬磁性材料，我们可以把它用作记忆元件。（原因）

Soft iron is magnetically soft, *the hysteresis effect being small*. 软铁是软磁性材料，因为磁滞效应小。（原因）

A change of velocity, *the mass being constant*, must mean a change in momentum. 如果质量不变，速度的变化就意味着动量的变化。（条件）

To explain this remarkable behavior, each electron is considered to possess an electric charge, *the charge being a numerical measure of the repulsion experienced between two electrons*. 为了解释这种奇特现象，可认为每一个电子带一个电荷——两个电子之间排斥力的数值量度。（附加说明）

The world is full of other kinds of waves, *including sound waves, seismic waves, radio waves, and X-rays*. 世界上充满其他种类的波，包括声波、地震波、无线电波和X射线。（附加说明）

A molecule of hydrogen has only two atoms, *each having one proton and one electron*. 氢分子仅有两个原子，每个原子有一个质子和一个电子。（附加说明）

An object can move uniformly in a straight line, *there being no cause to change that motion*. 如果没有改变物体运动状态的原因，那么物体会做匀速直线运动。（条件）

6. 分词复合结构

某些分词独立结构由介词 with 或 without 引出，形式是：

with(或 without)＋名词＋分词,这种结构在英语中称为"分词复合结构",在句中可作定语和状语,在专业文章中这种结构经常用来作为补充说明。其中 with 引导的分词结构中有时 with 可省略,分词结构前用逗号分隔。

The ferromagnetic materials can become paramagnetic, with the temperature *being above the Curie temperature*. 温度高于居里点温度时,铁磁质会变成顺磁质。(条件)

The volume of an ideal gas varies inversely proportional to pressure, with temperature *being constant*. 若温度不变,则理想气体的体积与压强成反比。(条件)

Maxwell pointed out that an object may be hot without the motion in it *being visible*. 麦克斯韦指出,即使看不见物体内部的分子运动,物体也可能是热的。(让步)

If we shake the end of the string, the string will take on the shape shown by the curve in the graph, with this shape *remaining the same but moving toward the right*. 如果我们摇动绳的一端,绳就会具有插图所示的曲线的形状,并保持不变的形状向右传播。(附加说明)

If something is moving, *with nothing touching it*, it will go on forever, moving at a uniform speed in a straight line. 运动中的物体,在没有受到任何外力触动时,将永远继续做匀速直线运动。(条件)

Ice, of relative density 0.9, floats in water *with nine-tenth submerged*. 冰的相对密度为 0.9,所以冰浮在水面上时,9/10 淹没在水里。(方式方法)

An atom of oxygen has eight protons and eight neutrons in its nucleus, *with eight electrons circling about that nucleus*. 一个氧原子核内有 8 个质子和 8 个中子,核外有 8 个电子绕着原子核旋转。(附加说明)

7. 非谓语动词短语代替从句

非谓语动词短语常用来代替从句而使句子简洁。例如:

The concept of time *which was considered as an absolute quantity in the Newtonian theory* received as a basically different interpretation in the theory of relativity *which was announced by Einstein in* 1905. 在牛顿理论中被认为是绝对量的时间概念,在爱因斯坦于 1905 年宣布的相对论中,得到了根本不同的解释。

可以用两个分词短语代替两个定语从句。请比较:

The concept of time *considered as an absolute quantity in the Newtonian theory* received as a basically different interpretation in the theory of relativity *announced by Einstein in* 1905.

16.2 专业英语阅读

16.2.1 Ampere's Circuital Law(安培环路定理)

In previous chapter we found that for highly symmetric charge distributions, we could calculate the electric field more easily using Gauss's law than Coulomb's law. A similar situation exists in magnetism. Ampere's law, which relates the tangential component of B summed around a closed curve L to the current I_{inside} that passes through the curve can be used to obtain an expression for the magnetic field in situations that have a high degree of symmetry. In mathematical form, **Ampere's Circuital Law** is

$$\oint_L \boldsymbol{B} \cdot d\boldsymbol{l} = \mu_0 \sum I_{\text{inside}} \quad (L \text{ is any closed curve}) \tag{16-1}$$

where I_{inside} is the net current that penetrates the area bounded by the curve L. Ampere's law holds for any curve L as long as the currents are continuous, that is, they do not begin or end at any finite point. It is useful in calculating the magnetic field $\boldsymbol{B}$ in situations that have a high degree of symmetry so that the line integral $\oint_L \boldsymbol{B} \cdot d\boldsymbol{l}$ can be written as the product of B and some distance. Ampere's law and Gauss's law are both of considerable theoretical importance, and both hold whether or not there is symmetry, but if there is no symmetry, neither is useful in calculating electric or magnetic fields.

16.2.2 Magnetic Field due to Varying Electric Field(与变化的电场相联系的磁场)

Ampere's law relates the line integral of the magnetic field around some closed curve L to the current that passes through any area bounded by that curve as Eq. (16-1).

Fig. 16-1

Maxwell recognized a flaw in Ampere's law. Fig. 16-1 shows two different surfaces bounded by the same curve L, which encircles a wire carrying current into a capacitor plate. The current through surface S_1 is I, but there is no current through surface S_2 because the charge stops on the capacitor plate. There is thus ambiguity in the phrase "the current through any surface bounded by the curve." Such a problem always arises when the current is discontinuous.

Maxwell showed that the law can be generalized to include all situations if the current I in the equation is replaced by the sum of the conduction current I and another term I_d, called **Maxwell's displacement current**, defined as

$$I_d = \varepsilon_0 \frac{d\phi_e}{dt} \tag{16-2}$$

where ϕ_e is the flux of the electric field through the same surface bounded by the curve L. The generalized form of Ampere's law is then.

$$\oint_L \boldsymbol{B} \cdot d\boldsymbol{l} = \mu_0(I + I_d) = \mu_0 I + \mu_0 \varepsilon_0 \frac{d\phi_e}{dt} \tag{16-3}$$

We can understand this generalization by considering again. Let us call the sum $I + I_d$ the generalized current. According to the argument just stated, the same generalized current must cross any area bounded by the curve L. Thus, there can be no net generalized current into or out of the closed volume. If there is a net true current I into the volume, there must be an equal net displacement current I_d out of the volume. In the volume in the

Fig. 16-1, there is a net conduction current I into the volume that increases the charge within the volume

$$I = \frac{dQ}{dt}$$

The flux of the electric field out of the volume is related to the charge by Gauss's law

$$\phi_{net} = \oint_s E_n dS = \frac{1}{\varepsilon_0} Q_{inside}$$

The rate of increase of the charge is thus proportional to the rate of increase of the net flux out of the volume

$$\frac{dQ}{dt} = \varepsilon_0 \frac{d\phi_{e,net}}{dt} = I_d$$

Thus, the net conduction current into the volume equals the net displacement current out of the volume. The generalized current is always continuous.

Maxwell's modification of Ampere's law shows that a changing electric flux produces a magnetic field whose line integral around a curve is proportional to the rate of change of the electric flux. We thus have the interesting reciprocal result that a changing magnetic field produces an electric field (Faraday's law) and a changing electric field produces a magnetic field (generalized form of Ampere's law). Note that there is no magnetic analog of a conduction current I. This is because the magnetic monopole, the magnetic analog of an electric charge, does not exist.

16.2.3 Effect on Magnetic Field Caused by Magnetic Media(磁介质对磁场的影响)

Materials fall into three categories-paramagnetic, diamagnetic, and ferromagnetic, according to the behavior of their magnetic moments in an external magnetic field. **Paramagnetism** arises from the partial alignment of the electron spins (in metals) or of atomic or molecular magnetic moments by an applied magnetic field in the direction of the field. In paramagnetic materials, the magnetic dipoles do not interact strongly with each other and are normally randomly oriented. In the presence of an external magnetic field, the dipoles are partially aligned in the direction of the field, thereby increasing the field. However, in external magnetic fields of ordinary strength at ordinary temperatures, only a very small fraction of the molecules are aligned because thermal motion tends to randomize their orientation. The increase in the total magnetic field is therefore very small. **Ferromagnetism** is much more complicated. Because of a strong interaction between neighboring magnetic dipoles, a high degree of alignment occurs even in weak external magnetic fields, causing a very large increase in the total field. Even when there is no external magnetic field, a ferromagnetic material may have its magnetic dipoles aligned, as in permanent magnets. **Diamagnetism** arises from the orbital magnetic dipole moments induced by an applied magnetic field. These magnetic moments are opposite the direction of the applied magnetic field so they decrease the total magnetic field B. This effect actually occurs in all materials, but because the induced magnetic moments are very small compared to the permanent magnetic moments, diamagnetism is masked by paramagnetic or ferromagnetic effects. Diamagnetism is thus observed only in materials that have no permanent magnetic moments.

16.2.4　Ferromagnetic Materials(铁磁质)

Ferromagnetism occurs in pure iron, cobalt, and nickel, and in alloys of these metals with each other. Ferromagnetism arises from a strong interaction between the electrons in a partially full band in a metal or between the localized electrons that form magnetic moments on neighboring atoms or molecules. This interaction, called the exchange interaction, lowers the energy of a pair of electrons with parallel spins.

Ferromagnetic materials have very large, positive values of magnetic susceptibility χ_m. In these substances, a small external magnetic field can produce a very large degree of alignment of the atomic magnetic dipole moments. In some cases, the alignment can persist even when the external magnetizing field is removed. This occurs because the magnetic dipole moments exert strong forces on their neighbors so that over a small region of space the moments are aligned with each other even when there is no external field. The region of space over which the magnetic dipole moments are aligned is called a **magnetic domain**. The size of a domain is usually microscopic. Within the domain, all the magnetic moments are aligned, but the direction of alignment varies from domain to domain so that the net magnetic moment of a macroscopic piece of ferromagnetic material is zero in the normal state. Fig. 16-2 illustrates this situation. The dipole forces that produce this alignment are predicted by quantum theory but cannot be explained with classical physics. At temperatures above a critical temperature, called the **Curie temperature**, thermal

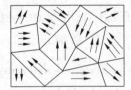

Fig. 16-2

agitation is great enough to break up this alignment, and ferromagnetic materials become paramagnetic.

When an external magnetic field is applied, the boundaries of the domains may shift or the direction of alignment within a domain may change so that there is a net macroscopic magnetic moment in the direction of the applied field. Since the degree of alignment is large for even a small external field, the magnetic field produced in the material by the dipoles is often much greater than the external field.

Fig. 16-3

It is interesting to note when the temperature of a ferromagnetic substance reaches or exceeds a critical temperature, called the Curie temperature, the substance loses its spontaneous magnetization and becomes paramagnetic. Below the Curie temperature, the magnetic moments are aligned and the substance is ferromagnetic. Above the Curie temperature, the thermal energy is large enough to cause a random orientation of dipoles, hence the substance becomes paramagnetic. For example, the Curie temperature for iron is 1043 K.

Glossary

highly symmetric	高度对称的	tangential component	切向分量
closed curve	闭合曲线	degree of symmetry	对称度
penetrate	穿过	bounded by…	以……为边界
finite point	有限点	line integral	线积分
encircle	环绕	discontinuous	不连续的
conduction current	传导电流	displacement current	位移电流
generalized Ampere's Law	广义安培环路定理	generalized current	广义电流
		modification	修正
magnetic monopole	磁单极	diamagnetic	抗磁的
magnetic medium	磁介质	ferromagnetic	铁磁的
paramagnetic	顺磁的	paramagnetism	顺磁性
magnetic moment	磁矩	electron spin	电子自旋
partial alignment	部分取向	randomly oriented	任意取向
magnetic dipole	磁偶极子	diamagnetism	抗磁性
ferromagnetism	铁磁性	induced magnetic moment	感生磁矩
orbital magnetic dipole moment	轨道磁偶极矩	permanent magnetic moment	固有磁矩
mask	v. 掩盖	cobalt	钴
iron	铁	alloy	合金
nickel	镍	parallel spin	平行自旋
exchange interaction	交换作用	magnetic domain	磁畴
magnetic susceptibility	磁化率	critical temperature	临界温度
quantum theory	量子理论	thermal agitation	热扰动
Curie temperature	居里温度		

16.3 专业英语常用表达法-16 用途 功能 目的

1. for 或动词不定式

for reference 供参考

a manual *for* technician 技工手册

solve the equation *for* x 解方程求 x

use the symbol Pb *for* lead 用符号 Pb 表示铅

What is the tool *for*? 这工具是做什么用的？

This is the very instrument *for* the experiment. 这是最适合做这个实验的仪器。

The institute is an international centre *for* physics research. 该机构是物理学研究的国

际中心。

The key lab is primarily a research establishment but also it is there *to welcome the public*. 这个重点实验室主要是一个科研机构，但同时也面向公众。

2．The function(或 purpose) is＋动词不定式

It has several functions and probably *the main one is to hide the structure of the instrument*. 它有好几个作用，主要的可能是为了把这台仪器的内部结构遮盖起来。

At the end we have a clear glass, *its function there is to give you a view of the circuit inside*. 在末端用的是透明玻璃，它的作用是使你看得见里边的电路。

3．用下列词语

be designed＋动词不定式(或 for 短语)

help＋动词不定式

have the function of

serve the purpose of

The building *is designed* primarily *for students* rather than teachers. 这座建筑是供学生而不是供教师使用的。

The cast glass *helps to express* the structure of the lab. 压铸玻璃有助于显露出实验室的结构。

It also *serves the purpose of* giving access over the roof for maintenance and for cleaning the glass. 还可以利用它到实验室顶部去进行维修和清洁玻璃。

Unit Five

LESSON 17

17.1 物理学专业英语中的长句分析(二)

在前几课中,介绍了关于复合句、从句、非谓语动词等知识,对这些知识的良好掌握是进行长句结构分析的基础。现在我们再结合实例来介绍一下长句结构分析的方法。

1. 物理学专业英语中长句的特点

由于物理专业内容的复杂性、综合性、多样性等因素,专业英语中长句用的较多,看起来较为复杂。特别是复合句式,在科技标准、专利规范、原理说明中尤为多见。有时,一个句子长达数行、数十行,包含几十个乃至上百个单词,或包含若干个从句和非谓语动词短语。它们互相制约、互相联系、互相依附,以至于形成从句中有短语、短语中带从句的复杂语言现象。

值得强调的是,在专业英语中多用一些过渡连词或短语来实现句子、段落和上下文的有效衔接,使陈述内容连贯一致,成为整体,或形成规范合理、紧凑连贯的语篇,最终达到准确表达内容的目的。

下面是专业英语中长句的几个特点:①修饰语多,特别是后置定语很长;②并列的成分多;③语言结构层次多;④指代关系复杂;⑤习惯搭配和成语经常出现。

2. 长句的分析方法

在分析长句时,不要因为句子太长而产生畏惧心理。采用我们前面介绍过的方法:抓住主干,添枝加叶(见 Lesson 9,物理学专业英语中的长句分析(一)),一般就会对长句子做出正确分析。无论是多么复杂的句子,它都是由一些基本的成分组成的。因此,首先我们要分析句子的基本成分,如主语、谓语、宾语、状语等,抓住主干部分,然后逐层分析各词意思以及相互间的逻辑、语法关系,再进行翻译。其次,要弄清英语原文的句法结构,找出整个句子的中心内容及其各层意思,然后分析几层意思之间的相互逻辑关系。最后,再按照汉语的特点和表达方式,正确地理解原文的意思。

根据专业英语长句的特点,在分析长句时,采用抓住主干,添枝加叶的方法,一般要进行下面几个步骤:

(1) 抓住主干:即通过形态识别,找出全句的主、谓、宾、表等主干成分,了解其"骨架含义",从整体上把握句子的结构。

(2) 查找分支:找出句中所有的谓语结构、非谓语动词、介词短语和从句的引导词。

(3) 辨别分支：分析从句和短语的功能。对于结构复杂，层次纷纭的主从复合句要抓住引导各种从句的连词，弄清各种从句的性质，如：是否为主语从句、宾语从句、表语从句等，若是状语从句，它是表示时间、原因、结果，还是表示条件等。

(4) 理清分支：分析词、短语和从句之间的相互关系，理解这些成分之间的逻辑关系和修饰关系，如：定语从句所修饰的先行词是哪一个等。

(5) 找寻叶子：注意插入语等其他成分，分析句子中是否有固定词组或固定搭配。

这种方法从分析英语句子结构入手，化繁为简，化长为短，化难为易，进而理解英语长句、难句的意思，从而使在英语长句、难句在理解、翻译过程中所遇到的困难得以解决。

下面就应用此方法对一些专业长句子进行分析：

例 1：Copernicus by announcing his heliocentric world system, may be said to have spoken the prologue preceding the rise of the curtain on modern physics revealing among the first actors, Galileo and Kepler. 哥白尼，由于宣布了他的太阳中心世界系统，可以认为已经为现代物理学的升幕作了个开场白，升幕后，最早出现的一批演员中有伽利略和开普勒。

句子主干是：Copernicus may be said to have spoken the prologue. 可以认为哥白尼已经作了个开场白。

逐个加上修饰语：

(1) by announcing his heliocentric world system（哥白尼）由于宣布了他的太阳中心世界系统（介词短语作方式状语）。

(2) preceding the rise of the curtain 在升幕之前（分词短语作状语）。

(3) on modern physics 为谁升幕？"为现代物理学"（介词短语作定语）。

(4) revealing among the first actors, Galileo and Kepler 升幕后，就"显露出了最早的一批演员（指现代物理学家），其中有伽利略和开普勒"（分词短语作状语）。

例 2：The general theory of relativity was proposed by Einstein in 1916 after nine years of grappling with the problem of formulating a theory of gravitation in agreement with the space-time symmetry of special relativity and with the experimental observation known since Galileo that all bodies, regardless of their mass, follow the same trajectory in a gravitational field.

为了提出一种引力理论能符合狭义相对论的时空对称要求，同时也与自从伽利略以来就知道的实验观测一致（即，一切物体在引力场中的运动都遵循相同的轨迹，与质量无关），爱因斯坦通过9年时间对此问题进行研究，于1916年提出了广义相对论。

句子主干是：The general theory of relativity was proposed by Einstein. 广义相对论是爱因斯坦提出来的。

(1) after nine years of grappling"在九年搏斗之后提出的……"（从 after 开始到句尾一个长长的介词短语作状语，修饰 proposed）。

(2) with the problem of formulating a theory of gravitation 搏斗的对象是"形成一个引力理论的问题"。

(3) in agreement with the space-time symmetry of special relativity 这个理论"符合狭义相对论的时空对称要求"。

(4) and with the experimental observation known since Galileo "还要符合自从伽利略以来就知道的实验观测"(划线的两个 with 是并列的成分,in agreement with 是固定搭配,在此引导定语修饰 a theory of gravitation)。

(5) that all bodies, regardless of their mass, follow the same trajectory in a gravitational field. 这个实验观察就是"一切物体在引力场中的运动都遵循相同的轨迹,与质量无关"(that 引导的从句作的 the experimental observation 的同位语)。

例3: Stated in words, Ohm's law says that the steady current through any portion of an electric circuit equals the potential difference across that portion of the circuit divided by the resistance of that portion of the circuit. 欧姆定律用文字表述为:电路中任一部分的稳恒电流强度等于这部分的电势差除以这部分的电阻。

句子主干是: Ohm's law says that…欧姆定律说的是……(从 that 开始到句尾是 that 引导的从句作宾语)。

宾语从句的主干是: the steady current equals the potential difference(主谓宾)。

(1) Stated in words 用文字表述(分词短语作状语)。

(2) the steady current through any portion of an electric circuit 电路中任一部分的稳恒电流强度(through 引导介词词组作定语修饰从句主语 steady current)。

(3) the potential difference across that portion of the circuit 电路中这部分的电势差(across 引导介词词组作定语修饰从句宾语 potential difference)。

(4) divided by the resistance of that portion of the circuit 除以这部分的电阻(分词短语作定语修饰从句宾语 potential difference)。

例4: The great challenge in the study of these novel processes is not so much how to solve a particular pattern by means of a particular method, as how to find new methods to furnish solutions to whole class of problems. 在研究这些新过程中的大难关主要不在于如何用某一个方法去解决某一个问题,而是在于如何去找到能使整个一类问题得到解决的新方法。

本句虽然很长,但却是只有一套主系表结构的简单句。句子主干是: The great challenge is not so much how to solve a particular pattern as how to find new methods. 大的难题主要不是如何解决某一特殊典型而是如何去找到新的方法。

可以更简化为 The challenge is not so much A as B 要克服的困难主要不是 A 而是 B。

not so much A as B 是一个固定词组,表示"不是 A 而是 B"。

(1) in the study of these novel processes 在研究这些新过程中(介词词组作定语修饰语)。

(2) how to solve a particular pattern by means of a particular method 如何用某一个方法去解决某一个问题(不定式短语作表语,by means of a particular method 作状语修饰 solve)。

(3) how to find new methods 如何找到新的方法(不定式短语作表语)。

(4) to furnish solutions to whole class of problems 能使整个一类问题得到解决(不定式短语作目的状语)。

例5: In order to present a sufficiently complete picture we feel it is necessary to connect theory, on the one hand, with a variety of applications from radar, sonar, speech, music, and medical signal processing, and on the other hand, with the digital component technology that is the main driving force for progress in this field as well as the overall field of computer design. 为了呈现一幅充实的全景图,我们认为有必要把理论,一方面,与雷达、声纳、话音、音乐及医学信号处理的多种应用相结合,另一方面,与数字分量技术相结合,这种技术是本领域及计算机设计全部领域的主要推动力。

句子主干是:We feel it is necessary. 我们觉得那有必要。

(1) In order to present a sufficiently complete picture 为了呈现一幅充实的全景图(目的状语)。

(2) 从 it is necessary 到句尾的从句是整个句子的宾语,前面省略的引导词 that。

(3) 从 to connect theory 到句尾是包含从句的 to 动词不定式短语,是宾语从句的实际主语,而前面的 it 是形式主语。

(4) 两个较长的以 with 引入的状语短语是平行的,由 on the one hand, on the other hand 引导,connect...with...是固定搭配。

(5) that is the main driving force for progress in this field as well as the overall field of computer design 是本领域及其计算机设计全部领域的主要推动力(该定语从句,修饰 technology,两个 field 是平行的,由 as well as 连接)。

(6) for progress in this field as well as the overall field of computer design(for 引导介词词组作定语修饰 force)。

例 6:While numerous basic advances were made during this period its most important characteristic is the development and the firm establishment of the experimental method as a means of scientific inquiry, as is well illustrated by Galileo's famous experiment of dropping two bodies of unequal weight from the leaning tower of Pisa, thereby proving by experiment the incorrectness of the assertion of Aristotle that the heavier body would fall more rapidly, an assertion which had been believed implicitly for nearly two thousand years. 这一时期取得非常多的基础进展,其最重要的特征是实验方法作为一种科学探索的方法得到发展和奠定,正如伽利略的著名比萨斜塔落体实验所展示的那样,通过实验证明了亚里士多德的、已经被盲目信奉了近两千年的、关于较重物体落得更快的论断的错误性。

句子主干是:its most important characteristic is the development and the firm establishment of the experimental method 其最重要的特征是实验方法得到发展和奠定。

(1) While numerous basic advances were made during this period 这一时期取得非常多的基础进展(状语从句)。

(2) as a means of scientific inquiry 作为一种科学探索的方法(定语,修饰 experimental method)。

(3) as is well illustrated by Galileo's famous experiment of dropping two bodies of unequal weight from the leaning tower of Pisa 正如伽利略的著名比萨斜塔落体实验所展示的那样(定语从句,修饰主句)。

(4) 从 thereby 到句尾,分词短语作状语。

(5) that the heavier body would fall more rapidly 较重物体落得更快(assertion of

Aristotle 的同位语从句)。

(6) which had been believed implicitly for nearly two thousand years (定语从句,修饰 an assertion)。

例 7: The physicist rightly dreads precise argument, since an argument that is convincing only if its precise loses all its force if the assumptions on which it is based are slightly changed, whereas an argument that is convincing though imprecise may well be stable under small perturbations of its underlying assumptions. 物理学家恐惧于那些精确无误的论断不无道理,因为某种只有在精确无误的条件下才令人置信的论断,一旦它赖以建立其上的假设稍有变化,便会失去它一部分的作用;而与此相反,一个尽管并不精确无误但却令人置信的论断,在其基本假设稍受干扰的情况下,仍然有可能是站得住脚的。

句子主干是: The physicist dreads precise argument. 物理学家恐惧于那些精确无误的论断。

此句中的主句和从句加在一起共有八个:

(1) 由 since 引导的是原因状语从句。

(2) 由 whereas 连接了两个长句子。

(3) whereas 后面的句子中的主语 an argument 之后又跟了一个定语从句 that is convincing though imprecise, 修饰 argument。

(4) since 从句中主语 an argument 由 that 引导的定语从句修饰。

(5) 定语从句中的 only if it is precise 是条件状语从句。

(6) since 从句中的 if the assumptions on which it is based are slightly changed 是条件状语从句。

(7) 定语从句 on which it is based 修饰主语 assumptions。

例 8: Thus, for instance, it may come as a shock to mathematicians to learn that the Schrödinger equation for the hydrogen atom is not a literally correct description of this atom, but only an approximation to a somewhat more correct equation taking account of spin, magnetic dipole, and relativistic effects; and that this corrected equation is itself only an imperfect approximation to an infinite set of quantum field-theoretical equations. 因此,举例来说,对数学家而言,了解到下述情形可能会令其惊愕不已,即薛定谔的氢原子方程式并非是对该原子做出的一种决然正确的描述,而仅仅是个近似值,趋近于一个在某种程度上更为正确的将自旋、磁性偶极子以及相对论效应考虑在内的方程式;而这个得以纠正的方程式就其本身而言也只是一个不完美的近似值,是趋近于无穷无尽的一整套量子场论方程式。

句子主干是: it may come as a shock to mathematicians 下述情形可能会令数学家惊愕不已。to learn that…;and that…是并列成分作句子的主语,两个 that 引导的都是 learn 的宾语从句。

例 9: Whether the experiment of dropping bodies of different weight from the leaning tower of Pisa was performed before a multitude, as some accounts have it; or whether the bodies were of lead or stone and what their weight were we do not know. 我们不知道比萨斜塔落体实验是否像某些记载那样在很多人目睹下进行,也不知道落体是铅制的还是石头

的、重量是多少。

句子主干是：we do not know whether…，or whether…两个 whether 引导的都是宾语从句。

掌握好专业英语中关于长句结构分析的方法在专业英语的学习中是非常重要的，它直接影响到读者对专业文献的阅读、理解和翻译。具有良好长句结构分析水平的读者，在专业文献的阅读、理解和相关翻译工作甚至专业写作中也会得心应手、游刃有余。

在接下来关于专业文献的阅读和翻译的部分中，关于长句结构分析的方法还会经常出现，读者也应该把提高长句结构分析水平一直贯穿在自己的专业英语学习过程当中。

17.2 专业英语阅读

17.2.1 Faraday's Law of Electromagnetic Induction（法拉第电磁感应定律）

In the early 1830s, Michael Faraday in England and Joseph Henry in America independently discovered that a changing magnetic field induces a current in a wire(Fig. 17-1). The two experiments shown in Fig. 17-1 have one thing in common. In both cases, an emf is induced in a circuit when the magnetic flux through the circuit changes with time. The emfs and currents caused by changing magnetic fields are called **induced emfs** and **induced currents**. The process itself is referred to as **magnetic induction**.

Fig. 17-1

When you pull the plug of an electric cord from its socket, you sometimes observe a small spark. Before the cord is disconnected, it carries a current, which produces a magnetic field encircling the current. When the cord is disconnected, the current abruptly ceases and the magnetic field around it collapses. The changing magnetic field produces an emf that tries to maintain the original current, resulting in a spark across the plug. Once the magnetic field reaches zero it is no longer changing, and the emf is zero.

Changing magnetic fields can result from changing currents or from moving magnets. The ends of a coil are attached to a galvanometer and a strong magnet is moved toward or away from the coil. The momentary deflection shown by the galvanometer during the motion indicates that there is an induced electric current in the coil-galvanometer circuit. A current is also induced if the coil is moved toward or away from the magnet, or if the coil is rotated in a fixed magnetic field. A coil rotating in a magnetic field is the basic element of a generator, which converts mechanical energy into electrical energy.

All of the various methods of magnetic induction can be summarized by a single relation known as **Faraday's law of induction**, which relates the induced emf in a circuit to the change in magnetic flux through the circuit.

Fig. 17-2

The flux of a magnetic field through a surface is defined similarly to the flux of an electric field. Let dS be an element of area on the surface and e_n be the unit vector perpendicular to the element (Fig. 17-2). The magnetic flux ϕ_m is then defined to be

$$\phi_m = \int_S \boldsymbol{B} \cdot \boldsymbol{e}_n dS = \int_S B_n dS \qquad (17\text{-}1)$$

The unit of magnetic flux is that of magnetic field times area, tesla-meter squared, which is called a **weber** (Wb)

$$1 \text{ Wb} = 1 \text{ T} \cdot \text{m}^2$$

Since B is proportional to the number of field lines per unit area, the magnetic flux is proportional to the number of lines through the area.

Experiments by Faraday, Henry, and others showed that if the magnetic flux through an area bounded by a circuit is changed by any means, an emf equal in magnitude to the rate of change of the flux is induced in the circuit. We usually detect the emf by observing a current in the circuit, but it is present even when the circuit is incomplete (not closed) and there is no current.

The magnetic flux through a circuit can be changed in many different ways. The current producing the magnetic field may be increased or decreased, permanent magnets may be moved toward the circuit or away from it, the circuit itself may be moved toward or away from the source of the flux, the orientation of the circuit may be changed, or the area of the circuit in a fixed magnetic field may be increased or decreased. In every case, an emf is induced in the circuit that is equal in magnitude to the rate of change of the magnetic flux.

Fig. 17-3 shows a single loop of wire in a magnetic field. If the flux through the loop is changing, an emf is induced in the loop.

$$\varepsilon = -\frac{d\phi_m}{dt} \qquad (17\text{-}2)$$

This result is known as **Faraday's law of induction** which states *the emf induced in a circuit is directly proportional to the time rate of change of magnetic flux through the circuit.*

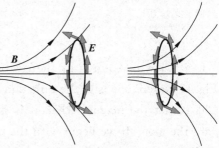

Fig. 17-3

The negative sign in Faraday's law has to do with the direction of the induced emf, which we will discuss shortly.

17.2.2　Lenz's Law(楞次定律)

The negative sign in Faraday's law has to do with the direction of the induced emf, which can be found from a general physical principle known as **Lenz's law**:

The polarity of the induced emf is such that it tends to produce a current that will create a magnetic flux to oppose the change in magnetic flux through the loop.

Note that we didn't specify just what kind of change causes the induced emf and current. We purposefully left the statement vague to cover a variety of conditions, which we will now illustrate.

Fig. 17-4 shows a bar magnet moving toward a loop that has a resistance R. Since **B** from the bar magnet is to the right, out of the north pole of the magnet, the movement of the magnet toward the loop tends to increase the flux through the loop to the right. (The magnetic field at the loop is stronger when the magnet is closer.) The induced current in the loop produces a magnetic field of its own. This induced current is in the direction shown, so the magnetic flux it produces is opposite that of the magnet. The induced magnetic field tends to decrease the flux through the loop. If the magnet were moved away from the loop, which would decrease the flux through the loop due to the magnet, the induced current would be in the opposite direction from that in Fig. 17-4. In that case, the current would produce a magnetic field to the right, which would tend to increase the flux through the loop. As we might expect, moving the loop toward or away from the magnet has the same effect as moving the magnet. Only the relative motion is important.

Fig. 17-4

Lenz's law is required by the law of conservation of energy. If the current in the loop in Fig. 17-4 were opposite the direction shown, the induced magnetic moment of the loop would attract the magnet when it is moving toward the loop and cause it to accelerate toward the loop. If we begin with the magnet a great distance from the loop and give it a very slight push toward the loop, the force due to the induced current would be toward the loop, which would increase the velocity of the magnet. As the speed of the magnet increases, the rate of change of the flux would increase, thereby increasing the induced current. This would further increase the force on the magnet. Hence, the kinetic energy of the magnet and the rate at which Joule heat is produced in the loop ($I^2 R$) would both increase with no source of energy. This would violate the law of conservation of energy.

Glossary

electromagnetic induction	电磁感应	emf (electromotive force)	电动势
magnetic flux	磁通量	induced emf	感生电动势
induced current	感应电流	magnetic induction	磁感应
plug	插头	socket	插座
encircle	环绕	cord	软线,电源线
galvanometer	检流计	deflection	偏转
coil	线圈	generator	发电机
Lenz's Law	楞次定律	polarity	极性

17.3 专业英语常用表达法-17 电磁学常用实验仪器2

air cooled motor 气冷马达/电动机
alternating accumulator 交流蓄电池
alternating current generator 交流发电机
alternating current meter 交流电流计
alternating current motor 交流电动机
alternating current rectifier 交流整流器
alternative switch 转换开关
alternator 交流发电机
arc lamp 弧光灯
arc rectifier 电弧整流器
arc welding generator 电焊机
armature coil 电枢线圈
armature type magneto 电枢式磁电机
armature 电枢;衔铁;磁舌
asynchronous generator 异步发电机
asynchronous motor 异步感应电动机
beam power amplifier 电子束功率放大器
cadmium nickel accumulator 镉镍蓄电池
cathode ray accelerator 阴极射线加速器
commutator ammeter 整流式安培计
conductivity meter 电导仪
copper-zinc accumulator 铜锌蓄电池
crest ammeter 巅值/峰值安培计
current amplifier 电流放大器
DC ammeter 直流电流计
DC amplifier 直流放大器
differential ammeter 差动安培计

diode   二极管
dust accumulator   集尘器
Edison accumulator   爱迪生蓄电池
electric arc lamp   电弧灯
electrodynamic ammeter   电动安培计
electromagnetic ammeter   电磁安培计
electron accelerator   电子加速器
electron microscope   电子显微镜
electrostatic actuator   静电激发器
feedback amplifier   回馈/反馈放大器
feedback relay amplifier   回馈继电放大器
helical accelerator   螺旋加速器
high-frequency ammeter   高频安培计
hydraulic accumulator   水压蓄电池
induction alternator   感应交流发电机
iron-nickel accumulator   铁镍蓄电池
optical ammeter   光学电流计
thermal expansion ammeter   热胀安培计
thermocouple ammeter   热电偶安培计
transistor   晶体管

LESSON 18

18.1 物理学专业英语文章的阅读与信息获得

当代科学技术发展迅速，物理学的发展也是日新月异，每天都会有大量的专业英语文章、科技新闻及其他专业资料发表在各类报刊和网络上，新的物理专业英语书籍也不断涌现，要想把这些英语专业文献资料都及时翻译成中文是不可能的。如果想要及时掌握最新的专业发展信息，把握住物理学及其相关领域的最新发展脉搏，最好的解决办法是直接阅读英语文献资料，获得第一手信息。

专业英语阅读活动的主要目的是从读物中获取所需要的信息，在阅读中培养从所读材料中获取信息的能力和技巧。阅读能力是一种综合性的能力，在阅读中既要了解语言点，更要分析读物的内容和作者的立场观点；既要求理解具体的事实，也要求理解抽象的概念；既要求理解文章的字面含义，也要求理解内容的深层次含义；既要求理解文中描述的具体细节，也要求理解语段或语篇之间的逻辑关系；既要分析字面意义，更要分析字里行间所隐含的意思。有时还必须根据整体意思，联系各个部分的内容，进行意义上的逻辑推理，才能理解真正的含义，进而达到对专业内容的理解。此外，专业资料中还常常包含若干辅助阅读部分（如插图、图形、图表等），在这些部分中仍然含有很多标记性词汇、符号、算式、数值等，都有助于对阅读内容的理解。只要有较好的英语基础，再掌握英语阅读的技巧，做到这一点并非难事。

18.1.1 浏览

浏览的主要目的是了解阅读内容的概貌。

在正式阅读前进行浏览,可以大概了解所需要的信息,决定该材料是否有读的必要,有时也能够激发阅读兴趣和欲望。

浏览的内容主要有:书名/标题和作者,因为书名或标题本身就点出了读物的中心和主题,作者信息也可以作为是否阅读的参考。书名或标题下的副标题或用特型字印刷的引子比标题更详细地提供了有关主要内容的信息,也是浏览的内容。浏览内容提要、摘要、关键词、目录、总结可以了解读物的主要内容。浏览前言、结束语或后记可以了解背景知识、作者意图、使用方法等。读文内小标题可以了解整体结构。浏览文中插图、表格、图片可以了解资料与自己所研究内容的相关程度。

18.1.2 略读

略读找出中心思想。中心思想是作者在文章中要表达的主要内容,是贯穿全文的核心。作者在文章中会努力通过各种支持材料和论述来阐明中心议题。因此,在进行专业资料的阅读时,首先要明确阅读时的主要目标,那就是寻找中心思想,明确 What is the main idea (subject) of this article/passage? What does this article/passage mainly (primarily) concerned? 在阅读中应自始至终把注意力集中在猎取所需信息上,努力抓住读物的中心内容、把握主要思想,这对于全文内容理解具有重要意义。抓住中心思想的方法是:阅读开头部分以了解主题、背景、意图;找出主要段落的主题句以了解读物的主要内容和整体结构;再读结尾部分以了解结论、用途、意义。"抓住中心"的指导思想要贯穿阅读全过程,始终保持清醒的头脑,不至于在攻克难词、难句、难概念的拼搏中迷失大方向,同时也能加深对读物的印象。

在寻找中心思想的过程中,要注意以下几个方面:

(1) 重视标题

物理学专业文献的标题和文学作品、故事、新闻的标题有显著的不同。专业文献的标题总是以最恰当、最简明词语的逻辑组合反映出文章最重要的内容。标题具有简明、准确、醒目的特点,也就是实话实说,用最少的词语反映出最为确切的论文内容。读者在阅读和检索文献时看懂标题也就知道了文献的最主要的内容。

(2) 细读摘要

国际上正式出版并对外发行的英文学术期刊都要求刊中的调查报告、实验方法或技术性文章、综述性文章、研究论文等在正文中附上英文摘要。摘要一般包括如下内容:陈述研究目的和研究内容及需要解决的问题;简要介绍研究所采用的方法和基本步骤;简要描述主要结果、主要结论及论文的价值。

(3) 抓住反映中心思想的句子

采用略读的方法浏览全文,理解文章主要内容。阅读时要注意抓住反映中心思想的句子,他们在文章中的位置不尽相同。但阅读时,文章的开头、结尾及段落的段首句和段尾句特别重要,因为其中往往包含文章的中心议题。

(4) 关注结果、结论与讨论部分

在物理学专业文献中,结果部分是对研究过程中所获取的数据的分析和对所观察到的现象的总结,是一篇专业文献的核心。结果部分会引发讨论,导出推理,最后给出结论。讨论内容一般从实验和观察的结果出发,从理论上对其分析、比较、阐述、推论和预测;推论中作者会提出自己的新见解,会着重讨论新发现、新发明和新的启示以及从中得出的结论。所以对这部分的认真阅读也是获得中心思想的捷径。

18.1.3 研读

为了领会和掌握所读材料的精神实质和内容细节以及作者的立场、观点、意图,就必须使用字斟句酌、边阅读边理解边深入思考的阅读方法,这种方法就是研读。研读时要求理解准确、透彻,不但要掌握文献的字面意义,而且还要深入理解作者的意图及文献的价值;不但要理解文献里的信息,而且还要通过分析、比较、联想等思维方法,用已有的知识、经验对这些信息进行理解和分析,把它们置入我们的知识系统,真正消化吸收所读的材料,丰富自己的知识,提高专业水平。研读不等于慢读,要注意培养按意群阅读的习惯,集中注意领会文献的信息,立足于读一遍就能理解全部内容,努力提高阅读速度。

在研读过程中,要尽量做到以下几点。

(1) 善于抓住段落的主题句和主要细节

为了对一个段落进行快速理解,从主题句出发,展开阅读是广泛运用并行之有效的手段。绝大多数段落都有一个主题句,而大多数主题句又安排在每一段的开头(有时也把主题句放在段尾或段内其他位置)。只要抓住了主题句就抓住了该段的段意。例如:

The law of charge conservation is one of the important characteristics of electric charge. In certain interactions among elementary particles, charged particles such as electrons are created or annihilated. However, in all these processes, equal amounts of positive and negative charge are produced or destroyed, so the net charge of the universe is unchanged. When two initially neutral objects are charged by being rubbed together, charge is not created in the process. The objects become charged because electrons are transferred from one object to the other. One object gains some amount of negative charge from the electrons transferred to it while the other loses an equal amount of negative charge and hence is left with a positive charge. That is, charge is conserved. The law of conservation of charge is a fundamental law of nature.

第一句"电荷守恒定律是电荷的重要特点之一"为此段的主题句,读完第一句就知道这一段的段意。

在抓住主题句后,接下来的阅读就是要抓住主要细节。除主题句外,段落还必须有把主题句扩展成段落的细节,有时,这些细节比主题句更有价值。必须指出,并不是所有的细节都同等重要,有些细节是主要的,而有些则是说明细节的"细节",称为次要细节。阅读时要注意区分主要细节和次要细节,注意掌握好重要细节。

为了说明"电荷守恒定律是电荷的重要特点"这个主题,作者列举了两个细节:In certain interactions... 和 When two initially neutral objects are charged by being rubbed together...。这些细节对电荷守恒定律的说明都是非常重要的,对理解主题也非常有帮助。

(2) 记住中心内容和主要细节

记住读过的主要内容对全文的理解大有好处,甚至对改善我们的知识结构、提高今后应用所学知识解决问题的能力都大有好处。方法主要包括:阅读时思想高度集中,努力加深第一印象,只围绕目的有重点地阅读和记忆,阅读过程中不时地停下来回想一下前面的内容,一边阅读一边思考、联想、推导、归纳、总结,把读物中的知识转化为大脑的知识,标记或摘录重点等。

(3) 区分对待事实、观点、推断和猜测

在阅读中,针对事实材料,要考虑材料的出处、来源数据的准确度和精确度,要衡量它们的价值和潜在用途。遇到某些观点时,要注意哪些是作者个人的观点,哪些是专家的证言,还要去分析判断这些观点正确与否,进而决定接受、部分接受、还是否定这些观点。在处理推论和猜测时,一方面要注意衡量这些推论所依据的是事实还是主观臆断,还要考虑所依据的事实是否充分;另一方面要注意衡量这些推论是否符合逻辑。总之,在阅读过程中要注意科学思维、进行正确的推论、做出合理的判断、得出合乎逻辑的结论,力求对内容全面准确地进行理解。

例如,下列的句子表达的就是事实,这些事实都可以得到证实。

In fact, the electric field of the source charge is present whether or not we introduce a test charge into the field. 事实上,不论检验电荷是否放入,场源电荷产生的电场都是存在的。

The case is the more the angle of incidence increases, the farther the refracted ray diverges from the normal. 实际情况是,入射角越大,反射线就偏离法线越远。

Ever since then, Einstein has never been back to the town where he was born. 从那以后,爱因斯坦再也没回过他出生的小镇。

表达事实的句子有时会包含如 in fact, actually, as a matter of fact, the case is, the truth is, the fact is that 等词句。

下列句子表达的是观点。

It sounds as if the argument is reasonable. 听起来好像论证得有道理。

Galileo's greatest glory was that in 1609 he was the first person to turn the newly invented telescope on the heavens to prove that the planets revolve around the sun rather than around the Earth. 伽利略最光辉的业绩在于他在1609年第一个把新发明的望远镜对准天空,以证实行星是围绕太阳旋转而不是围绕地球的。

I am afraid that the shock waves will be very strong in this case. 在这种情况下,恐怕冲击波会很强。

I think it best that you should explain the theorem in detail now. 我认为你最好现在把这个定理仔细解释一下。

I don't suppose that it is true. 我认为那不是真的。

表达观点的句子可能包含 as if, seem, sound, think 等表达观点的动词,还有诸如 great, too much, wonderful, boring, should, must 等一些用来表达通过判断所得出的感觉、感受的词汇。

下列句子表达的是推断,斜体部分就是推断的结果。

Since the weight depends on ***g***, *it varies with geographic location*. This is because ***g*** decreases with increasing distance from the center of the earth. 因为重量与重力加速度 ***g*** 有关，所以重量会随地理位置不同而变化。原因在于距离地心越远，***g*** 的数值会越小。

After the expansion, the gas occupies a greater volume than it did originally. *The gas molecules become more disordered* in that they are not as localized as they were originally. 膨胀后，气体占据比原来大的体积。气体分子变得更无序，因为分子已经不再局限在原来的空间。

下列句子表达的是猜测。

From what Maxwell stated, the displacement current was reasonable. 根据麦克斯韦所说，位移电流是合理的。

That the wave like this is nothing but a standing wave, I guess. 我猜测像这样的波就是驻波。

The experiment of dropping bodies of different weight from the leaning tower of Pisa was probably performed before a multitude, according to some accounts. 根据某些记载所述，比萨斜塔落体实验可能是在很多人目睹下进行的。

18.2 专业英语阅读

18.2.1 Induced emf and Induced Electric Field（感生电动势和感生电场）

Emf in a closed circuit is due to the change of the magnetic field going through the circuit. In essence, it is due to the change of magnetic flux through the closed circuit. According to Faraday's Law, we have

$$\varepsilon = -\frac{\mathrm{d}\phi_m}{\mathrm{d}t} \tag{18-1}$$

Since emf is the work done per unit charge, there must be a force exerted on the charge associated with the emf. We know that the current produced in the circuit is not due to Lorenz force, i.e. magnetic force. Maxwell thought it was due to electric force. But it is not electrostatic force produced by stationary charges. It is called **Nonelectrostatic Force**. The force per unit charge is the electric field ***E***, which in this case is induced by the changing magnetic flux. We can define it as **induced electric field E_i**. Induced electric field can exist independent of the conductor.

In general, the emf for any closed path can be expressed as the line integral of $\boldsymbol{E} \cdot \mathrm{d}\boldsymbol{l}$ over the path

$$\varepsilon = \oint_L \boldsymbol{E}_i \cdot \mathrm{d}\boldsymbol{l} \tag{18-2}$$

Compared with $\varepsilon = -\dfrac{\mathrm{d}\phi_m}{\mathrm{d}t}$, gives

$$\oint_L \boldsymbol{E}_i \cdot \mathrm{d}\boldsymbol{l} = -\frac{\mathrm{d}\phi}{\mathrm{d}t} = -\frac{\mathrm{d}}{\mathrm{d}t}\int_S \boldsymbol{B} \cdot \mathrm{d}\boldsymbol{S} = -\int_S \frac{\partial \boldsymbol{B}}{\partial t} \cdot \mathrm{d}\boldsymbol{S} \tag{18-3}$$

which means the line integral of the induced electric field over a closed path is *not zero*.

Therefore it is also called **vortex electric field**, which is generated by a changing magnetic field.

The electric fields that we studied previously resulted from static electric charges. These fields are conservative, meaning that the work done by the electrostatic field around a closed curve is zero. The electric field resulting from changing magnetic flux is not conservative. Its line integral around a closed curve equals the induced emf, which equals the rate of change of the magnetic flux.

The direction of induced electric field is the same as induced emf ε, which can be determined by Lenz's Law. See Fig. 18-1, the shape of the field lines is closed circles.

Fig. 18-1

We know that electrostatic field is conservative field, which has

$$\oint_L \bm{E}_s \cdot \mathrm{d}\bm{l} = 0$$

while the induced electric field is a nonconservative, time-varying field with

$$\oint_L \bm{E}_i \cdot \mathrm{d}\bm{l} = -\int_S \frac{\partial \bm{B}}{\partial t} \cdot \mathrm{d}\bm{S}$$

Therefore, the total electric field in space can be defined as

$$\bm{E} = \bm{E}_i + \bm{E}_s \tag{18-4}$$

As a result, we can get

$$\oint_L (\bm{E}_i + \bm{E}_s) \cdot \mathrm{d}\bm{l} = \oint_L \bm{E} \cdot \mathrm{d}\bm{l} = -\int_S \frac{\partial \bm{B}}{\partial t} \cdot \mathrm{d}\bm{S} \tag{18-5}$$

it is the general rule between magnetic and electric fields.

18.2.2 Eddy Currents(涡流)

In the examples we have discussed, the currents produced by a changing flux were set up in definite circuits. Often a changing flux sets up circulating currents, called **eddy currents**, in a piece of bulk metal like the core of a transformer. The heat produced by such current constitutes a power loss in the transformer. Consider a conducting slab between the pole faces of an electromagnet (Fig. 18-2). If the magnetic field **B** between the pole faces is changing with time (as it will if the current in the magnet windings is alternating current), the flux through any closed loop in the slab such as through the curve C indicated in the Fig. 18-2 will be changing. Since path C is in a conductor, there will be a current along the path. At the right in Fig. 18-2 we have indicated just one of the many closed paths that will contain currents if **B** varies.

The existence of eddy currents can be demonstrated by pulling a copper or aluminum sheet between the poles of a strong permanent magnet (Fig. 18-3). Part of the area enclosed by curve C in this figure is in the magnetic field, and part is outside the field. As the sheet is pulled to the right, the flux through this curve decreases (assuming that the flux into the paper is positive). According to Faraday's law and Lenz's law, a clockwise current will be induced around this curve. Since this current is directed upward in the region between the pole faces, the magnetic field exerts a force on the current to the left, opposing motion of the sheet. You can feel this force on the sheet if you try to pull a conducting sheet suddenly through a strong magnetic field.

Fig. 18-2   Fig. 18-3

Eddy currents are usually unwanted because power is lost in the form of heat generated by the current, and the heat itself must be dissipated. The power loss can be reduced by increasing the resistance of the possible paths for the eddy currents, as shown in Fig. 18-4(a). Here the conducting slab is laminated, that is, made up of small strips glued together. Because insulating glue separates the strips, the eddy currents are essentially confined to the strips. The large eddy-current loops are broken up, and the power loss is greatly reduced. Similarly if the sheet has cuts in it, as in Fig. 18-4(b), the eddy currents are lessened and the magnetic force is greatly reduced.

Eddy currents are not always undesirable. For example, they are often used to damp unwanted oscillations. With no damping present, sensitive mechanical balance scales used to weigh small masses might oscillate back and forth around their equilibrium reading many times. Such scales are usually designed so that a small piece of metal moves between the poles of a magnet as the scales oscillate. The resulting eddy currents dampen the oscillations so that equilibrium is quickly reached. Eddy currents also have a role in the magnetic braking systems of some rapid transit cars. A large electromagnet is positioned in the vehicle over the rails. When the magnet is energized by a current in its windings, eddy currents are induced in the rails by the motion of the magnet, and the magnetic forces provide a drag force on the car that stops it.

Fig. 18-4   Fig. 18-5

18.2.3 Mutual Induction(互感现象)

When two or more circuits are close to each other, as in Fig. 18-5, the magnetic flux through one circuit depends not only on the current in that circuit but also on the current in the nearby circuits. Let I_1 be the current in circuit 1 on the left in Fig. 18-5, and I_2 in circuit 2 on the right. The magnetic field at some point P is due partly to I_1 and partly to I_2. The contribution to the field at P from circuit 1 is proportional to the current in that circuit. We can therefore write the flux through circuit 2 due to circuit 1 proportional to the current I_1

$$\phi_{m2} = M_{2,1} I_1 \qquad (18\text{-}6)$$

where $M_{2,1}$ is called the **mutual inductance** of the two circuits. The mutual inductance depends on the geometrical arrangement of the two circuits. For instance, if the circuits are far apart, the flux through circuit 2 due to the current I_1 will be small and the mutual inductance will be small. An equation similar to Eq. (18-6) can be written for the flux through circuit 1 due to circuit 2

$$\phi_{m1} = M_{1,2} I_2 \qquad (18\text{-}7)$$

We can calculate the mutual inductance for two tightly wound concentric solenoids like the ones shown in Fig. 18-6. Let l be the length of both solenoids, and let the inner solenoid have N_1 turns and radius r_1 and the outer solenoid have N_2 turns and radius r_2. We will first calculate the mutual inductance $M_{2,1}$ by assuming that the inner solenoid carries a current I_1 and finding the magnetic flux ϕ_{m2} due to this current through the outer solenoid.

Fig. 18-6

The magnetic field due to the current in the inner solenoid is constant in the space within the solenoid and has magnitude

$$B_1 = \mu_0 (N_1/l) I_1 = \mu_0 n_1 I_1$$

The flux through the outer solenoid due to this magnetic field is therefore

$$\phi_{m2} = N_2 B_1 (\pi r_1^2) = \mu_0 n_2 n_1 l (\pi r_1^2) I_1$$

Note that the area used to compute the flux through the outer solenoid is not the area of that solenoid, πr_2^2, but rather is the area of the inner solenoid, πr_1^2, because the magnetic field due to the inner solenoid is zero outside the inner solenoid. The mutual inductance $M_{2,1}$ is thus

$$M_{2,1} = \frac{\phi_{m2}}{I_1} = \mu_0 n_2 n_1 l \pi r_1^2$$

Calculate the mutual inductance $M_{1,2}$ of the concentric solenoids in Fig. 18-6 in the same way we find

$$M_{1,2} = M_{2,1} = \mu_0 n_2 n_1 l \pi r_1^2$$

Note from above that $M_{1,2} = M_{2,1}$. It can be shown that this is a general result. We will therefore drop the subscripts for mutual inductance and simply write M.

18.2.4 Self-Induction(自感现象)

The magnetic flux through a circuit is related to the current not only in that circuit but also the currents in other nearby circuits. Consider a coil carrying a current I. The current produces a magnetic field $\boldsymbol{B}$ that varies from point to point, but B is proportional to I at every point. The magnetic flux through the coil itself is therefore also proportional to I

$$\phi_m = LI \tag{18-8}$$

where L is a constant called the **self-inductance** of the coil. The self-inductance depends on the geometric shape of the coil. The SI unit of inductance is the **henry** (H). From Eq. (18-8), we can see that the unit of inductance equals the unit of flux divided by the unit of current:

$$1\,\text{H} = 1\,\frac{\text{Wb}}{\text{A}} = 1\,\frac{\text{T} \cdot \text{m}^2}{\text{A}}$$

In principle, the self-inductance of any coil or circuit can be calculated by assuming a current I, finding $\boldsymbol{B}$ at every point, calculating the flux ϕ_m, and using $L = \phi_m/I$. In practice, the calculation may be very difficult. However, there is one case, that of the tightly wound solenoid, for which the self-inductance can be calculated directly. The magnetic flux through a solenoid of length l and N turns carrying a current I was shown as

$$\phi_m = \mu_0 N^2 IS/l = \mu_0 n^2 ISl$$

where $n = N/l$ is the number of turns per unit length and S is the area of the section of the solenoid. As expected, the flux is proportional to the current I. The proportionality constant is the self-inductance

$$L = \frac{\phi_m}{I} = \mu_0 n^2 Sl \tag{18-9}$$

The self-inductance of a solenoid is proportional to the square of the number of turns per unit length n and to the volume Sl. Thus, like capacitance, self-inductance depends only on geometric factors.

Glossary

induced emf	感生电动势	induced electric field	感生电场
nonelectrostatic force	非静电力	vortex electric field	涡旋电场
nonconservative field	非保守场	time-varying field	时变场
alternate	变化	alternative	交流电的,交变的
eddy currents	涡流	laminated	叠片(组成)的
mutual induction	互感现象	magnetic flux	磁通量
proportional to	正比于	tightly wound	紧密缠绕的
concentric solenoids	同芯螺线管	mutual inductance	互感(系数)
subscript	下标	self-induction	自感现象
self-inductance	自感系数	henry	亨利

18.3 专业英语常用表达法-18 物理学中常用数学运算

add/addition　加/加法
subtract/subtraction　减/减法
multiply/multiplication　乘/乘法
divide/division　除/除法
addend/augend　加数/被加数
subtrahend/minuend　减数/被减数
multiplier/multiplicand　乘数/被乘数
divisor/dividend　除数/被除数
numerator/denominator　分子/分母
sum/difference/product/quotient　和/差/积/商
perform an operation　进行 1 次运算
reduce a fraction　约分
reduce fractions to a common denominator　通分
cancel the denominator　消去分母
raise x to the nth power　x^n（取 x 的 n 次方）
extract the nth root of x　$\sqrt[n]{x}$（求 x 的 n 次根）
combine like terms　将同类项合并
cancel common terms　消去同类项
establish a formula　列出方程式
find the root to three decimals　求根至 3 位小数
rearrange the expression　重新排列表达式
bracket　加括号
remove parentheses　去括号
take a factor outside　拆出因子
factor (x^2-a^2)　分解(x^2-a^2)的因子
substitute B into A　将 B 代入 A
substitute A by B/substitute B for A　以 B 代 A
solve the equation for x　解方程式求 x 的值
remove a common factor　移出公因子、提取公因子
round off/half adjust/round　四舍五入
round up/down　按四舍五入法调高/调低为整数
differentiate a function implicitly　求一函数的隐微分
graph a function　用图表示出函数
9 and 12 can be cancelled out by 3　9 和 12 可用 3 来通约
dx (an increment of x considered as tending to zero) dee of x/dee x/differential x　x 的增量
$\dfrac{\mathrm{d}y}{\mathrm{d}x}$ the differential coefficient of y with respect to x; the first derivative of y with

respect to x, differentiate y with respect to x　对 x 求 y 的导数（微分）

$\dfrac{d^2 y}{dx^2}$ the second derivative of y with respect to x　对 x 求 y 的二阶导数（微分）

$\dfrac{d^n y}{dx^n}$ the nth derivative of y with respect to x　对 x 求 y 的 n 阶导数（微分）

$\dfrac{\partial y}{\partial u}$ the partial derivative of y with respect to u, where y is a function of u and another variable (or other variables)　对 u 求 y 的偏导数（偏微分）

$\int_a^b$ integral between limits a and b　在区间 $[a,b]$ 之间积分

LESSON 19

19.1　物理学专业英语阅读能力的培养

阅读能力是学习任何语言的基本技能之一。物理学专业英语的交际功能可以通过听、说、读和写四种语言技能来实现，其中说和写的技能属于主动性技能，比较难掌握，而听和读的技能属于被动性技能，相对容易掌握。阅读技能相对来讲是最容易掌握的技能。

对英语阅读技能和技巧的分类有不同的方法，但基本上可分为四种。第一种是精读(intensive reading skill)；第二种是泛读(extensive reading skill)；第三种是略读(skimming reading skill)；第四种是掠读(scanning reading skill)。每种阅读技能和技巧都有其特点和要求。

1. 精读技能

精读在四种阅读技能和技巧中要求最高，对所阅读的文章，要做到逐字细读，不但要了解文章的主题思想和内容，了解文章的文法结构，而且要掌握每个字词的意义和用法，必要时还需要把文章翻译成中文。精读阅读技能是学习专业英语的人、讲授专业英语的人或从事专业翻译的人员必须要掌握的技能。但对只需要查阅英语科技文献和信息的专业工作者，在多数情况下不需要使用精读技能。是否运用精读技能，不是看文章的长短，而在于是否需要对所阅读的英语资料做深度了解和研究。

下面以一段专业文献为例，简要说明通过精读要达到什么样的标准。

①In announcing that "every particle of matter in the universe attracts every other particle with a force inversely proportional to the square of the distance between the two particles", in showing that the one universal and comparatively simple law governs not only the motion of the planets round the sun and of the satellites round their planets but, probable, also the relative motions of all the heavenly bodies, Newton gave to the world a truth the importance of which in all branches of human thought can hardly be overestimated. ②Of value to science, of course, from microphysics to macrophysics. ③But consider the effect on man's concept of nature and of his relations thereto of realizing, indeed, of having proven to him, for the first time that the physical universe is governed by law, not by caprice; and if the physical universe, why not the biological universe, even the moral universe.

分析：这一段虽然比较长，但只有三个句子。第一句是一个复杂的长复合句，其主句是 Newton gave to the world a truth，In announcing that ... heavenly bodies 是该句的状语。the importance of which in all branches of human thought can hardly be overestimated 是定语从句修饰 a truth，the importance of which 实际上相当于 whose importance；这个定语从句中的 in all branches of human thought 是修饰 importance 的。第二句是一个简单句，可以认为是 It is of value to science...的缩写。第三句也是一个并列复合句，其主句是 But consider the effect ...why not ...the moral universe；on man's concept of nature and of his relations thereto 作定语修饰 effect；of nature and of his relations thereto 是 concept 的定语；of realizing, indeed, of having proven to him, for the first time that the physical universe is governed by law, not by caprice 也是 concept 的定语；that the physical universe is governed by law, not by caprice 是 realizing 的宾语从句；by law, not by caprice 是状语；if the physical universe 是状语从句的省略。其中分号以前的子句 But consider ...caprice 可以简化为 But consider the effect on man's concept of realizing that...；分号以后的子句 and if the physical universe, why not the biological universe, even the moral universe 相当于 if the physical universe is governed by law, why is the biological universe, even the moral universe, not so governed?

只有在了解了句子结构后，才能准确理解文章内容。该段文献的中文意思是：通过宣布"宇宙中的一个质点吸引另外一个质点的力反比于他们距离的平方"，表明一个普适的并且相对简单的定律不仅制约着行星绕太阳、卫星绕行星的运动，而且或许还制约着所有天体的相对运动，牛顿给世界一个真相，其重要性（在人类思想各分支中）是怎么过高评价都不过分的。这对于科学是非常有价值的，不论是微观物理学还是宏观物理学。但是，考虑一下对人类的观念造成的影响吧，对自然、对人类与自然的关系、人类第一次认识到（实际上已经获得了证实）物理的宇宙是由定律来制约，而不是由怪想制约的；如果物理的宇宙是这样，为什么生物的世界、道德的世界并非如此呢？

除此之外，也可以对文章的词汇含义、时态等做分析。不过，进行句子分析的目的是为了理解句子所包含的专业知识内容，千万要避免为分析而分析。只要懂得了句子的意思就应停止，不要无限制地分析下去。分析时首先应确定它是简单句还是复合句。如果是简单句，应先找出主语和谓语，然后重点分析其并列成分；如果是主从复合句，首先找出主句，然后再仔细地分析各个从句，判定它们的作用和与其他句子的关系。

精读技能不是一朝一夕就能学会的，它需要有比较全面的英语知识和专业背景，需要通过大量的阅读训练才能掌握好。

另外三种阅读技能和技巧，对需要通过英语及时了解大量物理专业信息的人们，更为实用，使用频率高，也比较容易掌握。熟练掌握了这三种英语阅读技能和技巧，对提高精读技能水平很有帮助。

2. 泛读技能

通过阅读大量的专业英语文章，可以扩大知识面、丰富专业词汇量、提高专业英语语感。为了快速提高专业英语水平，要坚持经常阅读一定数量的专业英语文章，一般每周要阅读

2～3 篇文章。专业人员工作忙，时间少，开始做泛读练习时，可以从 500 字开始，以后逐渐增加长度，一般控制在 2000～3000 字为宜。如果能坚持下去，一年以后，专业英语水平一定会有显著提高。

在做泛读练习时，要求虽然不像精读那样严格，但是必须要从头到尾把文章读完，对文章的关键词语和句子要有所理解。为了达到这样的要求，最好根据文章的内容或特点，事先提出一些问题，在阅读之后，回答这些问题，以巩固阅读效果。

下面一些问题可以作为参考。

（1）What is main theme of the article? 文章的主题思想是什么？

（2）How many paragraphs does this article have? 此文有几个段落？

（3）What is the topic sentence of each paragraph? 每段的主题句是什么？

（4）Pick up the sentences you are most interested and analyze them. 挑选出你最感兴趣的句子，并做分析。

（5）List the important and useful words and phrases. 记录下重要的和有用的单词和短语。

除了上面这些问题外，读者还要时刻记着几个问题：文章谈论的是谁？谁来谈论？与谁有关？（who），讨论什么内容？重点是什么？（what），什么时间？时效和期限如何？（when），在哪里？（where），文章写作的原因？为什么？（why），哪一类？（which），怎样进行？采取哪些方法和技术？（how）。总之，阅读时要保持头脑清晰，有针对性地阅读，做到随记要点。

3. 略读技巧

略读是一种快速阅读技巧，在查询大量英语文献时非常有用。略读是快速阅读文章，目的是了解文章主题思想。略读时不需要逐字去读，而是寻找文章内关键词语、主题句，从而了解文章的主题思想。在这个基础上，决定是否选取此资料，是否需要进一步精读。现以下面的短文为例，说明如何运用略读技巧，找出此文的主题思想。

Rutherford's Model

A student of Thomson, *Ernest Rutherford, did an experiment that radically changed his teacher's model of the atom.* A key tool in Rutherford's work was the newly discovered radioactivity, the spontaneous emission of fast-moving atomic particles from certain elements. Rutherford had previously shown that one of these radioactive products is a helium atom without its electrons. These particles have two units of positive charge and are known as *alpha particles.*

Rutherford bombarded materials with alpha particles and observed how the alpha particles recoiled from collisions with the atoms in the material. This procedure was much like determining the shape of an object hidden under a table by rolling rubber balls at it. Rutherford used the alpha particles as his probe because they were known to be about the same size as atoms. (One doesn't probe the structure of snowflakes with a sledgehammer.) The target needed to be as thin as possible to keep the number of collisions by a single alpha particle as small as possible, ideally only one. Rutherford chose gold because it could be made into a very thin foil.

The alpha particles are about 4 *times the mass of hydrogen atoms and* 7300 *times the mass of electrons*. Thomson's model predicted that the deflection of alpha particles by each atom (and hence by the foil) would be extremely small. The positive material of the atom was too spread out to be a very effective scatterer. Consider the following analogy. Use 100 kilograms of newspapers to make a wall one sheet thick. Glue ping-pong balls on the wall to represent electrons. If you were to throw bowling balls to the wall, you would clearly expect them to go straight through with no noticeable deflection.

Initially, Rutherford's results matched Thomson's prediction. However, when Rutherford suggested that one of his students look for alpha particles in the backward directions, he was shocked with the results. *A small number of the alpha particles were actually scattered in the backward direction!* Rutherford later described his feelings by saying, "It was almost as incredible as if you fired a 19-inch shell at a piece of tissue paper and it came back and hit you!"

On the basis of his experiment, *Rutherford proposed a new model in which the positive charge was not spread out but was concentrated in a very, very tiny spot at the center of the atom, which he called the nucleus*. Returning to our analogy, imagine what would happen if all the newspapers were crushed into a small region of space: Most of the bowling balls would miss the paper and pass straight through, but occasionally a ball would score of direct hit on the 100-kilogram ball of newspaper and recoil.

These experiments gave him an upper limit on the size of the gold nucleus. The nucleus has a diameter approximately 100,000 times smaller than its atom. This means that atoms are almost entirely empty space.

Rutherford's "solar system" model led to a new explanation for the emission of light from atoms. The orbiting electrons are accelerating, and accelerating charges radiate electromagnetic waves.

这篇短文约500字。用略读技巧,应该在3~5分钟内读完全文。文中用斜体字表示的,是阅读时应该注意的句子或词语。此文主题是介绍 Rutherford(卢瑟福)如何通过自己的实验否定了他的老师 Thomson(汤姆森)提出的关于原子的模型,最后提出了关于原子的"太阳系"模型。了解了短文的主题思想,就等于有了一条线索,能帮助读者更好地理解文章。略读是在大量英语文献中查找和选择所需要的资料时非常有用的阅读技巧。

4. 掠读技巧

掠读也是一种快速阅读技巧,与略读不同的是,它用来查询文章中的特定信息。人们在日常生活和工作中,都在自觉或不自觉地使用掠读技巧。例如,看文献的目录时,查找特定主题的文章;查字典时,查阅所需要的词汇;看文章时,查找特定的信息等。下面是一个国际会议的征稿通知,比如说对有关 Antennas(天线)方面的内容感兴趣,使用掠读的办法快速找出相关主题。掠读时,是找特定信息,所以只需要查看有 Antennas 一词的主题,其他完全不需要看,下面的内容应该在一分钟内就读完,迅速找到所有含 Antennas 一词的主题。

Call for Papers

ISAPE2008 offers a forum for antennas, propagation, and electromagnetic theory researchers to exchange ideas and experiences in the latest development and designs. You are invited to submit papers in all areas of antennas, propagation, electromagnetic theory, computational electromagnetics, and EMI.

Relevant topics of interest include the following:

Active and Integrated Antennas√	Non-linear electromagnetics
Adaptive and Smart Antennas√	Optical Technology in Antennas√
Antennas for Wireless Communications√	Radio Meteorology and Radio Astronomy
Aperture Antennas and Feeds√	Random Media and Rough Surfaces
Bio-electromagetics	Remote Sensing
Earth-Space and Terrestrial Propagation	SAR Polarimetry and Interferometry
EM fields in complex media	Scattering, Diffraction, and RCS
Geo-electromagnetics	Seismo-Electromagnetics
High-Frequency Techniques	Small Antennas√
Inverse Problems and Imaging	Time Domain Techniques
Ionospheric Propagation	Transient EM fields
Measurement Techniques	Tunnel Propagation
Millimeter and Optical Wave Propagation	Waveguiding Structures
Mobile and Indoor Propagation	Wire and Slot Antennas√

查找结果,一共有七条有关 Antennas 的相关主题,画有√ 的即是相关内容。

略读和掠读技巧对阅读的速度是有要求的,要越快越好。在训练这两种阅读技能时,最好用表计时,来督促自己不断提高阅读速度。

在了解了专业英语四种基本阅读技能和技巧后,实际学习中需要做的就是要通过练习,熟练掌握这些阅读技能。掌握了这些阅读技能后就等于有了得力助手,就可在浩如烟海的专业英语文献中,随心畅游,迅速查到自己所需要的资料。

19.2 专业英语阅读

19.2.1 Maxwell's Equations(麦克斯韦方程组)

Maxwell's equations, first proposed by the great Scottish physicist James Clerk Maxwell, relate the electric and magnetic field vectors E and B to their sources, which are electric charge, currents, and changing fields. These equations summarize the experimental laws of electricity and magnetism—the laws of Coulomb, Gauss, Biot-Savart, Ampere, and Faraday. These experimental laws hold in general except for Ampere's law, which does not apply to discontinuous currents such as those that occur when charging or discharging a capacitor. Maxwell was able to generalize Ampere's law with the invention of the displacement current. He was then able to show that the generalized laws of electricity and magnetism imply the existence of electromagnetic waves.

Maxwell's equations play a role in classical electromagnetism analogous to that of Newton's laws in classical mechanics. What's more, Maxwell's equations are of great theoretical importance. For example, Maxwell showed that these equations can be combined to yield a wave equation for the electric and magnetic field vectors E and B. Such electromagnetic waves are caused by accelerating charges, for example, the charges in an alternating current in an antenna. They were first produced in the laboratory by Heinrich Hertz in 1887. Maxwell showed that the speed of electromagnetic waves in free space should be

$$c = 1/\sqrt{\mu_0 \varepsilon_0} \qquad (19\text{-}1)$$

where ε_0, the permittivity of free space, is the constant appearing in Coulomb's and Gauss's laws and μ_0, the permeability of free space, is the constant appearing in the Biot-Savart law and Ampere's law. When the measured value of ε_0 and defined value of μ_0 are put into Eq. (19-1), the speed of electromagnetic waves is found to be about 3×10^8 m/s, the same as the measured speed of light. Maxwell noted this "coincidence" with great excitement and correctly surmised that light itself is an electromagnetic wave.

Maxwell's equations in medium are

$$\oint_S \boldsymbol{D} \cdot \mathrm{d}\boldsymbol{S} = q_{\text{free-inside}} \qquad (19\text{-}2\mathrm{a})$$

$$\oint_S \boldsymbol{B} \cdot \mathrm{d}\boldsymbol{S} = 0 \qquad (19\text{-}2\mathrm{b})$$

$$\oint_L \boldsymbol{E} \cdot \mathrm{d}\boldsymbol{l} = -\int_S \frac{\partial \boldsymbol{B}}{\partial t} \cdot \mathrm{d}\boldsymbol{S} \qquad (19\text{-}2\mathrm{c})$$

$$\oint_L \boldsymbol{H} \cdot \mathrm{d}\boldsymbol{l} = \int_S \left(\boldsymbol{j} + \frac{\partial \boldsymbol{D}}{\partial t} \right) \cdot \mathrm{d}\boldsymbol{S} \qquad (19\text{-}2\mathrm{d})$$

Eq. (19-2a) is Gauss's law. This law describes how electric field lines diverge from a positive charge and converge on a negative charge. Its experimental basis is Coulomb's law.

Eq. (19-2b), sometimes called Gauss's law for magnetism, states that the flux of the magnetic field vector B is zero through any closed surface. This equation describes the experimental observation that magnetic field lines do not diverge from any point in space or converge on any point; that is, it implies that isolated magnetic poles do not exist.

Eq. (19-2c) is Faraday's law; it describes how electric field lines encircle any area through which the magnetic flux is changing, and it relates the electric field vector E to the rate of change of the magnetic field vector B.

Eq. (19-2d) is Ampere's law modified to include Maxwell's displacement current. This law describes how the magnetic field lines encircle an area through which a current is passing or through which the electric flux is changing.

19.2.2 Electromagnetic Waves(电磁波)

Fig. 19-1 shows the electric and magnetic field vectors of an electromagnetic wave.

The electric and magnetic fields are perpendicular to each other and both are perpendicular to the direction of the propagation of the wave. Electromagnetic waves are thus **transverse waves**. The vectors E and B are in phase and their magnitudes are related by

$$E = cB \tag{19-3}$$

Fig. 19-1

where $c = 1/\sqrt{\mu_0 \varepsilon_0}$ is the speed of the wave. In general, the direction of propagation of an electromagnetic wave is the direction of the cross product $E \times B$.

Maxwell's equations imply that both E and B obey the wave equation similar to

$$\frac{\partial^2 y(x,t)}{\partial x^2} = \frac{1}{v^2} \frac{\partial^2 y(x,t)}{\partial t^2} \tag{19-4}$$

We consider only free space, in which there are no charges or currents, and we assume that the electric and magnetic fields E and B are functions of time and one space coordinate only, which we will take to be the x coordinate. Such a wave is called a **plane wave**, because field quantities are constant across any plane perpendicular to the x axis. For a plane electromagnetic wave traveling parallel to the x axis, the x components of the fields are zero, so the vectors E and B are perpendicular to the x axis and each obeys the wave equation

$$\frac{\partial^2 E}{\partial x^2} = \frac{1}{c^2} \frac{\partial^2 E}{\partial t^2}, \quad \frac{\partial^2 B}{\partial x^2} = \frac{1}{c^2} \frac{\partial^2 B}{\partial t^2} \tag{19-5}$$

where $c = 1/\sqrt{\mu_0 \varepsilon_0}$ is the speed of the waves, too. Eq. (19-5) are wave equations for E and B respectively.

The Electromagnetic Spectrum(电磁波谱)

The various types of electromagnetic waves—light, radio waves, X-rays, gamma rays, microwave, and others—differ only in wavelength and frequency, which are related to the speed c in the usual way, $f = c/\lambda$. The names corresponding to different parts of the electromagnetic spectrum usually associate with the various frequency and wavelength ranges. These ranges are often not well defined and sometimes overlap.

The human eye is sensitive to electromagnetic radiation with wavelengths from about 400 to 700 nm, the range called **visible light**. The shortest wavelengths in the visible spectrum correspond to violet light and the longest to red light, with all the colors of the rainbow falling between these extremes. Electromagnetic waves with wavelengths just beyond the visible spectrum on the short-wavelength side are called **ultraviolet ray**, and those with wavelengths just beyond the visible spectrum on the long-wavelength side are called **infrared waves**. Heat radiation given off by bodies at ordinary temperatures is in the infrared region of the electromagnetic spectrum. There are no limits on the wavelengths of electromagnetic radiation; that is, all wavelengths are theoretically possible.

Energy Carried by Electromagnetic Waves(电磁波的能量)

Mechanical waves carry energy. Electromagnetic waves also carry energy, and as they propagate through space they can transfer energy to objects placed in their path. The rate of flow of energy in an electromagnetic wave is described by a vector, called the **Poynting Vector**, defined by the expression

$$S = E \times H \tag{19-6}$$

where $H = \dfrac{B}{\mu_0 \mu_r} = \dfrac{B}{\mu}$, is the magnetic intensity vector. *The magnitude of the Poynting vector represents the rate at which energy flows through a unit surface area perpendicular to the flow and its direction is along the direction of wave propagation*, that is, in the same direction of the wave velocity, *c*. Thus, the Poynting vector represents *power per unit area*. The SI units of the Poynting vector are $J/s \cdot m^2 = W/m^2$.

Glossary

transverse wave	横波	in phase	同相
propagation	传播	wave equation	波方程
plane wave	平面波	wavelength	波长
visible spectrum	可见光谱	infrared wave	红外波
radiation	辐射	ultraviolet ray	紫外线
electromagnetic spectrum	电磁波谱	Poyngting vector	坡印亭矢量

19.3 专业英语常用表达法-19 数字的增加与倍数

1. 在表示增加的概念时,可以有两种说法,即"A 是 B 的 N 倍"或"A 比 B 大 N−1 倍",例如"A 是 B 的 3 倍"即是"A 比 B 大 2 倍"(请注意汉语的表达不同,数字不同,但意思相同)。而英语中虽然有几种句型来表示倍数的增加,但句中的倍数却没有数字上的变化。下面是英语表达倍数的常用句型(其中 N 指倍数):

  a. N+times+adj.+than
  b. N+times+as+adj.+as
  c. N+times+noun phrase
  d. verb (e.g. increase, grow, rise, be raised, multiply) (+by)+N+times
  e. verb (e.g. double, treble, quadruple)+noun

以上句型汉译的意思为"是……的 N 倍"或"增加了 N−1 倍"。请看下面的例句:

Aluminum has nearly 5 *times* the thermal conductivity of cast iron. 铝的导热率几乎是铸铁的 5 倍。

The resistivity of aluminum is 1.6 *times* that of copper. 铝的电阻率为铜的 1.6 倍。

The mass of the proton is 1836 *times* the mass of the electron. 质子的质量为电子质量

的 1836 倍。

Mercury weighs about 14 *times more than* water. 水银的重量约超过水的 14 倍。

Many planes can fly *several times faster than* sound. 许多飞机能以数倍于音速的速度飞行。

The Uranus is 14 *times as large as* the mass of the Earth. 天王星的质量是地球的 14 倍。

There is *four times as much* nitrogen *as* there is oxygen in air. 空气中的氮气比氧气多 3 倍。

The accuracy of the atomic clock is about *ten times as great as* that of the quartz clock. 原子钟的准确度约为石英钟的 10 倍。

The pinion rotates *five times as fast as* the gear. 小齿轮的转速为齿轮的 5 倍。

The resistance of the wire in circuit L_1 is *twice* the resistance of the wire in circuit L_2. L_1 电路导线的电阻为 L_2 电路导线的 2 倍。

Helium is *twice as heavy as* hydrogen. 氦有氢的 2 倍重。

If the second winding has *twice as many* turns *as* the first, the voltage will be twice as great. 如果第二个线圈的匝数比第一个线圈多 1 倍,电压也会提高 1 倍。

In a circuit of fixed resistance, if the voltage of the circuit *is doubled*, the current will also *double*. 在电阻固定的电路中,若电路电压增加 1 倍,则电流也会增加 1 倍。

2. 数字的增加还可以用分数或百分数来表示。这时的增长大多是净增长,可用汉语直接译为"增加几分之几","增加百分之几"。常用句型有:

a. 动词(如 increase,grow,jump,improve,exceed 等)+(by)+ 百分数,译为"上升了百分之……"

b. 百分数+形容词的比较级+than,译为"比……增百分之……"

c. 百分数+介词(up,over)+名词,译为"增百分之……"

例如:

New booster can *increase* the pay load *by* 120%. 新型推动器能使有效负载增加 120%。

Output of glass ceramics this year was 30 *percent higher than* last year. 今年玻璃陶瓷的产量比去年提高了 30%。

They note that the amount of carbon dioxide in the air has been *up* 13% in the last one hundred years. 他们注意到过去的 100 年里空气中二氧化碳的含量已增加了 13%。

3. 涉及 again 结构的译法

a. 在结构 as much/many...again as 与 again as much/many...as 中可译成"是……的 2 倍",或"比……多一倍"。例如:

The amount left was estimated to be *again as much as* all the aluminium that has been mined. 当时估计,剩余的铝储量是已开采量的 2 倍。

Pulley A turns *as fast again as* pulley B. A 滑轮转动比 B 滑轮快 1 倍。

b. 出现 again 的同时还出现 half,即 half as much/many...again as 或 half again as much/many...as 时,表示"是……一倍半","比……多一半"。

The videodisc is half *as wide again as* that one. 这个光盘比那个宽 0.5 倍。(或这个

光盘宽度是那个的 1.5 倍。)

The resistance of aluminum is approximately *half again as great as* that of copper for the same dimensions. 尺寸相同时,铝的电阻约为铜的 1.5 倍。

LESSON 20

20.1 物理学专业英语阅读时需要注意的问题

1. 阅读材料的选择

专业阅读是为了获取信息,有时就是为了提高专业英语水平。读者多数都是成年人,理解能力强,大多数具有专业背景,但外语水平可能不尽相同,专业词汇掌握的也可能有多有少。在选择阅读材料时要特别注意应用性和原汁原味,并且要有一定的深度。但在开始学习专业英语时,难度要适合自己的水平,不要超过了自己的理解能力。随着水平的提高,阅读材料的深度可以相应加深。

应用性和原汁原味的材料是指那些未经改编、未经简写的以英语为母语的人士在实际专业交流中所使用的话语,包括日常会话、学术杂志文章、专业书籍、通知、告示等。原始材料有语境、有上下文、有完整的结构、有作者的逻辑思维和立场观点,因此,从专业的意义上讲,应用性的原始材料可能更容易理解。

初学者可以选那些英美作者用简单词汇写成的文章,如科普文章、科学幻想、产品宣传材料等。比如下面这种程度的文章:

Most people would describe water as a colorless liquid. They would know that in very cold conditions it becomes a solid called ice, and that when heated on a fire it becomes a vapour called steam. But water, they would say, is a liquid.

We have learned that water is made up of two atoms of hydrogen and one atom of oxygen, which we describe by the formula H_2O. Chemically there is no difference between the gas, the liquid, and the solid, all of which are made of molecules with formula H_2O. And this is true of other chemical substances. Most of them can exist as gases or liquids or as solids. We may normally think of iron as a solid, but if we heat it in a furnace, it will melt and become a liquid, and at very high temperatures it will become a gas. We normally think of air as a mixture of gases, but at very low temperatures it becomes a liquid, and at lower temperatures still it becomes a white solid.

What, then, do we mean when we say that water is a liquid, air is a gas, and salt is a solid? We mean nothing more than that. This is the usual condition of things on our earth. On one of the outer planets all three substances would be solids, and on the sun all three would be gases. Most substances are only familiar to us in one state, because the temperatures required to turn them into gases are very high, or the temperatures necessary to turn them into solids are so low. Water is an exception in this respect, which is another reason why its three states have been given three different names.

对中等水平的读者,可选用科普杂志、百科全书或是用户手册上的文章,阅读面宜宽些。比如:

Chinese documents suggest that magnetism was recognized as early as about 2000 B. C. The ancient Greeks observed electric and magnetic phenomena possibly as early as 700 B. C. They found that a piece of amber, when rubbed, attracted pieces of straw or feathers. The existence of magnetic forces was known from observations that pieces of a naturally occurring stone called magnetite were attracted to iron. (The word *electric* comes from the Greek word for amber, *elektron*. The word *magnetic* comes from *Magnesia*, on the coast of Turkey where magnetite was found.)

In 1600, the Englishman William Gilbert discovered that electrification was not limited to amber but was a general phenomenon. Scientists went on to electrify a variety of objects, including chickens and people! Experiments by Charles Coulomb in 1785 confirmed the inverse-square law for the electrostatic force.

It was not until the early part of the 19th century that scientists established that electricity and magnetism are related phenomena. In 1820, Hans Oersted discovered that a compass needle, which is magnetic, is deflected when placed near an electric current. In 1831, Michael Faraday in England and, almost simultaneously, Joseph Henry in the United States showed that, when a wire loop is moved near a magnet (or, equivalently, when a magnet is moved near a wire loop), an electric current is observed in the wire. In 1873, James Clerk Maxwell used these observations and other experimental facts as a basis for formulating the laws of electromagnetism as we know them today. Shortly thereafter (around 1888), Heinrich Hertz verified Maxwell's predictions by producing electromagnetic waves in the laboratory. This achievement was followed by such practical developments as radio and television.

对英语水平较高的专业文献读者,可以选一些结合自己专业的英语原文资料、科研论文、专著等作为阅读材料。

2. 注重整体理解,避免只见树木不见森林

一开始,在进行专业英语阅读时,读者往往会过分小心仔细,总希望搞清每一个句子的意思;每遇到生词就会自觉或不自觉地去查字典,即使有时猜出了词义还觉得不放心,直到查了字典后才感觉踏实。有的读者在遇到长一些的句子就自觉不自觉地进行语法分析。还有的读者无论读什么样的文章,无论简单的还是复杂的,总是要在头脑里逐词逐句地翻译成中文后才能理解。这些习惯在专业英语阅读中应慢慢改掉。要在阅读中注重整体理解,理解掌握读物的主要内容,不需要彻底掌握读物中的每一个单词。始终记住阅读的目的是掌握读物的内容、接收读物所传递的信息,扩大词汇量和丰富语言知识是专业英语阅读的副产品。

3. 克服长难句障碍,读懂专业内容

在前面章节中,已经对专业英语中的长难句进行了介绍。应付这些长难句的有效方法之一就是我们介绍过的"抓住主干,添枝加叶"方法,能正确运用这种方法,一般对长句子就会做出正确分析。通过语法分析找出哪些是句子的主干,即句子的主语和谓语,哪些是修饰成分,找出各部分之间的关系。经过这样逐级逐层地分析,就能读懂长难句,最终理解文献中的专业知识内容。

4. 克服词汇障碍,提高阅读速度

扩大专业词汇量是提高专业阅读能力的一条切实可行的重要途径。要想流利地阅读专业文献资料,必须掌握大量的词汇,必须知道如何猜测生词词义。然而扩大词汇量的最佳途径就是经常地、广泛地、大量地阅读,把扩大专业词汇量变成经常的、自觉的行动。阅读和词汇既是互相牵制又是互相促进的,提高了一种能力,必然也会提高另一种能力。

尽管专业词汇量在不断扩大,但在进行专业阅读时,仍然还会遇到不少的生词,尤其是那些影响对文章理解的生词。生词不仅是一个拦路虎,而且给读者增加了压力,专业读者必须学会运用科学的猜词技巧,采用正确的方法来猜测生词的词义,这对阅读速度的提高有很大的帮助。下面就介绍一些猜测生词词义的方法。

(1) 根据释义猜测词义

在有些文章中,某些生词的词义在下文中可以得到解释或说明。这些解释有时以系表结构、定义、同位语形式出现。系表结构的句子有两种表意功能,一是表语说明主语的形状或特征,二是表语和主语是同位关系,即表语的内容等于主语的内容,后者往往是猜词的最好线索。这种结构有时用破折号、括号、冒号、引号等符号引出,还有时用 that is, that is to say, in other words 等引出。例如:

When two initially neutral objects are charged by being rubbed together, charge is not created in the process. The objects become charged because electrons are transferred from one object to the other. One object gains some amount of negative charge from the electrons transferred to it while the other loses an equal amount of negative charge and hence is left with a positive charge. That is, *charge is conserved*. The law of *conservation of charge* is a fundamental law of nature. 根据前面的解释说明,可以得出 *conserved* 和 *conservation* 具有"总量不变"的意思,实际上它们的意思就是"守恒"。

Capacitance, the ability to store electric charge, is one of the most common characteristics of electronic circuits. 由同位语我们可以很快猜出生词 *Capacitance* 的词义——电容量。

The *momentum* of an object is its velocity multiplied by its mass. 速度乘以质量就是 *momentum* 动量。

The most interesting problem centers on *inertia*—the property of matter that makes heavy things hard to get moving, but once moving, hard to stop. 破折号后面都是说明 *inertia*"惯性"的。

At the center of an atom is its *nucleus*, made up of particles called *protons and neutrons*. 位于原子中心的肯定是"原子核"*nucleus*,构成原子核的是"质子和中子"*protons and neutrons*。

(2) 根据上下文线索猜词义

某些生词的含义可以利用已知词汇的信息和未知词汇信息之间的联系以及生词前后表述的启发,弄清其含义。如:

Refraction refers to the change in direction of a wave at a boundary where it passes from one medium into another. For example, when light traveling in air is incident on a transparent material such as glass, it is partially reflected and partially transmitted. But the direction in which the transmitted light is propagated is different from the direction of the incident light, so the light is said to have been *refracted*, or bent. 根据 change in direction, the direction …is different from…和 bent 等词来判断, *refraction/refract* 有"改变方向、折"的意思, 再根据 wave at a boundary 和 transmit 等词和专业知识, 就可以判断出 *refraction/refract* 是表示"折射"。

Many quantities in physics have magnitude and direction. *Vectors* are quantities with magnitude and direction. Examples include velocity, acceleration, momentum, and force. Quantities with magnitude but no associated direction, for example, distance and speed, are called *scalars*. 从给出的例子包括"速度、加速度、动量和力"以及 quantities with magnitude and direction 就可以猜测到 *vector* 的意思应该是"矢量", 进一步也就知道了 *scalar* 的意思是"标量"。

The time it takes for a displaced object to execute a complete cycle of oscillatory motion—from one extreme to the other extreme and back—is called the *period T*. The unit of the period is second. The *reciprocal* of the period is the *frequency ν*, which is the number of cycle per second. 根据定义就会知道 *period* 是"周期", *frequency* 是"频率", 根据频率和周期的关系就会知道 *reciprocal* 的意思是"倒数"。

(3) 利用常识和经验猜词

某些文章的生词, 根据个人生活经验和基本常识也可以猜出。如:

Anyone who has observed a football moving in the air (or any object thrown in the air) has observed *projectile motion*. 根据常识可以推断: *projectile motion* 的意思是"被抛在空中的物体的运动", 也就是物理学中的抛体运动。

(4) 利用语义相反、对照信息猜词

有时文章在描述两件事物的不同特征时, 使用了截然相反的词, 形成鲜明的对照。这时可以给读者以暗示, 从而猜出生词的意思。如:

The major points of your plan are clear to me, but the technical details are still *hazy*. 计划的要点清楚, 而细节 *hazy*, 显然和 clear 的意思相反, 为"模糊"或"迷惑"的意思。

Suppose a person on a moving vehicle (observer A) throws a ball straight up in the air according to his frame of reference. According to observer A, the ball will move in a vertical path. On the other hand, a *stationary* observer (B), standing on the ground, will see the path of the ball as a parabola. 根据前面 on a moving vehicle 和后面的 standing on the ground 的意思相反的对比, 再根据 standing on the ground 是对 *stationary* 的进一步解释, 就可以猜到 *stationary* 的意思应该是"不动的、静止的"。

(5) 利用定语从句的功能猜词

定语从句是修饰和说明中心词的, 根据其提供的信息来猜测词义, 是一种猜词的好方法。如:

A space where there is no matter in any state is a *vacuum*. 根据定语从句的说明很容易得到 *vacuum* 的意思是"真空"。

Solids studied include crystals, solids whose molecules are in regular geometrical shapes, and *alloys*, which are combinations of different metals, such as copper and tin in bronze. 根据定语从句的说明和所举的例子青铜(包含铜与锡)，就可以猜出 *alloy* 的意思是"合金"。

(6) 根据复合词的各部分猜测词义

在物理学中，有些专业复合词汇的意思可根据其各部分的意思进行猜测。例如：

wavelength 波长，microwave 微波，voltmeter 伏特计，thundercloud 雷雨云，thunderstorm 雷暴，waveform 波形。

A substance that conducts electricity is a conductor. One that does not is an insulator. One that conducts electricity without resistance is a *superconductor*, possessing the property of *superconductivity*. 此句中的 *superconductor* 一词从上下文判断、从单词组合判断可以得到"超导体"，进一步可得出 *superconductivity* 是"超导性"。

(7) 根据前后缀猜测词义

可以充分利用前后缀知识来猜测专业词汇的意思。例如：

coaxial 同轴的，coexist 共存，concentric 同心的，uncharged 不带电的，redistribute 重新分配，equipotential 等电势的，nonslip 不滑的（防滑的），nondeforming 不变形的，interatomic 原子间的，intermolecular 分子间的，liquefy 液化，massless 无质量的，counterclockwise 逆时针的。

20.2 专业英语阅读：Introduction to Antennas（天线导言）

We studied the propagation characteristics of plane electromagnetic waves in source-free media without considering how the waves were generated. Of course, the waves must originate from sources, which in electromagnetic terms are time-varying charges and currents. In order to radiate electromagnetic energy efficiently in prescribed directions, the charges and currents must be distributed in specific ways. **Antennas** are structures designed for radiating electromagnetic energy effectively in a prescribed manner. Without an efficient antenna, electromagnetic energy would be localized, and wireless transmission of information over long distances would be impossible.

An antenna may be a single straight wire or a conducting loop excited by a voltage source, an aperture at the end of a waveguide, or a complex array of these properly arranged radiating elements. Reflectors and lenses may be used to accentuate certain radiation characteristics. Among radiation characteristics of importance are field pattern, directivity, impedance, and bandwidth. These parameters will be examined when particular antenna types are studied.

To study electromagnetic radiation, we must call upon our knowledge of Maxwell's equations and relate electric and magnetic fields to time-varying charge and current distributions. A primary difficulty of this task is that the charge and current distributions on antenna structures resulting from given excitations are generally unknown and very difficult to determine. In fact, the geometrically simple case of a straight conducting wire (linear antenna) excited by a voltage source in the middle has been a subject of extensive research for many years, and the exact charge and current distributions on a wire of a finite radius are extremely complicated even when the wire is assumed to be perfectly conducting. Fortunately, the radiation field of such an antenna is relatively insensitive to slight deviations in the current distribution, and a physically plausible approximate current on the wire yields useful results for nearly all practical purposes. We will examine the radiation properties of linear antennas with assumed currents.

By combining Maxwell's equations we can derive nonhomogeneous wave equations in E and in H. However, these equations tend to involve the charge and current densities in a complicated way. It is generally simpler to solve for the auxiliary potential functions A and V first. Using A and V, we can determine H and E. For harmonic time variation in a simple medium we have

$$H = \frac{1}{\mu} \nabla \times A \qquad (20\text{-}1)$$

and

$$E = -\nabla V - j\omega A \qquad (20\text{-}2)$$

The potential functions A and V are themselves solutions of nonhomogeneous wave equations. For harmonic time dependence the phasor retarded potentials are,

$$A = \frac{\mu}{4\pi} \int_{V'} \frac{J e^{-jkR}}{R} dv' \qquad (20\text{-}3)$$

$$V = \frac{\mu}{4\pi\varepsilon} \int_{V'} \frac{\rho e^{-jkR}}{R} dv' \qquad (20\text{-}4)$$

where $k = \omega\sqrt{\mu\varepsilon} = 2\pi/\lambda$ is the wavenumber. Of course, A and V are related by the Lorentz condition, for potentials, just as J and ρ are related by the equation of continuity, or

$$\nabla \cdot J = -j\omega\rho \qquad (20\text{-}5)$$

Hence there is no need for evaluating the integrals in both Eqs. (20-3) and (20-4). As a matter of fact, the relation of E and H are

$$E = \frac{1}{j\omega\varepsilon} \nabla \times H \qquad (20\text{-}6)$$

We follow three steps in the determination of electromagnetic fields from a current distribution: (1) determine A from J using Eq. (20-3); (2) find H from A using Eq. (20-1); and (3) find E from H using Eq. (20-6). Note that only Step 1 requires an integration and that Steps 2 and 3 involve only straightforward differentiation. This is the procedure we will use in finding the radiation pattern of antennas.

We will first study the radiation fields and characteristic properties of an elemental electric dipole and of a small current loop (or magnetic dipole). We then consider finite-length thin linear antennas, of which the half-wavelength dipole is an important special case. The radiation characteristics of a linear antenna are largely determined by its length and the manner in which it is excited. To obtain more directivity and other desirable properties, a number of such antennas may be arranged together to form an antenna array. The geometrical configuration, the spacings between the array elements, as well as the relative amplitudes and phases of the excitations in the elements all affect the field pattern of the array. Some basic properties of simple arrays will be considered.

When an antenna is used as a receiving device, its function is to collect energy from an incoming electromagnetic wave and deliver it to a receiver. Any antenna that is useful for radiation is also useful for reception. We will use the reciprocity theorem to show that the pattern, directivity, input impedance, effective height, and effective aperture of antenna are the same for transmitting as for receiving. We will define backscatter cross section and study the radar equation and the effect of wave propagation near the earth's surface. Finally, we will discuss such antenna types as traveling-wave antennas, Yagi-Uda antennas, helical antennas, broadband antennas and arrays, and aperture antennas.

Glossary

propagation	传播	characteristic	特征
plane electromagnetic wave	平面电磁波	source-free	无源
media	介质	source	源
time-varying charge	时变电荷	current	电流
radiate	辐射	electromagnetic energy	电磁能量
distribute	分布	wireless transmission	无线传输
conducting loop	导体环	voltage source	电压源
waveguide	波导	array	阵列
reflector	反射镜	lens	镜头
accentuate	加重	field pattern	场模式
impedance	阻抗	bandwidth	带宽
Maxwell's equations	麦克斯韦方程组	current distributions	电流分布
straight conducting wire	直导线	insensitive	不敏感
deviation	偏差	physically plausible	物理上似乎合理的
nonhomogeneous	非齐次的	current density	电流密度
auxiliary potential function	辅助势函数	phasor retarded potential	相量推迟势
wavenumber	波数	Lorentz condition	洛伦兹条件
continuity	连续性	electric dipole	电偶极子
current loop	电流环	magnetic dipole	磁偶极子
amplitude	振幅	phase	阶段
receiver	接收机	reciprocity theorem	互易定理
effective height	有效高度	effective aperture	有效孔径
transmit	传递	backscatter cross section	后向散射截面

traveling-wave antennas	行波天线	Yagi-Uda antennas	八木-宇田天线
helical antennas	螺旋天线	broadband antennas	宽频天线
aperture antennas	孔径天线		

20.3 专业英语常用表达法-20 分数 百分数 减少

1. 分数的表示法

(1) 分数可由基数词和序数词一起来表示。基数词作分子,序数词作分母,除了分子是"1"以外,其他情况下序数词都要用复数形式。

three fourths 或 three quarters 3/4　　　　one third 或 a third 1/3

a half 或 one half 1/2　　　　　　　　　　one quarter 或 a quarter 1/4

one and a half $1\frac{1}{2}$　　　　　　　　　　　one and a quarter $1\frac{1}{4}$

three and one fourth 或 three and one quarter $3\frac{1}{4}$

$1\frac{1}{2}$ hours (读作 one and a half hours,或者 an hour an a half)1.5 小时

$2\frac{3}{4}$ meters (读作 two and three-fourths meters) $2\frac{3}{4}$ m

4/5meter (读作 four fifths meter) $\frac{4}{5}$ m

5/6inch (读作 five sixths inch) $\frac{5}{6}$ in

Wire B has only *one half* as great a resistance as wire A. B 导线的电阻仅为 A 导线的 1/2。

By doubling the pressure we compressed the air to *one half of* its former volume. 通过把压强提高 1 倍,我们把空气压缩到其原体积的 1/2。

The new type of transistor operates about *one-third* faster than currently used devices. 新晶体管的操作速度比当前使用的器件约快 1/3。

If the radius of the coil were trebled, the field would be reduced to *one third* of its original strength. 假如线圈的半径增大到 3 倍,磁场强度会减少到其原强度的 1/3。

Nearly *three quarters* of the earth's surface is covered by water. 地表将近 3/4 为水所覆盖。

(2) 用…times,by a factor of…,或由-fold 构成的词。

当 times,by a factor of 或 -fold 与表示"减少"、"降低"、"小"、"少"这类词连用时,汉语习惯上常化作分数表达,一般不译作"减少……倍",而译作"减少……分之……"。例如:

Some steels can be drawn into wire *five times finer* than hair. 某些钢能被拉到头发丝的 1/5 那样细。

The moon has a mass nearly *one hundred times less* than the earth's. 月球的质量几乎是地球的 1%。

When the voltage is stepped-up by 10 times, the strength of the current is *stepped-down by 10 times.* 电压升高 10 倍,电流强度就会降低到 1/10。

During the next stroke, the air is compressed about *sixteen-fold*. 在下一冲程的过程里,空气被压缩到约为原体积的 1/16。

2．百分数的表示法

用基数词（整数或小数）＋percent（有时写成 per cent）。

fifty percent 50％

three percent 3％

zero point one two percent 0.12％

这里的 percent 前半部 per 表示"每一",后半部分 cent 表示"百",所以百分数中 percent 不用复数形式。

Water covers about *seventy percent* of the Earth's surface. 水覆盖地球表面的约 70％。

The world production of aluminum is only about *one per cent* of the world production of iron. 全世界的铝产量仅约为全世界铁产量的 1％。

3．"减少"的表示方法

英语所表示的"倍数减少",用汉语表示时,就不用"倍"来表达,而是采用分数或百分数表示,译为"减少到 1/n"或"减少了 ($n-1$)/n"。主要句型有(以 reduce 为例,n 表示倍数)：

reduce (by) n times   reduce by＋百分数/数字

be reduced n times   reduce n times as much/many…as

reduce by a factor of n n-fold reduction

reduce …n times n times less than

reduce to …(number)

例如：

When the space between the two conductors of a capacitor is occupied by a dielectric with the relative dielectric constant ε_r, it is found that the voltage between the plate *decreases by a factor of* ε_r. 如果电容器的两个极板间充满相对介电常数为 ε_r 的电介质,极板间的电压会减少到原来的 1/ε_r。

This kind of film *is twice thinner than* ordinary paper, but its quality is quite good. 这种胶片的厚度只是普通纸张的一半,可是质量相当好。

The instrument *is three times as* light as that one. 这个仪器比那个轻 2/3。或：这个仪器的重量是那个的 1/3。

The advantage of new-type equipment *is a 3-fold reduction* in volume. 新型设备的优点是体积小了 2/3。

当然,也可以使用"动词(decrease,reduce,come down,drop,fall,lower,cut 等)＋ to ＋百分数"、"百分数＋形容词的比较级＋than"、"百分数＋介词＋名词"的结构表示数量的减少,如：

By the year 2010, the annual rare earth output of the company is expected to *fall to* 35 *percent*. 预计到 2010 年,该公司的稀土年产量将下降 35％。

Unit Six

LESSON 21

21.1 物理学专业英语的翻译

21.1.1 翻译的总体原则

物理学专业英语是在物理学领域中进行国际学术交流的主要工具,而且其所涵盖的大量科技信息和专业术语在其他的学科中也有广泛的应用,因此在科技英语中占有重要的地位。总的来说,专业英语的翻译应力求客观、精确、通顺、简练,要充分注意其在词汇、句子、形态和文体方面的特点,以客观事物为中心,做到长而不乱,避免产生任何歧义。具体而言,翻译应力求用词上的准确明晰,论述上的逻辑严密,表述上的客观严谨,行文上的简洁通畅和修辞上的简单平实。词汇和结构是专业英语翻译的重点和难点,需要进行深入理解和反复推敲,同时注意知识的积累。只有在掌握与理解专业词汇和结构特点的基础上,恰当地使用翻译技巧,才能够达到翻译工作的基本要求。

整体上说,翻译过程包含三个阶段:理解、表述和校对。

理解包含对语法结构和逻辑关系的理解。掌握结构是基础,正确的逻辑分析才能够给出准确的翻译。由于物理学专业英语中长句较多,所以先进行结构分析会有助于理解逻辑关系。理解之后便是表述,无论采用直译还是意译,都应做到既忠实原文又表述得体。校对是必不可少的阶段,也是对前两个阶段的深化和推敲。物理学专业英语的翻译还有一个要点伴随始终,这就是专业的背景知识。语言是一种工具与桥梁,所传递的信息本身才是最重要的,优秀的译者必定要对所涉及的领域有足够的认识与理解。

翻译应首先力求正确与通达,然后才是行文的流畅、简洁和美感。因此翻译工作应遵循但不应拘泥于翻译的基本方法,应在"信"的基础上对译文进行调整与修饰,努力实现译文的"达"与"雅"。英语的各种基本翻译技巧均可以为物理学专业英语所用,例如直译、转换、省略、增补、合并、拆分等。在翻译中应将各种语法现象的基本翻译方法与翻译技巧相结合,对特殊或复杂的情况做恰当的处理,而不可一味套用固定的方法与结构。

在后面的篇幅中,我们将在专业术语、独立主格结构、名词化结构、分隔结构和长句这几个有代表性的方面,通过例子对物理学专业英语几种常见的翻译方法进行简单介绍,供读者参考。

21.1.2 物理学专业术语的翻译

词语是语言的基本要素,是信息的载体。物理学专业英语中大量使用专业术语,这些术语的意义较为固定和通用,是学术信息的载体。专业术语的翻译是准确理解专业文献的基础,更是专业写作时准确传递信息的关键。专业术语有一些基本的构成方式,了解这些方式有助于正确理解语义,同时有些词汇作为多义词在不同的语境中具有不同的含义,特别是在专业表述中有其特定的含义,需要进行认真的分析与选择。随着物理学的发展,新的专业词语也源源不断地产生,构成方式多种多样,构成的自由度也比以往更大,这就需要在平时的阅读中不断地总结和积累,并且在实际运用中以专业知识作为辅助。

1. 一般专业术语的翻译

(1) 音译

① 全部音译

物理学专业英语中很多材料的名称、物理量的计量单位(包括部分计量单位的前缀)、某些特殊方法等,通常均采用音译。例如:

ampere	安培(电流单位)
atto-	阿(托)(10^{-18})
farad	法拉(电容单位)
femto-	飞(母托)(10^{-15})
lux	勒克斯(光照度单位)
pico-	皮(可)(10^{-12})
pump	泵浦
roentgen	伦琴(辐射计量单位)
siemens	西门子(电导单位)
teflon	特氟隆

② 音译与意译结合

某些合成词包含人名、商标名或字母,一般名称和字母采取部分音译或直接保留,其余部分直译。例如:

Avogadro constant	阿伏伽德罗常数
Bose-Einstein condensate	玻色-爱因斯坦凝聚
Brinell hardness	布氏硬度
Bunsen burner	本生灯
Carnot engine	卡诺热机
Coriolis force	科里奥利力
β decay	β 衰变
Fahrenheit scale	华氏温标
Fermi level	费米能级
Photovoltaic	光生伏打效应
p-n junction	p-n 节
roentgen meter	伦琴计
Siemens heat	西门子热
Stokes' law	斯托克斯定律
Brookhaven National Laboratory	布鲁克海文国家实验室

这里要特别说明的是,除了为人们所熟知的著名科学家(历史人物)外,对于文献中的人名,应尽量采取保留英文拼写不变的方式,这可以提高译文的通用性,便于文献的检索和相关资料的查找。

(2) 形译与意译结合

某些物体、状态或方式是以其形状来命名的,在表示形状或状态时有些直接使用单词,有些则使用相似形象的英文字母,这类术语可以采取形译与意译相结合的方式来翻译,形译时可选择具有相应形状的汉字或物体。例如:

cross bit	十字钻头,X 形钻头
delta connection	三角形连接/△接法
D-iron	圆角槽铁
H-beam/T-beam	工字梁/丁字梁
I-shaped/I-section	工字形/工形截面
L-square/T-square	直角尺/丁字尺
thumbscrew	翼形螺钉
twist drill	螺丝钻,麻花钻
U-shaped magnet/U-trap	马蹄形磁铁(U 形磁铁)/虹吸管
Y-shaped network/Y-connection	星形电路/星形连接

(3) 组合+直译

很多专业术语是将几个单词直接组合在一起构成的,这类术语很多,构成方式也很多,例如:名词+名词,形容词+名词,分词+名词,名词+分词等。这些术语一般可采用直译的方式,直接将几个词的词义组合在一起,但为了做到翻译的准确与专业,应分析各单词之间的逻辑关系,选择最为恰当的表述。例如:

diffraction grating	衍射光栅(名词+名词)
condensation point	凝点(名词+名词)
beam current density	束流密度(名词+名词+名词)
constructive interference	相长干涉(形容词+名词)
computational physics	计算物理学(形容词+名词)
simple harmonic motion	简谐运动(形容词+形容词+名词)
convertible unsymmetrical anastigmat	可变半对称消相差镜组(形容词+形容词+名词)
alternating current	交流电(现在分词+名词)
heat resisting	耐热(的)(名词+现在分词)
battery-powered	电池供电的(名词+过去分词)

2. 缩略词的翻译

科技进步要求信息传递的通用、快捷,而缩略词通用性强,简洁明了,因此在专业文献中被广泛使用。缩略词的翻译一般采取音译,意译或保留原来的缩写部分不变的方式,但通用性不高的缩略形式应在文章中首次使用时予以说明。

(1) 音译

某些术语的构成和意译都比较复杂,因此其缩略形式和音译已经被广泛使用并当作固定词汇,这类缩略词可直接采用音译,而无须注明其完整形式。例如:

radar	雷达	radio detecting and ranging
laser	镭射（激光）	light amplification by stimulated emission of radiation
sonar	声纳	sound navigation and ranging

（2）意译或保留缩写形式

当缩略词的意译表述并不太复杂时，可以采取意译，但也可以在汉语表述中保留缩写形式不变，或仅在首次使用时给出意译进行解释，其后使用缩写形式。例如：

laser	激光，这是更为通用的译法
BCS theory	BCS 理论（Bardeen，Cooper，Schrieffer 建立的一种超导微观理论）
BSCCO	铋锶钙铜氧 bismuth strontium calcium copper oxide
CD	光盘 compact disc
CMOS	互补型金属氧化物半导体 complementary metaloxide semi-conductor
EDFA	掺铒光纤放大器 erbium-doped fibre anplifier
Fortran language	Fortran 语言 formula translation language
GPS	全球定位系统 global positioning system
IC	集成电路 integrated circuit
LCD	液晶显示器 liquid crystal display
LED	发光二极管 light emitting diode
LSI	大规模集成电路 large scale integration
NMR	核磁共振 nuclear magnetic resonance
SEM	扫描电镜 scanning electron microscope
SQUID	超导量子干涉仪 superconducting quantum interference device
STM	扫描隧道显微镜 scanning tunneling microscope
TBA	紧束缚近似 tight binding approximation
TEM	透射电镜 transmission electron microscope
WDM	波分复用 wavelength division multiplexing
XRD	X 射线衍射 X-ray diffraction
YBCO	钇钡铜氧 yttrium barium copper oxide

3．多义词的翻译

意译是物理学专业词汇翻译的一个重要方法，而正确的意译需要专业背景知识这个至关重要的因素，对于多义词的翻译更是如此。应根据文章所涉及的领域和背景、原词所涉及的概念或事实进行仔细推敲，正确选择符合句子含义或文章内容的科学概念，这些概念可能与非专业英语中的常用含义有所不同。例如：

argument	自变量
balance	天平
bank angle	自转角
bus	母线，总线
butterfly	蝶形突变
drum	鼓轮
family	族
finger	测厚规，指针

fork	音叉
grain	晶粒
hair	游丝
host	基质
moment	矩,力矩
monkey chatter	邻道干扰
normal	法线,垂直的,正交的
phosphors	荧光粉
plane	平面
spring	弹簧
transition	跃迁
work	功

21.2 专业英语阅读

21.2.1 The Nature of Light(光的本性)

Since the beginning of the present century, an increasing degree of uncertainty about the wave theory of light has been developing due to the discovery of the photoelectric effect, the quantum theory, and a number of allied phenomena, and due also to a detailed investigation into the nature and physical properties of the ether. Also, during this period a great deal has been learned about the structures of the atom which is not altogether limited to a wave picture of light. Hence the photon, or a light corpuscle, has been postulated.

Maxwell discovered that light is a wavelike disturbance in the electromagnetic field that travels at constant speed c in vacuum. Before Maxwell's insight shed light on the nature of light, philosophers debated its character, artists gloried in it, astronomers used it, and scientists were intrigued by it. Long before the idea of the electromagnetic field was born, people speculated about the nature and properties of light—the phenomenon that reveals all that we can see. The ancient Greeks thought light was fire, one of the four basic elements. Plato considered light to be streamers or filaments emitted by the eye. The Pythagoreans thought that light traveled from an object to one's eyes in the form of very fine particles, or corpuscles. The Greeks observed that objects cast sharp shadows and concluded that light travels in straight lines. As master geometers, the Greeks were also aware of the fact that the intensity of light decreases inversely as the square of the distance from the source. To them the particle description of light adequately fitted observations.

The particle theory remained essentially unchallenged until the seventeenth century. In 1678 Christian Huygens, a Dutch scientist, formally proposed that many of his predecessors had suspected—that light is a wavelike disturbance. Just as water waves travel form one point to another without water actually being moved from one point to the other, Huygens considered light to be waving in a medium he called the luminiferous aether. Huygens's ideas were not mere speculation. They commanded attention because he could describe many properties of light with the wave theory. The key to Huygens's theory of light was a geometric method of determining the shape of a wavefront at any time from knowledge of the wavefront at some earlier time.

A **wavefront** is the set of all points of equal phase. The phase of any wave is the argument in the functional form of the wave. For example, we learned that plane waves traveling with speed u can be described by an equation of the form $y(z, t) = f(z-ut)$.

The phase is $z-ut$, and a wavefront is the set of points in the zt plane satisfying $z-ut =$ constant, in this case a family of straight lines. A point source of light produces spherical wavefronts, as Fig. 21-1(a). Sufficiently far from the source, the radii of the spherical wavefronts are so large that the waves appear as plane waves, as shown in Fig. 21-1(b).

The general problem of following the propagation of electromagnetic waves is extremely complicated. Some of the simpler aspects of the problem are embodied in a fundamental principle enunciated by Huygens called **Huygens's Principle**: *Every point on a wavefront can be regarded as a new source of spherical waves that spread out in all directions with the same speed and frequency as the original wave.*

Fig. 21-2 (a) and (b) illustrate this principle for spherical and plane waves, respectively. Any point on a wavefront generates new spherical waves called wavelets. During the time interval equal to one period of the wave, each wavelet travels one wavelength. To construct the new wavefront, first draw wavelets as hemispheres of radius one wavelength from each point on the original wavefront. The surface tangent to all the wavelets represents the new wavefront that has moved one wavelength. Of course, in this construction we ignored wavelets moving backward toward the source, because they are not observed. It was not until 1826 that Fresnel showed that the disturbance did not propagate backward because of interference effects. In 1883 Kirchhoff proved by mathematical analysis that the secondary waves from the individual sources destroy one another by interference except at the wavefront itself, so the wave is propagated only in the direction away from its source.

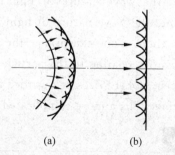

Fig. 21-1 (a) A point source of light creates spherical wavefronts. (b) Far from the source the wavefronts appears as planes

Fig. 21-2 Huygens's construction of wavefronts for (a) a spherical wave and (b) a plane wave

The ancients believed that light could be represented by straight lines called *rays*. In Huygens's construction, the rays are along the direction of propagation of the wavelets. They are lines perpendicular to the wavefronts.

21.2.2 The Wave-Particle Duality(波粒二象性)

A particle on the classical view is a concentration of energy and other properties in space and time, whereas a wave is spread out over a larger region of space and time. The question whether light are streams of particles (corpuscles) or waves is a very old one. This "either-or" formulation was classically natural and alien to the advanced "both-and" even the "neither-nor" solution of today. Early in the nineteenth century experiments were suggested and made to show that light is a wave motion. A key figure in this endeavour was Thomas Young, one of the most intelligent and clever scientists ever to live, who studied diffraction and interference of light already in 1803 with results that gave strong support to the wave theory of Christian Huygens as opposed to the particle or corpuscular theory of Isaac Newton. Further contributions were made by many other researchers, among them Augustin Jean Fresnel, who showed that light is a transverse wave.

Newton's theory of light had seemed suitable to explain the straight-line casting of sharp shadows of objects placed in a light beam. But wave theory was needed to explain interference where the light intensity can be enhanced in some places and diminished in other places behind a screen with a slit or several slits. The wave theory is also able to account for the fact that the edges of a shadow are not quite sharp.

The mathematical theory of electromagnetism by James Clerk Maxwell, set up in 1864, led to the view that light is of electromagnetic nature, propagating as a wave from the source to the receiver. Heinrich Hertz discovered experimentally the existence of electromagnetic waves at radio-frequencies in the 1880s. Maxwell died in 1879 and Hertz died only 37 years old in 1894, two years before Alfred Nobel's death.

At the end of the 19th century, which also is the time when the Nobel Prizes were instituted, the wave nature of light seemed definitely established. Thus the decisive research into the wave nature of light came too early to be considered for Nobel Prizes. However, there is one exception—the case of X-rays.

Discoveries relating to the particle nature of light belong to our century and thus one might expect Nobel Prizes be awarded for such achievements. This is almost true—but the Nobel archive tells a more complicated story as will be uncovered.

Glossary

photoelectric effect	光电效应	postulate	假定
wavelike	波状的	shed light on	阐明
intrigue	困惑	streamer	飘带
filament	细丝、长丝	emit	发射

Pythagoreans	毕达哥拉斯学派	corpuscle	微粒
geometer	几何学家	intensity of light	光的强度
luminiferous aether	传光的以太	wavefront	波前
argument	自变量	phase	相位
propagation	传播	embody	具体表达,使具体化
enunciate	系统阐明,明确表达	Huygens's Principle	惠更斯原理
wavelet	子波	hemisphere	半圆
Fresnel	菲涅尔	interference	干涉
Kirchoff	基尔霍夫	ray	（光）线
Thomas Young	托马斯·杨	diffraction	衍射
transverse wave	横波	enhance	加强
diminish	降低,减弱	slit	狭缝
Nobel Prizes	诺贝尔奖		

21.3 专业英语常用表达-21 光学常用实验仪器

Abbe refractometer 阿贝折射计
autocollimator 自准直仪
battery of lens 透镜组
biprism 双棱镜
blazed grating 闪耀光栅
concave lens 凹透镜
convex lens, positive lens 凸透镜
diaphragm 光阑
diffractometer 衍射仪
dispersion prism 色散棱镜
double-slit interferometer 双缝干涉仪
eye lens 接目镜
eyepiece 目镜
Fabry-Perot interferometer 法布里-珀罗干涉仪
Fourier grating 傅里叶光栅
Fresnel's biprism 菲涅耳双棱镜
grating 光栅
half wave plate 半波片
holographic grating 全息光栅
interferometer 干涉仪
laser 激光
lens 透镜
Michelson interferometer 迈克尔逊干涉仪
micrometer 显微镜
monochrometer 单色仪
multi-beam interferometer 多光束干涉仪
objective lens 物镜
optical bench 光具座
optical filter 滤光片
optical lever 光杠杆
optical table 光学平台
photometer 光度计
polarimeter 旋光仪
polaroid 偏振片
prism 棱镜
quarter wave plate 四分之一波片
Rayleigh refractometer 瑞利折射计
reading micrometer 读数显微镜
reflection grating 反射光栅
reflectometer 反射仪
refractometer 折射仪
scatterometer 散射仪
spectrometer 光谱仪/分光计
telescope 望远镜
thin lens, shallow lens 薄透镜
transmission grating 透射光栅
triple prism 三棱镜

vertometer 屈度计　　　　　　　　　X-ray diffractometer　X 射线衍射仪
white-light interferometer　白光干涉仪

LESSON 22

22.1 物理学专业英语中名词化结构的翻译

名词化现象是英语表达中的一种常见而又独特的语言现象,能够高度概括事物的本质,适合于表述现象、过程、性质、特征、原因和结果等,因此是物理学专业英语中重要的语法现象。其简洁、客观、正式、严密的表达可以充分的体现物理学科的严谨性、逻辑性和权威性,同时也可以简化复杂的句子结构。名词化结构同时具有名词和其他词性的功能,正确的翻译有利于信息的准确传递和对外文资料的正确理解。

名词化结构的翻译应考虑其不同的语法功能和结构特点,并结合专业知识的背景,使译文符合汉语的习惯与要求,在翻译中应先分析其地位、作用和与其他成分的关系。一些复杂的名词化结构实际上是浓缩的句子,翻译时要先理清主干和层次,并且应避免直接套用原文的结构,因为那样往往会造成译文的臃肿晦涩。只有将实际的内容、语境与翻译的方法、技巧进行良好的整合才能够得到恰当的译文。

22.1.1 动词名词化

在物理学专业英语中,动词的名词化结构最为常见,形式也比较丰富。这种名词化结构具有动词和名词的功能,名词特征使行文简洁,而动词含义则使事实表述准确,其中文词性和意义在翻译中可以灵活的处理。

1. 动作名词

动作名词指具有动词含义的名词。往往这类单词本身就具有动词和名词两种词性,翻译时应综合分析动作名词与其他成分之间的逻辑关系及其在句中的作用,将动作名词翻译为动词或是名词,并根据汉语表述的实际需要来选择通顺、易于理解的译文。

Electric current is the rate of charge *flow* past a given point in an electric circuit. 电流是单位时间内流经电路中某定点的电量。(*flow* 译为动词)

The *flow* of charge is from the positive to the negative plate when the capacitor is discharged. 放电时电荷的流动是从电容器的正极到负极。(*flow* 译为名词)或译为:放电时,电荷从电容器正极流向负极。

2. 动词的派生名词

动词的派生名词由动词加上 -ment,-tion,-ance,-ence,-sm,-y,-ity,-ness,-ability 等后缀构成,这种派生名词大量存在,在句中可与其他成分构成各种逻辑关系。

（1）派生名词＋介词＋名词

在这种结构中,如果介词后的名词在逻辑语义上是派生名词的主语,则可译为主谓结构;如果介词后的名词在逻辑语义上是派生名词的宾语,则可译为动宾结构。

The velocity *dependence of the air friction* may be very complicated so only some special cases can be treated analytically. 空气阻力随速度的变化非常复杂,因此只有一些特殊情况可以进行解析处理。(译为主谓结构,air friction 作 dependence 的逻辑主语)

The *formation of images* by lenses and eyes is on the base of the *refraction of light*. 镜头和眼睛通过光的折射成像。(formation of images 译为动宾结构,images 作 formation 的逻辑宾语;refraction of light 译为主谓结构,light 是 refraction 的逻辑主语)

The antirust paint has a *resistance to corrosion* by air or water. 防锈漆可以防止空气或水的腐蚀。(译为动宾结构,corrosion 作 resistance 的逻辑宾语)

The *superimposition of a small drift velocity by the applied electric field* on the free electron explains why the current is proportional to the voltage. 电流与电压成正比是由于外加电场在自由电子上叠加了一个很小的漂移速度。(句中有两层此类的名词化结构,其中 superimposition+of a small drift velocity 译为动宾结构,而 superimposition+by the applied electric field 则译为主谓结构)

(2) 介词+派生名词

这种介词短语形式的名词化结构在句中可以表示时间、原因、条件、目的、方式、让步等,因此可译成相应的状语成分或状语从句。

The formation of rainbow is due *to dispersion* of sunlight by water droplets in the atmosphere. 彩虹的形成是由于大气中的水滴对阳光的色散。(原因状语)

Ballistic curve is the actual trajectory *in presence of* air resistance. 弹道曲线是空气阻力存在情况下的实际轨迹。(条件状语)

The electric potential at any point in space produced by any number of point charges can be calculated *from the point charge expression by simple addition* since voltage is a scalar quantity. 既然电势是标量,多个点电荷在空间某点产生的电势就可以通过单个点电荷表达式的简单叠加来计算。(方式状语)

(3) 派生名词+短语或从句

此时派生名词前往往存在一个不表意的动词,与该派生名词构成动宾关系,因此这种结构中的派生名词往往译成动词。

The noise gives an *indication that* the signals are being disturbed. 噪声表明信号正受到干扰。(接从句)

The noise gives an *indication of* the disturbance to signals. 噪声表明信号正受到干扰。(接短语)

The existence of magnetic domains gives an *explanation to* the magnetic hysteresis. 磁畴结构的存在解释了磁滞现象。(注意其中 existence of magnetic domains 也是名词化结构,属于"派生名词+介词+名词"的情况)

The friction with air leads to the *decrescence of* the speed. 摩擦导致速率减小。(注意其中 friction with air 也是名词化结构,属于"派生名词+介词+名词"的情况)

(4) 名词+派生名词

英语中这种结构很多,应根据名词和派生名词的逻辑关系进行翻译。

① 如果前面的名词对派生名词起到修饰的作用,短语可改写为"派生名词+介词+名词"的形式,则可翻译成以派生名词为中心词的名词短语,前面的名词作为前置定语。

Once the cars are lifted to the top of the hill, gravity takes over and the remainder of the ride is an experience in *energy transformation*. 一旦车被开至山顶，重力就起主要的作用，其余的路程便是能量转化的过程。（斜体部分意为 transformation of energy）

Electrostatic shielding effectively reduces the *signal disturbance*. 静电屏蔽有效地减小了信号干扰。（斜体部分意为 disturbance to signal）

The number of significant digits does not change in the decimal *unit conversion*. 十进制的单位换算中有效数字位数不变。（斜体部分意为 conversion of unit）

② 如果名词在逻辑含义上是派生名词的宾语，则可以翻译成动宾短语。

Voltage division circuits are more often used in that case. 在这种情况下更多的使用分压电路。（voltage 是 division 的逻辑宾语）

Heat pump technology is effective for *energy efficiency improvement*. 热泵技术能够有效地提高能效。（energy efficiency 是 improvement 的逻辑宾语）

（5）动词（短语）+派生名词

这种用法中的动词一般没有明显的实际含义，只作为形式上的谓语，因此可以直接将动词的派生名词译为相应的谓语成分。值得一提的是，有很多这种形式的名词化结构已经成为了固定搭配，如 bear relation to, make use of, find application in, come into collision (with), give cause/rise to, give effect to, come into action, take into consideration 等。短语的含义均来自于名词化的动词，例如：

Laser spectroscopy has *led to advances* in the precision of the measurement of the spectral line frequencies. 激光光谱提高了谱线频率的测量精度。

The measurement of the sound velocity in some medium *bears close relation to* the temperature because of the changing state of the medium along with the temperature. 由于介质的状态随温度变化，因此声速的测量结果与温度密切相关。

The resultant external force *gives cause/rise to* the change of the velocity. 合外力导致速度的变化。

The hydrostatic weighing *makes use of* the Archimedean principle. 流体静力称衡法利用了阿基米德原理。

3. 动名词

动名词的动词性更强，一般可翻译成动词，但由于包含动名词的名词化结构往往可以改写为包含相应派生名词的名词化结构，因此亦可参照这些结构的翻译方法来翻译，并且根据动名词在句中所起的作用，以及与其他成分的关系来确定译文。

The function of the rheochord in the circuit is *current limiting*. 电路中滑线变阻器的作用是限流。

Heat pump technology is effective for *improving energy efficiency*. 热泵技术能够有效地提高能效。

Doing work and *transferring heat* are the two ways for *changing* the internal energy of a system. 做功与传热是改变系统内能的两种途径。

22.1.2　形容词名词化

形容词名词化结构在专业英语中使用的也较多，该结构具有名词词性，可以做主语、宾语、同位语等，既有形容词生动形象的表意功能，又满足科技文体表述严谨的要求。

1. 形容词的派生名词

物理学中有很多由形容词加上-ness,-ity,-ancy,-ency,-ce,-th,-ism 等词缀构成的派生名词，通常表示抽象概念，如状态、性质、程度、学科等，其中大部分已经被视作普通的名词，可直译为名词。

In physics, *intensity* is a measure of the time-averaged energy flux. 物理学中，强度是时均能流的量度。

In *electromagnetism*, *permeability* is the degree of magnetization of a material that responds linearly to an applied magnetic field. 在电磁学中，磁导率是材料对外磁场线性响应的磁化程度。

Electrical *conductance* is dependent on the electrical *conductivity* and the geometric dimensions of the conducting object. 电导与导体的电导率及几何尺寸有关。（句中 conductance 是动词的派生名词，conductivity 是形容词的派生名词，注意二者在词义上的区别，conductance 强调性质，而 conductivity 强调能力）

2. the＋形容词

在英语中，"the＋形容词"的结构通常用于表示具有相应特点的一类事物，而在物理学专业英语中，这种结构实际上通常是名词结构"the＋形容词＋名词"的省略形式，而且往往并列使用，其中的名词由于已经在句中被提及而省略，以避免表述上的重复，在翻译时可以酌情进行补充。

The combined uncertainty synthetically reflects the two kinds of errors, *the systematic* and *the random*. 合成不确定度综合地反映了系统误差与随机误差。（省略了 error）

In the center-of-mass system, the curvilinear motion has two velocity components, *the tangential* and *the normal*. 在质心坐标系中曲线运动有切向和法向两个速度分量。（省略了 component）

22.2　专业英语阅读

22.2.1　Reflection and Refraction（反射与折射）

The Huygens principle is not intuitively obvious, but it gained acceptance because it could be used to explain the laws of reflection and refraction, two phenomena concerning light that had been observed since antiquity. The ancient Greeks observed that when a ray of light is reflected by a mirror, the angle of incidence is equal to the angle of reflection. This is illustrated in Fig. 22-1(a), where θ_i denotes the angle of incidence and θ_r the angle of reflection, the angles between the light ray and a line perpendicular to the mirror. The law of reflection states that $\theta_i = \theta_r$.

Fig. 22-1 (a) Reflection of light, (b) Refraction of light

Fig. 22-1(b) illustrates the concept of refraction. When a light ray passes from one transparent medium, such as air, into another of different density, such as water, the ray is bent or *refracted*. When refraction takes place, the angle of incidence θ_i and the angle of refraction θ_t are different. (The subscript t in θ_t suggests transmitted light.) Ptolemy had observed that for a given pair of media, such as air and water, the ratio of the angles θ_i/θ_t is nearly constant. We now know this is true only for small angles. Kepler and others made numerous measurements in an attempt to find a relation that would hold for all angles. That relation, discovered experimentally in 1621 by a Dutch mathematician Willebrord Snell, is called **Snell's law** and states that for a given pair of media the ratio $\sin\theta_i/\sin\theta_t$ is constant.

Although the Huygens principle can be used to explain both these laws, they can be explained more simply by another principle stated by Fermat in 1657. This is called **Fermat's principle of least time** and it states that a ray of light traveling in any combination of media follows the path that minimizes its total travel time. The next two examples show how Fermat's principle implies both the law of reflection and Snell's law of refraction.

A convenient number that characterizes the behavior of light in a medium is the *index of refraction* of the medium, denoted by the symbol n. by definition, the index of refraction is the ration of the speed of light in vacuum to the speed of light in the medium,

$$n = c/v \qquad (22-1)$$

If light travels in a medium with index of refraction n_i and is refracted in a medium with index of refraction n_t, the general form of Snell's law of refraction is

$$n_i \sin\theta_i = n_t \sin\theta_t \qquad (22-2)$$

In general, n depends on the wavelength (and therefore the color) of the light. A vivid illustration of this property is the separation of white light into a rainbow of colors by a prism. This property of waves is known as **dispersion.** For air at standard temperature and pressure the index is nearly 1. It has very nearly the same value for all visible light.

Fig. 22-2 shows a number of rays from a point source in one medium of refractive index n_1 impinging on the surface of another medium of refractive index n_2, where $n_1 > n_2$. Snell's law implies

Fig. 22-2 The critical angle θ_c is the angle of incidence for which the angle of refraction is 90°. For angles greater than θ_c there is total internal reflection

where $\sin\theta_t > \sin\theta_i$ because $n_1/n_2 > 1$. For some incident angle θ_i less than 90° we have $\sin\theta_t = 1$ and hence $\theta_t = 90°$, which means the transmitted light travels parallel to the interface. This value of θ_i is called *critical angle* θ_c. When $\theta_i > \theta_c$, all the light is reflected, as shown in Fig. 22-2.

22.2.2 Interference of Light Waves(光波的干涉)

Despite Huygens's success in describing the propagation of light in terms of waves, many scientists advocated a corpuscular theory of light. Most notable among them was Isaac Newton who thought that light was best described as a stream of particles emitted by the light source. He objected to the wave theory because it did not explain why light travels in straight lines. In a lengthy dialogue with Huygens, Newton argued that if a hole is placed between a source of light and a screen, the patch of light on the screen has the same shape as the hole. One would expect this effect if light traveled in straight lines like tiny particles emitted by the source and absorbed by the screen. On the other hand, he argued, if light were truly a wave, it should bend around the hole and not produce a sharp shadow. Newton also asserted that because light travels through an evacuated glass container, light could not be a wave because waves require a medium in which to travel.

In response to Newton's objections, Huygens contended that if the wavelength of light is extremely small—much smaller than the dimensions of the object on which it shines, then bending of the waves would be too minute to observe and the object would cast sharp shadows. As far as light traveling in vacuum, Huygens replied that waves travel in the aether, a medium that permeates all of space and that is not removed when a container is evacuated.

The wave-particle controversy continued into the twentieth century when it was shown that light has the dual nature of both particles and waves. The first convincing experimental evidence for the wave nature of light appeared early in the nineteenth century in the classical investigations on interference by Thomas Young and Augustin Fresnel.

A physician by training, Young was also a self-educated linguist and natural philosopher. He made original studies of the eye while still in medical school, and his doctoral thesis dealt with the physics of sound as it relates to the human voice. In 1802, he found an ingenious way to demonstrated that light exhibits the phenomenon of interference.

When two waves encounter one another, their effects add according to the principle of superposition. If two waves are in phase at some point, they reinforce each other there, with crests adding on crests, thereby creating a stronger wave. This is called **constructive interference**. When two waves are exactly out of phase at some point, with crest arriving on top of trough, they can cancel each other and produce no light intensity at that point. This is called **destructive interference**.

Young demonstrated interference of light with two slits separated by a small distance and illuminated by light from a single source. He passed sun light through first the single slit, producing a narrow beam of light. He directed the light emerging from the single slit onto two narrow slits, and observed the result on a distant screen. The resulting interference pattern is a series of alternating bright and dark bands. Young never worked out a detailed mathematical description of interference. Instead, he drew elaborate diagrams of wave fronts to explain his observations. The task of rigorously establishing a theory was taken up later in the century by the French physicist Augustin Fresnel, who synthesized Huygens's wave description with the principle of interference. After his studies in interference, Young ventured to Egypt with Napoleon and deciphered the Rosetta Stone, which advanced the decoding of hieroglyphics.

Glossary

intuitively	直观地	antiquity	古代
angle of incidence	入射角	angle of reflection	反射角
transparent	透明的	transmitted light	透射光
Snell's law	斯涅尔定律	index of refraction	折射率
Fermat's principle of least time	费马最小时间原理	prism	棱镜
dispersion	色散	impinge	冲击,撞击
refractive index	折射率	critical angle	临界角
angle of refraction	折射角	corpuscular theory	微粒说
lengthy	冗长的	assert	主张
evacuated	真空的	objection	反对
contend	争辩,坚持认为	vacuum	真空
permeate	弥漫,渗透	controversy	争论,争议
dual nature	二象性	interference	干涉
ingenious	巧妙的,独创的	demonstrate	演示,证明

principle of superposition	叠加原理	in phase	同相
reinforce	加强	crest	波峰
constructive interference	相长干涉	out of phase	异相
trough	波谷	cancel	抵消
light intensity	光强	destructive interference	相消干涉
interference pattern	干涉图样	wave front	波前
rigorously	严格地	synthesize	综合,合成
decipher	破译	Rosetta Stone	罗塞塔石碑
hieroglyphics	象形文字		

22.3 专业英语常用表达-22 极值 约略数

1. 极值的表示

(1) 达到 as ...as + number

H. K. Onnes discovered in 1911 that the resistance of the mercury suddenly disappeared when cooled to a temperature *as low as* 268.98℃ below zero which was later called superconductivity. 昂内斯在1911年发现,当温度低至零下268.98℃时,水银的电阻突然消失,这一现象称为超导。

(2) 直到 up to + number

Under different conditions, the results of the experiment varied wildly from as little as 20 percent of normal *up to* as high as 90 percent of normal. 在不同的条件下,实验结果可以从正常值的20%变化到正常值的90%。

(3) 至少 at least + number

In order to obtain reliable data the experiment should be conducted *at least* 10 times under the same conditions. 为获得可靠的数据,应在相同条件下至少测量10次。

(4) 最大 at most + number

The magnetic field should be strictly controlled so that the deviation of the exciting current is *at most* 0.5A. 应严格控制磁场,以使励磁电流的偏差不超过0.5A。

(5) 最大值和最小值 *maximum* and *minimum* （用作形容词或名词）

Neither the *maximum* possible temperature nor the *minimum* one should be out of the range of the thermometer. （用作形容词）

Neither the *maximum* nor the *minimum* of the possible temperatures should be out of the range of the thermometer. （用作名词）

最高和最低温度均不可超过温度计的量程。

(6) 上限与下限 *the upper limit* and *the lower limit*

This is a new method for dynamic measurement of thermocouples protected by metal tube, which can be used to raise the *upper limit* of the temperature greatly. 这是一种动态测量带保护管的热电偶温度的新方法,可大大提高测温上限。

(7) 增至最大和减至最小 *to maximize* and *to minimize*

To minimize the error of the experimental result, the precisions of all the measuring apparatus should be upgraded to the appropriate level according to the principle of equipartition for the uncertainty. 为将测量结果的误差减至最小,所有测量仪器的精度应该按照不确定度均分原理提高到适当的等级。

2. 约略数的表示

(1) 以基数词的复数形式来表示：

the early/mid-/late 70s　70 年代初期/中期/晚期

the early/mid-/late 1970s　20 世纪 70 年代初期/中期/晚期

teens/twenties/fifties　十几/二十几/五十几

dozens of/scores of　数十/几十

hundreds of　数百/几百/成百上千

thousands of　数千/几千/成千上万

tens of thousands of　数万/几万

hundreds of thousands of　数十万/几十万

millions of　数百万/几百万

tens of millions of　数千万/几千万

millions and millions of　亿万

(2) 添加表示近似的词或短语来表示：

about(around/approximately/some/nearly/roughly/almost) three meters　大约 3 m

more than/over/above 40 grams　40 多克

less than/under/below 40 grams　不到 40 g

more than a quarter/one third　四分之一强/三分之一强

upward/upwards of 60　60 以上/多于 60

40 milliliters or so　40 ml 左右

20 seconds or more/or less　20 s 以上/以下

an hour more or less　1 h 左右

of the order of 3000 volts　约为 3000 V

(3) 以表示范围的短语来表示：

greater than/less than　大于/小于

be equal or greater than/be equal or less than　大于等于/小于等于

not more than/not less than　不大于/不小于

of the order of...　约为……

range from...to.../range between...and...　范围在……之间(谓语)

with a range of ...to ...　范围在……之间(定语或状语)

vary from ...to .../vary between ...and ...　从……变化至……

(4) "数量级"的表示：

order of magnitude, scale, level, order　数量级

one order/two orders of magnitude　一个/两个数量级

at the same level/at the same order (of magnitude)　在同一数量级上

the increase/decrease of three orders (of magnitude)　三个数量级的增加/减少

increase/decrease by one order of magnitude　增加/减少一个数量级
microscopic/astronomic scale　微观尺度/天文尺度的数量级
one order higher than …　比……高一个数量级
the scale of millisecond/the millisecond scale/the order of millisecond　毫秒数量级

LESSON 23

23.1 物理学专业英语中独立主格结构和分隔结构的翻译

23.1.1 独立主格结构的翻译

独立主格结构是一种很常见也很重要的语法现象，主要用于正式文体，可用于描绘事实，使行文紧凑简洁、表达清楚、形象具体，因此在专业文献中使用较多，其正确翻译在专业英语阅读与写作中都显得非常重要。

独立主格结构的实质是具有独立主语的非限定分句和无动词分句，属于从属结构，在意义上相当于一个从句，通常在句中充当状语，表示时间、条件、原因、结果、方式和伴随状况等。独立主格结构可位于句首或句末(偶见于句中)，通常用逗号(或破折号)与主句分开，其主语与主句的主语一般不同。多个独立主格结构可以同时存在，通常把表示概括意义的结构置于最后。在独立结构中作主语的名词词组有时可以省去限定词。

独立主格结构可以根据不同的标准来分类，例如按照结构中是否含有动词成分可以分为两种，一种采用与动词有关的现在分词、过去分词和不定式，而另一种则采用与动词无关的形容词和介词短语等；或按照独立结构在句中作状语所表示的不同含义进行分类，如表示时间、条件、原因、结果、方式和伴随状况等。各种分类方式并不能截然分开，无论是否采用动词，均可以表示各种状语含义。因此在翻译时，应在理解逻辑关系的基础上，根据所表示的含义译为相应的状语，或直接译为句子。

1. 含有动词成分的独立主格结构

对于这种类型的独立结构，首先要分析独立成分与主句间的逻辑关系，如果独立主格结构用于表示时间、条件、原因，可以增加相应的连词，翻译成状语从句；若独立主格结构表示方式或伴随状况，则一般用来对主句加以补充，可以直接译为一个独立或并列的句子。

(1) 主语＋现在分词

在逻辑上，主语与现在分词之间为主谓关系，独立结构中的现在分词一般表示正在进行的动作，当独立结构中的动作发生在主句谓语动作之前时，应采用完成时态的现在分词。

The atoms are grouped into tiny domains, each containing magnetically aligned atoms. 原子被分成很多微小的磁畴，每个磁畴都包含由于磁化而整齐排列的原子。(独立结构表示状态，译为一个并列的句子)

(2) 主语＋过去分词

在逻辑上，主语与过去分词之间为动宾关系，独立结构中的过去分词一般表示被动的关系或已经发生的动作。

The two balls stuck together after collision, *a way called perfectly inelastic collision*. 两个球在碰撞后粘在一起,这种碰撞称为完全非弹性碰撞。(独立结构表示方式,过去分词表示被动,译为一个并列的句子)

(3) 主语+动词不定式

在逻辑上,主语与动词不定式之间为主谓关系,独立结构中的不定式一般表示将要发生的动作,即独立结构中的动作发生在主句谓语动作之后。

In Compton scattering, there is a perfectly elastic collision between the incident photon and an atom, *the atom's energy to increase* and *the photon's energy to decrease*. 在康普顿散射中,入射光子与电子间发生完全弹性碰撞,原子的能量增加而光子的能量减少。(不定式表示结果,译为两个并列短句)

2. 不含动词成分的独立主格结构

(1) 主语+形容词

这种结构形式上没有动词介入,实质上相当于一个"主语+系动词+形容词"的系表结构中省略了系动词 being,翻译时可以直接表达独立主语所处的某种状态,或增加适当的动词来表示这种状态,译为状语或并列的句子均可。

The terminal posts of an apparatus are usually in different colors, *the positive red* and *the negative black*. 仪器的接线端通常使用不同的颜色,正极为红色,负极为黑色。(译为并列短句)

(2) 主语+介词短语

这种结构形式上同样没有动词介入,实质上相当于一个"主语+系动词+介词短语"的系表结构中省略了系动词 being,或是"主语+动词+介词短语"结构中省略了动词,在翻译时可以适当添加动词,译为状语或并列的句子。

The oscilloscope can be used to show the hysteresis loop of the ferromagnetic material, *the voltage proportional to the magnetic field into the channel* 1, *the voltage proportional to the magnetic induction into channel* 2, and scanning area set at *X-Y* position. 示波器可以用于显示铁磁材料的磁滞回线,与磁场成正比的电压输入通道1,与磁感应强度成正比的电压输入通道2,扫描范围设置为 X-Y 位置。(译为并列短句,注意最后一个独立主格结构 scanning area set at X-Y nosition 属于"名词+过去分词"的情况)

3. 由 with/without 引导的独立主格结构

一般来说,通常表示方式或伴随状况的独立主格结构可以转换为由 with 引导的介词词组,而表示否定意义的独立主格结构可转换为由 without 引导的介词词组。并且,在很多情况下 with 可以省略,并可同时省略 with 所引导的介词短语中的名词修饰语。

In the thermal radiation, vibrating and spinning molecules in one object give off electromagnetic radiation, *with the energy absorbed by molecules in another object*.

在热辐射过程中,物体中振动与自旋的分子发出电磁辐射,其能量被其他物体的分子所吸收。(表示结果,译为一个并列的句子,句中 with 可省略)

The two balls collide in a way of perfectly inelastic collision, *with most kinetic energy lost during the course*. 两球发生完全非弹性碰撞的过程中动能损失最多。(表示伴随的状

况,原来的主干部分译为状语,句中 with 可省略)或译为:两球的碰撞方式为动能损失最多的完全非弹性碰撞。(翻译时改变主语,独立主格成分译为定语)

The two balls collide in a way of perfectly elastic collision, *without any kinetic energy loss during the course.* 两球发生完全弹性碰撞,过程中没有动能损失。(表示伴随的状况,译为一个并列的句子,原句可以改为否定形式:…, no kinetic energy lost during the course.)或译为:两球的碰撞方式为动能守恒的完全弹性碰撞。(翻译时改变主语,独立主格成分译为定语)

4. It 引导的独立主格结构

主语 it 通常用于表示时间、距离、天气或自然现象等,此时结构中的 being 不能够省略。

It being a very long distance between the two stars in the universe, the measurement unit should be light year. 宇宙中两恒星间的距离非常大,因此必须使用光年作为度量单位。(增加连词,译为原因状语)

5. 倒装的独立主格结构

(1) there be 句型也可以在独立主格结构中出现,此时结构中的 being 不能够省略,there be 结构一般可以意译,翻译为状语或句子。

There being a torque on the rotor, the rotor exerts an equal but opposite torque on the engine. 由于转子受到力矩的作用,转子也对引擎施加一个等大而反向的力矩。(增加连词,译为原因状语从句)

(2) such 作为表语时,独立主格结构应采取倒装形式,此时结构中的 being 一般亦不能省略。

Such being the applied condition for the Gauss's law, the system should be highly symmetric in charge distribution. 高斯定律的适用条件就是这样,系统的电荷分布必须有较高的对称性。(译为一个并列的句子)或译为:高斯定律的适用条件是系统电荷分布的高度对称性。(主句的内容即为 such 所指的内容,因此可译为宾语)

23.1.2 分隔结构的翻译

英语是一种分析型语言,其句法关系主要通过功能词和语序(function word and word order)来体现,并且语序相对比较固定,即组成句子的成分在句中按其语法和语义关系都具有相对固定的位置,因而形成了五种基本句型,其语序叫做自然语序(natural word order)。但有时为了增强语言的表现力,自然语序往往被打破,形成一些变异结构,分隔结构(discontinuous structure)就属于其中的一种。分隔现象在科技文体中经常出现,其形式多样,结构复杂,而物理学专业英语往往具有较多的修饰成分且表现为长句,因此分隔结构更加常见,其正确翻译有助于对原文的理解。

英语的分隔结构是指在本应紧密相连的两个成分之间插入其他成分,从而使这两部分产生分隔的现象。起分隔作用的成分主要有三种:一是各种短语,如介词短语、不定式短语、分词短语等;二是各种从句,这也是最为常见的分隔结构;三是句中的附加成分,如插入语、同位语、独立主格结构等。分隔结构一般表现为以下几种情况:①主谓分隔;②动宾分隔;③系表分隔;④复合谓语或复合宾语的分隔;⑤先行词与修饰成分的分隔;⑥固定搭配的分隔。

根据分隔结构在句中所起的不同作用,分隔结构可以分为四种——结构性分隔、修饰性分隔、插入性分隔和倒装性分隔,各自具有不同的性质。结构性分隔可以起到使句子结构保持平衡匀称,避免头重脚轻的作用;修饰性分隔和插入性分隔主要起到说明、解释、补充和强调的作用;而倒装结构本身必定导致某些句子成分不在原来的位置上,从而造成成分的分隔。

在了解和掌握了分隔现象的常见形式之后,分隔结构的翻译应从句子本身入手,弄清句法结构和分隔成分的语法及语义作用,根据具体情况,灵活选取恰当的翻译方法,使译文准确表达原文的内容,准确传达原文的技术信息。以下就分隔结构的具体情况来介绍其翻译方法。

1. 主谓分隔

包含这种结构的句子其成分分析较为简单,分隔结构一般用于对主语进行说明或修饰。对于较长的分隔结构可以采用分译的方式,译为短句,而较短的分隔结构则可以采用合译的方式,译为定语,但有时也可以根据具体情况进行功能转换。例如:

Plastics, *such as nylon and artificial rubber*, are synthetic polymers. 诸如尼龙和人造橡胶这样的塑料是合成聚合物。(句中起说明作用的分隔结构比较短,因此可以采用合译,翻译为主语的定语)

Every substance in the world, *no matter how different it may seem from any other substance*, is made partly of electrons. 不管看起来与其他物质有多大的区别,世界上的各种物质都部分地由电子构成。(句中的分隔结构较长,为 no matter how 引导的让步状语从句,可采用分译)

Sensors *in a car tuned to radio signal from satellites* can locate the car precisely at any moment and warn of traffic jams. 汽车上的传感器能够随时精确地定位以及报告交通阻塞情况,这是由于可以接受卫星发出的无线电信号。(可以将句中作定语成分的分隔结构分译,并根据句意转换为原因状语从句)

Measurement, *which plays an important part in the physical experiment*, is not identical with all of the experiment. 在物理实验中起到重要作用的测量并不等同于物理实验的全部。或译为:测量并不等同于物理实验的全部,尽管它在物理实验中起到了重要的作用。(由于全句不太复杂,可以采取合译或分译)

2. 动宾分隔

动宾之间插入其他成分是比较明显的语序上的调整,因此这种分隔结构一般起到两种作用:一是由于宾语过长而将某些成分(如状语或宾语补足语)提前,此时恢复正常语序在句法上并不影响原句的意义,属于结构性分隔,因此在翻译时可进行灵活处理,此种情况较为多见;二是强调,即插入部分是原文想要强调的内容,在翻译时应保留原句的语序,即插入的成分仍紧邻动词。

Some object looks white because it sends back to *our eyes* all the colors in the light that reaches it. 某物体呈现白色是由于其将入射的各色光线均反射至我们眼中。(结构性分隔)

We call *conductors* those materials which allow electrons to pass easily. 我们把电子容易通过的材料称为导体。（结构性分隔）

Man has achieved remarkable success in the field of astronautics, the ultimate goal and purpose of which is to gain *for man himself* access to space and to other worlds. 人们在宇航方面已取得了惊人的成就，宇航的最终目标和意图就是使人类能够亲自进入太空并到达其他星球。（强调）

3. 系表分隔

这种结构的分隔原因与动宾分隔相似，翻译中亦可采用相同的方法处理。

The compensation method is, *compared with other ones*, a more accurate and visual one for the measurement of some physical quantities. 与其他方法相比，补偿法对于某些物理量的测量更为准确与直观。

4. 复合谓语／宾语的分隔

复合谓语分隔主要是因为在并列谓语动词之间、构成时态或语态的复合动词之间、to 与动词之间加入了状语成分，翻译时状语成分一般应紧随动词而不分开，但有时为了表示强调也可对语序做适当调整。复合宾语分隔在结构上与之类似，即在宾语和宾语补足语之间插入定语成分而形成分隔，翻译时也可采取相似的办法。

The dielectric can *obviously* weaken the electric field between the capacitor plates. 电介质可以明显地减弱电容器极板间的电场。

The capacitor in the circuit above is charged *from a battery* and discharged through a resistance R. 上述电路中的电容器通过电池充电，通过电阻 R 放电。

Laser *people all know* to be a very powerful device which can melt or destroy many kinds of materials known to man. 人们都知道，激光是一种非常强有力的装置，它能熔化或毁坏人们已知的很多种物质。（句中将宾语 laser 置于主谓结构之前，形成宾语和宾语补足语的分隔，是一种倒装式分隔，可用分译法进行翻译）

According to the equivalence principle, the effect produced by the gravity can *in no way* be distinguished from the effect produced by the acceleration. 根据等效原理，无法把万有引力所产生的效果与加速度所产生的效果区分开来。（介词短语 in no way 插入谓语 can be distinguished 中形成分隔，采用分译，移至谓语之前）

5. 先行词与修饰成分的分隔

这种分隔结构主要是指名词与其后置定语（或同位语）被谓语、状语或其他定语分隔，应根据句子的复杂程度选择分译或合译，若修饰成分过多，可将其中的部分修饰语转换为状语等进行翻译，以增强句子的表现力。

The beam of light is focused on the object *under the microscope* that is to be studied. 在显微镜下，光线聚焦在我们要研究的物质上。（修饰谓语动词的状语 under the microscope 在先行词和定语从句之间形成分隔，采用分译）

In experiments, another mode *is found* which is quite different from what we are familiar with. 实验中还会看到另外一种模式，它与我们所熟悉的模式有很大不同。（句中定语从句的先行词 mode 是本句的主语，且谓语 is found 较短，为平衡句子结构，避免头重脚

轻,将定语从句置于谓语之后构成分隔,采用分译)

There is nothing *in the energy conservation principle or in any other law of nature* that specifies for us the direction of heat flow. 在能量守恒原理或其他任何一条自然规律中,都没有给我们规定热量的流动方向。(名词 nothing 与其后置定语 that ... 被状语所分隔,采用分译)

Scientists have found some new methods *of making electronic circuits* by which many of the electronic devices have become quite small. 科学家们已经发现了一些新的制作电子电路的方法,而这些新方法使得电子器件变得非常小。(句中中心词 methods 由两个修饰成分修饰,一是 of making...,一是 by which...,很显然必定有一个修饰成分被分隔开,此时如果将修饰成分全部翻译为定语则显得过于臃肿,因此可根据句意和语境将其中一部分转换为其他成分,使句子表达更为顺畅)

6. 固定搭配的分隔

英语中有大量的固定搭配,这些固定用法中也可以存在分隔结构,在物理学专业英语中更是如此。这是由于物理学中的定义、规律与方法等往往存在着严格的限定条件,为了表明这些限定条件,能够更完整、更准确、更严谨地进行信息传递,专业英语中经常使用分隔结构,自然也包括对固定用法的分隔。对固定用法的正确辨识有利于我们准确地把握结构和理解文意,但同时也要求我们对分隔结构做恰当的处理,使翻译准确流畅。一般应保持固定搭配的原有含义不变,将起修饰和限定作用的插入部分译为状语或定语,并根据语境调整顺序,将该状语或定语放到合适的位置。

The capacitance of the capacitor depends *to some extent* on the magnitude of the dielectric constant of the dielectric in between the plates. 电容器的电容在一定程度上取决于极板间电介质的介电常数。(固定短语 depend on 被介词短语 to some extent 分隔,其目的在于限定动词,译为状语)

We should carefully distinguish velocity *which has both magnitude and direction* from speed which has only magnitude. 我们要注意把速度和速率区分开,因为速度既有大小又有方向,而速率只有大小。(由 which 引导的限制性定语从句造成了固定搭配 distinguish ... from 的分隔,翻译时可把定语从句分译)

The molecules of the gas meet with much more resistance *from the closely packed water molecules* to their free movement. 气体分子的自由运动受到了来自于紧密排列的水分子的更大的阻力。(定语分隔了名词 resistance 和介词 to 的固定搭配,插入成分译为定语)

分隔结构是极其常见的语法现象,正确翻译的要点仍是对句子主干的把握,然后将修饰成分以适当的方式添加上去,既要忠实于原文,又要避免歧义,力求表达流畅。

23.2 专业英语阅读:Bohr's Model(玻尔模型)

The model of atom proposed by Rutherford had several severe problems. It didn't account for the periodicity of the elements, it was unable to give any clue about the origins of the spectral lines, and it implied that atoms were extremely unstable. In 1913, the Danish theoretician Niels Bohr proposed a new model incorporating Planck's discrete energies and Einstein's photon into Rutherford's model.

Scientists are always using models when attempting to understand nature. The trick is to understand the limitations of the models. Bohr challenged the Rutherford model, stating that it was a mistake to assume the atom is just a scaled-down solar system with the same rules; electrons do not behave like miniature planets. Bohr proposed a new model based on three assumption, or postulates.

First, he proposed that the angular momentum of the electron is quantized. Only momenta L equal to whole-number multiples of a smallest angular momentum are allowed. This smallest angular momentum is equal to Planck's constant h divided by 2π. Bohr's first postulate can be written

$$L_n = n \frac{h}{2\pi} \qquad (23\text{-}1)$$

where n is a positive integer (whole number) known as quantum number.

In classical physics, the angular momentum L of a particle of mass m traveling at a speed v in a circular orbit of radius r is given by $L = mvr$. Therefore, the restriction on the possible values of the angular momentum puts restriction on the possible radii and speeds. Bohr showed that the only possible orbits are those for which the radii obey the relationship

$$r_n = n^2 r_1 \qquad (23\text{-}2)$$

where r_1 is the smallest radius and n is the same integer that appears in the first postulate. This means that the electrons cannot occupy orbits of arbitrary size, but only a certain discrete set of allowable orbits. The numerical value of r_1 is 5.3×10^{-11} meter.

There is also a definite speed associated with each possible orbit. This means that the kinetic energies are also quantized. Because the value of the electric potential energy depends on distance, the quantization of radii means that the potential energy also has discrete values. Therefore, there is a discrete set of allowable energies for the electron.

Bohr's second postulate states that an electron does not radiate when it is in one of the allowed orbits. This statement is contrary to the observation that accelerated charges radiate energy at a frequency equal to their frequency of vibration of revolution. Bohr challenged the assumption that this property is also true in the atomic domain. Radically breaking away from what was accepted, Bohr said that an electron has a constant energy when it is in an allowed orbit.

But light is produced by atoms. If light isn't radiated by orbiting electrons, how does an atom emit light? Bohr's third postulate answered this question: A single photon is emitted whenever an electron jumps down from one orbit to another. Energy conservation demands that the photon has energy equal to the difference in the energies of the two levels. It further demands that jumps up to higher levels can only occur when photons are absorbed. The electron is normally in the smallest orbit, the one with the lowest energy. If the atom absorbs a photon, the energy of the photon goes into raising the electron into a higher orbit. Furthermore, it is not possible for the atom to absorb part of the energy of the photon. It is all or nothing.

The electron in the higher orbit is unstable and eventually returns to the innermost orbit, or ground state. If the electron returns to the ground state in a single jump, it emits a new photon with energy equal to that of the original photon. Again, this is different from our common experience. When a ball loses its mechanical energy, its temperature rises—the energy is transferred to its internal structure. As far as we know, an electron has no internal structure. Therefore, it loses its energy by creating a photon.

Occasionally, the phrase "a quantum leap" is used to imply a big jump. But the jump needn't be big. There is nothing big about the quantum jumps we are discussing. A quantum leap simply refers to a change from one discrete value to another.

Ordinarily, an amount of energy is stated in joules, the standard energy unit. However, this unit is extremely large for work on the atomic level, and a smaller unit is customarily used. The electron volt (eV) is equal to the kinetic energy acquired by an electron falling through a potential difference of 1 volt. One electron volt is equal to 1.6×10^{-19} J. It requires 13.6 electron volts to remove an electron from the ground state of the hydrogen atom.

Bohr's explanation accounted for the existence of spectral lines, and his numbers even agreed with the wavelengths observed in the hydrogen spectrum. To illustrate Bohr's model, we draw energy level diagrams in Fig. 23-1. The ground state has the lowest energy and appears in the lowest position. Higher energy states appear above the ground state and are spaced to indicate the relative energy difference between the states.

Fig. 23-1 The energy-level diagram for the hydrogen atom

To see how Bohr's model gives the spectral lines, consider the energy level diagram. Suppose that the electron has been excited in the $n=4$ energy level. There are several ways that it can return to the ground state. If it jumps directly to the ground state, it emits the largest energy photon. The electron could also return to the ground state by making of a set of smaller jumps. It could go from the $n=4$ to the $n=2$ level and then from the $n=2$ to the ground level. The energies of these photons are smaller, so their lines occur at the end of the spectrum.

Bohr's scheme also explains the absorption spectrum. The absorption spectrum is obtained when white light passed through a cool gas before it is dispersed by a prism or a diffraction grating. In this case, the photons from the beam of white light are absorbed and later reemitted. Because the reemitted photons are distributed in all directions, the intensities of these photons are reduced in the original direction of the beam. This removal of the photons from the beam leaves dark lines in the continuous spectrum.

The solution to the mystery of the missing lines in the absorption spectrum is easy within Bohr's model. For an absorption line to occur, there must be electrons in the lower level. Then they can be kicked up one or more levels by absorbing photons of the correct energy. Because almost all the electrons in the atoms of the gas occupy the ground state, only the lines that correspond to jumps from this state show up in the spectrum. Jumps up from higher levels are extremely unlikely because electrons excited to a higher level typically remain there for less than a millionth of a second. Thus, there are fewer lines in the absorption spectrum than in the emission spectrum, in agreement with the observations.

Glossary

propose	提出	periodicity	周期性
element	元素	spectral lines	光谱线
theoretician	理论家	incorporate	包含,加入
discrete	不连续的	Einstein's photon	爱因斯坦的光子
Rutherford's model	卢瑟福模型	trick	技巧
scaled-down solar system	微缩的太阳系	miniature	小型的,微小的
postulate	假定	quantize	v. 量子化
whole-number	整数	Planck's constant	普朗克常量
integer	整数	quantum number	量子数
restriction	限制,约束	radiate	辐射
ground state	基态	quantum leap	量子跃迁
electron volt	电子伏特	hydrogen	氢
hydrogen spectrum	氢光谱	energy level diagram	能级图
excite	激发	absorption spectrum	吸收光谱
disperse	分散	diffraction grating	衍射光栅
continuous spectrum	连续光谱	emission spectrum	发射光谱

23.3 专业英语常用表达-23 距离 间隔

1. 空间距离与间隔

(1) 表示空间上的距离、间隔、范围等的常见词汇:

distance 距离、远离
extent 广度、宽度、长度、范围
gap 裂口、缺口、间隙
interstice 空隙、间隙、裂隙
interval 空间的间隔、空隙
length 长、长度,距离
pitch (螺旋的)螺距、(齿轮的)节距
play 间隙,(例如"back play 空程")
range 范围、区域、射程、距离

scope　范围、导弹的射程

separation　分隔、分开、分隔点、间隔、(导线的)间距

space　空白、距离、间隔

space length/spacing interval　间距、空间距离

spacing　间隔、(字间、行间等)空隙、空白

span　跨度、范围、全长、支点距、墩距、翼展

stretch　一段路程

way　路线、路途、路程

(2) 空间间隔的常见表达：

a distance of three kilometers/three kilometers' distance　3 km 的距离

be at a distance of three kilometers/be spaced at a distance of three kilometers/be spaced at an interval of three kilometers　在距离 3 km 处

the distance from A to B/the distance between A and B/the space interval between A and B　从 A 至 B 的距离

be 5cm (apart/away/distant/far) from point A　与 A 点相距 5 cm

be closely spaced　间距很小

be evenly spaced　等距

2. 时间距离与间隔

(1) 表示时间上的距离、间隔、范围等的常见词汇：

(time) interval　时间的间隔、间歇

distance　较长一段时间、时间上的间隔

duration　持续时间、期间

gap　时间的中断，间歇，间断

length　时间的长短、期间

space (of time)　(一段)时间、时间间隔

stretch　一段持续的时间

time lag　时间上的间隔、时滞

time limit　时限

time span/separation　时间跨度、时间间隔

cycle/period　周期

(2) 时间间隔的常见表达：

a time interval of two hours/two hours' time　2 h 的时间

two hours before/after ...　在……之前/之后 2 h

every five seconds/every other four seconds　每隔 4 s/每 5 s

every forth second　每个第四秒/每 3 s

The average *distance between* two apparatus should not be too small in case of errors caused by the mutual influence. 两仪器之间的平均距离不应过小，以免相互影响造成误差。

The screw rod goes forward *for a distance of the length of the pitch* each time it takes a turn. 螺栓每转一周可前进的距离为一个螺距。

The *time interval for* a particle to undergo a complete oscillation is called a *period*.
一个质点完成一次全振动所经历的时间为一个周期。

Half-life is *the period of time*, for a substance undergoing decay, to decrease by half.
半衰期是指某种衰变物质消耗至初始时的一半时所经历的时间。

LESSON 24

24.1 物理学专业英语中长句的翻译

由物理学科自身的特点所决定，物理学专业英语需要以准确的语言、严密的逻辑和严谨的结构来表述物理概念、规律和方法等，因此其中经常出现结构复杂、修饰限定成分较多的长句，对这些长句的准确把握也成为专业英语阅读与翻译的重点和难点。翻译是从一种语言向另一种语言的转换，除语法上的分析之外还要正确地理解原文的含义，这就需要把握两种不同语言的特点，利用语言知识来分析，利用专业知识来理解，完成合理顺畅的转换。

24.1.1 长句翻译的基本方法

从英汉两种语言的特点来看，"英语重形合，汉语重意合"。英语句子长，动词少，语序灵活，讲究平衡，而且句中有明确的连接词作为语法标志，各种成分通过句法组合为形式上的长句整体；而汉语句子短，动词多，语序比较固定，讲究对称，句中往往并无明确的连接成分，各个短句通过意义上的联系组合在一起。

语言上的差异、物理学的深奥和长句的复杂性，使物理学专业英语长句的理解与翻译成为专业英语学习中的难点，需要仔细推敲，谨慎处理。翻译长句很难一步到位，因此不可急于求成，应遵循一定的方法，逐层分析，逐步深入，正确分析语法结构，准确判断逻辑关系，灵活运用翻译技巧。为达到这些目的，可以将长句的翻译归纳为三个基本步骤：结构分析，部分翻译，整体组合。

1. 结构分析与部分翻译

正确的结构分析是进行准确翻译的前提和基础，具体的分析方法可参见前文（Lesson 9 & 17），即"抓住主干，添枝加叶"，这里不再赘述。分析的过程帮助我们弄清结构与关系，而句子的分析与理解是密不可分的，因此在结构分析的过程中，我们就已经基本完成了各个成分的翻译。

2. 确定对应关系，注意成分分隔

专业英语长句的复杂之处就在于其修饰成分繁多，关系复杂，往往表现为多个修饰成分的并列（一个中心词具有多个修饰语）或是嵌套（在一个语法单元中又出现其他的修饰成分），同时还存在成分分隔的现象。因此在找到了句子的各个成分之后，还应明确其间的关系，例如，定语（从句）所对应的中心词是什么，状语（从句）是表示时间、原因、结果，还是表示条件等。在这一过程中应特别注意成分分隔的现象，运用专业知识来帮助分析，正确理解各成分之间的对应关系。

3. 组合成分，调整语序，正确翻译

在完成了句子主干和各个单元的分析与翻译之后，最后一步就是根据各个成分之间的

逻辑关系进行组合与构建,形成完整的翻译。但直接组合后的译文很可能会晦涩难懂,这时可以在忠实原文含义的基础上根据汉语的语言习惯进行重新调整,使译文流畅并易于理解,在这一过程中可以使用一些翻译的技巧,例如顺译、倒译、转换、合并、拆解等。下面以实例进行分析。

(1) 简单句

In solid form, <u>the noble gases are held together</u> with Van der Waals forces resulting from the polarization of the electronic charge cloud on each atom.

分析:划线部分为句子主干,除 in solid form 这一状语之外,该简单句的谓语还具有一个由 with 引导的状语,在状语中,中心词 forces 又带有自己的修饰成分 resulting from…,其中又包含了两层分别由 of 和 on 引导的嵌套修饰成分。在翻译时,如果将 forces 的定语前置,则句子的主干显得不够明确,因此可将 forces 的定语以短句的形式来翻译。

译文:处于固态时,惰性气体通过范德瓦尔斯力结合在一起,而范德瓦尔斯力来源于每个原子的电子云极化。

<u>The value of electrical resistance</u> associated with a circuit element or appliance <u>can be determined</u> by measuring the voltage across it with a voltmeter and the current through it with an ammeter and then dividing the measured voltage by the current.

分析:划线部分为句子主干,associated with…appliance 为后置定语修饰主语,by 所引导的状语成分包含两个并列成分 measuring 和 dividing,而第一个成分中 measuring 的宾语是并列的 voltage 和 current(各自带有定语),方式状语是由 with 引导的短语。

译文:电路元件或电器的电阻值可以这样测量,用电压表测量两端的电压,用电流表测量其中的电流,然后用电压值除以电流值。

(2) 并列句

<u>Most crystalline materials</u> encountered in everyday life <u>are polycrystalline</u>, with the individual crystals being microscopic in scale, but <u>macroscopic single crystals can be produced</u> either naturally (e. g. diamonds) or artificially.

分析:划线部分为两个转折关系并列句的主干。第一个子句中,encountered in everyday life 是主语 materials 的后置定语,而 with…in scale 是表语 polycrystalline 的定语,其中又包含了分词结构 being microscopic in scale 来修饰 individual crystals。第二个子句中包含了并列状语 either…or…。

译文:大多数日常生活中所见的晶体材料是多晶体,其单晶体尺寸很微小,但宏观的单晶既可以天然形成(比如钻石)也可以人工合成。(将定语译为短句)

或者直接译为:大多数日常生活中所见的晶体材料是包含微小尺寸单晶体的多晶体,但宏观的单晶既可以天然形成(比如钻石)也可以人工合成。

<u>The ballistic pendulum is a classic example</u> of a dissipative collision in which conservation of momentum can be used for analysis, but <u>conservation of kinetic energy</u> during the collision <u>cannot be invoked</u> because the energy goes into inaccessible forms such as internal energy.

分析:宾语 example 后带有一个修饰语 of a dissipative collision,而 dissipative collision 又带有一个 in which 引导的定语从句,由 but 引导的第二个子句本身又是一个完整的因果

关系从句。

译文：冲击摆是耗散碰撞的典型例子，可以用动量守恒进行分析，但在碰撞过程中不能应用动能守恒，这是由于某些动能转变为不可见的形式，例如内能。

从译文可以看出，尽管第一个子句中宾语的定语并不算长，但是翻译为一个独立的句子能够更好的表明"动量守恒"与"动能守恒"之间的对照关系，并且为了反映这种对照关系，将动词 invoke 译成了"应用"。可见，在翻译的过程中既应考虑到整体的布局，又要注意细节，才能够更好地表达原文的含义。

（3）复合句

The bulk of solid-state physics theory and research is focused on crystals, largely because the periodicity of atoms in a crystal—its defining characteristic—facilitates mathematical modeling, and also because crystalline materials often have electrical, magnetic, optical, or mechanical properties that can be exploited for engineering purposes.

分析：该句是一个主从复合句，划双下划线的部分为主句的主干，of solid-state physics theory and research 用于限定主语 bulk。其从句为两个并列的原因状语从句，划单下划线的部分是第一个从句的主干，of atoms in a crystal 是 periodicity 的限定成分，its defining characteristic 作为插入语，可以理解为 the periodicity of atoms in a crystal 的同位语。划波浪下划线的部分是第二个从句的主干，that can be exploited for engineering purposes 是个定语从句，用于修饰 properties，同时 electrical, magnetic, optical, or mechanical 也是用于修饰 properties 的。

译文：固体物理学的理论和研究工作的主体都集中在晶体上，这主要是由于作为晶体基本特征的原子周期性便于进行数学模拟，同时也是由于晶体材料通常具有可供工程上开发利用的电学、磁学、光学或力学性质。

The net magnetization of ferromagnetic materials in response to an external magnetic field may actually occur more by the growth of the domains parallel to the applied field at the expense of other domains rather than the reorientation of the domains themselves as implied in the sketch, which is indicated by the microscopic evidence about magnetization.

分析：该句带有一个 which 引导的非限制性定语从句，划线部分为主句的主干。主语 the net magnetization 后带有由介词短语构成的较长的修饰语，而谓语 occur 后面又带有较长的状语。但相比之下，主语的修饰语稍短，因此直接译为前置定语，而将谓语的方式状语译为句子，并且为了将意思表达清楚，可拆开译为短句。注意句中的"evidence"一词译成了"观察结果"，这是根据语境（as implied in the sketch）及物理知识分析而得到的。

译文：磁化过程的微观观察结果表明，如图所示，铁磁材料响应外磁场造成的净磁化的产生，更多地是通过平行于外磁场的磁畴破坏其他磁畴而长大，而不是磁畴自身的重新取向。

24.1.2 长句的翻译技巧

长句的翻译过程可以概括为"解构"与"重构"两个基本过程。长句的分析是一个解构过程，将长句化整为零，逐层分析，帮助我们正确地理解句子内容，得到一个基本框架并了解各成分的含义。而将各种成分进行重新组合则是翻译的重构过程，通过重构最终得到贴切、通顺的译文。解构的过程需要语法知识和专业背景的辅助,而重构的过程则需要仔细推敲并运用一些翻译技巧,从而做到译文的流畅与通达,不仅使语序与表达方式符合汉语的语言习惯,而且使句意易于被理解。

长句的翻译的基本技巧包括:顺译、倒译、拆分和转换,但在实际的翻译中应综合考虑,灵活使用。

1. 顺译

有些长句的逻辑关系表述语序大致符合汉语的语言习惯,此时可按原文语序进行翻译,无须做太大的调整,这种译法为顺译。

Stephen later discerned several new characteristics of black holes and demonstrated that the amazing forces of the Big Bang would have created mini-black holes, each with a mass about that of a terrestrial mountain, but no larger than the subatomic proton.

本句为主从复合句,包含一个主语和两个谓语 discerned 及 demonstrated,按照原句的顺序进行翻译较为合理,可将独立主格成分 each...proton 译为句子。

全句可译为:后来,Stephen 又认识到黑洞一些新的特征,并证明大爆炸中令人震惊的巨大力量可能会产生很多微小的黑洞,每一个微小黑洞的质量相当于地球上一座大山的质量,但体积不大于亚原子内的质子。

2. 倒译

英语中有大量的修饰成分后置现象,其表述的逻辑顺序可能与汉语的习惯不同,此时可改变原文的语序,进行部分或者全句的倒译。例如可以将后置的定语从句置于被修饰的中心词之前,也可以将后置的状语从句前置,按照前因后果、先提出条件后交代结果的汉语表达习惯进行翻译。在包含主语从句、宾语从句和同位语从句等名词性从句的长句中,也可根据具体情况采用倒译的方式。

By assuming that the material contains immobile positive ions and an "electron gas" of classical, non-interacting electrons, the Drude model was able to explain electrical and thermal conductivity and the Hall Effect in metals, although it greatly overestimated the electronic heat capacity.

本句为主从复合句,包含一个 although 引导的让步状语从句和一个由 by 引导的方式状语。将 although 引导的让步状语从句提前更为符合汉语的语序,此外,对 classical, non-interacting electrons 的翻译可采用倒译,改变两个定语的语序,使翻译更为符合物理专业的表述习惯。注意在 electrical and thermal conductivity 中 electrical 后省略了 conductivity 一词。全句可译为:

尽管过分地估计了电子热容,通过假定材料包含固定不动的阳离子和无相互作用的经典"电子气",Drude 模型还是能够成功解释金属的电导性、热导性及霍尔效应的。

3. 拆分

由于英汉语言存在差异,英语多用长句,而汉语多用短句,因此拆分的方法在长句翻译中极其常见。结构复杂的英语长句直接翻译难于理解,并且繁多的修饰成分会使译文的句子冗长,采用拆分的方式可将多个修饰成分译为汉语的短句,使得句子结构简单,容易理解,表达通顺。拆分往往就意味着语序的改变,因此说翻译的方法并不唯一,应整合使用。

The mirages seen on hot days can be explained by the optic effect that the changing index of refraction of the air causes the light rays to bend and creates the appearance of specular reflections in the distance as directly from the surface of a pool of water.

分析:句子的主干(划线部分)很简单,但 optic effect 的同位语从句却比较繁琐,整个从句解释了主语 mirages 的成因,因此将同位语从句拆分为一个独立的句子进行翻译,同时将 as directly from the surface of a pool of water 也翻译为一个句子。

译文:炎热的天气中出现的海市蜃楼现象可以用光学效应来解释。空气折射率的改变引起了光线的偏折,从而导致了远处景物的镜面反射像的出现,这些反射像就好像从水面被直接反射的一样。

为了使句子更易于理解,添加了"远处景物"这一成分,此处只有了解物理光学的专业知识才能进行准确的增词翻译。

4. 转换

在翻译的过程中,由于采用倒译或拆分的方法,或是汉语表达的需要,往往会造成句子中某些成分的语法地位发生了改变,但从含义上来讲仍然是一致的。例如由宾语变为主语,由定语从句变为一个完整的短句等,这就是转换,在翻译中被大量的使用,在前面的例句中几乎都有体现。

Real crystals feature defects or irregularities in the ideal arrangements, and it is these defects that critically determine many of the electrical and mechanical properties of real materials.

译文:理想排布中的缺陷或不规则性是实际晶体的特点,而恰恰是这些缺陷决定了实际材料的电学和力学特性。

分析:由于采用了倒译,因此第一个子句中的 defects or irregularities 从宾语转换为主语,同样第二个子句中的 defects 从表语转换为主语。注意在翻译中省略了 determine 前的状语 critically 一词,这是由于通过"恰恰是……"的强调方式,使动词"决定"本身就可以表述出原文的含义。

长句的翻译方法是多种多样的,不必拘泥于某种特定的模式,在忠实于原文含义的前提下,可以根据具体的情况灵活地综合使用,同一个句子,也不局限于一种处理方法。严复先生所提出的"信、达、雅"三字翻译标准在专业英语中同样应该提倡,使专业语言的翻译在准确传递信息的基础上同样做到优美传神。

24.2 专业英语阅读:The Elementary Particles(基本粒子)

By 1948, the discovery of antiparticles and exchange particles had nearly tripled the number of known elementary particles. And the situation got worse. During the next seven years four other particles were discovered. Because the behavior of these particles did not match that of the known particles, they became known as the **strange particles.** The existence of the neutrino was confirmed in 1956. A second type of neutrino was discovered in 1962, and even a third type exists.

The 1960s also witnessed the discovery of another new phenomenon. Particles were discovered that live for such a short time that they decay into other particles before they travel distances that are visible even under a microscope. Typical lifetimes for these particles are 10^{-23} second (the unit it takes light to travel across a nucleus!)

Before long the number and variety of particles had become so large that physicists began calling the collection a zoo. The proliferation of new particles had once again destroyed the hope that the complex structures in nature could be built from a relative small number of simple building block. The number of "elementary" particles exceeded a few hundred. And the number continued to grow. Particle physicists began to feel organizational problems similar to those of zookeepers.

Much as zookeepers build order into their zoos by grouping the animals into families, particle physicists began grouping the elementary particles into families. Making families helps organize information and may result in new discoveries. When confronted with many seemingly unrelated facts, scientists often begin by looking for patterns. Mendeleev developed the periodic table of chemical elements using this technique. A Swiss mathematics teacher, Johann Balmer, decoded the data on the spectral lines of the hydrogen atom by arranging and rearranging the wave lengths. In the process he discovered a formula that gave the correct results. Both of these discoveries were empirical relationships, not results derived from fundamental understandings of nature. They served, however, to classify the data and provide some guidance for further experimental work.

Elementary particle physics was in a similar condition. Large amounts of data had been accumulated. Scientists were looking for patterns that might provide clues for the development of a comprehensive theory. Just as any collection of buttons can be classified in many ways—size, color, shape, and so forth—the elementary particles can be classified in different ways. (Of course, macroscopic attributes like color and size don't apply here.) One fruitful way is to group them according to the types of interaction in which they participate.

All particles participate in the gravitational interaction—even the massless photon because of the equivalence of mass and energy. Therefore, this interaction doesn't yield any natural divisions for the particles. Furthermore, gravitation is so small at the nuclear level that it usually isn't included in discussion of particle behavior.

The particles that participate in the strong interaction are called **hadrons**. This family includes most of the elementary particles. The hadrons are further divided into two subgroups according to their spin quantum numbers. The **baryons** have spins equal to 1/2, 3/2, 5/2...of the quantum unit of spin, while the **mesons** have the whole-number units of spin. The best known baryons are the neutron and proton. There are others but their lifetimes are extremely short, more than a billion times shorter than most of those common hadrons. The lepton family included the electron, the muon, the tau (discovered in 1977), and their associated neutrinos. The tau lepton is even more massive than the muon. The word **lepton** means "light particle" and refers to the observation that (with the exception of the tau) leptons are less massive than the hadrons. In fact, they appear to be pointlike, having no observable size and no evidence of any internal structure. All leptons and hadrons participate in the weak interaction. The only particles that fail to get list in the hadrons or lepton families are exchange particles.

The conservation laws provide insight into the puzzles of the elementary particles. We have already seen how the conservation laws were used to unravel beta decay. In some situations new conservation laws have been invented as a result of the experience of viewing many, many particle collisions. The success of the conservation laws has been responsible for a guiding philosophy: *If it can happen, it will*. That is, any process not forbidden by the conservation laws will occur. The classical laws of conserving energy (mass-energy), linear momentum, angular momentum (including spin), and electric charge are valid in the elementary particle realm. Any reaction or decay that occurs satisfies these laws. For instance, the neutron decays into a proton, an electron, and an antielectron neutrino via beta decay

$$n \to p + e^- + \bar{v}_e$$

but has never been observed to decay via

$$n \to p + e^+ + \bar{v}_e$$

The continual rise in the number of elementary particles once again raised the question of whether the known particles were the simplest building blocks. At the moment the leptons appear to the elementary; there is no evidence that they have any size of internal structure. The exchange particles also appear to be truly elementary for the same reasons. On the other hand, there is experimental evidence that the hadrons have some internal structure.

Particle physicists asked themselves: Is it possible to imagine a smaller set of particles with properties that could be combined to generate all the known hadrons? The most successful of the many attempts to build the hadrons is the quark model proposed by two American physicists, Murray Gell-Mann and George Zweig, in 1964. Their original model hypothesized the existence of three flavors of quark (and their corresponding antiquarks), now called the "up" (u), "down" (d), and "strange" (s) quarks. The strange quark has a strangeness number of -1, whereas the other quarks have no strangeness. Each quark has 1/2 unit of spin and a baryon number of 1/3.

Perhaps the boldest claim made in this model is the assignment of fractional electric charge to the quarks. There has never been any evidence for the existence of anything other than whole-number multiples of the charge on the electron. These fractional charges should (but apparently don't) make the quarks easy to find. Yet the scheme works. The quark model has had remarkable successes describing the overall characteristics of the hadrons. The antiquarks have signs opposite to their related quarks for the baryon number, charge, and other properties such as strangeness.

Glossary

antiparticle	反粒子	exchange particles	交换粒子
triple	3倍于,增至3倍	elementary particle	基本粒子
strange particle	奇异粒子	neutrino	中微子
decay	衰变	microscope	显微镜
lifetime	粒子寿命	proliferation	增加,激增
building block	结构单元,积木	zookeeper	动物园管理员
Mendeleev	门捷列夫	periodic table of chemical elements	元素周期表
Balmer	巴尔莫	decode	解释,破译
spectral line	光谱线	empirical relationship	经验关系
macroscopic attribute	宏观属性	gravitational interaction	引力相互作用
massless	无质量的	photon	光子
yield	产生	strong interaction	强相互作用
hadron	强子	spin quantum number	自旋量子数
baryon	重子	meson	介子
neutron	中子	proton	质子
lepton	轻子	muon	μ介子
tau	τ介子	massive	巨大的
pointlike	点状的	weak interaction	弱相互作用
unravel	阐明,解释	beta decay	β衰变
linear momentum	线动量	angular momentum	角动量
antielectron	正电子	quark model	夸克模型
three flavors of quark	夸克的三味	antiquark	反夸克
up quark	上夸克	down quark	下夸克
strange quark	奇异夸克	strangeness	奇异性

24.3 专业英语常用表达-24 位置 方位

1. 通过参照物表示物体相对位置

(1) 以 A 为参照物:

B is at the top of A.
C is in the middle of A.
D is at the bottom of A.
E is on the left of A and F is on the right of A.
B, C, D, E, and F are all inside of A.
G, H, M, and N are all outside of A.
M is over A and N is below A.
G and H are on either side/hand of A.

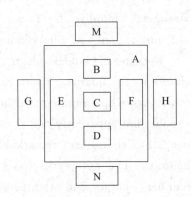

(2) 互为参照物：

B is above/over C.

B is diagonal above E/F.

D is below/under C.

E is to the left of C and F is to the right of C.

B, D, E, and F are all beside C.

G, E, C, F, and H are in the same line.

M, B, C, D, and N are in the same column.

C is between E and F/B and D.

2. 可用于方位表述的词语

above, beyond, on, on top, onto, up, upon, upwards, zenithward 在上,向上

below, beneath, down, downward, under, underneath 在下,向下

leftward, on the left (of), to the left (of), leftmost, on/to the left side (of) 在左,
　向左

rightward, on the right (of), to the right (of), rightmost, on/to the right side (of)
　在右,向右

on the east of, to the east of, eastward 在东边,向东

on the south of, to the south of, southward, southerly 在南边,向南

on the west, to the west, westward 在西边,向西

on the north of, to the north of, southward, northerly 在北边,向北

southeast/southwest 东南／西南

northeast/northwest 东北／西北

ahead, before, farther on, fore, forth, forward, further on, in front of, in the front
　of, straight ahead 在前,向前

at the rear of, backward, behind, hind, in back of, in the back (of), rearwards 在
　后,向后

exterior, external, out, out of, outer, outside, outward, without 在外,向外

in, inner, inside, interior, internal, into, inward, within 在内,向内

among, amid, at the center of, between, centered, in the center of, in the middle
　(of), inbetween, midst, toward the middle 居中,在中间

aside, alongside of, at the side of, beside, on both sides (of), on the side (of), to the
　side (of) 在旁边,在侧面

about, ambient, circumambient, circumjacent, environmental, around, all round,
　surrounding, enwrap, surround, encompass, encircle 在周围,围绕,周围的

atop, at the top of, on top, on (the) top of, top half, upper part （在）顶部

at the bottom (of), bottom side, bottom half, lower part （在）底部

along, alongside, following 沿着

across, athwart, thwart, passing, through, throughout, crossing, cross, traverse,
　span, intersect, penetrate, run through, cut through, bridging over 穿过,贯穿,

跨越

abreast, side by side, parallel, paratactic 平行, 并列

across from, opposite to, in opposite direction, face to face 相对, 相反

adjoin, be adjacent to, be close to, be contiguous to, be near, be next to, border on, bordering to, neighboring on, neighborhood, neighborhood, vicinal, vicinity 接近, 邻近

far, far beyond, far off, far from, away from, in the distance, at a distance, a long way off 远离, 在远处

horizontal, level, standard 水平的

vertical, normal, perpendicular, upright, erect, orthogonal 垂直的

oblique, lean, inclined, slant 倾斜的

upside down, bottom up, head over heel 颠倒的

(1) 注意:

above, over 都可表示"在……之上"。above 一般表示"在上面, 高于"但不一定垂直; over 表示"在……正上方", 强调垂直的关系。below, under, beneath 皆可表示"在……之下"。below 表示非垂直并且不与表面接触的下方; under 表示垂直并且不与表面接触的下方; beneath 则表示在某物之下, 几乎接触或接近。above 与 below 在意义上是相对的, 表示物体位置不垂直的上下关系; over 与 under 在意义上是相对的, 表示物体位置垂直的上下关系。

介词 beside 和 by 均表示"在……旁边", 可以替换, 相当于 next to。而 near 表示的距离与前两者稍远些。介词 beyond 在表示空间位置时, 指"在/向……那边", "在另一边"。

(2) 特定位置的表述

a: top left corner, upper-left

b: at the top, halfway across

c: top right corner, upper-right

d: halfway down left

e: the center, the middle

f: halfway down right

g: bottom left corner

h: at the bottom, halfway across

i: bottom right corner

3. 坐标的表示

(1) 地理坐标——经纬度

Beijing is located at 39.9°N and 116.4°E.

北京位于东经 116.4°, 北纬 39.9°。

(2) 直角坐标

Taking point O as the origin, the coordinate of point P is (36.9, 45.5) in unit of centimeter.

以 O 点为原点, P 点的坐标为 (36.9, 45.5) (单位: cm)。

Unit Seven

LESSON 25

25.1 物理学专业英语写作的一般知识

物理学专业英语的写作有其自己的特点,而且其书写的格式越来越规范和标准。专业英语的写作一般包括科研论文、科普文章、文摘、说明书、会议相关内容、成果汇报、申请报告等应用文体的写作。这些写作可分为两大部分:一是专业内容的阐述,即实验、研究、调查、设计、安排等工作,写作是这些内容的书面体现。如果这些工作本身没做好,没有值得写的实质内容,文章就会言之无物。二是语言文字的表达,即各种应用文体的写作。如果科研成果卓有成效,但是写作水平不尽如人意,就不能充分体现研究成果的价值,这会使科研成果的重要性大打折扣,甚至功亏一篑,以至于成果不能通过鉴定、论文不能得到发表等。所以对任何专业的人来说,专业写作的重要性是怎样强调也不为过的。

物理学专业英语的写作和普通的写作相比,具有内容难、要求严、起点高等特点。要想准确、清晰、流利地用英语来进行专业写作,要求写作者具备以下几点:第一,必须有较为扎实的专业英语术语和公共英语词汇基础;第二,必须掌握专业英语句子的构成,包括词汇、短语、从句、语态、时态、表达习惯等;第三,必须了解专业英语文体的写作习惯,了解各种应用文体的结构和特点;第四,要了解英语书面语与口语之间的异同,避免在书面表达中不恰当地使用口语习语。

写作可以说是最难掌握的语言技能,要想写得好就要多加练习。想要真正写出满意的专业文章,首先必须尽可能多读、多模仿本专业的那些优秀英语文章、论文、报告。从总体来看,以英语为母语的人写的论文语言更地道一些。其次,读论文时要力求读懂全部意思,尤其不要放过难点,因为感到难的地方往往是最需要补课的地方,不管从专业角度看还是从语言角度看都是如此,实在读不懂时应向内行请教。最后,将优秀专业英语文献中对写作有用的术语、表达方法和段落,特别是那些同汉语表达习惯不同,而自己又不会的地方记下来反复读、甚至背诵,模仿其中的短语、句型造句,或者改写其中的段落以表达自己的思想。对于提高专业英语的写作技能,这些方法都非常有效。

专业英语写作之所以是公认的最难掌握的语言技能,还因为它与层次条理、组织思想有着十分密切的关系。专业人员在用英语进行专业写作时,虽然在语言方面困难多一些,比如词不达意、搭配生硬、遣词造句捉襟见肘、甚至语法错误频出等。但是专业人员也有其自身的优势,比如能巧妙地借助母语思维、逻辑推理能力强、专业知识和经验丰富等。如果能够找到一种普遍适用的写作模式,在专业英语写作中就能从整体上进行把握,取得较为理想的效果。所幸的是,在专业学术文体的写作中的确存在着某些模式化、程式化的写作方法。在此我们尽可能简要地提供一些这样的写作模式和框架,提供一些语言素材,为专业人员的写作提供方便。

1. 文章的构成

物理学中的文章(article)从整体上看,主要包括引言(introduction)、正文(body)、结束语(conclusion)三大部分。

引言:一般比较简短,可以是一句话,也可以是一段话。主要用来引出文章的主题,介绍一下背景,或者某项研究或技术目前的状况,存在什么问题及本文想要说明的大致内容。

正文:文章的关键内容,一般可分为若干段落,每一段落都有自己的小主题。在每一段落中均应注意与前面提到内容的一致性和连贯性。在正文中应该用事实、论据或实验数据来阐明、发挥或论证作者在引言中提出的主题。

结束语:总结、概括全文的内容,特别是列出带有结论性的几条意见,或得出的结果,或是值得今后探讨的问题等。

2. 专业写作的一般步骤

在物理学及其相关领域,专业写作是一个确定主题、收集准备素材资料、获得数据、落笔拟写、修改草稿的文字加工过程。在已经明确拟写文章或论文的主题后,首先要围绕主题收集足够的资料、数据或证据,仔细审查,删去与主题无关或意义不大的材料,有时需要必要的理论推导,通过实验或计算得到准确的数据等,进而得到翔实的结果和最终结论。最后,把它们按逻辑顺序重新排列,写出一个提纲。提纲写好后,就可以写初稿了。这是一个组织素材,表达自己的思想和观点的过程。初稿写出后,根据主题、论据、逻辑、词法、语法还要不断修改与完善。

一篇专业文章或论文要完整顺畅、自成一体。文中所有的观点和论据都应与其主题或中心思想密切相关,千万不能跑题。文章是由段落构成的,在已经掌握了段落的写作之后,接下来要做的就是段落之间的自然过渡和有机衔接,最后形成一个完整有机的整体。

在内容的安排上,专业文章最主要的部分是中间的正文,这部分占全文的十分之七八较为适宜。而段落的安排要根据具体的需要来进行,可以按照重要性、时间顺序、空间顺序、逻辑顺序理论推导过程或实验进度等来安排。

专业文章一般由引言、正文和结论三部分组成。写作时还应该注意比例的掌握,主要的观点、论据、结果应该详细表述,次要的观点、论据则无须多说。开头和结尾的段落固然也很重要,但应该写得简短些。引言是文章开头部分的一段短文,也是文章主体部分的开端,它要向读者交代文章的主要写作意图和来龙去脉,引导读者阅读和理解全文,同时提供必要的背景知识,因此好的引言可以激发读者的阅读兴趣。正文部分提出作者的观点、论据、数据和结果,叙述要科学、准确、清楚、合乎逻辑。结尾部分阐明文章的结论、工作的意义、对未来的展望等内容,常以强劲有力的表达方法来加深读者的印象。

3. 专业英语写作常用文体类型

在物理学及其相关领域的专业写作中,常用的文体有:描写文、说明文、报告、学术论文、国际会议相关文字资料等。学习专业英语写作时,应该先从相对简单的描写文和说明文开始。写好描写文和说明文是进一步写作其他应用文体的基础。

在接下来几课的内容中,我们将对这些常见文体的写作方法进行介绍。

25.2 专业英语阅读:Waves and Particles(波与粒子)

Imagine the controversy de Broglie caused. Interference of light is believable because parts of the waves pass through each slit and interfere in the overlap region. But electrons don't split in half. Every experiment designed to detect electrons has found complete electrons, not half an electron. So how can electrons produce interference patterns?

The following series of thought experiments were proposed by physicist Richard Feynman to summarize the many, many experiments that have been conducted to resolve the wave-particle dilemma. Although they are idealized, this sequence of experiments gets at crucial factors in the issue.

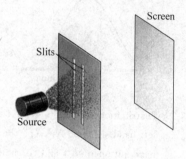

Fig. 25-1 The experimental setup for the thought experiment concerning the wave-particle dilemma

We will imagine passing various things through two slits and discuss the patterns that are produced on a screen behind the slits. In each case, there are three pieces of equipment: a source, two slits, and a detecting screen arranged as in Fig. 25-1.

In the first situation we shoot indestructible bullets at two narrow slits in a steel plate. Assume that the gun wobbles, so that the bullets are fired randomly at the slits. Our detecting screen is a sand box. We simply count the bullets in certain regions in the sand box to determine the pattern.

Imagine that the experiment is conducted with the right-hand slit closed. After 1 hour we sift through the sand and make a graph of the distribution of bullets. This graph is shown in Fig. 25-2(a). The curve is labeled N_L to indicate that the left-hand slit was open. Repeating the experiment with only the right-hand slit open yields the similar curve N_R shown in Fig. 25-2(b).

When both slits are opened, the number of bullets hitting each region during 1 hour is just the sum of the numbers in the previous experiments, that is, $N_{LR}=N_L+N_R$. This is just what we expect for bullets, or any other particles. This graph is shown in Fig. 25-2(c).

Now imagine repeating the experiment using water waves. The source is now an oscillating bar that generates straight waves. The detecting screen is a collection of devices that measure the energy (that is, the intensity) of the wave arriving at each region. Since these are waves, the detector does not detect the energy arriving in chunks, but rather in a smooth, continuous manner. The graphs in Fig. 25-3 show the average intensity of the waves at each position across the screen for the same three trials.

Fig. 25-2 Distribution of bullets with (a) the left-hand slit open N_L, (b) the right-hand slit open N_R, and (c) both slits open N_{LR}

Fig. 25-3 Intensity of water waves with (a) the left-hand slit open I_L, (b) the right-hand slit open I_R, and (c) Both slits open I_{LR}

Once again, the three trials yield no surprise. We expect an interference pattern when both slits are open. We see that the intensity with two slits open is not equal to the sum of the two cases with only one slit open, $I_{LR} \neq I_L + I_R$ but this is what we expect for water waves, or any other waves.

Both sets of experiments make sense, in part, because we used materials from the macroscopic world—bullets and water waves. However, a new reality emerges when we repeat these experiments with particles from the atomic world.

This time we use electrons as our "bullets". An electron gun shoots electrons randomly toward two very narrow slits. Our screen consists of an array of devices that can detect electrons. Initially the results are similar to those obtained in the bullet experiment: Electrons arrive as whole particles. The patterns produced with either slit open are the expected ones and are the same as those in Fig. 25-2((a) and (b)). The surprise comes when we look at the pattern produced with both slits open: We get an interference pattern like the one for waves!

Note what this means: If we look at a spot on the screen that has a minimum number of electrons and close one slit, we get an increase in the number of counts at that spot. Closing one slit yields more electrons! This is not the behavior expected of particles.

One possibility that was suggested to explain these results is that the electrons are somehow affecting each other. We can test this by lowering the rate at which the source emits electrons so that only one electron passes through the setup at a time. In this case, we might expect the interference pattern to disappear. How can an electron possibly interfere with itself? Each individual electron should pass through one slit or the other. How can it even know that the other slit is open? But the interference pattern doesn't disappear. Even though there is only one electron in the apparatus at a time, interference effects are observed after a large number of electrons are measured.

The set of experiments can be repeated with photons. The results are the same. The detectors at the screen see complete photons, not half photons. But the two-slit pattern is an interference pattern. Photons behave like electrons. Photons and electrons exhibit a duality of particle and wave behavior.

Glossary

controversy	争论，争议	de Broglie	德布罗意
slit	狭缝	overlap region	叠加区
thought experiment	思想实验	dilemma	进退两难的局面
indestructible	不能破坏的	wobble	摇晃
sift	详审	chunk	大块
array	排列，编队	duality	二象性

25.3 专业英语常用表达-25 近代物理及综合设计实验仪器

experiment facility of temperature characteristics of PN junction positive voltage drop
　　PN结正向压降温度特性实验仪
superconducting maglev demonstration unit　超导磁浮车演示装置
sensor experiment table　传感器实验台
plasma diagnosis experiment facility　等离子体诊断实验仪
electrical meter reform and calibration experiment facility　电表改装与校准实验仪
tester of charge-to-mass ratio of the electron　电子荷质比测定仪
comprehensive design-orientated dynamic experiment facility　动力学综合设计性实验
　　装置
multi-function microwave plasma experiment facility　多功能微波等离子体实验装置
multi-function vacuum experiment facility　多功能真空实验仪
Doppler effect and sound velocity comprehensive experiment facility　多普勒效应及声
　　速综合实验仪
Doppler effect experiment facility　多普勒效应实验仪
Franck-Hertz experiment facility　夫兰克-赫兹实验仪
solid measurement unit　固体测量装置
photosensor experiment facility　光电传感器实验仪
photoresistance characteristics experiment facility　光敏电阻特性实验仪
NMR experiment facility　核磁共振实验仪
glow plasma experiment facility　辉光等离子体实验仪
Young's modulus tester with Hall position sensor　霍尔位置传感器杨氏模量测定仪

AC circuit comprehensive experiment facility 交流电路综合实验装置
Planck constant tester/determinator 普朗克常数测定仪
atmosphere heat treatment program-controlled high-temperature furnace 气氛热处理程控高温炉
portable holograph experiment facility 轻便全息照相实验仪
sound velocity tester and signal source 声速测定仪及信号源
manual levitation force measurement unit 手动磁浮力测量装置
experiment facility of principle of digital electrical meter and design of universal meter 数字电表原理及万用表设计实验仪
double-grating weak vibration meter 双光栅微弱振动测量仪
temperature-sensing experiment facility 温度传感实验装置
physics design-orientated experimental modules 物理设计性实验模块
physics design-orientated experiment facilities 物理设计性实验装置
experiment facility of string vibration and sound 弦音实验仪
string vibration research experiment facility 弦振动研究实验仪
DC sputtering plasma experiment facility 直流溅射等离子实验装置
rotational inertia tester 转动惯量实验仪

LESSON 26

26.1 物理学专业英语的段落写作

段落是文章的缩影，写好段落是专业英语写作的关键一环。一个段落既是一篇文章的组成部分，也是一个相对独立的整体。只有写好了段落，才会成功地写出较好的文章。

要写好段落，首先要了解段落结构。段落是由表达单一中心思想的一组句子（包括主题句 topic sentence，支持句 supporting sentences 及结论句 concluding sentence）构成的，是文章结构的基本独立单位。一个好的段落，一般具有以下特点：首先，一个段落必须有一个中心，即主题思想，该中心由主题句特别是其中的主题词来表达。整个段落必须紧扣这个主题，这就是段落的统一性。其次，一个段落必须有若干支持句用来对主题句作具体阐述，使主题思想得到充分展开，主要通过列举事实、范例、援引等来阐述中心思想，从而给读者一个完整的感觉，这就是完整性。再次，段落有时还会有结论句，用来总结要点，提出供读者思考的一些见解，同时表明段落的结束，但有时也可能没有结论句。最后，一个段落不是杂乱无章的，而是有机的组合，句子的排列顺序必须合乎逻辑，从一个句子到另一个句子的过渡必须流畅，这就是连贯性。

26.1.1 主题句

主题句（topic sentence）是表达段落主题的句子。它用以阐明段落主题，要求全段其他文字都围绕它展开。请看下例：

The law of charge conservation is one of important characteristics of electric charge. In certain interactions among elementary particles, charged particles such as electrons are created or annihilated. However, in all these processes, equal amounts of positive and negative charge are produced or destroyed, so the net charge of the universe is unchanged. When two initially neutral objects are charged by being rubbed together, charge is not created in the process. The objects become charged because electrons are transferred from one object to the other. One object gains some amount of negative charge from the electrons transferred to it while the other loses an equal amount of negative charge and hence is left with a positive charge. That is, charge is conserved.

主题句(首句)中提出的"law of charge conservation"所指的内容,在展开句中逐一加以解释说明。从结构来看,这是一个比较典型的段落,它包括了主题句,支持句和结论句(即本段中的末句)。

1. 主题句的位置

主题句通常放在段落的开端,其特点是开门见山地摆出问题。其作用是使文章的结构更清晰,更具说服力,便于读者迅速地把握主题和了解全段的内容。主题句也可以放在段中起到承上启下的作用,或放在段尾起概括全段的作用。

2. 选好主题句中的关键词

段落的主题句对主题的限定主要是通过句中的关键词来表现的。关键词要尽量写得具体些,同时也必须是此段落中的核心词汇。如上句中的 charge conservation 就是关键词。准确地选择关键词是清楚地表达段落主题、写好段落主题句的重要前提之一。

3. 如何写好主题句的中心思想

主题句由两部分组成,即关键词和中心思想。关键词反映了中心思想的核心,中心思想的作用是导向和制约。所谓导向就是规定段落的发展脉络,所谓制约就是限制主题的覆盖范围,两者不可分割。没有导向,内容就会离题或偏题;没有制约,内容就可能超出一个段落所能容纳的范围。对于初学写作的人来说,"导向"的重要性容易理解,但如果由他们自己来构思一个主题句,就可能忽视"制约"这一面。例如:

There are two ways in which energy can be transferred between a system and its surroundings. One is work done by (or on) the system. This mode of energy exchange results in measurable changes in the macroscopic variables of the system, such as the pressure, temperature, and volume of gas. The other is heat transfer, which takes place at the microscopic level.

本段的主题句如果没有 in which 引出的定语从句,那么 two ways 不仅不能起制约作用,也不能起导向作用,而且句子本身也缺少了必要的内容,读起来也就使人觉得欠缺点什么。

因此,紧紧把握主题句中中心思想的导向和制约作用,是短文写作成功的关键之一。

26.1.2 段落的展开

在确定好了一个段落的主题句以后,接下来要做的就是进一步展开说明这个主题。要展开段落,就要准备好相关的例子、细节、数据、事实等材料,然后把这些材料按照一定的逻辑顺序安排好,这样一个段落的初稿准备就基本完成。最后,用一定的方法把本段落写出来。

1. 主要支持句

支持句也叫做展开句、论证句。主要支持句(major supporting statement)的特点是:围绕段落主题句展开的每一个支持句本身都不要求作进一步的说明或证明,句与句之间的关系是相互独立又是互相联系的。例如:

(主题句)There are two ways in which energy can be transferred between a system and its surroundings. (支持句1)One is work done by (or on) the system. This mode of energy exchange results in measurable changes in the macroscopic variables of the system, such as the pressure, temperature, and volume of gas. (支持句2)The other is heat transfer, which takes place at the microscopic level.

主题句指出系统和环境之间的能量交换有两种方式。然后用两个扩展句说明这两种方式。第一种是做功,第二种是热传递。

2. 次要支持句

次要支持句(minor supporting statement)是指对主要支持句作进一步的事实分析或举例说明。它从属于某一个或某几个支持句。例如:

(主题句)The law of charge conservation is one of important characteristics of electric charge. (主要支持句1)In certain interactions among elementary particles, charged particles such as electrons are created or annihilated. (主要支持句2)However, in all these processes, equal amounts of positive and negative charge are produced or destroyed, so the net charge of the universe is unchanged. (次要支持句1)When two initially neutral objects are charged by being rubbed together, charge is not created in the process. (次要支持句2)The objects become charged because electrons are transferred from one object to the other. (次要支持句3)One object gains some amount of negative charge from the electrons transferred to it while the other loses an equal amount of negative charge and hence is left with a positive charge. (结论句)That is, charge is conserved.

3. 主要支持句与次要支持句的关系

(1) 每个主要支持句都应该是对主题句中表示的主要思想的关键词的直接、明确的说明。

(2) 每个次要支持句都应该说明它的主要支持句。

(3) 含有讨论说明或分析的段落通常既要有主要支持素材,又要有次要支持素材。

4. 写好支持句的方法

主题句及关键词确定后,就要开始选择和主题有关的信息和素材了。实质上,根据关键词来选择每一个所需的支持性素材就是一个分类的过程。有一种常用的方法就是句子展开前加以设问,然后解答,即"设问-解答"的方法。下面我们通过举例来看一看这种分类过程是如何完成的:

When an object is heated or cooled, some of its physical properties change. Most solids and liquids expand when they are heated. A gas, if its pressure is kept constant, will also expand when it is heated, or, if its volume is kept constant, its pressure will rise. If an electrical conductor is heated, its electrical resistance changes.

假设：Topic sentence：When an object is heated or cooled, some of its physical properties change.

设问：Why can we put forward this topic idea?

解答：Because most solids and liquids expand when they are heated.

解答：Because a gas, if its pressure is kept constant, will also expand when it is heated, or, if its volume is kept constant, its pressure will rise.

解答：Because if an electrical conductor is heated, its electrical resistance changes.

从上面可以看出，三个支持句和关键词 physical properties change 是一致的。

当然，在写成段落时，没有必要在每个句子开头写上"because"，但是，在动笔展开句子时，头脑里要想着这个词，这种检验方法能帮助你把注意力集中在某个重心上，并围绕主题思想层层展开。

展开次要支持句的方法与展开主要支持句的方法类似，这里就不再赘述了。

26.1.3 段落展开的常用方法

无论是书面写作还是口语，良好的英文表达都应完整、连贯，各观点之间的过渡应流畅。在展开段落时，使用过渡词语是一个很好的方式，这些过渡词语让我们把两个观点更好地衔接在一起，使行文表达紧凑、流畅、条理清晰。

以下将介绍一些常用的段落展开方法，并介绍一些对应的过渡连词，方便读者参考。

1. 列举法

列举法是通过列举一系列的论据对主题句中提出的论点进行翔实、具体、全面地陈述或解释。列举的内容可能是同一对象呈现出的多种特性、变化，也可能是支持同一结论的各种依据、原因、理论、方法等。列举的顺序有很多种，可以按照所列各点内容的相对重要性、时间或空间等顺序进行。请看下面一段例文：

It was not until the early part of the 19th century that scientists established that electricity and magnetism are related phenomena. In 1820, Hans Oersted discovered that a compass needle, which is magnetic, is deflected when placed near an electric current. In 1831, Michael Faraday in England and, almost simultaneously, Joseph Henry in the United States showed that, when a wire loop is moved near a magnet (or, equivalently, when a magnet is moved near a wire loop), an electric current is observed in the wire. In 1873, James Clerk Maxwell used these observations and other experimental facts as a basis for formulating the laws of electromagnetism as we know them today. Shortly thereafter (around 1888), Heinrich Hertz verified Maxwell's predictions by producing electromagnetic waves in the laboratory. This achievement was followed by such practical developments as radio and television.

按照时间的顺序，作者列举了四点物理学发展史上的史实内容来详细说明物理学家发现 electricity and magnetism are related phenomena 的具体过程。该文条理清楚、脉络分明、内容连贯，从而使读者对整个段落的主题有了清晰的深入了解。

常用于列举法的过渡连接词有：

按逻辑次序展开的：first, second, first of all, to begin with, at first, finally, eventually, in the end, immediately, soon, next to, opposite to, in the middle of, on the left, afterward, then, next, for one thing, for another, finally, besides, moreover, one another, still another 等。

按空间顺序展开的：above, over, across from, around, also, adjacent to, close to, ahead of, below, beneath, beyond, down, further, here, in the distance, nearby, next to, on the left, on the right, opposite to, on top of, up, under 等。

按时间顺序展开的：first, second, etc. in the mean time, at the same time, after a while, after an interval, presently, soon, then, next, later, finally, eventually, thereupon, thereafter, after, afterward, at last 等。

由于要列举的各项内容之间的关系不尽相同，可以是并列、递进或对比等关系，因此使用恰当的过渡词语可以更为准确、清楚地表达这些关系，同时增加了内容的条理性，不致使某些方面被忽略。除了以上列举的一些常用的表示列举的过渡词语外，还可以根据具体内容之间的关系选择使用表达并列、附加、递进、转折、让步、对照等关系的连接词。

2. 举例和归纳法

通过举出具体事例来阐述、说明主题句内容的方法为举例法。严格地讲，举例法也可看作列举法的一种。它们的区别在于：列举法侧重罗列事实，所列事实力求全面；而举例法侧重通过举出典型事例来解释作者观点，事例可多可少。例如：

Capacitors find many applications in electrical circuits. Capacitors, for example, are used for tuning radio circuits and for "smoothing" the rectified current delivered by a power supply. For another example a capacitor is used to eliminate sparking when a circuit containing inductance is suddenly opened. Besides, the ignition system of every automobile engine contains a capacitor to eliminate sparking of the "points" when they open and close. Moreover, the efficiency of alternating current power transmission can often be increased by the use of large capacitors.

本段采用了四个事例来说明主题句中的关键词 applications，这四个例子分别由连接词 for example, for another example, besides 和 moreover 引出。

通过举一个或几个例子来展开段落，可以使中心句的抽象意思具体化，给读者留下清晰、明了的印象，可以增强说服力，这种方法是从概括到具体。

另一种通过举例或细节展开段落的方法是从具体到概括，即先铺叙细节，把归纳性的中心句放在段尾，即归纳法。比如：

If you stand along a highway and a car or truck approaches you with the horn blowing, the pitch (the perceived frequency) of the sound is higher as the vehicle approaches and lower as it recedes. You can also hear variations in the frequency of the motor noise when watching a racing car going around a track. A variation in the perceived sound frequency due to the motion of the sound source is an example of the Doppler effect.

作者通过列举 the vehicle approaches, it recedes 和 a racing car going around a track 等例子，最后归纳出了本段主题句(最后一句)，使得该文生动直观、容易理解。

可以看出,举例是一种相当好的展开段落、解释说明方法,因为物理学及其相关领域中需要举例说明的场合非常多,能够恰当地运用引导词可以更好地引起注意并加深印象。

举例时常用的连接词有:for example (instance), one example is, besides, furthermore, moreover, in addition, as an illustration, to illustrate, namely, that is, for one thing, a case in point 等。

3. 叙述法

叙述法发展段落主要是按照事物本身的时间、空间或逻辑的排列顺序,通过一些特定过渡连接词的使用,有层次、分步骤地表达主题。用这种方法展开段落,作者能够清楚连贯地交待事物的本末,从而可以使读者清晰、完整地理解文章的含义。例如:

The first capacitor was the Leyden jar, a glass container lined inside and out with gold foil. It was invented at the University of Leyden in the Netherlands by eighteenth-century experimenters who, while studying the effects of electric charges on people and animals, got the idea of trying to store a large amount of charge in a bottle of water. An experimenter held up a jar of water in one hand while charge was conducted to the water by a chain from a static electric generator. When he reached over to lift the chain out of the water with his other hand, he was knocked unconscious. After that Benjamin Franklin realized that the device for storing charge did not have to be jar-shaped and used foil-covered window glass, called Franklin panes. With several of these connected in parallel, he stored a large charge and attempted to kill a turkey with it. Instead, he knocked himself out. He later wrote, "I tried to kill a turkey but nearly succeeded in killing a goose."

这段是按照事物发展的先后顺序叙述 Franklin 发明电容器的过程。全文脉络清晰,叙述的层次感强,结构紧凑。

常用于叙述法中的过渡连接词有:first, at the beginning, to start with, after that, later, then, afterwards, in the end, finally 等。

4. 类比和对比法

将同类的事物按照某种特定的规则进行比较和分析是一种常用的方法。通过类比和对比,更容易阐明所述对象之间的异同和优缺点,可以让读者对事物有一个更加明了的认识。类比常用于指出同一范畴的事物之间或者几个人之间的相似之处,而对比则用于指出他们之间的不同之处。类比和对比均为写作中常用的方法,需要注意的是,进行类比或对比的两个对象的对比点应一致,顺序也应相同,否则就会相互脱离而构不成对比。例如:

Let us now introduce the idea of macroscopic and microscopic states. Suppose you toss N identical coins on the table, and half of them show Five-Fen and half show Emblem. This is a description of the large-scale or macroscopic state of the system of N coins. A description of the microscopic state of the system includes information about each individual coin: Coin 1 was Five-Fen, coin 2 was Emblem, coin 3 was Emblem, and so on. There can be many microscopic states that correspond to the same macroscopic description.

在这段文字中,作者通过宏观态和微观态描述对象方法的对比,使读者对宏观描述和微观描述有了一个基本的认识。

The properties of gases at low densities allow the definition of the ideal-gas temperature scale. If we compress such a gas while keeping its temperature constant, the pressure increases. Similarly, if a gas expands at constant temperature, its pressure decreases.

A ray incident on a surface is described by an angle of incidence. This is measured relative to a line perpendicular, or normal, to the reflection surface, a line commonly referred to as a normal. In like manner, the reflected ray is described by an angle of reflection.

通过这些类比和对比,两个对象之间的相似和不同之处就清晰地展现在读者面前。

表达类比的常用词语有:

compared with, even though, at the same time, not only... but also, meanwhile, similar to, similarly, at the same rate, as, like/alike, likewise, correspond to, correspondingly, resemble, resemblance, almost the same as, just as, in like manner, in the same way, to have...in common, common characteristics, to be parallel in..., both 等。

表达对比的常用词语有:

compared with, differ from, however, otherwise, still, nevertheless, even so, a larger (smaller) percentage than, less than, more than, unlike, in contrast to, in opposition to, on the contrary, on the opposite side, on the other hand, but, different from, although, while, in contrast to, in spite of, whereas, here...there..., the former...the latter..., some...others..., once...now...等。

比较法中有一种特殊的形式被称为比拟,它是指把属于两个不同范畴的事物的相似之处加以比较。比拟适用于解释抽象的思想,它能用具体的、人们熟知的事物来描述那些不易体会到的理论或设想,使人们对这一理论或设想有一个清楚明确的了解。比如用太阳系的例子来解释原子内部的结构。

Electrons orbit around the center or nucleus of the atom, much as planets in the solar system orbit around the sun. Electrons closer to the nucleus are held more tightly than those in the outer orbit. It is the electrons in the outermost orbit of certain kinds of atoms that can be made to flow as electric current.

5. 分类法

在阐述某一概念的段落中,常用分类法。根据事物的特点,通过对概念中所包括的事物进行分门别类,分别加以叙述,使读者有更为清晰的认识,如:

In this section we describe four specific kinds of thermodynamic processes that occur often in practical situations. These can be summarized briefly as "no heat transfer" or adiabatic, "constant volume" or isochoric, "constant pressure" or isobaric, and "constant temperature" or isothermal. For some of these we can use a simplified form of the first law of thermodynamics. An adiabatic process is defined as one with no heat transfer into or out of a system; An isochoric process is a constant-volume process; An isobaric process is a constant-pressure process. An isothermal process is a constant-temperature process.

在该段中为了说明主题句中的"four specific kinds of thermodynamic processes",作者将其分为"no heat transfer","constant volume","constant pressure" and "constant temperature",并逐一加以阐述。

采用这种方法的段落并没有明显的连接词,所述各项均为平行并列关系,所以没有明显的主次之分。需要注意的是,使用分类法展开段落时,要把握好类别的对应性,不要把不同类别的事物混淆在一起。

6. 因果分析法

在阐述某一现象的起因和最终导致的结果时,常采用因果分析法。分析原因和结果,要做到理由充足,逻辑合理。事件发生的原因和结果有时不止一个,所以在进行分析时,要尽量做到讨论全面和选材缜密。以原因和结果展开段落,主要有两种方法。第一种是先写出结果,再占用主要篇幅——写出原因。第二种是先叙述原因,再写出或预测其结果。例如:

Electric trains have many advantages over those drawn steam engines. There is no smoke to soil the passengers, clothes and the cushions in the trains. Because they carry no heavy loads of coal and water, these trains can start and stop with less waste of power. In a station they are silent: there is no steam to produce noise to deafen the passengers.

本段中,主题句提出了电气火车的优点,支持句则对产生这种现象的原因做出各种解释。

常用于因果分析法的连接词有:because, so, as a result, the reason is…, consequently, hence, therefore, accordingly, for this reason, owing to, because of, since, result in, the effect of, the consequence of, have an effect on, the reason for, seeing that, the cause of, It turns out that, now that, in that, for fear that, such…that, make…possible, due to, as, so that, so…that, out of, owe…to, thanks to 等。

7. 定义法

在物理学专业文章的写作中,定义法是必不可少的。为了避免对一个不熟悉的、多义的词或是术语、概念等产生疑问或误解,我们需要阐明它的定义。通过下定义,可以使读者对该事物有一个更直接的认识。

下定义的基本方式有四种:用一个同义词,或用一句话,或写一个段落,有的甚至写一篇论文。前两种方法通常用来给简单的术语和词汇下定义。比如:

The ratio of the charge to the potential is called the **capacitance** of the conductor. A useful device for storing charge and energy is the **capacitor**, which consists of two conductors, closely spaced but insulated from each other.

但是,我们常常会遇到含义复杂、意思抽象的词语或概念,这时就不得不用一个段落甚至一篇论文来阐明它的定义。可能还需运用举例、比较、比拟、分类和因果分析等方法才能使读者对其定义有一个明确完整的了解。例如:

In physics, a **model** is a simplified version of a physical system that would be too complicated to analyze in full detail. We invent a simplified version of a problem so that we can solve it simply and reasonably. For example, we neglect the size and shape of a car by representing it as a point object, or a particle, and we neglect air resistance by making the car move in a vacuum, we forget about the earth's rotation, and we make the weight constant.

这一段文字使我们了解了"model"的概念。仅仅通过第一句的定义,读者尚不能完全了解物理学中模型的概念,于是作者通过介绍引进"模型"的目的,再通过一个具体的例子"particle"使读者对于物理学中的模型有了一个清楚的了解。

常出现在定义法中的词语有:refer to, mean, call, to define, in definition, to explain, in explanation, by…is meant, in other words, to clarify, in clarification, to paraphrase 等。

以上,结合具体例子讨论了展开段落的几种方法。在实际写作中,我们往往不必拘泥于一种写作方法,而是将若干方法穿插在一起对主题句进行进一步的解释,从而使内容更加丰富有趣。

26.2 专业英语阅读

26.2.1 The Uncertainty Principle(测不准原理)

The interpretation that atomic particles are governed by probability left many scientists dissatisfied and hoping for some ingenious thinker to rescue them from this foolish predicament. The German physicist Werner Heisenberg showed that there was no rescue. He argued that there is a fundamental limit to our knowledge of the atomic world.

Heisenberg's idea—that there is an indeterminacy of knowledge—is often misinterpreted. The uncertainty is not due to a lack of familiarity with the topic, nor is it due to an inability to collect the required data such as the data needed to predict the outcome of a throw of dice, or the Kentucky Derby. Heisenberg was proposing a more fundamental uncertainty—one that results from the wave-particle duality.

Imagine the following thought experiment. Suppose you try to watch an electron moving through a room. The room is a complete vacuum, so there's no worry about the electron hitting gas molecules. To locate the electron you need something to carry information from the electron to your eyes. Suppose you use photons from a dim light bulb. Because this is a thought experiment, we can also assume that you have a microscope so sensitive that you will see the electron as soon as one photon bounces off the electron and enters the microscope.

You begin by using a bulb that emits low-energy photons. These have low frequencies and long wavelengths. The low energy means that the photon will not disturb the electron very much when it bounces off it. However, the long wavelength means that there will be lots of diffraction when the photon scatters from the electron. Therefore, you won't be able to determine the location of the electron very precisely.

To improve your ability to locate the electron, you now choose a bulb that emits more energetic photons. The shorter wavelength allows you to determine the electron's position relatively well. But the photon kicks the electron so hard that you don't know where the electron is going next. The smaller the wavelength, the better you can locate the electron, but the more the photon alters the electron's path.

Heisenberg argued that we cannot make any measurements on a system of atomic entities without affecting the system in this way. The more precise our measurements, the more we disturb the system. Furthermore, he argued, the measured and disturbed quantities come in pairs. The more precisely we determine one half of the pair, the more we disturb the other. In other words, the more *certain* we are about the value of one, the more *uncertain* we are about the value of the other. This is the essence of the uncertainty principle.

Two of these paired quantities are the position and momentum along a given direction. (Recall that the momentum for a particle is equal to its mass multiplied by its velocity.) As we saw in the thought experiment described above, the more certain your knowledge of the position, the more uncertain was your knowledge of the momentum. The converse is also true.

This idea is now known as Heisenberg's **uncertainty principle**. Mathematically, it says that the product of the uncertainties of these pairs has a lower limit equal to Planck's constant. For example, the uncertainty of the position along the vertical direction Δy multiplied by the uncertainty of the component of the momentum along the vertical direction Δp_y must always be greater than $\hbar/2$.

$$\Delta p_y \, \Delta y \geqslant \hbar/2$$

where $\hbar = h/2\pi$.

This principle holds for the position and component of momentum along the same direction. It does not place any restrictions on simultaneous knowledge of the vertical position and a horizontal component of momentum.

Another pair of variables that is connected by the uncertainty principle is energy and time, $\Delta E \Delta t \geqslant \hbar/2$. This mathematical statement tells us that the longer the time we take to determine the energy of a given state, the better we can know its value. If we must make a quick measurement, we cannot determine the energy with arbitrarily small uncertainty. Stated in another way, the energy of a stable state that lasts for a very long time is very well determined. However, if the state is unstable and exists for only a very short time, its energy must have some range of possible values given by the uncertainty principle.

26.2.2 Probability Waves(概率波)

Nature has an underlying rule governing this strange behavior. We need to unravel the mystery of why electrons (or photons for that matter) are always detected as single particles and yet collectively they produce wavelike distributions. Something is adding together to give the interference patterns. To see this we once again look at water waves.

There is something about water waves that does add when the two slits are open—the displacements (or heights) of the individual waves at any instant of time. Their sum gives the displacement at all points of the interference pattern; that is, $h_{12} = h_1 + h_2$. The maximum displacement at each point is the amplitude of the resultant wave at that point.

With light and sound waves we observe the intensities of the waves, not their amplitudes. Intensity is proportional to the square of the amplitude. It is important to note that the resultant, or total, intensity is not the sum of the individual intensities. The total intensity is calculated by adding the individual displacements to obtain the resulting amplitude of the combined waves and then squaring this amplitude. Thus, the intensity depends on the amplitudes of each wave and their relative phase. The intensity of the combined waves is larger than the sum of the individual intensities when the displacements are in the same direction and smaller when they are in opposite directions.

There is an analogous situation with electrons. The definition for a **matter-wave amplitude** (called a wave function) is analogous to that for water waves (this is usually represented by the symbol Ψ and pronounced "psi"). The square of the matter-wave amplitude is analogous to the intensity of a wave. In this case, however, the "intensity" represents the likelihood, or probability, of finding an electron at that location and time. There is one very important difference between the two cases. We can physically measure the amplitude of an ordinary mechanical wave, but there is no way to measure the amplitude of a matter wave. We can only measure the value of this amplitude squared.

These ideas led to the development of a new view of physics known as **quantum mechanics**, which are the rules for the behavior of particles at the atomic and subatomic levels. These rules replace Newton's and Maxwell's rules. A quantum-mechanical equation, called Schrödinger's equation after the Austrian physicist Erwin Schrödinger, is a wave equation that provides all possible information about atomic particles.

Glossary

probability	概率	predicament	困境
indeterminacy	不确定性	misinterpret	曲解
thought experiment	思想实验	dim light bulb	弱光灯泡
entity	实体	uncertainty principle	测不准原理
Planck's constant	普朗克常量	probability wave	概率波
underlying rule	潜规则	unravel	阐明,解释
collectively	全体地,共同地	intensity of the wave	波的强度
wavelike distribution	波状分布	interference pattern	干涉图样
matter-wave amplitude	物质波幅	wave function	波函数
likelihood	可能性	quantum mechanics	量子力学
Schrödinger's equation	薛定谔方程		

26.3 专业英语常用表达-26 一致 符合

常用动词有：
accord　符合，一致
coincide　一致，相符
fit　符合

agree　符合，一致
answer　符合
meet　符合，适合

常用名词有：
accord　一致，符合
coincidence　符合，一致
correspondence　符合，一致
congruence/congruency　一致，符合

agreement　符合，一致
consistence/consistency　一致(性)
conformity　符合，一致

常用形容词有：
consistent　一致的，符合的
congruous　一致的，全等的
corresponding　一致的，符合的

accordant　一致的
conformable　一致的，符合的

常用词组有：
answer to　适应，符合
be in agreement with...　与……相一致
be in accord with...　与……相一致
be in conformity with/to...　与……相一致
be/as consistent with...　与……相一致(协调)，符合……
bring...into accord with...　使……与……一致(相调和)
bring...into correspondence with...　使……与……一致起来
conform to...　(使)一致，(使)符合
conform M to N　使M与N一致
conform with　与……一致，与……符合
correspondence between M and N　M与N相符
correspond to/with...　符合于……
fit in with　符合，适应
fit...into...　使……符合……
fit...like a glove　完全符合……
tally with...　与……相符合，与……一致

例如：
answer a description　与描述相符
observations that *fit* the theory nicely　与理论完全相符的观测
consistence of composition　成分的一致性
consistency check　一致性检验
curve *fit*　曲线拟合
meet a criterion　符合标准

meet the specification 符合规格/规范

The lab *answers to* his description. 这实验室与他的描述相符。

The experimental results *agree/accord with* the theoretical calculations. 实验结果与理论计算相符合。

The actual experimental figures are *in agreement with/in accord with/in conformity with/consistent with* the estimated figures. 实验中的数字与估计数字相符合。

A contact lens *conforms to/is consistent with* the curvature of the eyeball. 接触透镜与眼球的曲率相符。

The theory does not *correspond to* the experimental facts. 这一理论与事实情况不符。

Our results *coincide with* those obtained by other professors. 我们的结果与其他一些教授所取得的结果相一致。

It is shown that the QCT(quasi-classical trajectory) calculated results *agree well with/show a good agreement with* the experimental data for the reaction. 结果表明,对于这种反应,利用准经典轨线法计算的结果与实验获得的数据吻合得很好。

LESSON 27

27.1 物理学专业英语中描写文和说明文的写作

27.1.1 描写文的英语写作

物理领域的描写文多数是在描述作者对于外在事物的观察,以及由各种感官知觉所形成的印象。因此,陈述的内容通常用于表明各种物体、现象、过程与事件的性质或状态,并且让读者也能通过这些细节的描述,去认识并体会作者所要呈现的外在事物的性质或状态。换言之,描写文在写作上必须要聚焦在事物的某项特点上,并且借助具体细节的刻画进一步清楚地呈现事物的特点。

描写文的写作要注意几个要点:

(1) 围绕主题,选好细节,使描写做到内容丰富、结构紧凑。

(2) 顺序恰当。

(3) 详略得当,重点突出。

(4) 努力运用客观、直观、形象的语言及恰当的形容词,并要避免重复单调地用词。把事物的外形、特征、性质等具体地描绘出来,使人产生身临其境、如睹其物的感受。

以下是一篇简短描写文的例子:

A Relay

A relay is a switching device for opening and closing one or more electrical circuits on receipt of an electrical signal.

A simple kind of relay consists of two parts: a switch in a high voltage circuit which is operated by a spring loaded armature and a low voltage electro-magnetic circuit.

The electro-magnetic circuit comprises a soft iron core shaped like a horseshoe. Each arm of the core has a coil wound around it. The coils are connected to each other and to a battery through an on/off switch.

以下是对静物进行描写时常用的表示方法：

above	在……上	below	在……下
over	在……上	underneath	在……下
at the front	在前面	at the back	在后部
to the left	在左边	to the right	在右边
on the left-hand side	在左手边	on the right-hand side	在右手边
in the middle	在中间	near	近
close to	靠近	apart	相隔
some distance from	相隔一段距离	upper	上面的
higher	更高的	lower	更低的
on top of	在……上面	at the top of	在……上部
at the foot of	在……底部	at the base of	在……底部
at the bottom of	在……底部	beside	在……旁边
alongside	在……旁边	on one side	在一边
on the other side	在另一边	front	前面
back	后面	rear	后面
upside down	颠倒的	inverted	颠倒的
inside	里面的	within	在……里面
outside	外面的	to be shaped like	形状像……
to be attached to	与……相连		

以下是对过程进行描写时的常用表达方法：

firstly	首先	first of all	首先
to begin with	首先	the first step is…	第一步是……
the first stage is…	第一阶段是……	at the first stage	在第一阶段
secondly	第二	next	其次；然后
then	然后；接着	subsequently	随后
after this	此后	the next step is…	下一步是……
in the next stage	在下一阶段中	in the following stage	在下面的阶段中
at the same time	同时	simultaneously	同时
finally	最后	eventually	最后
the last step is…	最后一步是……	in the last stage	在最后一阶段中

27.1.2 说明文的英语写作

说明文是对一个特定的主题提出解说和阐释，其主要目的是让本来对这一主题知之甚少的读者，在读完文章后能得到相当程度的了解。说明文中自然也不免掺杂叙述与描写的成分，但和描写文不同的是，说明文的叙述和描写侧重于提供精确完整的信息，让解说具备有力的证据，支持作者要阐明的观点。

物理专业中的说明文应用很多,各种仪器设备的使用说明、电器的操作手册、教科书、实验报告等,无一不是说明文。说明文是用说明的表达方式来解说事物,阐明事理,其主要特点有:功能性强、描写客观、分析理性、重逻辑、讲证据、推导过程严密、语言表达科学准确等。

说明文的种类有很多,物理学中常用的两种为事物说明文和事理说明文。

要写好说明文,应该注意以下几点:

(1) 抓住事物特点即本质特征。这样可以使读者获得全面、深刻的认识。

(2) 安排好说明顺序。说明文常用的顺序有三种:时间顺序;空间顺序;逻辑顺序。有时说明复杂的事物,常常将几种说明顺序结合运用。

(3) 恰当选择说明方法。要写好事物说明文,不仅要抓住特征,注意条理,而且要巧妙运用说明方法,像下定义、举例子、作比较、分类别、列数字、画图表、打比方等。这样就能类别清楚,层次分明,增强说明的直观性、形象性,使被说明事物的特征变得鲜明突出,可以把复杂的事物说得清楚、直观。

(4) 做到语言的准确、简明、通俗、生动。这是因为说明文的写作目的,是对事物作有条理的、客观的、科学的介绍和解释。

以下是一篇简短说明文的例子:

Cross Product (Vector Product)(叉积/矢积)

The cross product of two vectors A and B is defined to be a vector $C = A \times B$ whose magnitude equals the area of the parallelogram formed by the two vectors, as in Fig. 27-1 (a). The vector C is perpendicular to the plane containing A and B in the direction given by the right-hand rule, that is, as the fingers curl from the direction of A toward the direction of B, the direction of C is given by the thumb (Fig. 27-1 (b)). If ϕ is the angle between the two vectors and n is the unit vector that is perpendicular to each in the direction of C, the cross product of A and B is

Fig. 27-1

$$C = A \times B = (AB\sin\phi)n$$

If A and B are parallel, $A \times B$ is zero.

在描写文中列举的进行静物和过程描写时常用的表示方法,也同样可以在说明文中采用,在此不再重复列举。

27.2 专业英语阅读

27.2.1 Bose-Einstein Statistics(玻色-爱因斯坦统计)

In the early 1920s Satyendra Nath Bose, a professor of University of Dhaka was intrigued by Einstein's theory of light waves being made of particles called photons. Bose was interested in deriving Planck's radiation formula, which Planck obtained largely by guessing. In 1900 Max Planck had derived his formula by manipulating the math to fit the empirical evidence. Using the particle picture of Einstein, Bose was able to derive the radiation formula by systematically developing a statistics of massless particles without the constraint of particle number conservation. Bose derived Planck's Law of Radiation by proposing different states for the photon. Instead of statistical independence of particles, Bose put particles into cells and described statistical independence of cells of phase space. Such systems allow two polarization states, and exhibit totally symmetric wavefunctions.

He developed a statistical law governing the behavior pattern of photons quite successfully. However, he was not able to publish his work; no journals in Europe would accept his paper, being unable to understand it. Bose sent his paper to Einstein, who saw the significance of it and used his influence to get it published.

Fermi-Dirac and Bose-Einstein statistics apply when quantum effects are important and the particles are "indistinguishable". Quantum effects appear if the concentration of particles $(N/V) \geqslant nq$. Here nq is the quantum concentration, for which the interparticle distance is equal to the thermal de Broglie wavelength, so that the wavefunctions of the particles are touching but not overlapping. Fermi-Dirac statistics apply to fermions (particles that obey the Pauli exclusion principle), and Bose-Einstein statistics apply to bosons. As the quantum concentration depends on temperature; most systems at high temperatures obey the classical (Maxwell-Boltzmann) limit unless they have a very high density, as for a white dwarf. Both Fermi-Dirac and Bose-Einstein become Maxwell-Boltzmann statistics at high temperature or at low concentration.

Maxwell-Boltzmann statistics are often described as the statistics of "distinguishable" classical particles. In other words the configuration of particle A in state 1 and particle B in state 2 is different from the case where particle B is in state 1 and particle A is in state 2. This assumption leads to the proper (Boltzmann) distribution of particles in the energy states, but yields non-physical results for the entropy, as embodied in the Gibbs paradox. This problem disappears when it is realized that all particles are in fact indistinguishable. Both of these distributions approach the Maxwell-Boltzmann distribution in the limit of high temperature and low density, without the need for any ad hoc assumptions. Maxwell-Boltzmann statistics are particularly useful for studying gases. Fermi-Dirac statistics are most often used for the study of electrons in solids. As such, they form the basis of semiconductor device theory and electronics.

Bosons, unlike fermions, are not subject to the Pauli exclusion principle: an unlimited number of particles may occupy the same state at the same time. This explains why, at low temperatures, bosons can behave very differently from fermions; all the particles will tend to congregate together at the same lowest-energy state, forming what is known as a **Bose-Einstein condensate.**

B-E statistics was introduced for photons in 1920 by Bose and generalized to atoms by Einstein in 1924.

The expected number of particles in an energy state i for B-E statistics is:

$$n_i = \frac{g_i}{e^{(\varepsilon_i - \mu)/kT} - 1}$$

with $\varepsilon_i > \mu$ and where:

n_i is the number of particles in state i

g_i is the degeneracy of state i

ε_i is the energy of the ith state

μ is the chemical potential

k is Boltzmann's constant

T is absolute temperature

This reduces to Maxwell-Boltzmann statistics for energies $\varepsilon_i - \mu \gg kT$.

27.2.2 Fermi-Dirac Statistics(费米-狄拉克统计)

Before the introduction of Fermi-Dirac statistics (F-D statistics) in 1926, understanding some aspects of electron behavior was difficult due to seemingly contradictory phenomena. It was difficult to understand, for example, why electrons in a metal can move freely to conduct electric current, while their contribution in the same metal to the specific heat was negligible, as if there were considerably fewer electrons. It was also difficult to understand why the emission currents, generated by applying high electric fields to metals at room temperature, were almost independent of temperature.

The difficulty encountered by the electronic theory of metals at that time was due to considering that electrons were (according to classical statistics theory) all equivalent. In other words it was believed that each electron contributed to the specific heat an amount of the order of the Boltzmann constant k. This statistical problem remained unsolved until the discovery of F-D statistics.

F-D statistics was first published in 1926 by Enrico Fermi and Paul Dirac. According to an account, Pascual Jordan developed in 1925 the same statistics which he called Pauli statistics, but it wasn't published in a timely manner. Whereas according to Dirac, it was first studied by Fermi, and Dirac called it **Fermi statistics** and the corresponding particles **fermions**.

F-D statistics was applied in 1926 by Fowler to describe the collapse of a star to a white dwarf. In 1927 Sommerfeld applied it to electrons in metals and in 1928 Fowler and Nordheim applied it to field electron emission from metals. Fermi-Dirac statistics continues to be an important part of physics.

F-D statistics is a part of the science of physics that describes the energies of single particles in a system comprised of many particles (for example electrons) that obey the Pauli Exclusion Principle. It is named after Enrico Fermi and Paul Dirac, who each discovered it independently.

F-D statistics applies to identical particles with half-integer spin in a system in thermal equilibrium. Additionally, the particles in this system are assumed to have negligible mutual interaction. This allows the many-particle system to be described in terms of single-particle energy states. F-D statistics gives the distribution of particles over these states and includes the condition that no two particles can occupy the same state, which has a considerable effect on the properties of the system. Since Fermi-Dirac statistics applies to particles with half-integer spin, they have come to be called fermions. It is most commonly applied to electrons, which are fermions with spin 1/2. Fermi-Dirac statistics is a part of the more general field of statistical mechanics and uses the principles of quantum mechanics.

Glossary

Planck's Law of Radiation	普朗克辐射定律	quantum effects	量子效应
Fermi-Dirac statistic	费米-狄拉克统计	Bose-Einstein statistic	玻色-爱因斯坦统计
quantum concentration	量子浓度	indistinguishable	不可区分的
de Broglie wavelength	德布罗意波长	configuration	结构,位型,组态
condensate	凝聚	classical particles	经典粒子
temperature	温度	density	密度
photon	光子	white dwarf	白矮星
Pauli Exclusion Principle	泡利不相容原理	proper(Boltzmann)distribution	正常(玻耳兹曼)分布
Maxwell-Boltzmann statistic	麦克斯韦-玻耳兹曼统计	ad hoc	特定的,专门的
semiconductor device	半导体器件	congregate	使聚集,使集合
entropy	熵	Gibbs paradox	吉布斯佯谬
Bose-Einstein condensate	玻色-爱因斯坦凝聚	degeneracy	简并度
chemical potential	化学势	Boltzmann's constant	玻耳兹曼常数
specific heat	比热	fermions	费米子
emission current	发射电流	contradictory	矛盾的
identical particles	全同粒子	half-integer spin	半整数自旋
statistical mechanics	统计力学		

27.3 专业英语常用表达-27 状态 状况

at a complete standstill 处于完全停顿状态
at high temperature 在高温下
at/in/on/under… 处于……状态
at low concentration 在低密度(浓度)下
at rest 处于静止状态
at room temperature 在室温下
at the same electric potential 在相同电势下

at work　正在工作(运行)

bring/put…into/to…　使处于……状态

have a high density　具有高密度

in a good state of repair　维修良好,状态良好

in a stable state　处于稳定状态

in a state of disorder　处于杂乱(无序)状态

in a state of unstable equilibrium　处于非稳定平衡状态

in a suspended state　处于悬挂/暂停状态

in danger　处于危险状态,受到危险

in disrepair　失修

in equilibrium　处于平衡状态

in motion　处于运动状态

in operation　正在运行,在运行(工作)中

in poor condition　状况不佳

in progress　正在进行,在进行中

in suspension　吊着,悬浮着,悬着

in vacuum　在真空状态下

on fire　着火,在燃烧

on test　正在经受试验/测试

on the decrease　正在减少

on the increase　正在增长

under construction　正在建造中

under control　处于受控状态

under development　正在研制之中

under discussion　正在讨论中

under heat treatment　在热处理中

under investigation　在调查中

under study　在研究中

under way　正在进行

An object *at rest* will remain *at rest* and an object *in motion* will continue *in motion* with a constant velocity unless it experiences a net external force. 任何物体都保持静止的或沿一条直线做匀速运动的状态,除非作用在它上面的力迫使它改变这种状态。

Both Fermi-Dirac and Bose-Einstein become Maxwell-Boltzmann statistics *at high temperature* or *at low concentration*. 费米-狄拉克统计和玻色-爱因斯坦统计在高温或者低密度的情况下都会变为麦克斯韦-玻耳兹曼统计。

When no motion of charge occurs within the conductor, the conductor is *in electrostatic equilibrium*. 当导体内的电荷没有运动时,导体就处于静电平衡状态。

If an object is instantaneously *at rest*, is the force on it necessarily zero? 如果一个物体在某一瞬间是静止的,那么它所受到的外力是否必然为零呢?

Because the two spheres are connected by a conducting wire, the entire system is a single conductor and all points must be *at the same electric potential*. 由于这两导体球被导线连接，所以整个系统构成一个导体，因而所有各点处于电势相同的状态。

If a body is acted on by a number of forces and still remains stationary, the body is said to be *in equilibrium*. 如果一个物体受到数个力的作用而仍保持静止状态，我们说该物体处于平衡状态。

If the electric field were not zero, free charges in the conductor would accelerate *under the action of the electric force*. 如果电场不为零，导体内的自由电荷在电场力的作用下会加速运动。

The pig-iron comes out of the blast-furnace *in a molten state*. 生铁呈熔化状态流出高炉。

Metal which is hardened by cold-working may *be brought back to its original state/condition* by annealing. 通过冷加工而变硬的金属可通过退火恢复到它原来的状态。

The engine should be *under normal working conditions* during the test. 在试验时发动机应处于正常运行状态。

The surface of the liquid is *under a tension*. 液体的表面处在张力作用下。

LESSON 28

28.1 物理学专业科研论文的英语写作

著名物理学家法拉第指出："科学研究有三个阶段，首先是开拓，其次是完成，最后是发表。"科研论文写作是科学研究工作者毕生都要从事的工作。科研论文是创新性科学和技术研究工作取得成果的科学论述；是理论性、实验性或观测性新知识的科学记录。按照国际科学界的规定，任何一项科研成果的确立（尤其是基础理论研究成果），都必须以在公开学术刊物发表为依据。将研究成果撰写成论文，发表在专业学术期刊上就是把科技成果公之于世，确定科技成果的优先权。

专业学术期刊是进行科技信息交流的理想工具。目前国际上在物理学领域影响力比较大的、影响因子比较高的专业学术期刊大多是英文期刊。可是，一篇高质量的学术论文能否在国际知名学术期刊得到发表，并不仅仅取决于研究成果本身的质量与水平，也取决于科研论文的英文写作水平。英语写作上词不达意，错误百出的科研论文是不会得到发表的。

28.1.1 科研论文的组成部分

尽管物理学领域的专业学术期刊很多，各期刊要求的格式也不尽相同。但是，科研论文的一般框架结构都是基本相同的，一般包括九个部分：Title（标题），Authors and Affiliation（作者及所属单位），Abstract（摘要），Key Words（关键词），Introduction（引言），Body of the Paper（论文主体），Conclusion（结论），Acknowledgment（致谢），References（参考文献）。

28.1.2 英文标题的撰写方法

1. 标题的结构

标题又叫题目、题名。标题应以最恰当、最简明的词语的逻辑组合反映出文章中最重要的内容。英文标题常以名词短语(noun phrase)为主要形式,即标题基本上由一个或几个名词加上其前置和(或)后置定语构成。标题一般不使用介词短语的形式或从句的形式,但介词短语可作定语,如表示方法、条件等的 by,with 短语等。有时也用 on 引出介词短语,表示"论(关于)……"之意。短语型标题要确定好中心词,再进行前后修饰。各个词的顺序很重要,词序不当,会导致表达不够准确。标题一般不采用陈述句,因为标题主要起标示作用,而陈述句容易使标题具有判断式的语义;且陈述句不够精练和醒目,重点也不突出。少数情况(评述性、综述性和驳斥性)下可以用疑问句做标题,疑问句可用探讨性语气,易引起读者兴趣。

2. 标题的类型

报道型标题:常用于对某一领域的发展动态、新理论或实验进展等进行通报。例如:
Development of Nanophosphors—A review
解说型标题:对实验、方法、理论等解释或说明。例如:
An approach for solving Maxwell equations of electromagnetic field in chiral media
研究探索型:对方法、理论、观点等进行研究和探讨。
Quasi-Classical Trajectory Study of the Reaction Dynamics of Ca ($^1S_0$, ^3P) Atoms with $CHCl_3$
综合型标题:兼有以上三类特点。例如:
Quantum efficiency and surface passivation effect of nanocrystalline $Y_2O_3:Eu^{3+}$

3. 标题的字数

标题不应过长。国外科技期刊一般对标题字数有所限制。标题一般不超过两行,每行不超过 42 个印刷符号和空格。总的原则是,标题应确切、简练、醒目,在能准确反映论文特定内容的前提下,标题词数越少越好。若题目难以用一句话概括,还可以用副标题补充说明论文的特定实用信息和下层内容,使其更准确。

4. 标题中的冠词

科技论文标题中的冠词有简化的趋势,凡可用可不用的冠词均可不用。

5. 标题中的大小写

标题字母的大小写有以下 3 种格式:全部字母大写;每个词的首字母大写,但 3 个或 4 个字母以下的冠词、连词、介词全部小写;标题第 1 个词的首字母大写,其余字母均小写。

6. 标题中的缩略词语

已得到整个科技界或本领域科技人员公认的缩略词语,才可用于标题中,否则不要轻易使用。

28.1.3 作者及所属单位英译

1. 作者

作者的名字一定要用全名,中国人名按汉语拼音拼写。如:
Luo Keyan, Keyan Luo, Ke-yan Luo, KEYAN LUO.

2. 单位

单位名称要写全(由小到大),并附地址和邮政编码,确保联系方便。有些工作单位直接标在作者姓名下面。如：

Department of Physics，Dalian Maritime University，Dalian 116026，People's Republic of China．

也有不少杂志把工作单位写在论文第1页的脚注中。如：

The author is with the Department of Physics，Dalian Maritime University，Dalian 116026，People's Republic of China．

28.1.4 摘要

摘要的定义为："以提供文献内容梗概为目的，不加评论和补充解释，简明、确切地记叙文献重要内容的短文"。由于大多数检索系统只收录论文的摘要部分，或其数据库中只有摘要部分免费提供，并且有些读者只阅读摘要而不读全文或常根据摘要来判断是否需要阅读全文，因此摘要的清楚表达十分重要。好的英文摘要对于增加论文的被检索和引用机会、吸引读者、扩大影响起着不可忽视的作用。

由于摘要部分在科研论文书的写中具有重要作用，本书将在 LESSON 29 专门对摘要的英文写作进行论述，详细内容请参阅 29.1 物理学专业科研论文中摘要的英语写作。

28.1.5 关键词

根据联合国教科文组织的规定：全世界公开发表的科技论文，都必须附有英文关键词。关键词是为了适应文献索引工作，特别是计算机自动检索的要求，从文章中选取出来，用以表示全文主题信息的单词或术语。每篇文章选取 3~8 个词，置于摘要的下方。

28.1.6 引言

引言，又称导言、前言等，属于整篇论文的引论部分。引言的内容包括：说明本研究工作的起因、背景、目的、意义等；介绍或评价与本研究相关领域前人研究的历史、现状、成果及其相互关系；陈述本项研究的宗旨，包括研究目的、理论依据、方案设计、要解决的问题等。

1. 引言开头部分（对他人研究成果的评述）常用表达

Much work has been done on…

Somebody obtained very accurate results in…

By the late 1990's，researchers had started scientific work on…

In 2006×××and×××independently identified…

Current/Recent observations indicate that…

Recent observations indicate that…

The field of…has been one of steady growth during the past decade.

One of the most important aspects of…

The role of…is now well established.

As we know…

It has been proved that…

It was proved (reported) that…

There are few communications on the effect of…on…

Smith et al. (2000) reported that...

Most of the experiments were carried out...

It has been known long that...

It is well documented that...

According to the... theory,...

2. 引言中间部分（进展情况分析）的常用表达法

Recently, the so-called...has attracted considerable attention.

It has been shown that...

There has been increasing interest in...

As we know,...

As has been stated (proved) that...

This experiment has a significant impact on...

The method worked well at...

In recent years, more attention has been focused on...

The concept of...has been proposed and used by many authors during the last few years.

It was proved (reported) that...

Hayman (1999) pointed out that...

Sen showed that...

Two methods have been employed to estimate the...

Smith *et al*. (2000) reported that...

Several experiments on...

Based on the results of...

...were (was) discussed and reviewed.

In preliminary studies using...

The experiment on...was carried by...

In spite of the potential importance of...

We hypothesize that under conditions of...

The following questions need to be answered: ...

We have examined the effects of ...on...

Although increasingly more is known about...

As...can be..., several authors have investigated the role of...

A developmental study was undertaken to describe the...

Many studies have brought out that...

Many previous studies have shown that...

Some information is also available as to...

In the present study...was researched under conditions of...

We are also interested in...

In addition to our interest in understanding...

In addition to its role as a...

In contrast, the present author found previously that...

The results made by...have shown...

Recent evidence suggested that...

Recent experiments by...have suggested...

To meet this challenge, a great deal of effort focusing on...

...is (are) needed for better understanding...

At the present time...

However, it is becoming increasingly clear that...

3. 引言结尾部分(本项研究的宗旨)的常用表达法

The paper is organized as follows.

Our aim in this paper is to study...

To test specifically the ability of...

The primary objective of our study was to examine...

The goal of this study was to select...and to see whether...

The objective of the current study was therefore to examine the effects of... on...

This paper reports the growth response of...to...

This paper describes an experiment done to test the effects of... on...

Our objectives were (i)... (ii)...

28.1.7 正文

正文部分和摘要、引言部分相比，写作相对容易。只要英语表达正确，描述清晰就可以了。具体写作方法可参考 LESSON 26 中的"段落写作"部分。

学术论文的正文一般包括 Material and Method, Result, Discussion 三个部分。

Material and Method 部分主要描述研究课题的方法、思路、理论依据，理论的重要推导过程，研究过程中所使用的设备、仪器、软件、条件以及所用材料的性能等。

Result 部分公布有关数据和研究结果。

Discussion 部分对结果进行相关的讨论和分析。

28.1.8 结论段

结论段是对全文内容或相关研究课题的高度概括和理论总结。结论应该与论文的摘要、引言以及论文的主体相呼应。结论要简明扼要，重点说明通过研究得到了什么结果，解决了什么问题，有待改进之处等，同时提出以后的研究方向。

表示结论的常用词汇有：

To conclude, to sum up, to summarize, in summary, in all, in a word, in short, in brief, as has been noted.

常用句型有：

In conclusion,...

In summary,...

It is concluded that...
The results of the experiment indicated that...
The research work has brought about a discovery of...
The research conducted suggests that...
The fruitful work gives the explanation of...
The findings of the research have led to the conclusion that...
It is clear from the forgoing discussion that...
This demonstration/illustration/comparison shows...
The above results/data lead us to a conclusion that...
From the results we have obtained it can be concluded that...
On the basis of these results we conclude that...
All these data confirm the previous assumption that...
It has been proved that...is superior to that of the...
Studies and trials have led to the conclusion that...has substantial advantages over...for future development.

28.1.9 致谢

致谢应实事求是,并在征得被致谢者的书面同意后,提出其姓名和工作内容或说明贡献;标示出资助团体、组织及个人的全称;并且注明资助项目名称。如:"技术指导"、"参加实验"、"本项研究由…基金资助"等。

表达方式有:本文得到×××的帮助,本文承蒙×××详细审阅,谨此致谢等。

常用句型有:

The author(s) wish(es) to express sincere thanks to...
I'd like to thank...
Grateful acknowledgement of...
I would like to express my appreciation of...
Thanks must be given to...
Special thanks go to...
I offer my thanks to...
Particular recognition is due to...
His sincere thanks are offered to...
With a great sense of debt, we thank...

例如:

Technical support from Professor Baojiu Chen and data analysis by Dr. Li Yao are acknowledged.

The authors thank Professor Lihong Cheng (Department of..., ... University) for the helpful suggestions.

The authors are grateful to the support from Dr. Ying Shao (Department of..., ... University).

The research work is supported by the National Natural Science Foundation of China (Grant No. 10475036).

This work was supported by the Natural Science Foundation of Liaoning Province, China under Grant No. 10747111.

This work was supported by the Scientific Research Foundation of the Higher Education Institute of Liaoning Province, China (Grant No. 05L215).

致谢一般放在正文和参考文献之间,也有的放在文章首页的页脚处。

28.1.10 参考文献(References)

参考文献是学术论文必备的部分,一般附在论文之后。关于科技论文中参考文献的写作方式,不同的刊物要求不同。因此,作者在撰写论文时应首先决定该文在哪一种刊物上发表,然后再根据刊物的要求,按照规定的格式进行标注。

1. 参考书的一般书写顺序

顺序编号,作者姓名,书名,版次,出版社地点,出版社名称,出版年份。如:

References

[1] Zhong Haiyang, *et al*. University Physics. Dalian: Dalian Maritime University Press, 2006

[2] Lu Tan, Universe the Largest Subject of Physics. Changsha: Hunan Education Press, 1994

2. 期刊杂志上的一般书写顺序

作者姓名,文章标题(很多国际学术期刊不要求写),刊物名称(简写),年,卷(期)号,引用部分起(止)页码。如:

References

[1] R. N. Bhargava, D. Gallagher, X. Hong, A. Nurmikko, Phys. Rev. Lett. 1994, 72, 416-418.

[2] R. K. Jain, R. C. Lind, J. Opt. Soc. Am. 1983, 73, 647-651.

[3] A. I. Ekimov, A. L. Efros, A. A. Omushchenko, Solid State Commun. 1985, 56, 920-926.

也有按照如下顺序:作者姓名,刊物名称(简写),卷号(年),引用部分起(止)页码。如:

[1] A. Henglein, Chem. Rev. 89 (1989) 1861.

[2] R. Rosetti, S. Nakahara, L. E. Brus, J. Chem. Phys. 79 (1983) 1086.

[3] R. Rosetti, J. L. Ellison, J. M Gibson, L. E. Brus, J. Chem. Phys. 80 (1984) 552.

[4] L. E. Brus, J. Phys. Chem. 90 (1986) 2555.

如果引用的论文已经在发表当中,应在该文献的最后加上"印刷中"即"in press"字样。

各种学术期刊对于参考文献的书写顺序的要求可能会有少许的差异,但是所要求的主要内容都差不多。

28.2 专业英语阅读：Relativity（相对论）

When observers in different inertial reference systems describe the same events, their reports don't match. In the framework of classical relativity they disagree in their descriptions of the paths and on the values of an object's velocity, momentum, and kinetic energy. On the other hand, they agree on relative positions, lengths, time intervals, accelerations, masses, and forces. Even the laws of motion and the conservation laws are the same.

We never asked, or even thought to ask, whether some of these were actually the same for all reference systems or whether we had just assumed them to be the same. In classical relativity we assumed that the concepts of length, time, and mass were the same. But are they really the same?

Albert Einstein asked this question. He reexamined the process of describing events from different reference systems with an emphasis on the concepts of space and time. This led to the development of the special theory of relativity.

Einstein arrived at the special theory of relativity by setting forth two postulates, or conditions, that are assumed to be true. He then examined the effects of these postulates on our basic concepts of space and time. The predictions of special relativity were then compared with actual experimental measurements. The theory had to agree with nature to have any validity.

The First Postulate（第一假设）

The first postulate is related to the question of whether there exists an absolute space—some signpost in the Universe from which all motion can be regarded as absolute. This postulate says that there is no absolute space; any inertial reference system is just as good as any other. Einstein's first postulate is a reaffirmation of the Galilean principle of relativity.

The laws of physics are the same in all inertial reference systems.

As we discussed in the previous chapter, Galileo argued that a traveler in the hold of a ship moving with a constant velocity could not conduct experiments that would determine whether the ship was moving or at rest. However, the Galilean principle of relativity came into question near the end of the 19th century. A theory by the Scottish physicist James Clerk Maxwell describing the behavior of electromagnetic waves, such as light and radio, yielded unexpected results.

In Newton's laws, reference systems moving at constant velocities are equivalent to each other. If, however, one system accelerates relative to another, the systems are not equivalent. Because Newton's laws depend on acceleration and not on the velocity, acceleration of a reference system can be detected, but its velocity cannot.

In Maxwell's theory, however, the *velocity* of the electromagnetic waves appears in the equations rather than their acceleration. According to the classical ideas, the appearance of a velocity indicated that inertial systems were not equivalent. In principle, you could merely turn on a flashlight and measure the speed of light to determine how your reference system was moving.

Maxwell's equations and the Galilean principle of relativity were apparently in conflict. It seemed that the physics world view could not accommodate both. During his studies, Einstein had developed a firm belief that the principle of relativity must be a fundamental part of any physical theory. At the same time, he wasn't ready to abandon Maxwell's new ideas about light. He felt that the conflict could be resolved and that both the principle of relativity and Maxwell's equations could be retained.

Meanwhile, others were pursuing different options. If there were an absolute reference system in the Universe, it should be possible to find it. The key seemed to lie in the behavior of light. It is impossible, using experiments performed within inertial systems, to distinguish any one such system from any other; therefore, no experiment can establish whether a particular inertial system is uniformly moving or at "absolute rest". The concept of absolute rest thereby loses all significance; if it can never be determined, motion is relative, not absolute. The Principle of Relativity logically abolishes the concept of absolute rest and, along with it, the concept of absolute motion—motion is relative.

The Second Postulate(第二假设)

It is difficult (if not impossible) to re-create a creative process. Although Einstein mentioned the failure to find the ether in his 1905 paper, years late he indicated that his primary motivation in formulating the *Second Postulate* was his deep belief in the principle of relativity.

The Constancy of the Speed of Light: *Light propagates in free space with a speed c that is independent of the motion of the source.*

Now this much in itself is both orthodox and reasonable; after all, the speed of sound is independent of the motion of the source. A sound wave is launched into a medium, and the speed of the disturbance is only determined by the physical characteristics of the medium. The speed of the source is irrelevant. If light is a wave in the aether, this statement makes obvious sense.

Remember that the equations of Electromagnetic Theory—Maxwell's Equations—led to a wave equation that provided the speed of light in vacuum. Assuming Maxwell's Equation are right and given the First Postulate, it must be that this same wave equation is applicable in all inertial systems—the vacuum speed of light measured on Earth or inside a rocket ship must be the same, independent of any uniform relative motion. In Maxwell's theory, the speed of light is a constant, not a motion-dependent variable. In other words, *the speed of light measured with respect to an inertial system must be the same for all such systems.*

The fact that the speed of light is independent of the motion of the source is not at all troublesome, but is it also independent of the motion of the detector (i.e. the observer)? Certainly, the speed of sound is not; if the detector rushes toward the source, mobbing with respect to the air, the measured speed of sound increases. Just imaging two identical ships headed toward a motionless sound-emitting buoy, one steaming along at full speed and the other dead in the water. On both ships, the time it takes as blast of sound to sweep from bow to stern is measured, and the speed of the wave is computed in that inertial system. Clearly, for the ship moving toward the buoy, that time will be shorter (during the interval it takes the sound to traverse the ship, the stern will advance somewhat toward the pulse, shortening the effective length), and the wave speed will be determined to be faster.

But for the light wave, the conclusion is an astonishing one: *no matter how fast a light source moves toward or away from an inertial observer*, and *no matter how fast the observer moves toward or away from the source, the speed of the light passing from one to the other in vacuum will always be c—the speed of light is constant*; it is absolute.

The two postulates separately are innocent enough. It's when we mix them together, when we demand that they both apply at once, that things seem to become fantastic. The paradox of Einstein's youth is now no longer a paradox—one simply cannot travel next to a light beam and catch up to it. The spaceship could be rushing either toward or away from the source at any speed you like, say, 99% of c, and still the inertial observer aboard it will measure the speed of the beam to be c! This is one of the premier conclusions of the analysis; its disturbingly "illogical" nature suggests that our familiar, comfortable understanding of space and time requires revision.

Time Dilation(时间膨胀)

Time on a clock that is moving, at speed v, with respect to an inertial observer is seen to run slower than time on a clock that is stationary with respect to that observer.

$$\Delta t_M = \frac{\Delta t_S}{\sqrt{1 - v^2/c^2}}$$

This slowing down of time is known as **time dilation**, and it's usually a very small effect. A clock aboard a commercial plane flying at top speed for $\approx$ 70 000 years would lose about 1s compared to a clock on the ground.

The duration of an event Δt_S, as measured by an inertial observer who sees the event begin and end in one place is called the **proper time**; it's always shorter than the corresponding interval Δt_M, as measured by an observer who sees the event occur in a moving system.

Time dilation has been measured. Certain nuclei vibrate and emit gamma-rays with very precise frequencies. When a sample of such a substance is heated, the gamma-ray frequency is reduced. The atoms move around more rapidly, and with respect to an observer at rest in the laboratory, their nuclear clocks run more slowly.

Length Contraction(长度收缩)

A rod has one **proper length** measured by any observer at rest with respect to it, but it can also have different shorter lengths measured by people who are in uniform motion with respect to it.

$$L_M = L_S \sqrt{1 - v^2/c^2}$$

A moving observer measures an object to have a length (along the direction of motion) that is shorter than the length measured by an observer at rest with respect to the object (i.e., shorter than the proper length). This is the **length contraction**, and it applies only to the direction of motion; transverse distances are unaltered.

There is no absolute distance between Beijing and Shanghai; an atlas provides the proper distance as measure by people a rest with respect to the planet. But every traveler moving with regard to the surface sees his or her own version of that spatial interval, depending on his or her relative speed. Go fast enough, and Beijing and Shanghai can be a meter or two apart. As for the reality of all of this, the business is similar to what happens with the Doppler Effect. Run toward a source and the sound pitch increases. The wave itself doesn't physically change, but the perception of it certainly does change. What you hear and measure—the reality of the experience—most assuredly depends on how you move with respect to the source.

Glossary

classical relativity	经典相对论	special theory of relativity	狭义相对论
postulate	假定,基本原理	signpost	路标
reaffirmation	再肯定	yield	产生
Galilean principle of relativity	伽利略相对性原理	flashlight	闪光灯
accommodate	容纳	retain	保持
pursue	从事	abolish	废止
aether/ether	以太	formulate	阐明
constancy	恒久不变	orthodox	正统的,传统的
irrelevant	无关的	inertial systems	惯性系
motion-dependent	与运动有关的	mob	拥挤前进
buoy	浮筒	blast of sound	一阵声波
from bow to stern	从船首到船尾	paradox	佯谬,似非而是的论点
premier	第一的,首要的	disturbingly	令人不安地,动摇地
revision	修改,修正	time dilation	时间膨胀
proper time	固有时间	corresponding	对应的
length contraction	长度收缩	proper length	固有长度

atlas 地图,地图集
pitch 音调,音高标准
assuredly 确实地,确信地
spatial 空间的
perception 感知,感觉

28.3　专业英语常用表达-28　原因　理由

常用词语结构有：
-ed/-ing　短语或介词短语
by virtue of　由于……,因为……
on account of　由于……,因为……
for...　由于……,因为……
because/since/as...　因为……
owing to the fact that...　因为……
now that...　既然……,由于……
inasmuch as　因为……,由于……
for＋分句　因为……(不用于句首)
be attributed to...　归因于……
account for...　说明……的原因
result from...　由于……所引起
in view of the fact that...　因为……,考虑到……这一事实
due to the fact that...　因为……,由于……(这一事实)
because of　由于……,因为……
in view of　由于……,因为……
due to/owing to　由于……
from...　由于……
on account of the fact that...　因为……
seeing that...　鉴于……,由于……(的缘故)
in that...　因为……,原因在于……
insofar as...　因为……,由于……
arise from...　由于……而引起
be ascribed to...　归因于……
for the fact that...　是……的原因,说明……的原因
from the fact that...　由于……所引起,由于……产生

常用句型有：
The reason＋why 分句＋is＋that 分句　(……之所以)……的原因是……
This is/explains＋why 分句　这就是……的原因,这说明了为什么……
acceleration *due to* gravity　重力加速度
The radial or normal acceleration is *due to* the time rate of change in direction of the velocity vector.　法向加速度的产生是由于速度矢量的方向随时间的变化率。
Being negative, the electrons are attracted to the anode.　由于电子带负电,故被吸向

阳极。

Confined in a boiler, the steam from boiling water develops great pressure on the walls that confine it. 由于被密封在锅炉内，沸水所形成的蒸汽对封闭蒸汽的锅炉壁产生巨大的压力。

For many years, our standard of time was based on astronomical observations of the earth's rotation. *Because of/on account of/owing to/due to* the variations in the earth's rotation, in 1967 the 13th General Conference on Weights and Measures adopted an atomic standard for time. 过去很多年，我们的时间标准都是基于对地球转动的天文观察。由于地球转动的变化，1967年国际计量大会为时间采用了一种新的原子标准。

The microwaves in home ovens are tuned to the natural frequency of vibration of water molecules. The water molecules in food resonate with the oscillating electric field and absorb large amounts of energy, *accounting for* the rapid cooking times that make microwave ovens so convenient. 家用微波炉的微波波长已经预先设置为水分子的自然振动频率。微波炉之所以方便快捷就是因为食物中的水分子与电磁场共振并吸收了大量的热量所致。

Light travels a long way in a year, *for* its speed is 300 000 kilometers a second. 光在1年中能走很远的距离，因为光速是 300 000 km/s。

The difference between one element and another is *due to the fact that* they have different structures of atoms. 一种元素之所以不同于另一种元素是因为它们具有不同的原子结构。

This equation $r=r_0+v_0t+\frac{1}{2}at^2$ says that the displacement vector $r-r_0$ is the vector sum of a displacement v_0t, *arising from* the initial velocity of the particle, and a displacement $\frac{1}{2}at^2$, *resulting from* the uniform acceleration of the particle. 方程 $r=r_0+v_0t+\frac{1}{2}at^2$ 说明：位移矢量 $r-r_0$ 是位移 v_0t（由于粒子的初速度而产生）和位移 $\frac{1}{2}at^2$（由于匀加速度而产生）的矢量和。

This difference *results from* the fact that there are different numbers of neutrons in the two nuclei. 这种区别是由这两个核中的中子数不同引起的。

The reason why hard water does not lather readily with soap is that it contains calcium. 硬水之所以不容易起肥皂泡的原因是它含有钙。

This explains why gases are so easily compressed. 这说明了为什么气体那么容易被压缩。

Unit Eight

LESSON 29

29.1 物理学专业科研论文中摘要的英语写作

29.1.1 英文摘要

摘要是以提供文献内容梗概为目的,不加评论和补充解释,简明、准确地记述文献重要内容的短文。正式出版并对外发行的学术期刊等都要求刊中的调查报告、实验方法、技术性文章、综述性文章、研究论文等在正文中附上英文摘要。

1. 摘要的类型

根据内容的不同,摘要可分为以下三大类:信息性摘要、指示性摘要和报道—指示性摘要。

(1) 信息性摘要(informative abstract):也称报道性摘要或资料性摘要。其特点是全面、简要地概括论文的目的、方法、主要数据和结论,一般包括了原始文献某些重要内容的梗概。通常,阅读这种摘要可部分地取代阅读全文。

信息性摘要主要由以下三部分组成:

① 目的:主要说明作者写此文章的目的,或说明本文主要要解决的问题。

② 过程及方法:对作者的主要工作过程及所用的方法进行说明,也包括适用条件,使用的主要设备和仪器。

③ 结果:说明作者在此工作过程最后得到的结果和结论。如有可能,尽量提一句作者所得结果和结论的应用范围和应用情况。

信息性摘要多用于科技杂志或科技期刊的文章,也用于会议论文及各种专题技术报告。例如:

The reaction dynamics of the $Ca(^1S_0, ^3P) + CHCl_3 \rightarrow CaCl + CHCl_2$ has been studied by means of quasi-classical trajectory calculation based on a constructed extended London-Eyring-Polanyi-Sato potential energy surface. The vibrational distribution, reaction cross section and rotational alignment are all obtained, which are under detailed discussion for product CaCl. The calculated results show that the product CaCl vibrational population peaks are located at $v=13$ (for the ground state) and $v=12$ (for the excited states) at collision energy 2.302 kcal/mol. This product vibrational distribution agrees well with the experimental one in [Han et al, Chem. Phys. Lett. 178 (1991) 528]. The cross-section decreases thoroughly with the increasing of the collision energy. Rotational alignment $\langle P_2(J' \cdot K)\rangle$ are also obtained which deviating much from -0.5 and changing interestingly with collision energies from 1.5 kcal/mol to 20.6 kcal/mol.

（2）指示性摘要（indicative abstract）：也称为说明性摘要、描述性摘要（descriptive abstract）或论点摘要（topic abstract）。一般只用两三句话概括论文的主题，仅指出文献的综合内容，而不涉及论据和结论，多用于综述性文献、会议报告等。综述性文献最常用于介绍如某技术在某时期的综合发展情况，或某技术在目前的发展水平及未来展望等。总之这种文献是综述情况而不是某个技术工艺、某产品或某设备的研究过程。此类摘要可用于帮助读者决定是否需要阅读全文。例如：

Rare-earth doped materials are of crucial importance to optoelectronics, and are widely deployed in fiber amplifiers and solid-state lasers. This article summarizes the present state of the art in this rapidly growing field. Recent developments in the areas of rare-earth doped semiconductors and insulators are discussed and new classes of materials that open up new possibilities for extended functionality and greater optoelectronic integration are described. Nanostructured materials and wide bandgap semiconductors are of particular interest, though recent developments in more traditional material systems are highlighted. Emphasis is placed on erbium-doped materials, as these are of the greatest importance for telecommunications applications, but as range of other rare-earth ions are also discussed.

（3）报道—指示性摘要（informative-indicative abstract）：这种摘要结合了以上两种摘要的特点，以报道性摘要的形式表述文献中信息价值较高的部分，以指示性摘要的形式表述其余部分。在此不再举例说明。

29.1.2 摘要的基本结构和内容

摘要在本质上是一篇高度浓缩的论文，所以其构成与论文主体内容结构是对应的。传统的摘要多为一段式，在内容上大致包括引言、材料与方法、结果和结论、讨论等主要方面。摘要应包括以下内容梗概：

① 研究目的：研究工作的前提、目的和任务，所涉及的主题范围及需要解决的问题；
② 研究方法：所用的理论、条件、材料、手段、设备、程序、实验方法和基本步骤等；
③ 结果和结论：观察、实验的结果、重要数据、性能，由此得出的结论，以及结果的分析、比较、评价、应用；
④ 提出的问题：今后的课题、假设、启发、建议、预测等；
⑤ 其他：不属于研究、研制、调查的主要内容，但具有重要价值的信息。

一般地说，报道性摘要中②、③、④应相对详细，①和⑤则相对简略。指示性摘要则相反。

在确定了摘要的基本结构与内容后，就应该注重摘要写作中的细节问题了。选择适当词汇、时态和语态，是使摘要表达准确、符合英文语法修辞规则的前提。通常情况下，摘要中谓语动词的时态和语态都不是通篇一律的，而应根据具体内容有所变化，否则容易造成理解上的混乱。

1. 词汇的选择

学术论文摘要应该做到科学概念明确清晰,逻辑关系突出,文字简洁明了,内容正确无误。尤其是专业术语的表达上要符合英文习惯,体现专业英语的科学、准确、严谨的特征。

在用词方面应注意如下几个问题:

(1) 用词应力求简单,在表达同样意思时,尽量用短词代替长词,以常用词代替生僻词。当描述方法、步骤时,应该用狭义词代替广义词。例如,英文中有不少动词,do,run,get,take 等,虽简单常用,但其意义少则十几个,多则几十个,用这类词来描述研究过程,读者难免产生误解,这就要求根据具体情况,选择意义相对明确的词,诸如 perform,achieve 等,以便于读者理解。下表列出了一些例子。

日常使用的词	专业英语中的词	日常使用的词	专业英语中的词
about	approximately	turn on	complete
ask	inquire	take in	absorb
begin	commence	push in	insert
buy	purchase	push down	depress
carry	bear	put up	erect
change	transform	put together	aggregate
cheap	inexpensive	put out	extinguish
end	conclude	put in	add
finish	complete	wear away	erode
get	obtain	take away	remove
give	accord	send for	summon
have	posses	use up	consume
method	technique	carry out	perform
available	obtainable	come across	encounter
avoid	circumvent	make up	invent
quick	rapid		

(2) 能用名词作定语不要用动名词作定语,能用形容词作定语就不要用名词作定语。例如:用 measurement accuracy 不用 measuring accuracy 用 experimental results 不用 experiment results;可直接用名词或名词短语作定语的情况下,要少用 of 句型。例如用 measurement accuracy,不用 accuracy of measurement;用 camera curtain shutter,不用 curtain shutter of camera;用 equipment structure,不用 structure of equipment。

(3) 避免重复、删繁就简

像 true facts, basic essentials, cooperate together 等都是在写作时容易出现的重复叙述现象。同样的东西或者概念完全没有必要重复两次。

在删繁就简方面,能用一个词描述就不用词组。如用 increased 代替 has been found to

increase 用 the results show 代替 from the experimental results, it can be concluded that。
再如：

繁：The experiment was a very difficult one.

简：The experiment was very difficult.

像 in my opinion, I think that, one must admit that 等表现主观臆断的词汇，在学术论文中显得既不够严谨也不简练，应当避免。例：

不严谨：In my opinion, rare-earth doped materials are of crucial importance to optoelectronics.

较好：Rare-earth doped materials are of crucial importance to optoelectronics.

（4）避免口语化

口语化：There is another group of experts who examined the laser and found out the cause of the failure.

正式：Another group of experts examined the laser and found out the cause of the failure.

（5）专业术语要准确

准确选择专业词汇是摘要写作的一个关键问题。专业术语往往也是关键词，文献检索一般是从关键词开始的。如果用词不准确，那就可能造成文章在检索中被忽略，或造成对他人的误导。

在选择词汇时要充分考虑所叙述内容的专业范围，还要注意该词的语境。各个英语词汇在不同的应用条件下，具有不同的词义，具体选择哪一个，则要根据具体情况来决定。例如：resistance 阻力，电阻，耐久性；resistance to sparking 击穿电阻（电学）；resistance to heat 耐热性（材料科学）；resistance to wear 耐磨性（材料科学）。

在选择专业术语的时候，特别是跨学科的时候，确实会遇到很多难题。除了查阅专业工具书或者利用语料库以外，我们还可以借助于网络资源。例如我们可以利用 google 等搜索引擎的强大功能，实现翻译或者查找的目的。我们还可以有针对性地利用一些专业网站强大的检索功能，找到与自己的研究方向相同或者相近的文章，参考一下相关内容。另外，"中国知网"在线翻译助手（CNKI 翻译助手）等也都是专业工作者的好帮手。

2．英文摘要的时态

英文摘要时态的运用以简练为佳。

（1）一般现在时：用于说明研究目的、叙述研究内容、描述结果、得出结论、提出建议或讨论等；涉及公认事实、自然规律、永恒真理等，也要用一般现在时。摘要开头表示本文所"报告"或"描述"的内容，以及摘要结尾表示作者所"认为"的观点和"建议"的做法时，可采用一般现在时。

（2）一般过去时：用于叙述过去某一时刻的发现、某一研究过程（实验、观察、调查、研究等过程）。用一般过去时描述的发现、现象，往往是尚不能确认为自然规律、永恒真理，只是当时情况；所描述的研究过程也明显带有过去时间的痕迹。

（3）现在完成时和过去完成时：摘要中完成时用的相对较少。现在完成时把过去发生的或过去已完成的事情与现在联系起来，而过去完成时可用来表示过去某一时间以前已经完成的事情，或在一个过去事情完成之前就已完成的另一过去行为。说明某课题现已取得的成果,宜采用现在完成时。

3. 英文摘要的语态

采用何种语态,既要考虑摘要的特点,又要满足表达的需要。一篇摘要很短,尽量不要随便混用,更不要在一个句子里混用。

(1) 主动语态:摘要中谓语动词采用主动语态,有助于文字简洁、表达有力。

(2) 被动语态:在摘要的写作中一般都强调要多采用被动语态,理由是科技论文主要是说明事实经过,至于那件事是谁做的,无须一一说明。为强调动作承受者,采用被动语态为好;被动者无关紧要,也尽量用强调的事物作主语。

(3) 英文摘要的人称:过去,摘要的首句多用第三人称 This paper... 等开头,现在倾向于采用更简洁的被动语态或原形动词开头。例如：To describe...，To study...，To investigate...，To assess...，To determine...，行文时最好不用第一人称。

4. 注意事项

(1) 摘要一般不分段,但长篇报告或学位论文的摘要可以分段。摘要的字数视需要而定,一般 200～300 字;英文稿以 1000 印刷符号为宜,原则上不超过全文的 3‰。句型力求简单,通常应有 10 个左右意义完整、语句顺畅的句子。写论文摘要时,应尽量将文中的主要内容和这些内容的要素写入摘要中。

(2) 冠词的使用。主要是定冠词 the 易被漏用。the 用于表示整个群体、分类、时间、地名以及独一无二的事物、形容词最高级等较易掌握,而用于特指时常被漏用。这里有个原则,即当使用 the 时,听者或读者已经明确我们所指的是什么。

(3) 数词的使用。避免用阿拉伯数字作首词。

(4) 单复数的使用。一些名词单复数形式不易辨认,从而造成谓语形式出错,写作时应尽量避免。

(5) 使用短句。长句容易造成语义不清,但使用短句也要避免单调和重复。尽量采用-ing 分词和-ed 分词作定语,少用关系代词 which, who 等引导的定语从句。由于摘要的时态多采用一般过去时,使用关系代词引导的定语从句不但会使句式变得复杂,而且容易造成时态混乱。采用-ing 分词和-ed 分词作定语,在简化语句的同时,还可以减少时态判定的失误。

(6) 言简意赅。论文摘要的撰写应充分考虑论文的主要内容,尽量使用简洁的文字将论文的精华高度地概括出来。

29.1.3 英文摘要写作的常用表达方法

(1) 引言部分

回顾研究背景的常用词汇有 review, summarize, present, outline, describe 等。如：

This article *summarizes* the present state of transparent glass ceramics in this rapidly growing field.

This paper *outlines* some of the basic methods and strategies and *discusses* some related theoretical and practical issues.

阐明写作或研究目的的常用词汇有 purpose, attempt, aim 等。另外还可以用动词不定式充当目的状语来表达。如：

The aim is to help shipping industry carrying on the research of positioning analysis.

In order to study the quantum reaction dynamics of large molecular systems, the time-dependent quantum wave packet approach was used to study the $F+CD_4 \rightarrow CD_3+DF$ reaction systems.

介绍论文的重点内容或研究范围的常用的词汇有 study, present, include, focus, interest, emphasize, emphasis, attention 等。

Nanostructured materials and wide bandgap semiconductors *are of particular interest*.

Emphasis is placed on erbium-doped materials, as these are of the greatest importance for telecommunications applications.

（2）方法部分

介绍研究或实验过程的常用词汇有 test, study, investigate, examine, experiment, discuss, consider, analyze, analysis 等。

The influences of pretreatment of capillary and porogen solvent on porous structure and permeation were *investigated*.

We use N-body simulations *to investigate* the structure of dark halos in the standard cold dark matter cosmogony.

说明研究或实验方法的常用词汇有 perform, measure, estimate, calculate, by, with, using 等。

Baseline separation of several phenol compounds was *performed* on the monolithic column.

The single crystal structure was *determined* by X-ray diffraction.

Cross section and rate constant were *calculated* based on the MJ1 PES of the ground state.

介绍应用、用途的常用词汇有 use, apply, application 等。

The narrow bandwidth meets the requirements for future development of background suppressed latent fingerprint detection *for forensic applications*.

Our program *uses* a maximum likelihood approach and is based on version 3.3 of Felsenstein's dnaml program.

（3）结果部分

展示研究结果的常用词汇有 show, reveal, result, present, exhibit, achieve 等。

The calculated results *reveal* that the product CaCl vibrational population peaks are located at $v=13$（for the ground state）and $v=12$（for the excited states）at collision energy 2.302 kcal/mol.

The experimental results *show* that the proposed approach greatly improves the image retrieval's effect.

介绍结论的常用词汇有 summary, introduce, conclude 等，有时作者直接把结论写出，并不使用这些词汇。

It can be *concluded* that non-linear dynamic model concerning multi-factors should be the focus in near future research.

We *conclude* that the bottom ejecting cooling of piston is a powerful tool in the process of the design and improvement for the piston.

(4) 讨论部分

陈述论文的论点和作者的观点的常用词汇有 suggest, report, present, explain, expect, highlight, describe, discuss 等。

A general method of obtaining new double inverse scattering wave function from a double seed solution is *presented*.

The origin of the ultraviolet emission is *discussed* here with the help of temperature-dependent PL spectra.

用于阐明论证的常用词汇有 support, provide, indicate, identify, find, demonstrate, confirm, prove, clarify, verify 等。

Authors have successfully *demonstrated* that synthesis of PO from C_3H_6 and O_2 in DBD plasma.

The structure analysis *indicates* that there are a lot of hydrogen bonds in the crystal.

The experiment *proved* that the removal of the surfactant was a stepwise mechanism.

用于推荐和建议的常用词汇有 suggest, suggestion, recommend, recommendation, propose, necessity, necessary, expect 等，有时用 may, could 等词也能把意思表示出来。

IR absorption spectra and photoluminescence spectra *suggest* that the hybrid nanoparticles are promising materials for bioassay.

Our results *are a suggestion of* a new way to probe the position of fluorescent molecules in such photonic bandgap materials.

The electrospun SiO_2 nanofibers *could* be used for reinforcement of dental composites.

29.1.4 英文摘要写作中的常用句型

(1) 表明研究目的

The purpose of this paper is...

The primary goal of this research is...

The intention of this paper is to survey...

The overall objective of this study is...

The emphasis of this study lies in...

This paper aims at providing...

This paper presents.../reports.../describes.../discusses.../investigates.../deals with...

The objectives of this investigation are...

The aim of this investigation is to...

The purpose of the present study is to...

This paper is concerned with...

This paper is aimed at...
This paper is limited to...
The authors report...
The authors (writers) made observation on...
Investigation on... be carried out in...
...be evaluated and analyzed.

(2) 提出论据

The method used in this paper is known as...
The technique applied is referred to as...
The approach adopted widely is called...
This is a working theory based on the idea that...
The theory is characterized by...
Included in the experiment were...
This formula is verified by...
The experiment used consists of...
Experiments were performed to check...

(3) 说明研究方法

The experiment was performed using...
The approach is based on...
The present study was started in＋时间＋to (do)...
...be identified according to...
...be determined by...
...be based on the use of...
...be used to (do)...
...be collected from...
...be grown during...
...be observed by/using ...
...be studied by measuring...
...be characterized by...
Analysis of...by...revealed that...

(4) 表示研究结果与结论

The results indicate that...
Our results confirm that...
The study proves that...
The results demonstrate that...
The study reveals that...
The conclusion is that...
The results showed that...
The results can be summarized as follows.

We conclude: ①…②…③…
The comparison concludes that…
The results from the present investigation suggest that…
These findings regarding…suggest that…
These results support the findings found (observed) by…

29.2 专业英语阅读：Lasers(激光)

The understanding of the quantized energy levels in atoms and the realization that transitions between these levels involved the absorption and emission of photons led to the development of a new device that produced a special beam of light. Assume that we have a gas of excited atoms. Further assume that an electron drops from the $n=3$ to the $n=2$ level in the energy diagram in Fig. 29-1(a). A photon is emitted in some random direction. It could escape the gas, or it could interact with another atom with an electron in one of two ways. It could be absorbed by an atom with an electron in the $n=2$ level, exciting the electron to the $n=3$ level (Fig. 29-1(b)). This excited atom would then emit another photon at a random time in a random direction. On the other hand, the original photon could stimulate an electron in the $n=3$ level to drop to the $n=2$ level, causing the emission of another photon (Fig. 29-1(c)). This latter process is known as **stimulated emission**. Moreover, this new photon does not come out randomly. It has the same energy, the same direction, and the same phase as the incident photon; that is, the two photons are coherent. These photons can then stimulate the emission of further photons, producing a coherent beam of light.

The device that actually produces coherent beams of light is called a **laser**, which is an acronym for *light amplification by stimulated emission of radiation*. A laser produces a beam of light that is very different from that emitted by an ordinary light source such as a flashlight. The laser beam has a very, very narrow range of wavelengths, is highly directional, and can be quite powerful. The laser beam is a single color because all of the photons have the same energy. For instance, the helium-neon laser usually has a wavelength of 632.8 nanometers. The beam is highly directional because the stimulated photons move in the same direction as those doing the

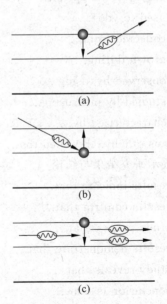

Fig. 29-1 (a) spontaneous emission (b) absorption (c) stimulated emission

stimulating. The fact that all of the photons have the same phase means that the amplitude of the resulting electromagnetic wave is very large. The intensity of a collection of coherent photons is obtained by adding the amplitudes and then squaring the sum. The intensity of a collection of incoherent photons is obtained by squaring the amplitudes and then adding these squares. The difference can be illustrated by considering a collection of five photons. In the laser beam we have $(2+2+2+2+2)^2 = 100$, while in the ordinary light beam we have $(2^2+2^2+2^2+2^2+2^2) = 20$. The effect is even more drastic for the very large number of photons in a laser beam. These factors combine to allow us to clearly see a 1-milliwatt laser beam shining on the surface of a 100 watt lightbulb.

Making a working laser was more complicated than the above description implies. A method had to be found for "building" a beam of many, many photons. This is done by putting mirrors at each end of the laser tube to amplify the beam by passing it back and forth through the gas of excited atoms. One of the mirrors is only partially silvered, so that a small part of the beam is allowed to escape (Fig. 29-2).

Fig. 29-2 A schematic of a simple laser

The construction of a laser was difficult because a photon is just as likely to be absorbed by an atom with an electron in the lower level as it is to cause stimulated emission of an electron in an excited level. Usually most of the excited atoms are in the lower energy state, so most of the photons are absorbed and only a few cause stimulated emission. Therefore, building a laser depends on developing a **population inversion**, a situation in which there are many more electrons in the excited state than in the lower energy state. This is usually done by exciting the atom's electrons into a metastable state that decays into an unpopulated energy state. A **metastable state** is a state in which the electrons remain for a long time. The electrons can be excited by using a flash of light, an electric discharge, or collisions with other atoms.

Lasers have a wide range of uses, from surveying to surgery. In surveying, the light beam defines a straight line, and by pulsing the beam the time for a round trip can be used to measure distances. This same method is used on a gigantic scale to determine the distance to the Moon to an accuracy of a few centimeters. A very short pulse (less than 1 nanosecond long) of laser light is sent through a telescope toward the Moon's surface. The beam is so well collimated that it only spreads out over an area a few kilometers in diameter. The Apollo astronauts left a panel of retroreflectors on the surface that reflects the light back to the telescope, allowing the round-trip time to be measured. These measurements serve as a test of the validity of the general theory of relativity because the theory predicts the detailed orbit of the Moon.

Laser "knives" are used in optometry and surgery. Two leading causes of blindness are glaucoma and diabetes. In treating glaucoma, a laser beam "drills" a small hole to relieve the high pressure that builds up in the eye. One of the complications of diabetes is the weakening of the walls of blood vessels to the point where they leak. The laser can be shined into the eye to cause coagulation to stop the bleeding. The energy in laser beams can also be used to weld detached retinas to the back of the eye. In laser surgery, the beam coagulates the blood as it slices through the tissue, greatly reducing bleeding. Laser beams can also be directed by fiber optics through tiny incisions to locations that would otherwise require major incisions and long healing times.

Lasers have widespread use in the marketplace. The audio and video information stored in the pits on CDs and videodiscs is read by laser beams. Likewise, the lasers at the checkout counters read the bar codes on the product identification labels, allowing the computer to print out a short description of the object and its current price. This has greatly reduced billing errors as well as the time required to check out.

Lasers have made practical holography possible and opened up a whole new research tool in holographic measurements.

Glossary

quantized energy levels	量子化能级	transition	跃迁
photon	光子	excited atom	受激发的原子
spontaneous emission	自发辐射	stimulated emission	受激辐射
acronym	首字母缩略词	amplification	放大
flashlight	闪光灯	helium-neon laser	氦-氖激光
coherent photon	相干光子	milliwatt	毫瓦
lightbulb	灯泡	silver	v. 镀银
population inversion	粒子数反转	excited state	激发态
metastable state	亚稳态	decay	衰减
unpopulation inversion	未占据的能态	surveying	测量
surgery	外科,外科学	collimated	准直的,平行的
retroreflector	回射器	general theory of relativity	广义相对论
optometry	视力测定,验光	glaucoma	绿内障,青光眼
diabetes	糖尿病	walls of blood vessels	血管壁
coagulation	凝结,凝结物	weld	焊接

detached retinas	脱落的视网膜	fiber optics	纤维光学
incision	切开，切口	bar code	条形码
product identification	产品识别	holography	全息摄影术，全息术
holographic	全息的		

29.3　专业英语常用表达-29　与物理学相关的词汇

applied physics	应用物理学	atmospheric physics	大气物理学
atomic physics	原子物理学	bubble physics	磁泡物理学
chemical physics	化学物理学	cloud physics	云物理学
computational physics	计算物理学	continuum physics	连续物理学
crystal physics	晶体物理学	earth physics	地球物理学
electron physics	电子物理学	environmental physics	环境物理学
experimental physics	实验物理学	health physics	保健物理学，放射卫生学
high-energy physics	高能物理学	infrared physics	红外物理学
low-temperature physics	低温物理学	marine physics	海洋物理学
mathematical physics	数学物理学	megagauss physics	兆高斯物理学
metal physics	金属物理学	molecular physics	分子物理学
nuclear physics	原子核物理学	oceanographic physics	海洋物理学
plasma physics	等离子物理学	quantum physics	量子物理学
radiation physics	辐射物理学	radio physics	无线电物理学
radioanalytical physics	放射分析物理学	reactor physics	反应堆物理（学）
relativistic physics	相对论物理学	semiconductor physics	半导体物理学
soil physics	土壤物理学	solar physics	太阳物理学
solid-state physics	固态物理学	statistical physics	统计物理学
surface physics	表面物理学	theoretical physics	理论物理学
thin-film physics	薄膜物理学	transistor physics	晶体管物理学
ultrasonic physics	超声物理学	vacuum physics	真空物理学
wood physics	木材物理学		

LESSON 30

30.1　物理学专业英语中报告的写作

　　在物理学及其相关领域的学习和工作中，会用到很多用途广泛的报告形式。工作中常用的有：提供项目进展情况的"进度报告（progress report）"，查证某些说法的"调查报告（investigation report）"，进行学术交流的"学术报告（academic report）"，对工作的开展提供建议的"建议书（recommendation report）"等。在学校中，报告已经成为常见的考核学生学习成果的方式，比如，实验报告、学期报告、专题报告、研究报告、科研论文报告、毕业论文报告等。尤其对于研究生而言，参加 seminar 进行 presentation 的机会很多，写报告更是一种要尽早掌握的技能。

物理领域中的各种英文工作报告力求准确、简洁、清晰。内容可以由文字和数据相结合，也可以由统计资料占主要篇幅。有时还用图示和表格辅助说明，使报告更加清楚。

30.1.1 报告的格式

报告主要由以下几部分组成：

1. Front Page 篇首

篇首主要包括以下几部分：

（1）Title page 标题页（封面）

（2）Preface 序言

（3）Abstract 报告摘要

（4）Table of contents 报告内容目录

2. Body 报告正文

（1）Introduction 引言

（2）Background 背景介绍

引言和背景介绍通常放在一起，放在报告的首段。一般是对于主题内容相关问题的阐述。在这里，要对所研究的问题进行明确的说明，介绍问题的起因、问题的相关主题和领域、解决问题的意义、期望解决的问题和达到的程度等内容。其中，通常有对相关问题过去研究状况的回顾，这些前期研究的基础可能是报告人自己的前期工作，也可能是其他研究者对这个问题的研究和贡献，同时对这些以前的研究贡献要有一些客观准确的评价。这么做的目的在于，首先能够让阅读报告的人清楚、迅速地了解报告所阐述问题的来龙去脉，其次也说明相关的研究具有良好的前期基础、调研广泛详细、有针对性、可信度高。

（3）Text (main body) with subsections 主体部分

这部分可以分章节阐述，含篇（Part）、章（Chapter）、节（Section），各章节分别设标题与小标题。

报告的这一部分通常包括 Procedure Section 过程部分、Result Section 结果部分和 Discussion Section 讨论部分。

Procedure Section 是报告最主要、最详尽的段落。其中可以包括详尽的资料、对研究过程具体翔实的描述、对仪器设备的说明、所采用的方法和手段、这些方法手段被采用的原因和优缺点、所做过的实验和试验、进行的观察和现象汇总等。在过程部分中所描述的内容，都具有可重现性，可以供别人重复和验证。

比如一个物理学的实验报告会有具体的操作步骤、采用的方法、观察的方式、获得的实验数据、实验室的环境条件（温度、湿度、气压等）。

一个科研过程的叙述，通常会复杂很多。一般地说，科研过程包括确定课题、调查研究、收集资料、分析和整理数据、进行推测或提出假设、检验和论证以及报告研究结果等步骤，每个阶段都有一些常用词语。现将部分过程常用英语表达列举如下：

① 描述调查研究和收集资料过程中的常用语：

investigate or conduct an investigation

visit or pay visits to people concerned
send out and collect questionnaires
take samples
collect information
gather data
obtain evidence
store sample(s)

② 进行整理、分析和比较过程的常用语：

organize/analyze data (findings, information, samples)

compare data (patterns, quantities, results, samples, values) A and B/compare A with B)/make a comparison between A and B

③ 在分析和比较的基础上得出初步结论，进行推测或提出假设等的常用语有：

a. 表示相同或类似

This is the same sort of pattern that people have got in...

This is the same sort of pattern that is going to be seen for...

The same thing will happen in... as well.

b. 表示差异

differ entirely (greatly, much, somewhat, widely)

entirely (qualitatively, quantitatively, slightly, vastly, very) different

big (considerable, huge, important, large, much, serious, slight, wide) difference(s)

c. 表示"证明，显示"等

常用 prove, reveal, show, suggest 等动词，其中 suggest 表示"把握不大，尚未得到证实"。例如：

The result is this extraordinary... showing huge variation. 结果就是，这个与众不同的……表明的差距是巨大的。

Laboratory evidence suggests, but does not prove, that...may be caused by...实验数据表明（虽然还未得到证实），……可能是……引起的。

They hope ... will reveal some of the causes of... 他们希望……揭示出……的某些成因。

④ 汇报科研工作和成果中，表示进度的常用词语有：just, now that, only, so far, still, 等；常用的说法有：

We're only just beginning to...

We're just about at that stage, or at the stage of...

We haven't begun yet to...

This is just getting the framework...

These are only some initial results...

The study is not yet completed (or not yet finished)...

Much remains to be done (to be discovered, to be looked for...)

Result Section 在报告中的地位非常重要。它是对研究或调查所获得结果的表述。在这里,要给出在问题段中提出的问题的最后具体解决方法及其相关的支持性材料。有时,所获得的结果导致的结论可能与最初的想法相悖,但应该把这种结果在报告中如实体现出来。如果所做的实验无法证明任何东西,或者获得的数据不完善或者与预想的相矛盾,那在报告中也要尽可能完整如实地阐述。

为了使结果能够清晰地展示,同时也能够对结果给予足够的强调,主要的结果应该采用鲜明直观的方式来表示,如目录、表格、坐标图、图解、示意图、照片等。

Discussion Section 中要对所获得的结果及所遇到的问题等进行讨论和建议。可以让读报告的人了解所得到的结果对问题的解决程度、所遇到的困难、以及其他的可能性等,这对以后的研究者也具有借鉴和指导作用,同时也可以为决策者提供一些建议和依据。

(4) Conclusion 结论

(5) Acknowledgments 致谢

(6) References 参考资料

第(4)、(5)、(6)部分的具体写作方式,与科研论文的英语写作部分中对应的内容相类似,读者可以参照对应的部分进行写作。

3. Appendixes 附录部分

附录部分是报告的最后一部分。这部分中的内容一般是那些不适合放在正文中、但仍然需要写在报告中的内容,例如比较大的数据表格、大的地图册、图纸、组织流程图表、背景知识等内容。不同的部分通常用字母表明顺序,例如 Appendix A,Appendix B 等。

30.1.2 报告写作的基本原则

(1) 明确报告的对象,分析他们的需要。不同的对象(如专家学者、管理人员、技术人员、检察视察人员等)需要的信息不同,在写作时要选择接受者希望得到的内容。

(2) 注意客观性和真实性。要如实报告研究、调查及其他活动的过程和结果,阐述事实本身,去除不相关的细节。

(3) 篇章结构要安排合理、富有逻辑性。报告分几大主要部分、几个小节,以及大标题和小标题各是什么,都要安排好并表示清楚。正式的报告更要讲究规范性,一般由标题、内容提要、目录、引言、正文和结束语等主要部分组成。简短的或非正式的报告也要确定好小节标题,要点要清晰、醒目。

(4) 篇章的组织模式一般按时间先后顺序来安排,也就是说,按研究或工作进行的先后顺序来组织篇章结构。或者按照各项工作的主次、重要性来组织。也可以将两者有机结合,如在某一段时间内做了几项工作,那就可以在时间总框架内,按主次来组织。

(5) 语言要简洁明了,直截了当。常用以下典型句型:

The reports provide the information about…

The reports present the findings of…

This report summarizes the results of…

(6) 如有必要可结合采用图表方式(如问卷、曲线图等)来表达调查结果。无论写什么报告,都要分析读者的要求和需要。作为项目的主管部门或出资赞助者,最想知道的信息是写报告人按照进度展开工作的情况和取得的阶段性成就、制造或生产出的样品或成品、收获、建议以及所取得的成果等。这些内容都要在报告中明确体现。

（7）在一份报告写完后，为了清楚和准确，除了要检查报告中陈述的技术资料外，还应该再检查一遍基本的语法和习惯性的表达是否准确。在复杂信息的表述中短句子比长句子更可取。也可以列出次序来打散文章中的长段并强调信息。尽可能用简单同时又不影响报告专业性的语言。虽然可以使用专业术语，但自抬身价的话应该避免。优秀的报告应该是一份为相关领域的读者准备的、有可读性并且有用的文件。

30.2 专业英语阅读：Spectroscopy（光谱学）

Isaac Newton showed that a glass prism could be used to split sunlight into a spectrum in 1666. Further studies by William Wollaston in 1802 revealed some black lines on the component colors of the solar spectrum. More detailed observations by Joseph von Fraunhofer resulted in 574 of these lines being mapped by 1815. These lines were named "Fraunhofer lines" in his honor. The image below shows a solar spectrum with Fraunhofer lines. Fraunhofer lines are dark absorption lines in the solar spectrum that can be seen when sunlight is passed through a prism to separate it into the colors of the rainbow. They occur because cooler gas, which is higher in the Sun's atmosphere, absorbs some colors of the light emitted by hotter gas lower in the Sun's atmosphere.

Fig. 30-1

Two key questions arise from studying these lines—what do they represent and how are they formed? The solutions to these questions were to take some time. Leon Foucault matched the lines produced by a sodium lamp with some of the dark lines in a solar spectrum in 1849. In 1857 Gustav Kirchoff and Robert Bunsen identified sodium in a solar spectrum. They found that a luminous solid or highly compressed hot gas could produce a continuous spectrum whilst a diffuse hot gas produced a spectrum with narrow bright lines on a black background.

Spectroscopy was originally the study of the interaction between radiation and matter as a function of wavelength. In fact, historically, spectroscopy referred to the use of visible light dispersed according to its wavelength, e.g. by a prism. Later the concept was expanded greatly to comprise any measurement of a quantity as function of either wavelength or frequency. Thus it also can refer to a response to an alternating field or varying frequency. A further extension of the scope of the definition added energy as a variable, once the very close relationship $E=h\nu$ for photons was realized. A plot of the response as a function of wavelength—or more commonly frequency—is referred to as a **spectrum**.

Spectrometry is the spectroscopic technique used to assess the concentration or amount of a given species. In this case, the instrument that performs such measurements is a **spectrometer** or **spectrograph**. Spectroscopy or spectrometry is often used in physical and analytical chemistry for the identification of substances through the spectrum emitted from or absorbed by them. It is also heavily used in astronomy and remote sensing. Most large telescopes have spectrometers, which are used either to measure the chemical composition and physical properties of astronomical objects or to measure their velocities from the Doppler shift of their spectral lines.

Two general types of spectra are now known, the continuous spectrum and the line spectrum. The continuous spectrum shows all the component colors of the rainbow. Line spectra appear in two forms, absorption spectra, showing dark lines on a bright background, and emission spectra with bright lines on a dark or black background. The first are like the solar spectrum and those from stars and the second are like those emitted from gas discharge tubes and some nebulae. These two types are in fact related and arise due to quantum mechanical interactions between electrons orbiting atoms and photons of light. Photons of light each have a specific frequency. The energy of a photon is a function of its frequency and is determined by $E=h\nu$, where ν is the frequency of the photon, E is the energy and h is Planck's constant which is equal to 6.626×10^{-34} J·s.

An electron orbits a nucleus in a stable energy level. If a photon of a specific frequency interacts with the electron, it can gain sufficient energy to "jump up" one or more levels. The photon is absorbed by the electron so cannot continue on to be detected by an observer. The electron then "de-excites" and jumps back down to a lower energy orbit, emitting a photon of specific frequency. This photon, however, could be emitted in any direction, not just in the same direction as the original incident photon. This is shown schematically in the diagram Fig. 30-2.

The Swiss school teacher, Johann Balmer in 1885 developed an empirical formula that determined the wavelengths of the four visible lines in hydrogen's spectrum. Five years later the Swedish physicist, Johannes Rydberg expanded Balmer's formula to apply to some other elements. The Danish physicist, Niels Bohr, finally provided an explanation as to how spectral lines formed in the 1920s. His work relied on quantum physics and the concept of energy shells or orbits for electrons.

The Balmer Series of visible lines for atomic hydrogen are caused by transitions from the $n=2$ orbit to and from higher orbits. The Lyman Series involves transitions down to the $n=1$ orbit and involve higher frequency photons in the UV region whilst the Paschen

Fig. 30-2

Series (to $n=3$) produces IR spectral lines. The number of spectral lines that can be produced is vast given the permutations of atoms, molecules and orbital transitions possible.

Glossary

spectroscopy	光谱学	solar	太阳的
Fraunhofer lines	夫琅和费谱线	prism	棱镜
sun's atmosphere	太阳大气	sodium lamp	钠灯
luminous	发光的	whilst	而
diffuse	扩散的	disperse	分散
comprise	包含	spectrometer	光谱仪,分光计
spectrograph	摄谱仪	remote sensing	遥感
composition	成分	astronomical	天文学的
continuous spectrum	连续光谱	absorption spectra	吸收光谱
emission spectra	发射光谱	gas discharge tube	气体放电管
nebulae	星云	de-excite	去激,发光
empirical formula	经验公式	Balmer Series	巴耳末系
Lyman Series	赖曼线系	UV region	紫外区
Paschen Series	帕邢系	IR spectral lines	红外光谱线
permutation	变换,排列	orbital transition	轨道跃迁

30.3 专业英语常用表达-30 导致 产生

可以表示"导致、产生、引起、造成"等含义的动词有：

bechance 发生,产生
create 引起,造成,是……的原因
engender 产生,引起,使出现,发生
excite 唤起,引起,诱发

generate 使形成,造成,引起,导致
incur 招致,引起,带来
initiate 使出现,使存在
invite 招致,引起

originate 发起,引起,导致
provoke 激起,引起,诱发
cause 引起,使发生,导致
elicit 导致,诱出
entail 引起,使成为必要
evoke 唤起,引起

give 产生,引起,带来
induce 引起,招致,感应
introduce 引导,引入,使开始
lead 促使,致使,引导
produce 产生,引起,导致
raise 唤起,激起,引起,招致

短语有：

be at the bottom of 是……的根本原因
bring about 带来,引起,导致,产生
call forth 唤起,使出现
come out of 由……产生,从……出来
draw forth 引起,引出,唤起
give occasion to 引起,使发生
issue in 导致,造成
lead up to 为……的先导,导致
open the door for 使成为可能,导致
result from 起因于,由……造成
set up 引起,导致
touch of 触发,引起

be creative of 产生
bring on 引起,导致,带来
come about 发生,产生
conduce to 引起,导致,有助于
give birth to 引起,产生,造成
give rise to 引起,导致,使发生
lead to 导致,引起,发生
open a door to 导致,使成为可能
result in 导致,造成,引起
set off 引起,激起
spark off 导致,引发,诱发

The increase in space between the molecules of a solid *causes* the expansion. 固体分子之间间隔的扩大导致了膨胀。

Rapid expansion of a gas *leads to* the decrease of the internal energy and the accompanying temperature reduction. 气体的迅速膨胀导致内能减少,温度下降。

The Lenz's law can be used to give the direction of the induced electromotive force (emf) and induced current *resulting from* electromagnetic induction. 楞次定律可以说明感生电动势和感生电流的方向,而二者均是由电磁感应所引起的。

The most common method to "pump" a gas laser, that is, to invert the population in the states that *give rise to* light amplification, is to use a gas discharge. "泵浦"气体激光(也就是对那些能产生光放大的状态进行粒子数反转)的最常见方法就是运用气体放电。

The results show that the ECR plasma source may *generate* stable, high density plasma with low electron temperature. 实验证明,ECR等离子体源能够稳定地产生电子温度较低的高密度等离子体。

Shock waves are *produced* when a body moving at hypersonic speeds compresses the air in front of it. 以高超音速运动的物体压缩它前面的空气时,会产生冲击波。

When reading a thermometer, it is essential to hold the instrument in an upright vertical position otherwise the reading error may be *introduced*. 对温度计读数时,一定要使温度计保持直立的位置,否则会引起读数误差。

LESSON 31

31.1 物理学专业英语中报告写作的实例

31.1.1 实验报告的写法

实验报告就是对一项实验的目的、仪器、过程、结果等情况进行记录、整理和总结的书面文字。

科学实验是开展科学活动最基本的方式和手段。而每次科学实验后，都应写出实验报告，对实验的目的、准备、过程、数据、现象、结果等进行客观的记录和总结。这是科学研究中必不可少的一环，写好实验报告，也是良好科学研究基本功的体现。

1. 撰写实验报告的一般方法

（1）报告的形式。实验报告一般有两种形式：一种是表格式，一种是叙述式。表格式的实验报告有固定的项目内容要求，一般是印制好了的，由实验者按表格填写就行了。

（2）数据记录。在进行实验之前，应确定好实验方法，拟定实验步骤，写在实验报告上。在实验的过程中，要按拟订的方法和步骤进行，对实验的过程进行认真的观察和记录，对实验数据作如实的反映，绝对容不得马虎，更不能擅自更改数据。

（3）结果分析。在进行分析时，首先要逐个检查、核实实验的数据和现象记录，再在此基础上进行分析，找出规律性的东西。

（4）语言表述。实验报告的语言应以客观、朴实、通俗为好，怎么符合实际就怎么表达。在词汇运用上也应坚持科学的态度。不要用华美的辞藻，也不要用夸张等修辞手法。

2. 物理实验报告的结构

物理实验报告一般包括如下部分：

（1）实验的编号和题目。

（2）对实验的介绍。通常包括三部分。

① 实验目的。这部分的内容主要是回答两个问题：Why are we doing the experiment? What problems are we trying to solve?

② 实验仪器。列出实验中使用的所有仪器及其型号。

③ 实验原理。写出实验所依据的原理、方法和需要验证的内容以及希望得到的结果，应写出必要的公式，画出必要的电路图、光路图和简明的原理图等。

以上的部分一般是在实验前通过预习而完成的，可根据实际的实验条件，通过查找资料完成。

（3）实验步骤。

① 清晰、简洁、明了地列出实验的每个步骤，并采用过去式和被动语态，如…solution was diluted by adding…，只需要写出主要的实验操作步骤，不需要写实验的准备过程。

② 写明实验的数据是如何获得的。

③ 列出用来记录实验数据的表格，表格内容要与实验步骤相对应，表格的行和列要写出对应栏目的内容，并标注单位。

(4) 数据记录。数据记录应如实、准确,正确保留有效数字。

(5) 数据的处理。列出计算公式,并代入数据计算出结果,并标注单位。注意标准偏差的单位与物理量的单位相同。最后要计算出实验的误差,给出物理量的数值区间。

(6) 结果与分析。简要归纳实验的结果(最后的物理量、化学量、数学量和相关的方程)、偏差(deviations)和误差(errors)。如果有需要,画出实验要求的作图和曲线等,并分析其所说明的事实。回答实验中提出的问题。

(7) 结论。结论通常回答 3 个问题:What did you do in the experiment? What does your data say? What did you learn? 在这部分中简短复述一下实验的目的和要解决的问题、实验是如何进行的、数据是如何获得的,并把数据或图表的内容进行简短概括,最后说明实验是否实现了预期的目的。

以下是一份实验报告的实例。

Measurement of Magnetization Curve of Ferromagnetic Material

Purpose

1. To understand the properties of the ferromagnetic material.
2. To observe the hysteresis loop of the ferromagnetic material.
3. To measure the practical magnetization curve of the ferromagnetic material.

Apparatus

Dual trace oscilloscope, AC millivoltmeter, experimental circuit, adjustable insulating transformer, wires

Principle

Ferromagnetic materials have a large and positive susceptibility to an applied magnetic field. They exhibit a strong attraction to magnetic fields and are able to retain their magnetic properties after the applied field being removed. Ferromagnetic materials' atoms have a net magnetic moment. They get their strong magnetic properties due to the presence of magnetic domains. In these domains, large numbers of atomic magnetic moments (10^{12} to 10^{15}) are aligned parallel so that the magnetic force within the domain is strong. When a ferromagnetic material is in the un-magnetized state, the domains are randomly organized and the net magnetic moment for the whole body is zero. When a magnetizing field is applied, the domains become aligned to produce a strong magnetic field.

As shown in Fig. 31-1 the ferromagnetic material is made into a ring with magnetizing coil of turns N_1 and secondary coil of turns N_2. The average circumference of the ring is l and the cross-sectional area is S. According to the Ampere's circuital theorem U_r is in proportion to the magnetic field H.

$$U_r = rlH/N_1 \qquad (31\text{-}1)$$

According to the law of electromagnetic induction the emf in the secondary coil is

$$\varepsilon_2 = -N_2 S dB/dt = RC dU_C/dt \Rightarrow U_C = N_2 SB/RC \qquad (31\text{-}2)$$

LESSON 31

Fig. 31-1 Circuit diagram

Since r, l, N_1, N_2, S and R are constants, the measurement of the magnetic field and magnetic induction can be realized by measuring the voltages across the resister and the capacitor. The numerical relationship is

$$H_m = (\sqrt{2}N_1/rl)U_r = 536U_r \text{(SI)} \qquad (31\text{-}3)$$

$$B_m = (\sqrt{2}RC/N_2S)U_C = 2.27U_C \text{(SI)} \qquad (31\text{-}4)$$

Procedure

1. Preparation

Connect the devices according to the circuit diagram. Set the range of the millivoltmeter as the maximum one. Turn on the power supply and adjust the oscilloscope to get an appropriate hysteresis loop on the fluorescent screen.

2. Measurement

Set the voltage of the adjustable insulating transformer at 100 V. Measure the magnitude of the effective voltage U_r and U_C for 12 times by AC millivoltmeter under different H_m controlled by the power. Reduce the output of the power by 5 V each time.

Data

The measured and calculated data are given in the following table.

No.	1	2	3	4	5	6	7	8	9	10	11	12
U_P/V	100	95	90	85	80	75	70	65	60	55	50	45
U_r/mV	87	83	79	77	73	69	67	63	59	57	54	51
U_C/mV	212	202	190	182	171	160	150	140	125	118	107	100
H_m/A/m	47	44	42	41	39	37	36	34	32	31	29	27
B_m/ 10^{-3} T	481	459	431	413	388	363	340	318	284	268	243	227

Analysis

The $B_m \sim H_m$ curve is plotted on the basis of the data (Fig. 31-2).

Conclusion

In the experiment the property of the ferromagnetic material was investigated by observing the hysteresis loop with the oscilloscope and by measuring the magnetization curve with the AC millivoltmeter. The hysteresis loop describes the hysteresis of the ferromagnetic material. From the data we can see that the magnetic induction changes nonlinearly along with the magnetic field. The experiment provides a method for the measurement of the magnetic field, and that is just the principle for the display of the hysteresis loop on the oscilloscope.

Fig. 31-2

31.1.2 观察(考察)报告的写法

观察报告就是通过对某个对象进行观察和记录、分析和研究而写成的一种书面文体。

写观察报告也是开展科研活动的基本功,许多科学研究都离不开观察。很多科学规律的发现,都是经过长期观察、随时记录、最后总结而获得的。观察报告就是对这种科学研究的记录、分析和总结,是开展科学研究的依据和基础。

以下是写观察报告的一般方法:

(1) 观察报告的格式一般具有标题、前言、主体和结尾几部分。标题要明确,可以通过标题大致了解观察的对象。前言部分应交代观察的对象、目的、方式等。主体部分应写清观察的过程、数据、分析及其结论。结尾部分写明观察者的姓名、观察日期等。

(2) 观察报告是一种科学研究报告,像一切科学报告一样,必须真实可靠。观察到的现象、过程、数据等,都必须准确、客观。

(3) 写观察报告应有客观的态度。无论是记录事实,还是叙述结论,都要忠实于客观实际,不必注入自己的感情,更不可使用自己主观的感情去代替或改变客观的现象,要力求写出事实的本来面目。

(4) 观察报告的结论。应从实际出发得出结论,不要捏造结论。

下面是一篇实地考察报告的实例:

To: Mr. XXX, president of YYY University

From: Mr. ABC, Dean of Studies

Subject: Buying Michelson interferometers and optical benches

Dear Mr. President:

Upon the request of the Equipment Division of the university, we have inspected the laboratories of the Physics Department and found its present equipments unsatisfactory to students, particularly to post graduates. Because there are just twenty Michelson interferometers in the laboratory, but there are almost ten times the students and 25 percent are postgraduates. The laboratory material is in such shortage that the situation has to be improved at once. In order to enhance the effect of experiments, it is hereby recommended that twenty Michelson interferometers and ten optical benches be bought and issued to the laboratories.

ABC (name of the writer)

在实地考察报告中，要求将所看到的状况实事求是地反映出来。这篇实地考察的例子就把实验室的状态如实地反映出来了。

31.1.3 工作报告的写法

英文工作报告在写作方法上要注意客观性和真实性。要如实报告工作、活动的过程和结果。要阐述事实本身，在不相关的细节上少花笔墨。文章的组织模式一般按工作进行的先后顺序，或者按照各项工作的主次、重要性来安排。也可以将两者有机结合，如果在某一段时间内做了几项工作，就可以在时间的总框架内，按工作的主次来编排。

下面是一篇工作报告实例：

WORK-IN-PROGRESS REPORT FOR THE MONTH OF MARCH, 2008

From: John Smith, Head, Academic Department
To: Mr. Paul Johnson, Chairman Dalian Ever-Education Association
Ref: 0091963
Date: 2 April 2008

Ⅰ. Dalian XXX University

1. The number of the postgraduates for the month is:
Form 1: 32, Form 2: 30, Form 3: 50, Form 4: 38, Form 5: 34

2. The week starting from 16 March 2009 was scheduled as a "week".

3. Technical training was scheduled to begin on 16 March 2009 offered in the Physics Department of Dalian XXX University within the period 16 March 2009 to 1 May 2009. The person in charge of the program would be head of the Physics Department.

Ⅱ. Academic exchange

1. As one of the initiators, the Association has agreed to host the seminar "The fostering of talented postgraduates in YY city", to be held on 3 May 2009 in Dalian.

2. The Chairman has agreed to give a talk on behalf of the Association in a seminar on the exchange of talented postgraduates within North East of China, which is scheduled to be held on 1 July 2009 in Dalian.

(signature)

这是一份简短的工作报告，这类报告应注意言之有序，无论是说一件事的始末，或多件事的情况，都必须有条不紊，思路清晰，并且言之有据，引用的数据要准确，事实的真相要客观地陈述。

31.2 专业英语阅读：Superconductivity（超导电性）

Superconductors, without resistance to the flow of electricity, are one of the last great frontiers of scientific discovery. Not only have the limits of superconductivity not yet been reached, but the theories that explain superconductor behavior seem to be constantly under review. In 1911 superconductivity was first observed in mercury by Dutch physicist

H. K. Onnes. When he cooled it to the temperature of liquid helium, 4 K(−269℃), its resistance suddenly disappeared. Later, in 1913, he won a Nobel Prize in physics for his research in this area. This discovery of superconductivity was followed by the observation of other metals which exhibit zero resistivity below a certain critical temperature, such as niobium-nitride at 16 K in 1941, vanadium-silicon at 17.5 K in 1953, and the first commercial superconducting wire, an alloy of NbTi in 1962. High-energy particle-accelerator electromagnets made of copper-clad niobium-titanium were then developed in the 1960s at the Rutherford-Appleton Laboratory in the UK.

The fact that the resistance is zero has been demonstrated by sustaining currents in superconducting lead rings for many years with no measurable reduction. An induced current in an ordinary metal ring would decay rapidly from the dissipation of ordinary resistance, but superconducting rings had exhibited a decay constant of over a billion years! One of the properties of a superconductor is that it will exclude magnetic fields, a phenomenon called the **Meissner effect**. German researchers Walter Meissner and Robert Ochsenfeld discovered that a superconducting material will repel the magnetic field. A magnet moving by a conductor induces currents in the conductor. This is the principle on which the electric generator operates. But, in a superconductor the induced currents exactly mirror the field that would have otherwise penetrated the superconducting material, causing the magnet to be repulsed. The Meissner effect is also referred to as strong diamagnetism. The Meissner effect is so strong that a magnet can actually be levitated over a superconductive material.

The disappearance of electrical resistivity was modeled in terms of electron pairing in the crystal lattice by John Bardeen, Leon Cooper, and Robert Schrieffer in what is commonly called the BCS theory. A new era in the study of superconductivity began in 1986 with the discovery of high critical temperature superconductors. It was the first widely-accepted theoretical understanding of superconductivity advanced in 1957 and won them the 1972 Nobel Prize in physics. The mathematically-complex BCS theory explained superconductivity at temperatures close to absolute zero for elements and simple alloys. However, at higher temperatures and with different superconductor systems, the BCS theory has subsequently become inadequate to fully explain how superconductivity is occurring.

Another significant theoretical advancement came in 1962 when B. D. Josephson, a graduate student at Cambridge University, predicted that electrical current would flow between two superconducting materials even when they are separated by a non-superconductor or insulator. His prediction was later confirmed and won him a share of the 1973 Nobel Prize in Physics. This tunneling phenomenon is today known as the "Josephson effect" and has been applied to electronic devices such as the SQUID (superconducting quantum interference device), an instrument capable of detecting even the weakest magnetic fields.

The 1980's were a decade of unrivaled discovery in the field of superconductivity. In

1964 Bill Little of Stanford University had suggested the possibility of organic (carbon-based) superconductors. The first of these theoretical superconductors was successfully synthesized in 1980 by Danish researcher Klaus Bechgaard and three French team members.

A new era in the study of superconductivity began in 1986 with the discovery of high critical temperature superconductors, which is a truly breakthrough discovery in the field of superconductivity. Alex Müller and Georg Bednorz created a brittle ceramic compound that superconducted at the highest temperature then known, 30 K. What made this discovery so remarkable was that ceramics are normally insulators. They don't conduct electricity well at all. So, researchers had not considered them as possible high-temperature superconductor candidates. The synthesized brittle ceramic behaved in a not-as-yet-understood way. The discovery of this first of the superconducting copper-oxides won them a Nobel Prize the following year. It was later found that tiny amounts of this material were actually superconducting at 58 K, due to a small amount of lead having been added as a calibration standard—making the discovery even more noteworthy.

Superconductivity can be applied in many fields and the first application may be superconducting transmission lines. Since 10% to 15% of generated electricity is dissipated in resistive losses in transmission lines, the prospect of zero loss superconducting transmission lines is appealing. In prototype superconducting transmission lines at Brookhaven National Laboratory, 1000 MW of power can be transported within an enclosure of diameter 40 cm. This amounts to transporting the entire output of a large power plant on one enclosed transmission line. This could be a fairly low voltage DC transmission compared to large transformer banks and multiple high voltage AC transmission lines on towers in the conventional systems. The superconductor used in these prototype applications is usually niobium-titanium, and liquid helium cooling is required. Current experiments with power applications of high-temperature superconductors focus on uses of BSCCO in tape forms and YBCO in thin film forms. Current densities above 10,000 amperes per square centimeter are considered necessary for practical power applications, and this threshold has been exceeded in several configurations.

Another example of the application of the superconductivity may be the superconducting maglev train. While it is not practical to lay down superconducting rails, it is possible to construct a superconducting system onboard a train to repel conventional rails below it. The train would have to be moving to create the repulsion, but once moving would be supported with very little friction. There would be resistive loss of energy in the currents in the rails. It was reported that such superconducting trains would be much safer than conventional rail systems at 200 km/h according to the engineering assessment. A Japanese magnetically levitated train set a speed record of 321 mi/h in 1979 using superconducting magnets on board the train. The magnets induce currents in the rails below them, causing a repulsion which suspends the train above the track.

Glossary

superconductivity	超导电性	superconductor	超导体
frontiers	新领域,尖端	critical temperature	临界温度
niobium	铌	nitride	氮
vanadium	钒	silicon	硅
high-energy particle-accelerator	高能粒子加速器	electromagnet	电磁铁
copper-clad	包铜的	titanium	钛
dissipation	损耗	decay constant	衰变常数
Meissner effect	麦斯纳效应	electric generator	发电机
diamagnetism	抗磁性	levitate	浮在空中
tunneling phenomenon	隧道现象	SQUID(superconducting quantum interference device)	超导量子干涉仪
organic	有机的	carbon-based	碳基的
brittle ceramic	脆性陶瓷	transmission lines	输电线路
dissipate	v. 损耗	resistive loss	电阻损耗
prototype	原型	transformer bank	变压器组
Brookhaven National Laboratory	布鲁克海文国家实验室	helium	氦
BSCCO	铋锶钙铜氧	YBCO	钇钡铜氧
magnetically levitated train	磁悬浮列车	superconducting maglev train	超导磁悬浮列车

31.3 专业英语常用表达-31 概括 结论

表达"概括"与"结论"的表述在实际语境中可以整合使用。

1. 可用于表达概括含义的词语有:

above all　首先,最重要的是
all in all　总的来说
all things considered　总的来看
altogether　总之,总的看来
anyway　无论如何,总之
basically　总而言之
briefly=in brief　总之,简言之
by and large　总的来说,一般地说
first and last　整体来看,总的看来
generally speaking　一般说来

generally　一般地,概括地
given all that　综上所述
in a few words　总之,简单地说
in a nut shell　概括地说,简单来说
in a word　总而言之
in any case　无论如何,总之
in broad outline　概括地说
in fine　简言之,总之,最后
in general　总之,一般说来

in short   总之,简言之
in summary   总的说来,概括起来
in the lump   就整体而言
on the whole   总的来说,大体上
overall   总的来说,总体上
the long and the short of   总之,整体上……

to be brief   简言之
to have a run-through of   归纳起来……
to make a long story short   长话短说
to put it briefly   简言之
to sum up   总而言之,总之
to summarize   简言之,总之
to take/taking it all in all   总的来说

2. 可用于引出结论的词语有:

accordingly   因此,从而,相应地,于是
as a result   作为结果,因此,结果是
as is known (to all)   众所周知
as we have seen   正如我们所见
clearly   很明显,显然
final consideration   最后要考虑的
given all that   综上所述
in closing   最后,在结束前
in consequence   因此,结果
in the final analysis   归根结底
so   所以,因此
the point is   重点是
thus   因此,于是
to conclude   最后,总而言之
to draw a conclusion   得出结论

as/so far as I know   据我所知
as has been mentioned   正如所提到的
as we all know   众所周知
at last   最后
consequently   所以,因此
finally   最后
hence   所以,因此
in conclusion   最后,总之
in the end   最后
lastly   最后
taking all into consideration   全面考虑
therefore   所以,因此
to close by   最后,以……来结束
to conclude with   以……来结束

LESSON 32

32.1 物理学专业英语中科技报告的写作

科技报告一般包括以下部分:

(1) Covers and label 封皮与标题:科技报告一般有一个精致的封皮,在封皮上印有报告的题目、作者和单位。

(2) Transmittal letter 传送信(备忘录):传送信并不是装订在报告内一个部分(也有的要求装订在第一页),一般夹在封皮外,如果封皮有内兜就放在里边。常写着"Here's that report we agreed I'd write!",一般提及过去的合同或协议、报告的目的、报告主要内容等。也可以建议一下接受者阅读之后的进一步联系。

(3) Title page and descriptive abstract 标题页和描述性摘要:在标题页上写着报告的标题、报告的接受人和单位、报告的提交人和单位。在此页的底部,写着报告的描述性摘要(基本上是把备忘录中的主要内容复制过来)。

（4）Table of contents 目录：在目录部分列出报告主体部分的标题和对照页码。一级标题要全部大写，二、三级标题可以每个单词首字母大写。

（5）List of figures and list of tables 插图目录和表格目录：列出图表的名称和对应页码，不必列出图表的全标题，只写出主要内容即可。

（6）Informative Abstract 信息性摘要：全面、简要地概括论文的目的、方法、主要数据和结论。

（7）Body 报告正文

① Introduction 引言：主要介绍报告的背景，主要解决的问题，写报告的目的，给读者一个对报告主要内容的介绍。

② Main body 主体部分：报告的主要内容部分。

③ Conclusion 结论：最后概括得出整个报告的结论。

（8）Appendixes 附录：附上相关的支持性材料。

（9）Information sources 信息来源（参考文献）：在报告的最后列出报告中引用内容的来源及参考文献。

下面是一份科技报告的实例，为了方便读者了解各部分结构，我们用黑体标出了报告的各个部分（Section 1，Section 2…），在实际报告中这些文字并不出现。

Section 1　Covers and label 封皮与标题

这部分作者可以按照自己的想法来设计，也可以找专业机构来设计，在此不赘述。

Section 2　Transmittal letter 传送信（备忘录）

223 Research Lab，Science Building

High-Tech Area，Dalian 116026

December 9，2006

Mr. Hank Jones

Luming Technical Research Associates，Inc.

1307 Huangpu Road

High-Tech Area，Dalian 116026

Dear Mr. Jones：

　　In keeping with our agreement，I am submitting the enclosed report entitled *Report on DVD Technology and Applications*.

　　As we agreed，the purpose of this report is to provide potential investors with introductory information on DVD technology and applications. The report provides an explanation of the differences between CD and DVD technology. Additionally, the report describes the construction of a DVD and summarizes applications of the DVD.

　　I hope this report meets with your expectations.

　　Respectfully,

Lily York

Encl.：Technical background report on DVD technology

Section 3　Title page and descriptive abstract 标题页和描述性摘要

Report

on

DVD TECHNOLOGY AND APPLICATIONS

submitted to

Dr. Hank Jones

Luming Technical Research Associates，Inc.

1307 Huangpu Road

High-Tech Area，Dalian 116026

May 6，2006

By

Lily York

Consultants

This report examines digital versatile disc (DVD) technology as a possible avenue for research and development. DVD technology is described，and its characteristics are compared with those of CD. Product development and economic forecasts conclude the main discussion of the report.

Section 4　Table of contents 目录

TABLE OF CONTENTS

LIST OF FIGURES	iii
ABSTRACT	iv
I. INTRODUCTION	1
II. DVD TECHNOLOGY OVERVIEW	2
Development of DVD Technology	3
CD-ROM and DVD Comparison	3
Physical Characteristics	4
Data Structure Characteristics	4
Operating Characteristics	5
III. CONSTRUCTION OF A DVD	**6**
Process in DVD Construction	6

    Physical Formatting ·· 6
    Glass Mastering ··· 6
    Metallization ·· 7
    Electroplating ··· 7
    Molding ··· 7
    Sputtering ·· 8
    Bonding ··· 8
  Current DVD Research ··· 8

IV. DVD APPLICATIONS ·· 9
  DVD-ROM ·· 9
  DVD-Video ··· 9
  DVD-Audio ··· 9
  DVD-R ··· 9
  DVD-RAM ·· 9

V. CONCLUSION ··· 10

INFORMATION SOURCES ··· 11

Section 5 List of figures and list of tables 插图目录和表格目录

LIST OF FIGURES

Figure	Page
1. DVD Comparison ··	4
2. Data Structures ··	5
3. Physical Formatting ··	6
4. Glass Mastering ··	6
5. Metallization ···	7
6. Electroplating ··	7
7. Molding ···	7
8. Sputtering ··	8
9. Bonding ··	8

LIST OF TABLES

Table	Page
1. CD-ROM vs. DVD Specifications ··	3

Section 6　Informative Abstract 信息性摘要

ABSTRACT

Digital versatile disc (DVD) is a collection of new optical disc technologies that have the potential to significantly improve the quality of a number of consumer electronic and personal computer products. DVD was invented and tested by Toshiba Corporation to fulfill two primary goals: (1) to provide higher throughput and (2) to provide higher capacity than current CD-ROM technology.

A digital versatile disc is similar in many ways to the current CD; however, small differences between the two allow for DVD to be implemented in ways that a CD cannot. These differences allow for a capacity increase of up to 26 times and transfer rates up to 4 times faster than conventional CD-ROM. The major difference that provides these increases is the use of a shorter wave-length laser, which allows for decreased tolerances in the manufacturing process and the use of multiple layers of storage on each side of the disc. While surface storage is vastly different from that used in CD technology at the microscopic level, the advances allow the DVD to be the same exact size as the CD-ROM.

These advances brought about by DVD open up a wealth of products and possibilities in modern applications. Current applications include DVD-video, which is capable of displaying broadcast-quality feature-length movies on the surface of a single disc, and DVD-ROM, which can be used in computer applications to provide higher throughput and higher storage capacity on a single disc. Other applications, already developed but not in widespread use, include DVD-audio, high-capacity, high-quality audio disc; DVD-R, a write-once DVD format for high-capacity data storage in computing applications; and DVD-RAM, a multiple read-write format also used for high-capacity storage in computing applications.

Section 7　Body 报告正文

Report

on

DVD TECHNOLOGY AND APPLICATIONS

7.1　Introduction 引言

Ⅰ. **INTRODUCTION**

Digital Versatile Disc, or DVD is a collection of new optical disc technologies that have the potential to significantly improve the quality of a number of consumer electronics and personal computer products. These discs are capable of holding up to 17 gigabytes (GB) of data storage, with current research offering a potential for 15 times more storage. This technology is made available through advances in laser technology and advances in manufacturing processes for optical discs. A Digital Versatile Disc is basically a double density, double sided, compact disc. In addition, the laser used to read a DVD utilizes a shorter wavelength, allowing the storage surface of each of these layers to be more compact.

The purpose of this report is to present the format, creation, and current applications for DVD technology. To emphasize the advances afforded using this technology, a side by side comparison with current Compact Disc technology will be used. Motorola Research and Development is currently investigating the possibilities for implementation of a DVD Group to interact with current research and product groups. This report will give the introduction and background necessary to determine the feasibility of DVD integration into current marketing and research products. This report will provide a simplified explanation of the construction methods required for DVD replication, solely for the purpose of presenting the difference in construction needed to manufacture a DVD.

The four parts of this report will discuss (1) a technological overview of DVD, utilizing a comparison of CD vs. DVD technologies, (2) the construction of a DVD and (3) current applications utilizing DVD. The technological overview section will use a comparison of current CD specifications vs. DVD specifications to convey the advances made possible using DVD. The construction section explains the manufacture of a DVD to show the physical advantages of DVD for data storage and retrieval. Finally, the section covering current applications examines the five current formats for DVD specifications and how they are currently being used today.

7.2　Main body of the report 报告主体

II. DVD TECHNOLOGY OVERVIEW

Before getting into the details of manufacturing DVDs and their applications, consider their basic construction and comparisons to CD-ROMs.

Development of DVD Technology

Digital Versatile Disc (DVD) technology was pioneered in 1993 by the Toshiba Corporation to fulfill two primary technical goals, providing both higher throughput and higher capacity than current CD-ROM technology. While DVD optical discs are quite similar to CD-ROM optical discs, there are a number of key physical differences, as well as philosophical differences. CD-ROM technology was originally designed to accommodate high quality audio data, and a large quantity of textual data. While the use of CD-ROM has been extended to include video data, the format falls short of providing broadcast television quality video and cannot store full-length feature films. The DVD format was specifically designed to address each of these limitations.

Beyond the inception of DVD technology, advances have been developed by a group of ten consumer electronics companies, called the DVD Forum, who have agreed on the set technical specifications for each DVD format. Until recently, there were two competing groups of companies: one led by Sony, and the other by Toshiba, that were both trying to develop proprietary high-density optical disc formats. Fortunately, these two groups joined forces and agreed to form the DVD Forum. The DVD Forum has also actively encouraged participation from members of the entertainment and computer industries so that the DVD format will have a broad base of support in both the consumer and computer electronics areas.

As mentioned before, two of the primary goals of DVD are to provide both higher capacity and higher throughput than what current CD-ROM technology offers. To demonstrate the advances afforded using DVD, this section will reference the specifications of CD-ROM vs. DVD technology.

CD-ROM vs. DVD Comparison

Table 32-1 shows some of the key similarities and differences between the CD-ROM and DVD formats.

Table 32-1. CD-ROM vs. DVD Specifications.
Source: "DVD: The Dawn of a New Generation."July, 1998. *Computer User*

Category	CD-ROM	DVD
Disc Diameter	120mm	120mm
Disc Thickness	1.2mm	1.2mm
Disc Structure	Single Substrate	Two Bonded 0.6 mm Substrates
Laser Wavelengths	780nm(infrared)	650 and 635nm(red)
Track Pitch	1.6microns	0.74microns
Shortest Pit Length	0.83 microns	0.4 microns
Data Layers	1	2
Data Sides	1	2
Data Capacity	650 Mbytes	4.7-17.0GB
User Data Rate	1.4Mbits/sec	10.0Mbits/sec

The key features, which comprise the difference between CD and DVD technologies, are the physical characteristics, data structure characteristics, and operating characteristics.

Physical Characteristics. The physical characteristics of the optical discs including thickness, diameter and structure are nearly identical, with the only exception being the DVD possessing a double substrate with half the thickness of a conventional CD. This allows multiple layers of data to be stored within the same thickness of a conventional CD single layer, as seen in Fig. 32-1.

Data Structure Characteristics. The data structure characteristics of the optical discs include laser wavelength, track pitch, and pit length. All of these characteristics differ from CD to DVD and allow for the significant improvements in data capacity and throughput seen in the DVD operating characteristics. Using a red laser for DVD devices vs. a standard infrared laser used for current CD devices, provides a much smaller

Fig. 32-1 DVD Comparison. Source: Smith, James. DVD Handbook, p. 19

wavelength, allowing better selectivity and smaller data structures, as seen in Fig. 32-2. Data can be stored in half the length previously necessary using conventional CD technology.

Fig. 32-2 Data Structures. Source: Smith, James, DVD Handbook, p. 22

Operating Characteristics. The advances provided by the shorter wavelength laser and multi-layer structure, exponentially increase the throughput of DVD devices vs. CD devices. All DVD formats and playback devices will support a minimum throughput rate that is eight times faster than conventional CD-ROM, and many DVD playback devices will support even higher transfer rates. In addition, by doubling both the number of layers and the number of sides utilized, capacity of DVD has been increased to a maximum of 17.0 GB of memory, compared to 650 MB (megabytes) of storage on a standard CD-ROM, an increase of more than 26 times the capacity.

III. CONSTRUCTION OF A DVD

DVD construction is similar to traditional CD-ROM construction with a few added steps, and a much higher degree of manufacturing tolerance required.

Process in DVD Construction

Each of the following major manufacturing steps will be presented using an explanation followed with a diagram to show the actual progression of the disc construction:

Physical formatting. Analog signal is converted to a digital signal and compressed using DVD compression standards, then stored for transfer onto the DVD. (Fig. 32-3)

Fig. 32-3 Physical Formatting

Glass mastering. A glass base is coated with light-sensitive photoresist, which is then developed in a sodium silicate solution, using a laser to implant the digital signal. (Fig. 32-4)

Metallization. Nickel is evaporated on the surface of the master, providing a conductive layer for the electroplating phase. (Fig. 32-5)

Fig. 32-4 Glass Mastering   Fig. 32-5 Metallization

Electroplating. A wet process in which the master is bathed in nickel sulfamate and a stamper is applied to create the pattern required for multiple disc replication. (Fig. 32-6)

Molding. The previously created master is used as a base, giving a pattern pressed onto an injection molded polycarbonate substrate. (Fig. 32-7)

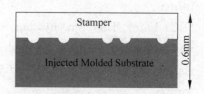

Fig. 32-6 Electroplating   Fig. 32-7 Molding

Sputtering. Similar to semiconductor sputtering, a metal layer is formed on the surface, aluminum for single layer, gold or silicon carbide for dual layer discs. (Fig. 32-8)

Bonding. Multiple layers are bonded together using either hot melt or ultraviolet processes. This bonding requires extreme precision to prevent the DVD from becoming unbalanced. (Fig. 32-9)

Fig. 32-8 Sputtering   Fig. 32-9 Bonding

The above processes provide the DVD with a variable number of readable substrates, allowing a maximum of two substrates per side, with a maximum of two sides. This manufacturing process is not a large departure from conventional CD-ROM manufacturing processes, requiring higher tolerances in the mastering phases of the process, addition of gold and silicon carbide in the sputtering process, and the addition of a bonding process.

Current DVD Research

Ongoing research in Tokyo performed by the Agency of Industrial Science and Technology has led to advances producing a DVD capable of holding 15 times as much data as current DVDs. This high memory density is achieved by adding an additional antimony film to the DVD, pinpointing the laser beam allowing up to 30 hours of moving images to be stored, using conventional DVD devices for playback.

IV. DVD APPLICATIONS

Given the technological advances made over CD-ROM, the applications for DVD are able to replace all conventional applications for optical disc use. Use of DVD is currently divided into five separate applications using six different DVD formats.

- *DVD-ROM*. High-capacity, high-throughput, read-only optical disc that can be used as a general-purpose computer storage device. This application is currently the most prevalent, with disc storage ranging from 4.7 to 17.0 GB, depending on format.
- *DVD-Video*. High capacity, high throughput, read-only optical disc that can be used for the interactive playback of high quality video, audio and graphic content. This application, similarly uses disc storage ranging from 4.7 to 17.0 GB, depending on the format.
- *DVD-Audio*. Similar to the DVD-Video, differing only in the compression and

storage of audio, rather than video.
- *DVD-R*. High capacity, high throughput, write once, optical disc used as a general-purpose computer storage device. This application currently is formatted to hold 3.8 GB of storage per side, although current advances promise to achieve 4.7 GB per side.
- *DVD-RAM*. High capacity, high throughput, read-write, used as a highly versatile storage medium for Michelson interferometers and other devices. This application currently uses its own format, allowing 2.6 GB of storage per side.

7.3　Conclusion 结论

V. CONCLUSION

In conclusion, this report gives the initial introduction to DVD technology required to determine whether to implement the technology in Motorola products in the future. Given the ease of implementation of this technology and potential growth in sales and revenues, DVD technology promises to afford many avenues of implementation. These implementations range from current video, audio, and computer applications to household combination cable modem and large data storage units for combined application in multiple use consumer electronics devices.

Section 8　Appendixes 附录（无）

Section 9　Information sources 信息来源（参考文献）

INFORMATION SOURCES

1. Boeler, Kurt. "DVD Systems Expanding." CNET-NEWS.COM. May 29, 1998.
2. Crawford, Albert. *Complete Guide to DVD*. New York: McGraw-Hill, 1997.
3. "DVD: The Dawn of a New Generation." *Computer User*. July 1998.
4. "DVD Gaining Momentum." *USA Today*. August 24, 1998.
5. "DVD Technology Advance." *Dow-Jones News*. June 19, 1998.
6. "DVD." *Encarta Encyclopedia*. 1998 Ed.
7. International Recording Media Association. "Optical Media Intelligence Report." July 1998.
8. Electronic Industries Association of Japan. "Optical Media Report." San Diego, CA: Toshiba Press, 1998.
9. Taylor, Jim. *DVD Demystified: Guide for DVD-Video and DVD-ROM*. New York: McGraw-Hill, 1998.

32.2　专业英语阅读

32.2.1　The Crystal Lattice（晶格）

Most solids have periodic arrays of atoms which form what we call a **crystal lattice.**

Amorphous solids and glasses are exceptions. The existence of the crystal lattice implies a degree of symmetry in the arrangement of the lattice, and the existing symmetries have been studied extensively. One of the implications of the symmetric lattice of atoms is that it can support resonant lattice vibration modes. These vibrations transport energy and are important in the thermal conductivity of non-metals, and in the heat capacity of all solids.

In mineralogy and crystallography, a crystal structure is a unique arrangement of atoms in a crystal. A crystal structure is composed of a **motif**, a set of atoms arranged in a particular way, and a lattice. Motifs are located upon the points of a lattice, which is an array of points repeating periodically in three dimensions. The points can be thought of as forming identical tiny boxes, called **unit cells**, that fill the space of the lattice. The lengths of the edges of a unit cell and the angles between them are called the **lattice parameters**. The symmetry properties of the crystal are embodied in its space group. A crystal's structure and symmetry play a role in determining many of its properties, such as cleavage, electronic band structure, and optical properties.

The crystal structure of a material or the arrangement of atoms in a crystal structure can be described in terms of its unit cell. The unit cell is a tiny box containing one or more motifs, a spatial arrangement of atoms. The unit cells stacked in three-dimensional space describe the bulk arrangement of atoms of the crystal. The crystal structure has a three dimensional shape. The unit cell is given by its lattice parameters, the length of the cell edges and the angles between them, while the positions of the atoms inside the unit cell are described by the set of atomic positions (x_i, y_i, z_i) measured from a lattice point.

Although there are an infinite number of ways to specify a unit cell, for each crystal structure there is a conventional unit cell, which is chosen to display the full symmetry of the crystal. However, the conventional unit cell is not always the smallest possible choice. A **primitive unit cell** of a particular crystal structure is the smallest possible volume one can construct with the arrangement of atoms in the crystal such that, when stacked, completely fills the space. This primitive unit cell will not always display all the symmetries inherent in the crystal. A Wigner-Seitz cell is a particular kind of primitive cell which has the same symmetry as the lattice. In a unit cell each atom has an identical environment when stacked in 3-dimension space. In a primitive cell, each atom may not have the same environment.

32.2.2 Lattice Vibrations(晶格振动)

The existence of a periodic crystal lattice in solid materials provides a medium for characteristic lattice vibrations. On the scale of the lattice spacing, these vibration modes are quantized, with the quantum of lattice vibration being called a phonon. Treating the lattice vibrations quantum mechanically led to the Einstein model and the Debye model of specific heat.

The Law of Dulong and Petit assumed that Maxwell-Boltzmann statistics and equipartition of energy could be applied even at low temperatures. Einstein recognized that for a quantum harmonic oscillator at energies less than kT, the Bose-Einstein statistics must be applied. This was the same conclusion that was drawn about blackbody radiation. In the Einstein treatment, the appropriate frequency in the expression had to be determined empirically by comparison with experiment for each element. The quantity $h\nu/k$ is sometimes called the **Einstein temperature**. Although the general match with experiment was reasonable, it was not exact. Debye advanced the treatment by treating the quantum oscillators as collective modes in the solid which are now called "phonons".

Einstein's oscillator treatment of specific heat gave qualitative agreement with experiment and gave the correct high temperature limit (the Law of Dulong and Petit). The quantitative fit to experiment was improved by Debye's recognition that there was a maximum number of modes of vibration in a solid. He pictured the vibrations as standing wave modes in the crystal, similar to the electromagnetic modes in a cavity which successfully explained blackbody radiation. The density of states for these modes, which are called "phonons", is of the same form as the photon density of states in a cavity.

In the BCS Theory of superconductivity, electron pairs in the low-temperature material couple by means of phonons to produce Cooper pairs. The phonon coupling produces a bound state which cannot be excited by the available thermal energy and therefore move without resistance through the crystal lattice.

Lattice vibrations can also interact with light to produce scattering called **Brillouin scattering**, which is used in laser spectroscopy. Scattering of light from acoustic modes is called Brillouin scattering. From a strictly classical point of view, the compression of the medium will change the index of refraction and therefore lead to some reflection or scattering at any point where the index changes. From a quantum point of view, the process can be considered one of interaction of light photons with acoustic or vibrational quanta (phonons). Two examples will provide some context for this phenomenon: Bragg type Brillouin scattering from standing wave acoustic modes and side-band phenomenon from interaction of laser radiation with water.

32.2.3　Band Theory of Solids(固体的能带论)

A useful way to visualize the difference between conductors, insulators and semiconductors is to plot the available energies for electrons in the materials. Instead of having discrete energies as in the case of free atoms, the available energy states form bands. Crucial to the conduction process is whether or not there are electrons in the conduction band. In insulators the electrons in the valence band are separated by a large gap from the conduction band, in conductors like metals the valence band overlaps the conduction band, and in semiconductors there is a small enough gap between the valence and conduction bands that thermal or other excitations can bridge the gap. With such a small gap, the presence of a small percentage of a doping material can increase conductivity dramatically.

An important parameter in the band theory is the **Fermi level**, the top of the available electron energy levels at low temperatures. The position of the Fermi level with the relation to the conduction band is a crucial factor in determining electrical properties.

Most solid substances are insulators, and in terms of the band theory of solids this implies that there is a large forbidden gap between the energies of the valence electrons and the energy at which the electrons can move freely through the material (the conduction band). For intrinsic semiconductors like silicon and germanium, the Fermi level is essentially halfway between the valence and conduction bands. Although no conduction occurs at 0K, at higher temperatures a finite number of electrons can reach the conduction band and provide some current. In doped semiconductors, extra energy levels are added. The increase in conductivity with temperature can be modeled in terms of the Fermi function, which allows one to calculate the population of the conduction band. In terms of the band theory of solids, metals are unique as good conductors of electricity. This can be seen to be a result of their valence electrons being essentially free. In the band theory, this is depicted as an overlap of the valence band and the conduction band so that at least a fraction of the valence electrons can move through the material.

Glossary

periodic array	周期性排列	crystal Lattice	晶格
amorphous solid	非晶固体	degree of symmetry	对称度
resonant Lattice vibration mode	晶格共振模式	thermal conductivity	热传导,导热性
non-metal	非金属	heat capacity	热容
mineralogy	矿物学	crystallography	结晶学
motif	型主	unit cell	晶胞,单胞
lattice parameter	晶格常数,点阵参数	space group	空间群
cleavage	解理	electronic band	电子带
stack	堆积	conventional unit cell	习用单胞
primitive unit cell	元胞,基本单胞	Wigner-Seitz cell	维格纳-赛茨晶胞
phonon	声子	law of Dulong and Petit	杜隆-珀蒂定律
equipartition of energy	能量均分	quantum harmonic oscillator	量子谐振子
Maxwell-Boltzmann statistics	麦克斯韦-玻耳兹曼统计	Bose-Einstein statistics	玻色-爱因斯坦统计
blackbody radiation	黑体辐射	collective mode	集体方式

standing wave	驻波	cavity	空腔
electron pair	电子对	Cooper pair	库伯对
bound state	束缚态	Brillouin scattering	布里渊散射
laser spectroscopy	激光光谱学	acoustic mode	声(学)模
side-band phenomenon	边带现象	discrete	分立的
conduction band	导带	valence	化合价
valence band	价带	doping material	掺杂物
Fermi level	费米能级	forbidden gap	禁隙
valence electron	价电子	intrinsic semiconductor	本征半导体,内禀半导体
silicon	硅	germanium	锗
doped semiconductor	掺杂半导体	overlap	重叠,交叠

32.3 专业英语常用表达-32 各种实验与试验

activation experiment　激活试验
acute experiment　急性实验
aerodynamic experiment　空气动力试验
aircraft reactor experiment　航空反应堆实验
analogue experiment　模拟实验
blank experiment　空转试验
bread board experiment　模拟板试验
breakthrough experiment　(离子交换)穿透/流穿实验
cascade experiment　串级/级联实验
check experiment　检查试验
choice experiment　选择实验
chronic experiment　慢性实验
cold gas blanket experiment　冷气体包层实验
comparative experiment　比较试验
competitive experiments　竞赛实验
complication/compound experiment　复合实验
computer-aided experiment　计算机辅助实验
confirmatory experiment　假说验证实验
contrast experiment　对比实验
controllable extensional experiment　可控延伸试验
controlled computational experiment　受控的计算试验
controlled experiment　对照实验
controlled experiment　有控制的对照实验
cookbook laboratory experiment　按作业指南进行的实验室实验

critical experiment　临界/极限试验
cross-over experiment　交叉实验
defect experiment　缺损实验
designed experiment　设计实验
destructive experiment　破坏试验
direct-current experiment　直流电试验
dishpan experiment　转盘实验
drag experiment　阻力试验
exponential experiment　指数实验
factorial experiment　析因实验
Faraday ice bucket experiment　法拉第冰桶试验
fast exponential experiment　快中子指数实验装置
Fellinger's experiment　费林格实验（氨吸收）
field experiment　野外/现场试验
Franck-Hertz experiment　弗兰克-赫兹实验
full-scale experiment　全尺寸实验
Gedanken experiment　想象实验
ground experiment　地面试验
group experiment　分组试验
high frequency experiment　高频实验
ice-pail experiment　冰桶实验
inclining experiment　倾斜试验
isolation experiment　隔离试验
laboratory experiment　实验室实验
large-scale experiment　大型试验，工业规模试验
lysimetric experiment　渗漏试验
model experiment　模型试验，模拟实验
molten salt reactor experiment　熔盐反应堆实验
natural experiment　自然实验
non-controllable extensional experiment　非可控延伸实验
numerical experiment　数值实验
open-syphon experiment　敞口虹吸实验
opposite experiment　对比实验
orientative experiment　定向试验
parity experiment　宇称实验
pedagogical experiment　教法实验
perfusion experiment　灌流实验
photo elastic experiment　光（测）弹性实验
photoelectric mixing experiment　光电混频实验

polarization experiment   极化实验
population experiment   群体试验
porous plug experiment   多孔塞实验
qualitative experiment   定性实验
quantitative experiment   定量实验
random experiment   随机试验
recoil experiment   反冲实验
reconstruction experiment   重组实验
routine experiment   例行试验
sensitivity experiments   灵敏性实验
simulated experiment   模拟实验
structure experiment   结构试验
synchronous altitude spin stabilized experiment   同步高度自旋稳定实验
tentative experiment   初步试验
tracer experiment   示踪/显迹实验
transition experiment   转换实验
transmission experiment   透射实验
triple-jet experiment   三(向)射流实验
two-part experiment   二部实验
two-stage experiment   两阶段实验
Wiener experiment   维纳实验
wind tunnel experiment   风洞试验

Unit Nine

LESSON 33

33.1 物理学国际学术会议用英语简介

国际学术会议,是国内外科研工作者之间面对面地进行学术交流的有效方式之一。参加学术会议,是一个了解学科发展动态,促进国际学术合作与交流的有效途径。随着我国科技的不断进步,我国在国际科学界的影响也在逐步扩大,有越来越多的国际学术会议在我国举行,我国的科研工作者有了更多的机会参加各类的学术交流活动,这为我们提供了能与国外学者进行交流、讨论与合作的良好条件。

物理学作为自然科学的一个重要分支,具有非常多的从业人员和科研工作者,每年物理学各分支领域的各种国际学术会议数量多、影响广、参加者众多。英语是物理学国际学术交流的重要工具,绝大多数国际学术会议都以英语作为工作语言。在学术交流过程中,良好的英语应用能力会让科研工作者准确地获取最新学术信息,了解相关领域的科研工作进展与成果,通过学术交流促进科研工作的进步,以避免重复性的工作。因此在国际学术会议交流过程中,英语应用能力显得至关重要。从获取国际学术会议的信息到进行准备并参加会议,整个过程包含了众多环节,除掌握相关的英语知识之外,对学术会议本身的了解也非常重要。因此国际学术会议英语是特定学术背景下的专业英语知识,涉及信息查询、信件交流、口语表达等多方面的内容和知识。以下针对这几个方面进行介绍。

1. 会议信息的来源(Sources for Conference Information)

获得国际学术会议信息的渠道多种多样,例如网络、专业性期刊、会议文献、专业机构或同行交流等。

1) 网络查询(Internet)

通过网络获得信息是一种最为快捷的方式,主要通过各种搜索引擎来实现,可以综合使用多种搜索引擎,扩大信息检索的范围。例如可搜索"限定词汇+表示会议的关键词"。其中限定词汇可包含主题(如 Nuclear Physics, Solid State Theory)、时间(如年份)、频率(如 annual 每年一次, biannual 每年两次, biennial 两年一次, triennial 三年一次)等。表示会议的词汇很多,所指会议各有侧重。例如:

(1) meeting 泛指各种会议,意义宽泛。

(2) conference 指关于一定主题的大型正式会议,就专门的学术问题进行研究。会议通常持续数天,包含演讲与讨论环节,研究成果通常以会议论文集的形式呈现。例如,

International Conference on Magnetics.

（3）symposium 指专题学术讨论会或报告会，就某一主题进行讨论的小型会议，与 conference 比较，symposium 的专业性更强。例如，The International Symposium on Nuclear Structure Physics.

（4）convention 指正式的、通常为定期的会议，与会代表通常为行业代表、政党或社团的成员、专业同行等。其中专业同行参加的专业性会议（professional convention）关注专业的进步与发展，通常由对某一主题感兴趣的协会或机构组织召开。例如，A Teachers' Convention.

（5）congress 指就某一问题、理念、政策或公共利益等进行讨论的大型国内或国际会议或代表大会，与会者通常来自不同的国家，或不同的独立组织机构。例如，The Annual Congress of Institute of Physics.

（6）forum 指论坛或演讲，用于交流观点或讨论问题，特别是较为重要的问题。学术论坛通常由专家发表演讲，听众参与讨论。例如，The Forum of Physics and Society.

（7）seminar 指学术研讨会，通常由大学或专业机构定期举办，每次涉及不同的主题，通常包括主要发言或演讲以及与会者参与的讨论。例如，A Seminar for the Theoretical Physics.

（8）colloquium 指学术报告会，通常邀请某一领域的专家学者做专题报告，参会者可以就报告主题进行提问、讨论或评价。例如，Physics and Astronomy Colloquium.

（9）workshop 指专题讨论会或讲习班，以针对某一主题的示范性讲授、讨论和交流为主要方式，主题所涉及的技术或信息针对性较强，旨在解决某一共性问题，或使参与者的能力得到提高。例如，The 2nd China-India Workshop on Solar Physics.

此外，国际上的重要学术机构经常会发布会议信息，因此也可以在专业学术机构的官方网站上查询相关的会议信息。例如，一些与物理学密切相关的国际学术机构有：

AIP　　　美国物理联合会 American Institute of Physics
APS　　　美国物理学会 American Physical Society
ASTM　　美国试验与材料协会 American Society for Testing and Materials
IEE　　　电气工程师学会（英国）Institute of Electrical Engineers
IEEE　　电子电气工程师学会（美国）Institute of Electrical and Electronics Engineers
IOP　　　物理学会（英国）Institute of Physics
SPIE　　光学工程师学会（美国）Society of Photo-optical Instrumentation Engineers

2）专业性期刊查询（Specialized Periodicals/Professional Journals）

包含会议信息的专业性期刊有两类。一类是某一领域的专业性学术期刊，其中经常会发布一些该领域的学术会议信息，例如 meeting notice, meeting information, announcements, invitations, call for papers, call for abstracts, circulars 等；另一类是专门用于发布会议信息的专业文献，例如：

我国的《国际科技会议和国际展览会预报》

美国的 World Meetings《世界会议》、Scientific Meetings《科技会议》和 World Convention Dates《世界集会日期》

英国的 Forthcoming International Scientific and Technical Conference《国际科技会议

预报》

日本的《国际学术会议一览》、《日本预定举办的国际会议一览表》

俄罗斯的《国际科学会议公报》

3) 会议文献查询(Conference Literature)

由于很多会议都会定期举行,因此通过以往的会议文献也可以预知新的会议信息。利用会议文献所提供的会议名称或缩写,会议主题和举办时间,可以通过网络或专业文献查询未来会议的具体信息。一般可按出版时间将会议文献分为会前文献(Pre-Conference Literature)、会间文献(Literature Generated During Conference)和会后文献(Post-Conference Literature)。会前文献如 Preprints 和 Advanced Abstracts 等;会间文献如 Meeting Minutes, Meeting Summary, Meeting Reports 等;会后文献如 Papers, Proceedings, Symposium, Colloquium Papers, Digests, Transactions, Records, Reports, Publications 等。

2. 国际学术会议的信息要点(Main Points of Conference Information)

一般来说,国际学术会议的主办机构会在媒体上发布会议公告(Public Announcement),其中包含会议的基本信息。往往在会议之前还会向与会者发出三轮通知(First/Second/Third Announcement),其内容各有侧重。总体上会议公告或通知包含以下几方面的信息:

1) 一般信息(General Information)

(1) 名称、时间、地点(Name, Dates, Locations/Venue)

会议名称包含会议的全称及缩写(Formal name and Short term),会议起止时间一般紧随名称后给出,地点一般指明城市或会议进行的具体地点。例如:

General Info

The 21st International Conference on Atomic Physics, ICAP 2008, will be held from July 27-August 1, 2008 in scenic New England, on the campus of the University of Connecticut, Storrs, Connecticut, USA.

Conference Announcement

2009 International Conference on Applied Physics and Mathematics(ICAPM 2009)

16 to 17 May 2009

Singapore, Singapore

(2) 简介(Conference/Introduction)

简介部分一般介绍会议的宗旨、作用或背景,也可以简要说明会议所涉及的领域与主题,起到宣传和邀约的作用。例如:

This ongoing series of conferences, held every even-numbered year since 1968, is devoted to fundamental studies of atoms, broadly defined.

This conference, first held in Lake Placid, NY in 1982, has traditionally been a forum for presenting the latest developments in spectroscopic research utilizing vibrational spectroscopy.

ChinaNANO 2009 is intended to stimulate discussions on the forefront of research in nanoscience and technology.

（3）会议主题（Topics/Themes/Scope）

常用的表述有：

Conference themes：

Topics：

Scope：

Topics covered include…

The conference will focus on…

The scope of the conference includes the following topics：

The conference will provide a forum to discuss…

The topics would include…

Recent research in… was covered, including the following topical areas：

Talks will encompass…, emphasizing…

The conference will cover all areas related to…, including…

The conference will include all areas of… In particular, the meeting will be arranged around four themes：

（4）重要日期（Important Dates）

会议信息中会对一些重要事项的开始或截止时间进行特别说明。例如：

Important Dates

Session Proposal Deadline	*Mar.10, 2009*
Session Proposal Acceptance Notice	*Mar.17, 2009*
Abstract Deadline	*Apr.30, 2009*
Abstract Acceptance Notice	*May.20, 2009*
Full paper Deadline	*Jul.7, 2009*
Registration Deadline	*Jul.20, 2009*
Conference Date	*Sep.18-20, 2009*

截止时间的常用表述为：

deadline for/of …

…deadline/due date

说明中的重要事项一般包括：

注册：Early (bird) registration（预注册，提前注册），Preconference registration（会前注册），Late registration（逾期注册），On-site registration（在线注册）

摘要或提案提交：Abstract submission, Proposal submission, Extended Abstract submission

论文提交：Paper submission, Paper manuscript submission, Submission of camera-ready papers, Final paper submission, Submission of full paper, Manuscript submission

录用通知：Author notification for abstract/full paper, Acceptance notification/notice, Notification/notice of acceptance

会议时间：Conference dates

2）征文（Call for Papers）

摘要 Abstract 和全文 Full Paper 的征文信息通常包括以下内容：

(1) 时间

截稿时间 Deadline for submission of abstract or final paper

录用通知发出时间 Notification of acceptance, Acceptance notification

(2) 语言

Language 语言, Official language 官方语言, Working language 工作语言, All manuscripts should be written in English. 所有稿件均需用英语撰写。

(3) 长度

maximum length for abstract or paper 摘要或论文的最大长度, limitation of pages 页数限制, maximum…words(…pages) in length 长度限制在……字(……页)之内, paper length is limited to…pages 论文长度应在……页之内

(4) 论文版式

DOC format(DOC 格式), PDF format(PDF 格式), Papers should be Word or PDF documents. (论文应为 Word 或 PDF 文件。)

(5) 排版格式

Conference template of paper 会议论文模板, Conference style 会议论文格式, Abstract or paper sample 摘要或论文样本

(6) 投稿数量

Limit of contributions per lead author 第一作者投稿数限制, Each presenting author can submit maximum two papers. 每位参会作者最多可投稿两篇。

(7) 提交方式

How to submit 如何提交, Online submission only 仅限在线提交, Submit electronically 电子提交, Submit on the web site 网站提交, Submit via e-mail to…通过电子邮件提交至……, Send the paper by e-mail 通过电子邮件提交论文, Only electronic submissions will be accepted. 只接受电子提交。

(8) 发表信息

All accepted papers will be included in the proceedings of…indexed by EI and ISTP. 所有被录用的论文将收入 EI、ISTP 检索的……论文集中。

(9) 发表要求

会议可能对论文的录用提出一些具体的要求，例如对论文原创性的要求。如：Papers and abstracts are accepted for review on the condition that the manuscript is original, has not been previously published or presented at a conference. 或是对注册或出席的要求如 Contributions will be included in the proceedings of…only if at least one of the authors of the paper is registered before…

3) 组织情况(Organization Information)

主办机构 Sponsors

承办机构 Organizer

协办机构 Co-Sponsors/Co-Organizer

赞助机构 Corporate Sponsors, Supporter

委员会 Committee(s)

名誉主席 Honorary chair

会议主席 General chair

联合主席 Co-chair

会议委员会 Conference committee

 组委会 Organization committee

  国际组委会 International organization committee

  国内组委会 Local organization committee

  组织主席 Organization chair

  执行组织主席 Executive organization chair

  组委会委员 Organization committee members

 程序委员会 Program committee/Academic committee/Science committee

  程序主席 Program chair

  执行程序主席 Executive program chair

  程序委员会委员 Program committee members

 秘书处 Secretariat

  秘书长 General secretary/Secretary general

  秘书 Secretary

  副秘书 Deputy secretary

 国际(技术)顾问委员会 International (technical) advisory committee/board

4) 注册信息 (Registration Information)

(1) 注册截止时间 (Deadline of registration)

(2) 注册费用 (Registration fees)

一般不同阶段注册所需的费用有所不同,信息中会注明 Early registration, Standard registration 和 Late registration 的不同费用标准;此外,不同身份的与会者注册费用亦有所不同,例如 Regular participant 和 Student participant 的费用不同, Author 和 Listener 的费用不同等。

(3) 支付方式 (Payment)

一般会议会提供几种不同的支付方式供选择,如信用卡 Credit card,支票 Check 或电汇 Wire transfer/Electronic transfer。

(4) 费用所含项目 (The registration fees include...)

信息中会明确列举注册费用所包含的项目和需要额外付费的项目。例如:

Admission to all sessions

A printed copy of the conference program

Proceedings CD

Coffee breaks

Daily conference lunch cocktail

An attendance and/or author certificate

An invoice of the registration fee

（5）注册说明（Registration note）

该项一般对参会或发表论文的必要条件进行说明。例如

Contributions will only be published at the conference publications if at least one of the authors of each accepted abstract is registered before...

It's necessary to be registered to get into the conference (as author or as general public).

（6）退款政策（Refund policy/Cancellation policy）

5）会议日程（Conference Program Information）

有关会议日程的信息会提前发布并不断地更新，例如，通过 Advanced program 和 Updated program 或 Program at a glance 等来提供会议日程的具体安排，如日期、时间、会场和主题（Date，Time，Room，Item）等。

6）膳宿及观光（Accommodations and Travel）

一般会提供关于会议地点 Venue、酒店预定 Hotel reservation、交通路线 Traffic route、可用交通方式 Transport available、天气 Weather、观光景点 Attractions、当地情况 Local information/About the city of...等方面的信息，为与会者提供方便。

7）联系方式（Contact Us/Correspondence）

提供有关会议各种事项的不同联系人及其联系方式，例如 Tel，E-mail，Website，Fax 等。

各种会议信息的要点、顺序与表达方式不尽相同，一般在会议网站或招贴海报上都可以查询到比较详尽的信息。以下我们将以 2009 年台湾高雄计算物理学国际会议的会议信息为例展示会议信息的表述方式。（信息内容来自互联网 http://www.ccp2009.tw/index.asp）

Conference on Computational Physics 2009, Taiwan

Invitation

CCP is the world's largest conference on computational physics. It is an annual event, rotating between the continents of Asia-Australia, Europe-Africa, and North and South America. In previous Asia-Australia rotations, it graced: Gyeongju, Korea 2006, Beijing, China 2003, and Brisbane, Australia 2000.

Scientists in any area of computational physics are welcome to participate. Subfields such as Condensed Matter, AMO, Plasma/Space, High Energy, QIS, Complex Systems, Education, and New Method for the major program.

Even in December, Taiwan has beautiful weather. The culture, cuisine and scenery will make the visit refreshing in addition to academic enriching.

Yours Truly,

J. Y. Hsu, Ph. D.

Professor, Department of Physics, NCKU, Tainan, Taiwan

Director, Institute of Space, Astrophysical and Plasma Sciences, NCKU, Tainan, Taiwan

Chairman, the Organizing Committee of the Conference on Computational Physics, 2009, Kaohsiung, Taiwan

Committees

Conference Organizers
    Conference Chair: ...
    Conference Vice Chair: ...
    Secretary General: ...
Advisory Committee members
    ...
Local Committee
    Co-Chair: ...
    Committee Members: ...
Program Committee
    Chair: ...
    Vice Chair: ...
    Committee for each topic: ...

Conference Information

Dates: December 15 (Tue)-19 (Sat) 2009

Venue: Grand Hi-Lai Hotel, Kaohsiung (No. 266, Cheng-Kung 1st Rd., Kaohsiung, Taiwan)

Official Language: English is the official language for CCP 2009.

Scientific Program

Program at a glance
    (Time schedule...)

Call for Abstracts

■ Scope

CCP 2009 provides an international forum for Computational Physics researchers throughout the world to exchange and share their experiences, new ideas, latest research results and future development suggestions on all aspects of Computational Physics. Authors are invited to submit manuscripts of research work in all areas of Computational Physics.

■ Topics of interest include, but are not limited to:

Condensed Matter Physics(凝聚态物理)
Atom, Molecules and Optics (AMO)(原子、分子与光学)
Plasma/Space Physics(等离子/空间物理)
High Energy Physics(高能物理)
Quantum Information Science (QIS)(量子信息科学)
Complex Systems(复杂系统)
    —Statistical Physics(统计物理)

——Biological Physics(生物物理)
——Nonlinear Physics(非线性物理)
——Bio-Material(生物材料)
Physics Education(物理教育)
New Methods/New Facilities(新方法/新设备)
——Petaflop Supercomputers(千兆浮点超级计算机)
——GPU Supercomputing(图形处理单元超级运算)
——Algorithms(算法)
Others

■ Important Dates

Abstract Submission Start: April 16, 2009
Abstract Submission Due: August 15, 2009
Notification of Acceptance: September 15, 2009
Camera Ready Submission Due: September 30, 2009
Early Bird Registration: October 31, 2009
Full Paper Submission Deadline: March 1, 2010

■ Abstract Submission

Papers/Posters presenting original and unpublished work are invited and will be evaluated based on originality, significance, technical soundness, and clarity of exposition.

Submitted abstract should be formatted in a one-column WORD format and should not exceed one page including figures and references. One author of each accepted paper will be expected to present the paper at the conference.

Submissions (oral/poster) will be refereed by Scientific Committees and the chosen papers will be published in Computer Physics Communications (CPC) together with the invited papers.

Before submitting your abstract, please make sure the abstract is prepared according to the instructions.

■ Type of Presentation

ORAL: Presenting author will be notified of acceptance by September 15, 2009.
POSTER: On 90 cm(W)×180 cm(H) bulletin board.

Registration

■ How to Register

ONLY on-line registration will be made at the conference website. If on-line registration is not available, please contact the conference secretariat (ccp2009.service@elitepco.com.tw).

This registration will be accepted ONLY upon receiving of payment. Registration Acknowledgement will be sent to you via e-mail within three days after a completion of your on-line registration. The confirmation of registration will be sent via e-mail within

3 weeks upon clearance of payment.

On-line registration will be available before 24:00 (GMT+8), Dec. 08, 2009. Registration after the deadline will be processed on-site with **CASH** (**NTD**) upon arrival.

■ Registration Fees

	Registration Fee		
Category	Early-bird Registration (paid before Oct. 31, 2009)	Regular Registration (Nov. 01, 2009 to Dec. 8, 2009)	On-Site Registration (on & after Dec. 9, 2009)
Academician	EUR 350	EUR 385	NTD 18,500
Non-academician	EUR 400	EUR 440	NTD 21,500
Student	EUR 175	EUR 195	NTD 9,500
Retired Professor	EUR 100		NTD 4,500

Note:

Registration as students must send a proof of status to the conference secretariat after registering. At least one author of each accepted paper is required to register and present the paper at the conference. Authors must complete all registration process and all the payment before 24:00(GMT+8), Sep. 30, 2009. Online registration will be closed after 24:00(GMT+8), Dec. 8, 2009. On-site registration only accepts CASH(NTD). Thank you.

	Additional Purchase	
Item	Regular	On-Site
Conference Tour	EUR 12/per person	NTD 500 per person
Accompany Person	EUR 65/per person	NTD 3,500 per person
Banquet Ticket	EUR 40 each	NTD 1,800 each
Welcome Reception Ticket	EUR 30 each	NTD 1,500 each
Abstract Book	EUR 40 each	NTD 1,800 each
Lunch Coupon	EUR 5/per day	NTD 200 per day

■ Full Program delegates are entitled to:

Admission to all speeches, technical sessions, symposiums, Opening Ceremony, exhibition.

Admission to Welcome Reception, banquet, coffee breaks and lunch.

Conference kit includes: badge, program, and abstract book.

...

■ Important Dates:

Early Bird Registration: 24:00 (GMT+8), October 31, 2009

Deadline for Hotel Accommodation: 24:00 (GMT+8), November 15, 2009

Last Day for All Cancellations with 75% Refund: 24:00 (GMT+8), November 15, 2009

■ Confirmation of Registration

You will receive confirmation of registration via Email after the online registration is completed. If you fail to receive emailed registration confirmation, please do not hesitate to contact the secretariat.

■ Letter of Invitation

Participants may request invitation letter from CCP 2009 Secretariat. The invitation is issued only for the purpose of entry visa application and is not a commitment from the CCP 2009 organizers to provide financial aid to any applicant or their accompanying persons. Expenses incurred are the personal responsibility of the applicant.

■ Cancellation & Refund

All cancellations and refund requests must be made in writing to the secretariat. For cancellations postmarked on or before 24:00(GMT+8), November 15, 2009, 75% of the registration fee will be refunded. For cancellations on or after 24:00(GMT+8) November 16, 2009, no fees will be refunded. Refunds will be issued after the meeting.

…

33.2 专业英语阅读：Errors of Observation(测量数据的误差)

1. Definitions of Simple Terms(简单术语的定义)

(i) **The mean.** A number of results from an experiment are usually averaged to give the mean value. For example, $\bar{x}$ is a mean of a number n of determinations where the values recorded are $x_1, x_2, x_3, \cdots, x_n$ and

$$\bar{x} = \frac{x_1 + x_2 + x_3 + \cdots + x_n}{n} \tag{33-1}$$

It is important to record also the variability of these observations. Thus the experimenter should be able to state that the value is the mean value (e.g. $\bar{x}$) plus or minus a parameter which denotes the variability of the observations due to random errors.

This variability is best expressed as the **standard deviation of the mean**, s_m which is defined later. The final results of experiment would therefore be expressed as

$$\bar{x} \pm s_m \tag{33-2}$$

where $\bar{x}$ is the mean value.

(ii) **The error.** The term error has two main meanings. It may be the difference between the experimental results and the true value, where this is known. For example, the precision work that has been done on the measurement of the speed of light waves a value of 2.99793×10^8 m/s. In a comparatively simple student's experiment the mean result is 3.05×10^8 m/s. The error is simply stated to be $(3.05 - 2.99793) \times 10^8 = 5.207 \times 10^6$ m/s.

In many cases of experimental work, the true result is not known. The error, or standard error is then best expressed as $\pm s_m$, where s_m is the standard deviation of the mean of n observations.

Random errors are minor experimental or accidental errors due to errors of judgment, or mildly fluctuating conditions which cannot be controlled. There are many causes of such fluctuations.

Systematic errors are constant errors which cause all results to be incorrect by roughly the same amount in the same direction. Care must be taken in the interpretation of systematic error.

(iii) **Probability.** A measured value may be less than, or greater than a certain figure. In general, the deviations of individual observations from the mean value $\bar{x}$ may be plotted to give a **Gaussian distribution curve**, also known as a **normal distribution**.

This Gaussian distribution will be obtained if the number n of observations is large. In many experiments time forbids that n is a large number. The plotted curve may then well depart from the Gaussian distribution. Provided the number of observations is adequate, however, the Gaussian distribution may be assumed and used as a standard of judgment. A feature of this distribution is that 68% of all observations lie between $\bar{x}$ and $\bar{x} \pm s$ and 95% of all observations lie between $\bar{x}$ and $\bar{x} \pm 2s$ where s is the standard deviation.

(iv) **Populations** and **samples.** A population is involved when the number of observations is very large, ideally infinity. In practice, samples are encountered in which the number of observation is finite. An important use of statistics is to test the significance of a sample value in comparison with the certainty of a population value.

2. The Calculation of Error(误差的计算)

To assess the random error, there are two possibilities.

(a) The range w could be taken as the difference between the largest and the smallest value recorded. This is simple but useless because it uses only two observations, both of which might be gross mistakes.

(b) The preferred alternative is to utilize the **variance** s^2 of sample, which is sum of the squares of the differences between the observations and their mean divided by $(n-1)$, where n is the number of observations, i.e.

$$s^2 = \frac{\sum(x-\bar{x})^2}{n-1} \qquad (33\text{-}3)$$

s is known as the **standard deviation**; $\bar{x}$ is the sample mean.

The variance of the population is given by

$$\sigma^2 = \frac{\sum(x-\mu)^2}{N} \qquad (33\text{-}4)$$

where μ is the population mean, and $n = N$ is now a very large number; but in experimentation we are concerned exclusively with samples rather than populations because the number of observations is limited, so Eq. (33-3) is the important expression.

The **standard deviation** has been called the **standard error** of an individual observation.

The standard deviation of a mean of n observations may be shown to be s_m, where

$$s_m = s/\sqrt{n} \qquad (33\text{-}5)$$

Experimental results should be reported in such way that the accuracy of the mean is known. If s and n are given, s_m can be calculated, and using knowledge of the Gaussian or normal distribution, the probability of obtaining a certain error is known. The calculation of s may be simplified by using in place of Eq. (33-3) the relationship

$$s^2 = \left[\left(\sum x\right)^2 - \frac{1}{n}\sum x^2\right]/(n-1) \qquad (33\text{-}6)$$

The normal or Gaussian distribution concerns a population (i.e. a very large number) for which the mean and the variance are known, but all experimental data is based on small samples (i.e. n is small) and as the true variance is unknown, a slightly different error distribution has to be used: this is the t distribution. t has its own probability distribution, any specified value of t being exceeded by a calculable probability, and tables are available to give t values for various conventional probability levels. This provides a method of testing whether a mean found from experimentally determined values differs significantly from any proposed value. In this case, the statistic t is defined from

$$t = (\text{measured value} - \text{true value})/s_m \qquad (33\text{-}7)$$

and this must exceed certain values listed in the statistic t table to establish a significant difference. To illustrate the process, we will revert to the experiment.

3. Random and systematic error(随机误差与系统误差)

Random error is easy to assess. Systematic error is a most difficult problem because, if the true result is not known, it is only by repeating experiments using different apparatus in various combinations, or by comparison with the results of other workers, or by intelligent appraisal of the design of the experiment in relation to sources of error, that progress can be made. For example, in the determination of the fundamental physical constants many systematic errors were undetected and, indeed, Professor Birge spent 20 years examining original records to reduce or eliminate errors.

Systematic errors are not revealed by one observer making repeated observations: it is hopeless to rely on statistics when the design of the experiment or the apparatus is faulty. A few examples are (i) wrong calibration of a ruler, or scale of an electrical instrument, thermometer etc., (ii) a stop-watch or other timing device which runs fast or slow, (iii) failure to take into consideration some fact such as, for example, the contact potential difference between two metals in such an experiment as determining the Planck constant from the minimum wavelength in the continuous X-ray spectrum, (iv) unexpected changes such as change of dimensions of a container, a photographic film or a diffraction grating replica due to mechanical loading, or immersion in a liquid or changes of temperature, pressure or even humidity, (v) in photometry, a photoelectric cell may pass current in the absence of light, (vi) personal errors may give a biased results because an observer may under-estimate or over-estimate consistently.

In experiments when the true result is unknown, systematic errors may pass unnoticed. For example, a student can readily determine whether such errors are involved in finding, for example, the local gravitational acceleration but even the experienced research scientist can be ignorant of the systematic error involved in, say, measuring the pressure of a gas at a value of about 10^{-3} Pa.

Random errors are generally taken to be reading errors and errors due to fluctuating experimental or environmental conditions. A single observer making repeated measurements may not obtain the same value each time, even though he is confident of each observation.

4. The Propagation of Error(误差的传递)

The reliability of a mean value of a series of observations is discussed. Most experimental work involves making measurements of a number of parameters and combining these in a variety of ways depending on the nature of the experimental work. In the combination of these measurements error is propagated.

The assumption is sometimes made that errors in each variable parameter used in a compound relation will always combine to give the worst possible result. In much experimental work a more realistic value of the error of a result derived from errors in measured parameters is obtained by using methods which allow positive errors in one variable to counteract errors in another.

Glossary

mean	平均值,平均数	average	v. 求……的平均数
determination	测量值	variability	变化性
parameter	参数,参量	denote	表明,指示
observation	观测数据	random error	随机误差
standard deviation	标准偏差	error	误差
true value	真值	precision	精确性,精度
comparatively	相对地	accidental error	偶然性误差
mildly	适度地,略微地	systematic error	系统误差
constant error	常差	probability	概率
Gaussian distribution curve	高斯分布曲线	normal distribution	正态分布
adequate	足够的,充足的	population	总体,总数
sample	抽样,样本	statistics	统计学
gross mistake	粗大的错误	variance	方差
sample mean	采样平均	population mean	总平均
accuracy	精度,准确度	t distribution	t-分布
combination	组合	appraisal	估量,评价
physical constant	物理常数	rely on	依靠
faulty	有错误的,有缺陷的	calibration	标定,校准

electrical instrument	电表,电学仪器	thermometer	温度计
stop-watch	秒表,停表	timing device	计时装置
contact potential difference	接触势差	Planck constant	普朗克常量
dimension	容积	photographic film	感光胶片
diffraction grating	衍射光栅	replica grating	复制光栅
mechanical loading	机械载荷	immersion	浸没
humidity	湿度	photometry	光度测量(术)
photoelectric cell	光电管,光电池,光电元件	biased	有偏差的,有偏见的
gravitational acceleration	重力加速度	reading error	读数误差
propagation of error	误差的传递		

33.3 专业英语常用表达-33 与实验相关的词汇

实验　experiment, experimentation
做实验　make (do/perform/try/carry out) an experiment on (upon/in/with)...
实验者　experimenter
实验员　laboratory assistant, lab assistant, laboratory technician
实验站　experiment station/establishment

实验理论常用词汇:

测量　measure, measurement
等精度/非等精度测量　equal/unequal observations
直接/间接测量　direct/indirect measurement (observation)
直接/间接测量量　directly/indirectly measured quantity
真值　true value
理论值　theoretical value
测量值　measured value
测量列　series of observations
算术平均值　arithmetic mean
不确定度　uncertainty
A类/B类不确定度　Type A/Type B uncertainty
系统误差　systematic error
随机误差　random error
示值误差　indication error
相对误差　relative error
标准偏差　standard deviation
方和根　root-sum-square

置信概率　fiducial/confidence probability
置信区间　fiducial/confidence interval
有效数字　significant figures
单位换算　unit conversion
科学计数法　scientific notation
舍入　round off
四舍五入　half adjust
进位舍入　round up
不进位舍入　round down
零点修正　zero correction
数据处理　data processing
列表法　schedule method
作图法　graphing method
逐差法　termwise subtraction
最小二乘法　least square method
坐标纸　coordinate paper

LESSON 34

34.1　物理学国际学术会议的信件交流英语

学术交流是科研工作的一部分，对科研工作者有着重要的意义，通过交流可以获取信息，发现新的问题和思路，促进科研工作的进行。物理学国际学术会议涉及各种形式的学术交流，例如书面的信件沟通，口头的演讲与讨论等。学术交流一方面是会务信息的交流，例如参会者与会务组之间的交流，投稿人与编辑、审稿人之间的沟通等；另一方面就是科研成果的交流，具有不同学术背景的观点、思想相互碰撞与融合，可以拓宽学术思路，激发灵感，提高创新能力。

在学术交流的过程中信件交流是一种重要的方式，并且随着 E-mail 的出现，通信成为一种快捷有效的交流方式。国际学术会议由于涉及世界各地的参与者，因此信件——特别是电子邮件，已经成为主要的沟通方式。信函可以用于邀请与回复、咨询与解释、提出要求、表达感谢等。往往一次会议的结束，恰是新结识的同行之间进行深入学术交流的开始。

1. E-mail 的格式及注意事项（Format and Tips for Writing E-mail）

电子邮件在形式上不及打印函件正式和可靠，但由于传递快捷，在学术交流过程中被广泛采用。用于学术交流的 E-mail 应使用正式、礼貌的语言并注意写作的规范，良好的写作风格表明对对方的重视与尊重。电子邮件虽然简短，但仍需遵循一定的格式，也要注意信函礼仪。

1）E-mail 的基本格式（Format for Writing E-mail）
（1）邮件标题（Heading）
收件人地址 To Address/Recipient's Address

信件发出前应仔细核对收件地址是否正确。

发件人地址 From Address/Sender's Address

对方所看到的来信地址通常会带有一个系统自动生成的签名,如果想通过签名给对方留下明确印象,可以修改该签名。

标题 Subject Line

标题便于收件人查阅邮件,因此一定要使用标题,并且应简短、明确、能够引起注意。例如第一次论文提交可以使用标题 *Paper submission*,再次提交时可改为 *Resubmission of revised paper*。回复邮件时可以使用 *Reply to...* 的形式,但若所回复的邮件有了新的主题,则应重拟标题。标题应尽量涉及具体的事件,以便提示信件的内容,不要使用 *Hello* 之类空洞的标题。

(2) 邮件正文(Text)

① 问候语 Salutation

恰当的问候语有助于建立良好的关系,E-mail 的问候语与打印函件的相同,位于首行,左对齐。较为正式的形式为 Dear+Title+Last name,使用冒号(也可使用逗号,不及冒号正式),例如 *Dear Professor Smith* 或 *Dear Mr. Smith*,常用的称呼有 *Mr.*, *Mrs.*, *Ms.*, *Dr.* 和 *Professor* 等。如果不知道对方的性别,可以用 Dear+First name+Last name,如 *Dear Attorney Smith*。如果不确定具体的收件人,可以用 Dear+Department 或 Dear Sir (or Madam),例如 *Dear Secretariat*。

② 正文 Body

E-mail 可以采用齐头格式(Block format 或 Full block style),即左对齐格式(left-justified),首行无缩进(比缩进格式更正式)。正文与问候语之间、正文各段落之间、结尾与签名之间均应为双行间隔(double space)。内容应清楚、简洁、切题、可读性强(Clear, Concise, To the point, Readable),一般一封邮件只包含一个主题,以免造成混乱或信息被忽略。

一般邮件(如咨询函)应首先进行简要的自我介绍,并说明写信的目的,然后进行详细说明,提供必要的支持性内容(如列举具体的问题)。最后应说明希望获得的信息或帮助,并对收件人的关注表示感谢。

若为回复性邮件则应首先重申邮件所回复的内容,或引用原信的内容(可以使用">+原文"表示引用),使收件人有的放矢,然后再进行具体解释。

③ 结尾辞 Closing

正文之后(双行间隔)通常是表示祝愿、敬意、感激或问候的结束语,Sincerely, Sincerely yours, Very truly yours, Yours truly, Yours respectfully 等是正式信件中常用的表达。

④ 签名 Signature

在结尾辞之后(双行间隔)为写信人的头衔(Courtesy title/academic title/professional title,可以省略)和全名(Full name),如有需要也可以包含其他信息如职务(Position)、单位(Organization)、电话(Telephone)和地址(Address)等。

⑤ 附件说明 Enclosure Notation

用于说明附件文件的数量与内容。例如单个附件:

Enclosure:*Paper with the title of...*

或多个附件:

Enc1：*Notification of acceptance*
Enc2：*Invoice*

2) 注意事项（Tips for Writing E-mail）

（1）注意正文与标题一样，不要采用全部大写的形式，这会造成阅读的困难并显得无礼，在英语中被称为"SHOUTING"。

（2）不要对邮件的字体等进行过多编辑，如果对方所使用的系统无法识别，则会导致信件格式甚至内容混乱；邮件发出前应核对拼写、语法、内容和地址是否正确。

（3）使用信件回复功能时，不要保留原信的全部内容，这会使信件打开较慢，应只保留必要的信息；注意正确地上传附件，并避免发送过大的附件。

（4）应给收件人足够的时间来回复，不要急于再次写信询问，注意语气礼貌，使用恰当的问候语和致谢语；在与他人首次通信时，有必要说明如何获知对方的邮件地址；不应随意泄露他人的邮件地址。

（5）应该注意，网络问题可能会导致电子邮件传递失败或内容泄露，因此若涉及重要或机密内容，应采取其他信息传递方式。

2. 会议信函的形式（Communication Letters）

用于物理学国际学术会议交流的信件一般包括：会议邀请函（invitation letter）、接受/拒绝函（letter of acceptance/declination）、咨询函（inquiry letters）、附信（cover letter）和致谢信（letter of thanks）等。

普通参会者所收到的邀请函意在对会议进行介绍并诚邀参加，一般可见于会议网站，内容可参见"学术会议信息"的部分。一般只有相关领域内知名的专家和学者等方可收到针对个人的会议邀请函，邀请其在会议中担任职务或进行学术报告等。受到邀请后，无论是否接受，均应尽快予以回复，并在回复信件中重述所受到的邀请、表达受邀的荣幸以及对邀请者的感谢。如接受邀请，则应明确说明是否能够参加会议，如因故无法接受邀请，应做出一定的解释并表示遗憾和歉意，信末一般可以重申谢意并预祝会议的成功。

尽管通过会议网站或会议通知可以获得国际会议的大部分信息，但参会者可能仍需就某些具体问题进行咨询，例如由于网络问题导致论文提交的延迟，有关注册费用的具体要求等。咨询信件的收件人可以是该项工作的具体负责人（如 Dear Professor...），在不清楚具体负责人的情况下也可以是某一部门（如 Dear Academic Committee）。咨询信件的主要内容应包含简单的自我介绍、明确的咨询事项、所希望的答复方式和致谢。信件的语气应礼貌，内容应尽量简短，如有必要应提供其他的联络方式。在得到答复之后应尽快回复，说明对所咨询问题是否已经清楚，并对所获得帮助表示感谢。

附信一般用于附加信息或提交文件（如摘要或论文），一般内容简短，只需说明附件的内容。致谢信用于在会后对会议的邀请、会议期间所提供的服务与帮助表示感谢，并可以加强同行之间的联系，为未来的学术交流活动创造更多机会。

3. 信件中的常用表达（Useful expressions for letter writing）

1) 信件开头

（1）首次写信

I have pleasure of introducing myself as...

It is my pleasure to introduce you that I am...

This is to introduce myself as...

I wish to introduce myself as...

Through the courtesy of..., we know that you are...

You have been introduced/recommended to me by Mr. Smith as...

I am writing to enquire about...

I am writing in connection with...

I am writing to you to draw/call/invite your attention to the fact that...

(2) 再次写信

I wish to refer you to our last letter of (date), concerning...

This is to refer to our previous letter dated...in which...

Reference is made to our letter of (date), regarding...

Referring to our letter dated...in connection with...

Further to our previous letter of (date), I wish to...

This is a follow-up to our letter dated...respecting...

With reference to your letter of...

I recently wrote to you about...

2) 信息提供

I have the opportunity of informing you that...

I take this opportunity to inform you that...

This is to inform you that...

Please be informed/advised that...

By this letter I wish to advise you that...

It may be of great interest to you to hear that...

I am pleased to announce/confirm...

It is with considerable pleasure/regrets that...

I will send all the details.

I'll let you know all the details.

I wish to inform/advise you with regret that...

I hereby inform/advise you with regret that...

I regret to inform you that...

3) 回信常用表达

I reply to your enquiry about...

Thank you for your letter of (date), concerning...

I have received (with thanks) your letter of (date), regarding...

I am in receipt of your letter dated...enclosing...

I acknowledge receipt of your letter dated...asking if...

I am pleased to have received your letter of (date)...

I refer to your letter of (date)...

Your letter of (date) has been received (with thanks)...

Your letter of (date) has just reached me.

From your letter dated...I learn that...

In reply to your letter of...

Replying to the question mentioned in your letter of (date), I wish to...

I have carefully considered your suggestions about...

4) 结束语

(1) 请求回复

I am waiting for a reply from you soon.

I am waiting for an early reply from you.

I request a prompt reply, please.

I am looking forward to your reply.

I look forward to hearing from you.

I look forward to seeing/meeting/getting together with you soon.

Please reply at an early date.

We look forward to receiving your reply.

I hope you will let me have your reply without delay.

I expect your favorable reply.

I hope that you will treat the matter as urgent and give me the reply the soonest possible.

If you have any comment on this matter, I shall be delighted to hear from you.

If you require any further information, feel free to contact me.

Please advise as necessary.

Should you need any further information, please do not hesitate to contact me.

I would very much appreciate an early reply.

(2) 表达感谢

Thank you very much for your invitation.

Thank you in advance for your kind invitation.

I extend my gratitude toward you for your invitation/answer/explanations/help...

Please accept my sincere gratitude for your valuable assistance in this matter.

I very much appreciate the efforts you have made in this connection.

I greatly appreciate...

Please accept my thanks for...

I am very much obliged to you for...

I would be most grateful if you could...

It would be nice if you could...

I'd be grateful if you could...

(3) 恳请留意/唤起注意

Your kind attention to this matter will be much appreciated.

I trust that you will give your due attention to this matter.

I shall appreciate your giving this matter your early/immediate attention.

I would appreciate your immediate attention to this matter.

I hope the above proposal will receive your particular attention.

I feel it my duty to remind you of this matter again.

5) 表达歉意

Please accept my apologies again.

I hope that this has not caused you any inconvenience.

I am extremely sorry for the inconvenience I have caused you.

With apologies once again.

I regret the trouble it may have caused you.

Once again, I apologize for any inconvenience.

I apologize for the delay in replying to your letter.

I'm terribly sorry not to have written sooner but…

6) 表达请求/要求

Could you send me the application form please?

Would you please inform the changed time?

May I ask you to send me…?

Is it possible for you to provide information for me to…?

You are kindly requested to…without delay.

I should like to call your attention to…

Would it be possible to telephone me as soon as possible?

7) 接受请求/要求/邀请

In accordance /compliance with your request, I send herewith…

As requested in your letter of (date), I…

Following your instructions, I have changed my format of my paper again.

At your request, I now have arranged…

I have duly noted your request that…

With regard to your request for…, I…

I have much pleasure in forwarding you…as desired…

Your request for…has been taken into my consideration.

It would give me great pleasure to attend…

8) 拒绝请求/要求/邀请

I regret being unable to meet your demand for…

I regret that I am unable to attend…

It is with much regret that I have to decline your request.

Unfortunately, I will not be able to attend…

Unfortunately, it is impossible for me to do what you request.

I am very sorry for having to turn down your request.

It is regrettable that I can do nothing to help you in this matter.

9) 表示确定

I can assure you of…

There is no doubt that…

You can feel certain that the task for me will be entirely satisfactory to you.

10) 请求理解

I should like to have your understanding about this matter.

I hope this will give you a clear understanding of the difficulty of the work.

11) 附件说明

I enclose herewith a copy of…for your reference.

I attach hereto a copy of…

Enclosed please find…

Enclosed is/are…

Enclosed you will find…

I am enclosing…

There is/are enclosed…

34.2　专业英语阅读：Experiment of Polarization of Light(光的偏振实验)

1. Introduction(引言)

This lab will address three concepts of wave polarization. We will conduct this experiment with light, but the general concepts apply to many other waves as well.

(1) Polarization(偏振)

Polarization occurs only in transverse waves. Examples of transverse waves are oscillations on a string, water waves, or the electromagnetic radiation we treat here. By definition, the oscillation is perpendicular to the direction of wave propagation in a transverse wave. Since in three-dimension space there are three independent dimensions, there are two possible perpendicular directions needed to describe any oscillatory motion perpendicular to the direction of motion. If you think about a transverse wave in a string, the oscillation could be up-and-down or left-and-right while the wave front propagates forward along the string. The two independent and perpendicular directions are called the two polarization states. (Or in coordinates, if a wave propagates along the z-axis, there are two polarizations perpendicular to the wave motion—one along the x-axis and the other along the y-axis.) Polarization cannot occur in longitudinal waves because the direction of oscillation has only one possibility, along the direction of motion.

You may argue that you can make oscillations happen on a string in more than just the two directions described above—and you are right! For example, you can make oscillations diagonally from the upper left to the lower right or you can even make circular oscillations by moving your hand continuously in a circle, producing a corkscrew pattern along the string. But no matter which wave you make, the oscillations can always be represented as two superimposed waves with displacements along the two mutually perpendicular polarization axes. Any vector can always be described by decomposing it into its x- and y- components. Here, the relevant vector is the oscillating displacement from the z-axis. The amplitudes of the resolved x and y components indicate how much of the wave is in each polarization state.

For electromagnetic radiation, the oscillating quantities are the electric (and magnetic) fields. These undulate perpendicular to the direction of the wave. Like waves in a string, electromagnetic waves are transverse waves and have polarization properties. The polarization state describes the axis along which the electric field in the wave oscillates. Visible light is electromagnetic radiation in a particular frequency-wavelength regime, with large frequency of oscillation(~ 1015 Hz) and small wavelength ($\sim 5 \times 10^{-7}$ m).

(2) Polarizer(起偏器)

Usually light is produced (e. g. incandescent light from a candle or a light bulb) by hot electrons and atoms, which are moving or are oriented in random directions, so that the wave is unpolarized. This means that the electric field associated with the wave oscillates in random directions (though always at right angles to the direction of the propagation of the light). So there is no favored direction for polarization. It is as if you were moving your hand in random directions at the end of a string. Note that this is very different from the cases of waves in a string described above. Even in circular polarization the oscillations were not random.

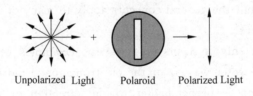

Fig. 34-1

A polarization filter, shown in Fig. 34-1, is a device with a specified direction, called the polarization axis. The filter absorbs all of the wave's incoming electric field perpendicular to the polarization axis and transmits the electric field parallel to the polarization axis. So no matter what the polarization of the light shining into a polarizer might be, the light coming out of the polarizer is always polarized in the direction specified by the polarization axis. An unpolarized wave just prior to the polarizer has an electric field (E) pointing randomly in all directions perpendicular to the wave direction, as shown in Fig. 34-2. The polarized wave after the polarizer has only half the energy content, and the E-field is oscillating solely along the polarization axis. This electric field has the same value as the component along that axis just before the polarizer.

(3) Malus Law(马吕斯定律)

Suppose a wave has linearly polarized light characterized by an electric field vector,

Fig. 34-2

E_0, at an angle, θ, relative to the direction of a polarizer. The electric field that is transmitted through the polarizer is $E = E_0 \cos\theta$, the component that was not absorbed. Since the energy intensity in the wave is proportional to E^2, then the intensity passing through two polarizers will be proportional to the square of the cosine of the angle θ between the two polarizing axes (Malus law).

$$I = I_{\max}\cos^2\theta \tag{34-1}$$

In this experiment, we use an incandescent unpolarized light source and then polarize it by first passing it through a polarizer. The electric field vector E_0 will then point along the same direction as the polarizing axis of the first polarizer. As the new polarized light falls on the second polarizer (analyzer), only the component of along the polarizing axis of the second polarizer will make it through unaffected.

As Fig. 34-3 illustrates, the electric field strength of only $E_0\cos\theta$ will make it through the second polarizer, so that the new intensity will be given by Eq. (34-1) above. A human eye or a photometer can detect this change in light intensity.

Fig. 34-3

2. Equipment(仪器)

(1) Linear Translator (A holder for the fiber optic cable that can be moved transversely in small increments, allowing a positioning with better than 0.1 mm precision.) (2) Photometer (Device to measure the total power contained in light impinging on it. It uses the photoelectric effect to convert the photons to electrons and various electron amplification techniques to produce a measurable electric current.) (3) Incandescent light source (4) Incandescentlight source power cord (5) Fiber optic cable (6) Holders (7) Polarization filters (8) Bench couplers and screws

3. Safety Note(安全提示)

Although the laser is of low intensity for most situations, it can be dangerous in certain circumstances unless used carefully. In particular, **DO NOT** use the laser in such a way that it can shine into any person's eye (The warning label on the laser states "**DO NOT stare into Beam!**"). When you are not actually using the laser, turn it off or close the beam shutter at the front of the laser.

4. Procedure(实验步骤)

(1) Make sure only the dim incandescent ceiling lights in the room are on.

(2) The linear translator should be placed at the far end of the track opposite the laser. Make sure that the linear translator is in the middle position (at 2.5 cm). Place the fiber-optic cable in the hole of the linear translator. Place the incandescent light source about 10~20 cm from the linear translator such that the light shines towards the linear translator.

(3) Place the polarizers in the holders. Rotate the polarizers such that the white mark on the holder aligns with the 0° angle reading on the polarizer. Place the two polarizers between the incandescent light source and the linear translator.

(4) Put the photometer to the lowest sensitivity (the 1000 setting) and use the zero adjust knob to make sure that the pointer is at the 0 position when the incandescent light source is turned off. Turn the incandescent light source back on and adjust the sensitivity of the photometer such that the needle is at the highest position without being at the maximum reading. The value of the sensitivity corresponds to the maximum value on the analog scale.

(5) Record this measurement as the intensity for 0° difference between the two polarizing axes. Measure the intensity for angles between 0° and 90° in increments of 10° degrees. If the readings become too small you may have to switch the photometer to a setting with a higher sensitivity.

(6) Plot the relative intensity (I divided by I_0, the intensity at 0°) vs. the $\cos^2$ of the angle between the axes of the polarizers.

(7) What is the general shape of your graph? What does this indicate? Did your line or curve pass through the origin? What reading do you obtain when the polarizers are at an angle of 90° relative to each other? (This is called the "noise" of your measuring device.) What reading would you expect if there was no noise? What is the signal to noise ratio? (The "signal" is the reading at 0°.) What does this tell you?

(8) If you had a lot of background light, how could you reduce the influence it would have on your results (by changing the setting or by changing your data analysis)?

(9) If you had aligned the 90° mark instead of the 0° mark of both polarizers with the white mark on the holder would your results have been any different? What relative intensity would you expect if the angle between the two polarizers was 180°? What for 270°?

(10) What are the main sources of error? Which do you think contributes most?

Glossary

polarization	偏振	polarization state	偏振态
diagonally	对角地	corkscrew	瓶塞钻
decompose	分解	undulate	波动,起伏
polarizer	起偏器	incandescent	白炽的

circular polarization	圆偏振	unpolarized	非偏振的,非极化的
filter	滤光片	polaroid	起偏振片
polarized light	偏振光	polarization axis	偏振轴
Malus law	马吕斯定律	light source	光源
analyzer	检偏器	photometer	光度计
linear translator	线性平移器	holder	支架
cable	电缆,多芯导线	increment	增量
positioning	定位	impinge	冲击
photoelectric effect	光电效应	power cord	电源线
coupler	耦合器	stare into	凝视
beam shutter	射束光闸	ceiling light	天花板灯

34.3 专业英语常用表达-34 观点 看法

1. 用于较为正式的书面语或口语中的常用句型

(1) 表述观点

from my point of view 依我之见,在我看来

in my (his/her) view 在我(他/她)看来

in my opinion 依我看,在我看来

I am of the opinion that... 我认为……

I am unconvinced that... 我认为/相信……不……(翻译时将否定放在宾语从句中)

I do not agree that... 我不同意……

I do not believe that... 我认为/相信……不……(翻译时将否定放在宾语从句中)

I hold the view/opinion that... 我认为……

I think/consider/find/feel/believe/suppose/presume/assume that... 我认为……

I would argue that... 我认为/我要说……

I would say that... 我认为/我要说……

It seems to me that... 我认为/我的看法是……

My view/opinion/belief/impression/conviction is that... 我认为/我的观点是/在我看来……

(2) 在文章中引入不同的观点

It is sometimes argued... 有时……

Of course, many/some people argue... 当然,很多人/有人主张……

While... 尽管……

Admittedly... 诚然/无可否认……

(3) 对观点进行解释说明

By this I mean... 我的意思是……

Here I'm referring to... 我指的是……

That is to say... 也就是说/换句话说/即/就是……

To be more precise,… 更确切地说/更准确地说/更具体地说……

2. 用于非正式口语中的常用句型

(1) 强调个人的观点看法

As for me/As to me,… 就我而言/依我之见/对我来说……
I feel… 我觉得……
In my eyes,… 在我看来……
To my mind,… 我认为/照我的看法……
I am under the impression that… 我的印象是……
I have the feeling that… 我感觉/我预感……
It is my impression that… 我觉得/我的印象是……
My impression is that… 我觉得/我的印象是……
My own feeling on the subject is that… 对这件事,我个人的观点是……

(2) 对所表达的观点非常肯定

I reckon… 我认为……
I am sure/I am certain that… 我确信/我确定……
I bet that… 我打赌/我相信……
I dare say that… 我敢说……
I form/adopt an opinion that… 我的想法是……
I have no doubt that… 我相信/我毫不怀疑/毫无疑问……
I'm quite convinced that… 我确信……
It goes without saying that… 不言而喻/毋庸置疑/不用说……

(3) 用于表达批评、否定的观点或对观点有所保留

As far as I'm concerned,… 就我而言/我的意见是/我认为……
If you ask me,… 依我看/据我看/我认为……
Speaking personally,… 就个人而言/从个人角度来说……
To be honest/frank (with you)… 老实说……
Generally speaking, I think… 一般说来/总的来说,我认为……
I'd just like to say… 我只想说……

(4) 表示猜测

I gather that… 我猜想……
I guess that… 我猜想……

3. 对观点表示赞同的常用语

A valid point. 可行的想法。/有效的建议。
Absolutely. I think that's a fantastic idea. 一点不错,我认为这是个极好的主意。
Exactly! 完全正确!
Fair enough! 说得对!/有道理!
He is quite right/absolutely right. 他是对的!/他完全正确!
He may be right. 他可能是对的。

I agree completely. 我完全同意。/我十分赞成。
I agree one hundred percent. 我百分之百地同意。
I agree wholeheartedly. 我非常赞成。/我完全同意。
I agree with you/him... 我赞成你的/他的……（观点）。
I agree. 我同意。/我赞成。
I am at one with him on that point. 我同意他的这一观点。
I approve of it. 我同意/我赞成。
I couldn't agree more. 我完全同意。
I guess I see what you mean. 我想我明白你的意思了。
I have come to the same conclusion. 我也有相同的结论。
I have no objection. 我没有异议。/我不反对。
I hold the same opinion. 我（与你）意见相同。
I quite agree. 我非常赞同。
I really think so. 我就是这么想的。
I share your view. 我也这么看。/我同意。
I think so. 我也这么想。/我想是的。
I think you're right. 我认为你是对的。
I'm in complete agreement. 我完全同意。
It is true. 的确。/是这样。
Just so! 正是如此。/正是这样。/一点不错。
Precisely! 正是这样！
Quite so! 正是如此！/的确是这样！/太对啦！
That's just it! 正是这样！/的确如此！
That's right. 对了。/没错。
That's true. 的确。/是这样。
We are of one mind on that question. 在这个问题上我们意见一致。
We are of the same mind on that question. 我们对这一问题看法一致。
Yes, of course! 是的，当然。
You're right there. 你是对的。

4. 对观点表示反对的常用语

I am afraid that is not quite true. 这恐怕不太对。
I disagree (completely). 我完全不能同意。/我着实不敢苟同。
I don't agree with what you say. 我不同意你的意见/你所说的。
I don't agree with you/him. 我不同意你的/他的观点。
I don't agree. 我不同意。/我不这样想。
I don't share your/his/her view. 我不同意你的/他的/她的观点。
I don't think it will work. 我想这难以实现。/我想这不管用。
I don't think so. 我不这样认为。
I don't think that's quite right. 我认为这不太对。

I take a different view. 我的观点不同。/我有不同的看法。
I think otherwise. 我不这样认为。/我不这样看。
I wouldn't say that. 我不这样认为。/我不这样想。
I'm afraid I can't agree with you there. 恐怕在这点上我不能同意你的意见。
Of course not! 当然不是!
On the contrary I think... 恰恰相反,我觉得……
That's not how I see it. 我并不这么看。
That's out of the question. 这是不可能的。
That's ridiculous. 这太荒唐了。
This argument does not hold water. 这种观点是站不住脚的。
You are/he is wrong. 你/他是错的。

LESSON 35

35.1 物理学国际学术会议口头报告

专题学术报告(Oral Presentation at Academic Conference)是学术会议中经常采用的一种有效交流方式,也是学术会议的重要环节。物理学所涉及的领域极为广泛,通过学术报告,可以了解相关学科的最新研究进展或整体发展。由于学术报告内容的专业性较强,并且要在有限时间内提供有独创性、有价值的信息,因此要求语言严谨,逻辑缜密,能够高效地传达思想。只有主题明确,着眼于听众需求的报告才能够取得良好的效果。而学术报告的效果,直接影响到听众对报告人科研成果的理解和对演讲者学术水平的认识。良好的演讲技巧可以让他人更好地了解报告人的科研工作,引起听众更多的兴趣,更好地促进学术交流。

35.1.1 口头报告的准备(Preparation for Oral Presentation)

学术会议上的报告多为论文陈述的形式(Paper Presentation),要求在有限的时间内将专业性很强的研究成果展示给大家,并通过支持材料说明研究成果的正确性。这在一定程度上需要通过语言技巧来说明论文的内容,因此只有进行充分的准备才能取得良好的效果。鉴于在撰写论文的过程中,我们已经对报告的内容有了比较深入的研究,因此准备工作的重点在于如何使报告能够顺利地进行,引起听众足够的兴趣。应根据报告的时间限制、听众对报告主题的了解程度等来确定报告的重点、详略程度、幻灯片的数量、演讲的方式等。

报告的内容与重点确定之后,为了保证信息的准确传递,报告的流畅进行,可以为报告撰写提纲或更为详细的脚本,并根据预演的效果进行修改和调整。

1. 大纲(Outline)

大纲可以确定报告的整体结构,帮助对报告的内容进行记忆,一般可以把每个要点写成单句的形式。报告一般有引言、正文和结束语三个部分,其作用均为传递信息,因此有这样一种说法,"*Tell them what you're going to say, tell them, and then tell them what you said.*"

(1) 引言(Introduction/Beginning)

该部分对报告的题目、主要内容和大纲结构进行介绍,让听众对报告的内容和重点有一

个整体的把握,效果良好的引言可以吸引听众的注意。一般结构为:
开场白(Opening remarks)
主题说明(Thesis statement/Introduction of topic)
要点预览(Preview of main points/Structure presenting)
目的(Purpose (if necessary))
(2) 正文(Body/Middle)

正文是报告的主体部分,对物理学科来说,主要包括问题提出,背景介绍,方法介绍(理论或实验)、结果陈述。由于所涉及的信息较多,可以对每部分内容进行一个小结,让听众对主要信息更明确;由于时间较短,对于比较详细的内容不能详述,可以向听众介绍相关内容在文章中的位置,或可以参考的资料等。正文部分的一般展开方式为:

Main Point 1
    Background (if necessary)
    Methodology (Theory or Experiments): Cover in short talks and refer people to the paper.
    Results: Cover key result well and explain to give insights.
    Brief summary of point 1 (if necessary)
Main Point 2
    Background (if necessary)
    Methodology (Theory or Experiments)…
    Results…
    Brief summary of point 2 (if necessary)
Main Point 3
    …

(3) 结束语(Conclusion/End)

结束语与报告的主题相呼应,使报告内容完整,其作用类似于引言,用于重申或强调报告的主要观点,让听众对报告的内容形成明确的认识。一般结构为:
预告结束(Forecast of end)
重申要点(Restatement or emphasis of main points)
结束语(Closing)

2. 脚本(Script)

报告的脚本比大纲更为详细(报告的文本形式),是在大纲基础上的内容扩充。可以写成详细的讲稿,也可以只写出提示性的要点内容和过渡语。

在撰写脚本的过程中应注意语言细节上的推敲,保证用词、表述、语法的准确,并注意报告的口语特点,使报告更容易被接受。例如尽量采用短句和口语化的词汇,对复杂的专业词汇应给以解释,注重采用亲和力强、更容易激发兴趣的说法,注意语言的生动性。

流畅的过渡使报告层次清楚、条理性强,在脚本中应设计好各个部分之间如何衔接,选择合适的过渡语。

一般演讲者的语速为每分钟 100~135 个单词,应根据报告时间来确定脚本的内容和详略,以保证主要的内容得到充分展示。同时可以准备一些备份的内容,以便在特殊情况下使用。

35.1.2 开始报告(Beginning a Presentation)

学术报告的时间宝贵,听众多为专家学者,对报告所涉及的领域有深入的了解,创新性的学术成果才是听众感兴趣的重点,因此在学术报告中应谨慎采用非学术演讲的开篇方式,一般可以在简单致谢与问候之后直接进入主题。引言部分确定了整个报告的基调,应简洁、清楚、容易记忆,一个成功报告的引言可以起到引起注意、声明主题和要点预览的多重作用。

1. 开场白(Opening Remarks)

(1) 对听众的称谓

称呼的一般顺序为:嘉宾,主席,主持人,代表。

Distinguished Guests (from...)

Respected/Honorary President Professor...

Mr. Chairman (Madam Chairman)

Mr. Chairman and Cochairman

Ladies and Gentlemen

Distinguished Colleagues

Fellow Delegates

(2) 对主持人的介绍表示感谢

I would like to thank Mr. Chairman for his gracious introduction.

Thank you very much, Mr. Chairman, for your very kind/gracious introduction.

Mr. Chairman, let me first of all thank you for your very kind introduction.

First I may thank for the generous introduction by Mr. Chairman.

I would like to thank Mr. Chairman for permitting me the privilege to speak to this audience. 其中 Mr. Chairman 可以具体为 Professor...或 Dr....等。

(3) 礼节性用语

Good morning/Good afternoon/Good evening.

It's a very great pleasure for me to be able to attend this conference.

I am honored to have been invited to speak at this conference.

I am very delighted/happy/glad/pleased/honored/privileged to be here (on this special occasion).

I appreciate the opportunity to be here (with you today/this morning/this afternoon).

It is a great pleasure to be given the honor as a speaker on this important topic.

It's an honor to have the opportunity to address such a distinguished audience.

I am very happy to have this chance to give my presentation.

I consider it a great honor to be asked to speak here.

2. 主题说明(Thesis Statement)

学术报告是学术信息交流的过程,而报告的主题则是信息的核心内容,整个报告的内容

都将围绕主题展开,主题介绍可以带领听众进入报告的主要内容,常用的表述如下:

I'd like to talk about some of our work in the field of…
I am here to present…to talk to you about…to speak about…
I'm going to talk/give a talk/speak about…
This presentation will investigate the…
I'd like to present/speak briefly about…
I'd like to provide an overview of…
My topic today will deal with…
I'd like to have a presentation concerning…
What I would like to present/talk about is…
I shall devote my talk to the…
I would like to concentrate on…
I want to confine/restrict/limit my talk to the point of…

3. 要点预览(Preview of Main Points)

说明主题之后,应把报告的大纲按照顺序告诉听众,帮助听众掌握内容的结构。介绍大纲的关键是条理分明、次序清楚,不要将内容展开说明。常用的表述有:

My talk consists of two parts. One is…, and the other is…
I would like to divide my presentation/talk into four parts.
My presentation will be given in three parts.
The subject can be viewed under the following three headings.
There are four major points to be covered in…
The effects of… will be shown by a comparison of… and…

I'll start with…	Next…	Finally…
Firstly…	Secondly…	Thirdly…(Last…)
To begin with…	Moving right along…	To close…
I'll open with…	Then I'll go on with…	And I'll wrap up with…
Step one is to…	Next step is to…	And the final step is to…
I shall first talk about…	Then I'll touch on…	And finally I'll discuss…
The first part deals with…	The second part concerns…	The last part relates to…

35.1.3 展开报告内容(Developing a Presentation)

引言部分已经确定了报告的主题,并且向听众展示了报告的整体结构,接下来就进入了报告的主体部分。其作用是对各个要点加以展开说明,使听众对主题有更深入的理解,重点就在于如何利用支持性材料来使观点更为客观、可信和深刻。这一目标要通过材料的逻辑结构和语言表述来实现。

1. 逻辑结构(Logical Structure)

材料组织方式的选择取决于材料之间的逻辑关系。常见的用于组织材料的逻辑结构很多,在使用中并不是截然分开的,可以结合或穿插在一起使用,最终目的是将观点阐述清楚,使听众形成明确的印象。常用的结构有以下几种：

（1）层次分解结构（Hierarchical Structure）

这种逻辑结构将主要观点逐层分解为小的主题，但在口语表述中采用这种结构时，通常层次不可过多，以免使听众对演讲的主题把握不清。

（2）顺序结构（Sequential Structure）

这是一种比较简单的结构，通过一系列相互关联的观点而最终得出结论。如时间顺序（Chronological Order）、空间顺序（Spatial Order）、因果顺序（Causal Order）、主题顺序（Topic Order）、问题导向顺序（Question Orientated Order）等均是比较常见的逻辑顺序。

（3）金字塔结构（Pyramid Structure）

这种结构首先概括性地阐明某一观点，然后逐步进行更为详细和深入的讨论，形成一种金字塔形逐步扩展的结构。可以说该结构的每一个层次都在讨论相同的主题，但深度和广度逐渐增大。这种结构有两个优点：一方面可以使听众对主题思想有比较深刻的印象和比较深入的理解，另一方面可以根据具体情况随时结束讨论，而不会影响报告的整体结构。

（4）三明治结构（Sandwich Structure）

三明治结构可以说是最为常见的一种结构，可以用在以上任一结构的某一个层次或环节当中。例如口头报告的"引言—主体—结束语"结构就属于这一类别。

2. 语言表述（Delivering）

语言是通过听觉和视觉来传递的，声音和符号可以看成语言传递的载体，不同载体的表述方式不同。文章和报告可以看作学术论文的两种不同载体，因此在表述方式上也有所不同。文章采用书面语体，而报告则采用口头语体，二者在语法、词汇和表现方式上均有所不同。对于相同的主题，文章的读者比报告的听众有更多的时间进行理解，因此学术报告所采用的语言表述应更能突出重点并且更易于理解。为了使学术报告的效果更好，帮助听众更好地理解报告的内容，在表述中除应保证语法正确之外，还应注意以下的方面：

（1）词汇和表达（Wording and Phrasing）

学术报告的用词应准确并且口语化，用词准确保证了学术的严谨性，使信息能够被准确无误地传递，避免歧义，而口语化的词汇可以使表述更为直观生动。抽象、难懂的词语，冗长、复杂的句式，过多修饰的间接表达都会增加理解的困难，并且会分散听众的注意力，因此应尽量避免。报告中应尽量使用具体、确切、简单的词语和结构简单、表达直接的短句，较为复杂的内容可以结合图片进行说明，让听众把注意力集中在报告的内容上面。具体应在以下几个方面加以注意：

① 使用口语词汇

学术报告毕竟是一种口头交流形式，使用口语词汇可以使表达更简单易懂，在修改报告脚本时应将一些正式的书面词汇换成较简单的口语词汇。平时应注意积累这类的词汇，留意口语中的常用表达。以下列举了一些这样的词汇：

Written Words	Spoken Words	Written Words	Spoken Words
accord	*give*	indistinct	*dim*
accordingly	*so*	inferior	*worse*
approximately	*about*	inform	*tell*

ascend	*climb*	inquire	*ask*
assist	*help*	intermittently	*on and off*
available	*obtainable*	nevertheless	*though*
bear	*carry*	obtain	*get*
cautious	*careful*	on account of	*because*
cease	*stop*	perspiration	*sweat*
center	*heart*	possess	*have*
circumvent	*prevent*	preserve	*keep*
commence	*begin*	rapid	*quick*
complete	*finish*	release	*free*
comprehension	*understanding*	remark	*say*
conclude	*end*	retain	*keep*
consume	*use*	sufficient	*enough*
contact	*touch*	superior	*better*
endeavor	*try*	technique	*method*
energetic	*lively*	thereafter	*from then on*
enquire	*ask*	transform	*change*
flame	*fire*	transparent	*clear*
heretofore	*before now*	vacant	*empty*
identical	*similar*	vision	*sight*
incorrect	*wrong*		

② 准确使用动词

学术报告要求用词准确直接，而很多动词短语有诸多含义，容易引起歧义，相比之下，动词具有更确切的词义，因此经常用动词代替相应的同义动词短语。如：

Verb Phrase	Verb	Verb Phrase	Verb
be made up of	*compose*	put out, go out	*extinguish*
break up	*rupture*	put together	*aggregate*
bring out	*introduce*	put up	*erect*
carry out	*perform*	put up with	*tolerate*
drive forward	*propel*	send for	*summon*
fill up	*occupy*	set fire (light) to	*ignite*
find out	*discover*	speed up	*accelerate*
go with	*accompany*	take ... into pieces	*dismantle*
keep up	*maintain*	take away	*remove*
look at (over)	*examine*	take in	*absorb*
make up	*invent*	turn into liquid	*liquefy*
make...weak	*weaken*	turn on	*complete*（接通）
push down	*depress*	turn upside down	*invert*
push in	*insert*	use up	*exhaust*

put in   add   wear away   erode

③ 专业术语的使用

专业词汇会给报告的理解带来一定的困难，使用时应特别注意。首先应注意报告中术语的一致性，用相同的术语来表示同一对象，并且应一直使用相同的单位制；对听众不熟悉的术语应给予清楚的定义或解释；如果报告中涉及较多的术语，可以在引言部分以列表的形式交代清楚。

④ 使用简单的短句

例如下面的几个句子在口语中理解起来就比较困难：

This peak is theorized to be resultant from two competing effects.

There are several known facts about spectrum having bearing on my interpretation of results.

The detecting and controlling systems are periodically testable to verify operability in the event that they are called upon to function.

换成下面的说法则更易于理解：

This peak is believed to result from two competing effects.

Several facts about spectrum influenced my interpretation of results.

In order to guarantee the normal function, the detecting and controlling systems are tested periodically.

⑤ 注意英汉语序的不同

英语和汉语属于完全不同的体系，各自在不同环境下发展，语序（词序）的差别很大，有时甚至相反，因此很多时候原意的非正确表达恰恰是由不正确的语序所导致的，在物理学专业英语中尤为如此。在阅读过程中，读者可以根据上下文来推敲原文的正确含义，但是在报告过程中，听众没有这样的时间。这就要求表达者特别注意语序的正确性，并且通过停顿、短句与重音使听众明了发言者所要表述的正确含义与要点。试通过以下例子来体会英汉语序的不同，并在口头表述中加以注意。

在这种情况下，有必要使用另外四个时钟脉冲。

In this case, it is necessary to apply four additional clock pulses.

近十年理论上的主要进展如下。

The main theoretical developments in this decade are as follows.

这是余下的主要限制因素。

This is the principle remaining limitation.

在触发器的许多应用场合都是这样。

It is so in many flip-flop applications.

在独立的章节中详细地给出了接收机每个部分的电路。

The circuits for each receiver section are presented in detail in separate chapters.

在这种情况下，电子向电池的正极运动。

In this case, the electron moves towards the positive battery terminal.

这一节讨论电路的预设计。

This section deals with preliminary circuit designs.

（2）常用的表达方式（Useful Expressions）

在报告中需要一定的词语和句式用于表示过渡、转折、比较、引用、强调等，以使报告的内容前后呼应，结构紧凑，逻辑性强，过渡流畅。以下介绍一些常用的表达方式：

① 引入正文（Introduction of the Body）

I want to start by...

The first topic I intend to discuss is...

Now, I would like to address myself to the first aspect of this problem.

Now I'd like to introduce the first point...

To begin with, I would like to talk about the background.

Now I'll review the first point...

First I would like to talk about the definition of some terms to be used in the presentation.

I think it would be best to start out by looking at some pictures.

Now I'm going to consider the first point...

It's time to discuss the first point...

I'd like to preface my presentation with...

The first point I would like to talk about is...

② 引入下一个要点（Introduction of Next Point）

Another fact that supports my main point is...

Following from this point is...

The second part of my presentation is...

The next point I'd like to bring up is...

Well, let's turn to/shift to/switch over to...

Turning to the next question, I'll talk about the theory/experiment...

Second, I'd like to talk about...

Here we come to the problem of...

So much/That's all for the...and now we can go on to the point of...

Let's leave/move away from the first problem and go into the next part.

I'd like to move on to the next topic.

Now let's turn our attention to...

This/That brings/leads us to my second point/the problem of...

③ 简述论点（Brief Discussion）

I would discuss this point without going into details.

I would offer/give a brief/short description of...

Let's go through this point briefly/succinctly.

Limited by the time available, I would skip over the details of this part.

My time is running short, so I would only give the outline of this part.

Time will not permit me to deal with all the sub-topics.

Time permits only an abstract of this problem.

④ 详述论点(Discussion in Detail)

I would like to go into the detail of this question.

I would deal with this part at length.

I would offer/give a detailed discussion about this point.

I would deal with the next point a little more extensively.

Since this part is important/difficult, I'd like to explain it in detail.

⑤ 论点的前后呼应(Coherence of Context)

I will provide some specific information about that in a minute.

I will talk about this in more detail after a moment.

I will return/come back to this point later on.

I will have more to say about that in a few minutes.

Now let's come back/return to what I said a moment ago.

This brings me back to the point...

Here I'd like to refer to the previous point...

⑥ 强调(Emphasis)

The crux of the matter is...

The next point is crucial.

Fundamentally (speaking), ...

Now I would like to address myself to the important part of my presentation.

Now I will concentrate on the point that...

It is necessary to explain the point that...

What will it lead to then?

⑦ 改变措辞(Rephrasing)

That is to say...

Let me put that in another way...

In other words, ...

As I have been saying...

⑧ 对幻灯片的说明(Caption of Slide)

常用动词：illustrate, indicate, describe, show, tell, demonstrate, depict, exhibit, present...

常用名词：slide, picture, curve, figure, table, chart, diagram, photo, bar, graph, flow chart, circuit diagram...

This slide illustrates...

On this slide, we can see...

The longest bar is...

This series of peaks shows...

The lowest point on the curve is...

This bar chart shows the growth of...

Please take a look at the screen/this slide/the picture.

⑨ 举例(Giving Examples)
Let me illustrate this by referring to…
A case in point is…
Take the case of…
A good example of this is…
I'd like to give an example to illustrate my point.
⑩ 口误的修正(Speech Error Correction)
当报告过程中发现自己表述有误或是不够确切时，可用诸如 excuse me，sorry，I mean，I am saying，or rather，or，to be exact，exactly，actually，more precisely，more accurately，more specifically，to be more specific 等插入语加以纠正，然后重新进行正确表述。上述的插入语除 excuse me 和 sorry 外，有些也可以用于引入其他的表达方式，或对前面并非错误的说法给予更好的解释。

（3）肢体语言(Body Language)
在报告中恰当地使用肢体语言可以获得更好的效果，因此声音、表情、站姿和手势都应得体。平淡的语调会令人感到乏味和疲倦，而富于变化的语速、音调和音量可使语言更为生动。注意在报告过程中要适当地停顿，这对报告的效果可以起到很好的作用。例如，要点陈述之前的短暂停顿既可以引起听众注意，也给报告者一定的时间来思考和组织语言，而陈述要点之后的停顿可以给听众一定的时间来理解。

眼神可以传达真诚和自信，报告中应尽可能多地与每位听众目光接触，目光在某一个方向上要停留几秒钟，使听众感觉到被注视。报告时的表情、手势和站姿都可以向听众传达想法和感受，因此应选择自然、得体的站姿和热情、自信的表情，并将表情、动作与语言恰当地配合。

35.1.4 结束报告(Ending a Presentation)

精彩的报告结尾可以成为点睛之笔，能够与主题和开篇形成良好的呼应，从而使整个报告结构完整，并有助于让听众对报告中的观点留下深刻的印象。因此，在结束语部分应对报告的主要观点进行总结性的重申与强调，或对主题的重要性给予评价，从而让听众明确什么是报告中最重要的信息(take-home message)。

首先应通过语言或借助幻灯片给听众一个报告即将结束的信号，以使大家重新集中注意力来关注最后一个部分。唐突的结尾会令人感到不完整或头重脚轻，并且报告的总结部分也不会得到充分的注意，但也不可赘述而令听众觉得啰嗦。常见的表达有：
Finally, I would like to finish the presentation with a few sentences.
In the introduction, I put forward a question…Now I hope it's clear that…
Now it is coming to the conclusion.
I would like to conclude with/close by…
Before I close, I'd like to say…
In a word/nutshell, …
In brief/short/closing/In conclusion/summary, …
To conclude/sum up/summarize,…

Given all that,…
Summing up,…
All in all,…
Overall…

在引起听众的充分注意之后,就应通过重述或总结来强调报告的要点或核心内容,这样报告才能够结构完整,前后呼应。在表达中应力求让听众回忆起报告中的要点内容,以加深印象。一般可以采用与报告的引言或主体部分相同的结构来重述观点,例如平行结构或层次分解的结构等,有时也可以直接利用报告的引言部分来进行总结和强调。

在报告的最后应对听众的关注给予感谢,也可以引入随后的讨论环节。常用的表达有:
Thank you for your attention/endurance.
That's all/So much for my speech. Thank you.
It has been a great pleasure for me to share my views with you. Thank you.
Well, that's it for my presentation. Thank you.
That's the end of my presentation. Thank you very much.

35.1.5 注意事项(Points for Attention)

(1) 事先进行充分的准备和演练,并要考虑到报告过程中可能出现的意外情况,由于意外情况或遗忘而造成的长时间停顿会使演讲的效果大打折扣。

(2) 准备讲稿或备忘卡片,以醒目的方式标出容易忘记的内容,报告中可以适当地参看,以免遗漏要点。但切忌阅读或背诵整个讲稿,这会使内容显得生硬和枯燥。

(3) 尽量保持较慢的语速,从容不迫地进行表达,发音清晰准确,语速、音调和音量富于变化。如果说错了要道歉并及时纠正,但不必过多地解释,然后继续报告的内容。

(4) 尽量避免语言的过多重复和不必要的解释,尽量减少 um、uh、eh 之类的语言。

(5) 分配好各个部分的时间,不要超时。如果时间紧张就应对剩余的部分作概括性的陈述而不具体展开,或将相对不重要的部分省略。

(6) 注重报告的口头表述与幻灯片的视觉辅助作用相结合,使听众理解起来更为容易。注意每页幻灯片的内容不可过多,以免分散听众的注意力,更不要朗读幻灯片上面的内容。

35.2 专业英语阅读：Measuring the Coefficient of Linear Expansion for Copper, Steel and Aluminum(铜、钢和铝的线性膨胀系数测量)

In this lab we will experimentally determine the coefficient of linear expansion for copper, steel and aluminum.

Pre-lab assignment

1. Read these lab instructions carefully. Study the relating section in textbook.

2. Prepare the first page of your lab report by writing out the title, objective, and the theory section for the lab.

3. Look up and list the accepted values for the linear expansion coefficient for copper, steel and aluminum.

Introduction

Most materials expand somewhat when heated through a temperature range that does not produce a change in phase. The added heat increases the average amplitude of vibration of the atoms in the material which increases the average separation between the atoms.

Suppose an object of length L undergoes a temperature change of magnitude ΔT. If ΔT is reasonably small, the change in length, ΔL, is generally proportional to L and ΔT. Stated mathematically:

$$\Delta L = \alpha L \Delta T \qquad (35\text{-}1)$$

where α is called the **coefficient of linear expansion** for the material.

For materials that are not isotropic, such as an asymmetric crystal for example, α can have a different value depending on the axis along which the expansion is measured. α can also vary somewhat with temperature so that the degree of expansion depends not only on the magnitude of the temperature change, but on the absolute temperature as well.

In this experiment, you will measure α for copper, aluminum, and steel. These metals are isotropic so that α need only be measured along one dimension. Also, within the limits of this experiment, α does not vary with temperature.

Fig. 35-1   Apparatus

Lab instructions

Measuring Length, L

Measure from the inner edge of the stainless steel pin on one end, to the inner edge of the angle bracket at the other end.

Mount the copper tube in the expansion base as shown in Fig. 35-1. The stainless steel pin on the tube fits into the slot on the slotted mounting block and the bracket on the tube presses against the spring arm of the dial gauge. Slide or push the tube to one side of the slide support. Drive the thumbscrew against the pin until the tube can no longer be moved. Use this as your reference point.

Measuring Room Temperature, T_{rm}

The temperature of the tube is monitored with a temperature dependent resistor (called a thermistor). There is a conversion chart on the computer which converts the measured resistance of the thermistor to the corresponding temperature of the thermistor.

1. Use one of the provided thumbscrews to attach the thermistor lug to the threaded hole in the middle of the copper tube. The lug should be aligned with the axis of the tube

so there is maximum contact between the lug and the tube. Place the foam insulator over the thermistor lug.

2. Plug the leads of your ohmmeter into the banana plug connectors labeled THERMISTOR in the center of the expansion base.

3. Measure and record R_{rm}, the resistance of the thermistor at room temperature.

Measuring Temperature and Length of Thermal Expansion, R_{hot} and L_{hot}

Use tubing to attach your steam generator to the end of the copper tube. Attach it to the end farthest from the dial gauge.

1. Turn the outer casing of the dial gauge to align the zero point on the scale with the long indicator needle hence making L_{ref} equal to zero. As the tube expands, the indicator needle will move in a counterclockwise direction.

2. Fill the copper boiler about 1/2 full with water and heat with a bunsen burner.

3. Attach the steam tube between the boiler and the copper expansion tube. Be careful with these steam tubes since they are delicate.

4. As steam begins to flow, watch the dial gauge and the ohmmeter. Record the distance the dial moves after the dial stabilizes, L_{hot}. (Each increment on the dial gauge is equivalent to 0.01mm of tube expansion.) When the thermistor resistance stabilizes record the resistance(R_{hot}). The thermistor takes longer to reach equilibrium than the tube hence make your measurement of L_{hot} before recording R_{hot}.

Calculating the Coefficient of Linear Expansion, α

Use the Conversion Program on the computer, to convert your thermistor resistance measurements, R_{rm} and R_{hot}, into temperature measurements, T_{rm} and L_{hot}.

1. Calculate ΔT using the formula $\Delta T = T_{hot} - T_{rm}$
2. Calculate ΔL using the formula $\Delta L = L_{hot} - L_{ref}$
3. Calculate α using Eq. (35-1).

Other Tubes

Repeat the experiment for the steel and aluminum tubes. When you finish with each tube, remove the tube from the apparatus, empty the condensation into a sink, and then blow out the tubes using the pressurized air on the tables. Be careful NOT to point the tubes towards anyone while blowing out the tubes.

Error analysis

Your lab report should include a determination of the final uncertainty in your measured values of α which is based on the individual uncertainties of the quantities measured using the rules in Errors and the Treatment of Data.

$\delta T_{rm}, \delta T_{hot}$: Using the computer, temperature measurements can be made to within 0.01℃. You may want to increase this uncertainty depending on how stable the thermistor is when reading R_{hot}. The uncertainty in the difference between two temperatures (ΔT) is readily determined using the sum rule.

δL: Using a good meter stick, length measurements normally have an uncertainty of

±0.0005 m (half a millimeter). Note that this assumes that you make very careful measurements.

$\delta L_{hot}, \delta L_{ref}$: Each increment on the dial gauge is equivalent to 0.01 mm. The uncertainty in the difference between two lengths (ΔL) is readily determined using the sum rule.

$\delta \alpha$: Now you must use the rules for propagation of errors to determine the uncertainty in α using the values of $\delta \Delta L, \Delta L, \delta \Delta T$ and ΔT above. As a challenge, and to prepare you for future labs, you should make an effort to determine this equation yourself using the rules laid out in Errors and the Treatment of Data. You can rely on your lab TAs or your professor for help if needed.

Lab report

In the results section of your report, state the results of your experiment in the form $\alpha = (x.xx \pm x.xx) \degree C^{-1}$. You should also address the following questions:

1. Look up the accepted values for the linear expansion coefficient for copper, steel, and aluminum. Compare these values with your experimental values. Do your results agree within their uncertainties?

2. If your result does not agree within uncertainties to the accepted values, suggest possible reasons for the discrepancy and how this error would affect your results. In particular state if the discrepancy is a result of random (statistical) or systematic error. If you don't understand the difference, then reread that section in Errors and the Treatment of Data. If your results indicate that systematic or random error(s) may be present, try to determine some possible sources of the error in the experiment. For each suggestion, determine if it would affect the result in the same direction as the discrepancy in your result.

Glossary

copper	铜	steel	钢
aluminum	铝	amplitude	振幅
separation	间距	isotropic	各向同性的
angle bracket	角铁	thermistor	热敏电阻
conversion chart	换算表	thumbscrew	翼形螺钉
lug	耳状手柄	threaded hole	螺纹孔
ohmmeter	欧姆表	banana plug	香蕉插头
bunsen burner	本生灯,煤气灯	condensation	冷凝液
sink	水槽	propagation of errors	误差传递
discrepancy	误差,差异		

35.3　专业英语常用表达-35　学术会议常用语

1. 有关会议一般信息

（1）名称

conference　会议,国际性学术研讨会
academic conference　学术会议
international conference　国际会议
symposium　专题研讨会,学术报告会
annual meeting/symposium/conference　年会
forum，international forum　论坛,国际论坛
workshop　研究会,讨论会

（2）日期

dates/important dates/key dates　重要日期

（3）地点

location/venue　地点,位置
conference location/venue　会议地点

（4）主题

issues/themes/(main) topics/scope of conference　会议主题
conference themes/topics　会议主题
topics of interests　会议主题,会议议题

2. 论文征稿、提交与录用

call for abstract/proposal/paper　摘要/提案/论文征集
paper deadline　论文截稿时间
deadline for abstract/full paper/proposal submission　摘要/全文/提案截止时间
submission deadline　提交截止时间
deadline extended　截止延期
date for notification of acceptance　录用通知发出时间
Paper acceptance/rejection will be informed by…　论文录用与否将在……前通知
deadline for authors notification　录用通知截止时间
camera ready version deadline　定稿截止时间

3. 会议注册

deadline/closing date for registration　注册截止日期
registration form　注册表
registration information　注册信息
registration fees and items　注册费用及项目
official invitation letter　官方邀请函
payment　支付方式
telegraphic transfer only　仅限电汇

bank transfer 银行汇款,银行转账
bank draft/check 银行汇票,银行支票

4. 会议进程及内容

conference schedule/program 会议时间表/程序
preliminary conference program 预备会议程序
final conference program 最终会议程序
opening ceremony/session 开幕式
closing ceremony/session 闭幕式
keynote session/parallel session/tutorial session 全体会议/分组会议/小组会议
keynote speech 主题报告
oral presentation 口头报告
poster presentation 招贴报告
tea/coffee break 茶歇
(buffet) lunch/(buffet) supper （简易）午餐/（自助）晚餐
(welcome) banquet （欢迎）宴会

5. 会议具体环节

opening 开始
introduction to speaker 报告人介绍
theme/paper presentation 主题报告
question and answer 讨论问答
comment on speaker 评论与致谢
closing 结束

LESSON 36

36.1 物理学国际学术会议的问答讨论环节口语

　　学术报告之后的问答讨论环节（Question and Answer Session）是同行之间进行交流的良好机会,双方可以针对报告中的具体问题进行探讨。对报告者而言,可以通过解答疑问来解释难点和强调重点;对提问者而言,则可以弄清疑问,或提出自己的不同见解。物理学涉及极其广泛的科学领域,对相同的问题有各种不同的研究方法,因此在讨论中科研工作者可以为彼此提供灵感、通过交流讨论解决疑难、提出新的思路和解决方案,使研究工作得到深化。

　　也正是基于这些益处,报告后的讨论环节可以看作一个微型的报告,与正式报告同样的重要。报告者应做好必要的准备,并在讨论过程中注意回答问题的内容、方式与语言。

1. 答问的方式与技巧

　　问答讨论环节可以让报告人通过互动及时地获得信息反馈,并可以把在讨论中获得的建设性建议用于下一步的工作,因此对科研工作有很大的促进作用。对于如此重要的环节,

报告人在报告之前应进行必要的准备,尽可能地保证这一环节完整、流畅地进行,一般应注意以下几点。

(1) 准备工作

学术报告的提问者往往是相关领域中的专家,对报告的内容非常熟悉,因此所提出的问题可能会有相当的深度、广度以及不可预见性,有时甚至直接指出研究工作中的不完善之处或漏洞所在。由于时间关系,回答者在现场一般没有充分的时间进行考虑,这就要求报告人要事先进行充分的准备。在报告前,报告人应将对问答环节的准备作为准备工作的一部分,进行深入考虑,全面地预测听众可能提出的问题,可以假设一些问题,并准备好最合适的解答。如果会议没有统一安排每个报告的问答环节,报告者在进行报告时就要预先告知听众随后的 Q&A Session,这样可以让听众对提问做好准备,并避免在报告中间被提问打断。

(2) 过程控制

在时间允许的情况下尽可能让每个想提问的人都有机会提问,不要让少数提问者的提问占据整个讨论环节,应按照提问者举手示意的顺序来请出提问者。在开始回答问题时,首先与提问者目光接触,然后转向其他所有听众,这样可以获得所有听众的注意。在回答完毕之后,可以再次通过目光了解提问者是否对回答表示满意。报告人应控制整个讨论过程,对于与主题无关的问题可以礼貌地回避(如"Actually, that question doesn't fit the context of our discussion.")。

(3) 答问方式

应首先仔细听清问题,在回答之前应将问题清楚地重复一遍,这可以保证对问题的正确理解,确保每个人都能听清楚问题,同时给自己一点时间来思考。表述答案前可做片刻停顿,这既引起了听众的注意,又表明了对答案的谨慎态度,同时也给了自己更多的思考时间。不要对问题进行评价,避免说类似"That was a great question."的话,如果想要对某一问题进行肯定,可以用"Thanks for asking that question."或者"I get asked that question by many people."等中性的表述,这可以让听众感到平等。回答问题时应尽可能简洁、切题。在回答中应尽可能多地提及报告中的内容,这有利于听众对报告内容加深印象,并有利于控制问答环节的主题。

(4) 问题的类型

对于寻求具体解释的一般性问题,可以简单地重复报告的内容来对问题进行说明或证明,或是澄清听众的误解。如果提问者对报告内容提出不同见解,可以通过资料、事实、数据等来证明自己的观点,但一定注意态度要礼貌谦和。对于过于复杂的深层问题无法进行简单回答时,可以在简略回答之后邀约提问者在其他时间进行讨论。对于听众的评价或是建议应表示感谢,但要控制时间,适时地打断发言并转入下一个问题。对不知道答案的问题应坦率地承认,不要回避或转换话题,并尽可能提供相关的书籍、资料或是该方面的专家以供参考。

(5) 时间的把握

为了能够巧妙地结束问答环节,可事先准备一段总结性的陈述用来重申报告主题并结束问答环节。注意在达到规定时间时应立刻结束讨论环节,在回答最后一个问题之前,就要礼貌地提示即将超时,并可以让其他提问者将问题留在会后进行讨论。

（6）提问者的礼仪

大型会议中问答环节的时间往往比较短暂，提问者应抓住机会参与讨论，同时应注意以下的方面。

如果为提问者准备了麦克风，则应在拿到麦克风后等待大家安静下来再进行提问；大声地表述，让提问者和听众都能够听清楚问题；不必解释提问的理由以免浪费时间，但如果适宜可以简要地介绍自己（一定要简要）；对所提的问题应做好准备，以保证问题的有效性（不要提那些答案显而易见的问题）；提问务必简短；每次尽量只提一个问题，把更多的机会留给其他的听众。

2．常用表达

（1）提问

I would like to ask/address/raise a question about…

I would like to know(whether)…

I would be glad to know(whether)…

I have a question about…

May I ask(a question about)…?

My question is/concerns/is concerned with…

What I would like to ask is…

What I am asking is…

I wonder if you would like to explain/comment on the point of…

I would be grateful/appreciate/obliged/for(to have) some explanation about…

I wonder if you would be kind enough to explain/comment on/give some examples for…

I wonder(What I am wondering is)…

I am curious about/interested in/keen on(whether/why/how/what/when)…

Could you please tell me whether/why/how/what/when…?

Do you mind showing me whether/why/how/what/when…?

I could not understand what you really mean by…

Do you have any ideas about…?

What do you think of/about…?

Could you back…up?

Could you give us an example about…?

Could you provide any example to prove what you have said about…?

Could you give any example that shows…?

（2）回答

① 对问题进行确认

Are you asking me the question about…?

I am not quite clear about the question? Do you mean…?

I am not quite sure what your question is. Could you address your question more specifically?

What do you mean by...?

I don't know whether I have understood your question correctly. Do you mean...?

② 肯定或否定的表示

Yes./No.

The answer is/I would say yes/no.

That is (not) correct/true/right.

Exactly!

Precisely!

I think so.

I think you're right.

You're right there.

I don't think so.

That is just what I mean.

That is not what I mean.

I(don't) believe/consider/suppose/regard the viewpoint is true.

Sure./Absolutely./Certainly./Definitely.

No, (absolutely/certainly/definitely) not.

I'm in complete agreement.

I (quite) agree.

I couldn't agree more.

③ 正面回答

My answer(to the question) is...

To answer this question, I would like to say that...

The direct/simple/brief answer to the question is...

Let me answer your question by some examples of...

I'd like to make a few comments on/explanation about...

I think I can give you a few general comments on/explanation about...

To comment on the question of you, I have made comparison between...and...

I'd like to present/offer/give/express/state my opinion on...

In my opinion, the conclusion can be supported by the experimental result that...

To answer your question, I'd like to repeat what I said just now.

I think this picture will be helpful for your understanding.

Here I'd like to explain it briefly.

My idea is on the basis of two points. The first is..., and the second is...

I will explain by some examples.

④ 非正面回答

Now I can only present some estimation about that.

As far as I know, little in-depth research has been carried out yet.

I can only provide/I have only a partial answer to that question.

That's one possible explanation, but not the only one.

I'm afraid it's a bit difficult for me to present some experimental data at the moment to support the theory since my idea is mainly out of theoretical consideration.

I'm afraid the question is too complicated to be answered with a few words. I'd like to discuss it with you after the session.

I think the answer to the question needs some further study.

I'm afraid the question is not within the field of the presentation.

I'm not sure if what you're saying has any relevance here.

I'm not sure if what you're saying has anything to do with our problem.

I'm not sure if what you're saying really matters in this case.

I'm not sure if what you're saying is relevant to our problem.

⑤ 无法回答时的表述

I'm sorry my experience/knowledge about your question is very limited so I think I cannot give a good answer to your question.

I'm sorry I really don't know the answer to the question.

Unfortunately I cannot answer the question at the moment.

I'm afraid I have no idea how to answer your question(about that).

Sorry, I am afraid I know little about that matter, so I don't think I can answer your question right now.

It's quite difficult for me to answer that question now.

I can't really recall; I'll have to get back to you on that.

I can't quite remember; I'll need to do a little checking and get back to you.

I can't fully remember; I'll have to check up on it.

I can't recall all the facts; I'll have to get back to you.

⑥ 回答之后表述

I wonder whether my answer is helpful to you.

Does that answer your question in a right way?

Is my explanation clear enough?

Is that what you wanted me to answer?

Would anyone like to add anything(to what I've said)?

Would anyone care to comment?

Would anyone like to give their ideas on this?

Would anyone care to add their thoughts(to the discussion)?

36.2 专业英语阅读：Franck-Hertz Experiment（夫兰克-赫兹实验）

Ⅰ. Introduction

By the early part of the twentieth century it was clear that isolated atoms absorb and emit electromagnetic radiation at characteristic frequencies. Bohr's atomic model suggested that this was due to an inherent quantization of the allowed energies of atomic electrons.

Given these ideas, it is reasonable to ask if other modes of energy transfer would also exhibit quantization. This was the question posed, and answered, by James Franck and Gustav Hertz (not Heinrich Hertz, of electromagnetic fame) in 1914.

Franck and Hertz bombarded isolated atoms with electrons and showed that the electrons lost discrete amounts of energy characteristic of each element. Further, they were able to show that electron bombardment at an appropriate energy led to optical emission at the known spectral frequency corresponding to that energy. Their results could be interpreted within the Bohr model as demonstrating excitation of one of the discrete energy levels, followed by a transition back to the ground state with emission of light. This is obviously a classic experiment, in the sense of being of key importance, but the adjective is otherwise unfortunate in that the experiment provided strong evidence against classical mechanics and in favor of the nascent quantum mechanics.

In our laboratory we will repeat Franck and Hertz's energy-loss observations, using mercury, and try to interpret the data in the context of modern atomic physics. We will not attempt the spectroscopic measurements, since the emissions are weak and in the extreme ultraviolet portion of the spectrum.

II. Theoretical considerations

It is well known that electrons can be boiled out of a hot metal filament. By applying a positive potential between the filament and a nearby electrode one can give the electrons any desired kinetic energy. If the electron subsequently hits a gas atom it may transfer energy to the atom. In this experiment we seek to measure that energy transfer. Because of the large mass difference between the electron and any atom, collisions which do not excite internal motions in the atom result in very small changes in electron energy. The energy loss we observe, therefore, is essentially a measure of the energy changes internal to the atom.

To a first approximation, the experiment can be understood by examining the idealized sketch in Fig. 36-1. Electrons are accelerated toward a grid through a sealed bulb containing a small amount of mercury. If the accelerating voltage is large enough, and there is no loss of energy in collisions, most electrons will pass through the grid and

Fig. 36-1 The drawing on the left shows the geometry and voltages used for the Franck-Hertz experiment. The graph shows the mechanical potential energy of an electron as a function of position within the tube. Note that both accelerating and retarding regions are present

continue up the retarding gradient to the collector electrode. The current meter measures this flow of electrons. Alternatively, electrons which have made an inelastic collision and reach the grid with small kinetic energy will be captured there, rather than at the collector. If we measure the collector current as a function of grid-filament voltage we can infer the probability of an inelastic collision as a function of electron energy.

With this geometry and our assumption of quantized atomic energy levels we should expect to see several dips in the collector current as we increase the accelerating voltage. Ignoring the retarding potential for the moment, the first dip will occur when electrons reach the grid with just enough energy to excite a mercury atom. The next dip will occur at twice this voltage, since an electron can then lose its energy midway from filament to grid and then be accelerated enough to collide again near the grid. At still higher voltages there can be additional collisions leading to more dips. The important point is that the whole array of equally-spaced dips will be due to the lowest energy transition that the electron can excite. In this picture, the only effect of the retarding potential is to shift the whole pattern to higher voltages.

If there were only one transition, this would be the whole story. Actually, though, mercury is multi-electron atom with a complicated excitation spectrum and electron impact is a violent process. As a result there are several competing processes, and the energy loss observed may not reflect the energy difference between the ground state and the first excited state of atomic mercury.

Several non-atomic factors also complicate the simple picture. First, electron impact can ionize the atom, as well as induce the intra-atomic transitions we have discussed so far. The free electron produced by the ionization event can then be accelerated and ionize another atom, eventually leading to creation of the conducting plasma in the tube. This causes a large increase in the collector current and, for the Hg vapor, a visible blue glow in the tube. The exact accelerating voltage at which breakdown occurs depends on the tube geometry, gas density and electron current, as well as the type of gas present. Once the gas has broken down the electrons are in a conducting medium and we can no longer interpret the collector current as a measure of the collision probability.

A more modest difficulty arises from other potentials in the apparatus. There is likely to be a difference in work function between the filament and collector plate. As you recall from the photoelectric effect, the work function is the minimum energy required to move an electron from a metal to the vacuum. This potential energy must be supplied when the electron leaves the filament and a similar energy is gained when the electron enters the collector. If the two potentials are not the same, the voltage scale will be shifted by a constant amount, of the order of $1 \sim 2$ volts. Since there are temperature gradients in the apparatus, there can also be thermoelectric voltage differences, amounting to a few tenths of a volt. Finally, the deliberately imposed retarding potential may vary somewhat from the nominal 1.2 V. Fortunately, constant offsets do not affect the voltage differences we want to measure.

III. Measurement and analysis

The laboratory is equipped with a mercury-filled tube in a small oven, power supplies and appropriate meters. Using this apparatus it is possible to plot the collector current as a function of filament to grid voltage, and to observe the effect of varying both the electron current and the gas density.

Most of the equipment is contained in two boxes. An electric oven is used to raise the temperature of the tube to 150~250℃ to produce the desired vapor pressure of mercury. The other box contains the voltage sources and a current-to-voltage amplifier for the collector signal. (Contrary to the diagram on the oven, it does not contain any electronics.) The manufacturer's operating instructions are available(in translation) for reference in the lab.

Fig. 36-2 Connection diagram for the NEVA Franck-Hertz apparatus. The circuitry inside the dashed lines is contained in the electronics box. The tube is housed in an oven, which is not shown

The apparatus should be wired as in Fig. 36-2. An X-Y recorder is used to directly plot the collector signal vs. accelerating voltage. The DMM provides for precise calibration of the accelerating voltage scale. An alternative procedure to display the data on an oscilloscope is given by the manufacturer but turns out to be less useful in practice.

Once the apparatus is wired you can proceed to make measurements as follows:

1. Stabilize the oven temperature at about 200℃. The thermostat provided allows large temperature swings so it is better to turn the control all the way up and use the variable transformer to set the input power level. Transformer settings in the range 80~90 will usually give the desired temperature.

2. Set the amplifier gain (Amplification) and zero-offset controls (0-Point) to mid-range. The filament current (Heating) should also be at mid-range initially. The accelerating voltage control is labeled U_B. It's switch should be set for DC(straight line) operation, not sweep(ramp line). Be sure the unit is switched on.

3. Adjust the gain on the X-Y recorder x-axis so that an accelerating voltage range of $0 \sim 40$ V can be displayed. Mark a couple of reference points on the chart at known voltages read on the DMM. Set the y-axis gain so that you can display the full range of the signal.

4. If you now sweep U_B slowly through its range you should get a curve with several relatively abrupt dips, terminated by an abrupt jump in the current when ionization occurs. At this point U_B will also decrease sharply due to a resistor that limits the arcing current.

5. Darken the room and closely observe the tube as you vary the voltage U_B. Can you explain the pattern of light emission you see in terms of the collector current you have just plotted?

Once you have verified that the apparatus is working, you can explore the effect of varying the filament current and the temperature. Obtain curves for low, medium and high values of the filament current at one temperature. Notice that the amplitude of the dips and the breakdown voltage both depend on these parameters, allowing you to observe different numbers of successive excitations. By varying the temperature over the range of about $150 \sim 250$℃ you can control the mercury vapor density over a wide range. This is of interest, since it should change the apparent excitation energy.

Ideally, your curves would show a sharp sawtooth pattern, dropping abruptly at each excitation point. Because of the spread in electron energies and the variation in collision probability with energy there will be some spread in the curves. It is probably reasonable to take the half-way point on the drop as an average for the excitation voltage. Find these points on each of your curves, and determine the corresponding U_B from the plot. Plot the values against sequential dip number, assigning serial number one to the lowest-voltage dip. A straight-line fit to this plot yields the apparent mercury excitation voltage.

Since the choice of the half-way point on the dip is essentially arbitrary, it could lead to a systematic error in the estimate of the excitation voltage. Explore this possibility by re-analyzing a few of the curves with some other choices for the excitation energy.

In your report you should present your data for the excitation voltage and any other observations you consider pertinent. Discuss the extent to which your data are consistent with the claims made in the reprint. Also, be sure to explain the tests you have made for systematic errors in the apparent excitation voltage.

Glossary

inherent	固有的,内在的	bombardment	轰击,碰撞
nascent	刚诞生的	extreme ultraviolet	远紫外
filament	灯丝	electrode	电极
grid	极板	mercury	水银
collector electrode	集电极	retarding potential	减速势

intra-atomic　　　　　　原子内的　　　　　sawtooth　　　　　　　　锯齿
sequential　　　　　　　连续的

36.3　专业英语常用表达法-36　双语教学课堂用语

提起注意：

Ready? /Are you ready for the class? /Are you all ready?

Be quiet, please. /Quiet, please. /Settle down.

Listen/Look/Watch carefully, please.

Please stop now. /Stop now, please. /Stop here, please.

复习：

Let's have a quick review of what we learned last time.

Let's review/do some review.

Do you remember what we learned in the last lesson?

Who can tell what we learned last time?

Last time we learned…and now we are going to revise/go over/review them.

开始学习新的内容：

Now, let's begin/start a new lesson.

Let's step into/move into a new chapter.

Let's move on to the next point/part/section/chapter/unit.

Now let's learn something new/different.

Now we will go on to the next exercise.

First of all, let's…/Next, let's…/For the last thing, let's…

提问：

Come up and write your answer on the blackboard.

Come and write it on the blackboard.

Please answer the following questions.

Please answer my question of…

Please read and put it into Chinese.

Who can tell me the answer to…?

In English, please.

Your turn, please. /It's your turn now. /Whose turn is it? /Next one, please.

Who hasn't answered yet?

What do you think about…?

Once more please. /Again please.

Pardon? I can't hear you clearly. Louder, please.

What do you mean by…?

鼓励：

Any volunteers?

Put your hand up, please. /Raise your hand, please. /Hand up, please.

Can you try to answer my question?

Try, please. /Try your best.

Think it over and try again.

Don't be nervous. /Take it easy.

You were almost right. /That's almost it. /You've almost got it.

You're on the right lines. /You're halfway there.

There's no need to rush. /There's no hurry. /We have plenty of time.

Go on. Have a/another try. /Have a go. /Have a guess.

Do you want a clue (hint)?

分组:

Let's do it one by one/in pairs/in group.

Discuss in a group. /Practice in groups. /In groups, please.

Get into/Form/Make groups of three/four...

Find a partner to discuss.

Work together with your partner.

Work in pairs.

Work in (groups of) threes/fours/fives.

Here are some tasks for you to work on in groups of four.

Everybody works individually. /Work independently.

Work by yourselves.

Ask your neighbor for help.

Work on the task together.

Ask others in the group/class.

讲解:

Any questions?

Do you understand? /Do you follow me? /Are you clear? /Is that clear?

Understand? /Got it? /Can you follow me?

Please look at the blackboard/picture/slide.

The theorem can be used to/be applied to/give explain to...

Pay attention to the application condition of the law.

Let's see some examples to the point.

Combining all the factors, we have...

Let me explain what I want you to do next.

The idea of this exercise is for you to...

This is a picture of...

Let me sum up.

Let's discuss something on the subject of...

As I said earlier,...

评价:

Very good. /God job. /Well done. /Excellent! /Jolly good. /A good answer. /Great!

Yes. /Fine. /Right. /Quite right. /That's right. /That's it. /That's correct. /That's OK.

That's quite right. /Yes, you've got it. /You've got the idea.

There's nothing wrong with your answer.

What you said was perfectly all right.

You didn't make a single mistake.

That's exactly the point.

That's just what I was looking for.

It depends. /It might be, I suppose. /In a way, perhaps. /Sort of, yes. /That's close.

That's more like it. /That's much better. /That's a lot better.

Not really. /Unfortunately not. /Not exactly.

I'm afraid that's not quite right. /Good try, but not quite right. /Not quite right. Try again.

That's not quite right, any other answers?

翻译练习

Unit One

1. Although a point is a geometrical concept quite different from everyday objects such as footballs and automobiles, we shall see that the actual motion of many objects is most easily described as the motion of a single point (the "center of mass"), plus the rotation of the object about that point.

2. **An interval of time.** The fundamental unit is the **second** (s), which by international agreement is defined as the duration of 9 192 631 770 periods of radiation corresponding to the transition between the two lowest energy levels in the atomic isotope cesium 133.

3. **An interval of length.** The fundamental unit is the **meter** (m), which is defined independently of the time interval. Before 1983, by international agreement the meter was defined as exactly 1 650 763.73 wavelengths of the orange light emitted from the isotope krypton 86. In November 1983, the length standard was defined as the distance that light travels in a vacuum in 1/299 792 458 second.

4. The cross product of two vectors $\boldsymbol{A}$ and $\boldsymbol{B}$ is defined to be a vector $\boldsymbol{C}=\boldsymbol{A}\times\boldsymbol{B}$ whose magnitude equals the area of the parallelogram formed by the two vectors. The vector $\boldsymbol{C}$ is perpendicular to the plane containing $\boldsymbol{A}$ and $\boldsymbol{B}$ in the direction given by the right-hand rule, that is, as your right hand fingers curl from the direction of $\boldsymbol{A}$ toward the direction of $\boldsymbol{B}$, the direction of $\boldsymbol{A}\times\boldsymbol{B}$ is given by your thumb. (注意定语从句、分词结构作定语的翻译)

5. For motion along a straight line, we choose a rectangular coordinate system that is oriented so that one of the axes (for example, the x axis) is along the line.

6. It is well known that all objects, when dropped, will fall toward the earth with nearly constant acceleration. In the idealized case, where air resistance is neglected, such motion is referred to as **free fall**.

7. In this section, we describe how observations made by different observers in different frames of reference are related to each other. We shall find that observers in different frames of reference may measure different displacements, velocities, and accelerations for a particle in motion. That is, two observers moving with respect to each other will generally not agree on the outcome of a measurement.

Unit Two

1. An object at rest will remain at rest and an object in motion will continue in motion

with a constant velocity (that is, constant speed in a straight line) unless it experiences a net external force (or resultant force).

2. The time rate of change of momentum of an object is equal to the resultant external force acting on the object.

3. If two bodies interact, the force exerted on body 1 by body 2 is equal to and opposite the force exerted on body 2 by body 1.

4. A force is conservative if the total work it does on a particle is zero when the particle moves around any closed path, returning to its initial position. From Fig. 6-5 we see that this definition implies that: The work done by a conservation force on a particle is independent of the path taken as the particle moves from one point to another.

5. In the past we saw that the net force acting on a system of particles is equal to the net force acting on the system because the internal forces (those exerted by the particles within the system on one another) cancel in pairs. The treatment of internal torques exerted by the particles within a system on one another leads to a similar result, that is, the net torque acting on a system equals the net external torque acting on the system.

6. Left to itself, a spring or a pendulum eventually stops oscillating because the mechanical energy is dissipated by frictional forces. Such motion is said to be damped. If the damping is large enough, as, for example, a pendulum submerged in molasses, the oscillator fails to complete even one cycle of oscillation. Instead it just moves toward the equilibrium position with a speed that approaches zero as the object approaches the equilibrium position. This type of motion is referred to as overdamped. If the damping is small enough that the system oscillates with an amplitude that decreases slowly with time-like a child on a playground swing when Mum stops providing a push each cycle-the motion is said to be underdamped. Motion with the minimum damping for nonoscillatory motion is said to be critically damped.

Unit Three

1. Suppose instead that we place the warm copper bar in a cool running stream. The bar cools until it stops contracting, at the point at which the bar and the water are in thermal equilibrium.

2. Suppose that we have two containers with identical volumes, each holding the same amount of the same kind of gas at the same temperature and pressure. If we consider the two containers as one system, we have twice the amount of gas at twice the volume, but at the same temperature and pressure.

3. Eq. (9-8), which relates the variables P, V, and T, is known as the **ideal-gas law**, and is an example of an **equation of state**. It describes the properties of real gases with low densities (and therefore low pressures). At higher densities, corrections must be made to this equation.

4. In some special cases the internal energy of a system depends only on its

temperature, not on its pressure or volume. The most familiar system having this special property is an ideal gas. For such system, if the temperature is constant, the internal energy is also constant; $\Delta E=0$, and $Q=W$, that is, any energy entering the system as heat Q must leave it again as work W done by the system. For most systems other than ideal gases the internal energy depends on pressure as well as temperature, so E may vary even when T is constant.

5. **Kelvin statement of the second law of thermodynamics**: *No system can take energy as heat from a single reservoir and convert it entirely into work without additional net changes in the system or its surroundings.*

6. **Clausius statement of the second law of thermodynamics**: *A process whose only net result is to transfer energy as heat from a cooler object to a hotter one is impossible.*

7. In the introduction, we alluded the essence of wave motion—the transfer of a disturbance through space without the accompanying transfer of matter. The propagation of the disturbance also represents a transfer of energy—thus, we can view waves as means of energy transfer. Two entries that depend on waves: mechanical waves and electromagnetic radiation. These are to be contrasted with another entry—matter transfer—in which the energy transfer is accompanied by a movement of matter through space.

Unit Four

1. The laws of electricity and magnetism play a central role in the operation of devices such as radios, televisions, electric motors, computers, high-energy particle accelerators, and a host of electronic devices used in medicine. More fundamental, however, is the fact that the interatomic and intermolecular forces responsible for the formation of solids and liquids are electric in origin. Furthermore, such forces as the pushes and pulls between objects in contact and the elastic force in a spring arise from electric forces at the atomic level.

2. Maxwell's contributions to the science of electromagnetism were especially significant because the laws he formulated are basic to all forms of electromagnetic phenomena. His work is comparable in importance to Newton's discovery of the laws of motion and the theory of gravitation.

3. Gauss's law, which relates the electric field on a closed surface to the net charge within the surface, is of fundamental importance in the study of electrostatic fields. In words, *Gauss's law states that in the electrostatic field in vacuum the net electric flux through any closed surface is equal to the net charge inside the surface divided by* ε_0.

4. In principle, Gauss's law is valid for all surfaces and all charge distributions. In practice, however, it can be used to calculate the electric field only for charge distributions that have high degrees of symmetry. For static charge distributions, Gauss's law and Coulomb's law are equivalent. However, Gauss's law is more general in that it is always

valid whether or not the charges are static.

5. The earliest known sources of magnetism were permanent magnets. One month after Oersted announced his discovery that a compass needle is deflected by an electric current, Jean Baptiste Biot and Felix Savart announced the results of their measurements of the force on a magnet near a long, current-carrying wire and analyzed these results in terms of the magnetic field produced by each element of the current. Andre-Marie Ampere extended these experiments and showed that current elements also experience a force in the presence of a magnetic field and that two currents exert forces on each other.

6. Diamagnetism arises from the orbital magnetic dipole moments induced by an applied magnetic field. These magnetic moments are opposite the direction of the applied magnetic field so they decrease the total magnetic field B. This effect actually occurs in all materials, but because the induced magnetic moments are very small compared to the permanent magnetic moments, diamagnetism is masked by paramagnetic or ferromagnetic effects. Diamagnetism is thus observed only in materials that have no permanent magnetic moments.

Unit Five

1. Experiments by Faraday, Henry, and others showed that if the magnetic flux through an area bounded by a circuit is changed by any means, an emf equal in magnitude to the rate of change of the flux is induced in the circuit.

2. This result is known as Faraday's law of induction which states the emf induced in a circuit is directly proportional to the time rate of change of magnetic flux through the circuit.

3. The negative sign in Faraday's law has to do with the direction of the induced emf, which can be found from a general physical principle known as Lenz's law.

4. The polarity of the induced emf is such that it tends to produce a current that will create a magnetic flux to oppose the change in magnetic flux through the loop.

5. With no damping present, sensitive mechanical balance scales used to weigh small masses might oscillate back and forth around their equilibrium reading many times. Such scales are usually designed so that a small piece of metal moves between the poles of a magnet as the scales oscillate. The resulting eddy currents dampen the oscillations so that equilibrium is quickly reached.

6. On the basis of his experiment, Rutherford proposed a new model in which the positive charge was not spread out but was concentrated in a very, very tiny spot at the center of the atom, which he called the nucleus.

7. These experimental laws hold in general except for Ampere's law, which does not apply to discontinuous currents such as those that occur when charging or discharging a capacitor.

8. Maxwell's equations, first proposed by the great Scottish physicist James Clerk

Maxwell, relate the electric and magnetic field vectors E and B to their sources, which are electric charge, currents, and changing fields.

9. To study electromagnetic radiation, we must call upon our knowledge of Maxwell's equations and relate electric and magnetic fields to time-varying charge and current distributions. A primary difficulty of this task is that the charge and current distributions on antenna structures resulting from given excitations are generally unknown and very difficult to determine. In fact, the geometrically simple case of a straight conducting wire (linear antenna) excited by a voltage source in the middle has been a subject of extensive research for many years, and the exact charge and current distributions on a wire of a finite radius are extremely complicated even when the wire is assumed to be perfectly conducting.

Unit Six

1. Early in the nineteenth century experiments were suggested and made to show that light is a wave motion. A key figure in this endeavour was Thomas Young, one of the most intelligent and clever scientists ever to live, who studied diffraction and interference of light already in 1803 with results that gave strong support to the wave theory of Christian Huygens as opposed to the particle or corpuscular theory of Isaac Newton.

2. The mathematical theory of electromagnetism by James Clerk Maxwell, set up in 1864, led to the view that light is of electromagnetic nature, propagating as a wave from the source to the receiver.

3. The Huygens principle is not intuitively obvious, but it gained acceptance because it could be used to explain the laws of reflection and refraction, two phenomena concerning light that had been observed since antiquity.

4. In response to Newton's objections, Huygens contended that if the wavelength of light is extremely small—much smaller than the dimensions of the object on which it shines, then bending of the waves would be too minute to observe and the object would cast sharp shadows.

5. Jumps up from higher levels are extremely unlikely because electrons excited to a higher level typically remain there for less than a millionth of a second. Thus, there are fewer lines in the absorption spectrum than in the emission spectrum, in agreement with the observations.

6. The 1960s also witnessed the discovery of another new phenomenon. Particles were discovered that live for such a short time that they decay into other particles before they travel distances that are visible even under a microscope.

7. Much as zookeepers build order into their zoos by grouping the animals into families, particle physicists began grouping the elementary particles into families. Making families helps organize information and may result in new discoveries.

8. Just as any collection of buttons can be classified in many ways—size, color,

shape, and so forth—the elementary particles can be classified in different ways. (Of course, macroscopic attributes like color and size don't apply here.) One fruitful way is to group them according to the types of interaction in which they participate.

Unit Seven

1. One possibility that was suggested to explain these results is that the electrons are somehow affecting each other. We can test this by lowering the rate at which the source emits electrons so that only one electron passes through the setup at a time.

2. Using the particle picture of Einstein, Bose was able to derive the radiation formula by systematically developing a statistics of massless particles without the constraint of particle number conservation.

3. He developed a statistical law governing the behaviour pattern of photons quite successfully. However, he was not able to publish his work; no journals in would accept his paper, being unable to understand it. Bose sent his paper to Einstein, who saw the significance of it and used his influence to get it published.

4. Before the introduction of Fermi-Dirac statistics (F-D statistics) in 1926, understanding some aspects of electron behavior was difficult due to seemingly contradictory phenomena. It was difficult to understand, for example, why electrons in a metal can move freely to conduct electric current, while their contribution in the same metal to the specific heat was negligible, as if there were considerably fewer electrons. It was also difficult to understand why the emission currents, generated by applying high electric fields to metals at room temperature, were almost independent of temperature.

5. Using the particle picture of Einstein, Bose was able to derive the radiation formula by systematically developing a statistics of massless particles without the constraint of particle number conservation.

6. He developed a statistical law governing the behaviour pattern of photons quite successfully. However, he was not able to publish his work; no journals in Europe would accept his paper, being unable to understand it. Bose sent his paper to Einstein, who saw the significance of it and used his influence to get it published.

7. Before the introduction of Fermi-Dirac statistics (F-D statistics) in 1926, understanding some aspects of electron behavior was difficult due to seemingly contradictory phenomena. It was difficult to understand, for example, why electrons in a metal can move freely to conduct electric current, while their contribution in the same metal to the specific heat was negligible, as if there were considerably fewer electrons. It was also difficult to understand why the emission currents, generated by applying high electric fields to metals at room temperature, were almost independent of temperature.

8. But for the light wave, the conclusion is an astonishing one: *no matter how fast a light source moves toward or away from an inertial observer, and no matter how fast the observer moves toward or away from the source, the speed of the light passing from one*

to the other in vacuum will always be c—the speed of light is constant; it is absolute.

9. Remember that the equations of Electromagnetic Theory—Maxwell's Equations—led to a wave equation that provided the speed of light in vacuum. Assuming Maxwell's Equation are right and given the First Postulate, it must be that this same wave equation is applicable in all inertial systems—the vacuum speed of light measured on Earth or inside a rocket ship must be the same, independent of any uniform relative motion.

Unit Eight

1. The understanding of the quantized energy levels in atoms and the realization that transitions between these levels involved the absorption and emission of photons led to the development of a new device that produced a special beam of light.

2. The device that actually produces coherent beams of light is called a **laser**, which is an acronym for *light amplification by stimulated emission of radiation*. A laser produces a beam of light that is very different from that emitted by an ordinary light source such as a flashlight. The laser beam has a very, very narrow range of wavelengths, is highly directional, and can be quite powerful. The laser beam is a single color because all of the photons have the same energy.

3. Most large telescopes have spectrometers, which are used either to measure the chemical composition and physical properties of astronomical objects or to measure their velocities from the Doppler shift of their spectral lines.

4. Superconductors, without resistance to the flow of electricity, are one of the last great frontiers of scientific discovery. Not only have the limits of superconductivity not yet been reached, but the theories that explain superconductor behavior seem to be constantly under review.

5. The fact that the resistance is zero has been demonstrated by sustaining currents in superconducting lead rings for many years with no measurable reduction. An induced current in an ordinary metal ring would decay rapidly from the dissipation of ordinary resistance, but superconducting rings had exhibited a decay constant of over a billion years!

6. Most solids have periodic arrays of atoms which form what we call a crystal lattice. Amorphous solids and glasses are exceptions. The existence of the crystal lattice implies a degree of symmetry in the arrangement of the lattice, and the existing symmetries have been studied extensively. One of the implications of the symmetric lattice of atoms is that it can support resonant lattice vibration modes. These vibrations transport energy and are important in the thermal conductivity of non-metals, and in the heat capacity of all solids.

Unit Nine

1. The normal or Gaussian distribution concerns a population (i. e. a very large number) for which the mean and the variance are known, but all experimental data is

based on small samples (i. e. n is small) and as the true variance is unknown, a slightly different error distribution has to be used: this is the t distribution.

2. Random error is easy to assess. Systematic error is a most difficult problem because, if the true result is not known, it is only by repeating experiments using different apparatus in various combinations, or by comparison with the results of other workers, or by intelligent appraisal of the design of the experiment in relation to sources of error, that progress can be made.

3. The assumption is sometimes made that errors in each variable parameter used in a compound relation will always combine to give the worst possible result. In much experimental work a more realistic value of the error of a result derived from errors in measured parameters is obtained by using methods which allow positive errors in one variable to counteract errors in another.

4. Usually light is produced (e. g. incandescent light from a candle or a light bulb) by hot electrons and atoms, which are moving or are oriented in random directions, so that the wave is unpolarized. This means that the electric field associated with the wave oscillates in random directions (though always at right angles to the direction of the propagation of the light).

5. Most materials expand somewhat when heated through a temperature range that does not produce a change in phase. The added heat increases the average amplitude of vibration of the atoms in the material which increases the average separation between the atoms.

6. For materials that are not isotropic, such as an asymmetric crystal for example, α can have a different value depending on the axis along which the expansion is measured. α can also vary somewhat with temperature so that the degree of expansion depends not only on the magnitude of the temperature change, but on the absolute temperature as well.

7. Their results could be interpreted within the Bohr model as demonstrating excitation of one of the discrete energy levels, followed by a transition back to the ground state with emission of light. This is obviously a classic experiment, in the sense of being of key importance, but the adjective is otherwise unfortunate in that the experiment provided strong evidence against classical mechanics and in favor of the nascent quantum mechanics.

Appendixes

附录1 物理专业所开设的课程名称汉英对照

BASIC 语言及应用　BASIC Language & Application
C 语言　C Language
C 程序设计　Program Design in C(Language)
FORTRAN 语言　FORTRAN Language
X 射线与电镜　X-ray & Electron Microscope
半导体材料　Semiconductor Materials
半导体物理　Semiconductor Physics
毕业设计　Graduation Project
毕业实习　Graduation Practice
变分法与张量　Calculus of Variations & Tensors
材料力学　Material Mechanics
常微分方程　Ordinary Differential Equations
场论　Field Theory
超导磁体及应用　Superconductive Magnet & Application
超导及应用　Superconductivity & Application
成像原理与技术　Principles & Technique of Imaging
传感器原理及应用　Fundamentals & Application of Sensors
磁性物理　Magnetophysics
大学物理　College Physics
大学物理实验　Experiment of College Physics
大学英语　College English
大学语文　College Chinese
单片机原理　Fundamentals of Single-Chip Computers
单片机原理及应用　Fundamentals & Applications of Single-Chip Computers
弹性力学　Elasticity
导波光学　Wave guiding Optics
德育　Moral Education
等离子体工程　Plasma Engineering

邓小平理论　Theory of Deng Xiaoping
低温固体物理　Low-Temperature Solid Physics
低温物理导论　Introduction to Low-Temperature Physics
低温原理　Low-Temperature Fundamentals
电磁场　Electromagnetic Fields
电磁场与电磁波　Electromagnetic Fields & Magnetic Waves
电磁场与微波技术　Electromagnetic Fields & Microwave Technology
电磁场中的数值方法　Numerical Methods in Electromagnetic Fields
电磁场中的数值计算　Numerical Calculation in Electromagnetic Fields
电磁学　Electromagnetics
电动力学　Electrodynamics
电工与电子技术　Electrotechnics & Electronic Technology
电工电子学　Electronics in Electrical Engineering
电工学　Electrotechnics
电路　Circuits
电路分析基础　Basis of Circuit Analysis
电路分析基础实验　Basic Experiment on Circuit Analysis
电路分析实验　Experiment on Circuit Analysis
电路和电子技术　Circuit and Electronic Technique
电路理论　Theory of Circuits
电路理论实验　Experiments in Theory of Circuits
电视接收技术　Television Reception Technology
电视原理　Principles of Television
电子材料与元件测试技术　Test Technology of

Appendixes

Electronic Materials and Elements
电子技术　Technology of Electronics
电子技术基础　Basic Electronic Technology
电子技术基础与实验　Basis & Experiment of Electronic Technology
电子线路　Electronic Circuits
电子线路实验　Experiment in Electronic Circuits
电子学　Electronics
法律基础　Fundamentals of Law
复变函数　Complex-Variables Functions
复变函数与积分变换　Functions of Complex Variables & Integral Transforms
傅里叶光学　Fourier Optics
概率论　Probability Theory
概率论与数理统计　Probability Theory & Mathematical Statistics
概率论与随机过程　Probability Theory & Stochastic Processes
高等数学　Advanced Mathematics
高分子物理　Polymer Physics
高分子物理实验　High Polymer Physics Experiment
高级英语听说　Advanced English Listening & Speaking
固体激光器　Solid-State Lasers
固体激光器件　Solid Laser Elements
固体激光与电源　Solid-State Laser & Power Units
固体物理　Solid State Physics
光波导理论　Optical Waveguide Theory
光电技术　Photoelectric Technology
光谱　Optical Spectrum
光谱分析　Spectral Analysis
光谱学　Spectroscopy
光纤传感器　Fiber Optical Sensors
光纤传感器基础　Fundamentals of Fiber Optical Sensors
光纤传感器及应用　Fiber Optical Sensors & Applications
光纤实验　Experiments in Optical Fiber
光纤原理与技术　Fiber Optical Operation & Technology
光学　Optics
光学信息导论　Introduction to Optical Infomation

红外物理　Infrared Physics
红外物理与技术　Infrared Physics & Technology
化学　Chemistry
画法几何及机械制图　Descriptive Geometry & Mechanical Graphing
汇编语言程序设计　Assembly Language Programming
积分变换　Integral Transforms
积分变换及数理方程　Integral Transforms & Mathematical Equations
激光基础　Basis of Laser
激光技术　Laser Technology
激光实验　Laser Experiments
激光原理　Principles of Laser
激光原理与技术　Laser Principles & Technology
计算方法　Computing Methods
计算机基础　Basis of Computer Engineering
计算机原理及应用　Principles & Applications of Computers
计算力学　Computational Mechanics
渐近方法　Asymptotical Methods
近代光学测试技术　Modern Optical Testing Technology
近代光学计量技术　Modern Optical Measuring Technology
近代物理实验　Experiment of Modern Physics
科技翻译　Scientific English Translation
科技史　History of Science & Technology
科技英语　Scientific English
科技英语基础　Elementary Scientific English
科技英语阅读　Readings of Scientific English
科学方法论　Scientific Methodology
科学技术史　History of Science & Technology
课程设计　Course Exercise
理论力学　Theoretical Mechanics
力学　Mechanics
力学实验　Experiment of Mechanics
量子力学　Quantum Mechanics
流体力学　Fluid Mechanics
模拟电路　Analog Circuitry
模拟电子技术　Analog Electronics Technique
模拟电子技术基础　Basis of Analogue Electronic Technique

模拟集成电路　Analog Integrated Circuitry
普通物理　General Physics
普通物理实验　Experiments of General Physics
热学　Thermology
热力学　Thermodynamics
热力学与统计物理　Thermodynamics & Statistical Physics
摄影技术　Techniques for Photography
生产实习　Production Practice
实验分析　Experimental Analysis
数据库原理及应用　Principles & Applications of Databases
数理方程　Mathematical Equations
数理方程积分变换　Integral Transforms of Mathematical Equations
数理方程与特殊函数　Equations of Mathmatical Physics & Special Functions
数理统计　Mathematical Statistics
数学分析　Mathematical Analysis
数学模型　Mathematical Models
数学物理方法　Methods of Mathematical Physics
数值分析　Numerical Analysis
数字电路　Digital Circuits
数字电路及微机原理　Digital Circuits & Microcomputer Principles
数字电子技术　Digital Electronic Technology
数字技术　Digital Techniques
随机过程与时序分析　Stochastic Processes & Time Series Analysis
体育　Physical Education
天线原理　Principle of Antennas
铁磁学　Ferromagnetics
铁电半导体　Ferro-Electric Semiconductor
统计物理　Statistical Physics
微波技术与天线　Microwave Techniques and Antennas

微机原理及应用　Principles & Applications of Microcomputers
物理学　Physics
物理光学　Physical Optics
物理光学实验　Optical-Physics Experiment
物理化学　Physical Chemistry
物理化学实验　Physical Chemistry Experiment
物理实验　Physical Experiment
误差理论　Theory of Error
显示技术　Display Technique
显示技术及装置　Display Technique & Equipment
线性代数　Linear Algebra
心理学　Psychology
信号变换与处理　Signal Conversion & Processing
信息光学　Information Optics
应用光学　Applied Optics
应用光学实验　Experiment of Applied Optics
应用物理实验　Experiment of Applied Physics
英语　English
英语泛读　Extensive English Reading
英语精读　Intensive English Reading
英语口语　Oral English Practice
英语听力　English Listening & Comprehension
英语写作　English Writing
英语语法　English Grammar
有限元法　Finite Element Methods
原子物理学　Atomic Physics
哲学　Philosophy
政治经济学　Political Economics
中国革命史　History of Chinese Revolutionary
专业实习　Specialty Practice
专业英语　Specialty English
专业英语阅读　Specialty English Reading
自然科学概论　Introduction to Natural Science
最优化方法　Optimigation Methods

附录2　教学教务管理常用词汇

在职进修班　in-service training course
进修班　class for advanced studies
短训班　short-term training course

专修科　special (training) course
自学考试　self-taught examination
教职员　teaching and administrative staff

Appendixes

教学人员	the faculty, teaching staff
大专院校校长	president, chancellor
教务长	dean of studies
(系)主任	chairman, chairperson, department head
副主任	vice-chairman, vice department head
教授	professor
副教授	associate professor
客座教授	visiting professor, guest professor
讲师	lecturer, instructor
助教	assistant, TA
专职教师	full-time teacher
兼职教师	part-time teacher
辅导员	assistant for political and ideological work
教研室/组	teaching and research section/group
教学组	teaching group
教员休息室	staff room, common room
母校	Alma Mater
校友	alumnus, alumna
学生会	students' union/association
高年级学生	upper/higher-grade student, student in senior grades
低年级学生	lower-grade student, student in junior grades
走读生	day student, non-resident student
住宿生	boarder
旁听生	auditor
研究生	graduate student, postgraduate (student)
应届毕业生	graduating student/pupil, this year's graduate
听课	to visit a class, to sit in on a class, to attend a lecture
公开课	open class
课程	course, curriculum
必修课	required/compulsory course
选修课	elective/optional course
基础课	basic course
专业课	specialized course
课程表	school timetable
课外活动	extracurricular activity
课外辅导	instruction after class
课外阅读	outside reading, after-class reading
课堂讨论	class discussion
(大学的)研究小组,讨论会	seminar
教学大纲	teaching program, syllabus
教学内容	content of a course
学习年限	period of schooling
学历	record of formal schooling
学年	school/academic year
学期	(school)term, semester
学分	credit
分数	mark, grade
五分制	the 5-grade marking system
百分制	100-mark system
学习成绩	academic record, school record
成绩单	school report, report card, transcript
基本框架	basic framework
办学效益	efficiency in school management
基础科学	the fundamentals basic science
学分制	credit system
三学期制	trimester system
双学士制	double bachelor's degree system
主副修制	system of a major field of specialization plus a minor field
教学、科研、生产的"三结合"	"3-in-1" combining teaching, research, and production
定向招生	oriented student recruitment
包分配	guarantee job assignment
示范试点	demonstration pilot project
动员	mobilize
多学科的	multidisciplinary
重点大学	key university
授予(学位)	confer
被授权	be authorized to do
博士后科研流动站	center for postdoctoral studies
专业	speciality
国家发明奖	National Invention Prize
国家自然科学奖	National Prize for Natural Sciences
国家科技进步奖	National Prize for Progress in Science and Technology
学术报告会,专题讨论会	symposium
毕业论文	thesis, dissertation
毕业实习	graduation field work/practice
毕业设计	graduation design/project
毕业典礼	graduation ceremony, commencement
毕业证书	diploma, graduation certificate
毕业鉴定	graduation appraisal

博士生导师	Ph. D advisor, doctoral advisor (supervisor)
授予某人学位	to confer a degree on sb.
补考	make up examination
奖学金	scholarship
（国家）助学金	(state)stipend/subsidy
领取助学金的学生	a grant-aided student
学费	tuition (fee)
资料中心	data center
国际文化交流	international cultural communication
CET-4	College English Test(Band 4)
CET-6	College English Test(Band 6)

附录 3　物理学一、二级学科名称英文词汇

1. 一级学科

物理学　Physics

2. 二级学科

理论物理　Theoretical Physics

粒子物理与原子核物理　Particle Physics and Nuclear Physics

原子与分子物理　Atomic and Molecular Physics

等离子体物理　Plasma Physics

凝聚态物理　Condensed Matter Physics

声学　Acoustics

光学　Optics

无线电物理　Radio Physics

附录 4　数学符号及英语表达

$\dfrac{1}{2}$　　a half *or* one half

$\dfrac{1}{3}$　　a third *or* one third

$\dfrac{2}{3}$　　two thirds

$\dfrac{1}{4}$　　a quarter *or* one quarter; a fourth *or* one fourth

$\dfrac{1}{10}$　　a tenth *or* one tenth

$\dfrac{1}{100}$　　a [one] hundredth

$\dfrac{1}{1000}$　　a [one] thousandth

$\dfrac{1}{1234}$　　one over a thousand two hundred and thirty-fourth

$\dfrac{3}{4}$　　three fourths *or* three quarters

$\dfrac{4}{5}$　　four fifths *or* four over five

$\dfrac{113}{300}$　　one hundred and thirteen over three hundred

$2\frac{1}{2}$	two and a half
$2\frac{7}{8}$	two and seven over eight *or* two and seven eighths
$3\frac{1}{8}$	three and one eighth
$4\frac{1}{3}$	four and a third
$125\frac{3}{4}$	a [one] hundred twenty-five and three fourths [quarters]
0.1	O point one *or* zero point one *or* nought point one
0.01	O point O one *or* zero point zero one *or* nought point nought one
0.25	nought point two five *or* point two five
0.045	decimal [point] nought four five
2.35	two point three five
$4.\dot{9}$	four point nine recurring
$3.03\dot{2}\dot{6}$	three point nought three two six, two six recurring
45.67	four five [forty-five] point six seven
38.72	three eight point seven two *or* thirty-eight decimal seven two
0.001	O point O O one *or* nought point nought nought one *or* zero point zero zero one *or* point nought nought one
$+$	plus; positive
$-$	minus; negative
$\pm$	plus or minus
$\mp$	minus or plus
$\times(\cdot)$	multiplied by; times
$\div$	divided by
$=$	is equal to; equals
$\equiv$	is identically equal to; be identical with; be equitvalent to
$\approx \cong$	is approximately equal to; approximately equals
( )	round brackets; parentheses
[ ]	square brackets
⟨ ⟩	angular brackets
{ }	braces
$\cap$	intersection
$\cup$	union
$\in$	is a member of (set)
$\subset$	is a subset of
$\sim$	difference
$*$	denotes an operation
$\Leftrightarrow$	is equivalent to
$\Rightarrow$	implies
{ } or Φ	empty set
$\rightarrow$	maps into

Appendixes

$\therefore$	therefore
$\because$	because
i or j	imaginary or square root of -1
π	pi; the ratio of the circumference of a circle to its diameter, approx. 3.14159
e or ε	① the base of natural logarithms, approx. 2.71828 ②the eccentricity of a conic section
$x!$	factorial x
$\log_n x$	log x to the base n
$\log_{10} x$	log x to the base 10($i.e.$ common logarithm)
$\log_e x$ or $\ln x$	log x to the base e($i.e.$ natural logarithm or Naperian logarithm)
M	modulus of common logarithms $\log_{10} e = 0.4343, (\log_{10} x = 0.4343 \times \log_e x)$
M^{-1}	$\log_e 10 = 2.3026, (\log_e x = 2.3026 \times \log_{10} x)$
x^n	$x \cdot x \cdot x \ldots$ to n factors; the nth power of x; x to the power n
$x^{\frac{1}{n}}$ or $\sqrt[n]{x}$	the nth root of x; x to the power one over n
$x \to a$	x approaches the limit a
θ	(the angle between the radius vector and the polar axis) the angle theta
$\sin^{-1} x$	(the principal value of the angle whose sine is x)arc sine of x
sinh	sinus hyperbolicus; the hyperbolic sine
$\sum$	the sum of the terms indicated; summation of; sigma
$\sum_{n=1}^{10} x_n$	sum over n from 1 to 10 of x_n
$\prod$	the product of the terms indicated
$\|x\|$	the absolute value of x
$\bar{x}$	the mean value of x; x bar
b'	b prime
b''	b double prime; b second prime
b'''	b triple prime
b_1	b sub one
b_2	b sub two
b_m	b sub m
$\dot{x}$	x dot
$\ddot{x}$	x two dots
b''_m	b double prime sub m
f or F	function
$f(x); F(x)$	function f(or F)of x
$y = f(x)$	y is a function of x
Δ	(finite difference or increment) delta
Δx or δx	(the increment of x) delta x
dx	(an increment of x considered as tending to zero) dee of x; dee x; differential x
$\frac{dy}{dx}$ or $D_x y$	the differential coefficient of y with respect to x; the first derivative of y with respect to x
$\frac{d^2 y}{dx^2}$	the second derivative of y with respect to x

Appendixes

Symbol	Reading
$\dfrac{d^n y}{dx^n}$	the nth derivative of y with respect to x
$\dfrac{\partial y}{\partial u}$	the partial derivative of y with respect to u, where y is a function of u and another variable (or variables)
$F'(x)$	the first derivative of function F of x with respect to x
∇	$\boldsymbol{i}\dfrac{\partial}{\partial x}+\boldsymbol{j}\dfrac{\partial}{\partial y}+\boldsymbol{k}\dfrac{\partial}{\partial z}$; del; nabla; vector differential operator
∇^n	nth del (nabla)
$\int$	integral
$\int_a^b$	integral between limits a and b; the integral from a to b
∞	infinity
$\mathbf{F}$	vector $\mathbf{F}$
$x+y$	x plus y
$(a+b)$	bracket a plus b bracket closed
$a=b$	a equals b; a is equal to b; a is b
$a\neq b$	a is not equal to b; a is not b
$a\pm b$	a plus or minus b
$a\approx b$	a is approximately equal to b
$a>b$	a is greater than b
$a\gg b$	a is much [far] greater than b
$a\geq b$	a is greater than or equal to b
$a<b$	a is less than b
$a\ll b$	a is much less than b
$a\leq b$	a is less than or equal to b
$a\perp b$	a is perpendicular to b
$x\to\infty$	x approaches infinity
$a\equiv b$	a is identically equal to b; a is of identity to b
$\angle a$	angle a
$a/\!/b$	a is parallel to b
$a\sim b$	the difference between a and b
$a\propto b$	a varies directly as b; a is proportional to b
$a\cap b$	a cap b; a meet b; a intersection b
$a\cup b$	a cup b; a join b; a union b
$1\times 1=1$	once one is one
$2\times 2=4$	twice two is four
$6\times 5=30$	six times [multiplied by] five equals [is equal to; are; makes; make] thirty
$30=6\times 5$	thirty is five times as large as six
$s=vt$	s equals [is equal to] v multiplied by t; s equals v times t
$1:2$	the ratio of one to two
$12\div 3=4$	12 divided by 3 equals [is] 4
$20:5=16:4$	the ratio of 20 to 5 equals the ratio of 16 to 4; 20 is to 5 as 16 is to 4

$a:b=c:d$	a is to b as c is to d
$a+b=c$	a plus b is[are; equals; is equal to]c
$c-b=a$	c minus b is [equals; is equal to] a; b from c leaves a
$v=\dfrac{s}{t}$	v equals s divided by t; v is s over t
$7+3<12$	7 plus 3 is less than 12
$12>7+3$	12 is greater than 7 plus 3
$72-16=56$	72 minus 16 is [equals; is equal to] 56 ;16 from 72 leaves 56
x^2	x square;x squared; the square of x; the second power of x;x to the second power
$5^2=25$	the second power of 5 is 25 ; 5 square is 25 ; the square of 5 is 25; 5 to the second power is equal to 25
y^3	y cube; y cubed; the cube of y; y to the third power; y to the third
y^{-10}	y to the minus tenth (power); y to the power (of) minus ten
$\sqrt{4}=\pm 2$	the square root of 4 is [equals] plus or minus 2
$\sqrt[3]{a}$	the cube root of a
$\sqrt[5]{x^2}$	the fifth root of x square
$\sqrt{518}$	the square root of five hundred and eighteen
$\sqrt[3]{930}$	the cubic root of nine hundred and thirty
$3x=5$	three times x equals 5
$\dfrac{x^3}{5}=y^2$	x raised to the third power divided by five equals y squared
$x^2+y^2=10$	x squared with y squared equals 10
$a=\dfrac{V_t-V}{t}$	a equals V sub t minus V all over (divided by)t
$(a+b-c\times d)\div e=f$	a plus b minus c multiplied by d, all divided by e equals f
$\left(8+6\dfrac{5}{8}-3.88\times 4\right)\div 2\dfrac{1}{2}$	eight plus six and five-eighths minus three decimal [point] eight eight multiplied by four, all divided by two and a half
$4567\div 23=198$ 余 13	23 into 4567 goes 198 times, and 13 remainder
$45+70+152=267$	45, 70 and 152 added together are 267
%	per cent
2%	two per cent
‰	per mille
5‰	five per mille
$\dfrac{3}{8}$%	three eighths (of one) per cent
0.3%	point three per cent
$\dfrac{1}{2}$ ton	half a ton
$\dfrac{2}{3}$ ton	two thirds of a ton
$\dfrac{3}{4}$ km	three quarters of a kilometer
1.75 km	one point seven five kilometers

Appendixes

60 mi/hr	sixty miles per hour
20°	twenty degrees
6′	①6 minutes ②6 feet
10″	①10 seconds ②10 inches
0℃	zero degree Centigrade [Celsius]
100℃	one [a] hundred degrees Centigrade
32°F	thirty-two degrees Fahrenheit

附录5 常用物理基本常量

物理常数 PHYSICAL CONSTANTS		符号	数 值
真空中光速	speed of light in vacuum	c	299 792 458 m/s
引力常量	gravitational constant	G	$6.672\ 59 \times 10^{-11}$ N·m²/kg²
阿伏伽德罗常量	Avogadro constant	N_A	$6.022\ 127 \times 10^{23}$ mol^{-1}
普适气体常量	universal gas constant	R	8.314 510 J/mol·K
玻尔兹曼常量	Boltzmann constant	k	$1.380\ 66 \times 10^{-23}$ J/K $8.617\ 39 \times 10^{-5}$ eV/K
理想气体摩尔体积	molar volume (STP)	V_m	$22.413\ 996 \times 10^{-3}$ m³/mol
基本电荷(元电荷)	electron charge magnitude	e	$1.602\ 176\ 53(14) \times 10^{-19}$ C
原子质量单位	atomic mass unit	u	$1.660\ 54 \times 10^{-27}$ kg
电子静止质量	electron mass	m_e	$9.109\ 39 \times 10^{-31}$ kg
电子荷质比	electron charge/mass ratio	e/m_e	$1.758\ 82 \times 10^{11}$ C/kg
质子静止质量	proton mass	m_p	$1.672\ 623 \times 10^{-27}$ kg 1.007 276 u
中子静止质量	neutron mass	m_n	$1.674\ 929 \times 10^{-27}$ kg 1.008 66 u
法拉第常量	Faraday constant	F	$9.648\ 53 \times 10^4$ C/mol
真空电容率	permittivity of vacuum	ε_0	$8.854\ 19 \times 10^{-12}$ C²/N·m²
真空磁导率	permeability of vacuum	μ_0	$1.256\ 64 \times 10^{-6}$ T·m/A
电子磁矩	electron magnetic moment	μ_e	$9.284\ 77 \times 10^{-24}$ J/T
质子磁矩	proton magnetic moment	μ_p	$1.410\ 618 \times 10^{-26}$ J/T
玻尔半径	Bohr radius	a_0	$5.291\ 77 \times 10^{-11}$ m
玻尔磁子	Bohr magneton	μ_B	$9.274\ 015 \times 10^{-24}$ J/T
核磁子	nuclear magneton	μ_N	$5.050\ 786\ 6 \times 10^{-27}$ J/T
普朗克常量	Planck constant	h	$6.626\ 068\ 76(52) \times 10^{-34}$ J·s $4.135\ 667\ 27(16) \times 10^{-15}$ eV·s
约化普朗克常量	reduced Planck constant	$\hbar$	$1.054\ 571\ 596(82) \times 10^{-34}$ J·s $6.582\ 118\ 89(26) \times 10^{-16}$ eV·s

续表

物理常量 PHYSICAL CONSTANTS		符号	数 值
精细结构常量	fine structure constant	α	$7.297\,352\,533 \times 10^3$
里德伯常量	Rydberg constant	R	$1.097\,373 \times 10^7$/m
电子康普顿波长	electron Compton wavelength	λ_{ec}	$2.426\,31 \times 10^{-12}$ m
质子康普顿波长	proton Compton wavelength	λ_{pc}	$1.321\,41 \times 10^{-15}$ m
热功当量	mechanical equivalent of heat		4.186 J/cal
标准大气压强	standard atmospheric pressure	1 atm	$1.013\,25 \times 10^5$ Pa
电子伏特	electron volt	1 eV	$1.602\,177\,33(49) \times 10^{-19}$ J
重力加速度(标准值)	acceleration due to gravity (standard)	g	$9.806\,65$ m/s^2
电子静止能量	electron rest energy	$m_e c^2$	0.510 999 06(15) J
理想气体体积(0℃, 1个大气压下)	volume of ideal gas (0℃ and 1 atm)		22.414 10(19) liter/mol

附录6 常用汉英物理学专业词汇表

BET 公式　BET formula
DLVO 理论　DLVO theory
HLB 法　hydrophile-lipophile balance method
pVT 性质　pVT property
ζ电势　zeta potential
阿伏加德罗常量　Avogadro number
阿伏加德罗定律　Avogadro law
阿伦尼乌斯电离理论　Arrhenius ionization theory
阿伦尼乌斯方程　Arrhenius equation
阿伦尼乌斯活化能　Arrhenius activation energy
阿马加定律　Amagat law
艾林方程　Erying equation
爱因斯坦光化当量定律　Einstein's law of photochemical equivalence
爱因斯坦-斯托克斯方程　Einstein-Stokes equation
安托万常数　Antoine constant
安托万方程　Antoine equation
昂萨格电导理论　Onsager's theory of conductance
半电池　half cell
半衰期　half-life period
饱和吸附量　saturated extent of absorption
饱和液体　saturated liquid
饱和蒸汽　saturated vapor

饱和蒸气压　saturated vapor pressure
爆炸界限　explosion limits
比表面功　specific surface work
比表面吉布斯函数　specific surface Gibbs function
比浓黏度　reduced viscosity
标准电动势　standard electromotive force
标准电极电势　standard electrode potential
标准摩尔反应焓　standard molar reaction enthalpy
标准摩尔反应吉布斯函数　standard Gibbs function of molar reaction
标准摩尔反应熵　standard molar reaction entropy
标准摩尔焓函数　standard molar enthalpy function
标准摩尔吉布斯自由能函数　standard molar Gibbs free energy function
标准摩尔燃烧焓　standard molar combustion enthalpy
标准摩尔熵　standard molar entropy
标准摩尔生成焓　standard molar formation enthalpy
标准摩尔生成吉布斯函数　standard molar formation Gibbs function
标准平衡常数　standard equilibrium constant
标准氢电极　standard hydrogen electrode
标准态　standard state
标准熵　standard entropy

标准压力　standard pressure
标准条件　standard condition
表观活化能　apparent activation energy
表观摩尔质量　apparent molar mass
表观迁移数　apparent transference number
表面　surfaces
表面过程控制　surface process control
表面活性剂　surfactant
表面超额　surface excess
表面张力　surface tension
表面质量作用定律　surface mass action law
玻意尔定律　Boyle law
玻意尔温度　Boyle temperature
玻意尔点　Boyle point
玻尔兹曼常量　Boltzmann constant
玻尔兹曼分布　Boltzmann distribution
玻尔兹曼公式　Boltzmann formula
玻尔兹曼熵定理　Boltzmann entropy theorem
玻色-爱因斯坦统计法　Bose-Einstein statistics
泊松　poise
不可逆过程　irreversible process
不可逆过程热力学　thermodynamics of irreversible processes
不可逆相变化　irreversible phase change
布朗运动　Brownian movement
查理定律　Charle law
产额　yield
敞开系统　open system
超电势　overpotential
沉降　sedimentation
沉降势　sedimentation potential
沉降平衡　sedimentation equilibrium
弛豫时间　relaxation time
触变性　thixotropy
粗分散系统　coarse disperse system
催化剂　catalyst
单分子层吸附　monomolecule layer absorption
单分子反应　unimolecular reaction
弹式热量计　bomb calorimeter
道尔顿定律　Dalton law
道尔顿分压定律　Dalton partial pressure law
德拜和法尔肯哈根效应　Debye and Falkenhagen effect
德拜立方公式　Debye cubic formula
德拜-休克尔极限公式　Debye-Huckel's limiting equation
等焓过程　isenthalpic process
等焓线　isenthalpic line
等概率定理　theorem of equal probability
低共沸点　lower azeotropic point
低共熔点　eutectic point
低共熔混合物　eutectic mixture
低会溶点　lower consolute point
低熔冰盐结晶　cryohydrate
第二类永动机　perpetual motion machine of the second kind
第三定律熵　third-law entropy
第一类永动机　perpetual motion machine of the first kind
缔合化学吸附　association chemical absorption
电池常数　cell constant
电池电动势　electromotive force of cells
电池反应　cell reaction
电导　conductance
电导率　conductivity
电动势的温度系数　temperature coefficient of electromotive force
电动电势　electrokinetic potential
电功　electric work
电化学　electrochemistry
电化学极化　electrochemical polarization
电极电势　electrode potential
电极反应　reaction on the electrode
电极种类　type of electrodes
电解池　electrolytic cell
电流效率　current efficiency
电迁移　electromigration
电迁移率　electromobility
电渗　electroosmosis
电渗析　electrodialysis
电泳　electrophoresis
丁达尔效应　Dyndall effect
定常流过程　steady flow process
定容摩尔热容　molar heat capacity under constant volume

定容温度计　constant volume thermometer
定态近似法　stationary state approximation
定压摩尔热容　molar heat capacity under constant pressure
定压温度计　constant pressure thermometer
定域粒子系统　localized particle system
动力(学)方程　kinetic equations
动力学控制　kinetic control
独立粒子系统　independent particle system
对称数　symmetry number
对应状态原理　principle of corresponding state
多方过程　polytropic process
多分子层吸附理论　adsorption theory of multi-molecular layers
二级反应　second-order reaction
二级相变　second-order phase change
法拉第常数　Faraday constant
法拉第定律　Faraday's law
反电动势　back E. M. F.
反渗透　reverse osmosis
反应分子数　molecularity
反应级数　reaction order
反应进度　extent of reaction
反应热　heat of reaction
反应速率　rate of reaction
反应速率常数　reaction rate constant
范德瓦耳斯常数　van der Waals constant
范德瓦耳斯方程　van der Waals equation
范德瓦耳斯力　van der Waals force
范德瓦耳斯气体　van der Waals gases
范托夫方程　van't Hoff equation
范托夫规则　van't Hoff rule
范托夫渗透压公式　van't Hoff equation of osmotic pressure
方均根速率　root-mean-square speed
非定域离子系统　non-localized particle systems
非基元反应　nonelementary reaction
非体积功　non-volume work
非依时化学计量反应　time-independent stoichiometric reactions
菲克第一扩散定律　Fick's first law of diffusion
沸点　boiling point
沸点升高　elevation of boiling point

费米-狄拉克统计法　Fermi-Dirac statistics
分布　distribution
分布数　distribution number
分解电压　decomposition voltage
分配定律　distribution law
分散系统　disperse system
分散相　dispersion phase
分体积　partial volume
分体积定律　partial volume law
分压　partial pressure
分压定律　partial pressure law
分子反应力学　mechanics of molecular reactions
分子间力　intermolecular force
分子蒸馏　molecular distillation
封闭系统　closed system
弗罗因德利希吸附经验式　Freundlich empirical formula of adsorption
负极点　negative pole
负吸附　negative absorption
复合反应　composite reaction
盖-吕萨克定律　Gay-Lussac law
甘汞电极　calomel electrode
感胶离子序　lyotropic series
杠杆规则　lever rule
高分子溶液　macromolecular solution
高共沸点　upper azeotropic point
高会溶点　upper consolute point
隔离法　isolation method
格罗塞斯-德雷珀定律　Grotthus-Draper's law
隔离系统　isolated system
功　work
功函　work content
共轭溶液　conjugate solution
共沸温度　azeotropic temperature
构型熵　configurational entropy
孤立系统　isolated system
固溶胶　solid sol
固相线　solid phase line
光反应　photoreaction
光化学第二定律　the second law of photochemistry
光化学第一定律　the first law of photochemistry
光敏反应　photosensitized reactions
光谱熵　spectrum entropy

广度性质　extensive property
广延量　extensive quantity
广延性质　extensive property
规定熵　stipulated entropy
过饱和溶液　oversaturated solution
过饱和蒸气　oversaturated vapor
过程　process
过渡态理论　transition state theory
过冷水　supercooled water
过冷液体　overcooled liquid
过热液体　overheated liquid
亥姆霍兹函数　Helmholtz function
亥姆霍兹函数判据　Helmholtz function criterion
亥姆霍兹自由能　Helmholtz free energy
焓　enthalpy
赫斯定律　Hess law
亨利常数　Henry constant
亨利定律　Henry law
恒沸混合物　constant boiling mixture
恒容摩尔热容　molar heat capacity at constant volume
恒容热　heat at constant volume
恒外压　constant external pressure
恒温方程　equation at constant temperature
恒压摩尔热容　molar heat capacity at constant pressure
恒压热　heat at constant pressure
化学动力学　chemical kinetics
化学反应计量式　stoichiometric equation of chemical reaction
化学反应计量系数　stoichiometric coefficient of chemical reaction
化学反应进度　extent of chemical reaction
化学计量式　stoichiometric equation
化学计量系数　stoichiometric coefficient
化学亲合势　chemical affinity
化学热力学　chemical thermodynamics
化学势　chemical potential
化学势判据　chemical potential criterion
化学吸附　chemisorption
环境　environment
环境熵变　entropy change in environment
挥发度　volatility

混合熵　entropy of mixing
混合物　mixture
活度　activity
活化控制　activation control
活化络合物理论　activated complex theory
活化能　activation energy
霍根-华森图　Hougen-Watson chart
基态能级　energy level at ground state
基尔霍夫公式　Kirchhoff formula
基元反应　elementary reaction
积分溶解热　integration heat of dissolution
吉布斯-杜安姆方程　Gibbs-Duhem equation
吉布斯-亥姆霍兹方程　Gibbs-Helmhotz equation
吉布斯函数　Gibbs function
吉布斯函数判据　Gibbs function criterion
吉布斯吸附公式　Gibbs absorption formula
吉布斯自由能　Gibbs free energy
极化电极电势　polarization potential of electrode
极化曲线　polarization curve
极化　polarization
极限摩尔电导率　limiting molar conductivity
价数规则　rule of valence
简并度　degeneracy
键焓　bond enthalpy
胶冻　jelly
胶核　colloidal nucleus
胶凝作用　gelatification
胶束　micelle
胶体　colloid
胶体分散系统　dispersion system of colloid
胶体化学　collochemistry
胶体粒子　colloidal particles
焦耳　Joule
焦耳-汤姆逊实验　Joule-Thomson experiment
焦耳-汤姆逊系数　Joule-Thomson coefficient
焦耳-汤姆逊效应　Joule-Thomson effect
焦耳定律　Joule law
接触电势　contact potential
接触角　contact angle
结晶热　heat of crystallization
节流过程　throttling process
节流膨胀　throttling expansion
节流膨胀系数　coefficient of throttling expansion

结线　tie line
界面　interface
界面张力　interfacial tension
浸湿　immersion wetting
浸湿功　immersion wetting work
精馏　rectification
聚电解质　polyelectrolyte
聚沉　coagulation
聚沉值　coagulation value
绝对反应速率理论　absolute reaction rate theory
绝对熵　absolute entropy
绝对温标　absolute temperature scale
绝热过程　adiabatic process
绝热式热量计　adiabatic calorimeter
绝热指数　adiabatic index
卡诺定理　Carnot theorem
卡诺循环　Carnot cycle
开尔文公式　Kelvin formula
柯诺瓦洛夫-吉布斯定律　Konovalov-Gibbs law
科尔劳施离子独立运动定律　Kohlrausch's law of independent migration of ions
可逆电池　reversible cell
可逆反应　reversible reactions
可逆过程　reversible process
可逆过程方程　reversible process equation
可逆体积功　reversible volume work
可逆相变　reversible phase change
克拉珀龙方程　Clapeyron equation
克劳修斯不等式　Clausius inequality
克劳修斯-克拉珀龙方程　Clausius-Clapeyron equation
控制步骤　control step
库仑计　coulometer
扩散控制的　diffusion-controlled
拉普拉斯方程　Laplace's equation
拉乌尔定律　Raoult law
兰格缪尔-欣谢尔伍德机理　Langmuir-Hinshelwood mechanism
兰格缪尔吸附等温式　Langmuir absorption isotherm formula
冷冻系数　coefficient of refrigeration
冷却曲线　cooling curve
离解化学吸附　dissociation chemical adsorption
离解热　heat of dissociation

离解压力　dissociation pressure
离子的标准摩尔生成焓　standard molar enthalpy of formation of ions
离子电迁移率　mobility of ions
离子迁移数　transport number of ions
离子独立运动定律　law of the independent migration of ions
离子气氛　ionic atmosphere
离子强度　ionic strength
理想混合物　perfect mixture
理想气体　ideal gas
理想气体绝热指数　adiabatic index of ideal gases
理想气体微观模型　micromodel of ideal gas
理想气体反应的等温方程　isothermal equation of ideal gaseous reactions
理想气体绝热可逆过程方程　adiabatic reversible process equation of ideal gases
理想气体状态方程　state equation of ideal gas
理想稀溶液　ideal dilute solution
理想液态混合物　perfect liquid mixture
粒子　particle
粒子的配分函数　partition function of particles
连串反应　consecutive reaction
链载体　chain carrier
链反应　chain reaction
量热熵　calorimetric entropy
量子统计法　quantum statistics
量子产率　quantum yield
临界参数　critical parameter
临界常数　critical constant
临界点　critical point
临界胶束浓度　critical micelle concentration
临界摩尔体积　critical molar volume
临界温度　critical temperature
临界压力　critical pressure
临界状态　critical state
零级反应　zero-order reaction
流动电位　streaming potential
流动功　flow work
笼效应　cage effect
路易斯-兰德尔逸度规则　Lewis-Randall rule of fugacity
露点　dew point

露点线　dew-point line
麦克斯韦关系式　Maxwell relation
麦克斯韦速率分布　Maxwell distribution of speeds
麦克斯韦能量分布　Maxwell distribution of energy
毛细管凝结　capillary condensation
毛细现象　capillary phenomenon
米凯利斯常数　Michaelis constant
摩尔电导率　molar conductivity
摩尔反应焓　molar reaction enthalpy
摩尔混合熵　molar entropy of mixing
摩尔气体常数　molar gas constant
摩尔热容　molar heat capacity
摩尔溶解焓　molar dissolution enthalpy
摩尔稀释焓　molar dilution enthalpy
内扩散控制　internal diffusions control
内能　internal energy
内压力　internal pressure
能级　energy level
能级分布　energy-level distribution
能量均分原理　principle of the equipartition of energy
能斯特方程　Nernst equation
能斯特热定理　Nernst heat theorem
凝点　freezing point
凝点降低　lowering of freezing point
凝点曲线　freezing point curve
凝胶　gel
凝聚态　condensed state
凝聚相　condensed phase
浓差超电势　concentration overpotential
浓差极化　concentration polarization
浓差电池　concentration cells
帕斯卡　pascal
泡点　bubble point
泡点线　bubble-point line
配分函数　partition function
碰撞截面　collision cross section
碰撞数　number of collisions
偏摩尔量　partial molar quantity
平衡常数(理想气体反应)　equilibrium constant for reaction of ideal gases
平动配分函数　partition function of translation
平衡分布　equilibrium distribution

平衡态　equilibrium state
平衡态近似法　equilibrium state approximation
平衡状态图　equilibrium state diagram
平均活度　mean activity
平均活度系数　mean activity coefficient
平均摩尔热容　mean molar heat capacity
平均质量摩尔浓度　mean mass molarity
平均自由程　mean free path
平行反应　parallel reaction
破乳,脱乳,反乳化　demulsification
铺展　spreading
普遍化范德瓦尔斯方程　universal van der Waals equation
其他功　the other work
汽化热　heat of vaporization
气溶胶　aerosol
气体常数　gas constant
气体分子运动论　kinetic theory of gases
气体分子运动论的基本方程　fundamental equation of kinetic theory of gases
汽相线　vapor line
迁移数　transport number
潜热　latent heat
强度量　intensive quantity
强度性质　intensive property
亲水溶胶　hydrophilic sol
氢电极　hydrogen electrode
区域熔化　zone melting
热　heat
热爆炸　heat explosion
热泵　heat pump
热功当量　mechanical equivalent of heat
热函　heat content
热机　heat engine
热机效率　efficiency of heat engine
热力学　thermodynamics
热力学第二定律　the second law of thermodynamics
热力学第三定律　the third law of thermodynamics
热力学第一定律　the first law of thermodynamics
热力学基本方程　fundamental equation of thermodynamics
热力学概率　thermodynamic probability
热力学能　thermodynamic energy

热力学特性函数　characteristic thermodynamic function
热力学温标　thermodynamic scale of temperature
热力学温度　thermodynamic temperature
热熵　thermal entropy
热效应　heat effect
熔点曲线　melting-point curve
熔化热　heat of fusion
溶胶　sol
溶解焓　dissolution enthalpy
溶液　solution
溶胀　swelling
乳化剂　emulsifier
乳状液　emulsion
瑞利公式　Rayleigh equation
润湿　wetting
润湿角　wetting angle
萨克尔-泰特洛德方程　Sackur-Tetrode equation
三相点　triple point
三相线　triple-phase line
熵　entropy
熵判据　entropy criterion
熵增原理　principle of entropy increase
渗透压　osmotic pressure
渗析法　dialytic process
生成反应　formation reaction
升华热　heat of sublimation
势电解质　potential electrolyte
舒尔策-哈代规则　Schulze-Hardy rule
松弛力　relaxation force
速率方程　rate equation
速率控制步骤　rate determining step
塔费尔公式　Tafel equation
态-态反应　state-state reaction
唐南平衡　Donnan equilibrium
淌度　mobility
特鲁顿规则　Trouton rule
特性黏度　intrinsic viscosity
体积功　volume work
统计权重　statistical weight
统计热力学　statistic thermodynamics
统计熵　statistic entropy
途径　path
途径函数　path function

外扩散控制　external diffusion control
完美晶体　perfect crystal
完全气体　perfect gas
微观状态　microstate
韦斯顿标准电池　Weston standard battery
维恩效应　Wien effect
位力方程　virial equation
位力系数　virial coefficient
无热溶液　athermal solution
无限稀溶液　infinitely dilute dilution
物理化学　physical chemistry
物理吸附　physisorptions
吸附　absorption
吸附等量线　absorption isostere
吸附等温线　absorption isotherm
吸附等压线　absorption isobar
吸附剂　adsorbent
吸附量　extent of absorption
吸附热　heat of absorption
吸附质　adsorbate
析出电势　evolution/deposition potential
稀溶液的依数性　colligative property of dilute solution
稀释焓　dilution enthalpy
系统　system
系统点　system point
系统的环境　environment of system
相　phase
相变　phase change
相变焓　enthalpy of phase change
相变热　heat of phase change
相点　phase point
相对挥发度　relative volatility
相对黏度　relative viscosity
相律　phase rule
相平衡热容　heat capacity in phase equilibrium
相图　phase diagram
相倚粒子系统　system of phase-dependent particles
悬浮液　suspension
循环过程　cyclic process
压力商　pressure quotient
压缩因子　compressibility factor
压缩因子图　diagram of compressibility factor

亚稳态　metastable state
盐桥　salt bridge
盐析　salting out
盐效应　salt effect
阳极　anode
杨氏方程　Young's equation
液体接界电势　liquid junction potential
液相线　liquid phase lines
一级反应　first-order reaction
一级相变　first-order phase change
逸度　fugacity
逸度系数　coefficient of fugacity
阴极　cathode
荧光　fluorescence
永动机　perpetual motion machine
永久气体　permanent gas
有效能　available energy
逾压力　excess pressure
原电池　primary cell
约化摩尔体积　reduced molar volume
约化体积　reduced volume
约化温度　reduced temperature
约化压力　reduced pressure
增比黏度　specific viscosity
沾湿　adhesional wetting
沾湿功　work of adhesional wetting
真溶液　true solution
真实电解质　real electrolyte
真实气体　real gas
真实迁移数　true transference number
振动配分函数　partition function of vibration

振动特征温度　characteristic temperature of vibration
蒸气压下降　depression of vapor pressure
正常沸点　normal boiling point
正吸附　positive absorption
支链反应　branched-chain reaction
直链反应　straight-chain reaction
指前因子　pre-exponential factor
质量作用定律　mass action law
制冷系数　coefficient of refrigeration
中和热　heat of neutralization
轴功　shaft work
转动配分函数　partition function of rotation
转化率　rate of convertion
转化温度　conversion temperature
状态　state
状态方程　state equation
状态分布　state distribution
状态函数　state function
准静态过程　quasi-static process
准一级反应　pseudo-first order reaction
自催化　autocatalysis
自由度　degree of freedom
自由度数　number of degrees of freedom
自由焓　free enthalpy
自由能　free energy
自由膨胀　free expansion
组分数　component number
最概然分布　most probable distribution
最概然速率　most probable speed
最佳反应温度　optimal reaction temperature

附录7　常用英汉物理学专业词汇表

A

a. c. generator　交流发电机
aberration　光行差,像差
absolute index of refraction　绝对折射率
absolute refractive index　绝对折射率
absolute temperature scale　绝对温标
absolute zero　绝对零度
absorber　吸收体
absorbing power　吸收能力,吸收本领
absorptance　吸收比
absorption　吸收
absorption coefficient　吸收系数
absorption line　吸收线
absorption spectrum　吸收光谱,吸收谱
accelerate　加速
acceleration　加速度
acceleration due to gravity　重力加速度
acceleration-time graph　加速度-时间关系线图
accelerator　加速器
acceptor　受主,受体
acceptor doping　受主掺杂
acceptor impurity　受主杂质
accommodation　调节,调焦
accumulator　蓄电池
accuracy　准确度
acetate strip　醋酸酯条片
achromatic　消色差的
achromatic aberration　消色差
achromatic condenser　消色差聚光透镜
achromatic light　消色差光,白光
acoustic blur　声响模糊
acoustic board　吸音板,吸声板
acoustic navigation　声响导航,声学导航
acoustic pressure　声压
acoustics　声学
act on　施于
action　作用量,作用,作用力
action of point　尖端作用

activation　激活,活化
activation energy　激活能,活化能
active nucleus　活性核,放射性核
activity　活性,(放射性)活度
adapter　接合器
adder　加法器
adhesion　附着力,附着,黏附
adhesive force　附着力
adiabatic　绝热的
adiabatic expansion　绝热膨胀
adiabatic process　绝热过程
aerial　天线
aerial induction　天线调谐电感
aerial network　天线网络
aerodynamic force　气动力
aerodynamics　空气动力学
aerofoil　机翼
agent　剂
air blower　吹风器
air column　空气柱,气柱
air cushion　气垫
air damping　空气阻尼
air film　气膜
air track　气垫导轨
air wedge　气楔
alignment　对准,校整
alpha decay　α衰变
alpha particle　α粒子
alpha-particle scattering analogue　α粒子散射模拟
alternating current　交流电
alternating voltage　交变电压,交流电压
alternator　交流发电机
altimeter　高度表,测高仪
ammeter　安培计
amorphous　非结晶的,无定形的
ampere　安培,安
ampere-hour　安培小时,安时
amplification　放大,放大率
amplifier　放大器

amplify 放大
amplitude 振幅
amplitude modulation 调幅,振幅调制
amyl acetate 乙酸戊酯,醋酸戊酯
analogue 模拟
analogue experiment 模拟实验
analogue signal 模拟信号
analogue-to-digital conversion 模数转换
analyger 检偏振器
AND gate 与门
anemometer 风速计
aneroid barometer 无液气压计,空盒气压表
angle of contact 接触角
angle of deviation 偏向角
angle of diffraction 衍射角
angle of dip 倾角
angle of elevation 仰角
angle of emergence 出射角
angle of incidence 入射角
angle of inclination 倾角
angle of minimum deviation 最小偏向角
angle of projection 投射角
angle of reflection 反射角
angle of refraction 折射角
angle of twist 扭转角
angstrom 埃
angular acceleration 角加速度
angular aperture 孔径角
angular displacement 角位移
angular frequency 角频率
angular impulse 角冲量
angular magnification 角放大率
angular momentum 角动量,动量矩
angular motion 角向运动,角运动
angular speed 角速率
angular velocity 角速度
angular width 角宽度
annealing 退火
anode 阳极
anomalous expansion 反常膨胀
antenna 天线
anticlockwise moment 逆时针力矩
antifreeze agent 防冻剂

antinodal line 腹线
antinode 波腹
antiparticle 反粒子
antiphase 反相
aperture 孔径
apparent depth 视深
apparent expansion 表观膨胀,视膨胀
apparent frequency 表观频率,视频率
apparent loss in weight 表观失重
apparent weight 表观重量
Appleton layer 阿普尔顿层,F电离层
aqueous layer 水层
Archimedes principle 阿基米德原理
area 面积
argon 氩
armature 电枢
artificial disintegration 人工蜕变
artificial radioactivity 人工放射性
astable 非稳态的
astable circuit 非稳态电路
astable multivibrator 非稳态多谐振荡器
astigmatism 像散
astronomical telescope 天文望远镜
at infinity 在无穷远处
at rest 静止
atmosphere 大气,大气圈,大气压
atmospheric pressure （大)气压
atom 原子
atomic bomb 原子弹
atomic bond 原子键
atomic density 原子密度
atomic diameter 原子直径
atomic energy 原子能
atomic mass 原子质量
atomic mass unit 原子质量单位
atomic model 原子模型
atomic nucleus 原子核
atomic number 原子序数
atomic radius 原子半径
atomic separation 原子间距
atomic spacing 原子间距
atomic structure 原子结构
atomic theory 原子论

atomizer 原子化器
attenuation 衰减
attraction 吸引
attractive force 吸力
audible frequency range 听频范围
audible signal 可听信号
audio frequency 声频
autofocus 自动聚焦,自动调焦
avalanche 电子雪崩
average acceleration 平均加速度
average power 平均功率
average speed 平均速率
average velocity 平均速度
Avogadro constant 阿伏伽德罗常数/常量
Avogadro number 阿伏伽德罗数
Avogadro's law 阿伏伽德罗定律
axial 轴向的,沿轴的
axial field 轴向场
axial search coil 轴向探察线圈
axis 轴
axis of rotation 转轴

B

back e.m.f. 反电动势
background radiation 本底辐射
Bainbridge mass spectrometer 班布里奇质谱仪
balance 天平,秤,平衡
balance arm 平衡臂
balance point 平衡点
balanced bridge 平衡电桥
balanced force 平衡力
ball bearing 球轴承
ballistic galvanometer 冲击电流计,冲击检流计
ballistic pendulum 冲击摆
Balmer series 巴耳末系
band spectrum 带状谱
bandwidth 带宽
bar code 条码
bar magnet 磁棒,条形磁铁
bare wire 裸线
barium 钡
barometer 气压计
barrier 障碍物

barrier layer 阻挡层,势垒层
barrier potential difference 阻挡层电势差,阻挡层电位差
Barton's pendulum 巴尔通摆
base 基极
base current 基极电流
battery 电池(组)
battery charger 电池充电器
battery holder 电池座
beaker 烧杯
beam splitter 分束器,射束分离器
beat 拍
beat frequency 拍频
becquerel 贝可(勒耳)(放射性活度单位)
bel 贝尔,贝
bell jar 钟形罩
bench mat 实验台垫
Bernoulli theorem 伯努利定理
beryllium 铍
beta decay β衰变
beta particle β粒子
biasing circuit 偏压电路
biasing voltage 偏压
biconcave lens 双凹透镜
biconvex lens 双凸透镜
bifilar pendulum 双线摆
bifocal lens 双焦距透镜
big-bang model 大爆炸模型
bimetallic strip 双金属片
binary adder 二进加法器
binary system 二进制
binding 结合
binding energy 结合能
binoculars 双筒望远镜
Biot-Savart law 毕奥-萨伐尔定律
bipolar 双极的
birefraction 双折射
bistable 双稳态的
bistable circuit 双稳电路
bistable multivibrator 双稳态多谐振荡器
bit 比特(二进制信息单位)
black-body radiation 黑体辐射
block and tackle 滑轮组

Appendixes

block diagram　方框图
blocking capacitor　隔直流电容器
blooming　敷霜,表面加膜
Bohr atom　玻尔原子
Bohr radius　玻尔半径
Bohr theory　玻尔理论
boil　沸腾,煮沸
boiler　锅炉
boiling point　沸点
bolometer　辐射热计
Boltzmann constant　玻尔兹曼常数
bombardment　轰击
bond energy　键能
bonding　成键
Bourdon gauge　布尔东气压计
bow wave　头波,舶波
Boyle law　玻意尔定律
Brackett series　布喇开系,布喇开光谱
Bragg angle　布拉格角
Bragg diffraction　布拉格衍射
Bragg plane　布拉格平面
Bragg's law　布拉格定律
brake　制动器
breakdown potential　击穿电势,击穿电位
breaking point　断点
breaking strength　抗断强度
breaking stress　致断应力
breeder reactor　增殖反应堆
bremsstrahlung　轫致辐射
Brewster's law　布儒斯特定律
bridge circuit　桥式电路
bridge rectifier　桥式整流器
bright fringe　亮纹
brightness　亮度
brittle　脆的,易碎的
bromine　溴
Brownian movement　布朗运动
brush　电刷
bubble chamber　气泡室
bubble raft model　泡筏模型
buffer　缓冲器
buffer circuit　缓冲电路
bulk modulus　体积弹性模量

Bunsen burner　本生灯
buoyancy　浮力
burette　滴定管
burette stand　滴定管架
burglar alarm　防盗警报器,防盗警钟
buzzer　蜂鸣器
bypass　旁路
byte　字节

C

cable　电缆
cadmium sulphide　硫化镉
caesium　铯
calcite　方解石
calibrate　校准,标上刻度
caliper　测径器,卡钳
calorie　卡路里,卡
calorimeter　量热器,量能器
camera　照相机
candela　坎(德拉)
cantilever　悬臂
capacitance　电容
capacitance substitution box　换值电容箱
capacitive circuit　电容电路
capacitive component　电容性分量
capacitive coupling　电容耦合
capacitive discharge　电容性放电
capacitive reactance　容抗
capacitor　电容器
capacitor-input filter　电容输入滤波器
capacity　容量,电容
capillarity　毛细现象,毛细作用
capillary depression　毛细下降
capillary rise　毛细上升
capillary tube　毛细管
capsule　囊
capture　俘获
carbon　碳
carbon granule　碳颗粒
carbon paper disc　圆形碳纸
carbon-14 dating　碳14年代测定法
carburettor　化油器,汽化器
carrier　载波

carry　进位
castor oil　蓖麻油
cathode　阴极，负极
cathode ray　阴极射线
cathode ray deflection tube　阴极射线偏转管
cathode-ray oscilloscope　阴极射线示波器，示波器
cathode-ray tube　阴极射线管
cavity resonator　空腔共振器
celestial telescope　天体望远镜
cell　电池，细胞
Celsius temperature scale　摄氏温标
centimeter　厘米
centralized low-voltage power supply unit　集中式低压电源箱
center of curvature　曲率中心
center of gravity　重心
center of mass　质心
center of oscillation　振荡中心
center-tapped transformer　中心抽头变压器
centrifugal force　离心力
centrifuge　离心机
centripetal acceleration　向心加速度
centripetal force　向心力
Chadwick　查德威克
chain reaction　链式反应
change of state　物态变化
change-over switch　换向开关
characteristic　特性，特征
characteristic curve　特性曲线
characteristic line　特征线
characteristic spectrum　特征光谱，特征谱
charge　电荷，充电，起电
charge carrier　载荷子，载流子
charge conservation　电荷守恒
charge density　电荷密度
charge distribution　电荷分布
charge-to-mass ratio　荷质比
charged particle　带电粒子
charging by contact　接触起电
charging by friction　摩擦生电
charging by induction　感应起电
charging by sharing　授受起电
charging time constant　充电时间常量

Charles law　查理定律
choke　扼流（圈）
choke circuit　扼流电路
chromatic aberration　色差
chromatic dispersion　色散
cinefilm soundtrack　电影胶片声迹
circle of least confusion　最少模糊圆
circuit　电路
circuit board　电路板
circuit breaker　断路器
circuit symbol　电路符号
circular coil　环形线圈
circular motion　圆周运动
circular orbit　圆周轨道
circular pulse　圆形脉冲
circular wave　圆形波
circular wavefront　圆形波阵面，圆形波前
clamp　夹钳，夹紧
clap-echo method　拍掌-回声法
cleave　裂开
clinical thermometer　体温计
clip　夹子
clockwise moment　顺时针力矩
closed circuit　闭合电路
closed pipe　封闭管道
closed tube　连通管
closed-loop control system　闭合环路控制系统
closed-loop gain　闭合环路增益
closed-loop voltage gain　闭合环路电压增益
closely packed　密堆积的
cloud chamber　云室
cloud chamber track　云室径迹
coaxial　共轴的，同轴的
coaxial cable　同轴电缆，同轴线
cobalt　钴
code　编码，(代)码
coder　编码器
coefficient of dynamic friction　动摩擦系数
coefficient of friction　摩擦系数
coefficient of restitution　恢复系数
coefficient of static friction　静摩擦系数
coefficient of viscosity　黏性系数
coherent　相干的

cohesion　内聚力,内聚
cohesive force　内聚力
coil　线圈
collector　集电极,集电器,集极
collector current　集电极电流,集极电流
collimator　准直管,准直仪
collision　碰撞
color　颜色
color code　色码,色标
combinational logic　组合逻辑
common emitter　共发射极
common-mode voltage　共模电压
commutator　对易式换向器,交换子
compass　指北针,罗盘
complete circuit　完整电路
component　组件,分量,组分
component force　分力
compound microscope　复显微镜
compound pendulum　复摆
compressed gas　压缩气体
compressibility　可压缩性,压缩率
compressible fluid　可压缩性流体
compression　压缩
compression spring balance　压缩弹簧天平
concave　凹,凹面,凹面的
concave lens　凹透镜
concave mirror　凹镜,凹面镜
concentric capacitor　同心电容器
condensation　凝结,凝聚
condensation nucleus　凝结核,凝聚核
condensation point　凝点,凝结点
condenser　聚光器,电容器,冷凝器
conductance　电导
conductivity　电导率
conductor　导体
conical pendulum　锥摆
conjugate foci　共轭焦点
conservation of angular momentum　角动量守恒
conversation of charge　电荷守恒
conservation of energy　能量守恒
conservation of mechanical energy　机械能守恒
conservation of momentum　动量守恒
conservative force　保守力

conserved　守恒的
constant acceleration　恒(定)加速度
constant angular acceleration　恒(定)角加速度
constant angular velocity　恒(定)角速度
constant force　恒力
constant motion　恒速运动
constant pressure　定压,恒压
constant speed　恒速率
constant temperature　定温,恒温
constant velocity　恒速度
constant volume　定容
constant volume gas thermometer　定容气体温度计
constantan　康铜
constriction　压缩,收缩
constructive interference　相长干涉
contact angle　接触角
contact area　接触面积
contact force　接触力
continuity equation　连续性方程
continuous spectrum　连续光谱,连续谱
continuous wave　连续波
contract　收缩
control experiment　对照实验,比对实验
control grid　控制栅极
control rod　控制棒
control system　控制系统
convection　运流,对流
converge　会聚
convergent lens　会聚透镜
convergent mirror　会聚镜
convex　凸,凸面,凸面的
convex lens　凸透镜
convex mirror　凸镜,凸面镜
coolant　冷却剂
cooling by evaporation　蒸发制冷
cooling correction　冷却修正
cooling curve　冷却曲线
cooling effect　冷却效应
cooling system　冷却系统
coplanar forces　共面力
core　芯,核心
Coriolis force　科里奥利力

corkscrew rule 螺旋法则
corona discharge 电晕放电
corpuscular theory of light 光的微粒学说
correction 校正,修正
cosmic radiation 宇宙辐射
coulomb 库仑
Coulomb's law 库仑定律
count rate 计数率
counter 计数器
counterweight 平衡锤,配重
couple 力偶
coupled oscillation 耦合振荡
coupling 耦合
covalent bond 共价键
crane magnet 起重磁铁
creep 蠕变
crest 波峰
critical angle 临界角
critical damping 临界阻尼
critical mass 临界质量
critical point 临界点
critical temperature 临界温度
critical velocity 临界速度
crocodile clip 鳄鱼夹
cross-hairs 十字丝,叉丝
cross-sectional area 截面积
Crova's disc 克罗瓦盘
crystal 晶体
crystal diffraction 晶体衍射,晶体绕射
crystal lattice 晶格
crystal planes 晶面
crystalline 结晶的
crystallization 结晶
crystallography 晶体学
cubical expansivity 体积膨胀系数,体积膨胀率
curie 居里
Curie point 居里点
current 电流
current amplification 电流放大
current amplification factor 电流放大因素
current amplifier 电流放大器
current balance 电流天平
current density 电流密度

current gain 电流增益
current intensity 电流强度
current pulse 电流脉冲
current sensitivity 电流灵敏度
current stabilizer 稳流器
current transfer characteristic 电流转移特性
current-carrying conductor 载(电)流导体
current-voltage characteristic curve 电流-电压特性曲线
curved mirror 曲面镜
cyclotron 回旋加速器
cylindrical concave lens 柱面凹透镜
cylindrical concave mirror 柱面凹镜
cylindrical convex lens 柱面凸透镜
cylindrical convex mirror 柱面凸镜
cylindrical lens 柱面透镜
cylindrical mirror 柱面镜

D

D. C. generator 直流发电机
D. C. motor 直流电动机
Dalton law of partial pressures 道尔顿分压定律
damped harmonic motion 阻尼谐动
damped harmonic oscillation 阻尼谐振
damped oscillation 阻尼振荡
damping 阻尼
damping force 阻尼力
dark fringe 暗纹
data 数据
dating 年代测定
daughter nucleus 子核
daughter nuclide 子核素
de Broglie relation 德布罗意关系
de Broglie wave 德布罗意波
dead time 失效时间
decade capacitance box 十进电容箱
decade resistance box 十进电阻箱
decay 衰变
decay analogue 衰变模拟
decay constant 衰变常量
decay curve 衰变曲线
decay law 衰变定律
decay product 衰变产物

decelerate 减速
deceleration 减速度
decibel 分贝
decode 译码,解码
decoder 译码器,解码器
deflection 偏转
deflecting plate 偏转板
deflection system 偏转系统
deflection tube 偏转管
deformation 形变
degradation of energy 能量退降
degree 度
degree Celsius 摄氏度
degree of freedom 自由度
demagnetization 退磁
demonstration diode 演示用二极管
demonstration meter 演示电表
density 密度
depletion layer 耗尽层
depth of field 景深
derived quantity 导出量
derived unit 导出单位
destructive interference 相消干涉
detection 探测,检测
detector 探测器
detector of radiation 辐射探测器
deuterium 氘
deuteron 氘核
deviation 偏差
device 器件,设备
diamagnetism 抗磁性
diaphragm 光阑,膜片
diatomic molecule 双原子分子
dielectric 介电体.电介质,介电的
dielectric constant 介电常量
dielectric polarization 电介极化
dielectric strength 电介强度
differential equation 微分方程
differential input voltage 差动输入电压
diffracted ray 衍射线,绕射线
diffraction 衍射,绕射
diffraction grating 衍射光栅,绕射光栅
diffuse reflection 漫反射

diffusion 扩散,漫射
diffusion cloud chamber 扩散云室
digital 数字的
digital display 数字显示
digital signal 数字信号
digital-to-analogue conversion 数模转换
dimension 量纲,因次,维,大小
dimensional analysis 量纲分析,因次分析
diminish 缩小
diode 二极管
diode probe 二极管微波探测器
diopter 屈光度,焦度
dipole 偶极子
direct current 直流(电)
direction 方向,方位
direction of propagation 传播方向
directly heated cathode 直热式阴极
discharge 放电
disintegration 蜕变
dislocation 位错
dispersion 色散
dispersive power 色散能力,色散本领,色散率
displacement 位移,排量
displacement can 排水罐
displacement-time graph 位移-时间图
dissipative force 耗散力
distance 距离
distance-time graph 距离-时间图
distortion 失真,扭曲,畸变
disturbance 扰动
diverge 发散
diverging lens 发散透镜
diverging mirror 发散镜
division of amplitude 振幅分割
division of wavefront 波阵面分割,波前分割
domain 畴,域
domestic circuit 家居电路
donor 施主,给体
doped semiconductor 掺杂半导体
doping 掺杂
Doppler broadening 多普勒(谱线)增宽
Doppler effect 多普勒效应
Doppler shift 多普勒频移

dosage 剂量
dose 剂量
dose rate 剂量率
double pulley 双滑轮
double refraction 双折射
double slit 双缝
double-pole double-throw switch 双刀双掷开关
doublet 双重线
drag force 曳力
drift velocity 漂移速度
driver circuit 驱动电路
driver frequency 驱动频率
driving cell 驱动电池
driving force 驱动力
driving mirror 行车后视镜
dry battery 干电池组
dry cell 干电池
dual-trace oscilloscope 双迹示波器
ductile 延性的
Dulong-Petit law 杜隆-珀蒂定律
dynamic equilibrium 动态平衡
dynamic friction 动摩擦
dynamic resistance 动态电阻
dynamics 动力学
dynamo 发电机

E

earth 接地,地线
earthquake wave 地震波
ebonite 硬质胶
ebonite rod 硬质胶棒
echo 回声,回波
eddy current 涡电流,涡流
eddy-current damping 涡流阻尼
eddy-current loss 涡流损耗
effective mass 有效质量
efficiency 效率
effort 施力
Einstein mass-energy relation 爱因斯坦质能关系
elastic collision 弹性碰撞
elastic constant 弹性常数,弹性常量
elastic deformation 弹性形变
elastic hysteresis 弹性滞后

elastic limit 弹性极限
elastic strain energy 弹性应变能
elasticity 弹性
electric bell 电铃
electric charge 电荷
electric current 电流
electric field 电场
electric field intensity 电场强度
electric field line 电场线
electric field pattern 电场图形
electric furnace 电炉
electric line of force 电力线
electric motor 电动机
electric potential 电势,电位
electric power 电功率
electric shock 电震,电击
electrical appliance 电器
electrical conductivity 导电率
electrical energy 电能
electrical oscillation 电振荡
electrical potential energy 电势能,电位能
electrical resonance 电共振
electricity 电,电学
electrode 电极
electrolysis 电解
electrolyte 电解质
electrolytic 电解质的,电解的
electrolytic capacitor 电解质电容器
electromagnet 电磁铁,电磁体
electromagnetic coil 电磁感应圈
electromagnetic contact 电磁触点
electromagnetic force 电磁力
electromagnetic induction 电磁感应
electromagnetic moment 电磁矩
electromagnetic oscillation 电磁振荡
electromagnetic radiation 电磁辐射
electromagnetic spectrum 电磁(频)谱
electromagnetic wave 电磁波
electromagnetism 电磁学
electrometer 静电计
electromotive force 电动势
electron 电子
electron beam 电子束

Appendixes

electron cloud　电子云
electron diffraction　电子衍射,电子绕射
electron drift　电子漂移
electron energy level　电子能级
electron gun　电子枪
electron transition　电子跃迁
electron tube　电子管
electron-volt　电子伏特,电子伏
electronics　电子学
electrophorus　起电盘
electroscope　验电器
electrostatic bond　静电键
electrostatic field apparatus　静电场仪器
electrostatic precipitation　静电沉降
electrostatics　静电学
element　元素,元件
elliptic orbit　椭圆轨道
elongation　伸长度
emergent ray　出射线
emission　发射
emission line　发射(谱)线
emission spectrum　发射光谱,发射谱
emissivity　发射率
emit　发射
emitter　发射极,射极
emitter current　发射极电流,射极电流
enamelled wire　漆包线
encode　编码
encoder　编码器
end-correction　端部修正,管口校正量
end-on collision　同向碰撞,尾追碰撞
energetic particle　高能粒子
energy　能量,能
energy band　能带
energy conversion　能量转换
energy conversion efficiency　能量转换效率
energy input　能量输入
energy level　能级
energy output　能量输出
energy transfer　能量传递
enriched uranium　浓缩铀
equation of continuity　连续性方程
equation of state　物态方程

equation of uniformly accelerated motion　匀加速运动方程
equatorial orbit　赤道轨道
equilibrium　平衡
equilibrium condition　平衡条件
equilibrium spacing　平衡间距
equipartition of energy　能量均分
equipotential　等势的,等位的
equipotential line　等势线,等位线
equipotential surface　等势面,等位面
equivalent capacitance　等效电容
equivalent inductance　等效电感
equivalent resistance　等效电阻
erect　正立,直立的,竖立的
escape velocity　逃逸速度
ether　以太
evacuation　抽成真空
evaporation　蒸发
excess pressure　逾电压
excitation　激发
excitation energy　激发能
excitation potential　激发电势,激发电位
excitation voltage　激励电压、励磁电压
excited　受激的
excited energy level　受激能级
excited state　激发态
expansion　膨胀
expansivity　膨胀率
exponential change　指数式改变
exponential decay　指数式衰变
exposure　曝光(量),照射量
extension　伸长
external force　外力
external work　外功
extrahigh tension　超高电压
extranuclear structure　核外结构
extraordinary ray　非常光线
extrapolation　外推,外推法
extrinsic semiconductor　外赋半导体,非本征半导体
eye lens　接目镜
eyepiece　目镜

F

f-number　f 数,光圈数
f-stop　f 制光圈
far point　远点
farad　法拉
Faraday constant　法拉第常数,法拉第常量
Faraday law of electromagnetic induction　法拉第电磁感应定律
fast breeder reactor　快中子增殖反应堆
feedback　反馈
feedback amplifier　反馈放大器
feedback resistance　反馈电阻
ferromagnetic substance　铁磁性物质
ferromagnetism　铁磁性
fictitious force　虚假力
fidelity　保真性,保真度
field coil　场线圈
field-effect transistor　场效应晶体管
field intensity　场强
field line　场线
field magnet　场磁铁,场磁体
field of view　视场,视野
field strength　场强
figure of merit　优值,灵敏值,品质因数
filament　灯丝,丝极
filter capacitor　滤波电容器
filter circuit　滤波电路
filter pump　滤泵
final state　终态,末态
final velocity　末速度
fine-adjustment　微调,细调
fire alarm　火警警报器,火警钟
first law of thermodynamics　热力学第一定律
first-order spectrum　第一级光谱,第一级谱
fission　裂变
fission reactor　裂变反应堆
fixed point　定点
fixed pulley　定滑轮
fixed resistor　定值电阻器
flat coil　扁平线圈
flat solenoid　扁平螺线管
flat-bottomed flask　平底烧瓶

Fleming's left hand rule　弗林明左手定则
Fleming's right hand rule　弗林明右手定则
floating body　浮体
fluid　流体
fluid dynamics　流体动力学
fluorescence　荧光
fluorescent screen　荧光屏,荧光幕
flux　通量
flux density　通量密度
flyback　回扫
flywheel　飞轮
focal length　焦距
focal plane　焦面
focus　焦点,聚焦,调焦
focus control　聚焦控制
follower circuit　跟随电路
foot pump　脚踏泵
force　力
force constant　力常数,力常量
force polygon　力多边形
force resolution　力的分解
force triangle　力三角形
force-extension curve　施力-伸长曲线
forced oscillation　受迫振荡
former　框,线圈架,绕线模
forward biased　正向偏压
forward current　正向电流
fossil fuel　化石燃料
Foucault's rotating mirror method　傅科旋转镜法
frame of reference　参考坐标系,参考系
Franck-Hertz experiment　弗兰克-赫兹实验
Fraunhofer diffraction　夫琅禾费衍射,夫琅禾费绕射
Fraunhofer lines　夫琅禾费谱线
free electron　自由电子
free fall　自由下坠,自由下落
free falling body　自由落体
free oscillation　自由振荡
free path　自由程
free space　自由空间
freeze　凝固
freezing point　凝点
freon　氟利昂,二氯二氟甲烷

frequency 频率
frequency modulation 调频,频率调制
frequency response 频率响应
Fresnel biprism 菲涅耳双棱镜
Fresnel diffraction 菲涅耳衍射,菲涅耳绕射
friction 摩擦,摩擦力
friction-compensated 补偿摩擦的
frictionless motion 无摩擦运动
fringe 条纹
fringe pattern 条纹图,干涉图
fuel rod 燃料棒
fulcrum 支点
full adder 全加器
full-scale deflection 满标偏转
full-wave rectification 全波整流
full-wave rectifier 全波整流器
fundamental frequency 基频
fundamental mode of vibration 基振动模
fundamental note 基音
fundamental quantity 基本量
fundamental unit 基本单位
fuse 熔断器
fuse rating 熔断器额定值
fusion 熔化,聚变
fusion point 熔点
fusion reactor 聚变反应堆

G

G-clamp G-形钳
gain 增益
gain control 增益控制
galaxy 星系
Galileo telescope 伽利略望远镜
Galileo's thought experiment 伽利略假想实验
galvanometer 电流计,检流计
gamma radiation 伽玛辐射
gamma ray 伽玛射线
gap 隙
gas 气,气体
gas pressure 气体强压,气压
gaseous phase 气相
gaseous state 气态
gauge 规,计

Gauss theorem 高斯定理
Geiger counter 盖革计数器
Geiger-Marsden scattering experiment 盖革-马斯登散射实验
Geiger-Muller counter 盖革-米勒计数器
Geiger-Muller tube 盖革-米勒管
general gas equation 普适气体方程
general gas law 普适气体定律
generator 发电机
genetic effect 遗传效应
geometrical optics 几何光学
germanium 锗
ghost effect 叠影效应
glancing angle 掠射角
glass fiber 玻璃纤维
glycerine 甘油
gold foil 金箔
goldleaf electroscope 金箔验电器
gradient 梯度
graduated cylinder 量筒
Graham's law of effusion 格雷姆泻流定律
grain 粒,晶粒
gramophone record 唱片,唱碟
graph 图,线图,图表
graphical method 图解法
grating 光栅
grating spectrometer 光栅光谱仪,光栅分光计
gravitation 引力
gravitational constant 引力常量
gravitational field 引力场
gravitational mass 引力质量
gravitational potential 引力势
gravitational potential difference 引力势差
gravitational potential energy 引力势能
gravity 重力
grazing incidence 掠射
greenhouse effect 温室效应
grid 栅极
grid control 栅极控制
grid system 高压电网
groove 纹道,针槽,开槽
ground 接地
ground state 基态

guinea and feather experiment 硬币与羽毛实验

H

hair spring 游丝
half adder 半加器
half-life 半衰期
half-silvered mirror 半镀银镜
half-wave rectification 半波整流
half-wave rectifier 半波整流器
Hall effect 霍尔效应
Hall probe 霍尔探测器
Hall voltage 霍尔电压
hand stroboscope 手动式频闪仪
harmonic 谐音
harmonic motion 谐运动
harmonic oscillation 谐振荡
head-on collision 对头碰撞
heat 热,热量,加热,热学
heat absorbent 吸热剂
heat absorber 吸热器
heat absorption 吸热,热吸收
heat capacity 热容(量)
heat conduction 热传导
heat exchange 热交换,换热
heat flow 热流
heat gain 热增益,得热
heat insulation 热绝缘,隔热
heat loss 热损失,失热
heat-proof 耐热的,隔热的
heat pump 热泵
heat radiation 热辐射
heat reservoir 热库
heat sink 热壑,散热器
heat transfer 热传递,热转移
heater 热子,加热器
heat effect 热效应
heating element 加热元件
Helmholtz coils 亥姆霍兹线圈
henry 亨利,亨
hertz 赫兹,赫
high-dispersion prism 高色散棱镜
high tension 高电压
hole 空穴,孔

hollow plastic lens 空心塑料透镜
hollow plastic prism 空心塑料棱镜
hologram 全息图
holography 全息术,全息学
Hooke law 虎克定律
horizontal 水平的
horizontal component 水平分量
horizontal deflection 水平偏转
horseshoe magnet 蹄形磁铁
hot cathode 热阴极
hour 小时
Huygens principle 惠更斯原理
hydraulic press 水压机
hydroelectric power 水力发电
hydrogen bomb 氢弹
hygrometer 湿度计
hyperbolic orbit 双曲线轨道
hypothesis 假说,假设
hysteresis 滞后(效应)

I

ideal gas 理想气体
ideal gas equation 理想气体方程
ideal gas temperature scale 理想气体温标
ideal machine 理想机械
illuminate 照明,照亮
image 像,映像
image distance 像距
immerse 浸没
immersion heater 浸没式加热器
impact 碰撞
impedance 阻抗
impulse 冲量
impurity 杂质
in focus 焦点对准
in parallel 并联
in phase 同相
in series 串联
incident ray 入射线
incident wavefront 入射波阵面,入射波前
inclined plane 斜面
incoherent 非相干的
incompressible fluid 非压缩性流体

indicator 指示器
indirectly heated cathode 旁热式阴极
induced charge 感生电荷
induced current 感生电流
induced e. m. f. 感生电动势
induced voltage 感生电压
inducing charge 施感电荷
inducing current 施感电流
inductance 电感
inductance-capacitance-coupled circuit 感容耦合电路
inductance coil 电感线圈
induction 感应
induction heating 感应加热
inductive circuit 感性电路
inductive component 电感性分量
inductive reactance 感抗
inductor 电感器,感应器
inelastic collision 非弹性碰撞
inert gas 惰性气体
inertia 惯性
inertia balance 惯性秤
inertial frame 惯性坐标系,惯性系
inertial mass 惯性质量
infrared detector 红外探测器
infrared radiation 红外辐射
infrared ray 红外线
initial state 初态
initial velocity 初速(度)
input 输入
input bias current 输入偏压电流
input characteristic 输入特性
input current 输入电流
input offset current 输入补偿电流
input power 输入功率
input resistance 输入电阻
input voltage 输入电压
input-output voltage characteristic 输入-输出电压特性
instantaneous acceleration 瞬时加速度
instantaneous angular velocity 瞬时角速度
instantaneous current 瞬时电流
instantaneous power 瞬时功率
instantaneous speed 瞬时速率

instantaneous velocity 瞬时速度
instantaneous voltage 瞬时电压
insulation 绝缘
insulator 绝缘体
integrated circuit 集成电路
intensity 强度
intensity control 强度控制
intensity of current 电流强度
interaction (相)互作用
interatomic force 原子间力
interatomic potential 原子间势
interatomic separation 原子间距
intercept 截距,截段
interconversion 互换
interference 干涉
interference pattern 干涉图样
internal energy 内能
internal force 内力
internal resistance 内电阻
internal work 内功
international system of units 国际单位制,公制
interval 间隔
intrinsic semiconductor 本征半导体
inverse-square law 平方反比定律
inverted 倒的,反(向)的
inverter 反相器,逆变器
inverting input 倒相输入
ion 离子
ion-pair 离子偶,离子对
ionic bond 离子键
ionic structure 离子结构
ionization 电离
ionization chamber 电离室
ionization current 电离电流
ionization energy 电离能
ionization potential 电离电势,电离电位
ionization voltage 电离电压
ionize 电离
ionized atom 离子
ionized layer 电离层
ionizing power 电离能力,电离本领
ionizing radiation 电离辐射
ionosphere 电离层

iris　可变光阑,虹膜
iron core　铁芯
iron filings　铁粉
irreversible process　不可逆过程
isobar　等压线,同量异位素
isobaric expansion　等压膨胀
isobaric process　等压过程
isochronous oscillation　等时振荡
isotherm　等温线
isothermal process　等温过程
isotope　同位素
isovolumetric process　等容过程

J

Jaegers method　耶格法
jet propulsion　喷气推进
jockey　滑动触头
joule　焦耳
joulemeter　焦耳计
junction　结,接头
junction diode　结型二极管
junction transistor　结型晶体管

K

Kaleidoscope　万花筒
Kelvin　开尔文,开
Kelvin temperature scale　开氏温标
Kepler law　开普勒定律
key　电键
kilogram　千克
kilowatt　千瓦特,千瓦
kilowatt-hour　千瓦小时,千瓦时
kilowatt-hour meter　电表,千瓦时计
kinematics　运动学
kinetic energy　动能
kinetic friction　动摩擦
kinetic theory　（分子）动理论
kinetic theory model　（分子）动理论模型
kinetic theory of gases　气体分子运动论
Kirchhoff's law　基尔霍夫定律
kit　套件,成套工具
knife-edge　刃形支承,刃刃,刃口
kryton　氪

Kundt tube　孔脱管

L

lagging　隔热层保温套
laminar flow　层流
laminated　分层的,叠片的
laser　激光,激光器
laser beam　激光束
laser material　激光材料
latch　闩锁
latent heat　潜热
lateral　横向的,侧向的,旁向的
lateral inversion　横向倒置
lateral magnification　横向放大,横向放大率
lateral search coil　横向探察线圈
lattice　点阵,晶格
lattice spacing　点阵间隔,点阵间距
law　定律
law of conservation of momentum　动量守恒定律
law of reflection　反射定律
law of refraction　折射定律
lead　超前,铅
lead-acid accumulator　铅酸蓄电池
leakage current　漏泄电流
least distance of distinct vision　最小明视距离
Leclanche cell　勒克朗谢电池
length　长度
lens　透镜,晶状体
lens formula　透镜公式
lens holder　透镜座
lens marker's formula　透镜制造者公式
Lenz law　楞次定律
lever　杠杆
light　光,光学
light beam　光束,光柱
light-dependent resistor　光敏电阻器
light-emitting diode　发光二极管
light guide　光导
light pipe　（导）光管
light ray　光线
light-sensitive resistor　光敏电阻器
light source　光源
lightning　闪电

lightning conductor　避雷导线，避雷装置
lightning rod　避雷针
limiting angle　极限角
limiting friction　极限摩擦
line of action　作用线
line of force　力线
line spectrum　线状光谱，线状谱
linear air track　线性气垫导轨
linear electronics　线性电子学
linear expansivity　线性胀率
linear flow　线流
linear momentum　线动量
linear voltage amplification　线性电压放大率
linearly polarized wave　线偏振波
liquefaction　液化
liquid　液体
liquid crystal　液晶
liquid phase　液相
liquid pressure　液体压强
liquid-in-glass thermometer　玻璃管液体温度计
Lissajous figure　利萨如图形
live　载电，活线，火线
Lloyd mirror　劳埃德镜
load　负载，负荷
lodestone　磁石
logic gate　逻辑门
logic level　逻辑电平，逻辑级
logic-level indicator　逻辑电平指示器，逻辑级指示器
logic value　逻辑值
long sight　远视
long wave　长波
longitudinal magnification　纵向放大，纵向放大率
longitudinal wave　纵波
loop　回路，圈
Lorentz force　洛伦兹力
Lorentz rotating disc　洛伦兹旋转盘
loudness　响度
loudspeaker　扬声器
low-frequency A. C. generator　低频交流发电机
low voltage　低电压
low-voltage immersion heater　低压浸没式电热器
lower limit　下限
lycopodium powder　石松粉
Lyman series　莱曼系

M

Mach number　马赫数
machine　机械
macroscopic　宏观的
magnadur magnet　玛格纳多尔磁铁
magnet　磁铁，磁体
magnet keeper　磁铁衔铁
magnetic domain　磁畴
magnetic effect　磁效应
magnetic field　磁场
magnetic field board　磁场板
magnetic field intensity　磁场强度
magnetic field strength　磁场强度
magnetic flux　磁通量
magnetic flux density　磁通密度
magnetic flux linkage　磁链
magnetic force　磁力
magnetic hysteresis　磁滞
magnetic induction　磁感应强度，磁感应
magnetic line of force　磁力线
magnetic material　磁性材料
magnetic meridian　磁子午线
magnetic moment　磁矩
magnetic north pole　磁北极
magnetic permeability　磁导率
magnetic pole　磁极
magnetic saturation　磁饱和
magnetic screen　磁屏
magnetic shielding　磁屏蔽
magnetic south pole　磁南极
magnetic susceptibility　磁化率
magnetic tape　磁带
magnetic tape recorder　磁带录音机
magnetic torque　磁矩
magnetic track　磁迹，磁道
magnetism　磁学，磁性
magnetization　磁化
magnetize　磁化
magnetizing current　磁化电流
magnification　放大，放大率

magnified 放大的
magnifying glass 放大镜
magnifying power 放大率
magnitude 量,量值,大小
mains frequency 市电频率
mains immersion heater 市电浸没式加热器
mains supply 市电电源
majority carriers 多数载流子
malleable 可锻的
Maltese cross tube 马尔塔十字管
manometer 流体压强计
mass 质量
mass defect 质量亏损
mass number 质量数
mass spectrometer 质谱仪
mass-energy relation 质能关系
matter wave 物质波
maximum error 最大误差
mean free path 平均自由程
measurement 测量
mechanical advantage 机械效益
mechanical efficiency 机械效率
mechanical energy 机械能
mechanical oscillation 机械振荡
mechanical wave 机械波
mechanism 机制,机理
medium 介质
medium wave 中波
Melde's experiment 迈尔德实验
melting 熔化
melting point 熔点
meniscus 弯液面,弯月面
meniscus lens 弯月形透镜
mercury 汞,水银
metal fatigue 金属疲劳
metal grid 金属栅
metallic bond 金属键
metastable 亚稳的,介稳的
method of dimensions 维数法,因次法
method of no-parallax 无视差法
meter 米
meter bridge 滑线电桥,米尺电桥
meter rule 米尺

mica 云母
mica capacitor 云母电容器
microammeter 微安培计,微安表
microelectronics 微电子学
micrometer 测微器,千分尺
micrometer caliper 螺旋测微器
microphone 传声器
microscope 显微镜
microscopic 微观的
microwave 微波
microwave apparatus 微波仪器
microwave receiver 微波接收器
microwave transmitter 微波发送器
milliammeter 毫安表,毫安计
Millikan experiment 密立根实验
millimeter 毫米
minimum deviation 最小偏向
minority carrier 少数载流子
minute 分,分钟
mirage 蜃景,海市蜃楼
mirror (反射)镜
mirror formula 球面镜公式
mobility 迁移率
mode 模(式)
model eye 眼球模型
model power line 输电线模型
moderator 慢化剂,减速剂
modulation 调制,调节
module 模块,模数
modulus of elasticity 弹性模量
modulus of rigidity 刚性模量
molar gas constant 摩尔气体常数,摩尔气体常量
molar heat capacity 摩尔热容
molar volume 摩尔体积
mole 摩(尔)
molecular bombardment 分子轰击
molecular force 分子力
molecular motion 分子运动
molecular polarization 分子极化
molecular separation 分子间距
molecular structure 分子结构
molecule 分子
moment 矩

moment arm 矩臂,力臂
moment of couple 力偶矩
moment of dipole 偶极矩
moment of force 力矩
moment of inertia 转动惯量
moment of momentum = angular momentum 动量矩,角动量
momentum 动量
monatomic molecule 单原子分子
monochromatic light 单色光
motion 运动
motor 电动机
motor rule 电动机法则
movable pulley 动滑轮
moving-coil galvanometer 动圈式电流计,动圈式检流计
moving-coil loudspeaker 动圈式扬声器
moving-coil meter 动圈式电表
multiflash photography 多闪照相术
multimeter 万用电表,多用(电)表
multiple image 复像
multiple reflection 多次反射
multiplication process 倍增过程
multiplier 倍增器
multivibrator 多谐振荡器
musical quality 音品,音色
musical instrument 乐器
mutation 突变
multiple-slit interference 多缝干涉
mutual inductance 互感(系数)
mutual induction 互感(应)
mutually perpendicular 互相垂直的

N

n-type semiconductor n型半导体
NAND gate 与非门,非与门
naphthalene 萘(球),卫生球
natural frequency 固有频率
nature 本质
near point 近点
necking down 颈缩
negater 反相器,倒换器,非门
negative charge 负电荷

negative feedback 负反馈
negative ion 负离子
negative supply rail 负供电轨
negative terminal 负端钮,负极柱
net force 净力
network 网络
neutral 中性的,中线的
neutral equilibrium 中性平衡
neutral point 中性点
neutrino 中微子
neutron 中子
neutron number 中子数
newton 牛顿
Newton first law of motion 牛顿运动第一定律
Newton law of gravitation 牛顿万有引力定律
Newton ring 牛顿环
Newton second law of motion 牛顿运动第二定律
Newton third law of motion 牛顿运动第三定律
Newtonian fluid 牛顿流体
Newtonian mechanics 牛顿力学
nichrome wire 镍铬线,镍铬合金线
Nicol prism 尼科耳棱镜
nitrogen 氮
no-parallax 无视差
nodal line 节线
node 节点,结点
noise 噪声
noise level 噪声级
noise pollution 噪声污染
non-conservative force 非守恒力,非保守力
noninertial system 非惯性坐标系,非惯性系
non-inverting input 非反相输入
non-Newtonian fluid 非牛顿流体
non-ohmic conductor 非欧姆导体
non-ohmic resistor 非欧姆电阻器
NOR gate 或非门,非或门
normal 法线
normal incidence 正入射
normal reaction 法向反作用力
normal stress 法向应力
north pole 北极
NOT gate 非门
note 音,乐音,律音

nozzle 喷嘴
nuclear 核的
nuclear energy 核能
nuclear energy level 核能级
nuclear fission 核裂变
nuclear force 核力
nuclear fusion 核聚变
nuclear pile 核堆
nuclear radiation 核辐射
nuclear reaction 核反应
nuclear reactor 核反应堆
nuclear waste 核废料
nuclear weapon 核武器
nucleon 核子
nucleon number 核子数
nucleus （原子）核
nuclide 核素

O

object 物,物体
object distance 物距
objective 物镜
obstacle 障碍物
octave 八音度,倍频程
oersted 奥(斯特)
ohm 欧姆
Ohm's law 欧姆定律
ohmic conductor 欧姆导体
ohmic resistor 欧姆电阻器
ohmmeter 欧姆计
oil film 油膜
opaque 不透明的
open circuit 断开电路,开路
open pipe 开管
open tube 开管
open-loop control system 开环控制系统
open-loop voltage gain 开环电压增益
operating voltage 操作电压
operational amplifier 运算放大器
opposite phase 反相
optical center 光心
optical density 光学密度
optical fiber 光导纤维,光纤

optical flatness 光学平面度
optical illusion 光幻象,视错觉
optical instrument 光学仪器
optical path 光程
optical path difference 光程差
optical system 光学系统,光具组
optical thickness 光学厚度
optically anisotropic 光学各向异性的
optically denser medium 光密介质
optically isotropic 光学各向同性的
optically thinner medium 光疏介质
optics 光学
OR gate 或门
orbit 轨道
orbital electron 轨道电子
order of magnitude 数量级
ordinary ray 寻常光线
organic glass 有机玻璃
orientation 取向,定向
oscillation 振荡
oscillator 振荡器
oscillatory circuit 振荡电路
oscilloscope 示波器
Ostwald viscometer 奥斯特瓦尔德黏度计
out of focus 离焦
out of phase 异相(位)
output 输出
output characteristic 输出特性
output current 输出电流
output power 输出功率
output voltage 输出电压
overload 过载
overtone 泛音

P

p-type semiconductor p型半导体
pair production 偶生成
paraffin 石蜡
parallax 视差
parallel axis theorem 平行轴定理
parallel beam projector 平行光束投射器
parallel circuit 并联电路
parallel forces 平行力

parallel rays 平行光线
parallel resonance 并联共振
parallel resonance circuit 并联共振电路
parallel-plate capacitor 平行板电容器
parallelogram of forces 力平行四边形
paramagnetism 顺磁性
parameter 参量,参数
paraxial ray 傍轴光线
parent nucleus 母核
parent nuclide 母核素
parking orbit 驻留轨道
partial polarization 部分偏振
partial pressure 分压力
partially polarized wave 部分偏振波
particle 粒子
particle movement 粒子运动,质点运动
pascal 帕斯卡
Paschen series 帕邢系
path 路程
path difference 程差
peak value 峰值
peak voltage 峰值电压
peak-to-peak current 峰-峰电流
peak-to-peak voltage 峰-峰电压
pendulum 摆
penetrating power 贯穿本领,穿透本领
penetration depth 贯穿深度,穿透深度
percentage error 百分误差
perfectly elastic 完全弹性的
perfectly inelastic 完全非弹性的
perigee 近地点
perihelion 近日点
period 周期
periodic fading 周期性衰退
periodic motion 周期运动
periodic table 周期表
periscope 潜望镜
permanent magnet 永磁体
permeability 磁导率
permeability of vacuum 真空磁导率
permittivity 电容率,介电常数
permittivity of free space 真空电容率
perpendicular axis theorem 垂直轴定理,正交轴定理
perpendicular distance 垂直距离
Perrin tube 佩林管
phase 相,相位
phase angle 相角
phase constant 相位常量,初相位
phase difference 相差,相位差
phase lag 相位滞后
phase lead 相位超前
phasor 相(矢)量
phon 方(响度单位)
photo-timing gate 光控计时门
phototransistor 光电晶体管
photocell 光电池
photodiode 光电二极管
photoelasticity 光(测)弹性
photoelectric cell 光电池
photoelectric current 光电流
photoelectric effect 光电效应
photoelectric threshold 光电阈
photoelectron 光电子
photographic negative 照相底片
photographic plate 照相底板
photon 光子
photosensitive 光敏的
photosensitive surface 光敏面
physical optics 物理光学
physical property 物理性质
physical quantity 物理量
pick-up 拾音器,拾音
piston 活塞
pitch 螺距,俯仰,音调
Pitot tube 皮托管
pivot 支点,支枢
Planck constant 普朗克常数,普朗克常量
plane mirror 平面镜
plane of polarization 偏振面
plane polarization 平面偏振
plane-polarized wave 面偏振波
plane wave 平面波
planetary motion 行星运动
plano-concave lens 平凹透镜
plano-convex lens 平凸透镜

plastic deformation　塑性形变
platinum-resistance thermometer　铂阻温度计
plug　插头,插塞
plutonium　钚
point action　尖端作用
point charge　点电荷
point mass　点质量
point of application of force　施力点
point of incidence　入射点
point source　点源
pointer　指针
Poiseuille's formula　泊肃叶公式
Poisson ratio　泊松比
polar　极(性)的
polarity　极性
polarization　偏振,极化
polarization grille　偏振栅
polarized light　偏振光
polarized wave　偏振波
polarizer　起偏器,起偏镜
polarizing angle　起偏振角,偏振角
polarizing filter　起偏振滤波器,偏振滤波器
polaroid　偏振片
pole　极(点)
polonium　钋
polyatomic molecule　多原子分子
polyethylene　聚乙烯
polygon of forces　力多边形
polystyrene bead　聚苯乙烯珠
polystyrene cup　聚苯乙烯杯
polythene strip　聚乙烯片
positive charge　正电荷
positive feedback　正反馈
positive ion　正离子
positive supply rail　正供电轨
positive terminal　正端钮,正接线柱
potential barrier　势垒,位垒
potential difference　(电)势差,(电)位差
potential divider　分压器
potential energy　势能,位能
potential gradient　势梯度,位梯度
potentiometer　电势差计,电位差计
power　功率

power amplifier　功率放大器
power distribution　配电
power factor　功率因数
power generation　发电
power loss　功率损耗
power pack　电源箱
power rating　电功率额定值
power station　电力站,发电厂
power supply　电源,供电
power supply unit　供电设备,电源箱
power transistor　功率晶体管
power transmission　输电
pressure　压强,压力
pressure cooker　高压锅,加压蒸煮器
pressure gauge　压强表
pressure law　气压定律
pressuriyed water reactor　压水式反应堆
primary coil　原线圈
primary current　一次电流,原电流
primary voltage　一次电压,原电压
primary winding　初级绕组,原绕组
principal axis　主轴
principal focus　主焦点
principle　原理
principle of flotation　浮体原理
principle of moments　力矩原理
principle of superposition　叠加原理
prism　棱镜
prismatic periscope　棱镜潜望镜
probe　探头,探测器
progressive wave　前进波
projectile　抛体
projectile motion　抛体运动
projection　投影,投射
projector　投影仪,放映机
prong　音叉臂
proof plane　验电板
propagation　传播
propeller　推进器
property　性质
proportionality constant　比例常数,比例常量
protactinium　镤
protective screen　防护屏

proton　质子
proton number　质子数
pseudo-force　假力，赝力
pulley　滑轮
pulse　脉冲
pump　泵
pupil　光瞳，瞳孔
pure note　纯音
push-button switch　按钮开关
pyrometer　高温计

Q

Q-factor　品质因数
quality of note　音品，音质
quantity of electricity　电量
quantization　量子化
quantum　量子
quantum number　量子数
quarter-wave aerial　四分之一波天线
quartz　石英
quenching agent　猝灭剂
quiescent condition　宁静状态

R

radial acceleration　径向加速度
radial component　径向分量
radial field　辐向场，径向场
radiation　辐射
radiation hazard　辐射危害
radiation protection　辐射防护
radiator　散热器，辐射器，辐射体
radio frequency　射频，无线电广播频率
radio telescope　射电望远镜
radio wave　无线电波
radioactive　放射(性)的
radioactive decay　放射衰变
radioactive disintegration　放射性蜕变
radioactive fallout　放射性沉降物
radioactive isotope　放射性同位素
radioactive nucleus　放射性核
radioactive series　放射系
radioactive source　放射源
radioactive waste　放射性废物

radioactivity　放射性(活度)
radioisotope　放射性同位素
radiometer　辐射计
radionuclide　放射性核素
radiotherapy　放射治疗
radium　镭
radius of curvature　曲率半径
radius of gyration　回转半径，回旋半径
radon　氡
rail　路轨
random　无规的，随机的
random error　随机误差
random motion　无规运动，随机运动
random nature　无规性，随机性
random walk　无规行走，随机游动
range　范围，射程，量程
rarefaction　稀疏
rate of decay　衰变率
rate of disintegration　蜕变率
ratemeter　(率表)率计
rating　额定值
ray　射线，光线
ray box　光线箱
ray diagram　光线图
Rayleigh criterion　瑞利判据
reactance　电抗
reaction　反作用，反(作用)力，反应
reactive component　无功分量
reactor　反应堆
reactor core　反应堆堆芯
reading error　读数误差
real depth　实深
real expansion　实膨胀，真膨胀
real focus　实焦点
real gas　真实气体
real image　实像
real object　实物
real-is-positive convention　实正虚负约定
recoil　反冲，回复
rectification　整流
rectifier　整流器
rectilinear motion　直线运动
rectilinear propagation　直线传播

red shift　红移
reed　舌簧
reed relay　舌簧继电器
reed switch　舌簧开关
reference frame　参考系
reference level　参考级,参考水平
reflectance　反射比
reflected ray　反射线
reflected wavefront　反射波阵面,反射波前
reflecting telescope　反射望远镜
reflection　反射,反映
reflection grating　反射光栅
refracted ray　折射线
refracted wavefront　折射波阵面,折射波前
refracting angle　折射角
refracting telescope　折射望远镜
refraction　折射
refractive index　折射率
refrigerator　冰箱
regular reflection　规则反射
relative density　相对密度
relative motion　相对运动
relative permeability　相对磁导率
relative permittivity　相对电容率
relative velocity　相对速度
relativity　相对论,相对性
relay　继电器
relay coil　继电器线圈
relay contact　继电器触点
rem　雷姆
remote control　遥控
repulsion　推斥,排斥
repulsive force　斥力
reservoir capacitor　存储电容器
reset switch　复位开关
resistance　电阻
resistance coil　电阻线圈
resistance substitution box　换值电阻箱
resistance thermometer　电阻温度计
resistive component　电阻分量,有功分量
resistivity　电阻率
resistor　电阻器
resolution　分解,分辨,分辨率

resolution of force　力的分解
resolution of vector　矢量的分解
resolving power　分辨本领
resonance　共振,共鸣
resonance tube　共鸣管
resonant frequency　共振频率
resonator　共振器
response time　响应时间
restoring couple　恢复力偶
restoring force　恢复力
restoring torque　恢复转矩
resultant　合量,合的
resultant displacement　合位移
resultant force　合力
resultant vector　合矢量
resultant velocity　合速度
retard　减速
retardation　减速度
retort stand　铁支架,铁架
reverberation　混响
reverberation time　混响时间
reverse bias　反向偏压
reverse current　反向电流
reversibility of light　光的可逆性
reversible process　可逆过程
reversing switch　倒向开关
revolution　旋转,转数
Reynolds number　雷诺数
rheostat　变阻器
right-angled fork track　直角分叉径迹
right-hand grip rule　右手握拳定则
right-hand screw rule　右手螺旋定则
rigid body　刚体
rigidity　刚性,刚度,刚度系数
ring circuit　环形电路
ripple　纹波
ripple tank　水波槽,波动箱
rocket　火箭
rolling　滚动
rolling friction　滚动摩擦
root-mean-square value　方均根值
rotary thermometer　转动式温度计
rotary-type potentiometer　旋转电势差计,旋转电

位差计
rotating platform 旋转台
rotating vector 转动矢量
rotation 旋转,自转,转动
rotational energy 转动能
rotational motion 旋转运动
rotor 转子
rubber tubing 橡胶管
rule 定则,法则
ruling 刻度,划线
runway 跑道
Rutherford scattering 卢瑟福散射
Rutherford's atomic model 卢瑟福原子模型
Rydberg constant 里德伯常数,里德伯常量

S

safety device 安全装置
satellite 卫星
satellite communication 卫星通讯,卫星通信
saturated vapour 饱和蒸汽,饱和汽
saturated vapour pressure 饱和蒸气压,饱和气压
saturation 饱和
saturation current 饱和电流
sawtooth voltage 锯齿波电压
scalar 标量
scalar product 标(量)积
scale 标度,比例尺,音阶
scaler 定标器
scan 扫描
scattering 散射
scattering analogue 散射模拟
scattering angle 散射角
scintillation 闪烁
screen 屏,幕
screened lead 屏蔽引线
screw 螺旋,螺钉
screwdriver 螺钉起子,螺丝刀
screw jack 螺旋起重器
sealed radioactive source 密封放射源
search coil 探察线圈
second 秒
second law of thermodynamics 热力学第二定律
second-order spectrum 第二级光谱,第二级谱

secondary coil 副线圈
secondary current 二次电流
secondary emission 次级发射
secondary voltage 二次电压
secondary winding 二次绕组,次级绕组
Seebeck effect 塞贝克效应
selective absorption 选择吸收
self-inductance 自感(系数)
self-induction 自感(应)
semicircular glass block 半圆玻璃块
semiconductor 半导体
semiconductor diode 半导体二极管
sensitivity 灵敏度
sensor 感应器,传感器
sequential logic 顺序逻辑
series circuit 串联电路
series resonance circuit 串联共振电路
series-wound motor 串绕电动机
set switch 设定开关
shaft (转)轴
shear force 切变应力
shear modulus 剪模量,剪切模量
shear strength 切变强度,剪切强度
shear stress 切应力,剪切应力
shearing force 剪切力
shock waves (冲)击波,激波
short circuit 短路
short sight 近视
shortwave 短波
shunt 分流器,分路
shunt-wound motor 并励电动机,并绕电动机
shutter 快门
sievert 希沃特
sign convention 符号约定
signal generator 信号发生器
significant figure 有效数字
silicon 硅
simple harmonic motion 简谐运动
simple pendulum 单摆
simulation 模拟
single-phase A.C. generator 单相交流发电机
single pulley 单滑轮
single slit 单缝

single trace oscilloscope 单迹示波器
single-pole double-throw switch 单刀双掷开关
sinusoidal wave 正弦波
slab-shaped magnet 平板形磁铁
slide projector 幻灯片放映机
slide-wire potentiometer 滑线电势差计,滑线电位差计
sliding contact 滑动接触
sliding friction 滑动摩擦
slinky spring 软弹簧
slip ring 集电环,滑环
slit 缝,狭缝
slope 斜率
slotted weight 有槽砝码
smoke cell 烟雾盒
smoothing 平波,平流
smoothing capacitor 平波电容器,平流电容器
smoothing choke 平波扼流圈,平流扼流圈
smoothing circuit 平波电路,平流电路
Snell law 斯涅耳定律
socket 插座
sodium lamp 钠灯
soft iron 软铁
soft iron core 软铁芯
solar cell 太阳能电池
solar energy 太阳能
soldering iron 烙铁
solenoid 螺线管
solid 固体
solid phase 固相
solid state 固态
solidification 凝固
solidifying point 凝固点
sonar 声呐
sonic boom 声爆,声震
sonometer 弦音计
sound 声音
sound intensity 声强(度)
sound intensity level 声强级
soundproofing 隔音,隔音法,消声
sound track 声迹,声道
sound wave 声波
south pole （指）南极

spark 火花
spark counter 火花计数器
specific charge 荷质比,比电荷,比荷
specific heat (capacity) 比热(容)
specific heat (capacity) at constant pressure 定压比热(容)
specific heat (capacity) at constant volume 定容比热(容)
specific latent heat 比潜热
specific latent heat of fusion 熔解比潜热
specific latent heat of vaporization 汽化比潜热
spectacles 眼镜
spectral analysis 光谱分析
spectral line （光）谱线
spectral order 光谱级
spectrometer （光）谱仪,分光计
spectroscopy 光谱学,光谱术
spectrum 谱,光谱,波谱
spectrum tube 光谱管
specular reflection 镜(面)反射
speed 速率
speed of light 光速
speed of sound 声速,音速
speed-time graph 速率-时间图
spherical aberration 球(面像)差
spherical lens 球面透镜
spherical mirror 球面镜
spherical wave 球面波
spherically symmetric 球对称的
spin 自旋
spiral 螺线,螺旋形
spiral spring 螺旋弹簧
spirit level 气泡水平仪
spontaneous 自发的
spontaneous disintegration 自发蜕变
spontaneous emission 自发发射
spring 弹簧,簧片,发条
spring balance 弹簧秤
square wave 方波
squarer 方波产生器
stable equilibrium 稳定平衡
stable state 稳(定状)态
stackable plug 叠加式插头

standard atmospheric pressure　标准大气压
standard cell　标准电池
standard deviation　标准偏差,标准差
standard error　标准误差
standing wave　驻波
starter　起动器
starting resistance　起动电阻
starting voltage　起动电压
state　态
states of matter　物态
static equilibrium　静态平衡
static friction　静摩擦
static resistance　静态电阻
statics　静力学
stationary wave　定态波
stator　定子
steady flow　定常流(动)
steady state　定常态
steam　水蒸气,蒸汽
steam engine　蒸汽机
steam point　汽点
steam turbine　汽轮机
steel yoke　钢轭
step-down transformer　降压器
step-up transformer　升压器
stereophonic　立体声的
stiffness　刚度,劲度
stimulated absorption　受激吸收
stimulated emission　受激发射
Stokes' law　斯托克斯定律
stop watch　停表
stop clock　停钟
stopping potential　遏止电势,遏止电位
storage battery　蓄电池(组)
storage capacitor　存储电容器
stored energy　储能
straight pulse　直线脉冲
straight wave　直线波
straight wavefront　直线波阵面,直线波前
strain　应变
strain gauge　应变规
stray capacitance　杂散电容
streamline　流线

stress　应力
stress-strain curve　应力-应变曲线
stretch　伸长,拉紧
strobe frequency　闪频
stroboscope　频闪仪
stroboscopic photography　频闪照相术
strontium　锶
stylus　唱针
substation　分站,配电站,变电站
sublimation　升华
submerge　浸没
subsonic speed　亚声速,亚音速
summing amplifier　加法放大器
superconductivity　超导(电)性
superconductor　超导体
supercooling　过冷
superficial expansivity　面膨胀系数,面膨胀率
superposition　叠加
supersaturation　过饱和
supersonic speed　超声速,超音速
surface charge density　表面电荷密度
surface energy　表面能
surface tension　表面张力
susceptibility　磁化率
sweep　扫描,扫掠
sweep rate　扫描速率
switch　开关,电键
switch off　截断,关闭
switch on　接通,开启
symbol　符号
synchronization　同步
syringe　针筒,注射器
system　系统
systematic error　系统误差

T

tangential acceleration　切向加速度
tangential component　切向分量
tape chart　纸带图表
tapping key　簧片按键
telephone receiver　电话听筒
telescope　望远镜
telescope mount　望远镜座

television 电视
temperature 温度
temperature coefficient of resistance 电阻温度系数
temperature difference 温差
temperature gradient 温度梯度
temperature scale 温标
tempering 回火
temporary magnet 暂时磁铁,暂时磁体
tensile force 拉力,张力
tensile strain 拉(伸)应变
tensile strength 抗张强度
tensile stress 拉(伸)应力
tension 张力
terminal 端钮,接线柱
terminal speed 终极速率
terminal velocity 终极速度
terrestrial telescope 地面望远镜
tesla 特斯拉
test charge 检验电荷
test tube 试管
theory 理论
thermal capacity 热容量
thermal conductivity 热导率
thermal equilibrium 热平衡
thermal radiation 热辐射
thermal reactor 热中子反应堆
thermal transmission 传热,热传递
thermionic diode 热离子二极管
thermionic emission 热离子发射
thermistor 热敏电阻器
thermistor thermometer 热敏电阻温度计
thermo-electromotive force 温差电动势,热电动势
thermocouple 温差电偶,热电偶
thermocouple thermometer 温差电偶温度计,热电偶温度计
thermodynamic temperature 热力学温度
thermoelectric effect 温差电效应,热电效应
thermometer 温度计
thermometer bulb 温度计泡
thermometric property 测温性质
thermometry 计温学,测温法

thermonuclear reaction 热核反应
thermopile 温差电堆
thermostat 恒温器
thin film 薄膜
Thomson's atomic model 汤姆逊原子模型
thorium 钍
three-pin plug 三脚插头
threshold frequency 阈频(率)
threshold intensity 阈强度
threshold of hearing 听觉阈
threshold voltage 阈电压
thrust 推力
thyratron 闸流管
ticker tape 纸带
ticker-tape timer 纸带打点计时器
tidal energy 潮汐能
time 时间
time base 时基
time-base control 时基控制
time constant 时间常数
time interval 时距
time switch 定时开关,计时开关
timer 定时器,计时器
timer-scaler 计时-计数器
toroid 环状线圈
toroidal coil 环状线圈
toroidal rheostat 环形变阻器
torque 转矩
Torricelli's theorem 托里拆利定理
Torricellian vacuum 托里拆利真空
torsion 扭转
torsion constant 扭转常量
torsional force 扭力
torsional moment 扭矩
torsional oscillation 扭转型振荡
torsional pendulum 扭摆
torsional strength 抗扭强度
torsional stress 扭(转)应力
total internal reflection 全(内)反射
trace 迹,示踪
tracer 示踪物,示踪剂
track 径迹
train of waves 波列

trajectory 轨道,轨迹
transducer 换能器,传感器
transformation 变换
transformer 变压器
transient current 瞬态电流
transient state 暂态,瞬态
transient voltage 瞬态电压
transistor 晶体管
transition 跃迁,过渡
transition energy 跃迁能
translation 平移
translational energy 平动动能
translucent screen 半透明屏,半透明幕
transmission 透射,输电,传输
transmission cable 输电缆
transmission grating 透射光栅
transmittance 透射比
transmitted ray 透射光线
transmutation 嬗变,转变
transparent 透明的
transverse 横向的
transverse magnification 横向放大,横向放大率
transverse wave 横波
travelling microscope 移测显微镜,读数显微镜
travelling wave 行波
triangle of force 力三角形
triangular prism 三棱镜,三角棱镜
trigger 触发,触发器
trigger input 触发输入
triode 三极管
triple-beam balance 三杆式天平,三臂秤,三梁天平
triple point 三相点,三态点
tripod stand 三脚架
tritium 氚
trolley 小车
trough 波谷
truth table 真值表
tune 调谐
tungsten filament 钨丝
tuning fork 音叉
turbine 涡轮
turbulent flow 湍流

turn 匝,转,转动
turn off 断开,关闭
turn on 接通,开启
turn ratio 匝(数)比
turntable 转盘
twist 扭曲
two-way switch 双向开关

U

ultimate tensile stress 极限拉伸应力
ultrahigh frequency 超高频
ultraviolet radiation 紫外辐射
ultraviolet ray 紫外线
ultrasonic 超声,超音
ultrasonic wave 超声波,超音波
unbalanced force 不平衡力
unidirectional circuit 单向电路
unidirectional current 单向电流
uniform 均匀的
uniform acceleration 匀加速度
uniform electric field 均匀电场
uniform magnetic field 均匀磁场
uniform motion 匀速运动
uniform speed 匀速率
uniform velocity 匀速度
uniformly accelerated motion 匀加速运动
unit 单位,单元
unit mass 单位质量
unit temperature 单位温度
universal gas constant 普适气体常量
universal gravitational constant 万有引力常量
universal stand 普用支架
unpolarized light 非偏振光
unpolarized wave 非偏振波
unstable equilibrium 不稳定平衡
unsteady state 非稳态
unstretched length 原长
upper limit 上限
upthrust 浮力
uranium 铀
uranium ore 铀矿
uranyl nitrate 硝酸双氧铀

V

vacuum 真空
vacuum discharge 真空放电
vacuum pump 真空泵
vacuum tube 真空管
valence electron 价电子
valve 电子管,阀,活门
Van de Graaff generator 范德格拉夫起电机
van der Waals' force 范德瓦耳斯力
vaporization 汽化
vapour 蒸汽,汽
vapour density 蒸汽密度,汽密度
vapour pressure 蒸汽压,气压
variable gain 可变增益
variable motion 变速运动
variable resistor 变阻器,可变电阻
variable speed 可变速率
variable velocity 可变速度
variation 变化
vector 矢量
vector addition 矢量加法
vector product 矢积
velocity 速度
velocity ratio 速度比
velocity-time graph 速度-时间图
Venturi meter 文丘里流量计
vernier 游标
vernier microscope 游标显微镜
vertical 垂直的
vertical component 垂直分量
vertical deflection 垂直偏转
very high frequency 甚高频
vibration 振动
vibration generator 激振器
vibrator 振动器
virtual earth 虚接地
virtual focus 虚焦点
virtual image 虚像
virtual object 虚物,虚物体
viscosity 黏度,黏性
viscous 黏(性)的
viscous flow 黏性流(动),黏滞流
viscous force 黏性力,黏力
viscous resistance 黏性阻力
visibility 可见度
visible light 可见光
visible spectrum 可见光谱
visual angle 视角
volt 伏特,伏
voltage 电压
voltage amplification 电压放大(率)
voltage comparator 电压比较器
voltage divider 分压器
voltage drop 电压降
voltage gain 电压增益
voltage rating 电压额定值
voltage regulator 调压器
voltage stabilizer 稳压器
voltmeter 伏特计,电压表
volume 体积,容积
vortex 涡旋
vulcanization 硫化

W

water vapour 水蒸气,水汽
water wave 水波
watt 瓦特,瓦
watt-meter 瓦特计,功率表
wave 波
wave motion 波动
wave number 波数
wave pattern 波动图样
wave source 波源
wave speed 波速(率)
wave train 波列
wave velocity 波速度
wave-particle duality 波粒二象性
waveform 波形
wavefront 波阵面,波前
waveguide 波导
wavelength 波长
wavelet 子波
weber 韦伯
wedge 楔
weight 重量,砝码,权(重)

weightlessness　无重状态,失重
Weston cadmium cell　韦斯顿镉电池
Wheatstone bridge　惠斯通电桥
wheel-and-axle　轮轴
white light　白光
wig-wag machine　摇摆机
Wilson cloud chamber　威尔逊云室
wind power　风力,风功率
wind tunnel　风洞
winding　绕组,绕
wire gauge　线规
wire gauze　铁丝网
wiring　接线,布线
work　功
work function　逸出功,功函数

X

X-ray　X射线
X-ray diffraction　X射线衍射
X-ray spectrum　X射线谱
X-shift　水平移
xenon　氙
xenon stroboscope　氙光频闪仪
XOR gate　异或门

Y

Y-shift　垂直移
yield point　屈服点
yield strength　屈服强度
Young modulus　杨氏模量
Young's double slit experiment　杨氏双缝实验
Young's interference fringes　杨氏干涉条纹

Z

Zener diode　齐纳二极管
zero correction　零点校正
zeroth law of thermodynamics　热力学第零定律
zeroth order　零级

参 考 文 献

1. 仲海洋. University Physics. 大连：大连海事大学出版社，2006
2. 董益坤，魏汝尧. 科技英语. 济南：山东大学出版社，2001
3. 吴朔平. 科技英语速成读本. 北京：新时代出版社，1982
4. 清华大学《英汉技术辞典》编写组编. 英汉技术辞典. 北京：国防工业出版社，1978
5. 科技英语学习. 上海交通大学出版社
6. Serway & Jewett. Principles of Physics (Third Edition)(物理学原理). 北京：清华大学出版社，2004
7. Richard P. Olenick, Tom M. Apostol & David L. Goodstein. Beyond the Mechanicai Universe(影印版). 北京：北京大学出版社，2001
8. Hugh D. Young & Roger A. Freedman. 西尔斯物理学. 北京：机械工业出版社，2003
9. David K. Cheng. 电磁场与电磁波（第二版）. 北京：清华大学出版社，2007
10. Online Technical Writing：Report Format and Final Production，http://www.io.com
11. http://www.ccp2009.tw/index.asp
12. http://www.EnMajor.com，ESP 理论与实践
13. 曾蕾，林泽铨，傅晓玲. 国际学术会议英语. 重庆：重庆大学出版社，2004
14. 叶云屏，邢清清，张剑. 科技英语读写：方法与实践. 北京：高等教育出版社，2007
15. 魏汝尧. 致用科技英语. 北京：国防工业出版社，2007
16. 马新英，孙学涛，林易. 科技英语教程. 北京：国防工业出版社，2005
17. 闫文培. 实用科技英语翻译要义. 北京：科学出版社，2008
18. 郑福裕，徐威. 英文科技论文写作与编辑指南. 北京：清华大学出版社，2008
19. 任胜利. 英语科技论文撰写与投稿. 北京：科学出版社，2004
20. 胡庚申. 国际会议交流英语. 北京：高等教育出版社，2000
21. Larry D. Kirkpatrick & Gerald F. Wheeler. Physics. USA：Saunders College Publishing，1998
22. Stephen Pople. Advanced Physics Through Diagrams. 上海：上海外语教育出版社，2000
23. R. M. Whittle & J. Yarwood. Experimental Physics for Students. London：Chapman and Hall，1973